CONTENTS

vi-vii	WORLD Countries
viii-ix	WORLD Cities
x-xi	WORLD Languages
xii-xiii	WORLD Economic Groups
xiv-xv	WORLD International Organisations
xvi	SYMBOLS
1	Arctic Ocean

NORTH AMERICA

2-3	North America
4-5	Canada West
6-7	Canada East
8-9	USA West
10-11	USA East
12	USA Alaska
13	Canada West
14-15	Canada Southeast, USA Northeast
16	USA Washington - New York - Boston
17	USA Southeast
18-19	USA South-Central
20	USA Northwest
21	USA Southwest
22	USA San Francisco & Los Angeles
23	Mexico Central
24-25	Mexico & Central America
26-27	Caribbean

SOUTH AMERICA

28	South America
29	South America South
30	South America Central
31	South America Northeast
32-33	South America North
34	Central Argentina
35	Brazil Southeast

EUROPE

36-37	Europe
38-39	Scandinavia
40-41	British Isles
42-43	England & Wales
44	Scotland North
45	Ireland
46	The Low Countries
47	Switzerland & Italy North
48-49	France
50-51	Spain & Portugal
52-53	Italy
54-55	The Balkans
56-57	Germany & Austria
58-59	Europe East-Central
60-61	European Russia, Ukraine & Baltic States

ASIA

62	Asia North
63	Russian Federation East
64-65	Russian Federation West
66-67	Asia South
68-69	Asia East

COLLINS

WORLD

POCKET

ATLAS

HarperCollins*Publishers*

Bartholomew
A Division of HarperCollins Publishers
Duncan Street, Edinburgh EH9 1TA

©Bartholomew 1993

First published by Bartholomew 1993
Reprinted 1994
ISBN 0 00 448036 8

Printed in Hong Kong

GH 7453

70-71	Asia Southeast
72-73	China Central
74	Japan & Korea
75	Japan Central
76-77	Burma, Thailand, Indo-China, Malaysia & Singapore
78	Indonesia Central
79	Philippines
80-81	Middle East
82-83	India & West China
84-85	India Northwest & Pakistan
86	India Northeast & Bangladesh
87	India South & Sri Lanka

AFRICA and THE MIDDLE EAST

88-89	Africa
90-91	Iran and The Gulf
92-93	Turkey, Syria & Iraq
94	Israel & Lebanon
95	Africa Northeast
96-97	Africa West
98-99	Africa Central
100-101	Africa South
102-103	Atlantic Ocean

OCEANIA

104-105	Australasia
106-107	Australia
108-109	Australia Southeast
110-111	New Zealand
112	Antarctica
113-192	Index

WORLD Countries

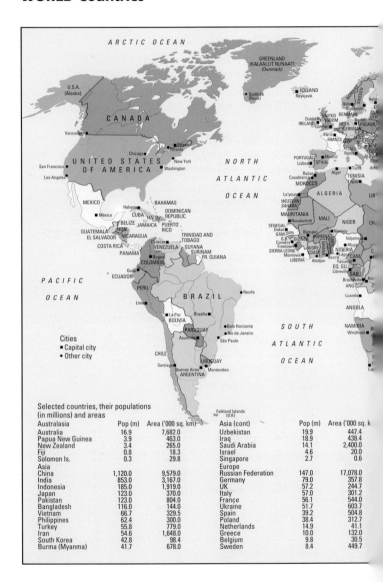

Cities
- ■ Capital city
- ● Other city

Selected countries, their populations (in millions) and areas					
Australasia	Pop (m)	Area ('000 sq. km)	**Asia (cont)**	Pop (m)	Area ('000 sq. k
Australia	16.9	7,682.0	Uzbekistan	19.9	447.4
Papua New Guinea	3.9	463.0	Iraq	18.9	438.4
New Zealand	3.4	265.0	Saudi Arabia	14.1	2,400.0
Fiji	0.8	18.3	Israel	4.6	20.0
Solomon Is.	0.3	29.8	Singapore	2.7	0.6
Asia			**Europe**		
China	1,120.0	9,579.0	Russian Federation	147.0	17,078.0
India	853.0	3,167.0	Germany	79.0	357.8
Indonesia	185.0	1,919.0	UK	57.2	244.7
Japan	123.0	370.0	Italy	57.0	301.2
Pakistan	123.0	804.0	France	56.1	544.0
Bangladesh	116.0	144.0	Ukraine	51.7	603.7
Vietnam	66.7	329.5	Spain	39.2	504.8
Philippines	62.4	300.0	Poland	38.4	312.7
Turkey	55.8	779.0	Netherlands	14.9	41.1
Iran	54.6	1,648.0	Greece	10.0	132.0
South Korea	42.8	98.4	Belgium	9.8	30.5
Burma (Myanma)	41.7	678.0	Sweden	8.4	449.7

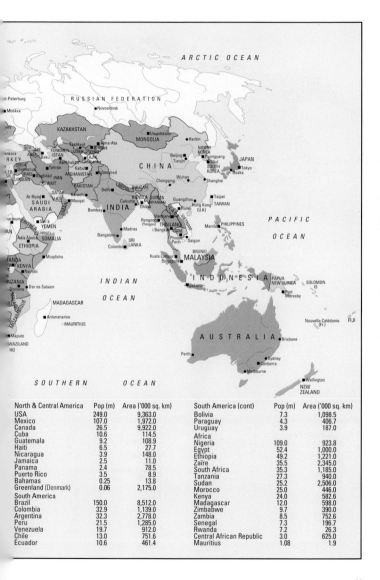

North & Central America	Pop (m)	Area ('000 sq. km)	South America (cont)	Pop (m)	Area ('000 sq. km)
USA	249.0	9,363.0	Bolivia	7.3	1,098.5
Mexico	107.0	1,972.0	Paraguay	4.3	406.7
Canada	26.5	9,922.0	Uruguay	3.9	187.0
Cuba	10.6	114.5	Africa		
Guatemala	9.2	108.9	Nigeria	109.0	923.8
Haiti	6.5	27.7	Egypt	52.4	1,000.0
Nicaragua	3.9	148.0	Ethiopia	49.2	1,221.0
Jamaica	2.5	11.0	Zaire	35.5	2,345.0
Panama	2.4	78.5	South Africa	35.3	1,185.0
Puerto Rico	3.5	8.9	Tanzania	27.3	940.0
Bahamas	0.25	13.8	Sudan	25.2	2,506.0
Greenland (Denmark)	0.06	2,175.0	Morocco	25.0	446.0
South America			Kenya	24.0	582.6
Brazil	150.0	8,512.0	Madagascar	12.0	598.0
Colombia	32.9	1,139.0	Zimbabwe	9.7	390.0
Argentina	32.3	2,778.0	Zambia	8.5	752.6
Peru	21.5	1,285.0	Senegal	7.3	196.7
Venezuela	19.7	912.0	Rwanda	7.2	26.3
Chile	13.0	751.6	Central African Republic	3.0	625.0
Ecuador	10.6	461.4	Mauritius	1.08	1.9

WORLD Cities

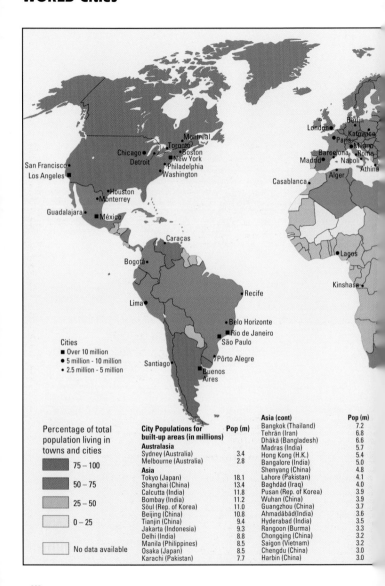

Cities
- ■ Over 10 million
- ● 5 million - 10 million
- ● 2.5 million - 5 million

Percentage of total population living in towns and cities

	75 – 100
	50 – 75
	25 – 50
	0 – 25
	No data available

City Populations for built-up areas (in millions)	Pop (m)
Australasia	
Sydney (Australia)	3.4
Melbourne (Australia)	2.8
Asia	
Tokyo (Japan)	18.1
Shanghai (China)	13.4
Calcutta (India)	11.8
Bombay (India)	11.2
Sôul (Rep. of Korea)	11.0
Beijing (China)	10.8
Tianjin (China)	9.4
Jakarta (Indonesia)	9.3
Delhi (India)	8.8
Manila (Philippines)	8.5
Osaka (Japan)	8.5
Karachi (Pakistan)	7.7

Asia (cont)	Pop (m)
Bangkok (Thailand)	7.2
Tehrān (Iran)	6.8
Dhākā (Bangladesh)	6.6
Madras (India)	5.7
Hong Kong (H.K.)	5.4
Bangalore (India)	5.0
Shenyang (China)	4.8
Lahore (Pakistan)	4.1
Baghdād (Iraq)	4.0
Pusan (Rep. of Korea)	3.9
Wuhan (China)	3.9
Guangzhou (China)	3.7
Ahmadābād(India)	3.6
Hyderabad (India)	3.5
Rangoon (Burma)	3.3
Chongqing (China)	3.2
Saigon (Vietnam)	3.2
Chengdu (China)	3.0
Harbin (China)	3.0

Asia (cont)	Pop (m)	Europe (cont)	Pop (m)	South America	Pop(m)
...i-pei (Taiwan)	3.0	Katowice (Poland)	3.4	São Paulo (Brazil)	17.4
...an (China)	2.9	Berlin (Germany)	3.2	Buenos Aires (Argentina)	11.5
...gapore (Singapore)	2.7	Roma (Italy)	3.1	Rio de Janeiro (Brazil)	10.7
...kara (Turkey)	2.6	Kiyev (Ukraine)	2.6	Lima (Peru)	6.2
...njing (China)	2.6	**North & Central America**		Bogotá (Colombia)	4.9
...ndung (Indonesia)	2.5	México (Mexico)	20.2	Santiago (Chile)	4.7
...ian (China)	2.5	New York (U.S.A.)	16.2	Caracas (Venezuela)	4.1
...gu (Rep. of Korea)	2.5	Los Angeles (U.S.A.)	11.9	Belo Horizonte (Brazil)	3.6
...ope		Chicago (U.S.A.)	7.0	Pôrto Alegre (Brazil)	3.1
...skva (Russ. Fed.)	8.8	Philadelphia (U.S.A.)	4.3	Recife (Brazil)	2.5
...s (France)	8.5	Detroit (U.S.A.)	3.7	**Africa**	
...don (U.K.)	7.4	San Francisco (U.S.A.)	3.7	Cairo (Egypt)	9.0
...nbul (Turkey)	6.7	Toronto (Canada)	3.5	Lagos (Nigeria)	7.7
...ano (Italy)	5.3	Guadalajara (Mexico)	3.2	Alexandria (Egypt)	3.7
...drid (Spain)	5.2	Houston (U.S.A.)	3.0	Kinshasa (Zaïre)	3.5
...kt-Peterburg (Russ. Fed.)	5.1	Monterrey (Mexico)	3.0	Casablanca (Morocco)	3.2
...oli (Italy)	3.6	Montréal (Canada)	3.0	Alger (Algeria)	3.0
...nai (Greece)	3.4	Washington (U.S.A.)	2.9		
...celona (Spain)	3.4	Boston (U.S.A.)	2.8		

WORLD Languages

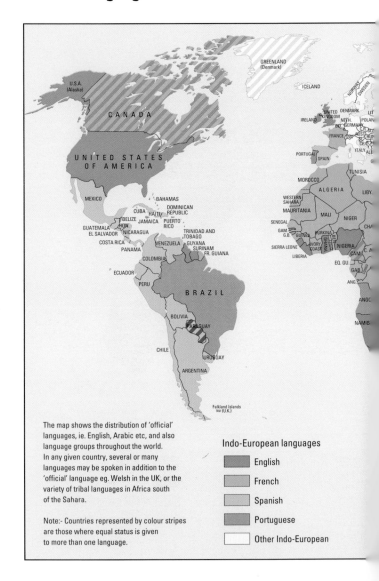

The map shows the distribution of 'official'
languages, ie. English, Arabic etc, and also
language groups throughout the world.
In any given country, several or many
languages may be spoken in addition to the
'official' language eg. Welsh in the UK, or the
variety of tribal languages in Africa south
of the Sahara.

Note:- Countries represented by colour stripes
are those where equal status is given
to more than one language.

Indo-European languages

- English
- French
- Spanish
- Portuguese
- Other Indo-European

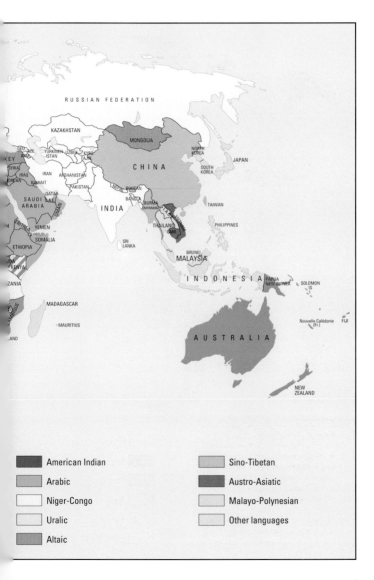

RUSSIAN FEDERATION

KAZAKHSTAN

MONGOLIA

NORTH KOREA

JAPAN

CHINA

SOUTH KOREA

GEO AZE
ARM
TURKMEN
-ISTAN
UZBEK KYRG
TAJI

KEY

SYRIA IRAQ
JORDAN

AFGHANISTAN

IRAN

KUWAIT

QATAR

SAUDI
ARABIA

UAE

OMAN

PAKISTAN

NEPAL BHUTAN

BANGLA

BURMA

MYANMAR

TAIWAN

INDIA

THAILAND LAOS

VIETNAM

CAM

PHILIPPINES

ERITREA

YEMEN

DJIBOUTI

SRI
LANKA

ETHIOPIA

SOMALIA

BRUNEI

MALAYSIA

KENYA

I N D O N E S I A

PAPUA
NEW GUINEA

SOLOMON
IS

ZANIA

MADAGASCAR

MAURITIUS

Nouvelle Calédonie
(Fr.)

FIJI

LAND

A U S T R A L I A

NEW
ZEALAND

	American Indian		Sino-Tibetan
	Arabic		Austro-Asiatic
	Niger-Congo		Malayo-Polynesian
	Uralic		Other languages
	Altaic		

WORLD Economic Groups

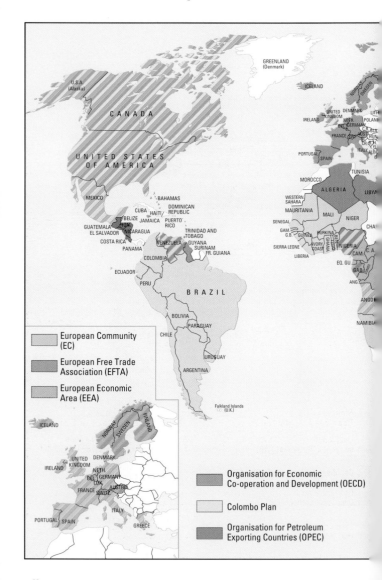

Legend:
- European Community (EC)
- European Free Trade Association (EFTA)
- European Economic Area (EEA)
- Organisation for Economic Co-operation and Development (OECD)
- Colombo Plan
- Organisation for Petroleum Exporting Countries (OPEC)

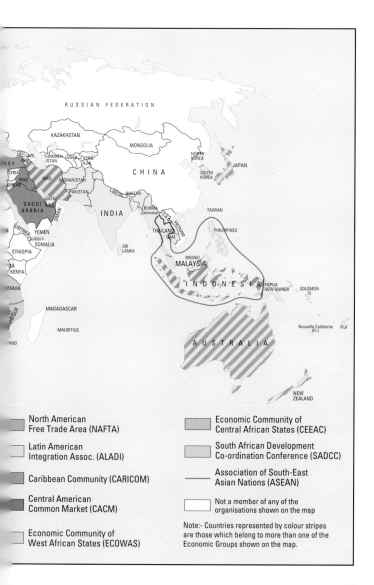

North American
Free Trade Area (NAFTA)

Latin American
Integration Assoc. (ALADI)

Caribbean Community (CARICOM)

Central American
Common Market (CACM)

Economic Community of
West African States (ECOWAS)

Economic Community of
Central African States (CEEAC)

South African Development
Co-ordination Conference (SADCC)

Association of South-East
Asian Nations (ASEAN)

Not a member of any of the
organisations shown on the map

Note:- Countries represented by colour stripes
are those which belong to more than one of the
Economic Groups shown on the map.

WORLD International Organisations

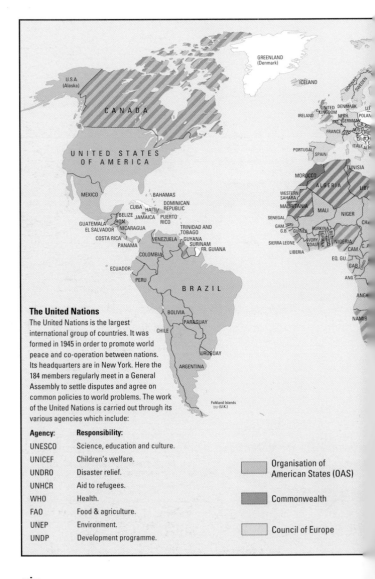

The United Nations

The United Nations is the largest international group of countries. It was formed in 1945 in order to promote world peace and co-operation between nations. Its headquarters are in New York. Here the 184 members regularly meet in a General Assembly to settle disputes and agree on common policies to world problems. The work of the United Nations is carried out through its various agencies which include:

Agency:	Responsibility:
UNESCO	Science, education and culture.
UNICEF	Children's welfare.
UNDRO	Disaster relief.
UNHCR	Aid to refugees.
WHO	Health.
FAO	Food & agriculture.
UNEP	Environment.
UNDP	Development programme.

Organisation of American States (OAS)

Commonwealth

Council of Europe

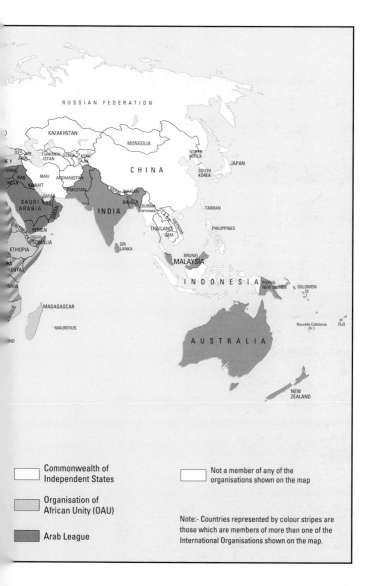

RUSSIAN FEDERATION

KAZAKHSTAN

MONGOLIA

GEO
RGIA
EY
TURKMEN-
ISTAN
UZBEK
ISTAN
KYRG-
TAJIK
NORTH
KOREA
JAPAN

SYRIA
IRAQ
IRAN
AFGHANISTAN
CHINA
SOUTH
KOREA

KUWAIT
PAKISTAN
NEPAL
BHUTAN
TAIWAN

QATAR
UAE
BANGLA
BURMA
MYANMAR

SAUDI
ARABIA
OMAN
INDIA
LAOS
VIETNAM
PHILIPPINES

ERITREA
YEMEN
DJIBOUTI
SOMALIA
THAILAND
CAM.

ETHIOPIA
SRI
LANKA

KENYA
BRUNEI
MALAYSIA

ANIA
INDONESIA
PAPUA
NEW GUINEA
SOLOMON
IS

MADAGASCAR

MAURITIUS
Nouvelle Calédonie
(Fr.)
FIJI

IND
AUSTRALIA

NEW
ZEALAND

	Commonwealth of Independent States		Not a member of any of the organisations shown on the map

Organisation of
African Unity (OAU)

Arab League

Note:- Countries represented by colour stripes are
those which are members of more than one of the
International Organisations shown on the map.

SYMBOLS

BOUNDARIES

~~	International
— — — —	International under Dispute
· · · · · ·	Cease Fire Line
————	Autonomous or State
————	Administrative
— — — —	Maritime (National)

LETTERING STYLES

CANADA	Independent Nation
FLORIDA	State, Province or Autonomous Region
Gibraltar (U.K.)	Sovereignty of Dependent Territory
Lothian	Administrative Area
LANGUEDOC	Historic Region
Loire **Vosges**	Physical Feature or Physical Region

TOWNS AND CITIES

Square Symbols denote capital cities. Each settlement is given a symbol according to its relative importance, with type size to match.

■	●	**New York**	Major City
■	●	**Montréal**	City
□	○	Ottawa	Small City
■	●	**Québec**	Large Town
□	○	St John's	Town
□	○	Yorkton	Small Town
□	○	Jasper	Village
			Built-up-area

LAKE FEATURES

	Permanent
	Seasonal

OTHER FEATURES

~~	River
·~·~·~·	Seasonal River
=	Pass, Gorge
~~	Dam, Barrage
~~	Waterfall, Rapid
————	Aqueduct
· · · · ·	Reef
▲ *4231*	Summit, Peak
· *.217*	Spot Height, Depth
◡	Well
◬	Oil Field
▲	Gas Field
—·—·— *Gas / Oil*	Oil/Natural Gas Pipeline
Gensbok Nat. Pk	National Park
UR	Historic Site
————	Main Railway
————	Other Railway
– – – –	Under Construction
—•—···—•—	Rail Tunnel
– · – · – ·	Rail Ferry
·····•·····	Canal
⊕	International Airport
✦	Other Airport

For pages 102-103, 104-105 only:

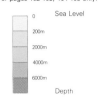

0	Sea Level
200m	
2000m	
4000m	
6000m	Depth

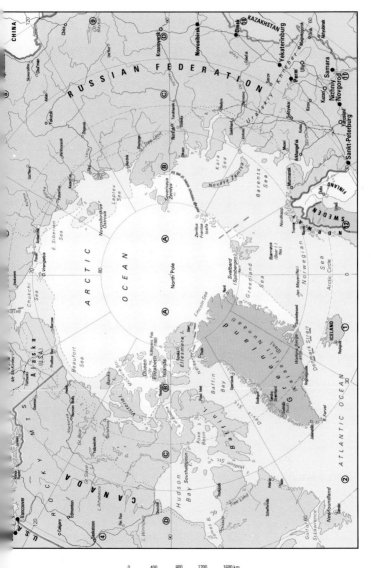

0   400   800   1200   1600 km
0   400   800 mls

NORTH AMERICA

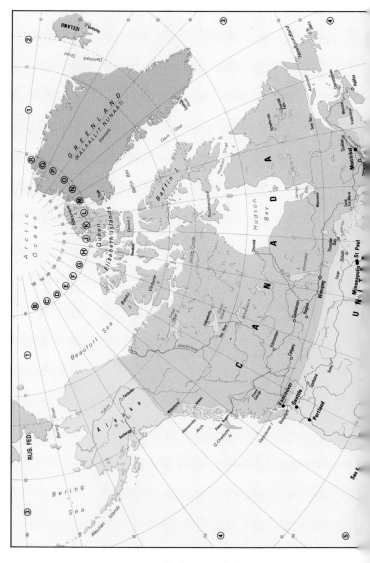

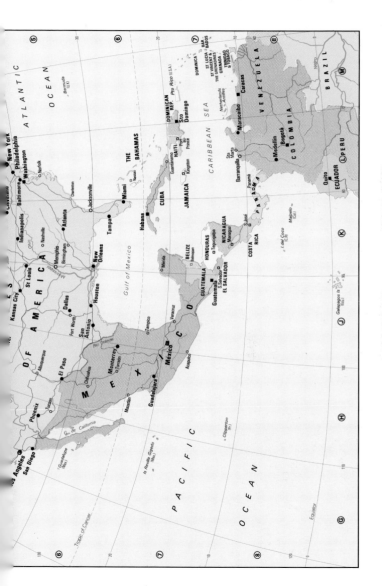

3

CANADA WEST

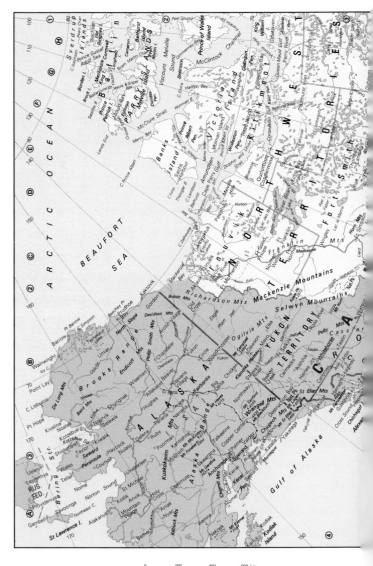

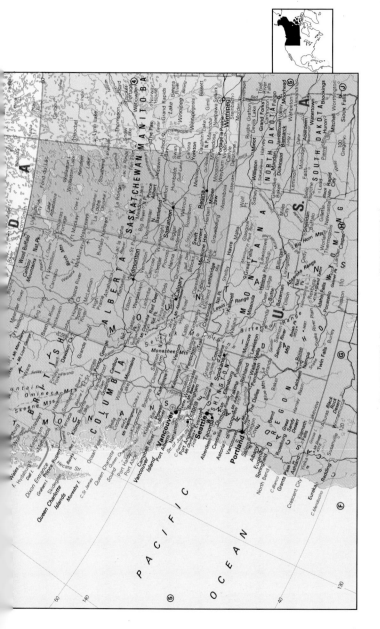

CANADA EAST

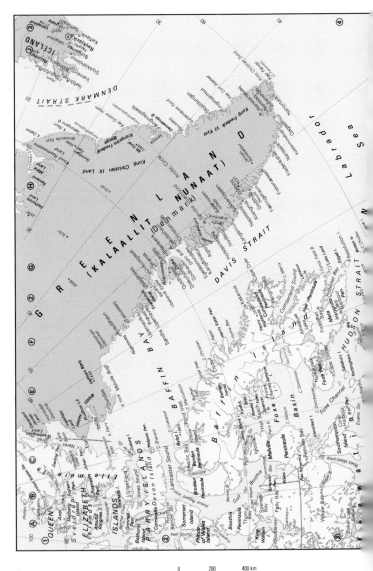

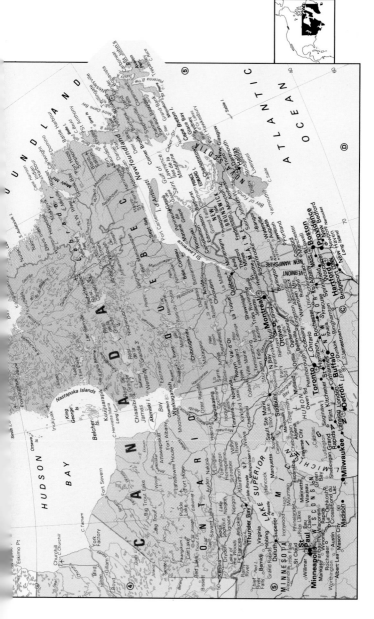

7

USA WEST

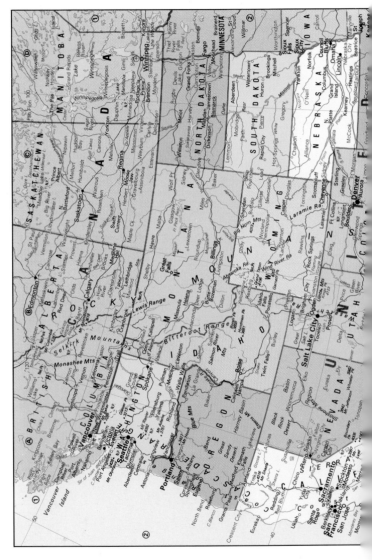

0   100   200   300   400km
0   100   200 mls

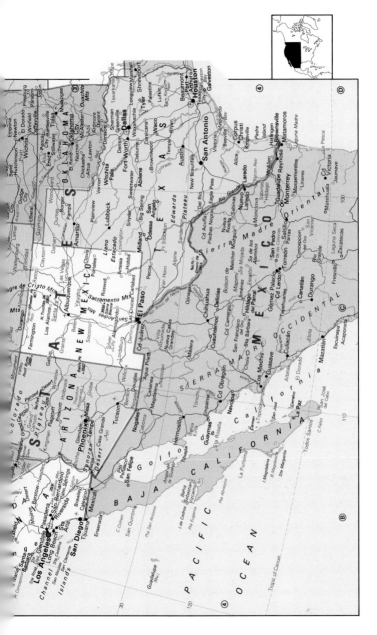

9

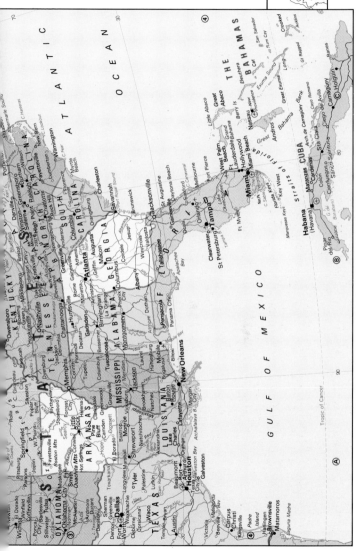

ATLANTIC OCEAN

THE BAHAMAS

Little Abaco
Great Abaco
Grand Bahama
Berry Is
Nassau New Providence
Great Bahama Bank
Andros
Eleuthera
Cat
San Salvador
Rum Cay
Long
Great Exuma
Crooked
Acklins
Gt Ragged
Exuma Sound

Albemarle Sound
C Hatteras
C Lookout
Portsmouth
Washington
Goldsboro
Greensboro
New Bern
C Fear
Wilmington
Fayetteville
Myrtle Beach
Lumberton
Charleston
Florence
Sumter
Wilmington
Danville
Durham
Raleigh
Chapel Hill
High Point
Winston-Salem
Greensboro
NORTH CAROLINA
SOUTH CAROLINA
Columbia
Anderson
Charlotte
Gastonia
Greenville
Spartanburg
Bristol
Middlesboro
KENTUCKY
Bowling Green
Owensboro
Paducah
Cairo
Cape Girardeau
Sikeston
TENNESSEE
Nashville
Knoxville
Chattanooga
Cleveland
Huntsville
Memphis
Dyersburg
Jackson
Corinth
Tupelo
Columbus
Decatur
Florence
Gadsden
Birmingham
Bessemer
Tuscaloosa
ALABAMA
Anniston
Rome
Marietta
Atlanta
Athens
Gainesville
Augusta
Macon
Columbus
Griffin
La Grange
GEORGIA
Albany
Waycross
Valdosta
Savannah
Brunswick
Jacksonville
St Augustine
Gainesville
Ocala
Daytona Beach
Sanford
Orlando
Melbourne
Ft Pierce
West Palm Beach
Hollywood
Ft Lauderdale
Miami
Miami Beach
Key West
Florida Keys
Clearwater
St Petersburg
Tampa
FLORIDA
Tallahassee
Cordele
Dothan
Panama City
Pensacola
Mobile
Biloxi
Hattiesburg
Laurel
Meridian
MISSISSIPPI
Jackson
Greenville
Greenwood
Clarksdale
Vicksburg
Natchez
Brookhaven
McComb
Bogalusa
LOUISIANA
Baton Rouge
New Orleans
Lafayette
Lake Charles
Morgan City
Alexandria
Natchitoches
Shreveport
Monroe
Bastrop
El Dorado
Camden
Hope
Hot Springs
Pine Bluff
Little Rock
Conway
Searcy
Helena
Forrest City
Blytheville
ARKANSAS
Ouachita Mtrs
Boston Mtrs
Fayetteville
Fort Smith
Muskogee
Durant
OKLAHOMA
Oklahoma City
Norman
Ada
Ardmore
Lawton
Stillwater
Ponca City
Bartlesville
Tulsa
Wichita
Winfield
Coffeyville
Parsons
Joplin
Springfield
W Plains
Rolla
El Dorado
Pittsburg
Sherman
Denton
Fort Worth
Dallas
Waxahachie
Tyler
Longview
Marshall
Texarkana
Palestine
Lufkin
TEXAS
Waco
Temple
Austin
Bryan
Beaumont
Port Arthur
Orange
Houston
Galveston
Victoria
Corpus Christi
Beeville
Kingsville
Padre Island
Brownsville
Harlingen
Matamoros
Sierra Madre

GULF OF MEXICO

Tropic of Cancer

Straits of Florida
CUBA
Habana (Havana)
Matanzas
Cárdenas
Pinar del Río
Colón
Cienfuegos
Sta Clara
Sancti Spíritus
Ciego de Ávila
Camagüey
Holguín
Banes

11

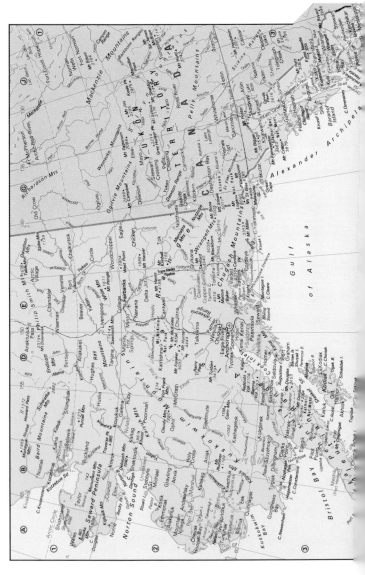

0   100   200 km
0   100 mls

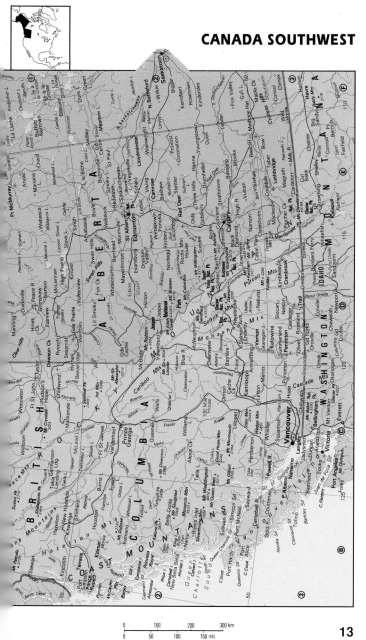

0   100   200   300 km
0   50   100   150 mls

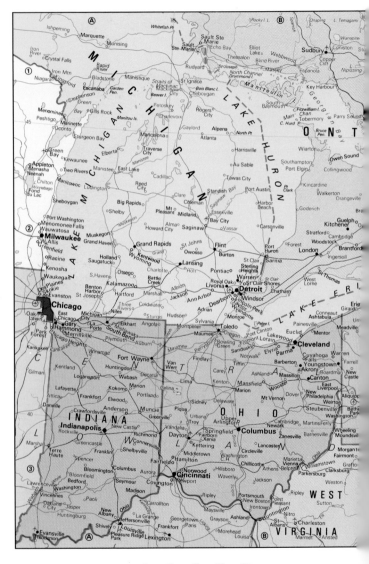

| 0 | 50 | 100 | 150 | 200 km |

| 0 | 50 | 100 mls |

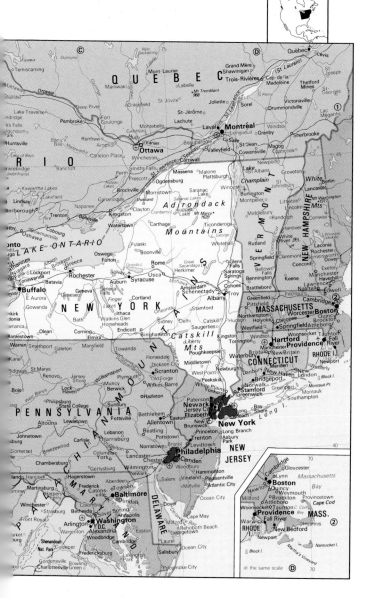

QUEBEC

St. Laurent

Québec
Lévis
St. Joseph

Grand'Mère
Shawinigan
Trois-Rivières
Cap-de-la-
Madeleine
Thetford
Mines
St.
Georges

Mont-Laurier
Maniwaki
Labelle
Mt Tremblant
St Jovite
St-Jérôme
Joliette
Sorel
Drummondville
Victoriaville
Lac
Mégantic

Réo.
Rackatoang
75

O N T A R I O

Deep River
Fort
Coulonge
Pembroke
Renfrew
Amprior
Carleton Place
Winchester
Lachute
Montebello
Buckingham
Gatineau
Ottawa
Laval Montréal
Longueuil Granby
Sherbrooke

St-Jean
Cowansville
Windsor
Magog
Newport
Dixville

Beauharnois
Valleyfield

Lawrence Seaway
Cornwall
Massena
Malone
Plattsburgh

St Albans
St Johnsbury
Groveton

White
Mts
Berlin
Lancaster

NEW HAMPSHIRE

Perth
Smiths Falls
Prescott
Brockville
Morristown
Ogdensburg

Lake
Champlain
Burlington
Middlebury
Montpelier
Randolph

Littleton
Mt Washington
6288
Conway

Laconia
Rochester
Dover

Kingston
Napanee
Clayton
Cranberry L
Tupper
Lake

Adirondack

Mountains
Mt Marcy
1629
Ticonderoga
L George
Whitehall
Rutland

Hanover
White
River Jct.

Concord

Exeter
Manchester
Nashua
Lowell

LAKE ONTARIO

Oswego
Fulton
Rome
Herkimer
Great
Sacandaga L

Glens
Falls
Saratoga
Springs

Bellows
Falls
Claremont

Keene

Brattleboro
Greenfield
Pittsfield
Northampton
Holyoke
Westfield
Springfield

Fitchburg
Cambridge Boston
Worcester
Chicopee
Amherst

MASSACHUSETTS

Rochester
Geneva
Seneca Falls
Auburn
Syracuse
Solvay
Oneida L.
Utica
Mohawk R.
Amsterdam
Schenectady Troy
Cohoes
Albany

Batavia
Buffalo
E. Aurora
Gowanda
Geneseo
Bath
Finger
Lakes
Cortland
Oneonta
Stamford

Hudson
Catskill
Saugerties

Torrington
Windsor
Hartford
New Britain
Waterbury
Meriden

Providence
Attleboro
Taunton
Fall River

RHODE I.
Westerly

Olean
Corning
Elmira
Watkins Glen
Horseheads
Endicott
Binghamton
Liberty

Catskill
Mts
Poughkeepsie
Middletown
West Point
Newburgh
Peekskill
White Plains

New Haven
New London
Block I.

CONNECTICUT

Bridgeport
Norwalk
Stamford
Greenwich
Greenport
Montauk Pt
Montauk
Southampton

Honesdale
Dickson City
Scranton
Old Forge
Wilkes-Barre
Berwick
Hazleton

Paterson
Jersey City
Newark
Elizabeth
New
Brunswick
Long I.
Bay
Shore

PENNSYLVANIA
Bethlehem
Allentown

New York
Long Beach
Asbury
Park
Long Branch

Princeton
Trenton
Levittown
Reading
Pottstown
Norristown

NEW
JERSEY

40

Lancaster
Columbia
Chester
Bristol
Philadelphia
Camden
Woodbury

Hammonton
Vineland
Pleasantville
Atlantic City

Gettysburg
York
Wilmington
Newark
Salem
Millville

Ocean City

DELAWARE

Baltimore
Dundalk
Aberdeen
Towson

Dover
Milford

Cape May
Rehoboth Beach
Georgetown

Bethesda
Silver Spring
Arlington
Washington
D.C.
Alexandria
Woodbridge

Annapolis
Cambridge
Laurel
Salisbury

Ocean City
Pocomoke City

Cambridge
Gloucester
Lynn
Boston
Quincy
Weymouth
Brockton
Provincetown
Cape Cod

MASS.

Milford
Woonsocket
Attleboro
Taunton Cape Cod
Providence Bay
Warwick
Fall River
New Bedford
Hyannis

RHODE
Newport
Block I.
Martha's Vineyard
Nantucket I.

at the same scale

70
70

15

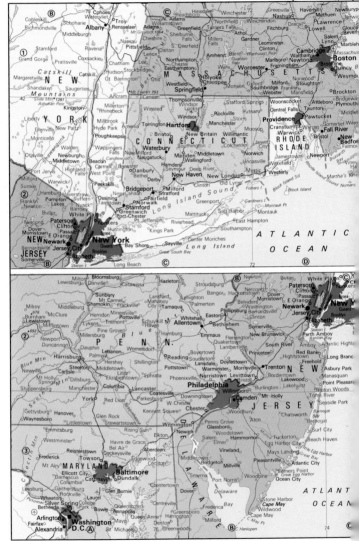

0 25 50 75 100 km
0 25 50 mils

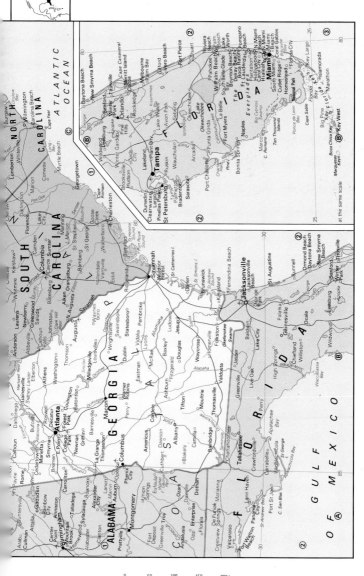

USA SOUTH-CENTRAL

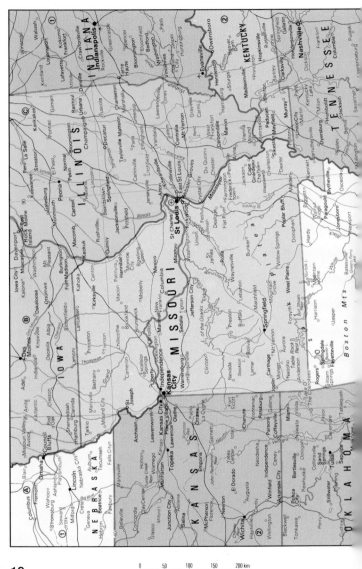

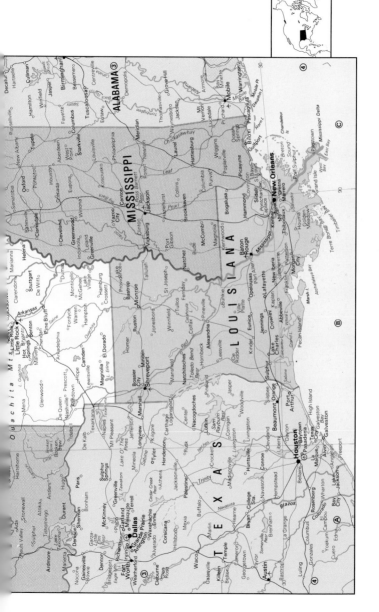

USA NORTHWEST

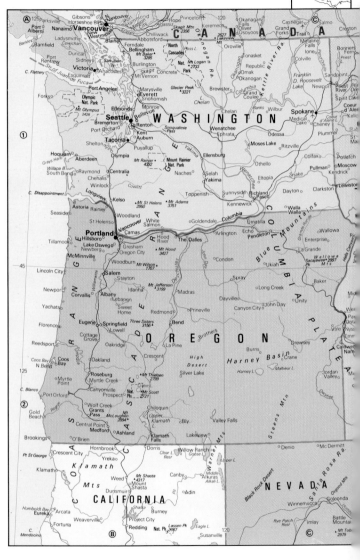

USA San Francisco & Los Angeles

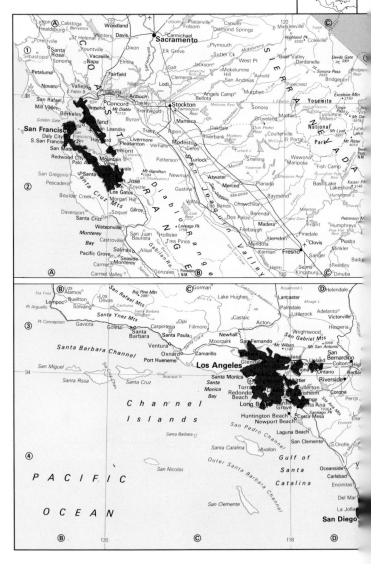

0   25   50   75   100 km
0   25   50 mls

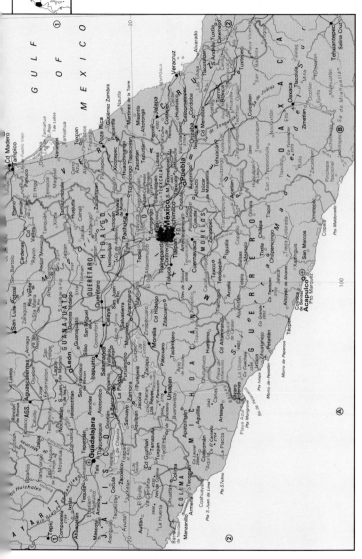

MEXICO CENTRAL

23

MEXICO & CENTRAL AMERICA

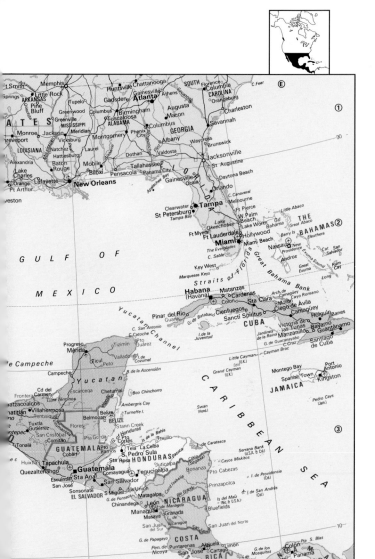

Ft Smith
Memphis
Huntsville Chattanooga
SOUTH
Florence
C. Fear
Springs
Little Rock
Tupelo
Gadsden
Athens
Columbia
Orangeburg
E

ARKANSAS
Pine
Bluff
Greenwood
Columbus
Birmingham
Augusta
Macon
CAROLINA
Charleston
①

reveport
Monroe
Jackson
Greenville
Tuscaloosa
ALABAMA
Columbus
GEORGIA
Savannah

LOUISIANA
MISSISSIPPI
Meridian
Montgomery
Albany

Vicksburg
Natchez
Hattiesburg
Laurel
Dothan
Waycross
Brunswick

Alexandria
Baton
Rouge
Mobile
Tallahassee
Panama City
Valdosta
Jacksonville
St Augustine
30

Lake
Charles
Lafayette
Biloxi
Pensacola
Apalach. Bay
Gainesville
Ocala
Daytona Beach

Orange
Pt Arthur
New Orleans
Orlando
C. Canaveral

veston

G U L F   O F
Clearwater
St Petersburg
Tampa Bay
Tampa
Ft Pierce
W Palm
Beach
Lake Worth
C. Canaveral
Melbourne

Ft Myers
Lake
Okeechobee
Gd
Bahama
Little Abaco
Great Abaco
THE
BAHAMAS
②

M E X I C O
Ft Lauderdale
Hollywood
Miami Beach
Berry Is.
New
Providence
Nassau
Eleuthera

The Everglades
Miami
Andros
Great
Exuma
Cat
San
Salvador

C. Sable
Exuma Sound

Key West
Marquesas Keys
Straits of Florida
Great Bahama Bank
Rum
Cay

Long

Habana
(Havana)
Matanzas
Cardenas
Arch. de
Camagüey
Cayo Romano

G U L F   O F
Pinar del Rio
Guane
Colon
Cienfuegos
Sta Clara
Morón
Ciego de Avila
Camagüey
Holguín

M E X I C O
Yucatan
G. de Batabanó
Sancti Spiritus
CUBA
Victoria de
las Tunas
Banes
Bayamo
G. Guantánamo

C. San Antonio
C. Catoche
I.de la
Juventud
Jardines
de la Reina
Manzanillo
Sta
Cruz
G. de Guacanayabo
Santiago
de Cuba

Progreso
Mérida
Tizimin
Juárez
Cayman Brac
Port
Antonio

Valladolid
I. de
Cozumel
Little Cayman
(U.K.)
Montego Bay
Spanish Town
Kingston

Campeche
Ticul
Peto
Grand Cayman
(U.K.)
JAMAICA

de Campeche
Y u c a t a n
B. de la Ascensión
Pedro Cays
(Jam.)

Cd del
Carmen
Escárcega
Chetumal
Bco Chinchorro
C A R I B B E A N
③

Los Términos
Ambergris Cay

atzacoalcos
Villahermosa
Frontera
Turneffe I.
Swan
(Hond.)
Serrana Bank
(U.S.A. & Col.)

o
Pto
Tuxtla
Gutiérrez
San Cristóbal
Comitán
Flores
Belmopan
BELIZE
Belize
Stann Creek
G. of
Honduras
Pto
Cortés
de la Bahía
Trujillo
C. de Caratasca

Tonalá
GUATEMALA
Pta Gorda
Tela
La Ceiba
S. Pedro
Sula
de Caratasca
S E A

Huixtla
Tapachula
Cobán
Pto
Barrios
Sta Rosa
HONDURAS
Juticalpa
Cayos Miskitos

Quezaltenango
Guatemala
Comayagua
Tegucigalpa
Coco o Segovia
Bonanza
Pto Cabezas

Escuintla
Sta Ana
San Salvador
Matagalpa
Grande
I. de Providencia
(Col.)

San José
EL SALVADOR
S Miguel La Unión
Chinandega
León
L. de Managua
NICARAGUA
I. de San Andrés
(Col.)

Sonsonate
G. de Fonseca
Masaya
Managua
L. de
Nicaragua
San Juan del Norte

San Juan
del Sur
Granada
COSTA
San Juan

G. de Papagayo
Pen. de
Nicoya
Puntarenas
Alajuela
San José
Cartago
Limón
G. de los
Mosquitos
Colón
Pta S. Blas
Panamá

RICA
La Chorrera
Arch. de
las Perlas
④

Pen. de Osa
David
Santiago
Chitré
Golfo
de
Panamá

G. Dulce
Pto
Armuelles
Pto Cortés
de
Chiriquí
Pen.
de Azuero
Pta
Solano

90
D
E

25

CARIBBEAN

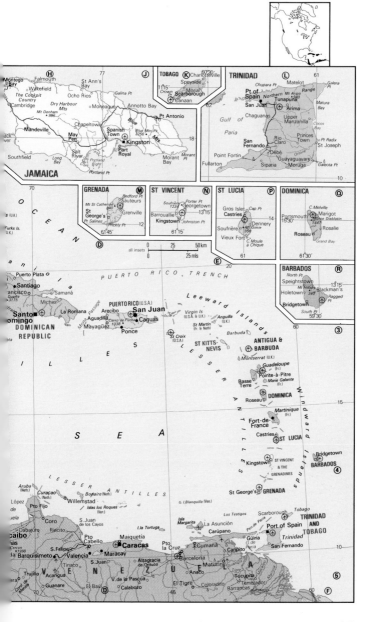

JAMAICA

TOBAGO

TRINIDAD

GRENADA
ST VINCENT
ST LUCIA
DOMINICA

BARBADOS

all insets
0   25   50 km
0   25 mls

PUERTO RICO TRENCH

Leeward Islands

DOMINICAN
REPUBLIC

PUERTO RICO (U.S.A.)
San Juan

ANTIGUA &
BARBUDA
Montserrat (U.K.)

Guadeloupe (Fr.)
Pointe-à-Pitre
Basse-Terre
Marie Galante

Roseau DOMINICA

Martinique (Fr.)
Fort-de-France
Castries ST LUCIA

Kingstown ST VINCENT
& THE
GRENADINES

St George's GRENADA

Bridgetown
BARBADOS

C   A   R   I   B   B   E   A   N   S   E   A

LESSER   ANTILLES

Aruba (Neth.)   Curaçao (Neth.)
Bonaire (Neth.)
Willemstad   Isles los Roques (Ven.)

I.Blanquilla (Ven.)

Los Testigos
Isla
Margarita La Asunción
I.la Tortuga

Scarborough   Tobago
Port of Spain TRINIDAD
AND
TOBAGO
Trinidad
San Fernando

VENEZUELA

27

SOUTH AMERICA

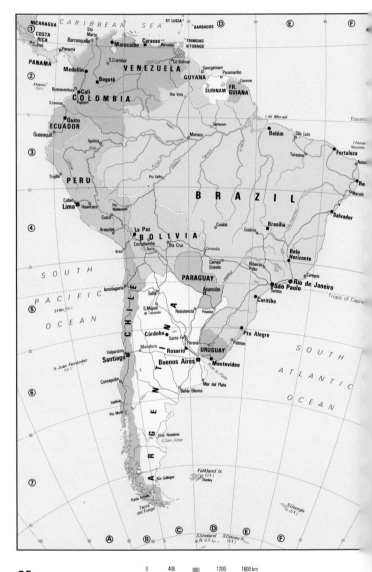

| 0 | 400 | 800 | 1200 | 1600 km |
| 0 | 400 | | 800 mls | |

Brasília · Ceres · Jaraguá · Pirenópolis · Anápolis · Goiânia · GOIÁS · Goiás · Rio Verde · Novas · Catalão · Itumbiara · Uberlândia · Uberaba · Ituiuba · Mineiros · Jataí

SÃO PAULO · Franca · Ribeirão Preto · Araraquara · Bauru · Marília · Assis · Sorocaba · Campinas · Jundiaí · Santos · São Paulo · Piracicaba · Limeira

PARANÁ · Londrina · Maringá · Cascavel · Toledo · Guarapuava · Ponta Grossa · Curitiba · Paranaguá

SANTA CATARINA · Joinville · Blumenau · Florianópolis · Lajes · Tubarão · Criciúma

RIO GRANDE DO SUL · Passo Fundo · Cruz Alta · Sta Maria · N. Hamburgo · Caxias do Sul · Porto Alegre · Pelotas · Bagé

MATO GROSSO · Cuiabá · Cáceres · Rondonópolis

MATO GROSSO DO SUL · Corumbá · Aquidauana · Campo Grande · Dourados · Jardim · Ponta Porã

BRAZIL · Planalto de Mato Grosso

BOLIVIA · Trinidad · Santa Cruz · Cochabamba · Sucre · Potosí · Oruro · La Paz · Tarija · Villamontes · Camiri

PARAGUAY · Asunción · Concepción · San Pedro · Pedro J. Caballero · Pilar · Filadelfia · Fuerte Olimpo

CHACO · GRAN CHACO · Formosa · Resistencia · Corrientes · Posadas · Encarnación

ARGENTINA · Salta · Jujuy · San Salvador · Orán · Tucumán · Santiago del Estero · Catamarca · La Rioja · Córdoba · Santa Fe · Paraná · Concordia · Rafaela

CHILE · Antofagasta · Iquique · Tocopilla · Calama · Copiapó · La Serena · Coquimbo · Ovalle · Arica · Tacna · Mejillones

CORDILLERA DE LOS ANDES · Desierto de Atacama

Arequipa · Nazca · Moquegua · Juliaca

Tropic of Capricorn

Islas Juan Fernández · Alejandro Selkirk · Robinson Crusoe

0   200   400   600 km
0   100   200   300 mls

C. Maguariпho
B. de Marajó
I. de Marajó
Salinópolis
Bragança
Pará
Capanema
Belém
Abaetetuba
Pinheiro
Alcântara
São Luís
Rosário
Parnaíba
Camocim
Acaraú
Monção
Chapadinha
Itapipoca
Caucaia
Bacabal
Coroatá
Sobral
Piripiri
Sta
Quitéria
Fortaleza (Ceará)
Codó
Caxias
Campo
Maior
Nova
Russas
Canindé
Aracati
Teresina
Castelo
Crateús
Quixadá
Areia Branca
Mombaça
Acopiara
Patu
Mossoró
PARÁ
MARANHÃO
Grajaú
Floriano
Oeiras
Picos
J. do Norte
Crateús
Sá
Sousa
Patos
Caicó
Natal
Imperatriz
PIAUI
PARAÍBA
Cabedelo
João Pessoa
Campina Grande
Marabá
Pto Franco
Carolina
Balsas
S.Raimundo
Nonato
Paulistana
Ouricuri
Salgueiro
Talhada
Limoeiro
Caruaru
Recife
(Pernambuco)
Araguaína
Petrolina
Juazeiro
Garanhuns
Palmares
Araguaia
Sen.do Bonfim
Cach. do
Afonso
Propriá
Penedo
Maceió
BRAZIL
TOCANTINS
Barra
Jacobina
Lagarto
Arapiraca
SERGIPE
Aracajú
Estância
BAHIA
Ibotirama
R.deJacuípe
Serrinha
Barreiras
Bom Jesus
da Lapa
Iaçu
Feira de S.
Cachoeira
Castro
Alves
Salvador (Bahia)
Valença
Caetité
Jequié
Ipiaú
Ilhéus
GOIÁS
Januária
Vitória da
Conquista
Itabuna
Ceres
Formosa
Jaraguá
Brasília
Porteirinha
Itapetinga
Canavieiras
Anápolis
Pirenópolis
São Francisco
Salinas
Belmonte
ATLANTIC
OCEAN
Goiânia
Montes Claros
Araçuaí
Pôrto Seguro
Caldas
Novas
Paracatu
Piraporá
Sa do Chifre
Itamaraju
Rio Verde
João
Pinheiro
Teófilo Otôni
Nanuque
Itumbiara
Quandira
Catalão
Diamantina
Gov.
Valadares
São Mateus
Araguari
Patos
de Minas
Corinto
Barragem de
São Simão
MINAS
GERAIS
Itabira
ESPIRITO
Fabriciano
Linhares
Uberlândia
Uberaba
Sete Lagoas
Manhuaçu
Cariacica
SANTO
Barragem Água
Araxá
Belo
Horizonte
Carátinga
Colatina
Vila Velha
Franca
Divinópolis
Con.
Lafaiete
Ponte Nova
Vitória
R. Preto
Barretos
Passos
S.João del Rei
Carangola
Cachoeiro de Itapemirim
Catanduva
Ribeirão Prêto
Poços de
Caldas
Lavras
Barbacena
Itaperuna
Araraquara
São Carlos
Pocos de
Caldas
Juiz
de Fora
S.João da Barra
SÃO PAULO
Marília
Limeira
Mantiqueira
Volta
Redonda
Nova
Friburgo
Campos
Bauru
Piracicaba
Jundiaí
Campinas
Barra
Mansa
Petrópolis
Magé
Sorocaba
São Paulo
Niterói
Itapeva
Itapetininga
Santos
Rio de Janeiro
Tropic of Capricorn
Itararé
Juquiá
São Vicente
Itanhaém
Iguape
Curitiba
Paranaguá
São Francisco do Sul

SOUTH AMERICA NORTH

GRENADA
I. de Margarita
St George's
La Asunción de Paria
Carúpano Güiria
mana
Trinidad
Cariaco
Caripito
Maturín
aco
Trucupita
Tigre
Barrancas
Cd Bolívar
Orinoco
Cd Guayana
Upata
Mabaruma
Cd Piar
Emb de
Gur
La Paragua
El Dorado
UELA
Salto
del Ángel
La Gran
Roraima
2780
Sabana
Sta Elena
Sa Pacaraima
Bonfim
Boa Vista
Lethem
RORAIMA
Caracaraí
ucuara
Branco
Negro
Tefé
Z O N A S
A S I L
Madeira
 brea
Humaitá
Prainha
Porto Velho
Aripuanã
rá-Mirim
Rondônia
O N D Ô N I A
Serra dos
Guaporé
Vilhena
I A
Itenez
inidad
Mato Grosso
M A T O   G R O S S O

The Grenadines
Tobago
TRINIDAD
AND
TOBAGO
Port of
Spain
San Fernando

A T L A N T I C

O C E A N

Charity
Suddie
Leguan I.
V-en Hoop
Georgetown
Bartica
New Amsterdam
Linden
Nieuw Amsterdam
Nieuw Nickerie
Paramaribo
Totness
Marienburg
Albina
Apoera
Witagron
Blommesteinmeer
Sinnamary
I du Diable (Devil's I.)
Kourou
Cayenne
GUYANA
SURINAM
Juliantop
1280
FRENCH
GUIANA
Cabo Orange
Oiapoque

Sa Tumucumaque
Serra Tumucumaque
Amapá
Ilha de Maracá
Sa do Navio
Macapá
Pto Santana
C. Maguarinho
Salinópolis
Bragança
Capanema
I. de Marajó
B. de Marajó
Pará
Belém
Abaetetuba
Cametá
AMAPÁ

Oriximiná
Óbidos
Amazonas
Santarém
Monte
Alegre
Manaus
Manacapuru
Careiro
Itacoatiara
Aveiro
Altamira
Tucuruí
Itaituba
Pimenta
P A R Á
Xingu
Tocantins
Maicurú
Paru
Tapajós

Jacareacanga
S. Félix
Marabá
Imperatriz
Pto
Franco
Araguaína
Carolina

Serra do Cachimbo
Cachimbo
C. do Araguaia

Sa dos Caiabis
Teles Pires
Sa   d o s   p a r e c i s
São Félix
TOCANTINS
Tocantins
Ilha do Bananal

Sa Formosa
Pto Artur
G R O S S O
Aruanã
G O I Á S
Araguaia
Uruaçu

33

CENTRAL ARGENTINA

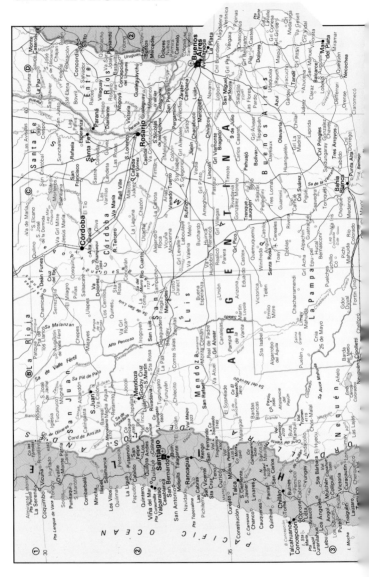

0   100 km
0   50 mls

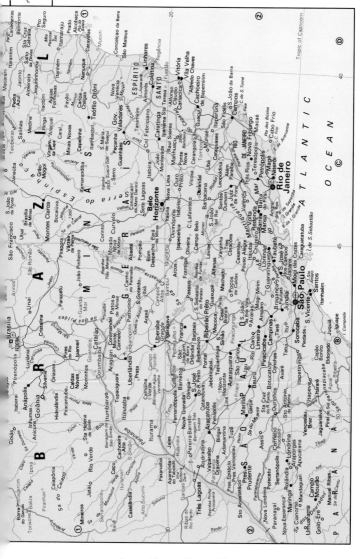

EUROPE

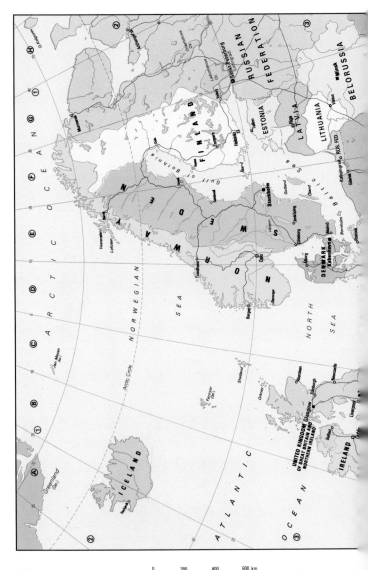

0   200   400   600 km
0   100   200   300 mils

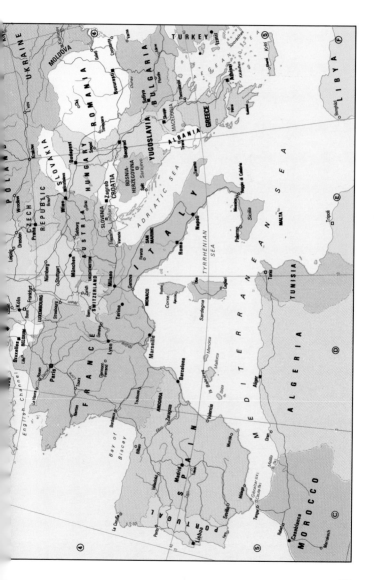

SCANDINAVIA

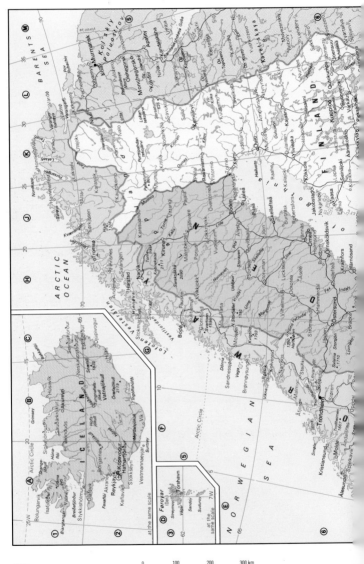

| 0 | 100 | 200 | 300 km |
| 0 | 50 | 100 | 150 mils |

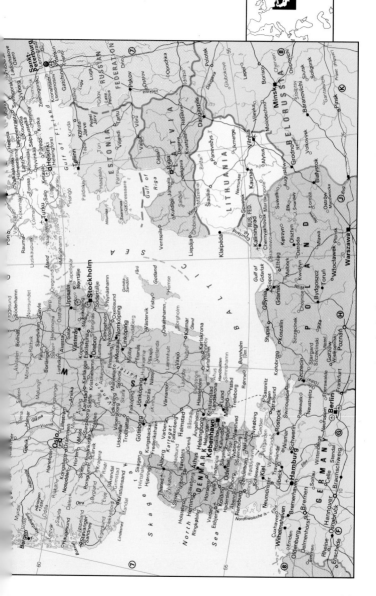

BRITISH ISLES

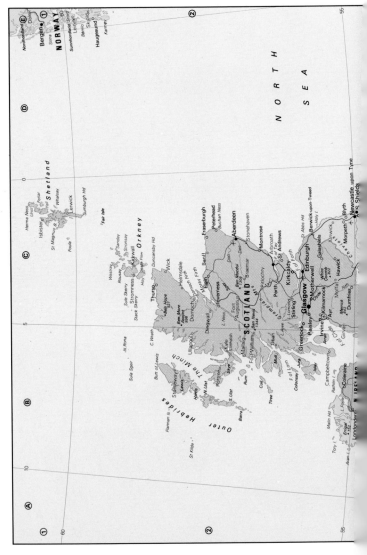

0   50   100   150   200 km
0   50   100 mils

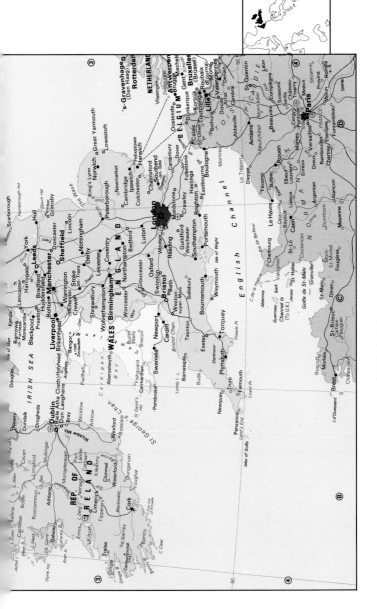

ENGLAND & WALES

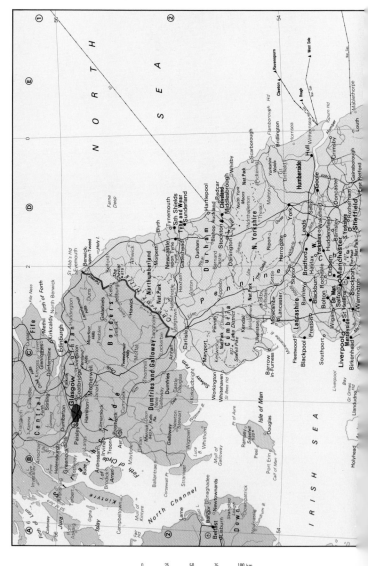

0   25   50   75   100 km
0   25   50 mls

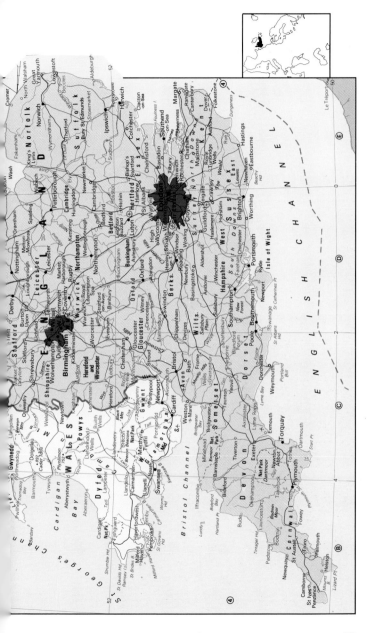

43

SCOTLAND NORTH

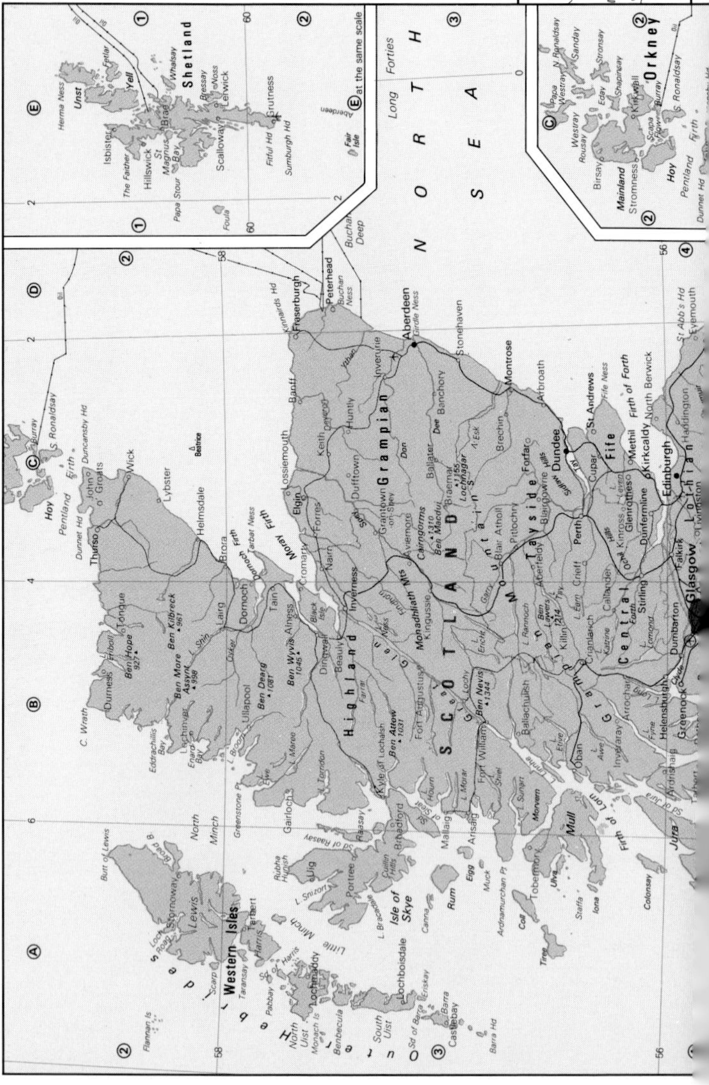

NORTH SEA

Shetland — Unst, Yell, Whalsay, Bressay, Lerwick, Hillswick, Scalloway, Sumburgh Hd, Fitful Hd, Hermaness, Foula, Papa Stour, The Faether, Fair Isle

Orkney — Mainland, Hoy, Stromness, Kirkwall, Scapa Flow, Pentland Firth, Dunnet Hd, Westray, Sanday, Stronsay, Rousay, North Ronaldsay, South Ronaldsay, Papa Westray, Eday, Burray

Long Forties

Buchan Deep

Peterhead, Fraserburgh, Buchan Ness, Kinnairds Hd, Rattray Hd, Aberdeen, Girdle Ness, Stonehaven, Montrose, Arbroath, St Andrews, Fife Ness, Firth of Forth, North Berwick, Dunbar, Eyemouth, St Abb's Hd, Haddington, Edinburgh, Firth of Forth

Hoy, Duncansby Hd, S Ronaldsay, Pentland Firth, Wick, Thurso, Lybster, Helmsdale, Brora, Dornoch Firth, Tain, Cromarty Firth, Cromarty, Nairn, Inverness, Lossiemouth, Buckie, Keith, Elgin, Huntly, Turriff, Banff, Dufftown, Don, Dee, Ballater, Banchory, Brechin, Forfar, Blairgowrie, Perth, Dundee, Glenrothes, Kirkcaldy, Dunfermline, Methil, Stirling, Falkirk, Glasgow, Greenock, Dumbarton, Helensburgh

GRAMPIAN
HIGHLAND
TAYSIDE
CENTRAL
SCOTLAND
Lothian
Fife

Cairngorms, Monadhliath Mts, Grampian Mts, Ben Macdui 1310, Ben Nevis 1344, Ben Lawers, Ben Alder, Loch Ness, Loch Linnhe, Loch Lomond, Loch Tay, Loch Rannoch, Loch Ericht, Loch Laggan, Loch Shiel, Loch Awe, Loch Fyne

Western Isles, Outer Hebrides, Lewis, Harris, North Uist, Benbecula, South Uist, Barra, Castlebay, Lochboisdale, Lochmaddy, Stornoway, Butt of Lewis, Tarbert, North Minch, Little Minch

Isle of Skye, Portree, Rum, Eigg, Muck, Canna, Coll, Tiree, Mull, Tobermory, Iona, Staffa, Colonsay, Jura, Islay, Oban, Fort William, Mallaig, Kyle of Lochalsh, Gairloch, Ullapool, Lochinver, Kinlochbervie, Durness, C. Wrath, Tongue, Scourie, Lochcarron, Torridon

Ben Hope 927, Ben Klibreck 961, Ben More Assynt 998, Ben Dearg, Ben Wyvis 1046, Ben Attow 1031

SCALE

| 0 | 25 | 50 | 75 | 100 km |
| 0 | 25 | | 50 mls | |

at the same scale

IRELAND

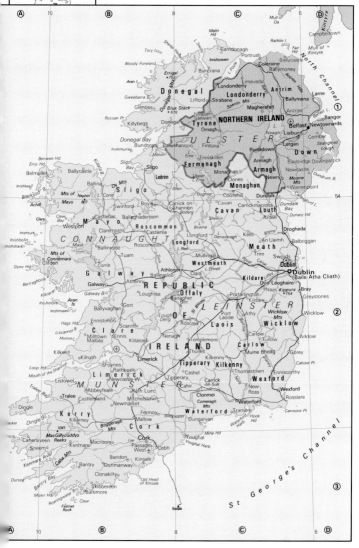

THE LOW COUNTRIES

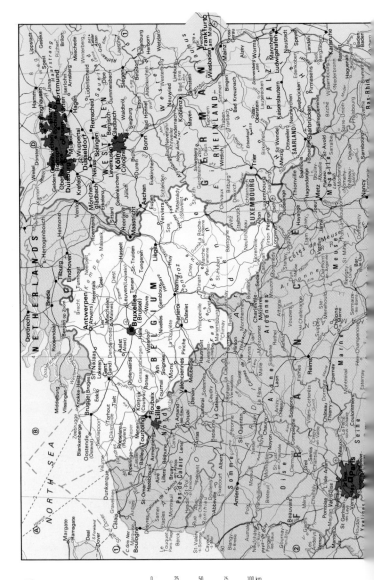

FRANCE

0   50   100   150   200 km
0   50   100 mls

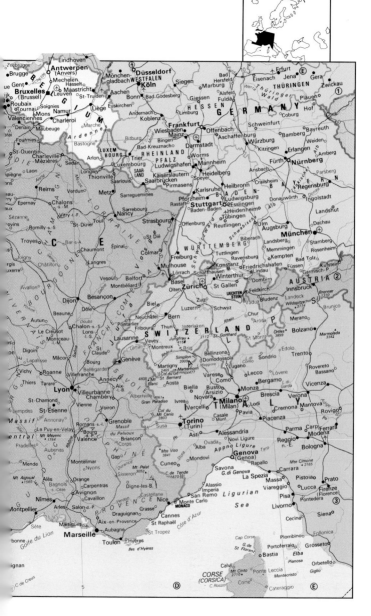

49

SPAIN & PORTUGAL

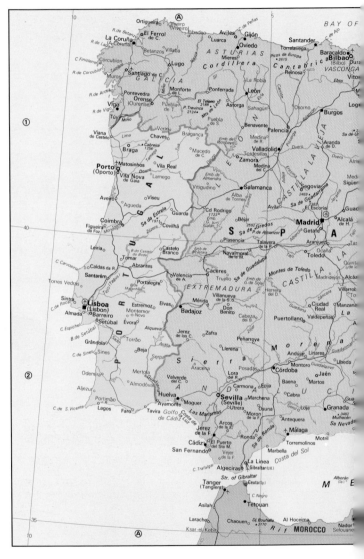

0   50   100   150   200 km
0   50   100 mls

4 Y
Capbreton
Biarritz
tian.
Bayonne
Irún
Tolosa
Pamplona
NAVARRA
Tafalla
horta
faro
zona
Alagón
Zaragoza
tayud
Daroca
Monreal
del C.
de Albarracín
Teruel
enca
N
N
cotilla
el P.
Roda
Albacete
Almansa
Hellín
RCIA
Cieza
Caravaca
Murcia
Totana
Lorca
Aguilas
Vera
Gata

Dax
Mont-de-Marsan
Adour
GAS
Orthez
Pau
Oloron-Ste-Marie
Lourdes
Tafalla
Jaca
Sa de Guara
Huesca
Barbastro
Lérida
(Lleida)
Alcañiz
Caspe
Tortosa
Amposta
Vinaroz
Benicarló
Torreblanca
Castellón de la P.
Villarreal
Segorbe
Sagunto
Valencia
Alcira
Játiva
Gandia
Onteniente
Denia
Villena
Alcoy
Benidorm
Elda
Alicante
Elche
Orihuela

Auch
Toulouse
Vignemale
3298
P. de Aneto
3404
Monteny
2883
ANDORRA
Andorra
La Vella
Puigcerdá
Sa del Codi
CATALUÑA
Vich
(Vic)
Sabadell
Tarrasa
Barcelona
Reus
Tarragona
Villanueva y G.
(Vilanova i la Geltrú)
Golfo
de
San Jorge
C. de Tortosa
Is Columbretes
Golfo de
Valencia
Valencia
Ibiza
S. Antonio
Abad
Ibiza
Formentera
C. de la Nao
Costa Blanca
C. de Palos
G. de
Mazarrón
Cartagena

Albi
Castres-
s./A.
Béziers
Carcassonne
Narbonne
Sète
Golfe du Lion
Perpignan
ROUSSILLON
C. de Creus
Figueras
(Figueres)
Gerona
(Girona)
San Feliu de G.
Costa Brava
C. de Formentor
C. de Caballería
Mallorca
Alcudia
Capdepera
Palma
de Mallorca
Manacor
Santañy
Cabrera
ISLAS BALEARES
(BALEARIC ISLANDS)
(Sp.)

Nîmes
Montpellier
Arles
Salon-d.-P.
Aix-en-Provence
Martigues
Marseille
Aubagne
Toulon
Hyères

Menorca
Ciudadela
Mahón
C. Binibeca

M E D I T E R R A N E A N   S E A

Alger
(Algiers)
Harrach
Dellys
Bejaia
(Bougie)
Cherchell
Boufarik
Blida
Tizi Ouzou
Djurdjura
Ténès
Miliana
Médéa
Bir
Rabalou
Bouira
Beni
Mansour
Kherrata
Sétif
Bosquet
Dahra
Chellf
Ech Cheliff
Ksar El
Boukhari
Aïn
Oussera
Chettab
Bj bou
Arréridj
Mts du Hodna
M'Sila
Mostaganem
Massif de l'Ouarsenis
A L G E R I A
Barikaï
C. Ferrat
Arzew
Relizane
Mina
Mohammadia
Sig
Oran
Mers el Kébir
Beni-Saf
Aïn
Témouchent
Mascara
Tiaret
Plat. du Sersou
Z. Chergui
Oued
Bou Saâda
Chott
el Hodna
Monts des
Ouled Naïl
Sidi-bel-Abbès
Frenda
Z. Gharbi

① 40 ② 36 ③

51

ITALY

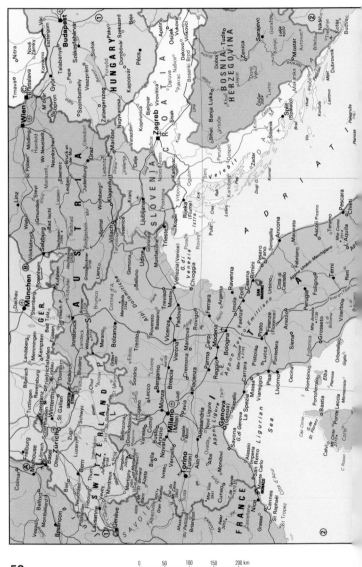

0   50   100   150   200 km
0   50   100 mls

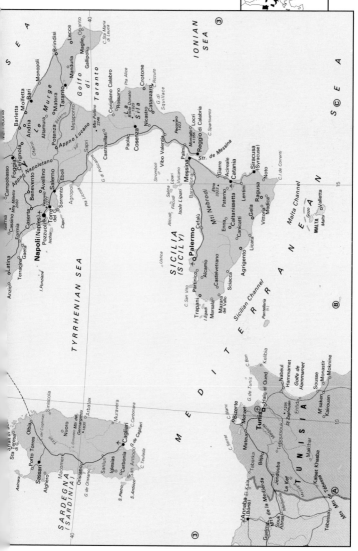

TYRRHENIAN SEA

MEDITERRANEAN SEA

IONIAN SEA

SARDEGNA
(SARDINIA)

SICILIA
(SICILY)

TUNISIA

Le Murge

Appno Napoletano

Appno Lucano

La Sila

Mti Nebrodi

Golfo di Taranto

Str. de Messina

Sicilian Channel

Malta Channel

Brindisi
Lecce
Maglie
C. Sta Maria di Leuca
Monopoli
Manduria
Bari
Molfetta
Barletta
Andria
Altamura
Matera
Taranto
Corigliano Calabro
Rossano
Pta Alice
Crotone
C. Rizzuto
G. di Squillace
Catanzaro
Nicastro
C. Spartivento
Reggio di Calabria
Messina
Giarre
Acireale
Catania
Siracusa (Syracuse)
Noto
Lentini
Paternò
Etna 3323
Gioia Tauro
Palmi
Vibo Valentia
Cosenza
Paola
Castrovillari
Mte Pollino 2248
Potenza
Benevento
Avellino
Eboli
Salerno
Sorrento
Capri
Torre del Greco
Napoli (Naples)
Pozzuoli
Ischia
Foggia
Cerignola
Campobasso
Caserta
Cassino
Formia
Gaeta
Terracina
Latina
Anzio
I. Ponziane
Vesuvio

Stromboli
Isole Lipari
Salina
Lipari
Vulcano
Filicudi
Alicudi
Panarea
Ustica

Cefalù
Palermo
Monreale
Bagheria
Termini
Alcamo
Castellammare
C. San Vito
Trapani
I. Egadi
Marsala
Mazara del Vallo
Sciacca
Agrigento
Licata
Gela
Vittoria
Ragusa
Modica
Canicattì
Caltanissetta
Enna
Caltagirone
C. le Correnti

Pantelleria (It.)

MALTA
Gozo
Malta
Valletta

Sassari
Porto Torres
Alghero
Olbia
Sorso
Nuoro
Mti del Gennargentu 1834
Oristano
G. di Oristano
Iglesias
Carbonia
S. Pietro
S. Antioco
C. Teulada
Cagliari
G. de Cagliari
Muravera
Arbatax
Macomer
Sanluri
Alamos
Capoterra
Strait of Bonifacio
Str. di Bonifacio

Bizerte
Tunis
Menzel
Mateur
La Goulette
Nabeul
Hammamet
Golfe de Hammamet
Kelibia
C. Bon
Sousse
Monastir
Moknine
M'saken
Kairouan
Enfidha
Zaghouan
Dj. Zaghouan
Djebibina
Béja
Tabarka
Jendouba
Le Kef
Ksar Kasba
Maktar
Medjerda
Mts de la Medjerda
Kasserine
Mts Khmir
Souk Ahras
Guelma
Annaba (Bône)
El Kala
Tébessa
Mts Tébessa
C. Serrat
C. blanc
G. de Tunis
G. de Gabès

40
40
15
10

A

B

C

3

1

2

3

THE BALKANS

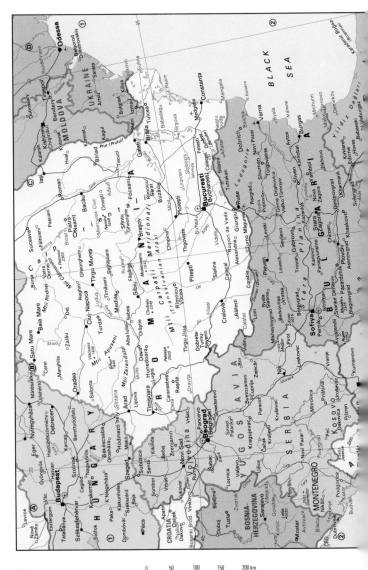

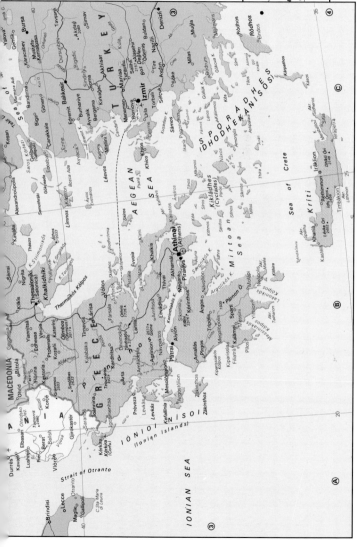

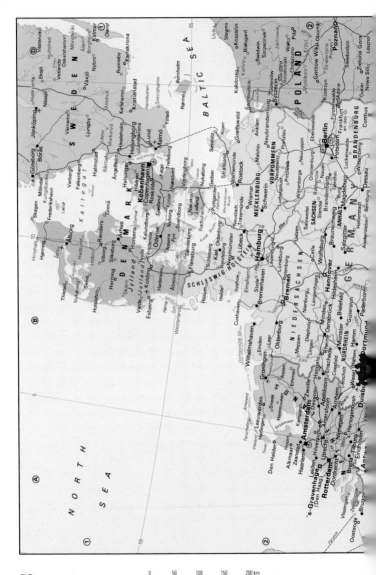

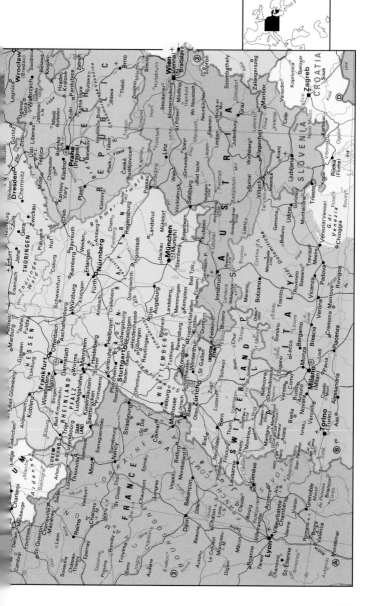

EUROPE EAST-CENTRAL

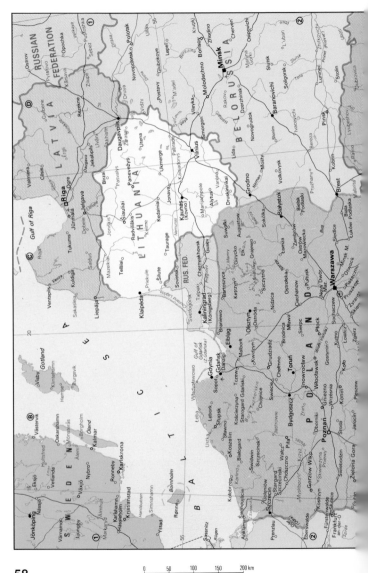

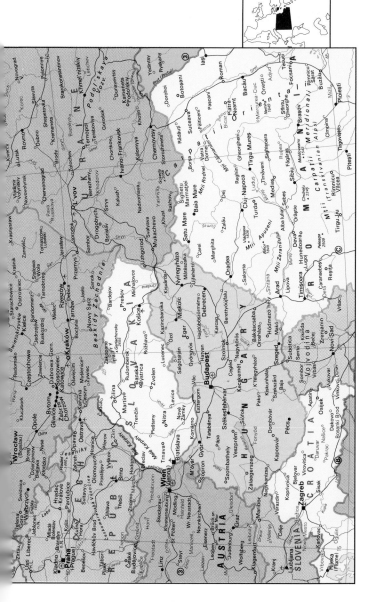

59

EUROPEAN RUSSIA, UKRAINE & BALTIC STATES

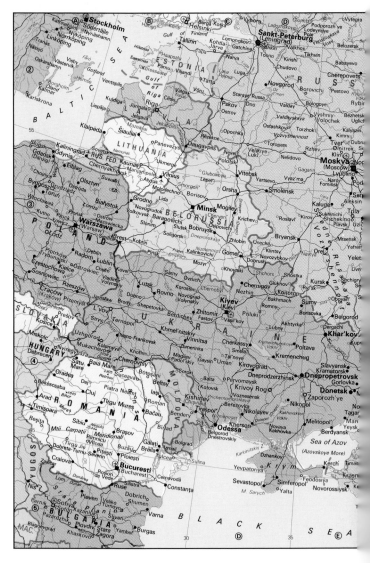

0	100	200	300	400 km
0		100		200 mls

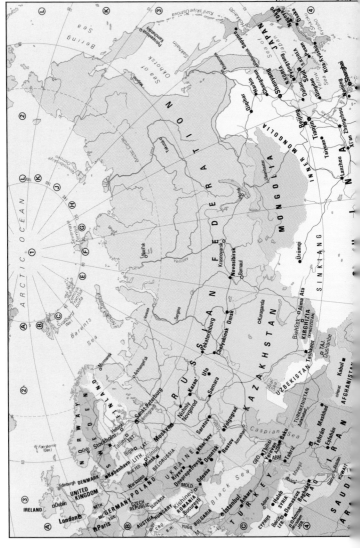

0	600	1200	1800 km
0	300	600	900 mls

RUSSIAN FEDERATION EAST

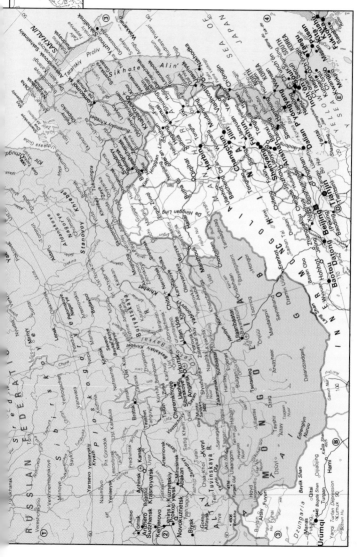

RUSSIAN FEDERATION WEST

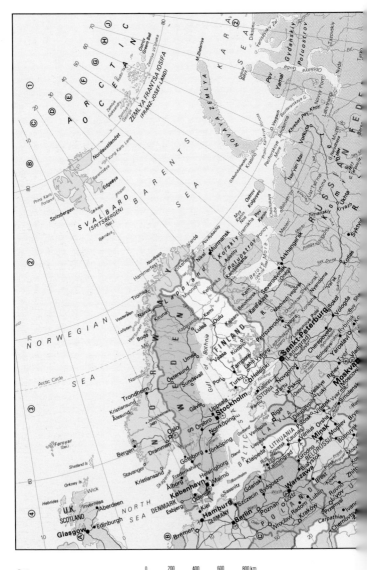

0	200	400	600	800 km
0		200	400 mls	

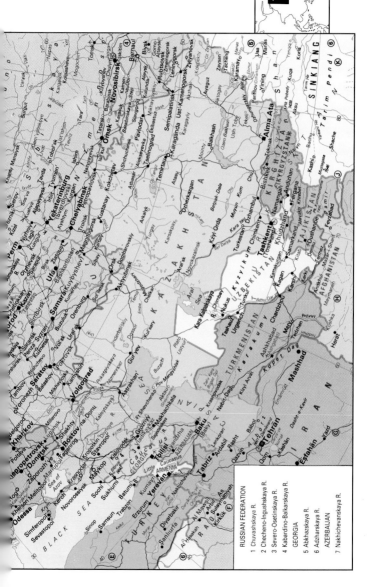

RUSSIAN FEDERATION
1 Chuvashskaya R.
2 Checheno-Ingushskaya R.
3 Severo-Osetinskaya R.
4 Kabardino-Balkarskaya R.
GEORGIA
5 Abkhazskaya R.
6 Adzharskaya R.
AZERBAIJAN
7 Nakhichevanskaya R.

ASIA SOUTH

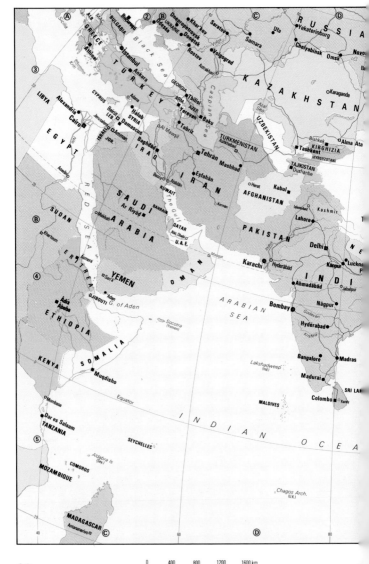

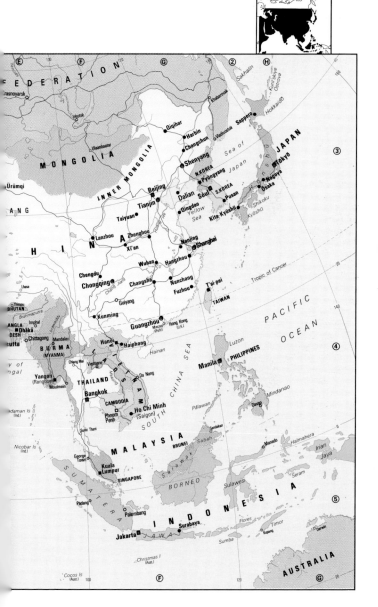

RUSSIAN FEDERATION

Krasnoyarsk

Irkutsk

Ulaanbaatar

MONGOLIA

Ürümqi

INNER MONGOLIA

Qiqihar

Harbin

Changchun

Shenyang

Beijing

Tianjin

Taiyuan

Lanzhou

Zhengzhou

Xi'an

Dalian

Qingdao

Yellow Sea

Nanjing

Shanghai

Wuhan

Hangzhou

Chengdu

Chongqing

Changsha

Nanchang

Fuzhou

Guiyang

Kunming

Guangzhou

Macau (Port.)

Hong Kong (U.K.)

C H I N A

CHANG

Lhasa

BHUTAN

Thimphu

Brahmaputra

BANGLA DESH

Dhaka

Calcutta

Chittagong

BURMA (MYANMA)

Mandalay

Chiang Mai

Vientiane

Yangon (Rangoon)

Moulmein

THAILAND

Bangkok

CAMBODIA

Phnom Penh

Surat Thani

Hanoi

Haiphong

Hainan

Da Nang

Ho Chi Minh (Saigon)

LAOS

VIETNAM

Andaman Is (Ind)

Bay of Bengal

Nicobar Is (Ind)

George Town

Kuala Lumpur

SINGAPORE

SUMATERA

Padang

Palembang

M A L A Y S I A

BORNEO

BRUNEI

Sarawak

Sabah

Sandakan

Jakarta

J A W A

Surabaya

I N D O N E S I A

Christmas I (Aust.)

Cocos Is (Aust.)

N.KOREA

Pyongyang

Seoul

S.KOREA

Pusan

Kita-Kyushu

Kyushu

Shikoku

Sea of Japan

Vladivostok

Khabarovsk

Sakhalin

Kuril'skiye Ostrova

Hokkaido

Sapporo

J A P A N

Tokyo

Nagoya

Osaka

PACIFIC OCEAN

Tropic of Cancer

T'ai-pei

TAIWAN

Luzon

Manila

PHILIPPINES

Mindanao

Davao

Palawan

SOUTH CHINA SEA

Manado

Halmahera

Sulawesi

Seram

Irian Jaya

Flores

Timor

Sumba

Kupang

Darwin

AUSTRALIA

Huang He

Chang Jiang

67

ASIA EAST

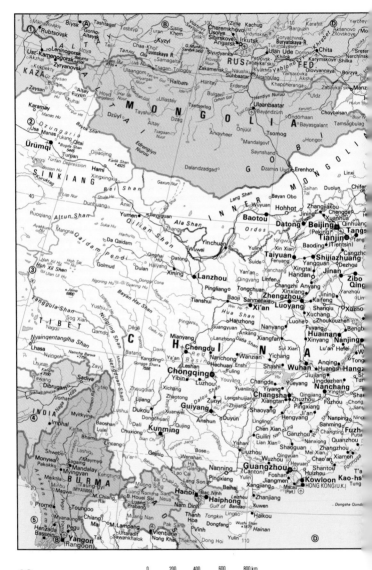

0   200   400   600   800 km

0   200   400 mls

69

ASIA SOUTHEAST

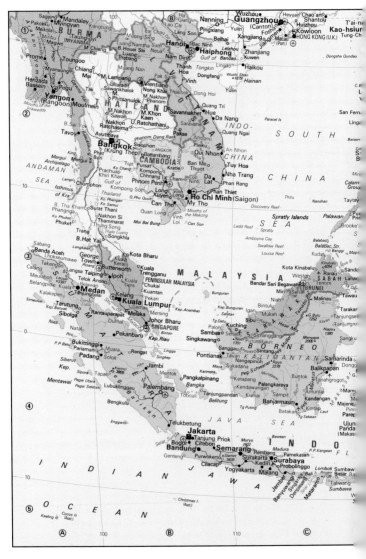

0	200	400	600	800 km
0	200		400 mls	

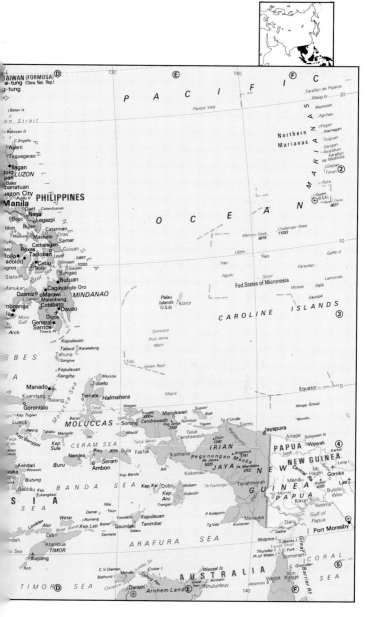

CHINA CENTRAL

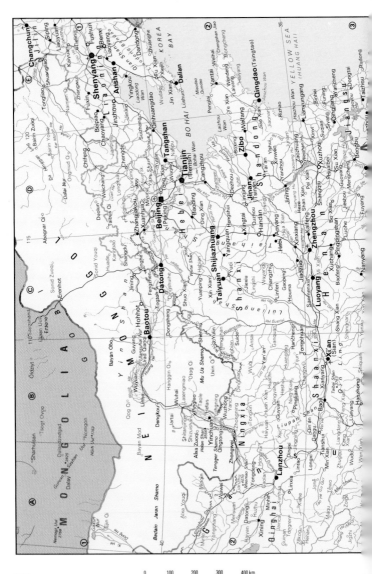

0 100 200 300 400 km
0   100   200 mls

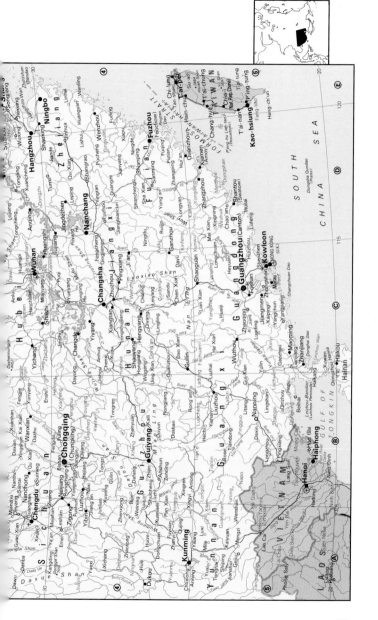

73

JAPAN & KOREA

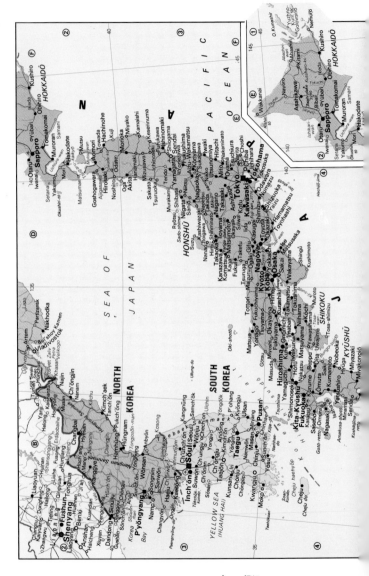

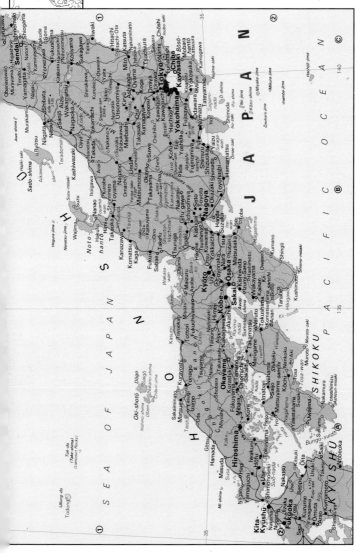

BURMA, THAILAND, INDO-CHINA, MALAYSIA & SINGAPORE

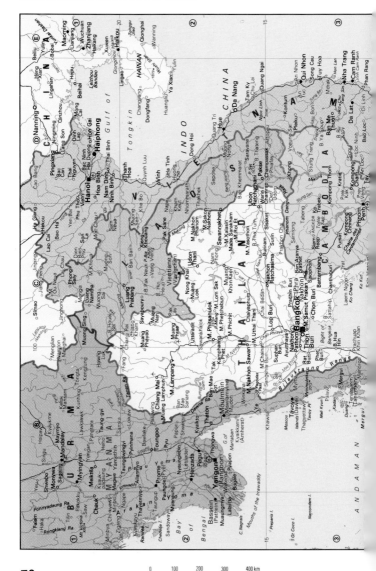

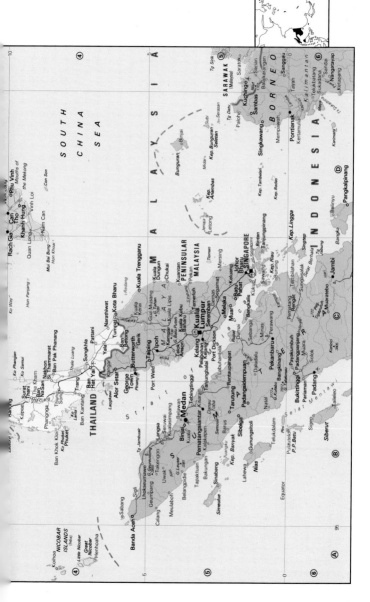

77

INDESIA CENTRAL

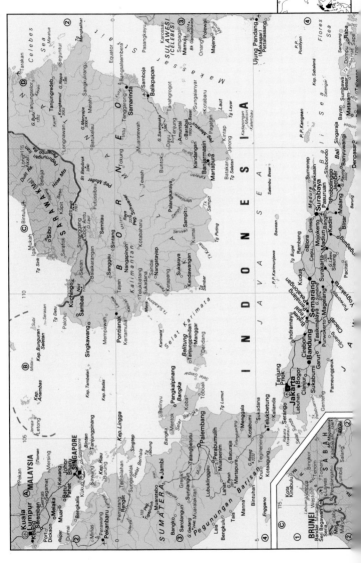

PHILIPPINES

MIDDLE EAST

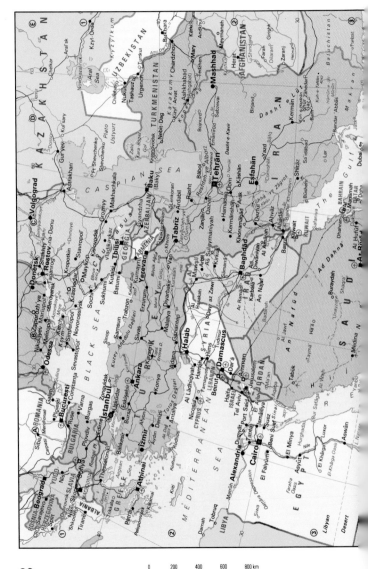

0   200   400   600   800 km
0   200   400 mls

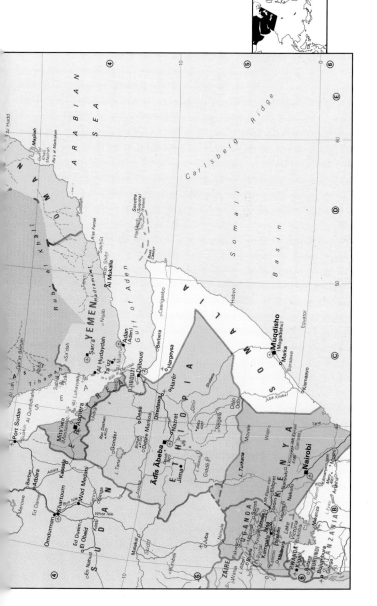

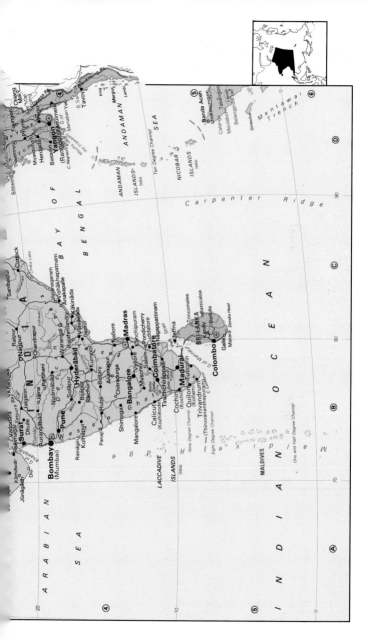

INDIA NORTHWEST & PAKISTAN

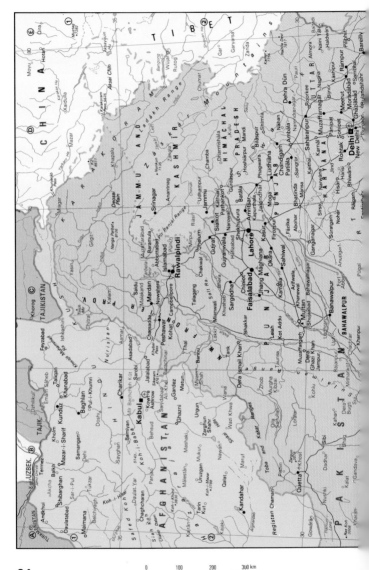

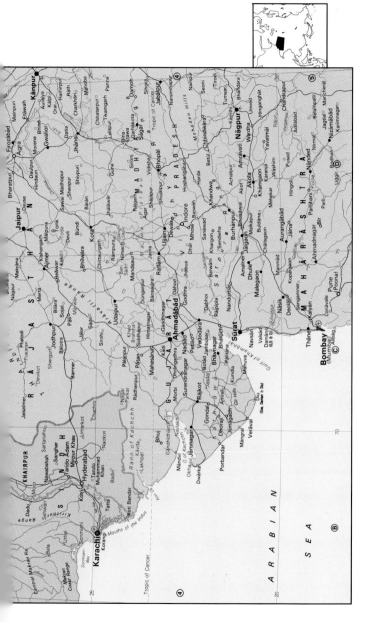

INDIA NORTHEAST & BANGLADESH

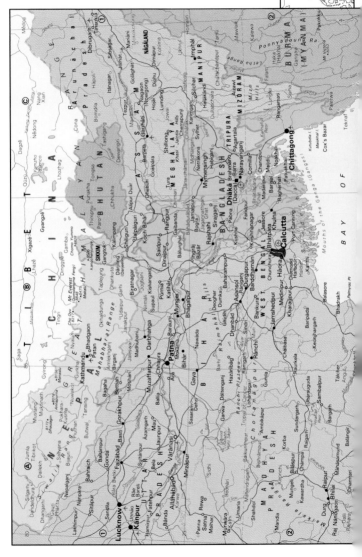

0	100	200	300 km
0	50	100	150 mls

INDIA SOUTH & SRI LANKA

Ⓐ Bombay (Mumbai)
Lonavale
Pune MAHARASHTRA
Ahmadnajar
Parbhani
Purna
Nānded
Belampalli
Sironcha
Jagdalpur
Kotapad
Ⓒ
Bir
Parli
Nirmal
Danlewara
Mahad
Wai
Bārāmati
Daund
Udgir
Bodhan
Nizāmābād
Bījāpur
Sukma
Bhandān
Phaltan
Chiplun
Satāra
Lātur
Jagtial
Mancherāl
Karimnagar
Wai
Barsi
Bīdar
Siddipet
Warangal
Pandharpur
Homnābād
Akalkot
Sangareddi
Yellandu
Bhadrāchalam
Karād
Vite
Solāpur
Gulbarga
Tāndur
Bhongir
Khammam
Kottagudem
Sāngli
Shāhābād
Nalgonda
Sunāpet
Rājahmundry
Miraj
Bijāpur
Yādgir
Hyderābād
Mahbūbnagar
Vijayawāda
Kākinada
Kolhāpur
Ichalkaranji
Narāyanpet
ANDHRA
Guntur
Yanam
Jamkhandi
Shorāpur
Wanparti
Tenāli
Bhimavaram
Bāgalkot
Rāichur
Nārasarāopet
Machilipatnam
Mālvan
Belgaum
Guledagudda
Gajendragarh
Kurnool
PRADESH
Chilakalūrūpet
Bāpatla
Vengurla
Panaji Goa
Daman
Koppal
Adoni
Dhone
Nandyāl
Chirāla
Madgaon
KARNATAKA
Gadag
Bellary
Guntakal
Giddalūr
Ongole
Kārwār
Hubli
Hospet
Gooty
Proddatūr
Kani Giri
Kondukūr
Sirsi
Hāveri
Kottūru
Tādpatri
Kavali
Kumta
Rānibennūr
Hirihar
Swammalli
Rāyadrug
Anantapur
15
Bhatkal
Dāvangere
Kalyandurg
Dharmavaram
Cuddapah
Nellore
Coondapoor
Shimoga
Chitradurga
Kadiri
Venkatagiri
Gudūr
Udupi
Kārkal
Bhadrāvati
Tarikere
Sira
Hindupur
Tirupati
Sri Kālahasti
Pulicat L.
Mangalore
Chikmagalūr
Kādūr
Arsikere
Tumkūr
Chik Ballāpur
Chittoor
Arakkonam
Madras
Kāsaragod
Hole Narsipur
Hassan
Tiptūr
Dod Ballāpur
Kolār
Gold Fields
Āmhūr
Vellore
Kānchipuram
Ⓐ
Cannanore
Mahe
Madiken
Nanjangūd
Mandya
Bangalore
Krishnagiri
Tiruppattūr
ⓐ
Tellicherry
Chāmrājnagar
Mysore
Dharmapuri
Javadi Hills
Tindivanam
Pondicherry
Badagara
Ootacamund
Doda Betta
2636
Mettur
Salem
Tiruvannāmalai
Villupuram
Cuddalore
Calicut
(Kozhikode)
Nilgiri Hills
Coonoor
Erode
Vriddhāchalam
Beypore
Coimbatore
Tiruppur
TAMIL NADU
Chidambaram
Ponnāni
Shoranur
Pālghāt
Pollāchi
Tiruchchirāppalli
Kumbakonam
Karāikāl
Trichūr
(Thrissur)
Animalai Hills
Pālani
Thanjāvūr
Nāgappattinam
Mannārgudi
Cochin
(Kochi)
Bodināyakkanūr
Dindigul
Pudukkottai
Pt Calimere
Kodikkarai
Ernākulam
Kambām
Vembanad L.
Kottayam
Virudunagar
Madurai
Paramakudi
Pt Pedro
10
Alleppey
Aruppukkottai
Rāmanāthapuram
Jaffna
Kāyankulam
Puliyangudi
Rājapālaiyam
Mullaittvu
Quilon
(Kollam)
Tenkāsi
Tuticorin
Talaimannār
Mannar
Vavuniya
Trincomalee
Trivandrum
(Thiruvananthapuram)
Tirunelveli
Palayānkottai
Gulf of Mannār
Havanakulam
Anurādhapura
Nāgercoil
Tiruchchendūr
Kanniyākumari
C.Comorin
Puttalam
Batticaloa
Ⓒ
Degree Channel
SRI LANKA
Chilaw
Dambulla
CEYLON
Matale
Kurunegala
Degree Channel
Negombo
Gampola
Kandy
Badulla
DIVES
Colombo
Dehiwala-Mt Lavinia
Moratuwa
Adam's Pk
2243
Nuwara-Eliya
Ratnapura
Opanake
Ambalangoda
Galle
Hambantota
Ⓐ
Ⓑ
Matara
Dondra Hd

Coromandel Coast
Palk Strait

Degree Channel

0   100   200   300 km
0   50   100   150 mls

87

AFRICA

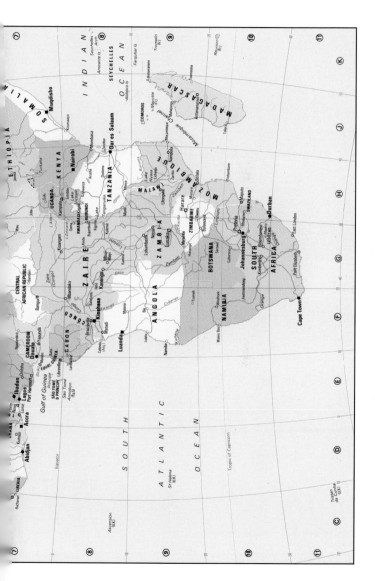

IRAN & THE GULF

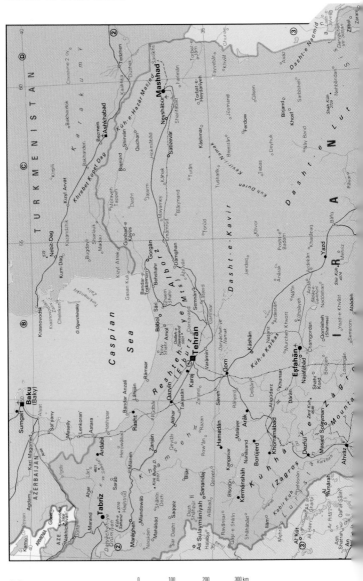

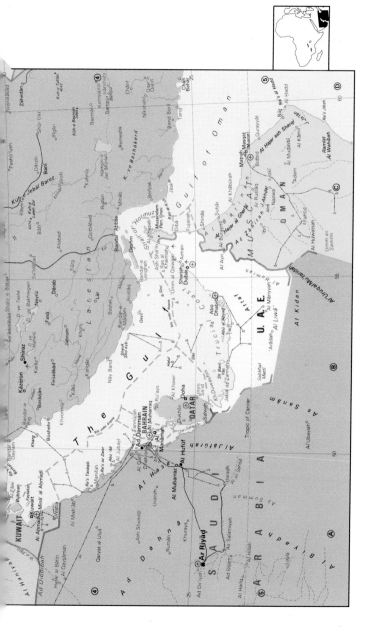

91

TURKEY, SYRIA & IRAQ

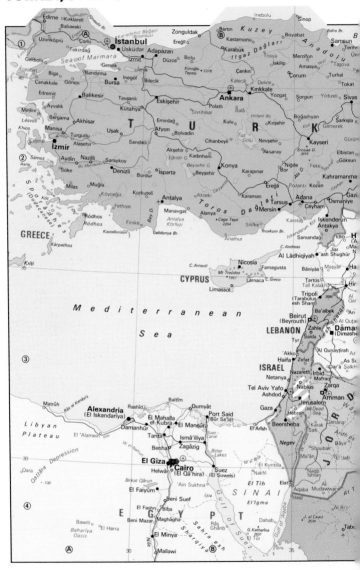

0   100   200   300 km
0   50   100   150 mls

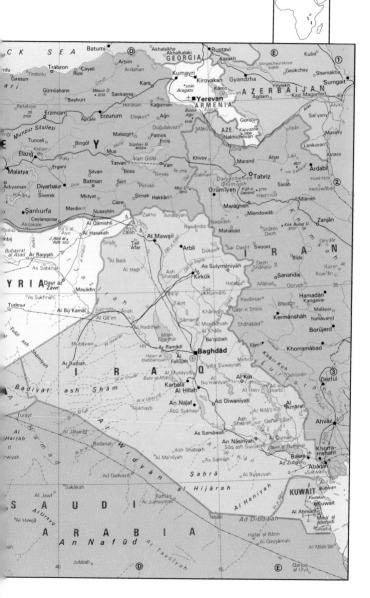

ISRAEL & LEBANON

CYPRUS

°Paleokhóno Larnaca
Lefkara   Larnaca
         Bay
                        C. Greco
      ∘Zygi
Limassol   C. Kítí
  Akrotiri Bay
     C. Gáta

MEDITERRANEAN

SEA

Tártus∘ ∘Duraykish
     Arwad°   An
                 Nasirah Tall Bisāh
            Hamīdīyah Tall Kalakh (CHEVALIERS) Hir
                  Kleiat°   Ooubayat Shnisri
                         Halba   Al Qusayr
El Mína°
Tripoli °Zghorta   El Hermel
(Tarābulus esh Shām)   Qornet es
Batroun° Amioune   Saouda °3088
     Deir el ∘   Dayr al
Jubail° Kartaba 'Ahmar
BYBLOS °   °Rhazīr Ba'albek° °2659 An Nab
LEBANON   Bikfaya °2628   Yabrūd°
  Jounié°   Rayak°
Beirut °Ba'abda   Az   Qutayfah
(Beyrouth) Aley° Zahle °Zabdāni
Damour°   'Ayn al Fijah
Beit ed Dine° Mechgharab At∘ Dūma Adhr
       Saïda°   Baradā   'Tall
       (Sidon) Jezzine Qatana°   Damasc
                 Rachaiya°   (Dimashq)
    Hâsbaiya° °Jash Shaykh
              (Mt Hermon) °Al Kiswah
  Mariayoun° °w w w Al Hijan
Tyr° Q.Shemona Baniyas∘ Dayr 'Alī°
(Tyre, Sour) Jouai'ya° °Mas'adah SYRIA
                CEASE FIRE Ghabāghib∘ °Burāc
Enn Nâqoûra°   LINES 1974
          Benni Al Qunaytirah   Mismīya°
         Jbail °1208   As Sanamayn°
Nahariya° °Ma'alot °Hama'an   °Khabab
      °Akko Tarshīha Qushnīyah∘   Al Lajāh Sha
      (Acre) Rama∘ (Safad)° Kafr Kannā Nawa° °863
B.of Haifa °Q. Yam   Kare Kenneret   °Izra Shahbe
Haifa∘ °Shefar'ām (Sea of Galilee) °Shaykh As Suwayda°
(Hefa) °Q.   Tiberias° °Fiq Miskin
       'Ata   Tasil∘
°'Atlit Mt Nazareth°   Ma'agan° °W. az Zayd Busr
    Carmel Afula°   Irbid∘ ash
Zikhron Ya'aqov°   Deir Abu Ramtha∘
CAESAREA°   °MEGIDDO Said∘
Pardes Hanna °ARMAGEDDON Beyt Husn∘ °Mafraq °Sabha
Hadera°   Jenin° Shean °Ajlūn J. Umm ed
Netanya° °Qabatiya   Tubas∘ °1247 Darā °Jarash Sabha°
       °Tulkarm   Zarqa∘ Es Samra°
ISRAEL °Sabastiya   Ba'al Hazor Karana∘
Herzliya° Kefar Sava° Nablus° °1016 Suweilin° °Amman
Ramat Gan∘°Petah Tiqwa   Salt∘   Marka∘ Sahāb∘
Tel Aviv° °Lod   °Ramallah   Wadi es Sir∘ Naur∘
Yafo (Jaffa)° Rishon le Zion Jericho   Qasr el Kharana°
  °Holon   °Ramla (Arīha) Mādabā° Dab'a°
Ashdod°   °Latrun °Jerusalem (El Quds)   Khan ez Zabib
         Beit Jala° (Yerushalayim)
Ashqelon°   Bethlehem°   liza° Qasr el Kharana°
         °Qiryat (Bayt Lahm)
Gaza° °Gat °Bet   Hebron° °Ei Ged
Gaza Strip Sederot°GIVRIN (El Khalil) °Dhībān
     °Dura °Yatta °Dhālniya Khan ez Zabib
Khan Yunis° Ofaqim° °Edh   Mazra°   Rabba∘
Rafah°   °Nevatim   MEZADA° El Lisan∘ Qatrāna°
        Zeelim°   °Arad
       HALUZA°   Dimona° °Sedom Karak° Manzil∘
            MAMSHIT° °Tel Meise   Qa'el Jafr
Reviwim°   San°   Mazar°
      SHIVTA°   °Yeroham °Ed Dabba JORD
Qeziot° °Sede   Oron°   Tafila°
       Boger °AVEDAT Hasa° Qa el Jinz
      El Quseima N e g e v °Rashādiya Jurf ed Darāwīsh
                  Dana°
G.Maghāra   G.Libni   892   Mizpe °En °1641
735 ▲ 735 ▲ G.Halâl Ramon Negev J.el Ata'ta° °1082
Bîr Hasana°   Har Ramon° Shaubak°
           Har Saggi Har Hakipa° Nill∘
E G Y P T   ▲1006   467▲ Jum Suwwana° °Unaisa
          PETRA∘
Bîr Gifgâfa°   C
Ras Burûn°
Sabkhet° El 'Arîsh Bîr Lahfân°
el Bardawil   W. Haridin
                Abu 'Aweigila
NIZANA°
G.Maghāra °Bir Gifgâfa

EGYPT

94

```
   0    25    50    75   100 km
   ├────┼────┼────┼────┤
   0        25        50 mils
```

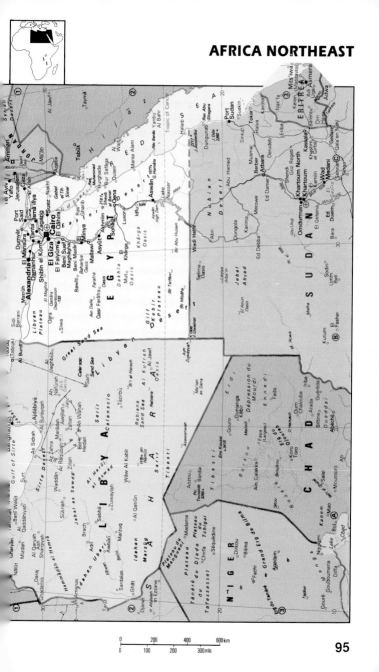

AFRICA WEST

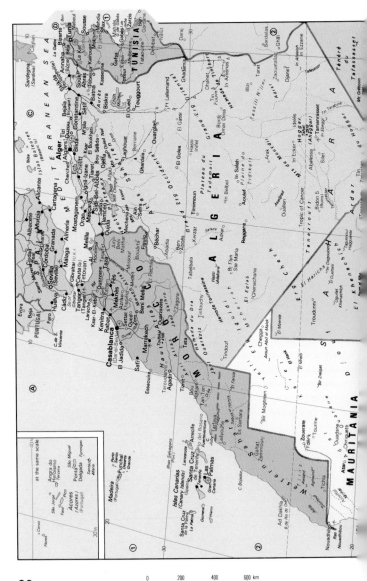

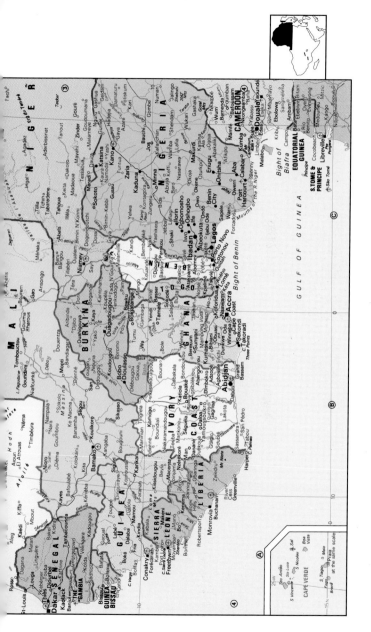

AFRICA CENTRAL

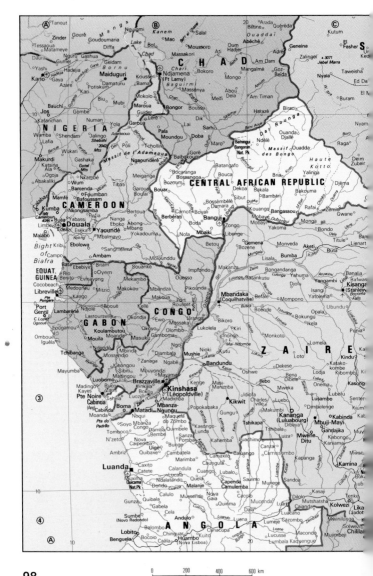

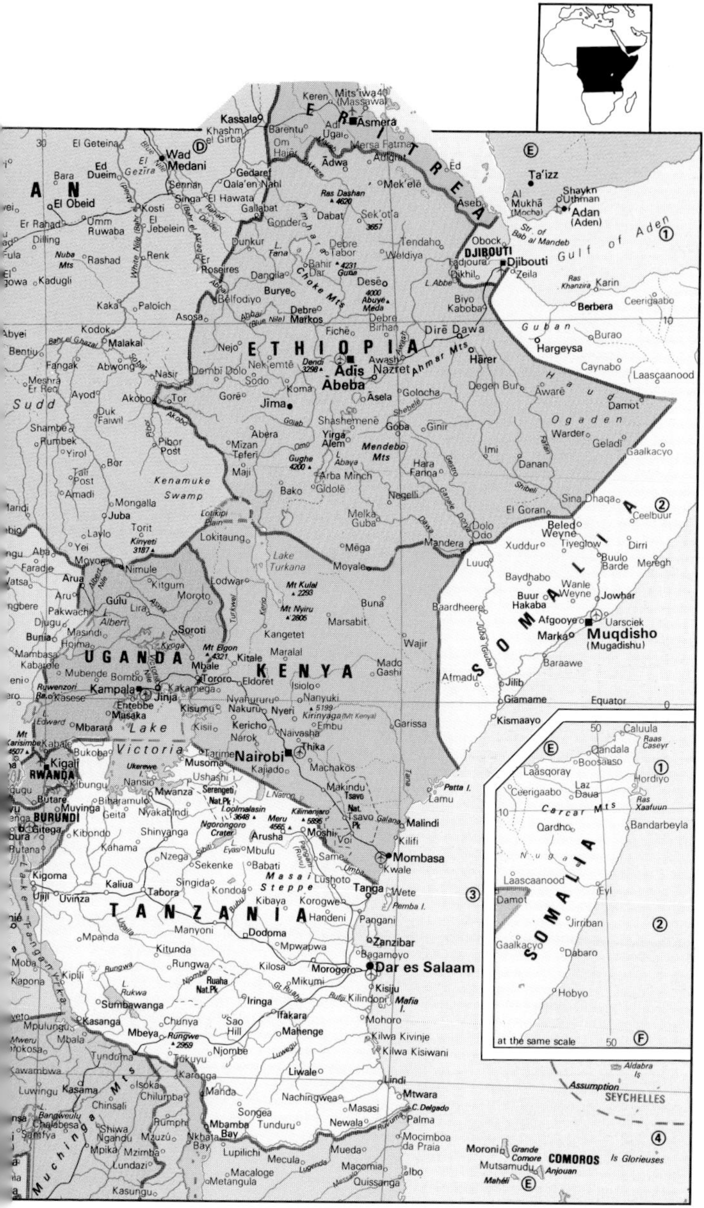
E R I T R E A
E T H I O P I A
DJIBOUTI
S O M A L I A
U G A N D A
K E N Y A
T A N Z A N I A
RWANDA
BURUNDI
SEYCHELLES
COMOROS
Kassala
Keren
Mits'iwa (Massawa)
Asmera
Wad Medani
El Geteina
Ed Dueim
El Obeid
Kosti
Gedaref
Sennar
Aseb
Mek'ele
Ras Dashan 4620
Gonder
L. Tana
Bahir Dar
Dese
Djibouti
Zeila
Berbera
Hargeysa
Dire Dawa
Harer
Adis Abeba
Nazret
Jima
Ta'izz
Adan (Aden)
Al Mukhā (Mocha)
Gulf of Aden
Str. of Bab al Mandeb
Ogaden
Haud
Sudd
Kenamuke Swamp
Juba
Lake Turkana
Lokitaung
Moyale
Mandera
Marsabit
Beled Weyne
Muqdisho (Mugadishu)
Marka
Kismaayo
Equator
Gulu
Lira
Soroti
Mt Elgon 4321
Kampala
Entebbe
Jinja
Kitale
Eldoret
Nakuru
Kisumu
Lake Victoria
Nairobi
Thika
Machakos
Garissa
Lamu
Malindi
Mombasa
Kilimanjaro 5895
Arusha
Moshi
Tanga
Pemba I.
Zanzibar
Dar es Salaam
Dodoma
Tabora
Kigoma
Ujiji
Mwanza
Kigali
Bujumbura
Iringa
Mbeya
Masai Steppe
Mafia I.
Kilwa Kivinje
Kilwa Kisiwani
Lindi
Mtwara
Songea
Lake Tanganyika
Muchinga Mts
Moroni
Grande Comore
Anjouan
Mohéli
Mutsamudu
Is Glorieuses
Aldabra Is
Assumption
Caluula
Qandala
Boosaaso
Laasqoray
Ceerigaabo
Carcar Mts
Qardho
Bandarbeyla
Laascaanood
Eyl
Damot
Jirriban
Gaalkacyo
Dabaro
Hobyo
at the same scale

AFRICA SOUTH

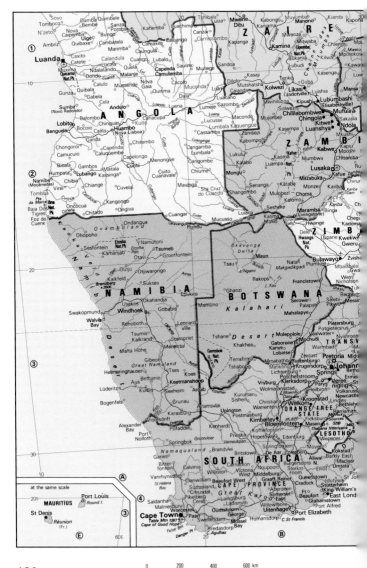

0   200   400   600 km

0   100   200   300 mls

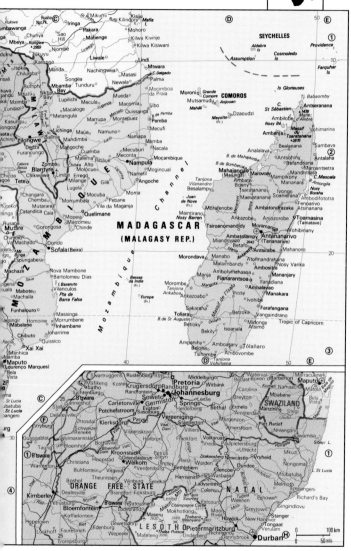

ATLANTIC OCEAN

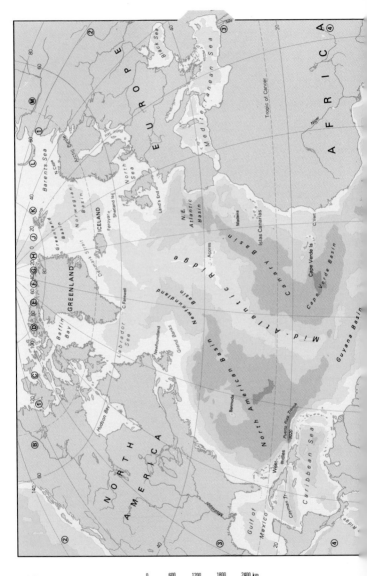

0	600	1200	1800	2400 km
0		600		1200 mls

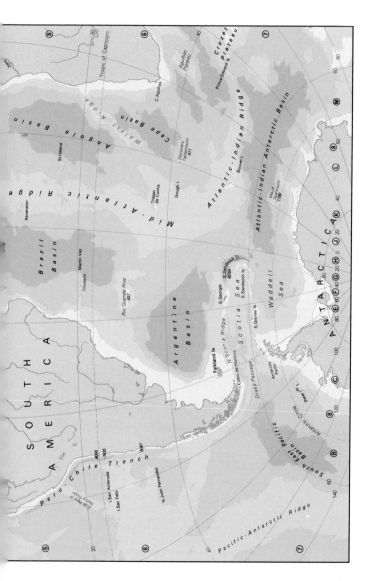

SOUTH AMERICA

ANTARCTICA

Peru-Chile Trench
6066
7635
6897

San Pablo
Island Ridge
I.San Ambrosio
I.San Felix
Is Juan Fernandez

Cabo de Hornos
Drake Passage
Falkland Is
N Scotia Ridge
Scotia Sea
S.Orkney Is
S.Georgia
S.Sandwich Tr.
8264
S.Sandwich Is

Argentine Basin

Rio Grande Rise
637

Trindade
Martin Vaz

Brazil Basil

Ascension

St Helena

Angola Basin

Mid-Atlantic Ridge

Tristan
da Cunha

Gough I.

Bouvet I.

Maud
Seamount
1789

Atlantic-Indian Antarctic Basin

Atlantic-Indian Ridge

Discovery
Tablemount
411

Walvis Ridge
Cape Basin

C.Agulhas
Agulhas
Plateau

Prince Edward Is
Crozet
Plateau

Tropic of Capricorn

Weddell Sea

Antarctic
Penin.

Peter I Is

Antarctic Circle

South East Pacific

Pacific-Antarctic Ridge

103

AUSTRALASIA

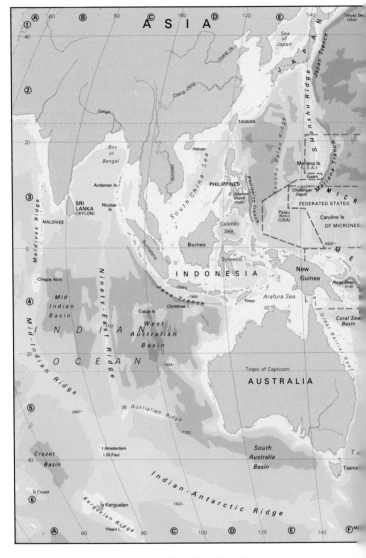

0   600   1200   1800   2400 km

0   600   1200 mls

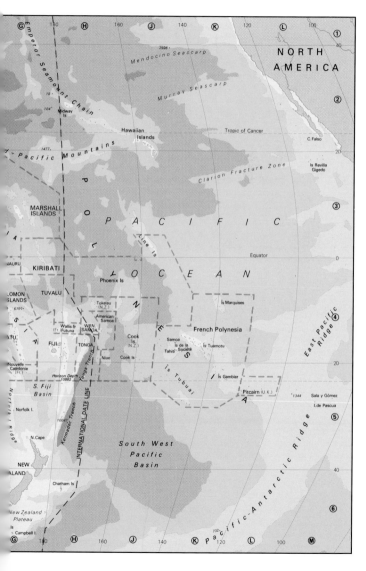

NORTH AMERICA

Emperor Seamount Chain

Mendocino Seascarp

2926

Murray Seascarp

104°

Midway Is

Hawaiian Islands

Tropic of Cancer

C.Falso

Pacific Mountains

1477.

Clarion Fracture Zone

Is Revilla Gigedo

MARSHALL ISLANDS

P   A   C   I   F   I   C

I   A

Line Is

Equator

NAURU

KIRIBATI

O   C   E   A   N

Phoenix Is

SOLOMON ISLANDS

TUVALU

6150·

Tokelau (N.Z.)

Is Marquises

Wallis & (Fr.) Futuna

American Samoa

WtN. SAMOA

French Polynesia

VANU ATU

FIJI

TONGA

Cook Is. (N.Z.)

Samoa Is de la Société

Is Tuamotu

Tahiti

Nouvelle Calédonie (Fr.)

Niue

Cook Is

Horizon Depth 10882

Is Tubuai

Is Gambier

S. Fiji Basin

Norfolk I.

10047.

INTERNATIONAL DATE LINE

Pitcairn (U.K.)

·1344

Sala y Gómez

I.de Pascua

N.Cape

Kermadec Trench

Tonga Trench

East Pacific Ridge

NEW ZEALAND

South West Pacific Basin

Chatham Is

New Zealand Plateau

Pacific-Antarctic Ridge

Campbell I.

732·

105

AUSTRALIA

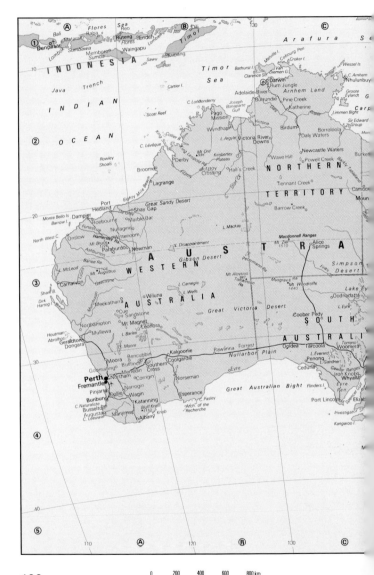

0   200   400   600   800 km
0   200   400 mils

AUSTRALIA SOUTHEAST

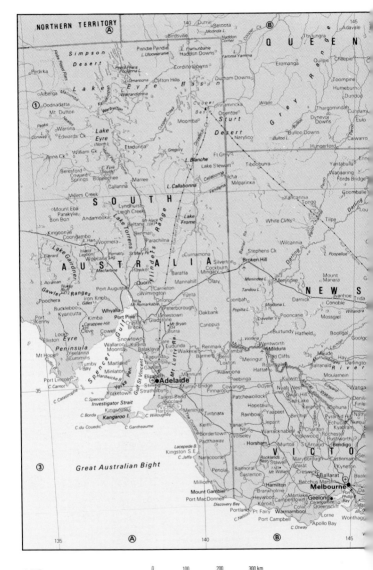

0	100	200	300 km
0	50	100	150 mls

Augathella C
914 Mt Hutton
Morven Mitchell Injune
Eurombah Taroom Mundubbera Biggenden Maryborough
Goynah
Muckadilla Wandoan Goondah
Mungallala Roma Wallumbilla Miles Chinchilla Kingaroy Wonbah Gympie
Surat Jackson Condamine Jandowae Dalby Kilcoy Maroochydore
Jandowae Toogoolawah Caloundra
Glenmorgan Tara Meandarra Oakey Crows Nest Caboolture
Moreton I.
St George Millmerran Clifton Pittsworth Toowoomba Ipswich Redcliffe
Bollon Mt Domville Allora Boonah N. Stradbroke I.
641 Warwick Beaudesert Brisbane
Dirranbandi Thallon Talwood Goondiwindi Inglewood Killarney Gold Coast
Hebel Boggabilla Stanthorpe Texas Tweed Heads
Mungindi New Angledool Yetman Croppa Ck Murwillumbah
Goodooga Ashley Mullumbimby
Lightning Ridge Collarenebri Pokataroo Gravesend Warialda Deepwater C. Byron
Narran L. Bingara Inverell Glen Innes Casino Lismore
Burren Jct Rowena Glencagh Woodburn
Bellata Ben Lomond Yamba
Walgett Wee Waa Namoi Emmaville Dorrigo C. Maclean
Narrabri 1505 Naradhan Barraba Guyra Grafton
Kaputar Manilla Round Mtn
Gwabegar Boggabri Uralla 1615 Bellingen Coff's Harbour
Coonamble Baradine Quirindi Armidale Dorrigo
Coonabarabran Mullaley Walcha Nambucca Heads
Gulargambone Werris Ck Black Sugarloaf Macksville
Gilgandra 1494 Kempsey Smoky C.
Nyngan Warren Coolah Quirindi Nundle Wauchope Port Macquarie
Nevertire Dunedoo Murrurundi Walcha Kendall
Trangie Merriwa Scone Gloucester Taree
Narromine Wellington Muswellbrook C. Hawke
Dubbo Dunggog Forster Sugarloaf Pt
Mudgee Singleton Dunggog
Trundle Peak Hill Mt Corcudgy Kurri Kurri Maitland Port Stephens
Parkes Mendooran Kandos 1274 Cessnock Raymond Terrace
Bogan Gate Orange Portland Morisset Newcastle
Forbes Cowra Blayney Lithgow Wyong Tuggerah L.
Canowindra Katoomba Richmond L. Macquarie
Grenfell Cowra Burragorang Windsor Port Jackson
Young Bathurst Camden Parramatta
Boorowa Crookwell Sydney
Temora Wyalong Campbelltown
Cootamundra Murrumburrah Goulburn Bowral Wollongong
Junee Burrinjuck Port Kembla
Coolamon Gundagai L. George Nowra Shellharbour
Wagga Tumut Canberra Jervis B.
ACT Queanbeyan
Barlow Holbrook Ulladulla
Hume Tumbarumba Queanbeyan Batemans Bay
Albury Wodonga Tumut Moruya
Mt Kosciusko Cabramurra
Bright 2230 Cooma Cobargo
Mt Bogong Nimmitabel Bega
Bombala Merimbula
Delegate
Orbost Genoa Eden
Bairnsdale Cann River C. Howe
Sale Bemm River Lakes Entrance Pt Hicks

QUEENSLAND

NEW SOUTH WALES

PACIFIC OCEAN

30

155

1

2

3

C

C

B

Wilson's Promontory C
145E
Wickham Bass Strait Furneaux
King I. Naracoopa C. Frankland Flinders I. Group
Currie Whitemark Lady Barron 40S
Stokes Pt Grassy Cape Barren I.
Hunter Is Stanley Banks Strait
C. Grim Smithton Wynyard Burnie C. Portland
Marrawah Ulverstone George Gladstone
Devonport Penguin Town Bridport Eddystone Pt
Deloraine Latrobe Scottsdale St Marys
Waratah Longford 1573 St Helens
Rosebery 1617 Mt Ossa Ben Lomond
Queenstown Derwent Br Oatlands Freycinet
Strahan Frenchmans Cap Tunbridge Peninsula
1444 Jamieson Maria I.
Macquarie Hbr TASMANIA Spring Bay
New Norfolk C. Bay
Maydena Sorell Tasman Pen
Huonville Hobart C. Pillar
Geeveston Bruny I.
Port Davey
S.W. Cape S.E. Cape

at the same scale

4

150

155

35

109

NEW ZEALAND

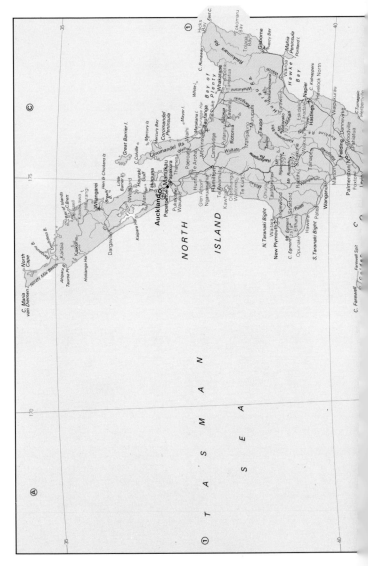

| 0 | 50 | 100 | 150 | 200km |
| 0 | | 50 | | 100 mls |

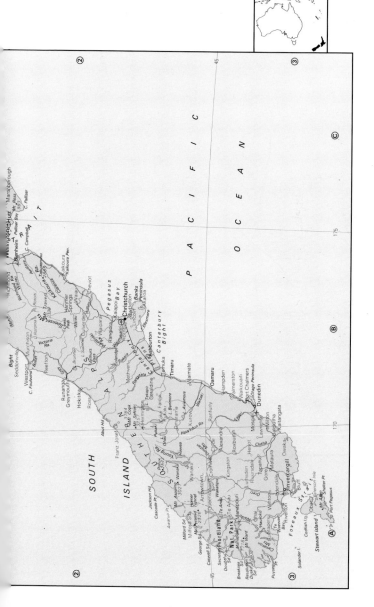

SOUTH ISLAND

PACIFIC OCEAN

SOUTHERN ALPS

Foveaux Strait

Stewart Island

Christchurch

Dunedin

Invercargill

Greymouth

Timaru

Oamaru

Wellington

Blenheim

ANTARCTICA

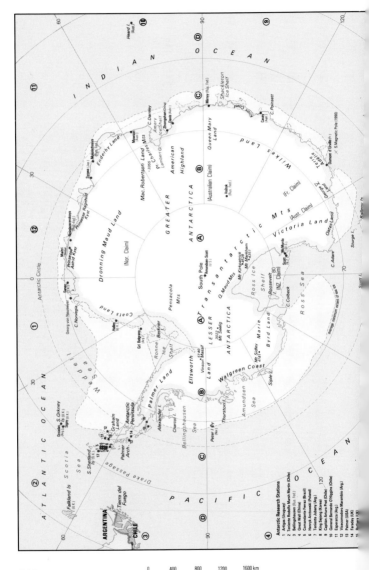

Antarctic Research Stations
1 Artigas (Uruguay)
2 Teniente Rodolfo Marsh Martin (Chile)
3 Bellingshausen (Rus. Fed.)
4 Great Wall (China)
5 Comandante Ferraz (Brazil)
6 Henryk Arctowski (Poland)
7 Teniente Jubany (Arg.)
8 King Sejong (Korea)
9 Capitan Arturo Prat (Chile)
10 General Bernardo O'Higgins (Chile)
11 Esperanza (Arg.)
12 Vicecomodoro Marambio (Arg.)
13 Palmer (USA)
14 Faraday (UK)
15 Rothera (UK)

Index

In the index, the first number refers to the page, and the following letter and number to the section of the map in which the index entry can be found. For example, 48C2 **Paris** means that Paris can be found on page 48 where column C and row 2 meet.

Abbreviations used in the index

Afghan	Afghanistan	Hung	Hungary	Pol	Poland	Arch	Archipelago
Alb	Albania	Ind	Indonesia	Port	Portugal	B	Bay
Alg	Algeria	Irish Rep	Ireland	Rom	Romania	C	Cape
Ant	Antarctica	Leb	Lebanon	Russian Fed	Russian	Chan	Channel
Arg	Argentina	Lib	Liberia		Federation	Gl	Glacier
Aust	Australia	Liech	Liechtenstein	S Arabia	Saudi Arabia	I(s)	Island(s)
Bang	Bangladesh	Lux	Luxembourg	Scot	Scotland	Lg	Lagoon
Belg	Belgium	Madag	Madagascar	Sen	Senegal	L	Lake
Bol	Bolivia	Malay	Malaysia	S Africa	South Africa	Mt(s)	Mountain(s)
Bulg	Bulgaria	Maur	Mauritania	Switz	Switzerland	O	Ocean
Burk	Burkina	Mor	Morocco	Tanz	Tanzania	P	Pass
Camb	Cambodia	Mozam	Mozambique	Thai	Thailand	Pen	Peninsula
Can	Canada	Neth	Netherlands	Turk	Turkey	Plat	Plateau
CAR	Central African Republic	NZ	New Zealand	USA	United States	Pt	Point
Den	Denmark	Nic	Nicaragua		of America	Res	Reservoir
Dom Rep	Dominican Republic	N Ire	Northern Ireland	Urug	Uruguay	R	River
El Sal	El Salvador	Nig	Nigeria	Ven	Venezuela	S	Sea
Eng	England	Nor	Norway	Viet	Vietnam	Sd	Sound
Eq Guinea	Equatorial Guinea	Pak	Pakistan	Yugos	Yugoslavia	Str	Strait
Eth	Ethiopia	Par	Paraguay	Zim	Zimbabwe	V	Valley
Fin	Finland	PNG	Papua New Guinea				
Germ	Germany	Phil	Philippines				

A

57B2 **Aachen** Germany
46C1 **Aalst** Belg
38K6 **Äänekoski** Fin
47C1 **Aarau** Switz
47B1 **Aare** *R* Switz
72A3 **Aba** China
99D2 **Aba** Nig
99D2 **Aba** Zaire
91A3 **Ābādān** Iran
90B3 **Ābādeh** Iran
96B1 **Abadla** Alg
35B1 **Abaeté** Brazil
35B1 **Abaeté** *R* Brazil
31B2 **Abaetetuba** Brazil
72D1 **Abagnar Qi** China
97C4 **Abakaliki** Nig
63B2 **Abakan**
　Russian Fed
97C3 **Abala** Niger
96C2 **Abalessa** Alg
32C6 **Abancay** Peru
90B3 **Abarqū** Iran
74E2 **Abashiri** Japan
74E2 **Abashiri-wan** *B*
　Japan
71F4 **Abau** PNG
99D2 **Abaya** *L* Eth
99D1 **Abbai** *R* Eth
99E1 **Abbe** *L* Eth
48C1 **Abbeville** France
19B4 **Abbeville** Louisiana,
　USA
17B1 **Abbeville** S Carolina,
　USA
45B2 **Abbeyfeale** Irish Rep
47C2 **Abbiategrasso** Italy
20B1 **Abbotsford** Can
84C2 **Abbottabad** Pak
61H3 **Abdulino**
　Russian Fed
98C1 **Abéché** Chad
39F7 **Åbenrå** Den
99D2 **Abeokuta** Nig
43B3 **Aberaeron** Wales

15C3 **Aberdeen** Maryland,
　USA
100B4 **Aberdeen** S Africa
44C3 **Aberdeen** Scot
8D2 **Aberdeen** S Dakota,
　USA
8A2 **Aberdeen**
　Washington, USA
4J3 **Aberdeen L** Can
44C3 **Aberfeldy** Scot
43C4 **Abergavenny** Wales
43B3 **Aberystwyth** Wales
81C4 **Abhā** S Arabia
90A2 **Abhar** Iran
97B4 **Abidjan** Ivory Coast
18A2 **Abilene** Kansas, USA
9D3 **Abilene** Texas, USA
43D4 **Abingdon** Eng
7B4 **Abitibi** *R* Can
7C5 **Abitibi,L** Can
61F5 **Abkhazskaya**
　Respublika, Georgia
84C2 **Abohar** India
97C4 **Abomey** Benin
98B2 **Abong Mbang** Cam
79A4 **Aborlan** Phil
98B1 **Abou Deïa** Chad
91A4 **Abqaiq** S Arabia
50A2 **Abrantes** Port
99C1 **Abri** Sudan
106A3 **Abrolhos** *Is* Aust
8B2 **Absaroka Range** *Mts*
　USA
91B5 **Abū al Abyad** *I* UAE
91A4 **Abū 'Ali** *I* S Arabia
91B5 **Abū Dhabi** UAE
95C1 **Abu Hamed** Sudan
97C4 **Abuja** Nig
33D5 **Abunã** Brazil
32D6 **Abunã** *R* Bol
93D3 **Abū Sukhayr** Iraq
111B2 **Abut Head** *C* NZ
95C3 **Abu 'Urug** *Well*
　Sudan
99C1 **Abuye Meda** *Mt* Eth
99C1 **Abu Zabad** Sudan
99D2 **Abwong** Sudan

56B1 **Åby** Den
94B3 **Aby 'Aweigila** *Well*
　Egypt
99C2 **Abyei** Sudan
24B2 **Acámbaro** Mexico
24B2 **Acaponeta** Mexico
24B3 **Acapulco** Mexico
31D2 **Acaraú** Brazil
32D2 **Acarigua** Ven
24C3 **Acatlán** Mexico
23B2 **Acatzingo** Mexico
97B4 **Accra** Ghana
85D4 **Achalpur** India
29B4 **Achao** Chile
47D1 **Achensee** *L* Austria
46E2 **Achern** Germany
41A3 **Achill I** Irish Rep
63B2 **Achinsk** Russian Fed
53C3 **Acireale** Italy
26C2 **Acklins** *I*
　Caribbean S
32C6 **Acobamba** Peru
29B2 **Aconcagua** *Mt* Chile
31D3 **Acopiara** Brazil
88B4 **Açores** *Is* Atlantic O
　A Coruña = La Coruña
47C2 **Acqui** Italy
108A2 **Acraman,L** Aust
　Acre = 'Akko
32C5 **Acre** State, Brazil
22C3 **Acton** USA
23B1 **Actopan** Mexico
19A3 **Ada** USA
50B1 **Adaja** *R* Spain
91C5 **Adam** Oman
35A2 **Adamantina** Brazil
98B2 **Adamaoua** Region,
　Nig/Cam
47D1 **Adamello** *Mt* Italy
16C1 **Adams** USA
87B3 **Adam's Bridge** India/
　Sri Lanka
13D2 **Adams L** Can
87C3 **Adam's Peak** *Mt*
　Sri Lanka
81C4 **'Adan** Yemen

92C2 **Adana** Turk
60D5 **Adapazari** Turk
112B7 **Adare,C** Ant
108B1 **Adavale** Aust
47C2 **Adda** *R* Italy
91A4 **Ad Dahna'** Region,
　S Arabia
96A2 **Ad Dakhla** Mor
81C4 **Ad Dālī'** Yemen
91B4 **Ad Damman**
　S Arabia
91A4 **Ad Dibdibah** Region,
　S Arabia
91A5 **Ad Dilam** S Arabia
91A5 **Ad Dir'iyah** S Arabia
93D3 **Ad Diwaniyah** Iraq
93D3 **Ad Duwayd** S Arabia
106C4 **Adelaide** Aust
4J3 **Adelaide Pen** Can
22D3 **Adelanto** USA
　Aden = 'Adan
81C4 **Aden,G of** Yemen/
　Somalia
97C3 **Aderbissinat** Niger
94C2 **Adhra** Syria
71E4 **Adi** *I* Indon
52B1 **Adige** *R* Italy
99D1 **Adigrat** Eth
85D5 **Ādilābād** India
20B2 **Adin** USA
15D2 **Adirondack Mts** USA
99D2 **Ādīs Ābeba** Eth
95C3 **Adi Ugai** Eritrea
93C2 **Adiyaman** Turk
54C1 **Adjud** Rom
4E4 **Admiralty I** USA
6B2 **Admiralty Inlet** *B*
　Can
87B1 **Adoni** India
48B3 **Adour** *R* France
96C2 **Adrar** *Mts* Alg
96A2 **Adrar** Region, Maur
96A2 **Adrar** Alg
96A2 **Adrar Soutouf**
　Region, Mor
98C1 **Adré** Chad
95A2 **Adri** Libya
47E2 **Adria** Italy

Adrian

14B2 Adrian Michigan, USA
52B2 Adriatic S S Europe
99D1 Adwa Eth
97B4 Adzopé Ivory Coast
55B3 Aegean S Greece
80E2 Afghanistan Republic, Asia
99E2 Afgooye Somalia
97C4 Afikpo Nig
38G6 Afjord Nor
96C1 Aflou Alg
99E2 Afmadu Somalia
99E2 Afolle Region, Maur
94B2 Afula Israel
92B2 Afyon Turk
95A3 Agadem Niger
97C3 Agadez Niger
96B1 Agadir Mor
85D4 Agar India
86C2 Agartala India
20B1 Agassiz Can
97B4 Agboville Ivory Coast
93E1 Agdam Azerbaijan
75B1 Agematsu Japan
48C3 Agen France
90A3 Agha Jari Iran
96A2 Aghwinirt Well Mor
47D2 Agno R Italy
47E1 Agordo Italy
48C3 Agout R France
85D3 Agra India
93D2 Agri Turk
53C2 Agri R Italy
53B3 Agrigento Italy
55B3 Agrinion Greece
34A3 Agrio R Chile
53B2 Agropoli Italy
61H2 Agryz Russian Fed
6E3 Agto Greenland
27D3 Aguadilla Puerto Rico
24B1 Agua Prieta Mexico
24B2 Aguascalientes Mexico
23A1 Aguascalientes State, Mexico
35C1 Aguas Formosas Brazil
50A1 Agueda Port
96C3 Aguelhok Mali
50B2 Aguilas Spain
23A2 Aguililla Mexico
100B4 Agulhas,C S Africa
79C4 Agusan R Phil
Ahaggar = Hoggar
93E2 Ahar Iran
110B1 Ahipara B NZ
85C4 Ahmadabad India
87A1 Ahmadnagar India
99E2 Ahmar Mts Eth
46D1 Ahr R Germany
46D1 Ahrgebirge Region, Germany
23A1 Ahuacatlán Mexico
23A1 Ahualulco Mexico
39J7 Ahus Sweden
90B2 Ahuvan Iran
90A3 Ahvaz Iran
26A4 Aiajuela Costa Rica
47B1 Aigle Switz
47B2 Aiguille d'Arves Mt France
47B2 Aiguille de la Grand Sassière Mt France
75B1 Aikawa Japan
17B1 Aiken USA
73A5 Ailao Shan Upland China
35C1 Aimorés Brazil
96B1 Ain Beni Mathar Mor
95B2 Ain Dalla Well Egypt
51C2 Ain el Hadjel Alg
95A3 Ain Galakka Chad
48B3 Ain Sefra Alg
92B4 'Ain Sukhna Egypt
75A2 Aioi Japan
96B2 Aioun Abd el Malek Well Maur
97B3 Aioun El Atrouss Maur
30C2 Aiquile Bol
97C3 Air Desert Region Niger

13E2 Airdrie Can
46B1 Aire France
42D3 Aire R Eng
46C2 Aire R France
6C3 Airforce I Can
47C1 Airolo Switz
4E3 Aishihik Can
12G2 Aishihik L Can
46B2 Aisne Department, France
49C2 Aisne R France
71F4 Aitape PNG
58D1 Aiviekste R Latvia
72B2 Aixa Zuogi China
49D3 Aix-en-Provence France
47A2 Aix-les-Bains France
86B2 Aiyar Res India
55B3 Aiyion Greece
55B3 Aiyna / Greece
86C2 Aizawl India
100A3 Aizeb R Namibia
74E3 Aizu-Wakamatsu Japan
52A2 Ajaccio Corse
23B2 Ajalpan Mexico
23A1 Ajana Mexico
74E2 Ajigasawa Japan
94B2 Ajlun Jordan
91C4 Ajman UAE
85C3 Ajmer India
9B3 Ajo USA
23A2 Ajuchitan Mexico
55C3 Ak R Turk
75B1 Akaishi-sanchi Mts Japan
87B1 Akalkot India
111B2 Akaroa NZ
75A2 Akashi Japan
61J3 Akbulak Russian Fed
93C2 Akçakale Turk
96A2 Akchar Watercourse Maur
55C3 Akdağ Mt Turk
98C2 Aketi Zaïre
93D1 Akhalkalaki Georgia
93D1 Akhalsikhe Georgia
55B3 Akharnaí Greece
12C3 Akhiok USA
92A2 Akhisar Turk
58D1 Akhiste Latvia
95C2 Akhmim Egypt
61G4 Akhtubinsk Russian Fed
60D4 Akhtyrka Ukraine
75A2 Aki Japan
7B4 Akimiski I Can
74E3 Akita Japan
96A3 Akjoujt Maur
94B2 'Akko Israel
4E3 Aklavik USA
97B3 Aklé Aouana Desert Region Maur
99D2 Akobo Sudan
99D2 Akobo R Sudan
84B1 Akoha Afghan
87B1 Akola India
85D4 Akot India
6D3 Akpatok I Can
55B3 Akra Kafirévs C Greece
55B3 Akra Maléa C Greece
38A2 Akranes Iceland
55C3 Akra Sidheros C Greece
55B3 Akra Spátha C Greece
55B3 Akra Tainaron C Greece
10B2 Akron USA
94A1 Akrotiri B Cyprus
84D1 Aksai Chin Mts China
92B2 Aksaray Turk
61H3 Aksay Kazakhstan
84D1 Aksayquin Hu L China
92B2 Aksehir Turk
92B2 Akseki Turk
63D2 Aksenovo Zilovskoye Russian Fed
68D1 Aksha Russian Fed
82C1 Aksu China

61H5 Aktau Kazakhstan
65J5 Aktogay Kazakhstan
61J4 Aktumsyk Kazakhstan
65G4 Aktyubinsk Kazakhstan
38B1 Akureyri Iceland
Akyab = Sittwe
65K5 Akzhal Kazakhstan
11B3 Alabama State, USA
11B3 Alabama R USA
17A1 Alabaster USA
93C2 Ala Dağlari Mts Turk
61F5 Alagir Russian Fed
47B2 Alagna Italy
31D3 Alagoas State, Brazil
31D4 Alagoinhas Brazil
51B1 Alagón Spain
93E4 Al Ahmadi Kuwait
25D3 Alajuela Costa Rica
12B2 Alakanuk USA
38L5 Alakurtti Russian Fed
93E3 Al Amārah Iraq
21A2 Alameda USA
23B1 Alamo Mexico
9C3 Alamogordo USA
9C3 Alamosa USA
39H6 Aland / Fin
92B2 Alanya Turk
17B1 Alapaha R USA
65H4 Alapayevsk Russian Fed
92A2 Alaşehir Turk
68C3 Ala Shan Mts China
4C3 Alaska State, USA
4D4 Alaska,G of USA
12C3 Alaska Pen USA
4C3 Alaska Range Mts USA
52A2 Alassio Italy
12D1 Alatna R USA
61G3 Alatyr' Russian Fed
108B2 Alawoona Aust
91C5 Al 'Ayn UAE
82B2 Alayskiy Khrebet Mts Tajikistan
49D3 Alba Italy
92C2 Al Bāb Syria
51B2 Albacete Spain
50A1 Alba de Tormes Spain
93D2 Al Badi Iraq
54B1 Alba Iulia Rom
54A2 Albania Republic, Europe
106A4 Albany Aust
17B1 Albany Georgia, USA
15D2 Albany New York, USA
8A2 Albany Oregon, USA
7B4 Albany R Can
34B2 Albardón Arg
91C5 Al Batinah Region, Oman
71F5 Albatross B Aust
95B1 Al Baydā Libya
11C3 Albemarle Sd USA
50B1 Alberche R Spain
108A1 Alberga Aust
46B1 Albert France
5G4 Alberta Province, Can
99D2 Albert,L Uganda/Zaïre
10A2 Albert Lea USA
99D2 Albert Nile R Uganda
49D2 Albertville France
48C3 Albi France
33G2 Albina Suriname
14B2 Albion Michigan, USA
15C2 Albion New York, USA
92C4 Al Bi'r S Arabia
91A5 Al Biyadh Region, S Arabia
50B2 Alborán / Spain
39G7 Alborg Den
93D3 Al Bū Kamāl Syria
47C1 Albula R Switz
9C3 Albuquerque USA
91C5 Al Buraymi Oman

95A1 Al Burayqah Libya
95B1 Al Burdi Libya
107D4 Albury Aust
93E3 Al Buşayyah Iraq
50B1 Alcala de Henares Spain
53B3 Alcamo Italy
51B1 Alcaniz Spain
31C2 Alcântara Brazil
50B2 Alcaraz Spain
50B2 Alcázar de San Juan Spain
51B2 Alcira Spain
35D1 Alcobaça Brazil
50B1 Alcolea de Pinar Spain
51B2 Alcoy Spain
51C2 Alcudia Spain
89J8 Aldabra Is Indian O
63E2 Aldan Russian Fed
63E2 Aldanskoye Nagor'ye Upland Russian Fed
43E3 Aldeburgh Eng
48B2 Alderney I UK
43D4 Aldershot Eng
19B3 Aledo USA
30E4 Alegrete Brazil
34C2 Alejandro Roca Arg
30H6 Alejandro Selkirk I Chile
63G2 Aleksandrovsk Sakhalinskiy Russian Fed
65J4 Alekseyevka Kazakhstan
60E3 Aleksin Russian Fed
58B1 Alem Sweden
35C2 Além Paraiba Brazil
49C2 Alençon France
21C4 Alenuihaha Chan Hawaiian Is
Aleppo = Halab
6D1 Alert Can
49C3 Alès France
52A2 Alessandria Italy
64B3 Alesund Nor
12C3 Aleutian Range Mts USA
4E4 Alexander Arch S Africa
100A3 Alexander Bay S Africa
17A1 Alexander City USA
112C3 Alexander I Ant
111A3 Alexandra NZ
29G8 Alexandra,C South Georgia
6C2 Alexandra Fjord Can
95B1 Alexandria Libya
11A3 Alexandria Louisiana, USA
10A2 Alexandria Minnesota, USA
10C3 Alexandria Virginia, USA
55C2 Alexandroúpolis Greece
13C2 Alexis Creek Can
94B2 Aley Leb
65K4 Aleysk Russian Fed
93D3 Al Fallūjah Iraq
51B1 Alfaro Spain
54C2 Alfatar Bulg
93E3 Al Fāw Iraq
35B2 Alfensas Brazil
55B3 Alfiós R Greece
47D2 Alfonsine Italy
35C2 Alfonzo Cláudio Brazil
35C2 Alfredo Chaves Brazil
61J4 Alga Kazakhstan
34B3 Algarrobo del Aguila Arg
50A2 Algeciras Spain
96C1 Alger Alg
96B2 Algeria Republic, Africa
53A2 Alghero Sardegna
Algiers = Alger
15C1 Algonquin Park Can
91C5 Al Hadd Oman
93D3 Al Hadithah Iraq
92C3 Al Hadithah S Arabia

93D2 Al Haḍr *Iraq*
91C5 Al Hajar al Gharbi *Mts Oman*
91C5 Al Hajar ash Sharqi *Mts Oman*
93C3 Al Hamad *Desert Region Jordan/ S Arabia*
93E4 Al Hanīyah *Desert Region Iraq*
91A5 Al Harīq S Arabia
93C3 Al Harrah *Desert Region S Arabia*
95A2 Al Harūj al Aswad *Upland Libya*
91A4 Al Hasa, *Region, S Arabia*
93D2 Al Hasakah *Syria*
93C4 Al Hawjā' S Arabia
93E3 Al Hayy *Iraq*
94C2 Al Hijānah *Syria*
93D3 Al Hillah *Iraq*
91A5 Al Hillah S Arabia
96B1 Al Hoceima *Mor*
91A4 Al Hufūf S Arabia
91B5 Al Humrah, *Region, UAE*
91C5 Al Huwatsah *Oman*
90A2 Alīābad *Iran*
91C4 Alīabad *Iran*
55B2 Aliákmon *R Greece*
93E3 Al al Gharbi *Iraq*
87A1 Alībāq *India*
51B2 Alicante *Spain*
9D4 Alice *USA*
106C3 Alice Springs *Aust*
53B3 Alicudi *I Italy*
84D3 Aligarh *India*
90A3 Aligüdarz *Iran*
84B2 Ali-Khel *Afghan*
55C3 Alimnía *I Greece*
86B1 Alīpur Duār *India*
14B2 Aliquippa *USA*
22B2 Aliṣal *USA*
93C3 Al' Isawiyah S Arabia
100B4 Aliwal North S Africa
95B2 Al Jaghbūb *Libya*
93D3 Al Jālamīd S Arabia
95B2 Al Jawf *Libya*
93C4 Al Jawf S Arabia
93D2 Al Jazīrah *Desert Region Syria/Iraq*
50A2 Aljezur *Port*
91A4 Al Jubayl S Arabia
91C5 Al Kāmil *Oman*
93D2 Al Khābūr *R Syria*
91C5 Al Khābūrah *Oman*
93D3 Al Khālis *Iraq*
91C4 Al Khasab *Oman*
91B4 Al Khawr *Qatar*
95A1 Al Khums *Libya*
91B5 Al Kidan, *Region, S Arabia*
94C2 Al Kiswah *Syria*
56A2 Alkmaar *Neth*
95B2 Al Kufrah Oasis *Libya*
93E3 Al Kūt *Iraq*
92C2 Al Lādhiqīyah *Syria*
86A1 Allahābad *India*
94C2 Al Lajāh *Mt Syria*
12D1 Allakaket *USA*
76B2 Allanmyo *Burma*
95C2 'Allaqi' *Watercourse Egypt*
17B1 Allatoona L *USA*
15C2 Allegheny *R USA*
10C3 Allegheny Mts *USA*
17B1 Allendale *USA*
111A3 Allen,Mt *NZ*
15C2 Allentown *USA*
87B3 Alleppey *India*
49C2 Aller *R France*
47D1 Allgäu *Mts Germany*
81C3 Al Lith S Arabia
91B5 Al Liwā *Region, UAE*
109D1 Allora *Aust*
14B2 Alma *Michigan, USA*
82B1 Alma Ata *Kazakhstan*
50A2 Almada *Port*
81 Al Madīnah = Medina
71F2 Almagan *I Pacific O*
91B4 Al Manāmah *Bahrain*
93D3 Al Ma'niyah *Iraq*

21A1 Almanor,L *USA*
51B2 Almansa *Spain*
13B1 Alma Peak *Mt Can*
91B5 Al Māriyyah *UAE*
95B1 Al Marj *Libya*
 Almaty = Alma Ata
93D2 Al Mawsil *Iraq*
50B1 Almazán *Spain*
35C1 Almenara *Brazil*
50B2 Almería *Spain*
61H3 Al'met'yevsk *Russian Fed*
56C1 Älmhult *Sweden*
93E3 Al Miqdādiyah *Iraq*
112C3 Almirante Brown *Base Ant*
34A1 Almirante Latorre *Chile*
55B3 Almirós *Greece*
91A4 Al Mish'āb S Arabia
50A2 Almodôvar *Port*
84D3 Almora *India*
91A4 Al Mubarraz S Arabia
92C4 Al Mudawwara *Jordan*
91C5 Al Mudaybi *Oman*
91B4 Al Muharraq *Bahrain*
81C4 Al Mukalla *Yemen*
81C4 Al Mukhā *Yemen*
91B3 Al Musayyib *Iraq*
44B3 Alness *Scot*
93E3 Al Nu'māniyah *Iraq*
42D2 Alnwick *Eng*
71D4 Alor *I Indon*
77C4 Alor Setar *Malay*
 Alost = Aalst
107E2 Alotau *PNG*
106B3 Aloysius,Mt *Aust*
34C3 Alpachiri *Arg*
14B1 Alpena *USA*
47B2 Alpes du Valais *Mts Switz*
52B1 Alpi Dolomitiche *Mts Italy*
47B2 Alpi Graie *Mts Italy*
9C3 Alpine *Texas, USA*
47C1 Alpi Orobie *Mts Italy*
47B2 Alpi Pennine *Mts Italy*
47C1 Alpi Retiche *Mts Switz*
47D1 Alpi Venoste *Mts Italy*
52A1 Alps *Mts Europe*
95A1 Al Qaddāhiyah *Libya*
94C1 Al Qadmūs *Syria*
93D3 Al Qā'im *Iraq*
93C4 Al Qalībah S Arabia
93D2 Al Qāmishli *Syria*
95A1 Al Qaryah ash Sharqīyah *Libya*
92C3 Al Qaryatayn *Syria*
91A4 Al Qatīf S Arabia
95A2 Al Qaţrūn *Libya*
91A4 Al Qaysāmah S Arabia
94C2 Al Quatayfah *Syria*
50A2 Alqueva *R Port*
92C3 Al Qunayţirah *Syria*
81C4 Al Qunfidhah S Arabia
93E3 Al Qurnah *Iraq*
94C1 Al Quşayr *Syria*
92C3 Al Qutayfah *Syria*
56B1 Als *I Den*
49D2 Alsace *Region, France*
57B2 Alsfeld *Germany*
42C2 Alston *Eng*
38J5 Alta *Nor*
29D2 Alta Gracia *Arg*
27D5 Altagracia de Orituco *Ven*
68A2 Altai *Mts Mongolia*
17B1 Altamaha *R USA*
33G4 Altamira *Brazil*
23B1 Altamira *Mexico*
53C2 Altamura *Italy*
68C1 Altanbulag *Mongolia*
71D4 Altape *PNG*
24B2 Altata *Mexico*
63A3 Altay *China*
63B3 Altay *Mongolia*
63A2 Altay *Mts*

 Russian Fed
47C1 Altdorf *Switz*
46D1 Altenkirchen *Germany*
34B3 Altiplanicie del Payún *Plat Arg*
47B1 Altkirch *France*
101C2 Alto Molócue *Mozam*
10A3 Alton *USA*
15C2 Altoona *USA*
34B2 Alto Pencoso *Mts Arg*
35A1 Alto Sucuriú *Brazil*
23B2 Altotonga *Mexico*
23A2 Altoyac de Alvarez *Mexico*
82C2 Altun Shan *Mts China*
20B2 Alturas *USA*
9D3 Altus *USA*
91B5 Al'Ubaylah S Arabia
93C4 Al Urayq *Desert Region S Arabia*
91B5 Al'Ūruq al Mu'taridah *Region, S Arabia*
9D2 Alva *USA*
23B2 Alvarado *Mexico*
19A3 Alvarado *USA*
39C6 Alvdalen *Sweden*
19A4 Alvin *USA*
38J5 Alvsbyn *Sweden*
80B3 Al Wajh S Arabia
85D3 Alwar *India*
93D3 Al Widyān *Desert Region Iraq/S Arabia*
72A4 Alxa Yougi *China*
93E2 Alyat *Azerbaijan*
39J8 Alytus *Lithuania*
46E2 Alzey *Germany*
23B2 Amacuzac *R Mexico*
99D2 Amadi *Sudan*
6C3 Amadjuak L *Can*
74B4 Amakusa-shotō *I Japan*
39G7 Amål *Sweden*
63D2 Amalat *R Russian Fed*
55B3 Amaliás *Greece*
85D4 Amalner *India*
69E4 Amami *I Japan*
69E4 Amami gunto *Arch Japan*
100C4 Amanzimtoti S Africa
33G3 Amapá *Brazil*
33G3 Amapá State, *Brazil*
9C3 Amarillo *USA*
60E5 Amasya *Turk*
23A1 Amatitan *Mexico*
 Amazonas = Solimões
32D4 Amazonas State, *Brazil*
28C3 Amazonas *R Brazil*
84D2 Ambāla *India*
87C3 Ambalangoda *Sri Lanka*
101D3 Ambalavao *Madag*
98B2 Ambam *Cam*
101D2 Ambanja *Madag*
1C7 Ambarchik *Russian Fed*
32B4 Ambato *Ecuador*
101D2 Ambato-Boeny *Madag*
101D2 Ambatolampy *Madag*
101D2 Ambatondrazaka *Madag*
57C3 Amberg *Germany*
25D3 Ambergris Cay *I Belize*
86A2 Ambikāpur *India*
101D2 Ambilobe *Madag*
101D3 Amboasary *Madag*
101D2 Ambodifototra *Madag*
101D3 Ambohimahasoa *Madag*
71D4 Ambon *Indon*
101D3 Ambositra *Madag*
101D3 Ambovombe *Madag*
98B3 Ambriz *Angola*
98C1 Am Dam *Chad*

64H3 Amderma *Russian Fed*
24B2 Ameca *Mexico*
23B2 Amecacameca *Mexico*
34C2 Ameghino *Arg*
56B2 Ameland *I Neth*
16C2 Amenia *USA*
112B10 American Highland *Upland Ant*
105H4 American Samoa *Is Pacific O*
17B1 Americus *USA*
101G1 Amersfoort S Africa
112C10 Amery Ice Shelf *Ant*
55B3 Amfíklia *Greece*
55B3 Amfissa *Greece*
63F1 Amga *Russian Fed*
63F1 Amgal *R Russian Fed*
69F2 Amga *Russian Fed*
69F1 Amgun' *R Russian Fed*
99D1 Amhara *Region Eth*
7D5 Amherst *Can*
16C1 Amherst *Massachusetts, USA*
 Amherst = Kyaikkami
87B2 Amhūr *India*
48C2 Amiens *France*
75B1 Amino *Japan*
94B1 Amioune *Leb*
89K8 Amirante Is *Indian O*
86B1 Amlekhgan *Nepal*
92C3 Amman *Jordan*
38K6 Ämmänsaario *Fin*
56B2 Ammersfoort *Neth*
90B2 Amol *Iran*
55C3 Amorgós *I Greece*
7C5 Amos *Can*
 Amoy = Xiamen
101D3 Ampanihy *Madag*
25B2 Amparo *Brazil*
51C1 Amposta *Spain*
85D4 Amrávati *India*
85C4 Amreli *India*
84C2 Amritsar *India*
56A2 Amsterdam *Neth*
101H1 Amsterdam S Africa
15D2 Amsterdam *USA*
98C1 Am Timan *Chad*
88L3 Amu Darya *R Uzbekistan*
6A2 Amund Ringes I *Can*
4F2 Amundsen S *Can*
112B4 Amundsen S *Ant*
80E Amundsen-Scott *Base Ant*
78D3 Amuntai *Indon*
63D2 Amur *R Russian Fed*
33E2 Anaco *Ven*
8B2 Anaconda *USA*
20B1 Anacortes *USA*
55C3 Anáfi *I Greece*
93D3 'Anah *Iraq*
21B3 Anaheim *USA*
87B2 Anaimalai Hills *India*
83C4 Anakapalle *India*
12E1 Anaktuvuk P *USA*
101D2 Analalava *Madag*
92B2 Anamur *Turk*
75A2 Anan *Japan*
87B2 Anantapur *India*
84D2 Anantnag *India*
31B5 Anápolis *Brazil*
90C3 Anār *Iran*
90B3 Anārak *Iran*
71F2 Anatahan *I Pacific O*
30D4 Añatuya *Arg*
74B3 Anbyon *N Korea*
22C4 Anacpa Is *USA*
4D3 Anchorage *USA*
30C2 Ancohuma *Mt Bol*
32B6 Ancón *Peru*
52B2 Ancona *Italy*
16C1 Ancram *USA*
29B4 Ancud *Chile*
34A3 Andacollo *Arg*
108A1 Andado *Aust*
32C6 Andahuaylas *Peru*
38F6 Andalsnes *Nor*
50A2 Andalucia *Region, Spain*
17A1 Andalusia *USA*

Andaman Is

83D4	Andaman Is Burma
83D4	Andaman S Burma
108A2	Andamooka Aust
38H5	Andenes Nor
47C1	Andermatt Switz
57B2	Andernach Germany
14A2	Anderson Indiana, USA
18B2	Anderson Missouri, USA
17B1	Anderson S Carolina, USA
4F3	Anderson R Can
87B1	Andhra Pradesh State, India
55B3	Andikíthira I Greece
65J5	Andizhan Uzbekistan
65H6	Andkhui Afghan
74B3	Andong S Korea
51C1	Andorra Principality, SW Europe
51C1	Andorra-La-Vella Andorra
43D4	Andover Eng
35A2	Andradina Brazil
12B2	Andreafsky I Greece
92B2	Andreas,C Cyprus
53C2	Andria Italy
11C4	Andros I The Bahamas
55B3	Andros I Greece
87A2	Androth I India
50B2	Andújar Spain
100A2	Andulo Angola
97C4	Anécho Togo
97C3	Anéfis Mali
34B3	Añelo Arg
63C2	Angarsk Russian Fed
38H6	Ange Sweden
24A2	Angel de la Guarda I Mexico
79B2	Angeles Phil
39G7	Angelholm Sweden
109C1	Angellala Creek R Aust
22B1	Angels Camp USA
71E4	Angemuk Mt Indon
48B2	Angers France
76C3	Angkor Hist Site Camb
41C3	Anglesey I Wales
19A4	Angleton USA
6G3	Angmagssalik Greenland
101D2	Angoche Mozam
29B3	Angol Chile
14B2	Angola Indiana, USA
100A2	Angola Republic, Africa
103H6	Angola Basin Atlantic O
12H3	Angoon USA
48C2	Angoulême France
96A1	Angra do Heroísmo Açores
35C2	Angra dos Reis Brazil
34C3	Anguil Arg
27E3	Anguilla I Caribbean S
26B2	Anguilla Cays Is Caribbean S
86B2	Angul India
99C2	Angumu Zaire
56C1	Anholt I Den
73C4	Anhua China
72D3	Anhui Province, China
12C2	Aniak USA
35B1	Anicuns Brazil
46B2	Anizy-le-Château France
4C3	Anjak USA
48B2	Anjou Region, France
101D2	Anjouan I Comoros
101D2	Anjozorobo Madag
74B3	Anju N Korea
72B3	Ankang China
92B2	Ankara Turk
101D2	Ankaratra Mt Madag
101D3	Ankazoabo Madag
101D2	Ankazobe Madag
56C2	Anklam Germany
76D3	An Loc Viet

73B4	Anlong China
73C3	Anlu China
18C2	Anna USA
96C1	'Annaba Alg
92C3	An Nabk S Arabia
92C3	An Nabk Syria
108A1	Anna Creek Aust
80C3	An Nafūd Desert S Arabia
93D3	An Najaf Iraq
42C2	Annan Scot
15C3	Annapolis USA
86A1	Annapurna Mt Nepal
14B2	Ann Arbor USA
94C1	An Nasirah Syria
93E3	An Nãsiriyah Iraq
47B2	Annecy France
47B1	Annemasse France
76D3	An Nhon Viet
17A1	Anniston USA
89E8	Annobon I Eq Guinea
49C2	Annonay France
27J1	Annotto Bay Jamaica
73D3	Anqing China
72B2	Ansai China
36C1	Ansbach Germany
26C3	Anse d'Hainault Haiti
72E1	Anshan China
73B4	Anshun China
97C3	Ansongo Mali
14B3	Ansted USA
92C2	Antakya Turk
101E2	Antalaha Madag
92B2	Antalya Turk
92B2	Antalya Körfezi B Turk
101D2	Antananarivo Madag
112C1	Antarctic Circle Ant
112C3	Antarctic Pen Ant
50B2	Antequera Spain
96B2	Anti-Atlas Mts Mor
7D5	Anticosti, I. d' Can
27E3	Antigua I Caribbean S
	Anti Lebanon = Jebel esh Sharqi
21A2	Antioch USA
19A3	Antlers USA
30B3	Antofagasta Chile
45C1	Antrim County, N Ire
45C1	Antrim N Ire
45C1	Antrim Hills N Ire
101D2	Antseranana Madag
101D2	Antsirabe Madag
101D2	Antsohihy Madag
20B1	An Tuc Viet
46C1	Antwerpen Belg
45C2	An Uaimh Irish Rep
84C3	Anupgarh India
87C3	Anuradhapura Sri Lanka
	Anvers = Antwerpen
4B3	Anvik USA
63B3	Anxi China
72C2	Anyang China
72A3	Anyêmaqên Shan Upland China
47C2	Anza R Italy
13E1	Anzac Can
65K4	Anzhero-Sudzhensk Russian Fed
53B2	Anzio Italy
74E2	Aomori Japan
52A1	Aosta Italy
97B3	Aoukâr Desert Region Maur
96C2	Aoulef Alg
95A2	Aozou Chad
30E3	Apa R Brazil/Par
11B4	Apalachee B USA
17B2	Apalachicola USA
17A2	Apalachicola B USA
23B2	Apan Mexico
64E3	Apatity Russian Fed
32C3	Apaporis R Colombia
35A2	Aparecida do Taboado Brazil
79B2	Aparri Phil
54A1	Apatin Croatia

64E3	Apatity Russian Fed
24B3	Apatzingan Mexico
56B2	Apeldoorn Neth
35B2	Apiaí Brazil
33F2	Apoera Surinam
108B3	Apollo Bay Aust
79C4	Apo,Mt Mt Phil
17B2	Apopka,L USA
30F2	Aporé R Brazil
10A2	Apostle Is USA
10A2	Apostle L USA
23A1	Apozol Mexico
11B3	Appalachian Mts USA
52B2	Appennino Abruzzese Mts Italy
52A2	Appennino Ligure Mts Italy
53C2	Appennino Lucano Mts Italy
53B2	Appennino Napoletano Mts Italy
52B2	Appennino Tosco-Emiliano Mts Italy
52B2	Appennino Umbro-Marchigiano Mts Italy
47C1	Appenzell Switz
42C2	Appleby Eng
14A2	Appleton Wisconsin, USA
30F3	Apucarana Brazil
23B1	Apulco Mexico
32D2	Apure R Ven
32C6	Apurimac R Peru
92C4	'Aqaba Jordan
92B4	'Aqaba,G of Egypt/ S Arabia
90B3	'Aqdã Iran
30E3	Aquidauana Brazil
23A2	Aquila Mexico
86A1	Ara India
17A1	Arab USA
81D4	Arabian S Asia/ Arabian Pen
31D4	Aracaju Brazil
30E3	Aracanguy, Mts de Par
31D2	Aracati Brazil
30F3	Araçatuba Brazil
50A2	Aracena Spain
31C5	Araçuai Brazil
94B3	Arad Israel
60B4	Arad Rom
98B2	Arada Chad
91B5	'Arãdah UAE
106C1	Arafura S Indon/Aust
30F2	Aragarças Brazil
51B1	Aragón Region, Spain
50B1	Aragón R Spain
33G6	Araguaia R Brazil
31B3	Araguaiana Brazil
31B5	Araguari Brazil
35B1	Araguari R Brazil
75B1	Arai Japan
96C2	Arak Alg
90A3	Arak Iran
76A2	Arakan Yoma Mts Burma
87B2	Arakkonam India
65G5	Aral Sea Kazakhstan/ Uzbekistan
80E1	Aral'sk Kazakhstan
	Aral'skoye More = Aral S
40B2	Aran I Irish Rep
50B1	Aranda de Duero Spain
23A1	Arandas Mexico
50B1	Aranjuez Spain
75A2	Arao Japan
97B3	Araouane Mali
29E2	Arapey R Urug
31D4	Arapiraca Brazil
35A2	Araporgas Brazil
30G4	Ararangua Brazil
31B6	Araraquara Brazil
35B2	Araras Brazil
107D4	Ararat Aust
93D2	Ararat Armenia
93E2	Aras R Azerbaijan
75C1	Arato Japan
32D2	Arauca R Ven

34A3	Arauco Chile
32C2	Arauea Colombia
85C4	Arãvalli Range Mts India
31B5	Araxá Brazil
99D2	Arba Minch Eth
53A3	Arbatax Sardegna
93D2	Arbil Iraq
47A1	Arbois France
39H6	Arbrá Sweden
44C3	Arbroath Scot
47A1	Arc France
47B2	Arc R France
48B3	Arcachon France
17B2	Arcadia USA
20B2	Arcata USA
23A2	Arcelia Mexico
26B2	Archipiélago de Camaguey Arch Cuba
29B6	Archipiélago de la Reina Adelaida Arch Chile
29B4	Archipiélago de los Chones Arch Chile
32B2	Archipiélago de las Perlas Arch Panama
35B2	Arcos Brazil
50A2	Arcos de la Frontera Spain
6B2	Arctic Bay Can
1C1	Arctic Circle
4E3	Arctic Red Can
4E3	Arctic Red R Can
4D3	Arctic Village USA
54C2	Arda R Bulg
65F6	Ardabil Iran
93D1	Ardahan Turk
39F6	Ardal Nor
96C2	Ardar des Iforas Upland Alg/Mali
45C2	Ardee Irish Rep
90B3	Ardekan Iran
46C2	Ardennes Department, France
57A2	Ardennes Region, Belg
90B3	Ardestan Iran
92C3	Ardh es Suwwan Desert Region Jordan
50A2	Ardila R Port
109C2	Ardlethan Aust
9D3	Ardmore USA
44A3	Ardnamurchan Pt Scot
46A1	Ardres France
44B3	Ardrishaig Scot
42B2	Ardrossan Scot
27D3	Arecibo Puerto Rico
31D2	Areia Branca Brazil
21A2	Arena,Pt USA
39F7	Arendal Nor
30B2	Arequipa Peru
52B2	Arezzo Italy
52B2	Argenta Italy
49C2	Argentan France
46B2	Argenteuil France
28C7	Argentina Republic, S America
103F7	Argentine Basin Atlantic O
48C2	Argenton-sur-Creuse France
54C2	Arges R Rom
84B2	Arghardab R Afghan
55B3	Argolikós Kólpos G Greece
46C2	Argonne Region, France
55B3	Árgos Greece
55B3	Argostólion Greece
22B3	Arguello,Pt USA
106B2	Argyle,L Aust
56C1	Arhus Den
100A3	Ariamsvlei Namibia
50B1	Arián zón R Spain
34C2	Arias Arg
97B3	Aribinda Burkina
30B2	Arica Chile
84C2	Arifwala Pak
	Arís = Jericho
27L1	Arima Trinidad
35B1	Arinos Brazil

116

33F6 **Arinos** R Brazil
23A2 **Ario de Rosales** Mexico
27L1 **Aripo,Mt** Trinidad
33E5 **Aripuana** Brazil
33E5 **Aripuana** R Brazil
44B3 **Arisaig** Scot
87B2 **Ariskere** India
13B2 **Aristazabal I** Can
34B3 **Arizona** Arg
9B3 **Arizona** State, USA
39G7 **Arjang** Sweden
61F3 **Arkadak** Russian Fed
19B3 **Arkadelphia** USA
65H4 **Arkalyk** Kazakhstan
11A3 **Arkansas** State, USA
11A3 **Arkansas** R USA
18A2 **Arkansas City** USA
64F3 **Arkhangel'sk** Russian Fed
41B3 **Arklow** Irish Rep
47D1 **Arlberg P** Austria
49C3 **Arles** France
19A3 **Arlington** Texas, USA
15C3 **Arlington** Virginia, USA
20B1 **Arlington** Washington, USA
97C3 **Arlit** Niger
57B3 **Arlon** Belg
Armageddon = Megiddo
45C1 **Armagh** County, N Ire
45C1 **Armagh** N Ire
61F5 **Armavir** Russian Fed
23A2 **Armenia** Colombia
32B3 **Armenia** Colombia
65F5 **Armenia** Republic, Europe
107E4 **Armidale** Aust
13D2 **Armstrong** Can
7C3 **Arnaud** R Can
92B2 **Arnauti** C Cyprus
56B2 **Arnhem** Neth
106C2 **Arnhem,C** Aust
106C2 **Arnhem Land** Aust
22B1 **Arnold** USA
15C1 **Arnprior** Can
46E1 **Arnsberg** Germany
100A3 **Aroab** Namibia
47C2 **Arona** Italy
12B2 **Aropuk L** USA
52A1 **Arosa** Switz
97A3 **Arquipélago dos Bijagós** Arch Guinea-Bissau
93D3 **Ar Ramādi** Iraq
42B2 **Arran** I Scot
93C2 **Ar Raqqah** Syria
95A2 **Ar Rāqūbah** Libya
49C1 **Arras** France
96A2 **Arrecife** Canary Is
34C2 **Arrecifes** Arg
23A1 **Arriaga** Mexico
93E3 **Ar Rifa't** Iraq
93E3 **Ar Rihāb** Desert Region Iraq
91A5 **Ar Riyād** S Arabia
44B3 **Arrochar** Scot
111A2 **Arrowtown** NZ
23B1 **Arroyo Seco** Mexico
91B4 **Ar Ru'ays** Qatar
91C5 **Ar Rustaq** Oman
93D3 **Ar Rutbah** Iraq
47D2 **Arsiero** Italy
49D2 **Arsizio** Italy
61G2 **Arsk** Russian Fed
55B3 **Árta** Greece
23A2 **Arteaga** Mexico
63B2 **Artemovsk** Russian Fed
63D2 **Artemovskiy** Russian Fed
9C3 **Artesia** USA
111B2 **Arthurs P** NZ
112C2 **Artigas** Base Ant
29E2 **Artigas** Urug
4H3 **Artillery L** Can
48C1 **Artois** Region, France
112C2 **Arturo Prat** Base Ant
93D1 **Artvin** Turk

99D2 **Aru** Zaire
33G6 **Aruanã** Brazil
27C4 **Aruba** I Caribbean S
86B1 **Arun** R Nepal
86C1 **Arunāchal Pradesh** Union Territory, India
87B3 **Arupukkottai** India
99D3 **Arusha** Tanz
98C2 **Aruwimi** R Zaire
68C2 **Arvayheer** Mongolia
47B2 **Arve** R France
7C5 **Arvida** Can
38H5 **Arvidsjaur** Sweden
39G7 **Arvika** Sweden
21B2 **Arvin** USA
94B1 **Arwad** I Syria
61F2 **Arzamas** Russian Fed
84C2 **Asadabad** Afghan
75A2 **Asahi** R Japan
74E2 **Asahi dake** Mt Japan
74E2 **Asahikawa** Japan
86B2 **Asansol** India
95A2 **Asawanwah** Well Libya
61K2 **Asbest** Russian Fed
15D2 **Asbury Park** USA
103H5 **Ascension** I Atlantic O.
57B3 **Aschaffenburg** Germany
56C2 **Aschersleben** Germany
52B2 **Ascoli Piceno** Italy
47C1 **Ascona** Switz
99E1 **Aseb** Eritrea
96C2 **Asedjirad** Upland Alg
99D2 **Asela** Eth
38H6 **Åsele** Sweden
54B2 **Asenovgrad** Bulg
46C2 **Asfeld** France
61J2 **Asha** Russian Fed
17B1 **Ashburn** USA
111B2 **Ashburton** NZ
106A3 **Ashburton** R Aust
92B3 **Ashdod** Israel
19B3 **Ashdown** USA
11B3 **Asheville** USA
109D1 **Ashford** Aust
43E4 **Ashford** Eng
Ashgabat = Ashkhabad
74D3 **Ashikaga** Japan
75A2 **Ashizuri-misaki** Pt Japan
65G6 **Ashkhabad** Turkmenistan
10B3 **Ashland** Kentucky, USA
18A1 **Ashland** Nebraska, USA
14B2 **Ashland** Ohio, USA
8A2 **Ashland** Oregon, USA
109C1 **Ashley** Aust
16B2 **Ashokan Res** USA
94B3 **Ashqelon** Israel
93D3 **Ash Shabakh** Iraq
91C4 **Ash Sha'm** UAE
93D2 **Ash Sharqāt** Iraq
93E3 **Ash Shatrah** Iraq
81C4 **Ash Shihr** Yemen
91A4 **Ash Shumlul** S Arabia
14B2 **Ashtabula** USA
18A1 **Ashton** USA
10C3 **Atlantic City** USA
16B2 **Atlantic Highlands** USA
92C3 **'Así** R Syria
47D2 **Asiago** Italy
53A2 **Asinara** I Medit S
65K4 **Asino** Russian Fed
42B6 **Askaig** Turk
39G7 **Askersund** Sweden
84C1 **Asmar** Afghan
95C3 **Asmera** Eritrea
75A2 **Aso** Japan
99D1 **Asosa** Eth
111A2 **Aspiring,Mt** NZ
93C2 **As Salamiyah** Syria
91A5 **As Salamiyah** S Arabia
92C2 **As Salmān** Syria
93D3 **As Salmān** Iraq
86C1 **Assam** State, India

93E3 **As Samāwah** Iraq
91B5 **As Sanām** Region, S Arabia
94C2 **As Sanamayn** Syria
56B2 **Assen** Neth
56B1 **Assens** Den
95A1 **As Sidrah** Libya
5H5 **Assiniboia** Can
5G4 **Assiniboine,Mt** Can
30F3 **Assis** Brazil
93C3 **As Sukhnah** Syria
93E2 **As Sulaymānīyah** Iraq
91A5 **As Summan** Region, S Arabia
99E3 **Assumption** I Seychelles
92C3 **As Suwaydā'** Syria
93D3 **As Suwayrah** Iraq
93E2 **Astara** Azerbaijan
52A2 **Asti** Italy
55C3 **Astipálaia** I Greece
50A1 **Astorga** Spain
8A2 **Astoria** USA
61G4 **Astrakhan'** Russian Fed
50A1 **Asturias** Region, Spain
30E4 **Asunción** Par
99D2 **Aswa** R Uganda
80B3 **Aswân** Egypt
95C2 **Aswân High Dam** Egypt
95C2 **Asyût** Egypt
92C3 **Az Zilaf** Syria
97C4 **Atakpamé** Togo
71D4 **Atambua** Indon
6E3 **Atangmik** Greenland
96A2 **Atar** Maur
65J5 **Atasu** Kazakhstan
95C3 **Atatisk Baraji** Res Turk
95C3 **Atbara** Sudan
65H4 **Atbasar** Kazakhstan
11A4 **Atchafalaya B** USA
10A3 **Atchison** USA
16B3 **Atco** USA
23A1 **Atenguillo** Mexico
52B2 **Atessa** Italy
46B1 **Ath** Belg
13E2 **Athabasca** Can
5G4 **Athabasca** R Can
5H4 **Athabasca L** Can
45B2 **Athenry** Irish Rep
Athens = Athinai
14B3 **Athens** Ohio, USA
19A3 **Athens** Texas, USA
55B3 **Athínai** Greece
45C1 **Athlone** Irish Rep
16C1 **Athol** USA
55B2 **Áthos** Mt Greece
45C2 **Athy** Irish Rep
98B1 **Ati** Chad
7A5 **Atikoken** Can
61F3 **Atkarsk** Russian Fed
18B2 **Atkins** USA
23B2 **Atlacomulco** Mexico
11B3 **Atlanta** Georgia, USA
14B2 **Atlanta** Michigan, USA
18A1 **Atlanta** Iowa, USA
10C3 **Atlantic City** USA
16B2 **Atlantic Highlands** USA
103H8 **Atlantic Indian Basin** Atlantic O
103H7 **Atlantic Indian Ridge** Atlantic O
96C1 **Atlas Saharien** Mts Alg
4E4 **Atlin** Can
4E4 **Atlin L** Can
94B2 **'Atlit** Israel
23B2 **Atlixco** Mexico
11B3 **Atmore** USA
101D3 **Atofinandrahana** Madag
12D3 **Atognak I** USA
19A3 **Atoka** USA
23A1 **Atotonilco** Mexico
23B2 **Atoyac** R Mexico
32B2 **Atrato** R Colombia

91B5 **Attaf** Region, UAE
81C3 **At Tā'if** S Arabia
94C2 **At Tall** Syria
17A1 **Attalla** USA
7B4 **Attauapiskat** Can
7B4 **Attauapiskat** R Can
93D3 **At Taysīyah** Desert Region S Arabia
14A2 **Attica** Indiana, USA
46C2 **Attigny** France
15D2 **Attleboro** Massachusetts, USA
76D3 **Attopeu** Laos
92C4 **At Tubayq** Upland S Arabia
34B3 **Atuel** R Arg
39H7 **Atvidaberg** Sweden
22B2 **Atwater** USA
49D3 **Aubagne** France
46C2 **Aube** Department, France
49C3 **Aubenas** France
17A1 **Auburn** Alabama, USA
21A2 **Auburn** California, USA
14A2 **Auburn** Indiana, USA
18A1 **Auburn** Nebraska, USA
15C2 **Auburn** New York, USA
20B1 **Auburn** Washington, USA
48C2 **Auch** France
110B1 **Auckland** NZ
105G6 **Auckland Is** NZ
48C3 **Aude** R France
7B4 **Auden** Can
47B1 **Audincourt** France
109C1 **Aughathella** Aust
57C3 **Augsburg** Germany
106A4 **Augusta** Aust
11B3 **Augusta** Georgia, USA
18A2 **Augusta** Kansas, USA
10D2 **Augusta** Maine, USA
12D3 **Augustine I** USA
58C2 **Augustów** Pol
106A3 **Augustus,Mt** Aust
106A3 **Aumale** France
50A2 **Auraiya** India
85D5 **Aurangābād** India
96C1 **Aurès** Mts Alg
48C3 **Aurillac** France
8C3 **Aurora** Colorado, USA
10B2 **Aurora** Illinois, USA
14B3 **Aurora** Indiana, USA
18B2 **Aurora** Mississippi, USA
100A3 **Aus** Namibia
14B2 **Au Sable** USA
10A2 **Austin** Minnesota, USA
21B2 **Austin** Nevada, USA
9D3 **Austin** Texas, USA
106C3 **Australia** Fed State/ Monarchy
107D4 **Australian Alps** Mts Aust
37E4 **Austria** Federal Republic, Europe
46A1 **Authie** R France
24B3 **Autlan** Mexico
49C2 **Autun** France
49C2 **Auvergne** Region, France
49C2 **Auxerre** France
46B1 **Auxi-le-Châteaux** France
49C2 **Avallon** France
22C4 **Avalon** USA
7E5 **Avalon Pen** Can
35B2 **Avaré** Brazil
90D3 **Avaz** Iran
94B3 **Avedat** Hist Site Israel
33F4 **Aveiro** Brazil
50A1 **Aveiro** Port
47A1 **Avellaneda** Arg
53B2 **Avellino** Italy
46B1 **Avesnes-sur-Helpe** France

117

Avesta

39H6 Avesta Sweden
52B2 Avezzano Italy
44C3 Aviemore Scot
111B2 Aviemore,L NZ
47B2 Avigliana Italy
49C3 Avignon France
50B1 Avila Spain
50A1 Aviles Spain
47D1 Avisio R Italy
108B3 Avoca R Aust
43C4 Avon County, Eng
43D4 Avon R Dorset, Eng
43D3 Avon R Warwick, Eng
43C4 Avonmouth Wales
17B2 Avon Park USA
46B2 Avre R France
54A2 Avtovac Bosnia-Herzegovina
94C2 A'waj R Syria
74D4 Awaji-shima B Japan
99E2 Aware Eth
111A2 Awarua Pt NZ
99E2 Awash Eth
99E2 Awash R Eth
75B1 Awa-shima I Japan
111B2 Awatere R NZ
95A2 Awbāri Libya
98C2 Aweil Sudan
95B2 Awjilah Libya
94C2 Axel Norway
6A2 Axel Heiburg I Can
43C4 Axminster Eng
75B1 Ayabe Japan
29E3 Ayacucho Arg
32C6 Ayacucho Peru
65K5 Ayaguz Kazakhstan
82C2 Ayakkum Hu L China
50A2 Ayamonte Spain
63F2 Ayan Russian Fed
32C6 Ayauiri Peru
92A2 Aydin Turk
92A2 Áyios Evstrátios I Greece
43D4 Aylesbury Eng
13D2 Aylmer,Mt Can
94C2 'Ayn al Fijah Syria
93D2 Ayn Zálah Iraq
95B2 Ayn Zuwayyah Well Libya
99D2 Ayod Sudan
107D2 Ayr Aust
42B2 Ayr Scot
42B2 Ayr R Scot
42B2 Ayre,Pt of Eng
54C2 Aytos Bulg
76C3 Ayutthaya Thai
23A1 Ayutla Mexico
55C3 Ayvacik Turk
55C3 Ayvalik Turk
86A1 Azamgarh India
97B3 Azaouad Desert Region Mali
97D3 Azare Nig
92C2 A'Zaz Syria
65F5 Azerbaijan Republic, Russian Fed
32B4 Azogues Ecuador
Azores = Açores
98C1 Azoum R Chad
60E4 Azov, Sea of Russian Fed/Ukraine
Azovskoye More = Azov, Sea of
96B1 Azrou Mor
34D3 Azucena Arg
32A2 Azuero,Pen de Panama
29E3 Azul Arg
94C2 Az-Zabdāni Syria
91C5 Az Zāhirah Mts Oman
95A2 Az Zahra Iraq
96A2 Azzeffal R Maur
93E3 Az Zubayr Iraq

B

94B2 Ba'abda Leb
92C3 Ba'albek Leb
94B3 Ba'al Hazor Mt Israel

99E2 Baardheere Somalia
54C2 Babadag Rom
92A1 Babaeski Turk
32B4 Babahoyo Ecuador
81C4 Bāb al Mandab Str Djibouti/Yemen
71D4 Babar I Indon
99D3 Babati Tanz
60E2 Babayevo Russian Fed
14B2 Baberton USA
13B1 Babine R Can
5F4 Babine L Can
90B2 Bábol Iran
79B2 Babuyan Chan Phil
79B2 Babuyan Is Phil
31C2 Bacabal Brazil
71D4 Bacan I Indon
60C4 Bacău Rom
76D1 Bac Can Viet
108B3 Bacchus Marsh Aust
82B2 Bachu China
4J3 Back R Can
12J2 Backbone Ranges Mts Can
76D1 Bac Ninh Viet
79B3 Bacolod Phil
79B3 Baco,Mt Phil
87B2 Badagara India
72A1 Badain Jaran Shamo Desert China
50A2 Badajoz Spain
51C1 Badalona Spain
93D3 Badanah S Arabia
46D2 Bad Bergzabern Germany
46D1 Bad Ems Germany
47C1 Baden Switz
57B3 Baden-Baden Germany
57B3 Baden-Württemberg State, Germany
57C3 Badgastein Austria
22C2 Badger USA
57B2 Bad-Godesberg Germany
57B2 Bad Hersfeld Germany
46D1 Bad Honnef Germany
85B4 Badin Pak
52B1 Bad Ischl Austria
93C3 Badiyat ash Sham Desert Region Jordan/Iraq
57B3 Bad-Kreuznach Germany
46D1 Bad Nevenahr-Ahrweiler Germany
47C1 Bad Ragaz Switz
57C3 Bad Tolz Germany
87C3 Badulla Sri Lanka
50B2 Baena Spain
97A3 Bafatá Guinea-Bissau
4H2 Baffin Region Can
6C2 Baffin B Greenland/Can
6C2 Baffin I Can
98B2 Bafia Cam
97A3 Bafing R Mali
97A3 Bafoulabé Mali
98B2 Bafoussam Cam
90C3 Bāfq Iran
60E5 Bafra Burun Pt Turk
91C4 Bāft Iran
98C2 Bafwasende Zaire
86A1 Bagaha India
87B1 Bāgalkot India
99D3 Bagamoyo Tanz
29F2 Bagé Brazil
93D3 Baghdad Iraq
86B2 Bāghelkhand Bang
91C3 Bāghin Iran
84B1 Baghlan Afghan
49C3 Bagnols-sur-Cèze France
97B3 Bagoé R Mali
Bagu = Pegu
79B2 Baguio Phil
86B1 Bahadurābād India
11C4 Bahamas,The Is Caribbean S
86B2 Baharampur India
92A4 Bahariya Oasis Egypt

84C3 Bahawalpur Pak
84C3 Bahawalpur Province, Pak
85C3 Bahawathagar Pak
Bahia = Salvador
31C4 Bahia State, Brazil
29D3 Bahia Blanca Arg
29D3 Bahia Blanca B Arg
34A3 Bahia Concepción B Chile
35C2 Bahia da Ilha Grande B Brazil
24B2 Bahia de Banderas B Mexico
24C2 Bahia de Campeche B Mexico
25D3 Bahia de la Ascension B Mexico
24B3 Bahia de Petacalco B Mexico
96A2 Bahia de Rio de Oro B Mor
35C2 Bahia de Sepetiba B Brazil
29C6 Bahia Grande B Arg
9B4 Bahia Kino Mexico
24A2 Bahia Magdalena B Mexico
24A2 Bahia Sebastia Vizcaino B Mexico
99D1 Bahar Dar Eth
86A1 Bahraich India
80D3 Bahrain Sheikdom, Arabian Pen
93D3 Bahr al Milh L Iraq
98C2 Bahr Aouk R Chad/CAR
Bahrat Lut = Dead S
98C2 Bahr el Arab Watercourse Sudan
99D2 Bahr el Ghazal R Sudan
98B1 Bahr el Ghazal Watercourse Chad
101H1 Baia de Maputo B Mozam
31B2 Baia de Marajó B Brazil
101D2 Baiá de Pemba B Mozam
31C2 Baia de São Marcos B Brazil
50A2 Baia de Setúbal B Port
31D4 Baia de Todos os Santos B Brazil
100A2 Baia dos Tigres Angola
60B4 Baia Mare Rom
98B2 Baiboukoum Chad
69E2 Baicheng China
101E2 Baie Antongila B Madag
7D5 Baie-Comeau Can
101D2 Baie de Bombetoka B Madag
101D2 Baie de Mahajamba B Madag
101D3 Baie de St Augustin B Madag
94B2 Baie de St Georges B Leb
10D2 Baie des Chaleurs B Can
7C4 Baie-du-Poste Can
72B3 Baihe China
72C3 Bai He R China
93D3 Ba'iji Iraq
86A2 Baikunthpur India
Baile Atha Cliath = Dublin
54B2 Băilesti Rom
46B1 Bailleul France
72A3 Baima China
17B1 Bainbridge USA
12B2 Baird Inlet USA
483 Baird Mts USA
72D1 Bairin Youqi China
72D1 Bairin Zuoqi China
107D4 Bairnsdale Aust
79B4 Bais Phil
54A1 Baja Hung
9B3 Baja California State, Mexico

24A1 Baja California Pen Mexico
61J2 Bakal Russian Fed
98C2 Bakala CAR
97A3 Bakel Sen
8C2 Baker Montana, USA
8B2 Baker Oregon, USA
6A3 Baker Foreland Pt Can
4J3 Baker L Can
4J3 Baker Lake Can
8A2 Baker,Mt USA
9B3 Bakersfield USA
90C2 Bakharden Turkmenistan
90C2 Bakhardok Turkmenistan
60D3 Bakhmach Ukraine
38C1 Bakkafloi B Iceland
99D2 Bako Eth
98C2 Bakouma CAR
65F5 Baku Azerbaijan
Baky = Baku
92B2 Balá I Phil
79A4 Balabac I Phil
70C3 Balabac Str Malay
70C4 Balabalangan Indon
108A2 Balaklava Aust
61G3 Balakovo Russian Fed
86A2 Balāngir India
61F3 Balashov Russian Fed
86B2 Balasore India
80A3 Balát Egypt
52C1 Balaton L Hung
45C2 Balbriggan Irish Rep
29E3 Balcarce Arg
54C2 Balchik Bulg
111B3 Balclutha NZ
18B2 Bald Knob USA
17B1 Baldwin USA
9C3 Baldy Peak Mt USA
Balearic Is = Islas Baleares
78C2 Baleh R Malay
79B2 Baler Phil
61H2 Balezino Russian Fed
106A1 Bali I Indon
92A2 Balikesir Turk
93C2 Balikh R Syria
78D3 Balikpapan Indon
79B2 Balintang Chan Phil
78C4 Bali S Indon
35A1 Baliza Brazil
84B1 Balkh Afghan
65J5 Balkhash Kazakhstan
44B3 Balachulish Scot
45B2 Ballaghaderreen Irish Rep
42B2 Ballantrae Scot
4G2 Ballantyne Str Can
87B2 Ballapur India
107D4 Ballarat Aust
44C3 Ballater Scot
112C7 Balleny Is Ant
86A1 Ballia India
109D1 Ballina Aust
41B3 Ballina Irish Rep
45B2 Ballinasloe Irish Rep
55A2 Balish Alb
45B1 Ballycastle Irish Rep
45C1 Ballycastle N Ire
45B1 Ballymena N Ire
45C1 Ballymoney N Ire
45B1 Ballyshannon Irish Rep
45B2 Ballyvaghan Irish Rep
108B3 Balmoral Aust
34C2 Balnearia Arg
84B3 Balochistān Region, Pak
100A2 Balombo Angola
109C1 Balonn R Aust
85C3 Bolotra India
86A1 Balrāmpur India
107D4 Balranald Aust
31B3 Balsas Brazil
23B2 Balsas Mexico
24B3 Balsas R Mexico
60C4 Balta Ukraine
39H7 Baltic S N Europe

92B3 Baltim Egypt
45B3 Baltimore Irish Rep
10C3 Baltimore USA
86B1 Bālurghāt India
61H4 Balykshi Kazakhstan
91C4 Bam Iran
98B1 Bama Nig
97B3 Bamako Mali
98C2 Bambari CAR
17B1 Bamberg USA
57C3 Bamberg Germany
98C2 Bambili Zaïre
35B2 Bambui Brazil
98B2 Bamenda Cam
13C3 Bamfield Can
98B2 Bamingui R CAR
98B2 Bamingui Bangoran National Park CAR
84B2 Bamiyan Afghan
91D4 Bampur Iran
91D4 Bampur R Iran
98C2 Banalia Zaire
97B3 Banamba Mali
76C3 Ban Aranyaprathet Thai
76C2 Ban Ban Laos
77C4 Ban Betong Thai
45C1 Banbridge N Ire
43D3 Banbury Eng
44C3 Banchory Scot
25D3 Banco Chinchorro Is Mexico
15C1 Bancroft Can
86A1 Banda India
70A3 Banda Aceh Indon
9784 Bandama R Ivory Coast
91C4 Bandar Abbās Iran
90A2 Bandar Anzali Iran
99F2 Bandarbeyla Somalia
91B4 Bandar-e Daylam Iran
91B4 Bandar-e Lengheh Iran
91B4 Bandar-e Māqām Iran
91B4 Bandar-e Rig Iran
90B2 Bandar-e Torkoman Iran
91A3 Bandar Khomeynī Iran
78C2 Bandar Seri Begawan Brunei
71D4 Banda S Indon
91C4 Band Boni Iran
35C2 Bandeira Mt Brazil
97B3 Bandiagara Mali
60C5 Bandirma Turk
45B3 Bandon Irish Rep
98B3 Bandundu Zaire
78B4 Bandung Indon
25E2 Banes Cuba
13D2 Banff Can
44C3 Banff Scot
5G4 Banff R Can
13D2 Banff Nat Pk Can
87B2 Bangalore India
98C2 Bangassou CAR
70C3 Banggi I Malay
95B1 Banghāzi Libya
76D2 Bang Hieng R Laos
78B3 Bangka I Indon
78A3 Bangko Indon
76C3 Bangkok Thai
82C3 Bangladesh Republic, Asia
84D2 Bangong Co L China
10D2 Bangor Maine, USA
45D1 Bangor N Ire
16B2 Bangor Pennsylvania, USA
42B3 Bangor Wales
78D3 Bangsalsembera Indon
76B3 Bang Saphan Yai Thai
79B2 Bangued Phil
98B2 Bangui CAR
100C2 Bangweulu L Zambia
77C4 Ban Hat Yai Thai
76C2 Ban Hin Heup Laos
76C1 Ban Houei Sai Laos
76B3 Ban Hua Hin Thai

97B3 Bani R Mali
97C3 Bani Bangou Niger
95A1 Bani Walid Libya
92C2 Bāniyās Syria
94B2 Baniyas Syria
52C2 Banja Luka Bosnia-Herzegovina
78C3 Banjarmasin Indon
97A3 Banjul The Gambia
77B4 Ban Kantang Thai
76D2 Ban Khemmarat Laos
77B4 Ban Khok Kloi Thai
71F5 Banks I Can
5E4 Banks I British Columbia, Can
4F2 Banks I Northwest Territories, Can
20C1 Banks L USA
111B2 Banks Pen NZ
109C4 Banks Str Aust
86B2 Bankura India
76B2 Ban Mae Sariang Thai
76B2 Ban Mae Sot Thai
76D3 Ban Me Thuot Viet
45C1 Bann R N Ire
76B2 Ban Na San Thai
84C2 Bannu Pak
34A3 Baños Maule Chile
76C2 Ban Pak Neun Laos
77C4 Ban Pak Phanang Thai
76D3 Ban Ru Kroy Camb
76B3 Ban Sai Yok Thai
76C3 Ban Sattahip Thai
59B3 Banská Bystrica Slovakia
85C4 Bānswāra India
77B4 Ban Tha Kham Thai
76D2 Ban Thateng Laos
76C2 Ban Tha Tum Thai
41B3 Bantry Irish Rep
41A3 Bantry B Irish Rep
76D3 Ban Ya Soup Viet
72C3 Banyuwangi Indon
72C3 Baofeng China
76C1 Bao Ha Viet
72B3 Baoji China
76D3 Bao Loc Viet
68A4 Baoshan China
72C1 Baotou China
87C1 Bāpatla India
46B1 Bapaume France
93D3 Ba'Qūbah Iraq
32J7 Baquerizo Moreno Ecuador
54A2 Bar Montenegro, Yugos
99D1 Bara Sudan
99E2 Baraawe Somalia
78D3 Barabai Indon
86A1 Bara Banki India
65J4 Barabinsk Russian Fed
65J4 Barabinskaya Step Steppe Kazakhstan/Russian Fed
50B1 Baracaldo Spain
26C2 Baracoa Cuba
94C2 Baradá R Syria
109C2 Baradine Aust
87A1 Bārāmati India
84C2 Baramula Pak
85D3 Bārān India
79B3 Barangas Phil
4E4 Baranof I USA
60C3 Baranovichi Belorussia
108A2 Baratta Aust
86B1 Barauni India
31C6 Barbacena Brazil
27F4 Barbados I Caribbean S
51C1 Barbastro Spain
101H1 Barberton S Africa
48B2 Barbezieux France
32C2 Barbōsa Colombia
27E3 Barbuda I Caribbean S
107D3 Barcaldine Aust
53C3 Barce = Al Marj
53C3 Barcellona Italy
51C1 Barcelona Spain

33E1 Barcelona Ven
107D3 Barcoo R Aust
34B3 Barda del Medio Arg
95A2 Bardai Chad
29C3 Bardas Blancas Arg
86B2 Barddhamān India
59C3 Bardejov Slovakia
47C2 Bardi Italy
47B2 Bardonecchia Italy
43B3 Bardsey I Wales
84D3 Bareilly India
64D2 Barentseya I Barents S
64E2 Barents S
95C3 Barentu Eritrea
86A2 Bargarh India
47B2 Barge Italy
63D2 Barguzin Russian Fed
63D2 Barguzin R Russian Fed
86B2 Barhi India
53C2 Bari Italy
51D2 Barika Alg
32C2 Barinas Ven
86B2 Baripāda India
86C2 Bari Sādri India
86C2 Barisal Bang
78C3 Barito R Indon
95A2 Barjuj Watercourse Libya
73A3 Barkam China
18C2 Barkley,L USA
13B3 Barkley Sd Can
100B4 Barkly East S Africa
106C2 Barkly Tableland Mts Aust
46C2 Bar-le-Duc France
106A3 Barlee,L Aust
106A3 Barlee Range Mts Aust
53C2 Barletta Italy
85C3 Barmer India
108B2 Barmera Aust
43B3 Barmouth Wales
42D2 Barnard Castle Eng
65K4 Barnaul Russian Fed
16B3 Barnegat USA
16B3 Barnegat B USA
6C2 Barnes Icecap Can
17B1 Barnesville Georgia, USA
18B3 Barnesville Ohio, USA
42D3 Barnsley Eng
43B4 Barnstaple Eng
97C4 Baro Nig
86C1 Barpeta India
32D1 Barquisimeto Ven
31C4 Barra Brazil
44A3 Barra I Scot
109D2 Barraba Aust
23A2 Barra de Navidad Mexico
35C2 Barra do Piraí Brazil
35A1 Barragem de São Simão Res Brazil
35A1 Barra do Garças Brazil
35B2 Barragem Agua Vermelha Res Brazil
50A2 Barragem do Castelo do Bode Res Port
50A2 Barragem do Maranhão Res Port
35A2 Barragem Três Irmãos Res Brazil
44A3 Barra Head Pt Scot
31C6 Barra Mansa Brazil
32B6 Barranca Peru
32C2 Barrancabermeja Colombia
33E2 Barrancas Ven
30E4 Barranqueras Arg
32C1 Barranquilla Colombia
44A3 Barra,Sound of Chan Scot
16C1 Barre USA
34B2 Barreal Arg
31C4 Barreiras Brazil
50A2 Barreiro Port

31D3 Barreiros Brazil
107D5 Barren,C Aust
12D3 Barren Is USA
31B6 Barretos Brazil
13E2 Barrhead Can
14C2 Barrie Can
13C2 Barrière Can
108B2 Barrier Range Mts Aust
107E4 Barrington,Mt Aust
27N2 Barrouaillie St Vincent and the Grenadines
4C2 Barrow USA
6A2 Barrow R Irish Rep
106C3 Barrow Creek Aust
106A3 Barrow I Aust
42C2 Barrow-in-Furness Eng
4C2 Barrow,Pt USA
6A2 Barrow Str Can
15C1 Barry's Bay Can
87B1 Barsi India
9B3 Barstow USA
49C2 Bar-sur-Aube France
33F2 Bartica Guyana
92B1 Bartin Turk
107D2 Bartle Frere,Mt Aust
9D3 Bartlesville USA
101C3 Bartolomeu Dias Mozam
58C2 Bartoszyce Pol
14C2 Barung I Indon
85D4 Barwah India
85C4 Barwani India
109C1 Barwon R Aust
61G3 Barysh Russian Fed
98B2 Basankusu Zaïre
34D2 Basavilbasa Arg
79B1 Basco Phil
52A1 Basel Switz
52C2 Basento R Italy
13E2 Bashaw Can
79B1 Bashi Chan Phil
61H3 Bashkortostan Russian Fed
52B1 Basilan I Phil
43E4 Basildon Eng
43D4 Basingstoke Eng
8B2 Basin Region USA
93E3 Basra Iraq
46D2 Bas-Rhin Department, France
76D3 Bassac R Camb
13E2 Bassano Can
52B1 Bassano Italy
47D2 Bassano del Grappa Italy
97C4 Bassari Togo
101C3 Bassas da India I Mozam Chan
76A2 Bassein Burma
27E3 Basse Terre Guadeloupe
97C4 Bassila Benin
22C2 Bass Lake USA
107D4 Bass Str Aust
39G7 Båstad Sweden
91B4 Bastak Iran
86A1 Basti India
52A2 Bastia Corse
57B3 Bastogne Belg
19B3 Bastrop Louisiana, USA
19A3 Bastrop Texas, USA
98A2 Bata Eq Guinea
78C3 Batakan Indon
82B2 Batala India
68B3 Batang China
98B2 Batangafo CAR
79B1 Batan Is Phil
35B2 Batatais Brazil
15C2 Batavia USA
109D3 Batemans Bay Aust
17B1 Batesburg USA
18B2 Batesville Arkansas, USA
19C3 Batesville Mississippi, USA
43C4 Bath Eng
15C2 Bath New York, USA
98B1 Batha R Chad
107D4 Bathurst Aust
7D5 Bathurst Can

119

Bathurst,C

4F2 Bathurst,C Can
106C2 Bathurst I Aust
4H2 Bathurst I Can
4H3 Bathurst Inlet B Can
97B3 Batié Burkina
90B3 Bātlāq-e-Gavkhūni Salt Flat Iran
109C3 Batlow Aust
93D2 Batman Turk
96C1 Batna Alg
11A3 Baton Rouge USA
94B1 Batroun Leb
76C3 Battambang Camb
87C3 Batticaloa Sri Lanka
13F2 Battle Eng
10B2 Battle Creek USA
7E4 Battle Harbour Can
20C2 Battle Mountain USA
78D2 Batukelau Indon
65F5 Batumi Georgia
77C5 Batu Pahat Malay
78A3 Baturaja Indon
94B2 Bat Yam Israel
71D4 Baubau Indon
97C3 Bauchi Nig
97B2 Bauges Mts France
7E4 Bauld,C Can
47B1 Baumes-les-Dames France
63D2 Baunt Russian Fed
31B6 Bauru Brazil
35A1 Baus Brazil
57C2 Bautzen Germany
78C4 Baween I Indon
95B2 Bawiti Egypt
97B3 Bawku Burma
76B2 Bawlake Burma
108A2 Bawlen Aust
17B1 Baxley USA
25E2 Bayamo Cuba
78D4 Bayan Indon
68C2 Bayandzürh Mongolia
68B3 Bayan Har Shan Mts China
72A1 Bayan Mod China
72B1 Bayan Obo China
47A2 Bayard F France
12J3 Bayard,Mt Can
63D3 Bayasgalant Mongolia
93D1 Baybay Phil
93D1 Bayburt Turk
10B2 Bay City Michigan, USA
19A4 Bay City Texas, USA
92B2 Bay Dağları Turk
64H3 Baydaratskaya Guba B Russian Fed
99E2 Baydhabo Somalia
48B2 Bayeux France
47D1 Bayerische Alpen Germany
57C3 Bayern State, Germany
92C3 Bâyir Jordan
63C2 Baykalskiy Khrebet Mts Russian Fed
63B1 Baykit Russian Fed
63B3 Baylik Shan Mts China/Mongolia
61J3 Baymak Russian Fed
79B2 Bayombong Phil
48B3 Bayonne France
57C3 Bayreuth Germany
19C3 Bay St Louis USA
15D2 Bay Shore USA
15C1 Bays,L of Can
68A2 Baytik Shan Mts China
 Bayt Lahm = Bethlehem
19B4 Baytown USA
50B2 Baza Spain
59D3 Bazaliya Ukraine
48B3 Bazas France
73B3 Bazhong China
91D4 Bazmān Iran
94C1 Bcharre Leb
16B3 Beach Haven USA
43E4 Beachy Head Eng
16C2 Beacon USA
101D2 Bealanana Madag
18B1 Beardstown USA

 Bear I = Bjørnøya
22B1 Bear Valley USA
8D2 Beatrice USA
44C2 Beatrice Oilfield N Sea
13C1 Beatton R Can
5F4 Beatton River Can
29E6 Beauchene Is Falkland Is
109D1 Beaudesert Aust
1B5 Beaufort S Can
100B4 Beaufort West S Africa
15D1 Beauharnois Can
44B3 Beauly Scot
21B3 Beaumont California, USA
11A3 Beaumont Texas, USA
49C2 Beaune France
48C2 Beauvais France
13F1 Beauval Can
12E1 Beaver R Alaska, USA
12E1 Beaver R Saskatchewan, Can
4D3 Beaver Creek Can
12E1 Beaver Creek USA
18C2 Beaver Dam Kentucky, USA
13E2 Beaverhill L Can
14A1 Beaver I USA
18B2 Beaver L USA
13D1 Beaverlodge Can
85C3 Beawar India
34B2 Beazley Arg
35B2 Bebedouro Brazil
43E3 Beccles Eng
54B1 Bečej Serbia, Yugos
96B1 Béchar Alg
12C3 Becharof L USA
11B3 Beckley USA
43D3 Bedford County, Eng
43D3 Bedford Eng
14A3 Bedford Indiana, USA
27M2 Bedford Pt Grenada
4D2 Beechey Pt USA
109C3 Beechworth Aust
109D1 Beenleigh Aust
92B3 Beersheba Israel
 Beér Sheva = Beersheba
94B3 Beér Sheva R Israel
9D4 Beeville USA
98C2 Befale Zaire
101D2 Befandriana Madag
109C3 Bega Aust
91B3 Behbehān Iran
12H3 Behm Canal Sd USA
90B2 Behshahr Iran
84B2 Behsud Afghan
69E2 Bei'an China
73B5 Beihai China
72D2 Beijing China
76E1 Beiliu China
73B4 Beipan Jiang R China
72E1 Beipiao China
 Beira = Sofala
92C3 Beirut Leb
68B2 Bei Shan Mts China
94B2 Beit ed Dine Leb
94B3 Beit Jala Israel
50A2 Beja Port
96C1 Beja Tunisia
96C1 Bejaia Alg
50A1 Béjar Spain
90C3 Bejestān Iran
59B3 Békéscsaba Hung
101D3 Bekily Madag
70A3 Bekasi Indon
61J2 Belaya R Ukraine
6A2 Belcher Chan Can
7C4 Belcher Is Can

84B1 Belchiragh Afghan
61H3 Belebey Russian Fed
99E2 Beled Weyne Somalia
31B2 Belém Brazil
32B3 Belén Colombia
34D2 Belén Urug
9C3 Belen USA
45D1 Belfast N Ire
101H1 Belfast S Africa
45D1 Belfast Lough Estuary N Ire
99D1 Belfodiyo Eth
42D2 Belford Eng
49D2 Belfort France
87A1 Belgaum India
56A2 Belgium Kingdom, N W Europe
60E3 Belgorod Russian Fed
60D4 Belgorod Dnestrovskiy Ukraine
95A2 Bel Hedan Libya
78B3 Belinyu Indon
78B3 Belitung I Indon
25D3 Belize Belize
25D3 Belize Republic, Cent America
48C2 Bellac France
5F4 Bella Coola Can
47C2 Bellagio Italy
19A4 Bellaire USA
47C1 Bellano Italy
87B1 Bellary India
109C1 Bellata Aust
47B2 Belledonne Mts France
8C2 Belle Fourche USA
49D2 Bellegarde France
17B2 Belle Glade USA
7E4 Belle I Can
48B2 Belle-Ile I France
7E4 Belle Isle,Str of Can
7C5 Belleville Can
18A2 Belleville Kansas, USA
20B1 Bellevue Washington, USA
109D2 Bellingen Aust
8A2 Bellingham USA
112C2 Bellingshausen Base Ant
112C3 Bellingshausen S Ant
52A1 Bellinzona Switz
32B2 Bello Colombia
107E3 Bellona Reefs Nouvelle Calédonie
22B1 Bellota USA
15D2 Bellows Falls USA
6B3 Bell Pen Can
52B1 Belluno Italy
29D2 Bell Ville Arg
31D5 Belmonte Brazil
25D3 Belmopan Belize
45B1 Belmullet Irish Rep
101D3 Belo-Tsiribihina Madag
64E3 Beloye More S Russian Fed
60E1 Beloye Ozero L Russian Fed
60E1 Belozersk Russian Fed
14B3 Belpre USA
108A2 Beltana Aust
19A3 Belton USA
59D3 Bel'tsy Moldova
16B2 Belvidere New Jersey, USA
98B3 Bembe Angola

97C3 Bembéréke Benin
10A2 Bemidji USA
39G6 Bena Nor
98C3 Bena Dibele Zaire
108C3 Benalla Aust
44B3 Ben Attow Mt Scot
50A1 Benavente Spain
44A3 Benbecula I Scot
106A4 Bencubbin Aust
8A2 Bend USA
44B3 Ben Dearg Mt Scot
60C4 Bendery Moldova
107D4 Bendigo Aust
57C3 Benešov Czech Republic
53B2 Benevento Italy
83C4 Bengal,B of Asia
96D1 Ben Gardane Tunisia
72D3 Bengbu China
78A2 Bengkalis Indon
78A3 Bengkulu Indon
100A2 Benguela Angola
92B3 Benha Egypt
44B2 Ben Hope Mt Scot
99C2 Beni Zaire
32D6 Béni R Bol
96B1 Beni Abbes Alg
51C1 Benicarló Spain
7A5 Benidji USA
51C2 Benidorm Spain
51C2 Beni Mansour Alg
95C2 Beni Mazar Egypt
96B1 Beni Mellal Mor
97C4 Benin Republic, Africa
97C4 Benin City Nig
95C2 Beni Suef Egypt
44B2 Ben Kilbreck Mt Scot
44B3 Ben Lawers Mt UK
109C4 Ben Lomond Mt Scot
44C3 Ben Macdui Mt Scot
44A3 Ben More Assynt Mt Scot
111B2 Benmore,L NZ
44B3 Ben Nevis Mt Scot
15D2 Bennington USA
94B2 Bennt Jbail Leb
98B2 Bénoué R Cam
9B3 Benson Arizona, USA
99C2 Bentiu Sudan
19B3 Benton Arkansas, USA
18C2 Benton Kentucky, USA
14A2 Benton Harbor USA
97C4 Benue R Nig
45B1 Benwee Hd C Irish Rep
44B3 Ben Wyvis Mt Scot
72E1 Benxi China
54B2 Beograd Serbia, Yugos
5J4 Berens R Can
5J4 Berens River Can
108A1 Beresford Aust
59C3 Berettyóújfalu Hung
58D2 Bereza Belorussia
59C3 Berezhany Ukraine
65G4 Berezniki Russian Fed
60D4 Berezovka Ukraine
64H3 Berezovo Russian Fed
92A2 Bergama Turk
52A1 Bergamo Italy
39F6 Bergen Nor
46C1 Bergen op Zoom Neth
48C3 Bergerac France
46D1 Bergisch-Gladbach Germany
12F2 Bering Gl USA

1C6 Bering Str USA/
Russian Fed
91C4 Berizak Iran
50B2 Berja Spain
8A3 Berkeley USA
112B2 Berkner I Ant
54B2 Berkovitsa Bulg
43D4 Berkshire County,
Eng
16C1 Berkshire Hills USA
13D2 Berland R Can
56C2 Berlin Germany
56C2 Berlin State,
Germany
15D2 Berlin New
Hampshire, USA
30D3 Bermejo Bol
30D4 Bermejo R Arg
3M5 Bermuda I Atlantic O
52A1 Bern Switz
16B2 Bernardsville USA
34C3 Bernasconi Arg
56C2 Bernburg Germany
47B1 Berner Oberland Mts
Switz
6B2 Bernier B Can
57C3 Berounka R
Czech Republic
108B2 Berri Aust
96C1 Berriane Alg
48C2 Berry Region, France
22A1 Berryessa,L USA
11C4 Berry Is The
Bahamas
98B2 Bertoua Camr
45B2 Berwghboy B
Irish Rep
15C2 Berwick USA
42C2 Berwick-upon-Tweed
Eng
43C3 Berwyn Mts Wales
101D2 Besalampy Madag
49D2 Besançon France
59C3 Beskidy Zachodnie
Mts Pol
93C2 Besni Turk
94B3 Besor R Israel
11B3 Bessemer USA
101D2 Betafo Madag
50A1 Betanzos Spain
94B3 Bet Guvrin Israel
101G1 Bethal S Africa
100A3 Bethanie Namibia
18B1 Bethany Missouri,
USA
18A2 Bethany Oklahoma,
USA
4B3 Bethel Alaska, USA
16C2 Bethel Connecticut,
USA
14B2 Bethel Park USA
15C3 Bethesda USA
94B3 Bethlehem Israel
101G1 Bethlehem S Africa
15C2 Bethlehem USA
48C1 Bethune France
101D3 Betioky Madag
108B1 Betoota Aust
98B2 Betou Congo
82A1 Betpak Dala Steppe
Kazakhstan
101D3 Betroka Madag
7D6 Betsiamites Can
86A1 Bettiah India
12D1 Bettles USA
47C2 Béttola Italy
85D4 Betul India
85D3 Betwa R India
46D1 Betzdorf Germany
12C3 Beverley,L USA
16D1 Beverly USA
21B3 Beverly Hills USA
97B4 Beyla Guinea
87B2 Beyrouth = Beirut
92B2 Beyşehir Turk
92B2 Beyşehir Gölü L Turk
94B2 Beyt Shean Israel
47C1 Bezau Austria
60E2 Bezhetsk
Russian Fed
49C3 Béziers France
90C2 Bezmein
Turkmenistan

63C2 Beznosova
Russian Fed
86B1 Bhadgaon Nepal
87C1 Bhadrāchalam India
86B1 Bhadrakh India
87B2 Bhadra Res India
87B2 Bhadrāvati India
84B3 Bhag Pak
86B1 Bhāgalpur India
84C2 Bhakkar Pak
82D3 Bhamo Burma
85D4 Bhandāra India
85D3 Bharatpur India
85C4 Bharūch India
86B2 Bhātiāpāra Ghat
Bang
84C2 Bhatinda India
87A2 Bhatkal India
86B2 Bhātpāra India
85C4 Bhāvnagar India
84C2 Bhera Pak
86A1 Bheri R Nepal
84C2 Bhilai India
85C3 Bhilwāra India
87C1 Bhimavaram India
85D3 Bhind India
84D3 Bhiwāni India
87B1 Bhongir India
85D4 Bhopal India
86B2 Bhubaneshwar India
85B4 Bhuj India
85D4 Bhusāwal India
82C3 Bhutan Kingdom,
Asia
71E4 Biak I Indon
52B2 Biala Podlaska Pol
58B2 Bialogard Pol
58C2 Bialystok Pol
38A1 Biargtangar C
Iceland
90C2 Biarjmand Iran
48B3 Biarritz France
47C1 Biasca Switz
92B4 Biba Egypt
74E2 Bibai Japan
100A2 Bibala Angola
57B3 Biberach Germany
97B4 Bibiani Ghana
54C1 Bicaz Rom
97C4 Bida Nig
87B1 Bidar India
91C5 Bidbid Oman
43B4 Bideford Eng
43B4 Bideford B Eng
96C2 Bidon 5 Alg
58C2 Bidzieta Pol
52A1 Biel Switz
59B2 Bielawa Pol
57B2 Bielefeld Germany
47B1 Bieler See L Switz
52A1 Biella Italy
58C2 Bielsk Podlaski Pol
76D3 Bien Hoa Viet
47B1 Bieno France
92A1 Biga Turk
55C3 Bigadiç Turk
19C3 Big Black R USA
18A1 Big Blue R USA
17B2 Big Cypress Swamp
USA
4D3 Big Delta USA
49D2 Bigent Germany
13F2 Biggar Can
5H4 Biggar Kindersley
Can
109D1 Biggenden Aust
12C3 Bigger,Mt Can
8C2 Bighorn R USA
76C3 Bight of Bangkok B
Thai
97C4 Bight of Benin B W
Africa
97C4 Bight of Biafra B
Cam
6C3 Big I Can
47C1 Bignasco Switz
97A3 Bignona Sen
21B2 Big Pine USA
17B2 Big Pine Key USA
14A2 Big Rapids USA
5H4 Big River Can
9C3 Big Spring USA
7A4 Big Trout L Can

7B4 Big Trout Lake Can
52C2 Bihać Bosnia-
Herzegovina
86B1 Bihār India
86B2 Bihar State, India
99D3 Biharamulo Tanz
60B4 Bihor Mt Rom
87B1 Bijāpur India
87C1 Bijāpur India
90A2 Bījār Iran
86A1 Bijauri Nepal
54A2 Bijeljina Bosnia-
Herzegovina
73B4 Bijie China
84C3 Bijnor India
84C3 Bijnot Pak
84C3 Bikāner India
94B2 Bikfaya Leb
69F2 Bikin Russian Fed
98B3 Bikoro Zaire
85C3 Bilara India
84D2 Bilaspur India
86A2 Bilaspur India
76B3 Bilauktaung Range
Mts Thai
50B1 Bilbao Spain
11B3 Biloxi USA
98C1 Biltine Chad
85D4 Bina-Etawa India
79B3 Binalbagan Phil
71D2 Bindura Zim
100B2 Binga Zim
101C2 Binga Mt Zim
109D1 Bingara Aust
57B3 Bingen Germany
15C2 Binghamton USA
78D1 Bingkor Malay
93D2 Bingöl Turk
72D3 Binhai China
13C2 Bin Island USA
78A3 Bintuhan Indon
78C2 Bintulu Malay
29B3 Bío Bió R Chile
102J4 Bioko I Atlantic O
87B1 Bīr India
95B2 Bir Abu Husein Well
Egypt
95B2 Bir al Harash Well
Libya
98C1 Birao CAR
86B1 Biratnagar Nepal
12E1 Birch Creek USA
108B3 Birchip Aust
5G4 Birch Mts Can
7A4 Bird Can
106C3 Birdsville Aust
106C2 Birdum Aust
86A1 Birganj Nepal
94A3 Bir Gifgāfa Well
Egypt
94A3 Bir Hasana Well
Egypt
35A2 Birigui Brazil
90C3 Birjand Iran
92B4 Birkat Qarun L Egypt
46D2 Birkenfeld Germany
43C4 Birkenhead Eng
60C4 Birlad R Rom
94A3 Bir Lahfān Well
Egypt
43C3 Birmingham Eng
11B3 Birmingham USA
95B2 Bir Misāha Well
Egypt
96A2 Bir Moghrein Maur
97C3 Birnin Kebbi Nig
97C3 Birni N'Konni Nig
69F2 Birobidzhan
Russian Fed
45C2 Birr Irish Rep
51C2 Bir Rabalou Alg
109C1 Birrie R Aust
44C2 Birsay Scot
61J2 Birsk Russian Fed

95B2 Bir Tarfâwi Well
Egypt
63B2 Biryusa Russian Fed
39J7 Biržai Lithuania
96B2 Bir Zreigat Well
Maur
48A2 Biscay,B of France/
Spain
17B2 Biscayne B USA
46D2 Bischwiller France
73B4 Bishan China
82B1 Bishkek Kirghizia
8B3 Bishop USA
42D2 Bishop Auckland Eng
43E4 Bishop's Stortford
Eng
86A2 Bishrāmpur India
96C1 Biskra Alg
79C4 Bislig Phil
8C2 Bismarck USA
90A3 Bisotūn Iran
97A3 Bissau Guinea-
Bissau
10A1 Bissett Can
5G4 Bistcho L Can
54C1 Bistrita R Rom
98B2 Bitam Gabon
57B3 Bitburg Germany
46D2 Bitche France
93D2 Bitlis Turk
55B2 Bitola Macedonia
56C2 Bitterfeld Germany
100A4 Bitterfontein S Africa
92B3 Bitter Lakes Egypt
8B2 Bitterroot Range Mts
USA
74D3 Biwa-ko L Japan
99E1 Biyo Kaboba Eth
65K4 Biysk Russian Fed
96C1 Bizerte Tunisia
52C1 Bj bou Arréridj Alg
52C1 Bjelovar Croatia
96B2 Bj Flye Ste Marie Alg
64C2 Bjørnøya / Barents S
12F1 Black R USA
18B2 Black R USA
10D3 Blackall Aust
42C3 Blackburn Eng
13E2 Black Diamond Can
5H5 Black Hills USA
44B3 Black Isle Pen Scot
27R3 Blackman's
Barbados
43C4 Black Mts Wales
43C3 Blackpool Eng
27H1 Black River Jamaica
8B2 Black Rock Desert
USA
65E5 Black S Asia/Europe
45A1 Blacksod B Irish Rep
109D2 Black Sugarloaf Mt
Aust
97B3 Black Volta R Ghana
41B3 Blackwater R
Irish Rep
18A2 Blackwell USA
54B2 Blagoevgrad Bulg
63E2 Blagoveshchensk
Russian Fed
20B1 Blaine USA
44C3 Blair Atholl Scot
44C3 Blairgowrie Scot
17B1 Blakely USA
108A1 Blanche,L Aust
34A2 Blanco R Arg
34B1 Blanco R Arg
8A2 Blanco,C USA
7E4 Blanc Sablon Can
43C4 Blandford Forum
Eng
46A2 Blangy-sur-Bresle
France
46B1 Blankenberge Belg
101C2 Blantyre Malawi
48B2 Blaye France
109C2 Blayney Aust
111B2 Blenheim NZ
96C1 Blida Alg
12H3 Blind River Can
108A2 Blinman Aust
78C4 Blitar Indon
15D2 Block I USA
16D2 Block Island Sd USA

Bloemfontein

101G1 **Bloemfontein** S Africa
101G1 **Bloemhof** S Africa
101G1 **Bloemhof Dam** *Res* S Africa
33F3 **Blommesteinmeer** *L* Surinam
38A1 **Blonduós** Iceland
45B1 **Bloody Foreland** *C* Irish Rep
14A3 **Bloomfield** Indiana, USA
18B1 **Bloomfield** Iowa, USA
10B2 **Bloomington** Illinois, USA
14A3 **Bloomington** Indiana, USA
16A2 **Bloomsburg** USA
78C4 **Blora** Indon
6H3 **Blosseville Kyst** *Mts* Greenland
57B3 **Bludenz** Austria
11B3 **Bluefield** USA
32A1 **Bluefields** Nic
26B3 **Blue Mountain Peak** *Mt* Jamaica
16A2 **Blue Mt** USA
109D2 **Blue Mts** Aust
27J1 **Blue Mts** Jamaica
8A2 **Blue Mts** USA
Blue Nile = Bahr el Azraq
99D1 **Blue Nile** *R* Sudan
4G3 **Bluenose** *L* Can
11B3 **Blue Ridge Mts** USA
13D2 **Blue River** Can
45B1 **Blue Stack** *Mt* Irish Rep
111A3 **Bluff** NZ
106A4 **Bluff Knoll** *Mt* Aust
30G4 **Blumenau** Brazil
49D2 **Blunder** Austria
20B2 **Bly** USA
12E3 **Blying Sd** USA
42D2 **Blyth** Eng
9B3 **Blythe** USA
11B3 **Blytheville** USA
97A4 **Bo** Sierra Leone
79B3 **Boac** Phil
72D2 **Boading** China
14B2 **Boardman** USA
63C3 **Boatou** China
33E3 **Boa Vista** Brazil
97A4 **Boa Vista** *I* Cape Verde
76E1 **Bobai** China
47C2 **Bóbbio** Italy
97B3 **Bobo Dioulasso** Burkina
60C3 **Bobruysk** Belorussia
17B2 **Boca Chica Key** *I* USA
32D5 **Bôca do Acre** Brazil
35C1 **Bocaiúva** Brazil
98B2 **Bocaranga** CAR
17B2 **Boca Raton** USA
59C3 **Bochnia** Pol
56B2 **Bocholt** Germany
46D1 **Bochum** Germany
100A2 **Bocoio** Angola
98B2 **Boda** CAR
63D2 **Bodaybo** Russian Fed
21A2 **Bodega Head** *Pt* USA
95A3 **Bodélé** *Region* Chad
38J5 **Boden** Sweden
47C1 **Bodensee** *L* Switz/ Germany
87B1 **Bodhan** India
87B2 **Bodināyakkanūr** India
43B4 **Bodmin** Eng
43B4 **Bodmin Moor** *Upland* Eng
38G5 **Bodø** Nor
55C3 **Bodrum** Turk
98C3 **Boende** Zaire
97A4 **Boffa** Guinea
76B2 **Bogale** Burma
19C3 **Bogalusa** USA
109C2 **Bogan** *R* Aust
97B3 **Bogandé** Burkina

6H3 **Bogarnes** Iceland
92C2 **Bogazlıyan** Turk
61K2 **Bogdanovich** Russian Fed
68A2 **Bogda Shan** *Mt* China
100A3 **Bogenfels** Namibia
109D1 **Boggabilla** Aust
109C2 **Boggabri** Aust
45B2 **Boggeragh Mts** Irish Rep
79B3 **Bogo** Phil
109C3 **Bogong,Mt** Aust
78B4 **Bogor** Indon
61H2 **Bogorodskoye** Russian Fed
32C3 **Bogotá** Colombia
63A2 **Bogotol** Russian Fed
86B2 **Bogra** Bang
72D2 **Bo Hai** *B* China
46B2 **Bohain-en-Vermandois** France
72D2 **Bohai Wan** *B* China
57C3 **Böhmer-Wald** *Upland* Germany
79B4 **Bohol** *I* Phil
79B4 **Bohol S** Phil
35A1 **Bois** *R* Brazil
14B1 **Bois Blanc** *I* USA
8B2 **Boise** USA
96A2 **Bojador,C** Mor
79B2 **Bojeador,C** Phil
90C2 **Bojnūrd** Iran
97A3 **Boké** Guinea
109C1 **Bokhara** *R* Aust
39F7 **Boknafjord** *Inlet* Nor
98B3 **Boko** Congo
76C3 **Bokor** Camb
98C3 **Bokungu** Zaire
98B1 **Bol** Chad
23A1 **Bolaános** Mexico
98B2 **Bolama** Guinea-Bissau
23A1 **Bolanos** *R* Mexico
48C2 **Bolbec** France
97B4 **Bole** Ghana
59B2 **Boleslawiec** Pol
97B3 **Bolgatanga** Ghana
60C4 **Bolgrad** Ukraine
34C3 **Bolivar** Arg
18B2 **Bolivar** Missouri, USA
18C2 **Bolivar** Tennessee, USA
30C2 **Bolivia** Republic, S America
38H6 **Bollnas** Sweden
38A1 **Bollon** Aust
32C2 **Bollvar** *R* Ven
52B2 **Bologna** Italy
60D2 **Bologoye** Russian Fed
69F2 **Bolon'** Russian Fed
61G3 **Bol'shoy Irgiz** *R* Russian Fed
74C2 **Bol'shoy Kamen** Russian Fed
Bol'shoy Kavkaz =Caucasus
61G4 **Bol'shoy Uzen** *R* Kazakhstan
9C4 **Bolson de Mapimi** *Desert* Mexico
43C3 **Bolton** Eng
92B1 **Bolu** Turk
38A1 **Bolungarvik** Iceland
92B2 **Bolvadin** Turk
52B1 **Bolzano** Italy
98B3 **Boma** Zaire
107B4 **Bombala** Aust
87A1 **Bombay** India
99D2 **Bombo** Uganda
35B1 **Bom Despacho** Brazil
86C1 **Bomdila** India
97A4 **Bomi Hills** Lib
31C4 **Bom Jesus da Lapa** Brazil
63E2 **Bomnak** Russian Fed
99C2 **Bomokandi** *R* Zaire
98C2 **Bomu** *R* CAR/Zaire
27D4 **Bonaire** *I* Caribbean S
12F2 **Bona,Mt** USA
25D3 **Bonanza** Nic

7E5 **Bonavista** Can
108A2 **Bon Bon** Aust
98C2 **Bondo** Zaire
97B4 **Bondoukou** Ivory Coast
Bône = 'Annaba
33E3 **Bonfim** Guyana
98C2 **Bongandanga** Zaire
98B1 **Bongor** Chad
19A3 **Bonham** USA
53A2 **Bonifacio** Corse
52A2 **Bonifacio,Str of** *Chan* Medit S
Bonin Is = Ogasawara Gunto
17B2 **Bonita Springs** USA
57B2 **Bonn** Germany
20C1 **Bonners Ferry** USA
12H1 **Bonnet Plume** *R* Can
13E2 **Bonnyville** Can
97A4 **Bonthe** Sierra Leone
99E1 **Booaaso** Somalia
108B2 **Booligal** Aust
108J1 **Boonah** Aust
15C2 **Boonville** USA
109C2 **Boorowa** Aust
6A2 **Boothia,G of** Can
6A2 **Boothia Pen** Can
98B3 **Booué** Gabon
108A1 **Bopeechee** Aust
99D2 **Bor** Sudan
92B2 **Bor** Turk
54B2 **Bor** Serbia, Yugos
8B2 **Borah Peak** *Mt* USA
39G7 **Borås** Sweden
91B4 **Borāzjān** Iran
108A3 **Borda,C** Aust
48B3 **Bordeaux** France
4G2 **Borden I** Can
6B2 **Borden Pen** Can
16B2 **Bordentown** USA
42C2 **Borders** Region, Scot
108B3 **Bordertown** Aust
96C2 **Bordj Omar Dris** Alg
87B2 **Borens River** Can
38A2 **Borgarnes** Iceland
9C3 **Borger** USA
39H7 **Borgholm** Sweden
47C2 **Borgosia** Italy
47D1 **Borgo Valsugana** Italy
59C3 **Borislav** Ukraine
61F3 **Borisoglebsk** Russian Fed
60C3 **Borisov** Belorussia
60E3 **Borisovka** Russian Fed
95A3 **Borkou** *Region* Chad
39H6 **Borlänge** Sweden
47C2 **Bormida** Italy
47D1 **Bormio** Italy
67F5 **Borneo** *I* Malay/ Indon
39H7 **Bornholm** *I* Den
55C3 **Bornova** Turk
98C2 **Boro** *R* Sudan
97B3 **Boromo** Burkina
60D2 **Borovichi** Russian Fed
108B2 **Borroloola** Aust
54B1 **Borsa** Rom
90A3 **Borūjed** Iran
90B3 **Borūjen** Iran
58B2 **Bory Tucholskie** Region, Pol
63D2 **Borzya** Russian Fed
73B5 **Bose** China
10G1 **Boshof** S Africa
54A2 **Bosna** *R* Bosnia-Herzegovina
37E4 **Bosnia-Herzegovina** Republic, Europe
75C1 **Bōsō-hantō** *B* Japan
Bosporus = Karadeniz Boğazi
51C2 **Bosquet** Alg
98B2 **Bossangoa** CAR
98B2 **Bossèmbélé** CAR
19B3 **Bossier City** USA
65K5 **Bosten Hu** *L* China
42D3 **Boston** Eng
10C2 **Boston** USA
11A3 **Boston Mts** USA
85C4 **Botād** India

54B2 **Botevgrad** Bulg
101G1 **Bothaville** S Africa
64C3 **Bothnia,G of** Sweden/Fin
100B3 **Botletli** *R* Botswana
60C4 **Botosani** Rom
100B3 **Botswana** Republic, Africa
53C3 **Botte Donato** *Mt* Italy
46D1 **Bottrop** Germany
35B2 **Botucatu** Brazil
7E5 **Botwood** Can
89D7 **Bouaké** Ivory Coast
98B2 **Bouar** CAR
96B1 **Bouârfa** Mor
98B2 **Bouca** CAR
51C2 **Boufarik** Alg
Bougie = Bejaia
97B3 **Bougouni** Mali
46C2 **Bouillon** France
96B2 **Bou Izakarn** Mor
46D2 **Boulay-Moselle** France
8C2 **Boulder** Colorado, USA
9B3 **Boulder City** USA
22A2 **Boulder Creek** USA
48C1 **Boulogne** France
98B2 **Boumba** *R* CAR
97B4 **Bouna** Ivory Coast
8B3 **Boundary Peak** *Mt* USA
97B4 **Boundiali** Ivory Coast
107F3 **Bourail** Nouvelle Calédonie
97B3 **Bourem** Mali
49D2 **Bourg** France
49D2 **Bourg de Péage** France
48C2 **Bourges** France
48C3 **Bourg-Madame** France
47B2 **Bourgogne** Region, France
47B2 **Bourg-St-Maurice** France
108C2 **Bourke** Aust
43D4 **Bournemouth** Eng
96C1 **Bou Saâda** Alg
98B1 **Bousso** Chad
97A3 **Boutilmit** Maur
103J7 **Bouvet I** Atlantic O
34D2 **Bovril** Arg
13E2 **Bow** *R* Can
107D2 **Bowen** Aust
19A3 **Bowie** Texas, USA
13E2 **Bow Island** Can
11B3 **Bowling Green** Kentucky, USA
18B2 **Bowling Green** Missouri, USA
14B2 **Bowling Green** Ohio, USA
14B2 **Bowling Green** Virginia, USA
12C2 **Bowmanville** Can
109C2 **Bowral** Aust
13C2 **Bowron** *R* Can
72D3 **Bo Xian** China
72D2 **Boxing** China
98B2 **Boyabat** Turk
5J4 **Boyd** Can
16B2 **Boyertown** USA
13E2 **Boyle** Can
41B3 **Boyle** Irish Rep
45C2 **Boyne** *R* Irish Rep
17B2 **Boynoton Beach** USA
98C2 **Boyoma Falls** Zaire
55C3 **Bozca Ada** *I* Turk
55C3 **Boz Dağlari** *Mts* Turk
8B2 **Bozeman** USA
Bozen = Bolzano
98B2 **Bozene** Zaire
98B2 **Bozoum** CAR
47B2 **Bra** Italy
52C2 **Brač** *I* Croatia
15C1 **Bracebridge** Can
95A2 **Brach** Libya
38H6 **Bräcke** Sweden
17B2 **Bradenton** USA

42D3 Bradford Eng
44E1 Brae Scot
44C3 Braemar Scot
50A1 Braga Port
34C3 Bragado Arg
50A1 Bragana Port
31B2 Bragança Brazil
35B2 Bragança Paulista
  Brazil
86C2 Brahman-Baria Bang
86B2 Brahmani R India
86C1 Brahmaputra R India
7E5 Braie Verte Can
60C4 Bräila Rom
10A2 Brainerd USA
97A3 Brakna Region, Maur
5F4 Bralorne Can
14C2 Brampton Can
33E3 Branco R Brazil
100A3 Brandberg Mt
  Namibia
56C2 Brandenburg
  Germany
56C2 Brandenburg State,
  Germany
101G1 Brandfort S Africa
8D2 Brandon Can
100B4 Brandvlei S Africa
57C2 Brandys nad Lebem
  Czech Republic
58B2 Braniewo Pol
10B2 Brantford Can
108B3 Branxholme Aust
7D5 Bras D'Or L Can
35C1 Brasila de Minas
  Brazil
32D6 Brasileia Brazil
31B5 Brasilia Brazil
54C1 Brasov Rom
78D1 Brassay Range Mts
  Malay
59B3 Bratislava Slovakia
63C2 Bratsk Russian Fed
15D2 Brattleboro USA
56C2 Braunschweig
  Germany
97A4 Brava I Cape Verde
9B3 Brawley USA
45C2 Bray Irish Rep
6C3 Bray I Can
13D2 Brazeau R Can
13D2 Brazeau,Mt Can
28D4 Brazil Republic,
  S America
103G5 Brazil Basin
  Atlantic O
9D3 Brazos R USA
98B3 Brazzaville Congo
57C3 Brdy Upland
  Czech Republic
111A3 Breaksea Sd NZ
110B1 Bream B NZ
78B4 Brebes Indon
44C3 Brechin Scot
46C1 Brecht Belg
59B3 Břeclav
  Czech Republic
43C4 Brecon Wales
43C4 Brecon Beacons Mts
  Wales
43B3 Brecon Beacons Nat
  Pk Wales
56A2 Breda Neth
100B4 Bredasdorp S Africa
38H6 Bredbyn Sweden
61J3 Bredy Russian Fed
15C2 Breezewood USA
47C1 Bregenz Austria
47C1 Bregenzer Ache R
  Austria
38A1 Breiðafjörður B
  Iceland
47C2 Brembo R Italy
17A1 Bremen USA
56B2 Bremen Germany
56B2 Bremerhaven
  Germany
20B1 Bremerton USA
19A3 Brenham USA
57C3 Brenner P Austria/
  Italy
47D2 Breno Italy
47D2 Brenta Italy
22B2 Brentwood Eng

52B1 Brescia Italy
  Breslau = Wrocław
47D1 Bressanone Italy
44E1 Bressay I Scot
48B2 Bressuire France
58C2 Brest Belorussia
48B2 Brest France
48B2 Bretagne Region,
  France
46B2 Breteuil France
16B2 Breton Woods USA
110B1 Brett,C NZ
109C1 Brewarrina Aust
16C2 Brewster New York,
  USA
20C1 Brewster
  Washington, USA
101G1 Breyten S Africa
52C1 Brežice Slovenia
98C2 Bria CAR
49D3 Briançon France
49C2 Briare France
21B2 Bridgeport
  California, USA
15D2 Bridgeport
  Connecticut, USA
19A3 Bridgeport Texas,
  USA
22C1 Bridgeport Res USA
16B3 Bridgeton USA
27F4 Bridgetown
  Barbados
7D5 Bridgwater Can
16D2 Bridgwater USA
43C4 Bridgwater B Eng
42D2 Bridlington Eng
109C4 Bridport Aust
47B1 Brienzer See L Switz
46C2 Briey France
52A1 Brig Switz
8B2 Brigham City USA
109C3 Bright Aust
43D4 Brighton Eng
46E1 Brilon Germany
55A2 Brindisi Italy
19B3 Brinkley USA
107E3 Brisbane Aust
15D2 Bristol Connecticut,
  USA
43C4 Bristol Eng
15D2 Bristol Pennsylvania,
  USA
16D2 Bristol Rhode Island,
  USA
11B3 Bristol Tennessee,
  USA
12B3 Bristol B USA
43B4 Bristol Chan Eng/
  Wales
4D3 British Mts USA
5F4 British Columbia
  Province, Can
6B1 British Empire Range
  Mts Can
101G1 Brits S Africa
100B4 Britstown S Africa
48C2 Brive France
59B3 Brno Czech Republic
17B1 Broad R USA
7C4 Broadback R Can
44A2 Broad Bay Inlet Scot
44B3 Broadford Scot
5H4 Brochet Can
4G2 Brock I Can
15C2 Brockport USA
16D1 Brockton USA
15C2 Brockville Can
6B2 Brodeur Pen Can
42B2 Brodick Scot
58B2 Brodnica Pol
60C3 Brody Ukraine
19B3 Broken Bow
  Oklahoma, USA
19B3 Broken Bow L USA
107D4 Broken Hill Aust
47C2 Broni Italy
38G6 Brønneysund Nor
16C2 Bronx Borough, New
  York, USA
79A4 Brooke's Point Phil
18B2 Brookfield Missouri,
  USA
11A3 Brookhaven USA

20B2 Brookings Oregon,
  USA
8D2 Brookings South
  Dakota, USA
16D1 Brookline USA
16C2 Brooklyn Borough,
  New York, USA
5G4 Brooks Can
12C3 Brooks,L USA
12A1 Brooks Mt USA
4C3 Brooks Range Mts
  USA
17B2 Brooksville USA
109D1 Brooloo Aust
106B2 Broome Aust
44C2 Brora Scot
20B2 Brothers USA
95A3 Broulkou Chad
13E3 Browning USA
9D4 Brownsville USA
9D3 Brownwood USA
46B1 Bruay-en-Artois
  France
106A3 Bruce,Mt Aust
14B1 Bruce Pen Can
59B3 Brück an der Mur
  Austria
  Bruges = Brugge
46B1 Brugge Belg
46D1 Brühl Germany
78C2 Brunei Sultanate,
  S E Asia
52B1 Brunico Italy
111B2 Brunner,L NZ
11B3 Brunswick Georgia,
  USA
18B2 Brunswick
  Mississippi, USA
29B6 Brunswick,Pen de
  Chile
109C4 Bruny I Aust
61F1 Brusenets
  Russian Fed
26A3 Brus Laguna
  Honduras
  Brüssel = Bruxelles
56A2 Bruxelles Belg
9D3 Bryan USA
108A2 Bryan,Mt Aust
60D3 Bryansk
  Russian Fed
19B3 Bryant USA
59B2 Brzeg Pol
93E4 Bübiyan I Kuwait/
  Iraq
99D3 Bubu R Tanz
32C2 Bucaramanga
  Colombia
44D3 Buchan Oilfield N
  Sea
97A4 Buchanan Lib
44D3 Buchan Deep N Sea
6C2 Buchan G Can
40C2 Buchan Ness Pen
  Scot
7E5 Buchans Can
44D3 Buchans Can
34C2 Buchardo Arg
  Bucharest = Bucureşti
47C1 Buchs Switz
43D3 Buckingham Eng
12B1 Buckland USA
12B1 Buckland R USA
108A2 Buckleboo Aust
98B3 Buco Zau Congo
54C2 Bucureşti Rom
59B3 Budapest Hung
84D3 Budaun India
43B4 Bude Eng
19B3 Bude USA
61F5 Budennovsk
  Russian Fed
54A2 Budva Montenegro,
  Yugos
98A2 Buéa Cam
22B3 Buellton USA
34B2 Buena Esperanza Arg
32B3 Buenaventura
  Colombia
23A2 Buenavista Mexico
29E2 Buenos Aires Arg
29D3 Buenos Aires State,
  Arg
18B2 Buffalo Mississippi,
  USA

10C2 Buffalo New York,
  USA
8C2 Buffalo South
  Dakota, USA
19A3 Buffalo Texas, USA
8C2 Buffalo Wyoming,
  USA
101H1 Buffalo R S Africa
13E2 Buffalo L Alberta,
  Can
5G3 Buffalo L Northwest
  Territories, Can
5H4 Buffalo Narrows Can
17B1 Buford USA
54C2 Buftea Rom
59C2 Bug R Pol/Ukraine
32B3 Buga Colombia
90B2 Bugdayli
  Turkmenistan
61H3 Bugulma
  Russian Fed
61H3 Buguruslan
  Russian Fed
93C2 Buhayrat al Asad Res
  Syria
41C3 Builth Wells Wales
34A2 Buin Chile
99C3 Bujumbura Burundi
98C3 Bukama Zaïre
99C3 Bukavu Zaïre
80E2 Bukhara Uzbekistan
78C2 Bukit Batubrok Mt
  Indon
70B4 Bukittinggi Indon
99D3 Bukoba Tanz
78D3 Buku Gandadiwata
  Mt Indon
71E4 Bula Indon
79B3 Bulan Phil
84D3 Bulandshahr India
100B3 Bulawayo Zim
55C3 Buldan Turk
85D4 Buldana India
68C2 Bulgan Mongolia
54B2 Bulgaria
  Republic, Europe
47B1 Bulle Switz
111B2 Buller NZ
109C3 Buller,Mt Aust
106A4 Bullfinch Aust
108B1 Bulloo R Aust
108B1 Bulloo Downs Aust
108B1 Bulloo L Aust
18B2 Bull Shoals Res USA
34A3 Bulnes Chile
71F4 Bulolo PNG
101G1 Bultfontein S Africa
98C2 Bumba Zaïre
76B2 Bumphal Dam Thai
99D3 Buna Kenya
106A4 Bunbury Aust
45C1 Buncrana Irish Rep
107E3 Bundaberg Aust
109D2 Bundarra Aust
85D3 Bündi India
45B1 Bundoran Irish Rep
109C1 Bungil R Aust
98B3 Bungo Angola
75A2 Bungo-suidō Str
  Japan
70B3 Bunguran I Ind
99D2 Bunia Zaïre
18B2 Bunker USA
19B3 Bunkie USA
17B2 Bunnell USA
78C3 Buntok Indon
71D3 Buol Indon
94B2 Burag Syria
98C1 Buram Sudan
99E2 Burao Somalia
79B3 Burauen Phil
80C3 Buraydah S Arabia
21B3 Burbank USA
109C2 Burcher Aust
92B2 Burdur Turk
63F3 Bureinskiy Khrebet
  Mts Russian Fed
56C2 Burg Germany
54C2 Burgas Bulg
17C1 Burgaw USA
47B1 Burgdorf Switz
100B4 Burgersdorp S Africa
50B1 Burgos Spain
58B1 Burgsvik Sweden

Burhaniye

55C3 Burhaniye Turk
85D4 Burhānpur India
79B3 Burias I Phil
76C2 Buriram Thai
35B1 Buritis Brazil
13B2 Burke Chan Can
106C2 Burketown Aust
97B3 Burkina Republic, Africa
15C1 Burks Falls Can
8B2 Burley USA
10A2 Burlington Iowa, USA
16B2 Burlington New Jersey, USA
10C2 Burlington Vermont, USA
20B1 Burlington Washington, USA
83D3 Burma Republic, Asia
20B2 Burney USA
16A2 Burnham USA
107D5 Burnie Aust
42C3 Burnley Eng
20C2 Burns USA
5F4 Burns Lake Can
82C1 Burqin China
108A2 Burra Aust
109D2 Burragorang,L Aust
44C2 Burray I Scot
109C2 Burren Junction Aust
109C2 Burrinjuck Res Aust
60C5 Bursa Turk
80B3 Bur Safâga Egypt
Bûr Sa'id = Port Said
14B2 Burton USA
43D3 Burton upon Trent Eng
38J6 Burtrask Sweden
108B2 Burtundy Aust
71D4 Buru Indon
99C3 Burundi Republic, Africa
78A2 Burung Indon
63D2 Buryatskaya Respublika, Russian Fed
99D1 Burye Eth
61H4 Burynshik Kazakhstan
43E3 Bury St Edmunds Eng
91B4 Büshehr Iran
98B3 Busira R Zaire
58C2 Buskozdroj Pol
94C2 Buşrá ash Shām Syria
106A4 Busselton Aust
49D2 Busto Italy
52A1 Busto Arsizio Italy
79A3 Busuanga I Phil
98C2 Buta Zaire
34B3 Buta Ranquil Arg
99C3 Butare Rwanda
42B2 Bute I Scot
69E2 Butha Qi China
14C2 Butler USA
8B2 Butte USA
77C4 Butterworth Malay
40B2 Butt of Lewis C Scot
6D3 Button Is Can
79C4 Butuan Phil
71D4 Butung I Indon
61F3 Buturlinovka Russian Fed
86A1 Butwal Nepal
99E2 Buulo Barde Somalia
99E2 Buur Hakaba Somalia
61F2 Buy Russian Fed
72B1 Buyant Ovvo Mongolia
61G5 Buynaksk Russian Fed
63D3 Buyr Nuur L Mongolia
93D2 Büyük Ağri Mt Turk
92A2 Büyük Menderes R Turk
54C1 Buzau Rom
54C1 Buzau R Rom
61H3 Buzuluk Russian Fed

16D2 Buzzards B USA
54C2 Byala Bulg
54B2 Byala Slatina Bulg
4H2 Byam Martin Chan Can
4H2 Byam Martin I Can
Byblos = Jubail
94B1 Byblos Hist Site, Leb
58B2 Bydgoszcz Pol
39F7 Bygland Nor
6C2 Bylot I Can
109C2 Byrock Aust
22B2 Byron Aust
109D1 Byron,C Aust
59B2 Bytom Pol

C

30E4 Caacupé Par
100A2 Caála Angola
13B2 Caazapa Sd Can
30E4 Caazapá Par
79B2 Cabanatuan Phil
31E3 Cabedelo Brazil
50A2 Cabeza del Buey Spain
34C3 Cabildo Arg
34A2 Cabildo Chile
32C1 Cabimas Ven
98B3 Cabinda Angola
98B3 Cabinda Province, Angola
27C3 Cabo Beata Dom Rep
51C2 Cabo Binibeca C Spain
53A3 Cabo Carbonara C Sardegna
34A3 Cabo Carranza C Chile
50A2 Cabo Carvoeiro C Port
9B3 Cabo Colnett C Mexico
32B2 Cabo Corrientes C Colombia
24B2 Cabo Corrientes C Mexico
26B3 Cabo Cruz C Cuba
50B1 Cabo de Ajo C Spain
51C1 Cabo de Caballeria C Spain
51C1 Cabo de Creus C Spain
50A2 Cabo de Gata C Spain
29C7 Cabo de Hornos C Chile
51C2 Cabo de la Nao C Spain
50A1 Cabo de Peñas C Spain
50A2 Cabo de Roca C Port
51C2 Cabo de Salinas C Spain
35C2 Cabo de São Tomé C Brazil
50A2 Cabo de São Vicente C Port
50A2 Cabo de Sines C Port
51C1 Cabo de Tortosa C Spain
29C4 Cabo Dos Bahias C Arg
50A2 Cabo Espichel C Port
9B4 Cabo Falso C Mexico
51B2 Cabo Ferrat C Alg
50A1 Cabo Finisterre C Spain
51C1 Cabo Formentor C Spain
35C2 Cabo Frio Brazil
35C2 Cabo Frio C Brazil
26A4 Cabo Gracias a Dios Honduras
31B2 Cabo Maguarinho C Brazil
50A2 Cabo Negro C Mor
109D1 Cabooolture Aust
33G3 Cabo Orange C Brazil
21B3 Cabo Punta Banda C Mexico
101C2 Cabora Bassa Dam Mozam

24A1 Caborca Mexico
24C2 Cabo Rojo C Mexico
23B1 Cabos Mexico
29C6 Cabo San Diego C Arg
32A4 Cabo San Lorenzo C Ecuador
53A3 Cabo Teulada C Sardegna
50A2 Cabo Trafalgar C Spain
50B2 Cabo Tres Forcas C Mor
29C5 Cabo Tres Puntas C Arg
7D5 Cabot Str Can
50B2 Cabra Spain
50A1 Cabreira Mt Port
51C2 Cabrera I Spain
34A3 Cabrero Chile
51B2 Cabriel R Spain
23B2 Cacahuamilpa Mexico
54B2 Čačak Serbia, Yugos
23B2 C A Carillo Mexico
30E2 Cáceres Brazil
50A2 Cáceres Spain
18B2 Cache R USA
13C2 Cache Creek Can
30C4 Cachi Arg
33G5 Cachimbo Brazil
31D4 Cachoeira Brazil
35A1 Cachoeira Alta Brazil
31D3 Cachoeira de Paulo Alfonso Waterfall Brazil
29F2 Cachoeira do Sul Brazil
31C6 Cachoeiro de Itapemirim Brazil
22C3 Cachuma,L USA
100A2 Cacolo Angola
100A2 Caconda Angola
35A1 Caçu Brazil
100A2 Caculuvar R Angola
59B3 Čadca Slovakia
43C3 Cader Idris Mts Wales
10B2 Cadillac USA
79B3 Cadiz Phil
50A2 Cádiz Spain
48B2 Caen France
42B3 Caernarfon Wales
43B3 Caernarfon B Wales
94B2 Caesarea Hist Site Israel
31C4 Caetité Brazil
30C4 Cafayate Arg
92B2 Çaga Tepe Turk
79B2 Cagayan R Phil
79B4 Cagayan de Oro Phil
79B4 Cagayan Is Phil
53A3 Cagliari Sardegna
27D3 Caguas Puerto Rico
45B3 Caha Mts Irish Rep
45A3 Cahersiveen Irish Rep
45C2 Cahir Irish Rep
45C2 Cahone Pt Irish Rep
48C3 Cahors France
101C2 Caia Mozam
35A1 Caiapó R Brazil
35A1 Caiapônia Brazil
31D3 Caicó Brazil
26C2 Caicos Is Caribbean S
11C4 Caicos Pass The Bahamas
12C2 Cairn Mt USA
44C3 Cairngorms Mts Scot
107D2 Cairns Aust
92B3 Cairo Egypt
11B3 Cairo USA
108B1 Caiwarro Aust
32B5 Cajabamba Peru
32B5 Cajamarca Peru
27D5 Calabozo Ven
52B2 Calafat Rom
29B6 Calafate Arg
79B3 Calagua Is Phil
51B1 Calahorra Spain
48C1 Calais France

30C3 Calama Chile
32C3 Calamar Colombia
79A3 Calamian Group Is Phil
98B3 Calandula Angola
70A3 Calang Indon
95B2 Calanscio Sand Sea Libya
79B3 Calapan Phil
54C2 Calarasi Rom
51B1 Calatayud Spain
22B2 Calaveras Res USA
79B3 Calbayog Phil
19B4 Calcasieu L USA
86B2 Calcutta India
50A2 Caldas da Rainha Port
31B5 Caldas Novas Brazil
30B4 Caldera Chile
8B2 Caldwell USA
29C5 Caleta Olivia Arg
9B3 Calexico USA
5C4 Calgary Can
17B1 Calhoun USA
17B1 Calhoun Falls USA
32B3 Cali Colombia
87B2 Calicut India
8B3 Caliente Nevada, USA
8A3 California State, USA
22C3 California Aqueduct USA
87B2 Calimera,Pt India
34B2 Calingasta Arg
22A1 Calistoga USA
108A1 Callabonna R Aust
108A1 Callabonna,L Aust
15C1 Callander USA
44B3 Callander Scot
108A1 Callanna Aust
32B6 Callao Peru
13E1 Calling L Can
23B1 Calnali Mexico
17B2 Caloosahatchee R USA
109D1 Caloundra Aust
23B2 Calpulalpan Mexico
53B3 Caltanissetta Italy
98B3 Caluango Angola
100A2 Calulo Angola
100A2 Caluquembe Angola
99F1 Caluula Somalia
13B2 Calvert I Can
52A2 Calvi Corse
23A1 Calvillo Mexico
100A4 Calvinia S Africa
25E2 Camagüey Cuba
25E2 Camagüey,Arch de Is Cuba
30B2 Camaná Peru
30C3 Camargo Bol
22C3 Camarillo USA
29C4 Camarones Arg
20B1 Camas USA
98B3 Camaxilo Angola
98B3 Cambatela Angola
76C3 Cambodia Republic, S E Asia
43B4 Camborne Eng
49C1 Cambrai France
43C3 Cambrian Mts Wales
14B2 Cambridge County, Eng
43E3 Cambridge Eng
27H1 Cambridge Jamaica
15C3 Cambridge Maryland, USA
15D2 Cambridge Massachussets, USA
110C1 Cambridge NZ
14B2 Cambridge Ohio, USA
4H3 Cambridge Bay Can
60E5 Cam Burun Pt Turk
11A3 Camden Arkansas, USA
109D2 Camden Aust
15D3 Camden New Jersey, USA
17B1 Camden South Carolina, USA
18B2 Cameron Missouri, USA

19A3 **Cameron** Texas, USA
4H2 **Cameron I** Can
111A3 **Cameron Mts** NZ
98A2 **Cameroon** Federal Republic, Africa
98A2 **Cameroon** *Mt* Cam
31B2 **Cametá** Brazil
79B4 **Camiguin** *I* Phil
79B2 **Camiling** Phil
17B1 **Camilla** USA
22B1 **Camino** USA
30D3 **Camiri** Bol
31C2 **Camocim** Brazil
98C3 **Camissombo** Angola
106C2 **Camooweal** Aust
34D2 **Campana** Arg
29A5 **Campana** *I* Chile
13B2 **Campania** I Can
111B2 **Campbell,C** NZ
13B2 **Campbell I** Can
105G6 **Campbell I** NZ
4E3 **Campbell,Mt** Can
84C2 **Campbellpore** Pak
5F5 **Campbell River** Can
7D5 **Campbellton** Can
109D2 **Campbelltown** Aust
42B2 **Campbeltown** Scot
25C3 **Campeche** Mexico
108B3 **Camperdown** Aust
31D3 **Campina Grande** Brazil
31B6 **Campinas** Brazil
35B1 **Campina Verde** Brazil
98A2 **Campo** Cam
53B2 **Campobasso** Italy
35B2 **Campo Belo** Brazil
35B1 **Campo Florido** Brazil
30D4 **Campo Gallo** Arg
30F3 **Campo Grande** Brazil
31C2 **Campo Maior** Brazil
30F3 **Campo Mourão** Brazil
35C2 **Campos** Brazil
35B1 **Campos Altos** Brazil
47D1 **Campo Tures** Italy
76D3 **Cam Ranh** Viet
5G4 **Camrose** Can
100A2 **Camucuio** Angola
27K1 **Canaan** Tobago
16C1 **Canaan** USA
100A2 **Canacupa** Angola
2F3 **Canada** Dominion, N America
29D2 **Cañada de Gomez** Arg
9C3 **Canadian** *R* USA
60C5 **Canakkale** Turk
34B3 **Canalejas** Arg
13D2 **Canal Flats** Can
24A1 **Cananea** Mexico
102G3 **Canary Basin** Atlantic O
Canary Is = Islas Canarias
23A2 **Canas** Mexico
24B2 **Canatlán** Mexico
11B4 **Canaveral,C** USA
31D5 **Canavieiras** Brazil
107D4 **Canberra** Aust
20B2 **Canby** California, USA
55C3 **Candarli Körfezi** *B* Turk
16C2 **Candlewood,L** USA
29E2 **Canelones** Urug
18A2 **Caney** USA
100A2 **Cangamba** Angola
100B2 **Cangombe** Angola
72D2 **Cangzhou** China
7D4 **Caniapiscau** *R* Can
53B3 **Canicattì** Italy
31D2 **Canindé** Brazil
92B1 **Çankiri** Turk
13D2 **Canmore** Can
44A3 **Canna** *I* Scot
87B2 **Cannanore** India
49D3 **Cannes** France
109C3 **Cann River** Aust
30F4 **Canoas** Brazil
13F1 **Canoe L** Can
9C3 **Canon City** USA
108B2 **Canopus** Aust

5H4 **Canora** Can
109C2 **Canowindra** Aust
45C2 **Cansore Pt** Irish Rep
43E4 **Canterbury** Eng
111B2 **Canterbury Bight** *B* NZ
111B2 **Canterbury Plains** NZ
77D4 **Can Tho** Viet
Canton = Guangzhou
19C3 **Canton** Mississippi, USA
18B1 **Canton** Missouri, USA
10B2 **Canton** Ohio, USA
12E2 **Canton** USA
20C2 **Canyon City** USA
12J2 **Canyon Range** *Mts* Can
20B2 **Canyonville** USA
98C3 **Canzar** Angola
76D1 **Cao Bang** Viet
31B2 **Capanema** Brazil
35B2 **Capão Bonito** Brazil
48B3 **Capbreton** France
24B2 **Cap Corrientes** *C* Mexico
52A2 **Cap Corse** *C* Corse
48B2 **Cap de la Hague** *C* France
15D1 **Cap-de-la-Madeleine** Can
6C3 **Cap de Nouvelle-France** *C* Can
51C2 **Capdepera** Spain
23A2 **Cap de Tancitiario** *C* Mexico
109C4 **Cape Barren I** Aust
103J6 **Cape Basin** Atlantic O
7E5 **Cape Breton I** Can
97B4 **Cape Coast** Ghana
15D2 **Cape Cod B** USA
6C3 **Cape Dorset** Can
17C1 **Cape Fear** *R* USA
18C2 **Cape Girardeau** USA
6B3 **Cape Henrietta Maria** Can
Cape Horn = Cabo de Hornos
104E3 **Cape Johnston Depth** Pacific O
35C1 **Capelinha** Brazil
4B3 **Cape Lisburne** USA
100A2 **Capelongo** Angola
15D3 **Cape May** USA
5F5 **Cape Mendocino** USA
98B3 **Capenda Camulemba** Angola
4F2 **Cape Perry** Can
100B4 **Cape Province** S Africa
48B2 **Cape Tatnam** Can
100A4 **Cape Town** S Africa
102G4 **Cape Verde** *Is* Atlantic O
102G4 **Cape Verde Basin** Atlantic O
12F3 **Cape Yakataga** USA
107D2 **Cape York Pen** Aust
46A1 **Cap Gris Nez** *C* France
26C3 **Cap-Haïtien** Haiti
31B2 **Capim** *R* Brazil
112C2 **Capitán Arturo Prat** *Base* Ant
27P2 **Cap Moule à Chique** *C* St Lucia
53C3 **Capo Isola de Correnti** *C* Italy
53C3 **Capo Rizzuto** *C* Italy
55A3 **Capo Santa Maria di Leuca** *C* Italy
53B3 **Capo San Vito** Italy
27P2 **Cap Pt** St Lucia
53B2 **Capri** *I* Italy
100B2 **Caprivi Strip** Region, Namibia
52A2 **Cap Rosso** *C* Corse
102H4 **Cap Vert** *C* Sen
32C4 **Caquetá** *R* Colombia
54B2 **Caracal** Rom

33E3 **Caracaraí** Brazil
32D1 **Caracas** Ven
35B2 **Caraguatatuba** Brazil
29B3 **Carahue** Chile
35C1 **Caraí** Brazil
35C2 **Carandaí** Brazil
31C6 **Carangola** Brazil
54B1 **Caransebeş** Rom
108A2 **Carappee Hill** *Mt* Aust
26A3 **Caratasca** Honduras
35C1 **Caratinga** Brazil
51B2 **Caravaca** Spain
35D1 **Caravelas** Brazil
18C2 **Carbondale** Illinois, USA
53A3 **Carbonia** Sardegna
7E5 **Carboear** Can
5G4 **Carcaion** Can
99E1 **Carcar Mts** Somalia
48C3 **Carcassonne** France
4E3 **Carcross** Can
22B2 **Cardel** Mexico
25D2 **Cárdenas** Cuba
23B1 **Cárdenas** Mexico
43C4 **Cardiff** Wales
43B3 **Cardigan** Wales
43B3 **Cardigan B** Wales
13E2 **Cardston** Can
54B1 **Carei** Rom
33F4 **Careiro** Brazil
34A2 **Carén** Chile
14B2 **Carey** USA
48B2 **Carhaix-Plouguer** France
29D3 **Carhué** Arg
31C6 **Cariacica** Brazil
5J4 **Caribou** Can
5G4 **Caribou Mts** Alberta, Can
5F4 **Caribou Mts** British Columbia, Can
79B3 **Carigara** Phil
46C2 **Carignan** France
33E1 **Caripito** Ven
15C1 **Carleton Place** Can
101G1 **Carletonville** S Africa
18C2 **Carlinville** USA
42C2 **Carlisle** Eng
15C2 **Carlisle** USA
34C3 **Carlos** Arg
35C1 **Carlos Chagas** Brazil
45C2 **Carlow** County, Irish Rep
45C2 **Carlow** Irish Rep
21B3 **Carlsbad** California, USA
9C3 **Carlsbad** New Mexico, USA
5H5 **Carlyle** Can
12G2 **Carmacks** Can
47B2 **Carmagnola** Italy
43B4 **Carmarthen** Wales
43B4 **Carmarthen B** Wales
22B2 **Carmel** California, USA
16C2 **Carmel** New York, USA
94B2 **Carmel,Mt** Israel
34D2 **Carmelo** Urug
22B2 **Carmel Valley** USA
9B4 **Carmen** *I* Mexico
29D4 **Carmen de Patagones** Arg
35C2 **Carmi** USA
21A2 **Carmichael** USA
35B1 **Carmo do Paranaiba** Brazil
50A2 **Carmona** Spain
106A3 **Carnarvon** Aust
100B4 **Carnarvon** S Africa
35D1 **Carncacá** Brazil
45C1 **Carndonagh** Irish Rep
106B3 **Carnegi,L** Aust
98B2 **Carnot** CAR
108A2 **Carnot,C** Aust
17B2 **Carol City** USA
31B3 **Carolina** Brazil
101H1 **Carolina** S Africa
17C1 **Carolina Beach** USA
104F3 **Caroline Is** Pacific O
60B4 **Carpathians** *Mts* E Europe

59D3 **Carpatii Orientali** *Mts* Rom
106C2 **Carpentaria,G of** Aust
83C5 **Carpenter Ridge** Indian O
49D3 **Carpentras** France
52B2 **Carpi** Italy
22C3 **Carpinteria** USA
17B2 **Carrabelle** USA
52B2 **Carrara** Italy
41B3 **Carrauntoohill** *Mt* Irish Rep
45C2 **Carrickmacross** Irish Rep
45B2 **Carrick on Shannon** Irish Rep
45C2 **Carrick-on-Suir** Irish Rep
108A2 **Carrieton** Aust
8D2 **Carrington** USA
50B1 **Carrión** *R* Spain
10A2 **Carroll** USA
17A1 **Carrollton** Georgia, USA
14A3 **Carrollton** Kentucky, USA
18B2 **Carrollton** Missouri, USA
18C2 **Carruthersville** USA
60E5 **Çarsamba** Turk
92B2 **Çarsamba** *R* Turk
8B3 **Carson City** USA
14B2 **Carsonville** USA
26B4 **Cartagena** Colombia
51B2 **Cartagena** Spain
32B3 **Cartago** Colombia
25D4 **Cartago** Costa Rica
111C2 **Carterton** NZ
18B2 **Carthage** Missouri, USA
15C2 **Carthage** New York, USA
19B3 **Carthage** Texas, USA
106B2 **Cartier I** Timor S
7E4 **Cartwright** Can
31D3 **Caruaru** Brazil
33E1 **Carúpano** Ven
46B1 **Carvin** France
34A2 **Casablanca** Chile
96B1 **Casablanca** Mor
35B2 **Casa Branca** Brazil
9B3 **Casa Grande** USA
52A1 **Casale Monferrato** Italy
47D2 **Casalmaggiore** Italy
34C3 **Casares** Arg
13C3 **Cascade Mts** Can/ USA
111A2 **Cascade Pt** NZ
8A2 **Cascade Range** *Mts* USA
30F3 **Cascavel** Brazil
53B2 **Caserta** Italy
112C9 **Casey** *Base* Ant
45C2 **Cashel** Irish Rep
34C2 **Casilda** Arg
107E3 **Casino** Aust
32B5 **Casma** Peru
51B1 **Caspe** Spain
8C2 **Casper** USA
61G4 **Caspian Depression** *Region* Kazakhstan
65G6 **Caspian S** Asia/ Europe
14C3 **Cass** USA
100B2 **Cassamba** Angola
46B1 **Cassel** France
12J3 **Cassiar** Can
4E3 **Cassiar Mts** Can
35A1 **Cassilândia** Brazil
53B2 **Cassino** Italy
22C3 **Castaic** USA
34B2 **Castaño** *R* Arg
47B2 **Castelfranco** Italy
49D3 **Castellane** France
34D3 **Castelli** Arg
51B2 **Castellón de la Plana** Spain
31C3 **Castelo** Brazil
53D3 **Castelo Branco** Port
48C3 **Castelsarrasin** France
53B3 **Castelvetrano** Italy
108B3 **Casterton** Aust

Castilla La Nueva

50B2 **Castilla La Nueva** Region, Spain
50B1 **Castilla La Vieja** Region, Spain
41B3 **Castlebar** Irish Rep
44A3 **Castlebay** Scot
42C2 **Castle Douglas** Scot
20C1 **Castlegar** Can
45B2 **Castleisland** Irish Rep
108B3 **Castlemain** Aust
45B2 **Castlerea** Irish Rep
109C2 **Castlereagh** Aust
48C3 **Castres-sur-l'Agout** France
27E4 **Castries** St Lucia
29B4 **Castro** Arg
30F3 **Castro** Brazil
31D4 **Castro Alves** Brazil
53C3 **Castrovillari** Italy
22B2 **Castroville** USA
111A2 **Caswell Sd** NZ
25E2 **Cat I** The Bahamas
79B3 **Catabalogan** Phil
32A5 **Catacaos** Peru
35C2 **Cataguases** Brazil
19B3 **Catalaõ** Brazil
35B1 **Catalão** Brazil
51C1 **Cataluña** Region, Spain
30C4 **Catamarca** Arg
30C4 **Catamarca** State, Arg
101C2 **Catanduca** Brazil
79B3 **Catanduanes** I Phil
31B6 **Catanduva** Brazil
53C3 **Catania** Italy
53C3 **Catanzaro** Italy
79B3 **Catarman** Phil
108A2 **Catastrophe,C** Aust
26C5 **Catatumbo** R Ven
16A2 **Catavissa** USA
23B2 **Catemaco** Mexico
49D3 **Cater** Corse
52A2 **Cateraggio** Corse
98E3 **Catete** Angola
97A3 **Catio** Guinea-Bissau
7A4 **Cat Lake** Can
13C3 **Catlegar** Can
107E3 **Cato I** Aust
25D2 **Catoche,C** Mexico
16A3 **Catoctin Mt** USA
15C3 **Catonsville** USA
34C3 **Catrilo** Arg
15D2 **Catskill** USA
15D2 **Catskill Mts** USA
32C2 **Cauca** R Brazil
31D2 **Caucaia** Brazil
32B2 **Caucasia** Colombia
65F5 **Caucasus Mts** Georgia
46B1 **Caudry** France
98B3 **Caungula** Angola
29B3 **Cauquenes** Chile
87B2 **Cauvery** R India
49D3 **Cavaillon** France
47D1 **Cavalese** Italy
97B4 **Cavally** R Lib
45C2 **Cavan** County, Irish Rep
45C2 **Cavan** Irish Rep
79B3 **Cavite** Phil
31C2 **Caxias** Brazil
32C4 **Caxias** Brazil
30F4 **Caxias do Sul** Brazil
98B3 **Caxito** Angola
17B3 **Cayce** USA
93D1 **Cayeli** Turk
33G3 **Cayenne** French Guiana
46A1 **Cayeux-sur-Mer** France
25E3 **Cayman Brac** I Caribbean S
26A3 **Cayman Is** Caribbean S
26A3 **Cayman Trench** Caribbean S
99E2 **Caynabo** Somalia
25E2 **Cayo Romana** I Cuba
25D3 **Cayos Miskitos** Is Nic
26A2 **Cay Sal** I Caribbean S
100B2 **Cazombo** Angola

Ceará = Fortaleza
31C3 **Ceara** State, Brazil
79B3 **Cebu** Phil
79B3 **Cebu** I Phil
16B3 **Ceciltton** USA
52B2 **Cecina** Italy
8B3 **Cedar City** USA
19A3 **Cedar Creek Res** USA
5J4 **Cedar L** Can
10A2 **Cedar Rapids** USA
17A1 **Cedartown** USA
24A2 **Cedros** I Mexico
106C4 **Ceduna** Aust
99E2 **Ceelbuur** Somalia
99E1 **Ceerigaabo** Somalia
53B3 **Cefalú** Italy
59B3 **Cegléd** Hung
100A2 **Cela** Angola
24B2 **Celaya** Mexico
Celebes = Sulawesi
70C3 **Celebes S** S E Asia
14B2 **Celina** USA
52C1 **Celje** Slovenia
56C2 **Celle** Germany
71E4 **Cendrawasih** Pen Indon
47C2 **Ceno** R Italy
19B3 **Center** USA
16C2 **Center Moriches** USA
17A1 **Center Point** USA
47D2 **Cento** Italy
44B3 **Central** Region, Scot
98B2 **Central African Republic** Africa
16D2 **Central Falls** USA
18C2 **Centralia** Illinois, USA
8A2 **Centralia** Washington, USA
20B2 **Central Point** USA
71F4 **Central Range** Mts PNG
16A3 **Centreville** Maryland, USA
78C4 **Cepu** Indon
71D4 **Ceram Sea** Indon
34C3 **Cereales** Arg
31B5 **Ceres** Brazil
100A4 **Ceres** S Africa
22B2 **Ceres** USA
48C2 **Cergy-Pontoise** France
53C2 **Cerignola** Italy
60C5 **Cernavodă** Rom
9C4 **Cerralvo** I Mexico
23A1 **Cerritos** Mexico
34B2 **Cerro Aconcagua** Mt Arg
23B1 **Cerro Azul** Mexico
34A3 **Cerro Campanario** Mt Chile
34C2 **Cerro Champaqui** Mt Arg
23A2 **Cerro Cuachaia** Mt Mexico
23B1 **Cerro de Astillero** Mexico
34B2 **Cerro de Olivares** Mt Arg
32B6 **Cerro de Pasco** Peru
27D3 **Cerro de Punta** Mt Puerto Rico
23A2 **Cerro El Cantado** Mt Mexico
34B3 **Cerro El Nevado** Mt Arg
23A2 **Cerro Grande** Mts Mexico
34A2 **Cerro Juncal** Mt Arg/Chile
23A1 **Cerro la Ardilla** Mts Mexico
34B1 **Cerro las Tortolas** Mt Chile
23A2 **Cerro Laurel** Mt Mexico
34A2 **Cerro Mercedario** Mt Arg
34A3 **Cerro Mora** Mt Chile
27C4 **Cerron** Mt Ven

34B3 **Cerro Payún** Mt Arg
23B2 **Cerro Penón del Rosario** Mt Mexico
34B2 **Cerro Sosneado** Mt Arg
23A2 **Cerro Teotepec** Mt Mexico
34B2 **Cerro Tupungato** Mt Arg
23B2 **Cerro Yucuyacau** Mt Mexico
47C2 **Cervo** R Italy
52B2 **Cesena** Italy
60B2 **Cèsis** Latvia
57C3 **Ceské Budejovice** Czech Republic
59B3 **Ceskomoravská Vysocina** Mts Czech Republic
55C3 **Cesme** Turk
107E4 **Cessnock** Aust
52C2 **Cetina** R Croatia
96B1 **Ceuta** N W Africa
92C2 **Ceyham** Turk
92C2 **Ceyhan** R Turk
93C2 **Ceylanpinar** Turk
Ceylon = Sri Lanka
63B2 **Chaa-Khol** Russian Fed
48C2 **Chaâteaudun** France
47B1 **Chablais** Region, France
34C2 **Chacabuco** Arg
32B5 **Chachapoyas** Peru
34B3 **Chacharramendi** Arg
87B3 **Chachran** Pak
30D4 **Chaco** State, Arg
98B1 **Chad** Republic, Africa
98B1 **Chad** L C Africa
34B3 **Chadileuvu** R Arg
8C2 **Chadron** USA
18C2 **Chaffee** USA
85A3 **Chagai** Pak
63F2 **Chagda** Russian Fed
84B2 **Chaghcharan** Afghan
104B4 **Chagos Arch** Indian O
27L1 **Chaguanas** Trinidad
91D4 **Chāh Bahār** Iran
76C2 **Chai Badan** Thai
76C3 **Chaine des Cardamomes** Mts Camb
98C4 **Chaine des Mitumba** Mts Zaire
76C2 **Chaiyaphum** Thai
84C2 **Chajari** Arg
84C2 **Chakwal** Pak
30B2 **Chala** Peru
100C2 **Chalabesa** Zambia
84A2 **Chalap Dalam** Mts Afghan
73C4 **Chaling** China
85C4 **Chālisgaon** India
12F1 **Chalkyitsik** USA
46C2 **Challerange** France
46C2 **Châlons sur Marne** France
49C2 **Chalon sur Saône** France
57C3 **Cham** Germany
84D2 **Chamba** India
85D3 **Chambal** R India
15C2 **Chambersburg** USA
49D2 **Chambéry** France
46B2 **Chambly** France
85A3 **Chambor Kalat** Pak
90B3 **Chamgordan** Iran
47B2 **Chamonix** France
86A2 **Champa** India
49C2 **Champagne** Region, France
101G1 **Champagne Castle** Mt Lesotho
47A1 **Champagnole** France
10B2 **Champaign** USA
18D2 **Champassak** Laos
10C2 **Champlain,L** USA
87B2 **Chamrajnagar** India
30B4 **Chañaral** Chile
34A3 **Chanco** Chile

4D3 **Chandalar** USA
4D3 **Chandalar** R USA
84D2 **Chandigarh** India
86C2 **Chandpur** Bang
85D5 **Chandrapur** India
91D4 **Chānf** Iran
101C2 **Changara** Mozam
74B2 **Changbai** China
69E2 **Changchun** China
73C4 **Changde** China
68E4 **Chang-hua** Taiwan
76D2 **Changjiang** China
73D3 **Chang Jiang** R China
74B2 **Changjin** N Korea
73C4 **Changsha** China
72E3 **Changshu** China
74B2 **Changwu** China
74B3 **Changyŏn** N Korea
72C2 **Changzhi** China
73E3 **Changzhou** China
48B2 **Channel Is** Europe
9B3 **Channel Is** USA
7E5 **Channel Port-aux-Basques** Can
76C3 **Chanthaburi** Thai
46B2 **Chantilly** France
18A2 **Chanute** USA
73D5 **Chaoan** China
73D3 **Chao'an** China
73D3 **Chao Hu** L China
76C3 **Chao Phraya** R Thai
72E1 **Chaoyang** China
31C4 **Chapada Diamantina** Mts Brazil
31C2 **Chapadinha** Brazil
23A1 **Chapala** Mexico
23A1 **Chapala,Lac de** L Mexico
61H3 **Chapayevo** Kazakhstan
30F4 **Chapecó** Brazil
27H1 **Chapeltown** Jamaica
78S **Chapleau** Can
61E3 **Chaplygin** Russian Fed
112C3 **Charcot I** Ant
80E2 **Chardzhou** Turkmenistan
48C2 **Charente** R France
98B1 **Chari** R Chad
98B1 **Chari Baguirmi** Region, Chad
84B1 **Charikar** Afghan
18B1 **Chariton** R USA
33F2 **Charity** Guyana
85D3 **Charkhāri** India
46C1 **Charleroi** Belg
18C2 **Charleston** Illinois, USA
18C2 **Charleston** Missouri, USA
11C3 **Charleston** S Carolina, USA
10B3 **Charleston** W Virginia, USA
98C3 **Charlesville** Zaire
107D3 **Charleville** Aust
49C2 **Charleville-Mézières** France
14A1 **Charlevoix** USA
14B2 **Charlotte** Michigan, USA
11B3 **Charlotte** N Carolina, USA
17B2 **Charlotte Harbor** B USA
10C3 **Charlottesville** USA
7D5 **Charlottetown** Can
27K1 **Charlotteville** Tobago
108B3 **Charlton** Aust
10C1 **Charlton I** Can
84C2 **Charsadda** Pak
107D3 **Charters Towers** Aust
48C2 **Chartres** France
29E3 **Chascomús** Arg
13D2 **Chase** Can
48B2 **Châteaubriant** France
48C2 **Châteaudun** France
48B2 **Châteaulin** France

48C2 Châteauroux France
46D2 Château-Salins France
49C2 Château-Thierry France
46C1 Châtelet Belg
48C2 Châtellerault France
43E4 Chatham Eng
7D5 Chatham New Brunswick, Can
16C1 Chatham New York, USA
14B2 Chatham Ontario, Can
13A2 Chatham Sd Can
12H3 Chatham Str Arg
49C2 Châtillon France
47B2 Châtillon Italy
16B3 Chatsworth USA
17B1 Chattahoochee USA
17A1 Chattahoochee R USA
11B3 Chattanooga USA
76A1 Chauk Burma
49D2 Chaumont France
46B2 Chaumont France
77D3 Chau Phu Viet
50A1 Chaves Port
61H2 Chaykovskiy Russian Fed
50B2 Chazaouet Alg
34C2 Chazón Arg
32C2 Chcontá Colombia
57C2 Cheb Czech Republic
65F4 Cheboksary Russian Fed
10B2 Cheboygan USA
74B3 Chech'on S Korea
85C3 Chech'en USA
18A2 Checotah USA
76A2 Cheduba I Burma
108B1 Cheepie Aust
96B2 Chegga Maur
100C2 Chegutu Zim
20B1 Chehalis USA
74B4 Cheju S Korea
74B4 Cheju do I S Korea
74B4 Cheju-haehyŏp Str S Korea
63F2 Chekunda Russian Fed
20B1 Chelan,L USA
90B2 Cheleken Turkmenistan
34B3 Chelforo Arg
80D1 Chelkar Kazakhstan
59C2 Chełm Pol
58B2 Chełmno Pol
43E4 Chelmsford Eng
43C4 Cheltenham Eng
65H4 Chelyabinsk Russian Fed
101C2 Chemba Mozam
57C2 Chemnitz Germany
84D2 Chenab R India/Pak
96B2 Chenachane Alg
20C1 Cheney USA
18A2 Cheney Res USA
72D1 Chengda China
73A3 Chengdu China
72E2 Chengshan Jiao Pt China
73C4 Chenxi China
73C4 Chen Xian China
73D3 Chen Xian China
32B5 Chepén Peru
34B2 Chepes Arg
48C2 Cher R France
23A2 Cheran Mexico
17C1 Cheraw USA
48B2 Cherbourg France
96C1 Cherchell Alg
63C2 Cheremkhovo Russian Fed
60E2 Cherepovets Russian Fed
60D4 Cherkassy Ukraine
61F5 Cherkessk Russian Fed
60D3 Chernigov Ukraine
60D2 Chernobyl Ukraine
60C4 Chernovtsy Ukraine
61J2 Chernushka Russian Fed

60B3 Chernyakhovsk Russian Fed
61G4 Chernyye Zemli Region, Russian Fed
18A2 Cherokees,L o'the USA
34A3 Cherquenco Chile
86C1 Cherrapunji India
60C3 Cherven' Belorussia
59C2 Chervonograd Ukraine
10C3 Chesapeake B USA
42C3 Cheshire County, Eng
16C1 Cheshire USA
64F3 Chéshskaya Guba B Russian Fed
21A1 Chester California, USA
42C3 Chester Eng
18C2 Chester Illinois, USA
16C1 Chester Massachusets, USA
15C3 Chester Pennsylvania, USA
17B1 Chester S Carolina, USA
16A3 Chester R USA
42D3 Chesterfield Eng
6A3 Chesterfield Inlet Can
16A3 Chestertown USA
25D3 Chetumal Mexico
13C1 Chetwynd Can
12A2 Chevak USA
111B2 Cheviot NZ
40C2 Cheviots Hills Eng/Scot
13D3 Chewelah USA
8C2 Cheyenne USA
86A1 Chhapra India
86C1 Chhatak Bang
85D4 Chhatarpur India
85D4 Chhindwāra India
86B1 Chhuka Bhutan
73E5 Chia'i Taiwan
100A2 Chiange Angola
76C2 Chiang Kham Thai
76B2 Chiang Mai Thai
47C1 Chiavenna Italy
74E3 Chiba Japan
86B2 Chibåsa India
100A2 Chibia Angola
7C4 Chibougamou Can
75A1 Chiburi-jima I Japan
101C3 Chibuto Mozam
10B2 Chicago USA
14A2 Chicago Heights USA
12G3 Chichagof I USA
43D4 Chichester Eng
75B1 Chichibu Japan
69G4 Chichi-jima I Japan
11B3 Chickamauga L USA
19C3 Chickasawhay R USA
9D3 Chickasha USA
12F2 Chicken USA
32A5 Chiclayo Peru
8A3 Chico USA
29C4 Chico R Arg
29C4 Chico R Arg
101C2 Chicoa Mozam
15D2 Chicopee USA
7C5 Chicoutimi Can
101C3 Chicualacuala Mozam
87B2 Chidambaram India
6D3 Chidley,L Can
17B2 Chiefland USA
99C3 Chiengi Zambia
47C1 Chieri Italy
46C2 Chiers R France
47C1 Chiesa Italy
47D2 Chiese R Italy
52B2 Chieti Italy
72D1 Chifeng China
12C3 Chiginagak,Mt USA
4C3 Chigmit Mts USA
23B2 Chignahuapán Mexico
12C3 Chignik USA
24B2 Chihuahua Mexico
87B2 Chik Ballápur India
87B2 Chikmagalúr India

12C2 Chikuminuk L USA
101C2 Chikwawa Malawi
76A1 Chi-kyaw Burma
87C1 Chilakalürupet India
23B2 Chilapa Mexico
87B3 Chilaw Sri Lanka
28B6 Chile Republic
34B2 Chilecito Mendoza, Arg
100B2 Chililabombwe Zambia
86B2 Chilka L India
13C2 Chilko R Can
5F4 Chilko L Can
13C2 Chilkotin R Can
34A3 Chillán Chile
34D3 Chillar Arg
18B2 Chillicothe Missouri, USA
14B3 Chillicothe Ohio, USA
13C3 Chilliwack Can
86B1 Chilmari India
101C2 Chilongozi Zambia
20B2 Chiloquin USA
24C3 Chilpancingo Mexico
43D4 Chiltern Hills Upland Eng
14A2 Chilton USA
101C2 Chilumba Malawi
69E4 Chi-lung Taiwan
101C2 Chilwa L Malawi
100C2 Chimanimani Zim
46C1 Chimay Belg
65G5 Chimbay Uzbekistan
32B4 Chimborazo Mt Ecuador
32B5 Chimbote Peru
65H5 Chimkent Kazakhstan
101C2 Chimoio Mozam
67E3 China Republic, Asia
China National Republic = Taiwan
25D3 Chinandega Nic
32B6 Chincha Alta Peru
109D1 Chinchilla Aust
101C2 Chinde Mozam
76B2 Chindwin R Burma
100B2 Chingola Zambia
100A2 Chinguar Angola
96A2 Chinguetti Maur
74B3 Chinhae S Korea
100C2 Chinhoyi Zim
12D3 Chiniak,C USA
84C2 Chiniot Pak
74B3 Chinju S Korea
23C2 Chinko R CAR
75B1 Chino Japan
101C2 Chinsali Zambia
52B1 Chioggia Italy
101C2 Chipata Zambia
101C3 Chipinge Zim
87A1 Chiplún India
43C4 Chippenham Eng
10A2 Chippewa Falls USA
32A3 Chira R Peru
87C1 Chirāla India
101C3 Chiredzi Zim
95A2 Chirfa Niger
32A2 Chiriqui Mt Panama
54C2 Chirpan Bulg
32A2 Chirripo Grande Mt Costa Rica
100B2 Chirundu Zim
100B2 Chisamba Zambia
7C4 Chisasibi Can
72B3 Chishui He R China
Chişinău = Kishinev
47B2 Chisone R Italy
61H2 Chistopol Russian Fed
63C2 Chita Russian Fed
100A2 Chitado Angola
100A2 Chitembo Angola
12F2 Chitina USA
12F2 Chitina R USA
87B2 Chitradurga India
84C1 Chitral Pak
32A2 Chitré Panama
86C2 Chittagong Bang
85C4 Chittaurgarh India
87B2 Chittoor India
100B2 Chiume Angola

47D1 Chiusa Italy
47B2 Chivasso Italy
100C2 Chivhu Zim
29D2 Chivilcoy Arg
100C2 Chivu Zim
75A1 Chizu Japan
29C3 Choele Choel Arg
34C3 Choique Arg
24B2 Choix Mexico
58B2 Chojnice Pol
99D1 Choke Mts Eth
48B2 Cholet France
23B2 Cholula Mexico
100B2 Choma Zambia
86B1 Chomo Yummo Mt China/India
57C2 Chomutov Czech Republic
63C1 Chona R Russian Fed
74B3 Ch'ŏnan S Korea
76C3 Chon Buri Thai
32A4 Chone Ecuador
74B2 Ch'ŏngjin N Korea
74B3 Chongju N Korea
74B3 Ch'ŏngju S Korea
100A2 Chongoroi Angola
73B4 Chongqing China
74B3 Chŏngŭp S Korea
74B3 Chŏnju S Korea
86B1 Chooyu Mt China/Nepal
59D3 Chortkov Ukraine
74B3 Ch'ŏrwŏn N Korea
59B2 Chorzow Pol
74E2 Choshi Japan
34A3 Chos-Malal Arg
58B2 Choszczno Pol
86A2 Chotanāgpur Region, India
96C1 Chott Melrhir Alg
22B2 Chowchilla USA
63D3 Choybalsan Mongolia
6A3 Chrantrey Inlet B Can
111B2 Christchurch NZ
101G1 Christiana S Africa
6D2 Christian,C Can
12H3 Christian Sd USA
6E3 Christianshab Greenland
104D4 Christmas I Indian O
65J5 Chu Kazakhstan
65J5 Chu R Kazakhstan
29C4 Chubut State, Arg
29C4 Chubut R Arg
60D2 Chudovo Russian Fed
Chudskoye Ozero = Peipus, Lake
4D3 Chugach Mts USA
12E2 Chugiak USA
75A1 Chūgoku-sanchi Mts Japan
29F2 Chui Brazil
29B3 Chuillán Chile
77C5 Chukai Malay
76D2 Chu Lai Viet
21B3 Chula Vista USA
12E2 Chulitna USA
63E2 Chulman Russian Fed
32A5 Chulucanas Peru
30C2 Chulumani Bol
65K4 Chulym Russian Fed
63A2 Chulym R Russian Fed
63B2 Chuma R Russian Fed
84D2 Chumar India
63F2 Chumikan Russian Fed
77B3 Chumphon Thai
74B3 Ch'unch'ŏn S Korea
86B2 Chunchura India
74B3 Ch'ungju S Korea
Chungking = Chongqing
99D3 Chunya Tanz
63C1 Chunya R Russian Fed
27L1 Chupara Pt Trinidad
30C3 Chuquicamata Chile
52A1 Chur Switz

Churāchāndpur

86C2 Churāchāndpur India
7A4 Churchill Can
7D4 Churchill R
Labrador, Can
7A4 Churchill R
Manitoba, Can
7A4 Churchill,C Can
7D4 Churchill Falls Can
5H4 Churchill L Can
84C3 Chūru India
23A2 Churumuco Mexico
61J2 Chusovoy
Russian Fed
61G2 Chuvashskaya
Respublika,
Russian Fed
68B4 Chuxiong China
76D3 Chu Yang Sin Mt
Viet
78B4 Cianjur Indon
47D2 Ciano d'Enza Italy
35A2 Cianorte Brazil
52E2 Ciechanów Pol
25E2 Ciego de Avila Cuba
32C1 Ciénaga Colombia
25D2 Cienfuegos Cuba
59B3 Cieszyn Pol
51B2 Cieza Spain
92B2 Cihanbeyli Turk
23A2 Cihuatlán Mexico
78B4 Cijulang Indon
78B4 Cilacap Indon
54C1 Cimpina Rom
51C1 Cinca R Spain
52C2 Cincer Mt Bosnia-
Herzegovina
10B3 Cincinnati USA
54B1 Cindrelu Mt Rom
55C3 Cine R Turk
46C1 Ciney Belg
34B3 Cipolletti Arg
4D3 Circle Alaska, USA
14B3 Circleville USA
78B4 Cirebon Indon
43D4 Cirencester Eng
47D2 Citadella Italy
24C3 Citlaltepetl Mt
Mexico
100A4 Citrusdal S Africa
52B2 Citta del Vaticano
Italy
52B2 Città di Castello Italy
24B2 Ciudad Acuña
Mexico
23A2 Ciudad Altamirano
Mexico
33E2 Ciudad Bolivar Ven
24B2 Ciudad Camargo
Mexico
25C3 Ciudad del Carmen
Mexico
23B1 Ciudad del Maiz
Mexico
51C1 Ciudadela Spain
33E2 Ciudad Guayana
Ven
24B3 Ciudad Guzman
Mexico
23A2 Ciudad Hidalgo
Mexico
24B1 Ciudad Juárez
Mexico
9C4 Ciudad Lerdo Mexico
24C2 Ciudad Madero
Mexico
23B2 Ciudad Mendoza
Mexico
24B2 Ciudad Obregon
Mexico
27C4 Ciudad Ojeda Ven
24B3 Ciudad Piar Ven
50B2 Ciudad Real Spain
50A1 Ciudad Rodrigo
Spain
24C2 Ciudad Valles
Mexico
24C2 Ciudad Victoria
Mexico
52B2 Civitavecchia Italy
93D2 Cizre Turk
43E4 Clacton-on-Sea Eng
5G4 Claire,L Can
14C2 Clairton USA
47A1 Clairvaux France

17A1 Clanton USA
100A4 Clanwilliam S Africa
45C2 Clara Irish Rep
34D3 Claraz Arg
45B2 Clare County,
Irish Rep
14B2 Clare USA
45A2 Clare I Irish Rep
15D2 Claremont USA
45A2 Claremorris Irish Rep
109D1 Clarence R Aust
111B2 Clarence R NZ
106C2 Clarence Str Aust
12H3 Clarence Str USA
19B3 Clarendon USA
7E5 Clarenville Can
5G4 Claresholm Can
15C2 Clarion
Pennsylvania, USA
24A3 Clarión I Mexico
15C2 Clarion R USA
105J3 Clarion Fracture Zone
Pacific O
11B3 Clark Hill Res USA
14B2 Clark,Pt Can
14B3 Clarksburg USA
11A3 Clarksdale USA
12C3 Clarks Point USA
20C1 Clarkston USA
18B2 Clarksville Arkansas,
USA
35A1 Claro R Brazil
29D3 Claromecó Arg
18A2 Clay Center USA
44D2 Claymore Oilfield
N Sea
13B3 Clayoquot Sd Can
9C3 Clayton New Mexico,
USA
15C2 Clayton New York,
USA
41B3 Clear C Irish Rep
41B3 Cleare,C USA
13D1 Clear Hills Mts Can
21A2 Clear L USA
20B2 Clear Lake Res USA
13D2 Clearwater USA
11B4 Clearwater USA
13E1 Clearwater R Can
13C2 Clearwater L Can
9D3 Cleburne USA
42E2 Cleeton Oilfield
North Sea
22B1 Clements USA
79A3 Cleopatra Needle Mt
Phil
107D3 Clermont Aust
46B2 Clermont France
46C2 Clermont-en-Argonne
France
49C2 Clermont-Ferrand
France
46D1 Clervaux Germany
47D1 Cles Italy
108A2 Cleve Aust
42D2 Cleveland County,
Eng
19B3 Cleveland
Mississippi, USA
10B2 Cleveland Ohio, USA
11B3 Cleveland
Tennessee, USA
19A3 Cleveland Texas,
USA
41B3 Clew B Irish Rep
45A2 Clifden Irish Rep
109D1 Clifton Aust
16B2 Clifton New Jersey,
USA
108A1 Clifton Hills Aust
13F3 Climax Can
18B2 Clinton Arkansas,
USA
5F4 Clinton Can
16C2 Clinton Connecticut,
USA
16D1 Clinton
Massachusetts, USA
19B3 Clinton Mississippi,
USA
18B2 Clinton Missouri,
USA

16B2 Clinton New Jersey,
USA
4H3 Clinton-Colden L Can
23A3 Clipperton I Pacific O
30C2 Clisa Bol
45B3 Clonakilty Irish Rep
107D3 Cloncurry Aust
45C1 Clones Irish Rep
45C2 Clonmel Irish Rep
10A2 Cloquet USA
12C2 Cloudy Mt USA
22C2 Clovis California,
USA
9C3 Clovis New Mexico,
USA
60B4 Cluj Rom
54B1 Cluj-Napoca Rom
47B1 Cluses France
47C2 Clusone Italy
111A3 Clutha R NZ
43C3 Clwyd County, Wales
6D2 Clyde Can
111A3 Clyde NZ
42B2 Clyde R Scot
23A2 Coahuayana Mexico
23A2 Coalcomán Mexico
13E2 Coaldale Can
21B2 Coaldale USA
21A2 Coalinga USA
33E5 Coari R Brazil
17A1 Coastal Plain USA
4E4 Coast Mts Can
8A2 Coast Ranges Mts
USA
42B2 Coatbridge Scot
23B2 Coatepec Mexico
16B3 Coatesville USA
15D1 Coaticook Can
6B3 Coats I Can
112B1 Coats Land Region,
Ant
25C3 Coatzacoalcos
Mexico
7C5 Cobalt Can
25B3 Cobán Guatemala
107D4 Cobar Aust
109C3 Cobargo Aust
45B3 Cobh Irish Rep
32D6 Cobija Bol
15D2 Cobleskill USA
51B2 Cobo de Palos C
Spain
7C5 Cobourg Can
107D2 Cobourg Pen Aust
57C2 Coburg Germany
32B4 Coca Ecuador
17B2 Coca USA
30C1 Cochabamba Bol
46D1 Cochem Germany
87B3 Cochin India
13E2 Cochrane Alberta,
Can
7B5 Cochrane Ontario,
Can
108B2 Cockburn Aust
16A3 Cockeysville USA
27H1 Cockpit Country,The
Jam
25D3 Coco R Honduras/
Nic
98A2 Cocobeach Gabon
27L1 Cocos B Trinidad
104C4 Cocos Is Indian O
23A1 Cocula Mexico
10C2 Cod,C USA
111A3 Codfish I NZ
7D4 Cod I Can
47E2 Codigoro Italy
31C2 Codó Brazil
47C2 Codogno Italy
8C2 Cody USA
56B2 Coesfeld Germany
8B2 Coeur d'Alene USA
9D3 Coffeyville USA
108A2 Coffin B Aust
109D2 Coff's Harbour Aust
23B2 Cofre de Perote Mt
Mexico
48B2 Cognac France
15D2 Cohoes USA
108B3 Cohuna Aust
29B5 Coihaique Chile
87B2 Coimbatore India
50A1 Coimbra Port

32A3 Cojimies Ecuador
107D4 Colac Aust
31C5 Colatina Brazil
112B6 Colbeck,C Ant
43E4 Colchester Eng
16C2 Colchester USA
47B1 Col de la Faucille
France
13E2 Cold L Can
52A1 Col du Grand St
Bernard P
Italy/Switz
47B2 Col du Lautaret P
France
52A1 Col du Mont Cenis P
France/Italy
14B2 Coldwater USA
12F1 Coleen R USA
14B2 Coleman Michigan,
USA
101G1 Colenso S Africa
45C1 Coleraine N Ire
111B2 Coleridge,L NZ
100B4 Colesberg S Africa
22C1 Coleville USA
21A2 Colfax California,
USA
19B3 Colfax Louisiana,
USA
20C1 Colfax Washington,
USA
24B3 Colima Mexico
23A2 Colima State, Mexico
34A2 Colina Chile
44A3 Coll I Scot
109C1 Collarenebri Aust
52A2 Colle de Tende P
France/Italy
12E2 College USA
17B1 College Park
Georgia, USA
16A3 College Park
Washington, USA
19A3 College Station
USA
106A4 Collie Aust
106B2 Collier B Aust
46A1 Collines de L'Artois
Mts France
46B2 Collines De Thiérache
France
14B2 Collingwood Can
110B2 Collingwood NZ
19C3 Collins Mississippi,
USA
4H2 Collinson Pen Can
107D3 Collinsville Aust
18C2 Collinsville Illinois,
USA
18A2 Collinsville
Oklahoma, USA
34A3 Collipulli Chile
49D2 Colmar France
35B2 Colômbia Brazil
32B3 Colombia Republic,
S America
15C3 Colombia USA
87B3 Colombo Sri Lanka
25D2 Colón Cuba
32B2 Colón Panama
29E2 Colonia Urug
34D2 Colonia del
Sacramento Urug
34B3 Colonia 25 de Mayo
Arg
29C5 Colonia Las Heras
Arg
44A3 Colonsay I Scot
23A1 Colontlán Mexico
27E5 Coloradito USA
8C3 Colorado State, USA
9B3 Colorado R Arizona,
USA
29D3 Colorado R
Buenos Aires, Arg
9D3 Colorado R Texas,
USA
9B3 Colorado Plat USA
8C3 Colorado Springs
USA
22D3 Colton USA
16A3 Columbia Maryland,
USA

128

19C3 **Columbia** Mississippi, USA
10A3 **Columbia** Missouri, USA
15C2 **Columbia** Pennsylvania, USA
11B3 **Columbia** S Carolina, USA
11B3 **Columbia** Tennessee, USA
13D2 **Columbia** *R* Can
8A2 **Columbia** *R* USA
5G4 **Columbia,Mt** Can
20C1 **Columbia Plat** USA
11B3 **Columbus** Georgia, USA
14A3 **Columbus** Indiana, USA
11B3 **Columbus** Mississippi, USA
8D2 **Columbus** Nebraska, USA
10B2 **Columbus** Ohio, USA
19A4 **Columbus** Texas, USA
20C1 **Colville** USA
4C3 **Colville** *R* USA
110C1 **Colville,C** NZ
4F3 **Colville L** Can
42C3 **Colwyn Bay** Wales
47E2 **Comacchio** Italy
22B1 **Comanche Res** USA
112C2 **Comandante Ferraz** *Base* Ant
25D3 **Comayagua** Honduras
34A2 **Combarbalá** Chile
45C2 **Comeragh** *Mts* Irish Rep
86C2 **Comilla** Bang
25C3 **Comitán** Mexico
46C2 **Commercy** France
48B2 **Committees B** Can
52A1 **Como** Italy
29C5 **Comodoro Rivadavia** Arg
23A1 **Comonfort** Mexico
87B3 **Comorin,C** India
101D2 **Comoros** *Is* Indian O
49C2 **Compiègne** France
23A1 **Compostela** Mexico
34B2 **Comte Salas** Arg
86C1 **Cona** China
97A4 **Conakry** Guinea
34B2 **Concarán** Arg
48B2 **Concarneau** France
35D1 **Conceição da Barra** Brazil
31B3 **Conceição do Araguaia** Brazil
35C1 **Conceiçao do Mato Dentro** Brazil
29B3 **Concepción** Chile
30E3 **Concepción** Par
29E2 **Concepción** *R* Arg
24B2 **Concepcion del Oro** Mexico
34D2 **Concepcion del Uruguay** Arg
9A3 **Conception,Pt** USA
35B2 **Conchas** Brazil
9C4 **Conchos** *R* Mexico
21A2 **Concord** California, USA
15D2 **Concord** New Hampshire, USA
29C2 **Concordia** Arg
8D3 **Concordia** USA
20B1 **Concrete** USA
109D1 **Condamine** Aust
107D4 **Condobolin** Aust
20B1 **Condon** USA
46C1 **Condroz** *Mts* Belg
17A1 **Conecuh** *R* USA
47E2 **Conegliano** Italy
89F8 **Congo** Republic, Africa
89F8 **Congo** *R* Congo **Congo,R = Zaïre**
14B1 **Coniston** Can
45B2 **Connaught** Region, Irish Rep
14B2 **Conneaut** USA

10C2 **Connecticut** State, USA
15D2 **Connecticut** *R* USA
15D2 **Connellsville** USA
45B2 **Connemara,Mts of** Irish Rep
14A3 **Connersville** USA
108B2 **Conoble** Aust
19A3 **Conroe** USA
35C2 **Conselheiro Lafaiete** Brazil
77D4 **Con Son** *Is* Viet **Constance,L = Bodensee**
60C5 **Constanta** Rom
96C1 **Constantine** Alg
12C3 **Constantine,C** USA
29B3 **Constitución** Chile
13F3 **Consul** Can
47E2 **Contarina** Italy
31C4 **Contas** *R* Brazil
23B2 **Contreras** Mexico
4H3 **Contuoyto L** Can
11A3 **Conway** Arkansas, USA
15D2 **Conway** New Hampshire, USA
17C1 **Conway** South Carolina, USA
108A1 **Conway,L** Aust
12C3 **Conwy** Wales
106C3 **Coober Pedy** Aust
110B2 **Cook** *Str* NZ
13B2 **Cook,C** Can
4C3 **Cook Inlet** *B* USA
105H4 **Cook Is** Pacific O
111B2 **Cook,Mt** NZ
107D2 **Cooktown** Aust
109C2 **Coolabah** Aust
108C1 **Cooladdi** Aust
109C2 **Coolah** Aust
109C2 **Coolamon** Aust
106B4 **Coolgardie** Aust
109C2 **Cooma** Aust
109C2 **Coonabarabran** Aust
109C2 **Coonamble** Aust
108B2 **Coonbah** Aust
108A2 **Coondambo** Aust
108C1 **Coongoola** Aust
87B2 **Coonoor** India
108B1 **Cooper Basin** Aust
106C3 **Cooper Creek** Aust
108B1 **Cooper Creek** *R* Aust
108A3 **Coorong,The** Aust
109D1 **Cooroy** Aust
20B2 **Coos B** USA
20B2 **Coos Bay** USA
107D4 **Cootamundra** Aust
45C1 **Cootehill** Irish Rep
23B2 **Copala** Mexico
23B2 **Copalillo** Mexico **Copenhagen = København**
30B4 **Copiapó** Chile
47D2 **Copparo** Italy
12F2 **Copper** *R* USA
4D3 **Copper Centre** USA
14B1 **Copper Cliff** Can **Coppermine = Qurlurtuuk**
4G3 **Coppermine** *R* Can **Coquihattville = Mbandaka**
30B4 **Coquimbo** Chile
54B2 **Corabia** Rom
17B2 **Coral Gables** USA
6B3 **Coral Harbour** Can
107D2 **Coral S** Aust/PNG
104F4 **Coral Sea Basin** Pacific O
107E2 **Coral Sea Island Territories** Aust
108B3 **Corangamite,L** Aust
33F3 **Corantijn** *R* Surinam/Guyana
46B2 **Corbeil-Essonnes** France
50A1 **Corcubion** Spain
11B3 **Cordele** USA
50A1 **Cordillera Cantabrica** *Mts* Spain
26C3 **Cordillera Central** *Mts* Dom Rep

79B2 **Cordillera Central** *Mts* Phil
34B2 **Cordillera de Ansita** Arg
32B5 **Cordillera de los Andes** *Mts* Peru
30C4 **Cordillera del Toro** *Mt* Arg
32C2 **Cordillera de Mérida** Ven
34A3 **Cordillera de Viento** *Mts* Arg
25D3 **Cordillera Isabelia** *Mts* Nic
32B3 **Cordillera Occidental** *Mts* Colombia
32B3 **Cordillera Oriental** *Mts* Colombia
108B1 **Cordillo Downs** Aust
29D2 **Córdoba** Arg
24C3 **Córdoba** Mexico
50B2 **Córdoba** Spain
29D2 **Córdoba** State, Arg
4D3 **Cordova** USA **Corfu = Kérkira**
109D2 **Coricudgy,Mt** Aust
53C3 **Corigliano Calabro** Italy
11B3 **Corinth** Mississippi, USA
31C5 **Corinto** Brazil
45B2 **Cork** County, Irish Rep
41B3 **Cork** Irish Rep
92A1 **Çorlu** Turk
31C5 **Cornel Fabriciano** Brazil
35A2 **Cornélio Procópio** Brazil
7E5 **Corner Brook** Can
109C3 **Corner Inlet** *B* Aust
15C2 **Corning** USA
7C5 **Cornwall** Can
43B4 **Cornwall** County, Eng
43B4 **Cornwall,C** Eng
4H2 **Cornwall I** Can
32D1 **Coro** Ven
31C2 **Coroatá** Brazil
30C2 **Coroico** Bol
35B1 **Coromandel** Brazil
87C2 **Coromandel Coast** India
110C1 **Coromandel Pen** NZ
110C1 **Coromandel Range** *Mts* NZ
22D4 **Corona** California, USA
13E2 **Coronation** Can
4G3 **Coronation G** Can
24C2 **Coronda** Arg
29B3 **Coronel** Chile
34D3 **Coronel Brandsen** Arg
34C3 **Coronel Dorrego** Arg
35C1 **Coronel Fabriciano** Brazil
30E4 **Coronel Oviedo** Par
29D3 **Coronel Pringles** Arg
34C3 **Coronel Suárez** Arg
34D3 **Coronel Vidal** Arg
30B2 **Coropuna** *Mt* Peru
109C3 **Corowa** Aust
49D3 **Corps** France
9D4 **Corpus Christi** USA
9D4 **Corpus Christi,L** USA
79B3 **Corregidor** *I* Phil
35A1 **Corrente** *R* Mato Grosso, Brazil
30E4 **Corrientes** Arg
30E4 **Corrientes** State, Arg
19B3 **Corrigan** USA
106A4 **Corrigin** Aust
107C2 **Corringe Is** Aust
109C3 **Corryong** Aust
52A2 **Corse** *I* Medit S
42B2 **Corsewall** *Pt* Scot **Corse = Corse**
9D3 **Corsicana** USA
52A2 **Corte** Corse
9C3 **Cortez** USA
52B1 **Cortina d'Ampezzo** Italy

15C2 **Cortland** USA
23A2 **Coruca de Catalan** Mexico
93D1 **Çoruh** *R* Turk
60E5 **Corum** Turk
30E2 **Corumbá** Brazil
31B1 **Corumba** *R* Brazil
35B1 **Corumbaiba** Brazil
20B2 **Corvallis** USA
96A1 **Corvo** *I* Açores
43C3 **Corwen** Wales
23B2 **Coscomatopec** Mexico
53C3 **Cosenza** Italy
101D1 **Cosmoledo** *Is* Seychelles
34C2 **Cosquin** Arg
51B2 **Costa Blanca** Region, Spain
51C1 **Costa Brava** Region, Spain
50B2 **Costa de la Luz** Region, Spain
50B2 **Costa del Sol** Region, Spain
22D4 **Costa Mesa** USA
25D3 **Costa Rica** Republic, Cent America
23B2 **Cotabato** Phil
30C3 **Cotagaita** Bol
49D3 **Côte d'Azur** Region, France
46C2 **Côtes de Meuse** *Mts* France
97C4 **Cotonou** Benin
32B4 **Cotopaxi** *Mt* Ecuador
43C4 **Cotswold Hills** *Upland* Eng
20B2 **Cottage Grove** USA
56C2 **Cottbus** Germany
108A3 **Couedic,C du** Aust
20C1 **Coeur d'Alene L** USA
46B2 **Coulommiers** France
15C1 **Coulonge** *R* Can
22B2 **Coulterville** USA
4B3 **Council** USA
8D2 **Council Bluffs** USA
58C1 **Courland Lagoon** *Lg* Lithuania/Russian Fed
47B2 **Courmayeur** Italy
13B3 **Courtenay** Can **Courtrai = Kortrijk**
48B2 **Coutances** France
43D3 **Coventry** Eng
50A1 **Covilhã** Spain
17B1 **Covington** Georgia, USA
19B3 **Covington** Louisiana, USA
109C2 **Cowal,L** Aust
108B3 **Cowangie** Aust
15D1 **Cowansville** Can
108A1 **Coward Springs** Aust
108A2 **Cowell** Aust
108C3 **Cowes** Aust
21B3 **Cowichan L** Can
20B1 **Cowlitz** *R* USA
109C2 **Cowra** Aust
30F2 **Coxim** Brazil
16C1 **Coxsackie** USA
86C2 **Cox's Bazar** Bang
22B2 **Coyote** USA
23A2 **Coyuca de Benitez** Mexico
59B2 **Chozov** Pol
100B4 **Cradock** S Africa
8C2 **Craig** USA
57C3 **Crailsheim** Germany
54B2 **Craiova** Rom
15D2 **Cranberry L** USA
5G5 **Cranbrook** Can
20C2 **Crane** Oregon, USA
16D2 **Cranston** USA
20B2 **Crater L** USA
20B2 **Crater Lake Nat Pk** USA
31C3 **Crateus** Brazil
31D3 **Crato** Brazil
14A2 **Crawfordsville** USA
17B1 **Crawfordville** USA
43D4 **Crawley** Eng
5H4 **Cree L** Can
46B2 **Creil** France

Crema

47C2 Crema Italy
52B1 Cremona Italy
46B2 Crépy-en-Valois France
52B2 Cres I Yugos
20B2 Crescent City USA
34C2 Crespo Arg
13D3 Creston Can
18B1 Creston USA
17A1 Crestview USA
108B3 Creswick Aust
47A1 Crêt de la Neige Mt France
Crete = Kriti
18A1 Crete USA
55B3 Crete,S of Greece
48C2 Creuse R France
43C3 Crewe Italy
44B3 Crianlarich Scot
30G4 Criciuma Brazil
44C3 Crieff Scot
12G3 Crillon,Mt USA
35B1 Cristalina Brazil
52C1 Croatia Republic, Europe
78D1 Crocker Range Mts Malay
19A3 Crockett USA
106C2 Croker I Aust
44C3 Cromarty Scot
43E3 Cromer Eng
111A3 Cromwell NZ
11C4 Crooked I The Bahamas
13C2 Crooked R Can
8D2 Crookston USA
109C2 Crookwell Aust
109D1 Croppa Creek Aust
11A3 Crossett USA
12G3 Cross Sd USA
53C3 Crotone Italy
19B3 Crowley USA
27K Crown Pt Tobago
109D1 Crows Nest Aust
107D2 Croydon Aust
43D4 Croydon Eng
104B5 Crozet Basin Indian O
4F2 Crozier Chan Can
30F4 Cruz Alta Brazil
25E3 Cruz,C Cuba
35C2 Cruz del Eje Arg
32C5 Cruzeiro Brazil
32C5 Cruzeiro do Sul Brazil
13C1 Crysdale,Mt Can
108A2 Crystal Brook Aust
18B2 Crystal City Missouri, USA
14A1 Crystal Falls USA
101C2 Cuamba Mozam
100B2 Cuando R Angola
100A2 Cuangar Angola
Cuango,R = Kwango,R
34C2 Cuarto R Arg
24B2 Cuauhtémoc Mexico
23B2 Cuautla Mexico
25D2 Cuba Republic, Caribbean S
100A2 Cubango R Angola
100A2 Cuchi R Angola
100A2 Cuchi R Angola
34C3 Cuchillo Có Arg
32D3 Cucuí Brazil
32C2 Cúcuta Colombia
87B2 Cuddalore India
87B2 Cuddapah India
106A3 Cue Aust
32B4 Cuenca Ecuador
51B1 Cuenca Spain
24C3 Cuernavaca Mexico
19A4 Cuero USA
30E2 Cuiabá Brazil
30E2 Cuiabá R Brazil
23B2 Cuicatlan Mexico
35C1 Cuieté R Brazil
44A3 Cuillin Hills Mts Scot
98B3 Cuilo R Angola
100A2 Cuito R Angola
100A2 Cuito Cunavale Angola
23A2 Cuitzeo Mexico
77D3 Cu Lao Hon I Viet

109C3 Culcairn Aust
109C1 Culgoa R Aust
24B2 Culiacán Mexico
79A3 Culion I Phil
17A1 Cullman USA
47A2 Culoz France
15C3 Culpeper USA
32J7 Culpepper I Ecuador
17B2 Culter Ridge USA
111B2 Culverden NZ
33E1 Cumaná Ven
10C3 Cumberland Maryland, USA
11B3 Cumberland R USA
6D3 Cumberland Pen Can
6D3 Cumbernauld Sd Can
42C2 Cumbria Eng
21A2 Cummings USA
108A2 Cummins Aust
42B2 Cumnock Scot
34A3 Cunco Chile
100A2 Cunene R Angola/Namibia
52A2 Cuneo Italy
107D3 Cunnamulla Aust
44C3 Cupar Scot
54B2 Cuprija Serbia,Yugos
27D4 Curaçao I Caribbean S
34A3 Curacautin Chile
34B3 Curaco R Arg
34A3 Curanilahue Chile
34A3 Curepto Chile
29B2 Curicó Chile
30G4 Curitiba Brazil
108A2 Curnamona Aust
100A2 Curoca R Angola
31C5 Curvelo Brazil
13D2 Cutbank R Can
17B1 Cuthbert USA
34B3 Cutral-Có Arg
86B2 Cuttack India
100A2 Cuvelai Angola
56B2 Cuxhaven Germany
14B2 Cuyahoga Falls USA
79B3 Cuyo Is Phil
32C6 Cuzco Peru
99C3 Cyangugu Zaïre
Cyclades = Kikládhes
13F3 Cypress Hills Mts Can
92B3 Cyprus Republic, Medit S
6D3 Cyrus Field B Can
59B3 Czech Republic Republic, Europe
59B2 Częstochowa Pol

D

76C1 Da I Viet
69E2 Da'an China
94C3 Dab'a Jordan
27C4 Dabajuro Ven
99E2 Dabaro Somalia
73B3 Daba Shan Mts China
99D1 Dabat Eth
85C4 Dabhoi India
73C3 Dabie Shan Mts China
97A3 Dabola Guinea
97B4 Dabou Ivory Coast
59B2 Dabrowa Gorn Pol
57C3 Dachau Germany
57C3 Dachstein Mt Austria
73A3 Dada He R China
17B2 Dade City USA
84B3 Dadhar Pak
85B3 Dadu Pak
68C3 Dadu He R China
79B3 Daet Phil
73B4 Dafang China
76B2 Daga R Burma
99E2 Dagabur Eth
97A3 Dagana Sen
65F5 Dagestanskaya Respublic, Russian Fed
79B2 Dagupan Phil
92B4 Dahab Egypt
63E3 Da Hinggan Ling Mts China

17B1 Dahlonega USA
85C4 Dāhod India
86A1 Dailekh Nepal
34C3 Daireaux Arg
69F4 Daitō Is Pacific O
106C3 Dajarra Aust
97B3 Dakar Sen
95B2 Dakhla Oasis Egypt
97C3 Dakoro Niger
54B2 Dakovica Serbia, Yugos
54A1 Dakovo Croatia
100B2 Dala Angola
97A3 Dalaba Guinea
72D1 Dalai Nur L China
68C2 Dalandzadgad Mongolia
79B3 Dalanganem Is Phil
76D3 Da Lat Viet
72A1 Dalay Mongolia
107E3 Dalby Aust
39F7 Dalen Nor
42C2 Dales,The Upland Eng
17A1 Daleville USA
9C3 Dalhart USA
4E2 Dalhousie,C Can
72E2 Dalian China
9D3 Dallas USA
20B1 Dalles,The USA
5E4 Dall I USA
86A2 Dalli Rajhara India
97C3 Dallol R Niger
97C3 Dallol Bosso R Niger
52C2 Dalmatia Region Bosnia-Herzegovina
69F2 Dal'nerechensk Russian Fed
97B4 Daloa Ivory Coast
73B4 Dalou Shan Mts China
86A2 Dāltenganj India
18C1 Dalton Georgia, USA
16C1 Dalton Massachusetts, USA
106C2 Daly R Aust
21A2 Daly City USA
106C2 Daly Waters Aust
85C4 Damān India
92B3 Damanhûr Egypt
71D4 Damar I Indon
98B2 Damara CAR
92C3 Damascus Syria
16A3 Damascus USA
74A2 Damaturu Nig
90B2 Damavand Iran
98B3 Damba Angola
87C3 Dambulla Sri Lanka
90B2 Damghan Iran
84D3 Damoh India
99D1 Damot Eth
99E2 Damot Eth
94B2 Damour Leb
106A3 Dampier Aust
94B3 Dana Jordan
22C2 Dana,Mt USA
97B4 Danané Lib
76D2 Da Nang Viet
79B3 Danao Phil
70A3 Danau Tobu L Indon
71D4 Danau Tuwuti L Indon
73A3 Danba China
15D2 Danbury USA
86A1 Dandeldhura Nepal
87A1 Dandeli India
108C3 Dandenong Aust
100A4 Danger Pt S Africa
99D1 Dangila Eth
6D1 Daniels Harbour Can
6D1 Daniel's Harbour Can
7E4 Dannebrog Øy I Greenland
110C2 Dannevirke NZ
87C1 Dantewara India
82B2 Danube = Donau
10B2 Danville Illinois, USA
11B3 Danville Kentucky, USA
16A2 Danville Pennsylvania, USA

11C3 Danville Virginia, USA
Danzig = Gdańsk
73C4 Dao Xian China
73B4 Daozhen China
79B4 Dapiak,Mt Phil
79B4 Dapitan Phil
68B3 Da Qaidam China
69E2 Daqing China
94C2 Dar'a Syria
91B4 Dārāb Iran
95A1 Daraj Libya
90B3 Dārān Iran
92C3 Dar'a Salkhad Syria
86B1 Darbhanga India
22C1 Dardanelle USA
18B2 Dardanelle,L USA
Dar-el-Beida = Casablanca
99D3 Dar es Salaam Tanz
110B1 Dargaville NZ
17B1 Darien USA
Darjeeling = Därjiling
86B1 Därjiling India
107D4 Darling R Aust
109C1 Darling Downs Aust
6C1 Darling Pen Can
108B2 Darlington Aust
17C1 Darlington USA
57B3 Darmstadt Germany
95B1 Darnah Libya
108B2 Darnick Aust
4A3 Darnley B Can
112C10 Darnley,C Ant
51B1 Daroca Spain
98C2 Dar Rounga Region, CAR
43C4 Dart R Eng
41C3 Dartmoor Moorland Eng
43C4 Dartmoor Nat Pk Eng
7D5 Dartmouth Can
43C4 Dartmouth Eng
107D1 Daru PNG
52C1 Daruvar Croatia
106C2 Darwin Aust
91B4 Daryacheh-ye Bakhtegan L Iran
91B4 Daryacheh-ye Mahārlū L Iran
90B3 Daryācheh-ye Namak Salt Flat Iran
90D3 Daryācheh-ye-Sistan Salt L Iran/Afghan
91B4 Daryacheh-ye Tashk L Iran
80C2 Daryacheh-ye Orūmiyeh L Iran
91C4 Dārzin Iran
91B4 Das I UAE
73C3 Dashennonglia Mt China
90C2 Dasht Iran
90B3 Dasht-e-Kavir Salt Desert Iran
90C3 Dasht-e Lut Salt Desert Iran
90D3 Dasht-e Naomid Desert Region Iran
85D3 Datia India
72A2 Datong China
72C1 Datong China
73A3 Datong He R China
79B4 Datu Piang Phil
39K7 Daugava R Latvia
60C2 Daugavpils Latvia
6D1 Daugaard Jensen Land Greenland
84A1 Daulatabad Afghan
85D3 Daulpur India
46D1 Daun Germany
87A1 Daund India
5H4 Dauphin Can
16A2 Dauphin USA
49D2 Dauphiné Region, France
97C3 Daura Nig
85D3 Dausa India
87B2 Dävangere India
79C4 Davao Phil
79C4 Davao G Phil
22A2 Davenport California, USA

10A2 Davenport Iowa, USA
32A2 David Panama
4D3 Davidson Mts USA
21A2 Davis USA
112C10 Davis Base Ant
7D4 Davis Inlet Can
6E3 Davis Str Greenland/ Can
61J3 Davlekanovo Russian Fed
47C1 Davos Switz
99E2 Dawa R Eth
73A4 Dawan China
84B2 Dawat Yar Afghan
Dawei = Tavoy
91B4 Dawhat Salwah B Qatar/S Arabia
76B2 Dawna Range Mts Burma
4E3 Dawson Can
17B1 Dawson Georgia, USA
107D3 Dawson R Aust
5F4 Dawson Creek Can
13D2 Dawson,Mt Can
12G2 Dawson Range Mts Can
73A3 Dawu China
73C3 Dawu China
48B3 Dax France
73B3 Daxian China
73B5 Daxin China
73A3 Daxue Shan Mts China
73C4 Dayang China
94C2 Dayr'Ali Syria
94C1 Dayr'Atiyah Syria
93D2 Dayr az Zawr Syria
10B3 Dayton Ohio, USA
19B4 Dayton Texas, USA
20C1 Dayton Washington, USA
11B4 Daytona Beach USA
73C4 Dayu China
78D3 Dayu Indon
72D2 Da Yunhe China
20C2 Dayville USA
73B3 Dazhu China
100B4 De Aar S Africa
26C2 Deadman's Cay The Bahamas
92C3 Dead S Israel/Jordan
46A1 Deal Eng
101G1 Dealesville S Africa
13B2 Dean R Can
13A2 Dean Chan Can
34C2 Deán Funes Arg
14B2 Dearborn USA
4F3 Dease Arm B Can
4E4 Dease Lake Can
48C2 Deauville France
97B4 Debakala Ivory Coast
12B2 Debauch Mt USA
27L1 Débé Trinidad
59C2 Debica Pol
58C2 Deblin Pol
97B3 Débo,L Mali
59C3 Debrecen Hung
99D2 Debre Birhan Eth
99D1 Debre Markos Eth
99D1 Debre Tabor Eth
11B3 Decatur Alabama, USA
17B1 Decatur Georgia, USA
10B3 Decatur Illinois, USA
14B2 Decatur Indiana, USA
48C3 Decazeville France
73A4 Dechang China
97B3 Dédougou Burkina
101C2 Deds a Malawi
42B2 Dee R Dumfries and Galloway, Scot
42C3 Dee R Eng/Wales
44C3 Dee R Grampian, Scot
15C1 Deep River Can
16C2 Deep River USA
109D1 Deepwater Aust
7E5 Deer Lake Can
8B2 Deer Lodge USA

34D3 Defferrari Arg
17A1 De Funiak Springs USA
68B3 Dêgê China
99E1 Degeh Bur Eth
106A3 De Grey R Aust
91B3 Deh Bid Iran
84B1 Dehi Afghan
96D1 Dehibat Tunisia
87B3 Dehiwala-Mt Lavinia Sri Lanka
90A3 Dehlorän Iran
84D2 Dehra Dün India
86A2 Dehri India
98C2 Deim Zubeir Sudan
94B2 Deir Abu Sa'id Jordan
94C1 Deir el Ahmar Leb
60B4 Dej Rom
19B3 De Kalb Texas, USA
63G2 De Kastri Russian Fed
98C3 Dekese Zaïre
98B2 Dekoa CAR
106B1 Dekusi Indon
9B3 Delano USA
10C3 Delaware State, USA
14B2 Delaware USA
15C2 Delaware R USA
109C3 Delegate Aust
47B1 Delémont Switz
101D2 Delgado C Mozam
84D3 Delhi India
15D2 Delhi New York, USA
92B1 Delice Turk
24B2 Delicias Mexico
90B3 Delijän Iran
47B1 Delle France
22D4 Del Mar USA
39F8 Delmenhorst Germany
4B3 De Long Mts USA
109C4 Deloraine Aust
5H5 Deloraine Can
17B2 Delray Beach USA
9C4 Del Rio USA
8B3 Delta USA
12E2 Delta R USA
12E2 Delta Junction USA
99D2 Dembi Dolo Eth
46C1 Denver R Belg
9C3 Deming USA
54C2 Demirköy Turk
49C1 Denain France
82A2 Denau Uzbekistan
42C3 Denbigh Wales
12B2 Denbigh,C USA
78B3 Dendang Indon
46C1 Dendermond Belg
46B1 Dendre R Belg
72B1 Dengkou China
72C3 Deng Xian China
Den Haag = 's-Gravenhage
27H1 Denham,Mt Jamaica
56A2 Den Helder Neth
51C2 Denia Spain
49C1 Denilquin Aust
107D4 Deniliquin Aust
20C2 Denio USA
9D3 Denison Texas, USA
12D3 Denison,Mt USA
92A2 Denizli Turk
39F7 Denmark Kingdom, Europe
1C1 Denmark Str Greenland/Iceland
27P2 Dennery St Lucia
78D4 Denpasar Indon
16B3 Denton Maryland, USA
9D3 Denton Texas, USA
107E1 D'Entrecasteaux Is PNG
47B1 Dents du Midi Mt Switz
8C3 Denver USA
98B2 Déo R Cam
86B2 Deoghar India
85C5 Deolali India
84D1 Deosai Plain India

95B3 Dépression du Mourdi Chad
19B3 De Queen USA
84C3 Dera Pak
84B3 Dera Bugti Pak
84C2 Dera Ismail Khan Pak
106B2 Derby Aust
16C2 Derby Connecticut, USA
43D3 Derby County, Eng
43D3 Derby Eng
18A2 Derby Kansas, USA
60E3 Dergachi Ukraine
19B3 De Ridder USA
Derna = Darnah
95C3 Derudeb Sudan
109C4 Derwent Bridge Aust
34B2 Desaguadero Arg
34B2 Desaguadero R Arg
30C2 Desaguadero R Bol
21B3 Descanso Mexico
20B2 Deschutes R USA
99D1 Desë Eth
29C5 Deseado Arg
29C5 Deseado R Arg
47D2 Desenzano Italy
96A1 Deserta Grande I/ Medeira
30C4 Desierto de Atacama Desert Chile
18B2 Desloge USA
10A2 Des Moines Iowa, USA
60D3 Desna R Russian Fed
29B6 Desolación I Chile
14A2 Des Plaines USA
56C2 Dessau Germany
12G2 Destruction Bay Can
46A1 Desvres France
21B3 Dete Rom
100B2 Dete Zim
10B2 Detroit USA
76D3 Det Udom Thai
73A3 Deva Rom
56B2 Deventer Neth
44C3 Deveron R Scot
85C3 Devikot India
22C2 Devil Postpile Nat Mon USA
22C1 Devils Gate P USA
Devil's Island = Isla du Diable
8D2 Devils Lake USA
12H3 Devils Paw Mt Can
43D4 Devizes Eng
85D3 Devli India
55B2 Devoll R Alb
43B4 Devon County, Eng
6A2 Devon I Can
107D5 Devonport Aust
86C1 Dewangiri Bhutan
85D4 Dewas India
101G1 Dewetsdorp S Africa
11B3 Dewey Res USA
19B3 De Witt USA
18C2 Dexter Missouri, USA
73A3 Deyang China
90C3 Deyhuk Iran
90A3 Dezful Iran
72D2 Dezhou China
90A2 Dezh Shāhpūr Iran
91B4 Dhahran S Arabia
86C2 Dhākā Bang
87B2 Dhamavaram India
86A2 Dhamtari India
86B2 Dhanbad India
86A1 Dhangarhi Nepal
86B1 Dhankuta Nepal
85B4 Dhar India
87B2 Dharmapuri India
84D2 Dharmshala India
97B3 Dhar Oualata Desert Region Maur
86A1 Dhaulagiri Mt Nepal
86B2 Dhenkänäi India
94B3 Dhibah Jordan
55C3 Dhikti Ori Mt Greece
55C3 Dhodhekánisos Is Greece
55B3 Dhomokós Greece
87B1 Dhone India

85C4 Dhoraji India
85C4 Dhrāngadhra India
86B1 Dhuburi India
85C4 Dhule India
22B2 Diablo,Mt USA
21A2 Diablo Range Mts USA
34C2 Diamante Arg
34B2 Diamante R Arg
31C5 Diamantina Brazil
107D3 Diamantina R Aust
86B2 Diamond Harbours India
22B1 Diamond Springs USA
91C4 Dibā UAE
98C3 Dibaya Zaïre
86C1 Dibrugarh India
8C2 Dickinson USA
15C2 Dickson City USA
93D2 Dicle R Turk
13E2 Didsbury Can
85C3 Didwāna India
97B3 Diebougou Burkina
46D2 Diekirch Lux
46D2 Diéma Mali
76C1 Dien Bien Phu Viet
56B2 Diepholz Germany
48C2 Dieppe France
46C1 Diest Belg
46D2 Dieuze France
7D5 Digby Can
49D3 Digne-les-Bains France
49C2 Digoin France
29B3 Digos Phil
71E4 Digul R Indon
86C1 Dihang R India
Dijlah = Tigris
49C2 Dijon France
98A2 Dik Chad
99E1 Dikhil Djibouti
46B1 Diksmuide Belg
18I Dikson Russian Fed
82A2 Dilaram Afghan
106B1 Dili Indon
76D3 Di Linh Viet
46E1 Dillenburg Germany
99C1 Dilling Sudan
12C3 Dillingham USA
8B2 Dillon USA
100B2 Dilolo Zaïre
Dimashq = Damascus
98C3 Dimbelenge Zaïre
97B4 Dimbokro Ivory Coast
54C2 Dimitrovgrad Bulg
61G3 Dimitrovgrad Russian Fed
94B3 Dimona Israel
86C1 Dimapur India
79C3 Dinagat I Phil
86B1 Dinajpur India
48B2 Dinan France
92B2 Dinar Turk
99D1 Dinder R Sudan
87B2 Dindigul India
72B2 Dingbian China
86B1 Dinggyê China
41A3 Dingle Irish Rep
41A3 Dingle B Irish Rep
97A3 Dinguiraye Guinea
44B3 Dingwall Scot
72A2 Dingxi China
72D2 Ding Xian China
76D1 Dinh Lap Viet
21C2 Dinuba USA
97A3 Diouloulou Sen
86C1 Diphu India
99E2 Dirê Dawa Eth
106A3 Dirk Hartog I Aust
95A3 Dirkou Niger
109C1 Dirranbandi Aust
99E2 Dirri Somalia
29G8 Disappointment,C South Georgia
20B1 Disappointment,C USA
106B3 Disappointment,L Aust
108B3 Discovery B Aust

Discovery Tablemount

103J7 Discovery Tablemount Atlantic O
47C1 Disentis Muster Switz
6E3 Disko Greenland
6E3 Disko Bugt *B* Greenland
6E3 Diskofjord Greenland
58D1 Disna *R* Belorussia
35B1 Distrito Federal Federal District, Brazil
85C4 Diu India
79C4 Diuat Mts Phil
31C6 Divinópolis Brazil
61F4 Divnoye Russian Fed
93C2 Divriği Turk
22B1 Dixon California, USA
5E4 Dixon Entrance *Sd* Can/USA
13D1 Dixonville Can
93E3 Diyālā *R* Iraq
65F6 Diyarbakir Turk
90A3 Diz *R* Iran
98B2 Dja *R* Cam
94C1 Djadi *R* Alg
95A2 Djado,Plat du Niger
98B3 Djambala Congo
96C2 Djanet Alg
50A2 Djebel Bouhalla *Mt* Mor
96C1 Djelfa Alg
98C2 Djéma CAR
97B3 Djenné Mali
97B3 Djibo Burkina
99E1 Djibouti Djibouti
99E1 Djibouti Republic, E Africa
98C2 Djolu Zaire
97C4 Djougou Benin
99D2 Djugu Zaire
38C2 Djúpivogur Iceland
51C2 Djurdjura *Mts* Alg
60E2 Dmitrov Russian Fed
Dnepr = Dnieper
60D4 Dneprodzerzhinsk Ukraine
60E4 Dnepropetrovsk Ukraine
60C3 Dneprovskaya Nizmennost' Region, Belorussia
Dnestr = Dniester
60D4 Dnieper *R* Ukraine
60D4 Dniester *R* Ukraine
60D2 Dno Russian Fed
98B2 Doba Chad
58C1 Dobele Latvia
34C3 Doblas Arg
71E4 Dobo Indon
54A2 Doboj Bosnia-Herzegovina
54B2 Dobreta-Turnu-Severin Rom
54C2 Dobrich Bulg
60D3 Dobrush Belorussia
31C5 Doce *R* Brazil
30D3 Doctor R P Peña Arg
87B2 Dod India
87B2 Doda Betta *Mt* India
Dodecanese = Sporádhes
9C3 Dodge City USA
99D3 Dodoma Tanz
75A1 Dōgo *I* Japan
97C3 Dogondoutchi Niger
93D2 Doğubayazit Turk
91B4 Doha Qatar
7C5 Dolbeau Can
46C2 Dôle France
43C3 Dolgellau Wales
47D1 Dolomitiche *Mts* Italy
99E2 Dolo Odo Eth
29E3 Dolores Arg
34D2 Dolores Urug
23A1 Dolores Hidalgo Mexico
4G3 Dolphin and Union Str Can
29E6 Dolphin,C Falkland Is
71E4 Dom *Mt* Indon
65G4 Dombarovskiy Russian Fed

38F6 Dombas Nor
46D2 Dombasle-sur-Meurthe France
54A1 Dombóvár Hung
27E3 Domfront France
27C3 Dominica *I* Caribbean S
27C3 Dominican Republic Caribbean S
6C3 Dominion,C Can
7E4 Domino Can
68D1 Domna Russian Fed
52A1 Domodossola Italy
78D4 Dompu Indon
29B3 Domuyo *Mt* Arg
109D1 Domville,Mt Aust
44C3 Don *R* Scot
61F4 Don *R* Russian Fed
45C1 Donaghadee N Ire
57C3 Donau *R* Germany
57C3 Donauwörth Germany
50A2 Don Benito Spain
42D3 Doncaster Eng
98B3 Dondo Angola
101C2 Dondo Mozam
87C3 Dondra Head *C* Sri Lanka
45B1 Donegal County, Irish Rep
40B3 Donegal Irish Rep
40B3 Donegal *B* Irish Rep
45B1 Donegal *Mts* Irish Rep
60E4 Donetsk Ukraine
73C4 Dong'an China
106A3 Dongara Aust
73A4 Dongchuan China
76D2 Dongfang China
74B2 Dongfeng China
70C4 Dongqala Indon
68D1 Donggi Cona *L* China
74A3 Dongguan China
73C5 Donghai Dao *I* China
72A1 Dong He *R* China
76D2 Dong Hoi Viet
73C5 Dong Jiang *R* China
95C3 Dongola Sudan
73D5 Dongshan China
68D4 Dongsha Qundao *I* China
72C2 Dongsheng China
72E3 Dongtai China
73C4 Dongting Hu *L* China
73B5 Dongzhi China
73D3 Dongzhi China
18B2 Doniphan USA
52C2 Donji Vakuf Bosnia-Herzegovina
38G5 Dönna *I* Nor
21A2 Donner P USA
46D2 Donnersberg *Mt* Germany
101C1 Donnybrook S Africa
Donostia = Saint Sebastian
22B2 Don Pedro Res USA
12D1 Dooneral,Mt USA
79B4 Dopolong Phil
73A3 Do Qu *R* China
47D2 Dora Baltea *R* Italy
49D2 Dorbirn Austria
43C4 Dorchester Eng
6C3 Dorchester,C Can
46C2 Dordogne *R* France
56A2 Dordrecht Neth
13F2 Dore L Can
13F2 Dore Lake Can
97B3 Dori Burkina
46B2 Dormans France
57B3 Dornbirn Austria
44B3 Dornoch Scot
44B3 Dornoch Firth *Estuary* Scot
38H6 Dorotea Sweden
109D2 Dorrigo Aust
20B2 Dorris USA
43C4 Dorset County, Eng
43C4 Dorsten Germany
56B2 Dortmund Germany
98C2 Doruma Zaire
63D2 Dosatuy Russian Fed
84B1 Doshi Afghan

22B2 Dos Palos USA
97C3 Dosso Niger
65G5 Dossor Kazakhstan
11B3 Dothan USA
49C1 Douai France
98A2 Douala Cam
109D1 Double Island Pt Aust
49D2 Double *R* France
111A3 Doubtful Sd NZ
97B3 Douentza Mali
9C3 Douglas Arizona, USA
42B2 Douglas Eng
17B1 Douglas Georgia, USA
8C2 Douglas Wyoming, USA
12A1 Douglas,C USA
13B2 Douglas Chan Can
12D3 Douglas,Mt Can
46B1 Doullens France
45C1 Doun County, N Ire
30F3 Dourados Brazil
50A1 Douro *R* Port
15C3 Dover Delaware, USA
43E4 Dover Eng
15D2 Dover New Hampshire, USA
16B2 Dover New Jersey, USA
14B2 Dover Ohio, USA
43D3 Dover *R* Eng
41D3 Dover,Str of UK/France
16B3 Downington USA
42B2 Downpatrick N Ire
13C2 Downton,Mt Can
75A1 Dōzen *I* Japan
96A2 Dr'aa *R* Mor
35A2 Dracena Brazil
16D1 Dracut USA
49D3 Draguignan France
101C3 Drakensberg *Mts* S Africa
101G1 Drakensberg *Mt* S Africa
103E7 Drake Pass Pacific/Atlantic O
55B2 Dráma Greece
39G7 Drammen Nor
38A1 Drangajökull Iceland
52A1 Drava *R* Slovenia
13D2 Drayton Valley Can
49C2 Dreaux France
57C2 Dresden Germany
20C2 Drewsey USA
54B2 Drin *R* Alb
54A2 Drina *R* Bosnia-Herzegovina/Serbia
58D1 Drissa *R* Belorussia
45C2 Drogheda Irish Rep
59C3 Drogobych Ukraine
112B12 Dronning Maud Land Region, Ant
30D3 Dr P.P. Pená Par
5G4 Drumheller Can
14B1 Drummond I USA
15D1 Drummondville Can
58C2 Druskininksi Lithuania
12G3 Dry B USA
7A5 Dryden Can
27H1 Dry Harbour Mts Jamaica
76B3 Duang *I* Burma
91C4 Dubai UAE
5H3 Dubawnt *R* Can
4H3 Dubawnt *L* Can
107D4 Dubbo Aust
45C2 Dublin County, Irish Rep
45C2 Dublin Irish Rep
17B1 Dublin USA
60E2 Dubna Russian Fed
60C3 Dubno Ukraine
15C2 Du Bois USA
13B2 Dubose,Mt Can
58D2 Dubrovica Ukraine
54A2 Dubrovnik Croatia
10A2 Dubuque USA

46D2 Dudelange Lux
1C10 Dudinka Russian Fed
43C3 Dudley Eng
97B4 Duékoué Ivory Coast
50B1 Duero *R* Spain
44C3 Dufftown Scot
52B2 Dugi Otok *I* Croatia
56B2 Duisburg Germany
93E1 Dükan Iraq
99D2 Duk Faiwil Sudan
91B4 Dukhān Qatar
73A4 Dukou China
68B3 Dulan China
34C2 Dulce *R* Arg
78C2 Dulit Range *Mts* Malay
86C2 Dullabchara India
10A2 Duluth USA
94C2 Dūmā Syria
78A2 Dumai Indon
79A3 Dumaran *I* Phil
9C3 Dumas USA
94C2 Dumayr Syria
42B2 Dumbarton Scot
42C2 Dumfries Scot
42B2 Dumfries and Galloway Region, Scot
86B2 Dumka India
15C1 Dumoine,L Can
112C8 Dumont d'Urville *Base* Ant
95C1 Dumyat Egypt
54C2 Dunărea *R* Rom
45C2 Dunary Head *Pt* Irish Rep
54B2 Dunav *R* Bulg
59D3 Dunayevtsy Ukraine
13C3 Duncan Can
16A2 Duncannon USA
44C2 Duncansby Head *Pt* Scot
45C1 Dundalk Irish Rep
16A3 Dundalk USA
45C1 Dundalk *B* Irish Rep
6D2 Dundas Greenland
4G2 Dundas Pen Can
71E5 Dundas Str Aust
11D1 Dundee S Africa
44C3 Dundee Scot
108B1 Dundoo Aust
42B2 Dundrum *B* N Ire
111B3 Dunedin NZ
17B2 Dunedin USA
109C2 Dunedoo Aust
44C3 Dunfermline Scot
85C4 Dungarpur India
45C2 Dungarvan Irish Rep
43E4 Dungeness Eng
109D2 Dungog Aust
99C2 Dungu Zaire
95C2 Dungunab Sudan
72B2 Dunhua China
68B2 Dunhuang China
46B1 Dunkerque France
10C2 Dunkirk USA
99D1 Dunkur Eth
97B4 Dunkwa Ghana
41B3 Dun Laoghaire Irish Rep
46B2 Dunmanway Irish Rep
26B1 Dunmore Town The Bahamas
44C2 Dunnet Head *Pt* Scot
42C2 Duns Scot
20B2 Dunsmuir USA
111A2 Dunstan Mts NZ
46C2 Dun-sur-Meuse France
72D1 Duolun China
18C2 Du Quoin USA
94B3 Dura Israel
49D3 Durance *R* France
24B2 Durango Mexico
50B1 Durango Spain
9C3 Durango USA
29E2 Durazno Urug
9D3 Durant USA
54A2 Duraykish Syria
101H1 Durban S Africa
46D1 Düren Germany
86A2 Durg India
86B2 Durgapur India
42D2 Durham County, Eng

42D2 **Durham** Eng
11C3 **Durham** N Carolina, USA
16D1 **Durham** New Hampshire, USA
108B1 **Durham Downs** Aust
54A2 **Durmitor** Mt Montenegro, Yugos
44B2 **Durness** Scot
55A2 **Durrës** Alb
108B1 **Durrie** Aust
45A3 **Dursey** I Irish Rep
55C3 **Dursunbey** Turk
110B2 **D'Urville I** NZ
90D2 **Dushak** Turkmenistan
73B4 **Dushan** China
82A2 **Dushanbe** Tajikistan
111A3 **Dusky Sd** NZ
56B2 **Düsseldorf** Germany
73B4 **Duyun** China
92B1 **Düzce** Turk
60C2 **Dvina** R Latvia
85B4 **Dwârka** India
6D3 **Dyer,C** Can
11B3 **Dyersburg** USA
43B3 **Dyfed** County, Wales
61F5 **Dykh Tau** Mt Russian Fed
108B1 **Dynevor Downs** Aust
68B2 **Dzag** Mongolia
63C3 **Dzamin Uüd** Mongolia
101D2 **Dzaoudzi** Mayotte
68C2 **Dzamin Uüd** Mongolia
68B2 **Dzavhan Gol** R Mongolia
80E1 **Dzhezkazgan** Kazakhstan
61F2 **Dzerzhinsk** Russian Fed
63E2 **Dzhalinda** Russian Fed
65J5 **Dzhambul** Kazakhstan
60D4 **Dzhankoy** Ukraine
Dzharkent = Panfilov
65H4 **Dzhezkazgan** Kazakhstan
84B1 **Dzhilikul'** Tajikistan
65J5 **Dzhungarsky Alatau** Mts Kazakhstan
59B2 **Dzierzoniow** Pol
63B3 **Dzül** Mongolia
82C1 **Dzungaria** Basin, China

E

7B4 **Eabamet L** Can
12F2 **Eagle** Alaska, USA
20B2 **Eagle L** California, USA
19A3 **Eagle Mountain L** USA
9C4 **Eagle Pass** USA
4E3 **Eagle Plain** Can
12E2 **Eagle River** USA
17B1 **Earlmart** USA
17B1 **Easley** USA
15C2 **East Aurora** USA
43E4 **Eastbourne** Eng
14A2 **East Chicago** USA
69E3 **East China Sea** China/Japan
83B4 **Eastern Ghats** Mts India
29E6 **East Falkland** I Falkland Is
11E1 **East Fork** R USA
21B2 **Eastgate** USA
16C1 **Easthampton** USA
16C2 **East Hampton** USA
14A2 **East Lake** USA
14B2 **East Liverpool** USA
100B4 **East London** S Africa
7C4 **Eastmain** Can
7C4 **Eastmain** R Can
17B1 **Eastman** USA
15C3 **Easton** Maryland, USA
15C2 **Easton** Pennsylvania, USA
16B2 **East Orange** USA

105L4 **East Pacific Ridge** Pacific O
17B1 **East Point** USA
42D3 **East Retford** Eng
11A3 **East St Louis** USA
1B7 **East Siberian S** Russian Fed
43E4 **East Sussex** County, Eng
17B1 **Eatonton** USA
10A2 **Eau Claire** USA
71F3 **Eauripik** I Pacific O
23B1 **Ebano** Mexico
98B2 **Ebebiyin** Eq Guinea
56C2 **Eberswalde** Germany
73A4 **Ebian** China
65K5 **Ebinur** L China
53C2 **Eboli** Italy
98B2 **Ebolowa** Cam
51B1 **Ebro** R Spain
92A1 **Eceabat** Turk
96C1 **Ech Cheliff** Alg
72D2 **Eching** China
2C4 **Echo** USA
4G3 **Echo Bay** Can
46D2 **Echternach** Lux
108B3 **Echuca** Aust
50A2 **Ecija** Spain
6B2 **Eclipse Sd** Can
32B4 **Ecuador** Republic, S America
99E1 **Ed** Eritrea
44C2 **Eday** I Scot
98C1 **Ed Da'ein** Sudan
95C3 **Ed Damer** Sudan
95C3 **Ed Debba** Sudan
44B2 **Eddrachillis** B Scot
99D1 **Ed Dueim** Sudan
109C4 **Eddystone Pt** Aust
98A2 **Edea** Cam
109C3 **Eden** Aust
42C2 **Eden** R Eng
101G1 **Edenburg** S Africa
111A3 **Edendale** NZ
46E2 **Edenkoben** Germany
46E1 **Eder** R Germany
6D3 **Edgell I** Can
64D2 **Edgeøya** I Barents S
16A3 **Edgewood** USA
94B3 **Edh Dhahiriya** Israel
55B2 **Edhessa** Greece
44C3 **Edinburgh** Scot
60C5 **Edirne** Turk
17B1 **Edisto** R USA
13D2 **Edith Cavell,Mt** Can
20B1 **Edmonds** USA
5G4 **Edmonton** Can
7D5 **Edmundston** Can
19A4 **Edna** USA
12H3 **Edna Bay** USA
52B1 **Edolo** Italy
94B3 **Edom** Region, Jordan
92A2 **Edremit** Turk
55C3 **Edremit Körfezi** B Turk
68B2 **Edrengiyn Nuruu** Mts Mongolia
5G4 **Edson** Can
34C3 **Eduardo Castex** Arg
12J2 **Eduni,Mt** Can
108B3 **Edward** R Aust
99C3 **Edward,L** Uganda/Zaire
108A1 **Edwards Creek** Aust
9C3 **Edwards Plat** USA
18C2 **Edwardsville** USA
12H3 **Edziza,Mt** Can
12B2 **Eek** USA
46B1 **Eeklo** Belg
10B3 **Effingham** USA
6E3 **Egedesminde** Greenland
12C2 **Egegik** USA
59C3 **Eger** Hung
16F1 **Egersund** Nor
16B3 **Egg Harbor City** USA
4G2 **Eglinton** I Can
110B1 **Egmont,C** NZ
110B1 **Egmont,Mt** NZ
92B2 **Eğridir Gölü** L Turk
95B2 **Egypt** Republic, Africa

50B1 **Eibar** Spain
49C2 **Eibeuf** France
46D1 **Eifel** Region, Germany
44A3 **Eigg** I Scot
83B5 **Eight Degree Chan** Indian O
106B2 **Eighty Mile Beach** Aust
108C3 **Eildon,L** Aust
56B2 **Eindhoven** Neth
47C1 **Einsiedeln** Switz
94B3 **Ein Yahav** Israel
57C2 **Eisenach** Germany
57C3 **Eisenerz** Austria
46D1 **Eitorf** Germany
72A1 **Ejin qi** China
23B2 **Ejutla** Mexico
110C2 **Eketahuna** NZ
65J4 **Ekibastuz** Kazakhstan
63F2 **Ekimchan** Russian Fed
92B3 **Ek Mahalla el Kubra** Egypt
39H7 **Eksjo** Sweden
10B1 **Ekwen** R Can
92A3 **El'Alamein** Egypt
92B3 **El'Arîsh** Egypt
94B2 **Elat** Israel
99B3 **El'Atrun Oasis** Sudan
93C2 **Elazig** Turk
53C2 **El Azraq** Jordan
52B2 **Elba** I Italy
92C2 **El Balyana** Egypt
32C2 **El Banco** Colombia
55B2 **Elbasan** Alb
27D5 **El Baül** Ven
57C2 **Elbe** R Germany
94C1 **El Bega'a** R Leb
14A2 **Elberta** USA
8C3 **Elbert,Mt** USA
17B1 **Elberton** USA
92C2 **Elbistan** Turk
58B2 **Elblag** Pol
29B4 **El Bolson** Arg
61F5 **Elbrus** Mt Russian Fed
Elburz Mts = Reshteh-ye Alborz
21B3 **El Cajon** USA
19A4 **El Campo** USA
51B2 **Elche** Spain
51B2 **Elda** Spain
32B3 **El Diviso** Colombia
96B2 **El Djouf** Desert Maur
18B2 **Eldon** USA
11A3 **El Dorado** Arkansas, USA
35B2 **Eldorado** Brazil
9D3 **El Dorado** Kansas, USA
24B2 **El Dorado** Mexico
33E2 **El Dorado** Ven
99D2 **Eldoret** Kenya
22C1 **Eleanor,L** USA
96B2 **El Eglab** Region, Alg
51B1 **El Escorial** Spain
93D2 **Eleşkirt** Turk
11C4 **Eleuthera** I The Bahamas
92B4 **El Faiyûm** Egypt
96B2 **El Farsia** Well Mor
98C1 **El Fasher** Sudan
92B4 **El Fashn** Egypt
50A1 **El Ferrol del Caudillo** Spain
99C1 **El Fula** Sudan
96C1 **El Gassi** Alg
99D1 **El Geteina** Sudan
99D1 **El Gezira** Region, Sudan
94B3 **El Ghor** V Israel/Jordan
10B2 **Elgin** Illinois, USA
44C3 **Elgin** Scot
92B3 **El Giza** Egypt
96C1 **El Golea** Alg
99D2 **Elgon,Mt** Uganda/Kenya
99E2 **El Goran** Eth
23A2 **El Grullo** Mexico

96B2 **El Guettara** Well Mali
96B2 **El Haricha** Desert Region Mali
92A4 **El Harra** Egypt
51C2 **El Harrach** Alg
99D1 **El Hawata** Sudan
23B1 **El Higo** Mexico
34A3 **El Huecu** Arg
92B4 **El'Igma** Desert Region Egypt
12B2 **Elim** USA
4H2 **Elira,C** Can
Elisabethville = Lubumbashi
39K6 **Elisenvaara** Fin
El Iskandariya = Alexandria
61F4 **Elista** Russian Fed
106C4 **Elizabeth** Aust
15D2 **Elizabeth** USA
11C3 **Elizabeth City** USA
17C1 **Elizabethtown** N Carolina, USA
16A2 **Elizabethtown** Pennsylvania, USA
96B1 **El Jadida** Mor
92C3 **El Jafr** Jordan
99D1 **El Jebelein** Sudan
96C1 **El Jem** Tunisia
58C2 **Elk** Pol
16B3 **Elk** R Maryland, USA
14B3 **Elk** R W Virginia, USA
95C3 **El Kamlin** Sudan
22B1 **Elk Grove** USA
El Khalil = Hebron
80B3 **El Khârga** Egypt
80B3 **El-Khârga Oasis** Egypt
14A2 **Elkhart** USA
96B2 **El Khenachich** Desert Region Mali
54C2 **Elkhovo** Bulg
14C3 **Elkins** USA
8B2 **Elko** USA
16B3 **Elkton** USA
99C1 **El Kuntilla** Egypt
99C1 **El Lagowa** Sudan
4H2 **Ellef Ringnes I** Can
8A2 **Ellensburg** USA
16B2 **Ellenville** USA
16B2 **Ellesmere** USA
111B2 **Ellesmere,L** NZ
16A3 **Ellicott City** USA
100B4 **Elliot** S Africa
7B5 **Elliot Lake** Can
94B3 **El Lisan** Pen Jordan
112B3 **Ellsworth Land** Region Ant
95B1 **El Maghra** Egypt
92B3 **El Mansûra** Egypt
16B3 **Elmer** USA
96B3 **El Merelé** Desert Region Maur
34B2 **El Milagro** Arg
94B1 **El Mina** Leb
92B4 **El Minya** Egypt
22B1 **Elmira** California, USA
10C2 **Elmira** New York, USA
96B2 **El Mreïtl** Well Maur
56B2 **Elmshorn** Germany
98C1 **El Muglad** Sudan
96B2 **El Mzereb** Well Mali
79A3 **El Nido** Phil
99D1 **El Obeid** Sudan
23A2 **El Oro** Mexico
96C1 **El Oued** Alg
9C3 **El Paso** USA
21A2 **El Porta** USA
22C2 **El Portal** USA
50A2 **El Puerto del Sta Maria** Spain
El Qâhira = Cairo
El Quds = Jerusalem
94B3 **El Quseima** Egypt
9D3 **El Reno** USA
4E3 **Elsa** Can
25D3 **El Salvador** Republic, Cent America
22D4 **Elsinore L** USA
34B3 **El Sosneade** Arg

Elsterwerde

57C2	**Elsterwerde** Germany
	El Suweis = Suez
50A1	**El Teleno** *Mt* Spain
110B1	**Eltham** NZ
33E2	**El Tigre** Ven
92B4	**El Tih** *Desert Region* Egypt
34C2	**El Tío** Arg
20C1	**Eltopia** USA
92B4	**El Tûr** Egypt
87C1	**Elūru** India
50A2	**Elvas** Port
32C5	**Elvira** Brazil
34A2	**El Volcán** Chile
14E3	**Ely** Eng
10A2	**Ely** Minnesota, USA
8B3	**Ely** Nevada, USA
14B2	**Elyria** USA
90B2	**Emāmrūd** Iran
84B1	**Emām Sāheb** Afghan
58B1	**Eman** *R* Sweden
61J4	**Emba** Kazakhstan
61J4	**Emba** *R* Kazakhstan
29C3	**Embalse Cerros Colorados** *L* Arg
51B2	**Embalse de Alarcón** *Res* Spain
50A2	**Embalse de Alcántara** *Res* Spain
50A1	**Embalse de Almendra** *Res* Spain
50A2	**Embalse de Garcia de Sola** *Res* Spain
33E2	**Embalse de Guri** *L* Ven
51B1	**Embalse de Mequinenza** *Res* Spain
50A1	**Embalse de Ricobayo** *Res* Spain
29E2	**Embalse de Rio Negro** *Res* Urug
29C3	**Embalse El Chocón** *L* Arg
29C4	**Embalse Florentine Ameghino** *L* Arg
50A1	**Embalse Gabriel y Galán** *Res* Spain
30D3	**Embarcación** Arg
5G4	**Embarras Portage** Can
47B2	**Embrun** France
99D3	**Embu** Kenya
56B2	**Emden** Germany
73D4	**Emei** China
107A3	**Emerald** Aust
7D4	**Emeri** Can
5J5	**Emerson** Can
21B1	**Emigrant P** USA
95A3	**Emi Koussi** *Mt* Chad
34B3	**Emilo Mitre** Arg
92B2	**Emirdağ** Turk
56B2	**Emmen** Neth
56B2	**Emmerich** Germany
20C2	**Emmett** USA
16A3	**Emmitsburg** USA
12B2	**Emmonak** USA
92A4	**Emory Peak** *Mt* USA
24A2	**Empalme** Mexico
101H1	**Empangeni** S Africa
30E4	**Empedrado** Arg
105G1	**Emperor Seamount Chain** Pacific O
18A2	**Emporia** Kansas, USA
56B2	**Ems** *R* Germany
23A1	**Emzacamican** Mexico
30E4	**Encarnación** Par
97B4	**Enchi** Ghana
22D4	**Encinitas** USA
35C1	**Encruzilhada** Brazil
106B1	**Endeh** Indon
13D2	**Enderby** Can
112C11	**Enderby Land** Region, Ant
15C2	**Endicott** USA
12D1	**Endicott Mts** USA
47D1	**Engadin** *Mts* Switz
79B2	**Engaño,C** Phil
94B3	**En Gedi** Israel

47C1	**Engelberg** Switz
78A4	**Enggano** *I* Indon
41C3	**England** Country, UK
7E4	**Englee** Can
14C3	**English Channel** Eng/France
97B3	**Enji** *Well* Maur
39H7	**Enköping** Sweden
53B3	**Enna** Italy
99C1	**En Nahud** Sudan
95B3	**Ennedi** *Region* Chad
109C1	**Enngonia** Aust
41B3	**Ennis** Irish Rep
19A3	**Ennis** Texas, USA
45C2	**Enniscorthy** Irish Rep
45C1	**Enniskillen** N Ire
45B2	**Ennistimon** Irish Rep
94B2	**Enn Nâqoûra** Leb
57C3	**Enns** *R* Austria
39F8	**Enschede** Neth
24A1	**Ensenada** Mexico
73B3	**Enshi** China
99D2	**Entebbe** Uganda
17A1	**Enterprise** Alabama, USA
20C1	**Enterprise** Oregon, USA
97C4	**Enugu** Nig
75B1	**Enzan** Japan
49C2	**Epernay** France
16A2	**Ephrata** Pennsylvania, USA
20C1	**Ephrata** Washington, USA
49D2	**Épinal** France
46A2	**Epte** *R* France
100A3	**Epukiro** Namibia
34C3	**Epu pel** Arg
90B3	**Equid** Iran
89D7	**Equator** Malt
98A2	**Equatorial Guinea** Republic, Africa
47C2	**Erba** Italy
46D2	**Erbeskopf** *Mt* Germany
34A3	**Ercilla** Chile
93D2	**Erciş** Turk
92C2	**Erciyas Dağlari** *Mt* Turk
74B2	**Erdaobaihe** China
72C1	**Erdene** Mongolia
68C2	**Erdenet** Mongolia
95B3	**Erdi** *Region* Chad
30F4	**Erechim** Brazil
92B1	**Ereğli** Turk
92B2	**Ereğli** Turk
68D2	**Erenhot** China
50B1	**Eresma** *R* Spain
46D1	**Erft** *R* Germany
57C2	**Erfurt** Germany
93C2	**Ergani** Turk
96B2	**Erg Chech** *Desert Region* Alg
95A3	**Erg du Djourab** *Desert* Chad
97D3	**Erg Du Ténéré** *Desert Region* Niger
92A1	**Ergene** *R* Turk
96B2	**Erg Iguidi** *Region* Alg
58D1	**Ergli** Latvia
98B1	**Erguig** *R* Chad
68D1	**Ergun'** *R* China/Russian Fed
63E2	**Ergun Zuoqi** China
95A2	**Eribia** Sudan
10C2	**Erie** USA
10B2	**Erie,L** Can/USA
42B2	**Erin Port** Eng
44A3	**Eriskay** *I* Scot
99D1	**Eritrea**
46D1	**Erkelenz** Germany
57C3	**Erlangen** Germany
19B3	**Erling,L** USA
101G1	**Ermelo** S Africa
87B3	**Ernakulam** India
87B2	**Erode** India
108B1	**Eromanga** Aust
96B1	**Er Rachidia** Mor
99D1	**Er Rahad** Sudan
101C2	**Errego** Mozam
40B2	**Errigal** *Mt* Irish Rep
41A3	**Erris Head** *Pt* Irish Rep

99D1	**Er Roseires** Sudan
94B2	**Er Rummân** Jordan
57C2	**Erzgebirge** *Upland* Germany
93C2	**Erzincan** Turk
65F6	**Erzurum** Turk
48C3	**Esara** *R* Spain
56B1	**Esbjerg** Den
9C4	**Escalón** Mexico
10B2	**Escanaba** USA
25C3	**Escárcega** Mexico
24C2	**Esch** Lux
21B3	**Escondido** USA
24B2	**Escuinapa** Mexico
25C3	**Escuintla** Guatemala
98B2	**Eséka** Cam
51C1	**Esera** *R* Spain
90B3	**Eşfahān** Iran
101H1	**Eshowe** S Africa
110C1	**Eskdale** NZ
38C1	**Eskifjörður** Iceland
39H7	**Eskilstuna** Sweden
4E3	**Eskimo L** Can
7A3	**Eskimo Point** Can
92B2	**Eskisehir** Turk
50A1	**Esla** *R* Spain
29A5	**Esmeralda** *I* Chile
32B3	**Esmeraldas** Ecuador
26B2	**Esmerelda** Cuba
49C2	**Espalion** France
14B1	**Espanola** Can
32J7	**Española** *I* Ecuador
106B4	**Esperance** Aust
34C2	**Esperanza** Arg
112C2	**Esperanza** *Base* Ant
35C1	**Espírito Santo** State, Brazil
101C3	**Espungabera** Mozam
29B2	**Esquel** Arg
20B1	**Esquimalt** Can
34D2	**Esquina** Arg
94C2	**Es Samra** Jordan
96B1	**Essaouira** Mor
96A2	**Es Semara** Mor
56B2	**Essen** Germany
33F3	**Essequibo** *R* Guyana
43E4	**Essex** County, Eng
14B2	**Essex** USA
57B3	**Esslingen** Germany
46B2	**Essonne** France
31D4	**Estância** Brazil
101G1	**Est** *R* S Africa
47D2	**Este** Italy
46B2	**Esternay** France
30D3	**Esteros** Par
5H5	**Estevan** Can
17B1	**Estill** USA
60B2	**Estonia** Republic, Europe
29B6	**Estrecho de Magallanes** *Str* Chile
50A2	**Estremoz** Port
59B3	**Esztergom** Hung
108A1	**Etadunna** Aust
46C2	**Etam** France
48C2	**Étampes** France
108A1	**Etamamiune,L** Aust
46A1	**Étaples** France
85D3	**Etāwah** India
99D2	**Ethiopia** Republic, Africa
23B2	**Etla** Mexico
53B3	**Etna** *Mt* Italy
12H3	**Etolin I** USA
12H3	**Etolin Str** USA
6C2	**Eton** Can
100A2	**Etosha Nat Pk** Namibia
100A2	**Etosha Pan** *Salt L* Namibia
17B1	**Etowah** *R* USA
46D2	**Ettelbruck** Lux
109C2	**Euabalong** Aust
14B2	**Euclid** USA
109C3	**Eucumbene,L** Aust
108A2	**Eudunda** Aust
19A2	**Eufala L** USA
17A1	**Eufaula** USA
8A2	**Eugene** USA
108C1	**Eulo** Aust
19B3	**Eunice** Louisiana, USA
46D1	**Eupen** Germany
93D3	**Euphrates** *R* Iraq

19C3	**Eupora** USA
48C2	**Eure** *R* France
20B2	**Eureka** Can
6B1	**Eureka** Can
8B3	**Eureka** Nevada, USA
6B2	**Eureka** *Sd* Can
108C3	**Euroa** Aust
109C1	**Eurombah** *R* Aust
101D3	**Europa** *I* Mozam Chan
57B2	**Euskirchen** Germany
13B2	**Eutsuk L** Can
13D2	**Evansburg** Can
6B1	**Evans,C** Can
7C4	**Evans,L** Can
6B3	**Evans Str** Can
14A2	**Evanston** Illinois, USA
8B2	**Evanston** Wyoming, USA
11B3	**Evansville** Indiana, USA
101G1	**Evaton** S Africa
106C4	**Everard,L** Aust
82C3	**Everest,Mt** China/Nepal
8A2	**Everett** Washington, USA
16C1	**Everett,Mt** USA
11B4	**Everglades,The** *Swamp* USA
43D3	**Evesham** Eng
98B2	**Evinayong** Eq Guinea
39F7	**Evje** Nor
47B1	**Evolène** Switz
50A2	**Évora** Port
37C2	**Evreux** France
55B3	**Évvoia** *I* Greece
98B3	**Ewo** Congo
22C1	**Excelsior Mt** USA
18B2	**Excelsior Springs** USA
21B2	**Exeter** California, USA
43C4	**Exeter** Eng
15D2	**Exeter** New Hampshire, USA
43C4	**Exmoor Nat Pk** Eng
43C4	**Exmouth** Eng
50A2	**Extremadura** Region, Spain
25E2	**Exuma Sd** The Bahamas
99D3	**Eyasi** *L* Tanz
42C2	**Eyemouth** Scot
99E2	**Eyl** Somalia
106B4	**Eyre** Aust
106C3	**Eyre Creek** *R* Aust
106C3	**Eyre,L** Aust
106C4	**Eyre Pen** Aust
79B3	**Eyte** *I* Phil
23A1	**Eztatlan** Mexico
55C3	**Ezine** Turk

F

4G3	**Faber L** Can
39G7	**Fåborg** Den
52B2	**Fabriano** Italy
99B3	**Fachi** Niger
95B3	**Fada** Chad
97C3	**Fada N'Gourma** Burkina
52B2	**Faenza** Italy
6J3	**Faeringehavn** Greenland
98B2	**Fafa** *R* CAR
99E2	**Fafan** *R* Eth
54C1	**Fǎgǎras** Rom
46C1	**Fagnes** Region, Belg
97B3	**Faguibine,L** *L* Mali
91C5	**Fahud** Oman
96A1	**Faial** *I* Acores
4D3	**Fairbanks** USA
14B3	**Fairborn** USA
8D2	**Fairbury** USA
16A3	**Fairfax** USA
21A2	**Fairfield** California, USA
16C2	**Fairfield** Connecticut, USA
14B3	**Fairfield** Ohio, USA
45C1	**Fair Head** *Pt* N Ire
40C2	**Fair Isle** *I* Scot

111B2 Fairlie NZ
14B3 Fairmont W Virginia, USA
13D1 Fairview Can
4E4 Fairweather,Mt USA
71F3 Fais I Pacific O
84C2 Faisalabad Pak
8C2 Faith USA
44E1 Faither,The Pen Scot
86A1 Faizābād India
43E3 Fakenham Eng
39G7 Fakōping Sweden
86C2 Falam Burma
24C2 Falcon Res Mexico/USA
97A3 Falémé R Mali/Sen
39G7 Falkenberg Sweden
42C2 Falkirk Scot
29D6 Falkland Is Dependency, S Atlantic
29E6 Falkland Sd Falkland Is
22D4 Fallbrook USA
8B3 Fallon USA
15D2 Fall River USA
18A1 Falls City USA
43B4 Falmouth Eng
27H1 Falmouth Jamaica
16D2 Falmouth Massachusetts, USA
100A4 False B S Africa
24A2 Falsterbo C Mexico
56C2 Falster I Den
54C1 Fălticeni Rom
39H6 Falun Sweden
92B2 Famagusta Cyprus
46C1 Fannene Region, France
76B2 Fang Thai
99D2 Fangak Sudan
73E5 Fang liao Taiwan
52B2 Fano Italy
112C3 Faraday Base Ant
99C2 Faradje Zaire
101D3 Farafangana Madag
95B2 Farafra Oasis Egypt
80E2 Farah Afghan
71F2 Farallon de Medinilla I Pacific O
97A3 Faranah Guinea
71F3 Faraulep I Pacific O
43D4 Fareham Eng
Farewell,C = Kap Farvel
107G5 Farewell,C NZ
110B2 Farewell Spit Pt NZ
8D2 Fargo USA
94B2 Fari'a R Israel
10A2 Faribault USA
86B2 Faridpur Bang
90C2 Farimān Iran
18B2 Farmington Missouri, USA
9C3 Farmington New Mexico, USA
22B2 Farmington Res USA
42D2 Farne Deep N Sea
13D2 Farnham,Mt Can
12H2 Faro Can
50A2 Faro Port
39H7 Fåro I Sweden
89K9 Farquhar Is Indian O
44B3 Farrar R Scot
14B2 Farrell USA
55B3 Fársala Greece
91B4 Fasā Iran
45B3 Fastnet Rock Irish Rep
60C3 Fastov Ukraine
86A1 Fatehpur India
13D1 Father Can
30F2 Fatima do Sul Brazil
101G1 Fauresmith S Africa
47B2 Faverges France
7B4 Fawn R Can
38H6 Fax R Sweden
38A2 Faxaflói B Iceland
95A3 Faya Chad
11A3 Fayetteville Arkansas, USA
11C3 Fayetteville N Carolina, USA

93E4 Faylakah I Kuwait
84C2 Fāzilka India
96A2 Fderik Maur
11C3 Fear,C USA
21A2 Feather Middle Fork R USA
48C2 Fécamp France
34D2 Federación Arg
34D2 Federal Arg
71F3 Federated States of Micronesia Is Pacific O
56C2 Fehmarn I Germany
32C5 Feijó Brazil
73C5 Feilai Xai Bei Jiang R China
110C2 Feilding NZ
100C2 Feira Zambia
31D4 Feira de Santan Brazil
92C2 Feke Turk
57B3 Feldkirch Austria
34D2 Feliciano R Arg
41D3 Felixstowe Eng
47D1 Feltre Italy
38G6 Femund L Nor
74A2 Fengcheng China
73B4 Fengdu China
72D1 Fenging China
73B3 Fengjie China
73B3 Feng Xian China
72C1 Fengzhen China
72C2 Fen He R China
101D2 Fenoarivo Atsinanana Madag
60E5 Feodosiya Ukraine
90C3 Ferdow Iran
46B2 Fère-Champenoise France
82B2 Fergana Uzbekistan
45C1 Fermanagh County, N Ire
45B2 Fermoy Irish Rep
47D1 Fermo Mt Austria
32J7 Fernandina I Ecuador
17B1 Fernandina Beach USA
103G5 Fernando de Noronha I Atlantic O
35A2 Fernandópolis Brazil
20B1 Ferndale USA
21B2 Fernley USA
52B2 Ferrara Italy
32B5 Ferreñafe Peru
19B3 Ferreira USA
96B1 Fès Mor
18B2 Festus USA
54C2 Feteşti Rom
92A2 Fethiye Turk
61H5 Fetisovo Kazakhstan
44E1 Fetlar I Scot
84C1 Feyzabad Afghan
101D3 Fianarantsoa Madag
99D2 Fiché Eth
101G1 Ficksburg S Africa
47D2 Fidenza Italy
55A2 Fier Alb
47D1 Fiera Di Primeiro Italy
44C3 Fife Region, Scot
44C3 Fife Ness Pen Scot
48C3 Figeac France
50A1 Figueira da Foz Port
51C1 Figueras Spain
Figueres = Figueras
96B1 Figuig Mor
105G4 Fiji Is Pacific O
30D3 Filadelfia Par
54B2 Filiaşi Rom
55B3 Filiatrá Greece
53B3 Filicudi I Italy
21B3 Fillmore California, USA
44B3 Findhorn R Scot
10B2 Findlay USA
13D2 Findlay,Mt Can
15C2 Finger Lakes USA
101C2 Fingoè Mozam
92B2 Finike Turk
106C2 Finke R Aust
108A1 Finke Flood Flats Aust
64D3 Finland Republic, N Europe

39J7 Finland,G of N Europe
5F4 Finlay R Can
5F4 Finlay Forks Can
108C3 Finley Aust
38H5 Finnsnes Nor
71F4 Finschhafen PNG
47C1 Finsteraarhorn Mt Switz
56C2 Finsterwalde Germany
45C1 Fintona N Ire
111A3 Fiordland Nat Pk NZ
94B2 Fiq Syria
93C2 Firat R Turk
22B2 Firebaugh USA
52B2 Firenze Italy
34C2 Firmat Arg
85D3 Firozābād India
84C2 Firozpur India
39H7 Firspång Sweden
42B2 Firth of Clyde Estuary Scot
44C3 Firth of Forth Estuary Scot
44A3 Firth of Lorn Estuary Scot
40C2 Firth of Tay Estuary Scot
91B4 Firūzābād Iran
100A3 Fish R Namibia
22C2 Fish Camp USA
16C2 Fishers I USA
6B3 Fisher Str Can
43B4 Fishguard Wales
6E3 Fiskenaesset Greenland
46B2 Fismes France
9B3 Flagstaff USA
42D2 Flamborough Head C Eng
8C2 Flaming Gorge Res USA
44A2 Flannan Isles Is Scot
12J2 Flat R Can
13E3 Flathead R USA
8B2 Flathead L USA
18B2 Flat River USA
16D2 Flattery,C USA
42C3 Fleetwood Eng
39F7 Flekkefjord Nor
69G4 Fleming Deep Pacific O
16B2 Flemington USA
56B2 Flensburg Germany
47B1 Fleurier Switz
106C4 Flinders I Aust
12J2 Flinders I Aust
107D2 Flinders R Aust
106C4 Flinders Range Mts Aust
5H4 Flin Flon Can
10B2 Flint USA
42C3 Flint Wales
11B3 Flint R USA
46B1 Flixecourt France
17A1 Florala USA
11B3 Florence Alabama, USA
18A2 Florence Kansas, USA
20B2 Florence Oregon, USA
11C3 Florence S Carolina, USA
32B3 Florencia Colombia
46C2 Florenville Belg
25D3 Flores Guatemala
71F2 Flores I Açores
106B1 Flores I Indon
34D3 Flores R Arg
70C4 Flores S Indon
31C3 Floriano Brazil
30G4 Florianópolis Brazil
25D2 Florida State, USA

29E2 Florida Urug
17B2 Florida B USA
17B2 Florida City USA
107E1 Florida Is Solomon Is
11B4 Florida Keys Is USA
11B4 Florida,Strs of USA
55B2 Flórina Greece
38F6 Florø Nor
47D1 Fluchthorn Mt Austria
54C1 Focsani Rom
53C2 Foggia Italy
97A4 Fogo I Cape Verde
48C3 Foix France
6C3 Foley I Can
52B2 Foligno Italy
43E4 Folkestone Eng
17B1 Folkston USA
52B2 Follonica Italy
22B1 Folsom USA
22B1 Folsom L L USA
5H4 Fond-du-Lac Can
10B2 Fond du Lac USA
48C2 Fontainebleau France
18B2 Fontenac USA
48B2 Fontenay-le-Comte France
52C1 Fonyód Hung
12D2 Foochow = Fuzhou
12D2 Draker,Mt USA
46D2 Forbach France
109C2 Forbes Aust
97C4 Forcados Nig
38F6 Forde Nor
108C1 Fords Bridge Aust
19B3 Fordyce USA
97A4 Forécariah Guinea
6G3 Forel,Mt Greenland
14B2 Forest Can
17B1 Forest Park USA
22A1 Forestville USA
44C3 Forfar Scot
46A2 Forges-les-Eaux France
20B1 Forks USA
52B2 Forlì Italy
51C2 Formentera I Spain
53B2 Formia Italy
96A1 Formigas I Açores
Formosa = Taiwan
30E4 Formosa Arg
31B5 Formosa Brazil
30D3 Formosa State, Arg
73D5 Formosa Str Taiwan/China
47D2 Fornovo di Taro Italy
38D3 Føroyar Is N Atlantic O
44C3 Forres Scot
106B4 Forrest Aust
11A3 Forrest City USA
107D2 Forsayth Aust
39J6 Forssa Fin
109D2 Forster Aust
18B2 Forsyth Missouri, USA
84C3 Fort Abbas Pak
7B4 Fort Albany Can
31D2 Fortaleza Brazil
44B3 Fort Augustus Scot
7B4 Fort Beaufort S Africa
21A2 Fort Bragg USA
8C2 Fort Collins USA
15C1 Fort Coulogne Can
27E4 Fort de France Martinique
17A1 Fort Deposit USA
10A2 Fort Dodge USA
106A3 Fortescue R Aust
7A5 Fort Frances Can
4F3 Fort Franklin Can
4F3 Fort Good Hope Can
108B1 Fort Grey Aust
44B3 Forth R Scot
7B4 Fort Hope Can
34B3 Fortín Uno Arg
4F3 Fort Liard Can
96C1 Fort Lallemand Alg
Fort Lamy = Ndjamena
11B4 Fort Lauderdale USA
4F3 Fort Liard Can

Fort Mackay

5G4 Fort Mackay Can
5G5 Fort Macleod Can
5G4 Fort McMurray Can
4E3 Fort McPherson USA
18B2 Fort Madison USA
8C2 Fort Morgan USA
11B4 Fort Myers USA
5F4 Fort Nelson Can
4F3 Fort Norman Can
17A1 Fort Payne USA
8C2 Fort Peck Res USA
11B4 Fort Pierce USA
4G3 Fort Providence Can
5G3 Fort Resolution Can
98B3 Fort Rousset Congo
5F4 Fort St James Can
13C1 Fort St John Can
13E2 Fort Saskatchewan
Can
18B2 Fort Scott USA
4E3 Fort Selkirk Can
7B4 Fort Severn Can
61H5 Fort Shevchenko
Kazakhstan
4F3 Fort Simpson Can
5G3 Fort Smith Can
4G3 Fort Smith Region,
Can
11A3 Fort Smith USA
9C3 Fort Stockton USA
20B2 Fortuna California,
USA
5G4 Fort Vermilion Can
17A1 Fort Walton Beach
USA
10B2 Fort Wayne USA
44B3 Fort William Scot
9C3 Fort Worth USA
12F2 Fortymile R USA
12E1 Fort Yukon USA
73C5 Foshan China
47B2 Fossano Italy
12G3 Foster,Mt USA
98B3 Fougamou Gabon
48B2 Fougères France
44D1 Foula I Scot
43C4 Foulness I Eng
111B2 Foulwind,C NZ
98B2 Foumban Cam
49C1 Fourmies France
55C3 Fournoí I Greece
97A3 Fouta Djallon Mts
Guinea
111B3 Foveaux Str NZ
43B4 Fowey Eng
13D2 Fox Creek Can
6B3 Foxe Basin G Can
6B3 Foxe Chan Can
6C3 Foxe Pen Can
41B3 Fox Valley Can
45B2 Foynes Irish Rep
100A2 Foz do Cuene
Angola
30F4 Foz do Iguaçu Brazil
16A2 Frackville USA
34B2 Fraga Arg
16D1 Framingham USA
31B6 Franca Brazil
49C2 France
Republic, Europe
10A2 Frances Can
12J2 Frances R Can
49D2 Franche Comté
Region, France
100B3 Francistown
Botswana
13B2 Francois L Can
14A2 Frankfort Indiana,
USA
11B3 Frankfort Kentucky,
USA
13A3 Frankfort S Africa
57B2 Frankfurt Germany
46E1 Frankfurt am Main
Germany
56C2 Frankfurt-an-der-Oder
Germany
57C3 Fränkischer Alb
Upland Germany
14A3 Franklin Indiana,
USA
19B4 Franklin Louisiana,
USA

16D1 Franklin
Massachusetts, USA
16B2 Franklin New Jersey,
USA
14C2 Franklin
Pennsylvania, USA
4F2 Franklin B Can
20C1 Franklin D Roosevelt
L USA
4F3 Franklin Mts Can
4J2 Franklin Str Can
111B2 Franz Josef Glacier
NZ
Franz-Joseph-Land =
Zemlya Frantsa Iosifa
5F5 Fraser R Can
44C3 Fraserburgh Scot
107E3 Fraser I Aust
13B2 Fraser L Can
47B1 Frauenfeld Switz
34D2 Fray Bentos Urug
40C2 Frazerburgh Scot
16B3 Frederica USA
56B1 Fredericia Den
15C3 Frederick Maryland,
USA
16B3 Fredericksburg
Virginia, USA
12H3 Frederick Sd USA
18B2 Fredericktown USA
7D5 Fredericton Can
6E3 Frederikshab
Greenland
39G7 Frederikshavn Den
15C2 Fredonia USA
39G7 Fredrikstad Nor
16B2 Freehold USA
26B1 Freeport The
Bahamas
19A4 Freeport Texas, USA
97A4 Freetown Sierra
Leone
57B3 Freiburg Germany
57C3 Freistadt Austria
106A4 Fremantle Aust
22B2 Fremont California,
USA
18A1 Fremont Nebraska,
USA
14B2 Fremont Ohio, USA
33G3 French Guiana
Dependency,
S America
109C4 Frenchmans Cap Mt
Aust
105J4 French Polynesia Is
Pacific O
24B2 Fresnillo Mexico
8B3 Fresno USA
22C2 Fresno R USA
47A1 Fretigney France
46B1 Frévent France
47A2 Freycinet Pen Aust
97A3 Fria Guinea
22C2 Friant USA
22C2 Friant Dam USA
52A1 Fribourg Switz
57B3 Friedrichshafen
Germany
6D3 Frobisher B Can
6D3 Frobisher Bay Can
5H4 Frobisher L Can
61F4 Frolovo Russian Fed
43C4 Frome Eng
108A1 Frome R Aust
43C4 Frome R Eng
106D4 Frome,L Aust
25C3 Frontera Mexico
15C3 Front Royal USA
53B2 Frosinone Italy
73C5 Fuchuan China
73E4 Fuding China
24B2 Fuerte R Mexico
30E3 Fuerte Olimpo Par
96A2 Fuerteventura I
Canary Is
72C2 Fugu China
68A2 Fuhai China
91C4 Fujairah UAE
75B1 Fuji Japan
73D4 Fujian Province,
China
69F2 Fujin China

75B1 Fujinomiya Japan
74D3 Fuji-san Mt Japan
75B1 Fujisawa Japan
75B1 Fuji-Yoshida Japan
63A3 Fukang China
74C3 Fukuchiyima Japan
74D3 Fukui Japan
74C4 Fukuoka Japan
74E3 Fukushima Japan
74C4 Fukuyama Japan
57B2 Fulda Germany
57B2 Fulda R Germany
73B4 Fuling China
27L1 Fullarton Trinidad
22D4 Fullerton USA
18C2 Fulton Kentucky,
USA
15C2 Fulton New York,
USA
46C1 Fumay France
75C1 Funabashi Japan
96A1 Funchal Medeira
35C1 Fundão Brazil
7D5 Fundy,B of Can
10C3 Funhalouro Mozam
72D3 Funing China
73B5 Funing China
73D4 Fuqing China
10C2 Furancungo Mozam
91C4 Fürg Iran
47C1 Furka P Switz
107D5 Furneaux Group Is
Aust
56C2 Fürstenwalde
Germany
57C3 Fürth Germany
74D3 Furukawa Japan
6B3 Fury and Hecla St
Can
74A2 Fushun Liaoning,
China
73A4 Fushun Sichuan,
China
74B2 Fusong China
73D5 Füssen Germany
72E2 Fu Xian China
72E1 Fuxin China
72D3 Fuyang China
72E1 Fuyuan China
73A4 Fuyuan Yunnan,
China
68A2 Fuyun China
73D4 Fuzhou China
56C1 Fyn I Den

G

99E2 Gaalkacyo Somalia
21B2 Gabbs USA
100A2 Gabela Angola
96D1 Gabe's Tunisia
22B2 Gabilan Range Mts
USA
98B3 Gabon Republic,
Africa
100B3 Gaborone Botswana
54C2 Gabrovo Bulg
91B3 Gach Sārān Iran
17A1 Gadsden Alabama,
USA
10A1 Gads L Can
53B2 Gaeta Italy
71F3 Gaferut I Pacific O
96C1 Gafsa Tunisia
60D2 Gagarin Russian Fed
97B4 Gagnoa Ivory Coast
7C4 Gagnon Can
61F5 Gagra Georgia
86B1 Gaibanda India
29C4 Gaimán Arg
17B2 Gainesville Florida,
USA
17B1 Gainesville Georgia,
USA
19A3 Gainesville Texas,
USA
42D3 Gainsborough Eng
108A2 Gairdner,L Aust
44B3 Gairloch Scot
16A3 Gaithersburg USA
81B1 Gajendragarh India
73D4 Ga Jiang R China
99D3 Galana R Kenya

103D5 Galapagos Is
Pacific O
42C2 Galashiels Scot
54C1 Galaţi Rom
4C3 Galena Alaska, USA
18B2 Galena Kansas, USA
27L1 Galeota Pt Trinidad
27L1 Galera Pt Trinidad
10A2 Galesburg USA
15C2 Galeton USA
61F2 Galich Russian Fed
50A1 Galicia Region, Spain
Galilee,S of =
Tiberias,L
27J1 Galina Pt Jamaica
99D1 Gallabat Sudan
47C2 Gallarate Italy
87C3 Galle Sri Lanka
51B1 Gállego R Spain
Gallipoli = Gelibolu
55A2 Gallipoli Italy
38J5 Gällivare Sweden
42B2 Galloway District
42B2 Galloway,Mull of C
Scot
8C3 Gallup USA
22B1 Galt USA
50A2 Galtat Zemmour Mor
25C2 Galveston USA
11A4 Galveston B USA
34C2 Galvez Arg
49D3 Galvi Corse
45B2 Galway County,
Irish Rep
41B3 Galway Irish Rep
41B3 Galway B Irish Rep
36B5 Gamba China
97B3 Gambaga Ghana
4A3 Gambell USA
97A3 Gambia R The
Gambia/Sen
97A3 Gambia,The
Republic, Africa
98B3 Gambona Congo
100A2 Gambos Angola
87C3 Gampola Sri Lanka
99E2 Ganale Dorya R Eth
15C2 Gananoque Can
Gand = Gent
100A2 Ganda Angola
98C3 Gandajika Zaïre
84B3 Gandava Pak
7E5 Gander Can
85C4 Gändhidhäm India
85C4 Gändhinagar India
85D4 Gändhi Sägar L
India
51B2 Gandia Spain
86B2 Ganga R India
85C3 Ganganar India
86C2 Gangaw Burma
72A2 Gangca China
82C2 Gangdise Shan Mts
China
Ganges = Ganga
86B1 Gangtok India
72B3 Gangu China
8C2 Gannett Peak Mt
USA
72B2 Ganquan China
108A3 Gantheaume C Aust
39K8 Gantsevichi
Belorussia
73D4 Ganzhou China
97C3 Gao Mali
72A2 Gaolan China
72C2 Gaoping China
97B3 Gaoua Burkina
97A3 Gaoual Guinea
72D3 Gaoyou Hu L China
73C5 Gaozhou China
49D3 Gap France
79B2 Gapan Phil
84D2 Gar China
109C1 Garah Aust
3103 Garanhuns Brazil
21A1 Garberville USA
35B2 Garça Brazil
35A2 Garcias Brazil
47D2 Garda Italy
9C3 Garden City USA
14A1 Garden Pen USA
34D3 Gardey Arg
84B2 Gardez Afghan

16C2 **Gardiners I** USA
16D1 **Gardner** USA
47D2 **Gardone** Italy
47D2 **Gargano** Italy
85D4 **Garñakota** India
61K2 **Gari** Russian Fed
100A4 **Garies** S Africa
99D3 **Garissa** Kenya
19A3 **Garland** USA
57C3 **Garmisch-Partenkirchen** Germany
90B2 **Garmsar** Iran
18A2 **Garnett** USA
8B2 **Garnett Peak** Mt USA
48C3 **Garonne** R France
44B3 **Garry** R Scot
78B4 **Garut** Indon
86A2 **Garwa** India
14A2 **Gary** USA
82C2 **Garyarsa** China
4H3 **Garza L** Can
19A3 **Garza-Little Elm** Res USA
90B2 **Gasan Kuli** Turkmenistan
48B3 **Gascogne** Region, France
18B2 **Gasconade** R USA
106A3 **Gascoyne** R Aust
98B2 **Gashaka** Nig
97D3 **Gashua** Nig
10D2 **Gaspé** Can
10D2 **Gaspé,C. de** Can
94A1 **Gata,C** Cyprus
60C2 **Gatchina** Russian Fed
42D2 **Gateshead** Eng
19A3 **Gatesville** USA
15C1 **Gatineau** Can
15C1 **Gatineau** R Can
109D1 **Gatton** Aust
86C1 **Gauháti** India
58C1 **Gauja** R Latvia
86A1 **Gauri Phanta** India
22B3 **Gaviota** USA
39H6 **Gävle** Sweden
108A2 **Gawler Ranges** Mts Aust
72A1 **Gaxun Nur** L China
86A2 **Gaya** India
97C3 **Gaya** Niger
14B1 **Gaylord** USA
109D1 **Gayndah** Aust
61H1 **Gayny** Russian Fed
60C4 **Gaysin** Ukraine
92B3 **Gaza** Israel
92C2 **Gaziantep** Turk
97B4 **Gbaringa** Lib
58B2 **Gdansk** Pol
58B2 **Gdańsk,G of** Pol
39K7 **Gdov** Russian Fed
58B2 **Gdynia** Pol
94A3 **Gebel Halâl** Mt Egypt
95C2 **Gebel Hamata** Mt Egypt
92B4 **Gebel Katherina** Mt Egypt
94A3 **Gebel Libni** Mt Egypt
94A3 **Gebel Maghâra** Mt Egypt
99D1 **Gedaref** Sudan
55C3 **Gediz** R Turk
56C2 **Gedser** Den
46C1 **Geel** Belg
108B3 **Geelong** Aust
109C4 **Geeveston** Aust
97D3 **Geidam** Nig
46D1 **Geilenkirchen** Germany
99D3 **Geita** Tanz
73A5 **Gejiu** China
53B3 **Gela** Italy
99E2 **Geladī** Eth
46D1 **Geldern** Germany
55C2 **Gelibolu** Turk
92B2 **Gelidonya Burun** Turk
46D1 **Gelsenkirchen** Germany
39F8 **Gelting** Germany

77C5 **Gemas** Malay
46C1 **Gembloux** Belg
98B2 **Gemena** Zaïre
92C2 **Gemerek** Turk
92A1 **Gemlik** Turk
52B1 **Gemona** Italy
100B3 **Gemsbok** Nat Pk Botswana
98C1 **Geneina** Sudan
34C3 **General Acha** Arg
34C3 **General Alvear** Buenos Aires, Arg
34B2 **General Alvear** Mendoza, Arg
34C2 **General Arenales** Arg
34D3 **General Belgrano** Arg
112B2 **General Belgrano** Base Ant
112C2 **General Bernardo O'Higgins** Base Ant
34D3 **General Conesa** Buenos Aires, Arg
30D3 **General Eugenio A Garay** Par
34D3 **General Guido** Arg
34C3 **General La Madrid** Arg
34C2 **General Levalle** Arg
30C4 **General Manuel Belgrano** Mt Arg
34D3 **General Paz** Buenos Aires, Arg
34C3 **General Pico** Arg
34C2 **General Pinto** Arg
34D3 **General Pirán** Arg
29C3 **General Roca** Arg
112C3 **General San Martin** Base Ant
79C4 **General Santos** Phil
34C3 **General Viamonte** Arg
34C3 **General Villegas** Arg
15C2 **Genesee** R USA
15C2 **Geneseo** USA
18A1 **Geneva** Nebraska, USA
15C2 **Geneva** New York, USA
Geneva,L of = LacLéman
52A1 **Genève** Switz
50B2 **Genil** R Spain
109C3 **Genoa** Aust
52A2 **Genova** Italy
32J7 **Genovesa** I Ecuador
46B1 **Gent** Belg
78B4 **Genteng** Indon
56C2 **Genthin** Germany
93E1 **Geokchay** Azerbaijan
100B4 **George** S Africa
7D4 **George** R Can
109C2 **George,L** Aust
17B2 **George,L** Florida, USA
15D2 **George,L** New York, USA
111A2 **George Sd** NZ
109C4 **George Town** Aust
15C3 **Georgetown** Delaware, USA
33F2 **Georgetown** Guyana
14B3 **Georgetown** Kentucky, USA
77C4 **George Town** Malay
27N2 **Georgetown** St Vincent and the Grenadines
17C1 **Georgetown** S Carolina, USA
19A3 **Georgetown** Texas, USA
97A3 **Georgetown** The Gambia
112C8 **George V Land** Region, Ant
112C12 **George Forster** Base Ant
17B1 **Georgia** State, USA

14B1 **Georgian B** Can
13C3 **Georgia,Str of** Can
106C3 **Georgina** R Aust
61F5 **Georgiyevsk** Russian Fed
57C2 **Gera** Germany
46B1 **Geraardsbergen** Belg
111B2 **Geraldine** NZ
106A3 **Geraldton** Aust
108J2 **Geraldton** Can
94B3 **Gerar** R Israel
4C3 **Gerdine,Mt** USA
12E2 **Gerdova Peak** Mt USA
77C4 **Gerik** Malay
60B4 **Gerlachovsky** Mt Pol
13C1 **Germansen Lodge** Can
56C2 **Germany** Republic, Europe
101G1 **Germiston** S Africa
46D1 **Gerolstein** Germany
51C1 **Gerona** Spain
46E1 **Geseke** Germany
99E2 **Gestro** R Eth
50B1 **Getafe** Spain
16A3 **Gettysburg** Pennsylvania, USA
93D2 **Gevas** Turk
55B2 **Gevgelija** Macedonia
47B1 **Gex** France
94C2 **Ghabāghib** Syria
96C1 **Ghadamis** Libya
90B2 **Ghaem Shahr** Iran
86A1 **Ghāghara** R India
97B4 **Ghana** Republic, Africa
100B3 **Ghanzi** Botswana
96C1 **Ghardaia** Alg
95A2 **Ghāt** Libya
84D3 **Ghāziābād** India
84C3 **Ghazi Khan** Pak
84B2 **Ghazni** Afghan
54C1 **Gheorgheni** Rom
88E4 **Ghudamis** Alg
90D3 **Ghurian** Afghan
95B2 **Gialo** Libya
99E2 **Giamame** Somalia
53C3 **Giarre** Italy
100A3 **Gibeon** Namibia
50A2 **Gibraltar** Colony, SW Europe
50A2 **Gibraltar,Str of** Spain/Africa
106B3 **Gibson Desert** Aust
20B1 **Gibsons** Can
87B1 **Giddalūr** India
99D2 **Gidole** Eth
57B2 **Giessen** Germany
17B2 **Gifford** USA
74D3 **Gifu** Japan
42B2 **Gigha** I Scot
52B2 **Giglio** I Italy
50A1 **Gijón** Spain
107D2 **Gilbert** R Aust
8D8 **Gilbert,Mt** Can
17C2 **Gile** Mozam
94B2 **Gilead** Region, Jordan
95B2 **Gilf Kebir Plat** Egypt
109C2 **Gilgandra** Aust
84C1 **Gilgit** Pak
84C1 **Gilgit** R Pak
108C2 **Gilgunnia** Aust
7A4 **Gillam** Can
108A2 **Gilles** L Aust
13B2 **Gill I** Can
14A1 **Gills Rock** USA
14A2 **Gilman** USA
22B2 **Gilroy** USA
8D1 **Gimli** Can
101H1 **Gingindlovu** S Africa
79C4 **Gingoog** Phil
99D2 **Ginir** Eth
55B3 **Gióna** Mt Greece
109C3 **Gippsland** Mts Aust
14B2 **Girard** USA
32C3 **Girardot** Colombia
44C3 **Girdle Ness** Pen Scot
93C1 **Giresun** Turk
85C4 **Gir Hills** India

98B2 **Giri** R Zaire
86B2 **Giridih** India
Girona = **Gerona**
48B2 **Gironde** R France
42B2 **Girvan** Scot
111C2 **Gisborne** NZ
46A2 **Gisors** France
99C3 **Gitega** Burundi
Giuba,R = **Juba,R**
54C2 **Giurgiu** Rom
46C1 **Givet** Belg
58C2 **Gizycko** Pol
55B2 **Gjirokastër** Alb
4J3 **Gjoatlaven** Can
39G6 **Gjøvik** Nor
7D5 **Glace Bay** Can
12G3 **Glacier Bay Nat Mon** USA
13E3 **Glacier Nat Pk** USA/Can
20B1 **Glacier Peak** Mt USA
6B2 **Glacier Str** Can
107E3 **Gladstone** Queensland, Aust
108A2 **Gladstone** S Aust, Aust
109C4 **Gladstone** Tasmania, Aust
14A1 **Gladstone** USA
38A1 **Gláma** Mt Iceland
39G6 **Gláma** R Nor
46D2 **Glan** R Germany
47C1 **Glärner** Mts Switz
47C1 **Glarus** Switz
18A2 **Glasco** USA
8C2 **Glasgow** Montana, USA
42B2 **Glasgow** Scot
16B3 **Glassboro** USA
43C4 **Glastonbury** Eng
61H2 **Glazov** Russian Fed
59B3 **Gleisdorf** Austria
110C1 **Glen Afton** NZ
16A3 **Glen Burnie** USA
101H1 **Glencoe** S Africa
9B3 **Glendale** Arizona, USA
22C3 **Glendale** California, USA
12E2 **Glenhallen** USA
109C1 **Glen Innes** Aust
109C1 **Glenmorgan** Aust
109D2 **Glenreagh** Aust
16A3 **Glen Rock** USA
19A3 **Glen Rose** USA
44C3 **Glenrothes** UK
15D2 **Glens Falls** USA
45B1 **Glenties** Irish Rep
19B3 **Glenwood** Arkansas, USA
8C3 **Glenwood Springs** USA
39F6 **Glittertind** Mt Nor
59B2 **Gliwice** Pol
9B3 **Globe** USA
58B2 **Głogów** Pol
38G5 **Glomfjord** Nor
109D2 **Gloucester** Aust
43C4 **Gloucester** Eng
16D1 **Gloucester** USA
58D1 **Glubokoye** Belorussia
60D3 **Glukhov** Russian Fed
59B3 **Glmünd** Austria
57C3 **Gmunden** Austria
58B2 **Gniezno** Pol
100A3 **Goabeg** Namibia
87A1 **Goa, Daman and Diu** Union Territory, India
86C1 **Goālpāra** India
99D2 **Goba** Eth
100A3 **Gobabis** Namibia
34C2 **Gobernador Crespo** Arg
34B3 **Gobernador Duval** Arg
72B1 **Gobi** Desert China/Mongolia
75B2 **Gobo** Japan
87B1 **Godag** India
87C1 **Godāvari** R India
14B2 **Goderich** Can
6E3 **Godhavn** Greenland
85C4 **Godhra** India
34B2 **Godoy Cruz** Arg

Gods L

7A4 **Gods** L Can
6E3 **Godthab** Greenland
Godwin Austen =
 K2
35B1 **Goianidra** Brazil
35B1 **Goiânésia** Brazil
35B1 **Goiânia** Brazil
35A1 **Goiás** Brazil
31B4 **Goiás** State, Brazil
35A2 **Goio-Erê** Brazil
99D2 **Gojab** R Eth
55C2 **Gökçeada** I Turk
55C3 **Gökova Körfezi** B
 Turk
92C2 **Gökova** Turk
63C3 **Gol** R Mongolia
86C1 **Golāghāt** India
93C2 **Gölbaşi** Turk
20C2 **Golconda** USA
20B2 **Gold Beach** USA
109D1 **Gold Coast** Aust
13D2 **Golden** Can
110B2 **Golden B** NZ
20B1 **Goldendale** USA
22A2 **Golden Gate** Chan
 USA
19B4 **Golden Meadow**
 USA
21B2 **Goldfield** USA
13B3 **Gold River** Can
56C2 **Goleniów** Pol
22C3 **Goleta** USA
52A2 **Golfe d'Ajaccio** G
 Corse
96D1 **Golfe de Gabes** G
 Tunisia
 Golfe de Gascogne =
 Biscay,Bay of
52A2 **Golfe de St Florent** G
 Corse
48B2 **Golfe de St-Malo** B
 France
49C3 **Golfe du Lion** G
 France
29B4 **Golfo Corcovado** G
 Chile
50B2 **Golfo de Almeira** G
 Spain
29B4 **Golfo de Ancud** G
 Chile
25D2 **Golfo de Batabano** G
 Cuba
50A2 **Golfo de Cadiz** G
 Spain
53A3 **Golfo de Cagliari** G
 Sardegna
24A1 **Golfo de California** G
 Mexico
25D4 **Golfo de Chiriqui** G
 Panama
25D3 **Golfo de Fonseca** G
 Honduras
26B2 **Golfo de
 Guacanayabo** G
 Cuba
32A4 **Golfo de Guayaquil**
 G Ecuador
26B5 **Golfo del Darien** G
 Colombia/Panama
32A2 **Golfo de los
 Mosquitos** G
 Panama
25D3 **Golfo del Papagaya**
 G Nic
51B2 **Golfo de Mazarrón** G
 Spain
25D4 **Golfo de Nicoya** G
 Costa Rica
53A2 **Golfo de Oristano** G
 Sardegna
25E4 **Golfo de Panamá** G
 Panama
25D3 **Golfo de Papagayo** G
 Costa Rica
27E4 **Golfo de Paria** G Ven
29B5 **Golfo de Penas** G
 Chile
49D3 **Golfo de St Florent**
 Corse
51C1 **Golfo de San Jorge** G
 Spain
24C3 **Golfo de
 Tehuantepec** G
 Mexico

32B3 **Golfo de Torugas** G
 Colombia
32B2 **Golfo de Uraba** G
 Colombia
51C2 **Golfo de Valencia** G
 Spain
27C4 **Golfo de Venezuela**
 G Ven
52A2 **Golfo di Genova** G
 Italy
53C3 **Golfo di Policastro** G
 Italy
53C3 **Golfo di Squillace** G
 Italy
53C2 **Golfo di Taranto** G
 Italy
52B1 **Golfo di Venezia** G
 Italy
25D4 **Golfo Dulce** G
 Costa Rica
29C5 **Golfo San Jorge** G
 Arg
29D4 **Golfo San Matias** G
 Arg
68B3 **Golmud** China
99E2 **Golocha** Eth
12B2 **Golovin B** USA
74F2 **Golovnino**
 Russian Fed
99C3 **Goma** Zaire
97D3 **Gombe** Nig
60D3 **Gomel** Belorussia
96A2 **Gomera** I Canary Is
24B2 **Gómez Palacio**
 Mexico
 Gonam R
 Russian Fed
90C2 **Gonbad-e Kávús**
 Iran
86A1 **Gonda** India
85C4 **Gondal** India
99D1 **Gonder** Eth
92A1 **Gönen** Turk
55C3 **Gonen** R Turk
73A4 **Gongga Shan** Mt
 China
72A2 **Gonghe** China
97D3 **Gongola** R Nig
22B2 **Gonzales** California,
 USA
19A4 **Gonzales** Texas, USA
34C3 **Gonzalez Chaves** Arg
13C2 **Good Hope Mt** Can
12B3 **Goodnews Bay** USA
109C1 **Goodooga** R Aust
42D3 **Goole** Eng
108C2 **Goolgowi** Aust
108A3 **Goolwa** Aust
106A4 **Goomalling** Aust
108C2 **Goombalie** Aust
109D1 **Goomeri** Aust
109D1 **Goondiwindi** Aust
7E4 **Goose Bay** Can
17C1 **Goose Creek** USA
20B2 **Goose L** USA
87B1 **Gooty** India
64H3 **Gora Munku Sardyk**
 Mt Mongolia/
 Russian Fed
64H3 **Gora Narodnaya** Mt
 Russian Fed
64G3 **Gora Tel'pos-iz**
 Russian Fed
54A2 **Goražde** Bosnia-
 Herzegovina
4D3 **Gordon** USA
13E1 **Gordon L** Can
15C3 **Gordonsville** USA
98B2 **Goré** Chad
99D2 **Gorë** Eth
111A3 **Gore** NZ
63F2 **Gore Topko** Mt
 Russian Fed
45C2 **Gorey** Irish Rep
90B2 **Gorgan** Iran
93E2 **Goris** Armenia
52B1 **Gorizia** Italy
 Gor'kiy = Nizniy
 Novgorod
61F2 **Gor'kovskoye
 Vodokhranilishche**
 Res Russian Fed

57C2 **Gorlitz** Germany
60E4 **Gorlovka** Ukraine
22C3 **Gorman** USA
54C2 **Gorna Orjahovica**
 Bulg
68A1 **Gorno-Altaysk**
 Russian Fed
69G2 **Gornozavodsk**
 Russian Fed
61F2 **Gorodets**
 Russian Fed
59C3 **Gorodok** Ukraine
59D3 **Gorodok** Ukraine
71F4 **Goroka** PNG
86A1 **Gorokhpur** India
101C2 **Gorongosa** Mozam
71D3 **Gorontalo** Indon
61K2 **Goro Yurma** Mt
 Russian Fed
45B2 **Gort** Irish Rep
63C2 **Goryachinsk**
 Russian Fed
59D3 **Goryn'** R Ukraine
59B2 **Góry Świetokrzyskie**
 Upland Pol
64G3 **Gory Tel'pos-iz'** Mt
 Russian Fed
39H8 **Gorzów Wielkopolski**
 Pol
74E2 **Goshogawara**
 Japan
52C2 **Gospić** Croatia
53B2 **Gostivar** Macedonia
58B2 **Gostynin** Pol
39G7 **Göteborg** Sweden
98B2 **Gotel** Mts Nig
39H7 **Gotland** I Sweden
74B4 **Gotō-retto** I Japan
39H7 **Gotska Sandón** I
 Sweden
74C3 **Götsu** Japan
98D3 **Goudoumaria** Niger
103H7 **Gough I** Atlantic O
109C2 **Goulburn** Aust
97B3 **Goumbou** Mali
97B3 **Goundam** Mali
98B1 **Gouré** Niger
97B3 **Gourma Rharous**
 Mali
46A2 **Gournay-en-Bray**
 France
95A3 **Gouro** Chad
71E5 **Gove Pen** Aust
60B4 **Goverla** Mt Ukraine
35C1 **Governador
 Valadares** Brazil
86A2 **Govind Ballabh Paht
 Sägar** L India
15C2 **Gowanda** USA
84B3 **Gowärän** Afghan
30E4 **Goya** Arg
98C1 **Goz-Beida** Chad
53B3 **Gozo** I Medit S
95C3 **Goz Regeb** Sudan
100B4 **Graaff-Reinet**
 S Africa
15C1 **Gracefield** Can
109D1 **Grafton** Aust
8D2 **Grafton** N Dakota,
 USA
14B3 **Grafton** W Virginia,
 USA
5E4 **Graham** L Can
13C1 **Graham** R Can
13E1 **Graham L** Can
100B4 **Grahamstown**
 S Africa
31B3 **Grajaú** Brazil
58C2 **Grajewo** Pol
55B2 **Grámmos** Mt
 Greece/Alb
44C3 **Grampian** Region,
 Scot
44B3 **Grampian** Mts Scot
32C3 **Granada** Colombia
25D3 **Granada** Nic
50B2 **Granada** Spain
15D1 **Granby** Can
96A2 **Gran Canaria** I
 Canary Is
30D4 **Gran Chaco** Region
 Arg
14A2 **Grand** R Michigan,
 USA

18B1 **Grand** R Missouri,
 USA
27Q2 **Grand B** Dominica
11C4 **Grand Bahama** I
 The Bahamas
7E5 **Grand Bank** Can
102F2 **Grand Banks**
 Atlantic O
97B4 **Grand Bassam** Ivory
 Coast
9B3 **Grand Canyon** USA
26A3 **Grand Cayman** I
 Caribbean S
13E2 **Grand Centre** Can
20C1 **Grand Coulee** USA
34B3 **Grande** R Arg
31C4 **Grande** R Bahia,
 Brazil
35B1 **Grande** R Minas
 Gerais/São Paulo,
 Brazil
13D2 **Grande Cache** Can
47A2 **Grande Chartreuse**
 Region, France
101D2 **Grande Comore** I
 Comoros
13D1 **Grande Prairie** Can
19A3 **Grande Prairie** USA
95A3 **Grand Erg de Bilma**
 Desert Niger
96B2 **Grand erg Occidental**
 Mts Alg
96C2 **Grand erg Oriental**
 Mts Alg
7C4 **Grande Rivière de la
 Baleine** R Can
20C1 **Grande Ronde** R
 USA
7D5 **Grand Falls** New
 Brunswick, Can
7E5 **Grand Falls**
 Newfoundland, Can
20C1 **Grand Forks** Can
8D2 **Grand Forks** USA
16B1 **Grand Gorge** USA
14A2 **Grand Haven** USA
19C3 **Grand Isle** USA
19B4 **Grand L** USA
15D1 **Grand Mère** Can
50A2 **Grândola** Port
5J4 **Grand Rapids** Can
14A2 **Grand Rapids**
 Michigan, USA
18B1 **Grand Rapids**
 Minnesota, USA
47B2 **Grand St Bernard** P
 Italy/Switz
8B2 **Grand Teton** Mt
 USA
8B2 **Grand Teton Nat Pk**
 USA
46A2 **Grandvilliers** France
25D1 **Grangeburg** USA
51C1 **Granollers** Spain
52A1 **Gran Paradiso** Mt
 Italy
47D1 **Gran Pilastro** Mt
 Austria/Italy
43D3 **Grantham** Eng
21B2 **Grant,Mt** USA
44C3 **Grantown-on-Spey**
 Scot
9C3 **Grants** USA
20B2 **Grants Pass** USA
48B2 **Granville** France
5H4 **Granville L** Can
35C1 **Grão Mogol** Brazil
49D3 **Grasse** France
21A2 **Grass Valley** USA
5H5 **Gravelbourg** Can
46B1 **Gravelines** France
100C3 **Gravelotte** S Africa
15C2 **Gravenhurst** Can
109D1 **Gravesend** Aust
12H3 **Gravina I** USA
12B2 **Grayling** USA
20B1 **Grays Harbor** B
 USA
14B3 **Grayson** USA
18C2 **Grayville** USA
57B3 **Graz** Austria
27H1 **Great** R Jamaica
11C4 **Great Abaco** I
 The Bahamas

106B4 Great Australian Bight G Aust
16B3 Great B New Jersey, USA
25E2 Great Bahama Bank The Bahamas
110C1 Great Barrier I NZ
107D2 Great Barrier Reef Is Aust
16C1 Great Barrington USA
4F3 Great Bear L Can
9D2 Great Bend USA
107D3 Great Dividing Range Mts Aust
42D2 Great Driffield Eng
16B3 Great Egg Harbor B USA
112B10 Greater Antarctic Region, Ant
26B2 Greater Antilles Is Caribbean S
43D4 Greater London Metropolitan County, Eng
43C3 Greater Manchester County, Eng
25E2 Great Exuma I The Bahamas
8B2 Great Falls USA
44B3 Great Glen V Scot
86B1 Great Himalayan Range Mts Asia
11C4 Great Inagua I The Bahamas
100B4 Great Karroo Mts S Africa
109C4 Great L Aust
100A3 Great Namaland Region, Namibia
42C3 Great Ormes Head C Wales
11C4 Great Ragged I The Bahamas
99D3 Great Ruaha R Tanz
15D2 Great Sacandaga L USA
8B2 Great Salt L USA
95B2 Great Sand Sea Libya/Egypt
106B3 Great Sandy Desert Aust
8A2 Great Sandy Desert USA
Great Sandy I = Fraser I
4G3 Great Slave L Can
16C2 Great South B USA
106B3 Great Victoria Desert Aust
112C2 Great Wall Base Ant
72B2 Great Wall China
43E3 Great Yarmouth Eng
94B1 Greco,C Cyprus
55B3 Greece Republic, Europe
15C2 Greece USA
8C2 Greeley USA
6B1 Greely Fjord Can
14A1 Green B USA
14A2 Green Bay USA
14A3 Greencastle Indiana, USA
16C1 Greenfield Massachusetts, USA
14A2 Greenfield Wisconsin, USA
13F2 Green Lake Can
6F2 Greenland Dependency, N Atlantic O
102H1 Greenland Basin Greenland S
1B1 Greenland S Greenland
42B2 Greenock Scot
16C2 Greenport USA
16B3 Greensboro Maryland, USA
11C3 Greensboro N Carolina, USA
15C2 Greensburg Pennsylvania, USA
44B3 Greenstone Pt Scot

18C2 Greenup USA
17A1 Greenville Alabama, USA
97B4 Greenville Lib
19B3 Greenville Mississippi, USA
16D1 Greenville N Hampshire, USA
14B2 Greenville Ohio, USA
17B1 Greenville S Carolina, USA
19A3 Greenville Texas, USA
43E4 Greenwich Eng
16C2 Greenwich Eng
16B3 Greenwood Delaware, USA
19B3 Greenwood Mississippi, USA
17B1 Greenwood S Carolina, USA
18B2 Greers Ferry L USA
108A1 Gregory,L Aust
107D2 Gregory Range Mts Aust
56C2 Greifswald Germany
64F3 Gremikha Russian Fed
56C1 Grenå Den
19C3 Grenada USA
27E4 Grenada I Caribbean S
109C2 Grenfell Aust
49D2 Grenoble France
27M2 Grenville Grenada
107D2 Grenville,C Aust
20B1 Gresham USA
78C4 Gresik Jawa, Indon
78A3 Gresik Sumatera, Indon
19B4 Gretna USA
111B2 Grey R NZ
12G2 Grey Hunter Pk Mt Can
7E4 Grey Is Can
16C1 Greylock,Mt USA
111B2 Greymouth NZ
107D3 Grey Range Mts Aust
45C2 Greystones Irish Rep
101H1 Greytown S Africa
101F1 Griekwastad S Africa
17B1 Griffin USA
108C2 Griffith Aust
107D5 Grim,C Aust
15C2 Grimsby Can
42D3 Grimsby Eng
38B1 Grimsey I Iceland
13H7 Grimshaw Can
39F7 Grimstad Nor
47C1 Grindelwald Switz
6A2 Grinnell Pen Can
6B2 Grise Fjord Can
61H1 Griva Russian Fed
39J7 Grobina Latvia
58C2 Grodno Belorussia
86A1 Gromati R India
56B2 Groningen Neth
106C2 Groote Eylandt I Aust
100A2 Grootfontein Namibia
100B3 Grootvloer Salt L S Africa
27P2 Gros Islet St Lucia
46E1 Grosser Feldberg Germany
52B2 Grosseto Italy
46E2 Gross-Gerau Germany
57C3 Grossglockner Mt Austria
47E1 Gross Venediger Mt Austria
12C3 Grosvenor,L USA
21A2 Groveland USA
21B2 Grover City USA
15D2 Groveton USA
61G5 Groznyy Russian Fed
58B2 Grudziądz Pol
100A3 Grünau Namibia
44E2 Grutness Scot
61F3 Gryazi Russian Fed

61E2 Gryazovets Russian Fed
29G8 Gryviken South Georgia
45A2 Gt Blasket I Irish Rep
35C2 Guaçuí Brazil
23A1 Guadalajara Mexico
50B1 Guadalajara Spain
107E1 Guadalcanal I Solomon Is
50B2 Guadalimar R Spain
51B1 Guadalope R Spain
50B2 Guadalqivir R Spain
24B2 Guadalupe Mexico
3G6 Guadalupe I Mexico
27E3 Guadeloupe I Caribbean S
50B2 Guadian R Spain
50A2 Guadiana R Port
50B2 Guadix Spain
32D6 Guajará Mirim Brazil
32C1 Guajira,Pen de Colombia
32B4 Gualaceo Ecuador
34D2 Gualeguay Arg
34D2 Gualeguaychú Arg
71F2 Guam I Pacific O
34C3 Guamini Arg
77C5 Gua Musang Malay
23A1 Guanajuato Mexico
23A1 Guanajuato State, Mexico
32D2 Guanare Ven
25D2 Guane Cuba
73C5 Guangdong Province, China
73A3 Guanghan China
72C3 Guanghua China
73A4 Guangmao Shan Mt China
73B5 Guangnan China
72B3 Guangyuan China
73D4 Guangze China
67F3 Guangzhou China
35C1 Guanhães Brazil
32D3 Guania R Colombia
27E5 Guanipa R Ven
26B2 Guantánamo Cuba
72D1 Guanting Shuiku Res China
73B5 Guanxi Province, China
73A3 Guan Xian China
32B2 Guapa Colombia
33E6 Guapore R Brazil/Bol
30C2 Guaqui Bol
32B4 Guaranda Ecuador
30F4 Guarapuava Brazil
35B2 Guaratinguetá Brazil
34A3 Guarda Port
35B1 Guarda Mor Brazil
9C4 Guasave Mexico
47D2 Guastalla Italy
25C3 Guatemala Guatemala
25C3 Guatemala Republic, Cent America
34C3 Guatraché Arg
32C3 Guaviare R Colombia
35B2 Guaxupé Brazil
27L1 Guayaguayare Trinidad
32A4 Guayaquil Ecuador
24A2 Guaymas Mexico
34D2 Guayquiraro R Arg
100B2 Guba Zaïre
99E2 Guban Region Somalia
79B3 Gubat Phil
56C2 Gubin Pol
87B2 Gudūr India
14B2 Guelph Can
26A2 Guenabacoa Cuba
98C1 Guéréda Chad
48C2 Guéret France
48B2 Guernsey I UK
23A2 Guerrero State, Mexico
99D2 Gughe Mt Eth
63C3 Gugigu China
71F2 Guguan I Pacific O
109C2 Guiargambone Aust

73C4 Guidong China
97B4 Guiglo Ivory Coast
73C5 Gui Jiang R China
43D4 Guildford Eng
73C4 Guilin China
47B2 Guillestre France
72A2 Guinan China
97A3 Guinea Republic, Africa
102H4 Guinea Basin Atlantic O
97A3 Guinea-Bissau Republic, Africa
97C4 Guinea,G of W Africa
26A2 Güines Cuba
97B3 Guir Well Mali
84C2 Guiranwala Pak
33E1 Güiria Ven
46B2 Guise France
79C3 Guiuan Phil
73B5 Gui Xian China
73B4 Guiyang China
73B4 Guizhou Province, China
85C4 Gujarat State, India
84C2 Gujrat Pak
87B1 Gulbarga India
58D1 Gulbene Latvia
87B1 Guledagudda India
80D3 Gulf,The S W Asia
109C2 Gulgong Aust
73B4 Gulin China
12E2 Gulkana USA
13E2 Gull L Can
13F2 Gull Lake Can
55C3 Güllük Körfezi B Turk
99D2 Gulu Uganda
109C1 Guluguba Aust
97C3 Gumel Nig
46D1 Gummersbach Germany
86A2 Gumpla India
93C1 Gümüşhane Turk
85D4 Guna India
99D1 Guna Mt Eth
109C3 Gundagai Aust
98B3 Gungu Zaïre
6H3 Gunnbjørn Fjeld Mt Greenland
109D2 Gunnedah Aust
87B1 Guntakal India
17A1 Guntersville USA
17A1 Guntersville L USA
87C1 Guntur India
77C5 Gunung Batu Putch Mt Malay
78D3 Gunung Besar Mt Indon
78D2 Gunung Bulu Mt Indon
78A3 Gunung Gedang Mt Indon
78C2 Gunung Lawit Mt Malay
78C4 Gunung Lawu Mt Indon
78D2 Gunung Menyapa Mt Indon
78D2 Gunung Niapa Mt Indon
78A3 Gunung Patah Mt Indon
78C4 Gunung Raung Mt Indon
78A3 Gunung Resag Mt Indon
78D3 Gunung Sarempaka Mt Indon
78C4 Gunung Sumbing Mt Indon
77C5 Gunung Tahan Mt Malay
78A2 Gunung Talakmau Mt Indon
100A2 Gunza Angola
72D3 Guoyang China
84D2 Gurdāspur India
84D3 Gurgaon India
86A1 Gurkha Nepal
92C2 Gürün Turk
31B2 Gurupi R Brazil

Guruve

100C2 **Guruve** Zim
72A1 **Gurvan Sayhan Uul**
 Upland Mongolia
61H4 **Gur'yev** Kazakhstan
97C3 **Gusau** Nig
58C2 **Gusev** Russian Fed
74A3 **Gushan** China
61F2 **Gus'khrustalnyy**
 Russian Fed
12G3 **Gustavus** USA
22B2 **Gustine** USA
11B3 **Guston** USA
56B2 **Gütersloh** Germany
18C2 **Guthrie** Kentucky,
 USA
18A2 **Guthrie** Oklahoma,
 USA
23B1 **Gutiérrez Zamora**
 Mexico
33F3 **Guyana** Republic,
 S America
102F4 **Guyana Basin**
 Atlantic O
72C1 **Guyang** China
48B3 **Guyenne** Region,
 France
9C3 **Guymon** USA
109D2 **Guyra** Aust
72B2 **Guyuan** China
109C2 **Gwabegar** Aust
85D3 **Gwalior** India
100B3 **Gwanda** Zim
98C2 **Gwane** Zaire
82A3 **Gwardar** Pak
45B1 **Gweebarra B**
 Irish Rep
89G9 **Gwelo** Zim
43C4 **Gwent** County,
 Wales
100B2 **Gweru** Zim
109C1 **Gwydir** R Aust
43C3 **Gwynedd** Wales
65F5 **Gyandzha**
 Azerbaijan
86B1 **Gyangzê** China
68B3 **Gyaring Hu** L China
64J2 **Gydanskiy Poluostrov**
 Pen Russian Fed
86B1 **Gyirong** China
6F3 **Gyldenløues**
 Greenland
109D1 **Gympie** Aust
59B3 **Gyöngyös** Hung
59B3 **Györ** Hung

H

38K6 **Haapajärvi** Fin
60B2 **Haapsalu** Estonia
56A2 **Haarlem** Neth
46D1 **Haarstrang** Region,
 Germany
25D2 **Habana** Cuba
86C2 **Habiganj** Bang
74D4 **Hachijö-jima** / Japan
75B1 **Hachiman** Japan
74E2 **Hachinohe** Japan
75B1 **Hachioji** Japan
16B2 **Hackettstown** USA
108A2 **Hack,Mt** Aust
42C2 **Haddington** Scot
108B1 **Haddon Corner** Aust
108B1 **Haddon Downs** Aust
97D3 **Hadejia** Nig
97C3 **Hadejia** R Nig
94B2 **Hadera** Israel
56B1 **Haderslev** Den
81D4 **Hadiboh** Socotra
4H2 **Hadley B** Can
73B5 **Hadong** Vietnam
81C4 **Haḍramawt** Region,
 Yemen
56C1 **Hadsund** Den
74B3 **Haeju** N Korea
91A4 **Hafar al Bātin**
 S Arabia
6D2 **Haffners Bjerg** Mt
 Greenland
84C2 **Hafizabad** Pak
86C1 **Häflong** India
38A2 **Hafnarfjörður** Iceland
12B3 **Hagemeister** I USA
56B2 **Hagen** Germany
15C3 **Hagerstown** USA
75A2 **Hagi** Japan

73A5 **Ha Giang** Vietnam
46D2 **Hagondange** France
45B2 **Hags Hd** C Irish Rep
46D2 **Haguenan** France
96A2 **Hagunia** Well Mor
69G4 **Haha-jima** / Japan
68B3 **Hah Xil Hu** L China
74A2 **Haicheng** China
76D1 **Hai Duong** Viet
94B2 **Haifa** Israel
94B2 **Haifa,B of** Israel
72D2 **Hai He** R China
73C5 **Haikang** China
76E1 **Haikou** China
80C3 **Ha'il** S Arabia
86C2 **Hailâkândi** India
63D3 **Hailar** China
74B2 **Hailong** China
69E2 **Hailun** China
38J5 **Hailuoto** I Fin
76D2 **Hainan** I China
12G3 **Haines** USA
12G2 **Haines Junction**
 Can
59B3 **Hainfeld** Austria
73B5 **Haiphong** Vietnam
26C3 **Haiti** Republic,
 Caribbean S
95C3 **Haiya** Sudan
72A2 **Haiyan** China
72B2 **Haiyuan** China
72D3 **Haizhou Wan** B
 China
59C3 **Hajdúböszörmény**
 Hung
75B1 **Hajiki-saki** Pt Japan
86C2 **Haka** Burma
21C4 **Hakalau** Hawaiian Is
93D2 **Hakkari** Turk
74E2 **Hakodate** Japan
 Hakwa = Haka
75B1 **Hakui** Japan
75B1 **Haku-san** Mt Japan
92C2 **Halab** Syria
93E3 **Halabja** Iraq
95C2 **Halaib** Sudan
94C1 **Halba** Leb
68B2 **Halban** Mongolia
56C2 **Halberstadt**
 Germany
79B3 **Halcon,Mt** Phil
39G7 **Halden** Nor
86B2 **Haldia** India
84D3 **Haldwäni** India
13C1 **Halfway** R Can
7D5 **Halifax** Can
42D3 **Halifax** Eng
6D1 **Hall Basin** Sd Can
6B3 **Hall Beach** Can
46C1 **Halle** Belg
56C2 **Halle** Germany
112B1 **Halley** Base Ant
39F6 **Hallingdal** R Nor
8D1 **Hall Pen** Can
106B2 **Hall's Creek** Aust
71D3 **Halmahera** I Indon
39G7 **Halmstad** Sweden
56B2 **Haltern** Germany
38J5 **Halti** Mt Nor
42C2 **Haltwhistle** Eng
91B4 **Halul** I Qatar
94B3 **Haluza** Hist Site
 Israel
75A2 **Hamada** Japan
96C2 **Hamada de Tinrhert**
 Desert Region Alg
96B2 **Hamada du Dra**
 Upland Alg
90A3 **Hamadan** Iran
96B2 **Hamada Tounassine**
 Region, Alg
92C2 **Hamāh** Syria
75B2 **Hamamatsu** Japan
39G6 **Hamar** Nor
87C3 **Hambantota**
 Sri Lanka
19B3 **Hamburg** Arkansas,
 USA
18A1 **Hamburg** Iowa, USA
16B2 **Hamburg**
 Pennsylvania, USA
56B2 **Hamburg** Germany
16C2 **Hamden** USA
39J6 **Hämeenlinna** Fin

106A3 **Hamersley Range**
 Mts Aust
74B2 **Hamgyong Sanmaek**
 Mts N Korea
74B2 **Hamhŭng** N Korea
64H1 **Hami** China
94B1 **Hamidiyah** Syria
108B3 **Hamilton** Aust
14C2 **Hamilton** Can
110C1 **Hamilton** NZ
14B3 **Hamilton** Ohio, USA
42B2 **Hamilton** Scot
22B2 **Hamilton,Mt** USA
38K6 **Hamina** Fin
86A1 **Hamirpur** India
56B2 **Hamm** Germany
95A2 **Hammādāh al Hamra**
 Upland Libya
38H6 **Hammerdal** Sweden
38J4 **Hammerfest** Nor
14A2 **Hammond** Illinois,
 USA
19B3 **Hammond** Louisiana,
 USA
16B3 **Hammonton** USA
111B3 **Hampden** NZ
43D4 **Hampshire** County,
 Eng
19B3 **Hampton** Arkansas,
 USA
91C4 **Hämün-e Jaz Mürian**
 L Iran
84B3 **Hamun-i-Lora** Salt L
 Pak
21C4 **Hana** Hawaiian Is
21C4 **Hanalei** Hawaiian Is
74C2 **Hanamaki** Japan
72C2 **Hanchuan** China
73C3 **Hanchuan** China
15C3 **Hancock** Maryland,
 USA
10B2 **Hancock** Michigan,
 USA
75B2 **Handa** Japan
72C2 **Handan** China
99D3 **Handeni** Tanz
72B2 **Hanggin Qi** China
39J7 **Hangö** Fin
73E3 **Hangzhou** China
73E3 **Hangzhou Wan** B
 China
111B2 **Hanmer Springs** NZ
13E2 **Hanna** Can
18B2 **Hannibal** USA
56B2 **Hannover** Germany
39G7 **Hanöbukten** B
 Sweden
76D1 **Hanoi** Viet
16A3 **Hanover** USA
29B6 **Hanover** I Chile
72B3 **Han Shui** China
73C3 **Han Shui** R China
85D3 **Hänsi** India
68D2 **Hantay** Mongolia
72B3 **Hanzhong** China
86B2 **Häora** India
38J5 **Haparanda** Sweden
86C1 **Häpoli** India
92C2 **Haqi** S Arabia
91A5 **Haradh** S Arabia
99E2 **Hara Fanna** Eth
75C1 **Haramachi** Japan
101C2 **Harare** Zim
98C1 **Harazé** Chad
14B2 **Harbor Beach** USA
85D4 **Harda** India
39F6 **Hardangerfjord** Inlet
 Nor
46D2 **Hardt** Region,
 Germany
108A2 **Hardwicke B** Aust
99E2 **Harer** Eth
99E2 **Hargeysa** Somalia
94B3 **Har Hakippa** Mt
 Israel
68B3 **Harhu** L China
78A3 **Hari** R Indon
75A2 **Harima-nada** B
 Japan
56B2 **Harlingen** Neth
9D4 **Harlingen** USA
43E4 **Harlow** Eng
94B2 **Har Meron** Mt Israel

20C2 **Harney Basin** USA
20C2 **Harney L** USA
38H6 **Härnösand** Sweden
63B3 **Har Nuur** L
 Mongolia
97B4 **Harper** Lib
12F2 **Harper,Mt** USA
15C3 **Harpers Ferry** USA
94B3 **Har Ramon** Mt Israel
7C4 **Harricanaw** R Can
16B3 **Harrington** USA
7E4 **Harrington Harbour**
 Can
44A3 **Harris** District Scot
18C2 **Harrisburg** Illinois,
 USA
16A2 **Harrisburg**
 Pennsylvania, USA
101G1 **Harrismith** S Africa
18B2 **Harrison** USA
15C3 **Harrisonburg** USA
7E4 **Harrison,C** Can
13C3 **Harrison** L Can
18B2 **Harrisonville** USA
44A3 **Harris,Sound of** Chan
 Scot
14B2 **Harrisville** USA
42D3 **Harrogate** Eng
94B3 **Har Saggi** Mt Israel
38H5 **Harstad** Nor
12G2 **Hart** R Can
39F6 **Härteigen** Mt Nor
16C2 **Hartford** Connecticut,
 USA
14A2 **Hartford** Michigan,
 USA
38G6 **Hartkjølen** Mt Nor
108A2 **Hart,L** Aust
43B4 **Hartland Pt** Eng
42D2 **Hartlepool** Eng
19A3 **Hartshorne** USA
17B1 **Hartwell Res** USA
101F1 **Hartz** R S Africa
68B2 **Har Us Nuur** L
 Mongolia
43E4 **Harwich** Eng
84D3 **Haryana** State, India
94B3 **Hasä** Jordan
94B2 **Häsbaiya** Leb
43D4 **Haselmere** Eng
75B2 **Hashimoto** Japan
90A2 **Hashtgar** Iran
90A2 **Hashtrūd** Iran
87B2 **Hassan** India
56B2 **Hasselt** Belg
96B2 **Hassi Inifel** Alg
96B2 **Hassi Mdakane** Well
 Alg
96C1 **Hassi Messaoud** Alg
108C3 **Hastings** Aust
43E4 **Hastings** Eng
8D2 **Hastings** Nebraska,
 USA
110C1 **Hastings** NZ
108B2 **Hatfield** Aust
12B1 **Hatham Inlet** USA
85D3 **Häthras** India
76D2 **Ha Tinh** Viet
108B2 **Hattah** Aust
11C3 **Hatteras,C** USA
19C3 **Hattiesburg** USA
59B3 **Hatvan** Hung
76D3 **Hau Bon** Viet
99E2 **Haud** Region, Eth
39F7 **Haugesund** Nor
110C1 **Hauhungaroa Range**
 Mts NZ
13F1 **Haultain** R Can
110B1 **Hauraki G** NZ
111A3 **Hauroko,L** NZ
47C1 **Hausstock** Mt Switz
96B1 **Haut Atlas** Mts Mor
98C2 **Haute Kotto** Region,
 CAR
46C1 **Hautes Fagnes** Mts
 Belg
46B1 **Hautmont** Belg
96B1 **Hauts Plateaux** Mts
 Alg
90D3 **Hauzdar** Iran
18B1 **Havana** USA
 Havana = Habana
87B3 **Havankulam**
 Sri Lanka

110C1 Havelock North NZ
43B4 Haverfordwest
      Wales
16D1 Haverhill USA
87B2 Haveri India
16C2 Haverstraw USA
59B3 Havlíčkův Brod
      Czech Republic
8C2 Havre USA
16A3 Havre de Grace USA
7D4 Havre-St-Pierre Can
54C2 Havsa Turk
21C4 Hawaii I Hawaiian Is
21C4 Hawaii Volcanoes
      Nat Pk Hawaiian Is
111A2 Hawea,L NZ
110B1 Hawera NZ
42C2 Hawick Scot
111A2 Hawkdun Range Mts
      NZ
110C1 Hawke B NZ
109D2 Hawke,C Aust
108A2 Hawker Aust
76B1 Hawng Luk Burma
93D3 Hawr al Habbaniyah
      L Iraq
93D3 Hawr al Hammār L
      Iraq
21B2 Hawthorne USA
108B2 Hay Aust
5G3 Hay R Can
46D2 Hayange France
4B3 Haycock USA
7A4 Hayes R Can
6D2 Hayes Halvø Region
      Greenland
12E2 Hayes,Mt USA
5G3 Hay River Can
18A2 Haysville USA
22A2 Hayward California,
      USA
86B2 Hazārībāg India
46B1 Hazebrouck France
19B3 Hazelhurst USA
4G2 Hazel Str Can
5F4 Hazelton Can
13B1 Hazelton Mts Can
6C1 Hazen L Can
94B3 Hazeva Israel
16D2 Hazleton USA
22A1 Healdsburg USA
108C3 Healesville Aust
12E2 Healy USA
108B6 Heard I Indian O
19A3 Hearne USA
10B2 Hearst Can
72D2 Hebei Province,
      China
109C1 Hebel Aust
72C2 Hebi China
72C2 Hebian China
94B3 Hebron Israel
18A1 Hebron Nebraska,
      USA
5E4 Hecate Str Can
12H3 Heceta I USA
73B5 Hechi China
73C5 Hechuan China
4G2 Hecla and Griper B
      Can
111C2 Hector,Mt NZ
38G6 Hede Sweden
39H6 Hedemora Sweden
20C1 He Devil Mt USA
56B2 Heerenveen Neth
46C1 Heerlen Neth
      Hefa = Haifa
73D3 Hefei China
73B4 Hefeng China
69F2 Hegang China
75B1 Hegura-jima I Japan
94B3 Heidan R Jordan
56B2 Heide Germany
101G1 Heidelberg
      Transvaal, S Africa
57B3 Heidelberg Germany
63E2 Heihe China
101G1 Heilbron S Africa
57B3 Heilbronn Germany
56C2 Heiligenstadt
      Germany
38K6 Heinola Fin
73B4 Hejiang China
6J3 Hekla Mt Iceland

76C1 Hekou Viet
73A5 Hekou Yaozou
      Zizhixian China
72B2 Helan China
72B2 Helan Shan Mt
      China
19B3 Helena Arkansas,
      USA
8B2 Helena Montana,
      USA
22D3 Helendale USA
71E3 Helen Reef I
      Pacific O
44B3 Helensburgh Scot
91B4 Helleh R Iran
51B2 Hellín Spain
20C1 Hells Canyon R USA
46D1 Hellweg Region,
      Germany
22B2 Helm USA
80E2 Helmand R Afghan
100A3 Helmeringhausen
      Namibia
46C1 Helmond Neth
44C2 Helmsdale Scot
74B2 Helong China
39G7 Helsingborg Sweden
      Helsingfors = Helsinki
56C1 Helsingør Den
38J6 Helsinki Fin
43B4 Helston Eng
92B4 Helwân Egypt
19A3 Hempstead USA
39H7 Hemse Sweden
72A3 Henan China
72C3 Henan Province,
      China
110B1 Hen and Chicken Is
      NZ
14A3 Henderson Kentucky,
      USA
9B3 Henderson Nevada,
      USA
19B3 Henderson Texas,
      USA
73E5 Heng-ch'un Taiwan
68B4 Hengduan Shan Mts
      China
56B2 Hengelo Neth
72B2 Hengshan China
72D2 Hengshui China
76D1 Heng Xian China
73C4 Hengyang China
77A4 Henhoaha Nicobar Is
43D4 Henley-on-Thames
      Eng
16B3 Henlopen,C USA
7B4 Henrietta Maria,C
      Can
18A2 Henryetta USA
112C2 Henryk Arctowski
      Base Ant
68C2 Hentiyn Nuruu Mts
      Mongolia
76B2 Henzada Burma
73B5 Hepu China
80E2 Herat Afghan
5H4 Herbert Can
110C2 Herbertville NZ
46E1 Herborn Germany
26A4 Heredia Costa Rica
43C3 Hereford Eng
43C3 Hereford & Worcester
      County, Eng
46C1 Herentals Belg
47B1 Héricourt France
18A2 Herington USA
111A3 Heriot NZ
47C1 Herisau Switz
15D2 Herkimer USA
44E1 Herma Ness Pen
      Scot
109C2 Hermidale Aust
111B2 Hermitage NZ
      Hermon,Mt = Jebel
      ash Shaykh
24A2 Hermosillo Mexico
16A2 Herndon
      Pennsylvania, USA
22C2 Herndon California,
      USA
46D1 Herne Germany
56B1 Herning Den

90A2 Herowābad Iran
50A2 Herrera del Duque
      Spain
17B2 Hershey USA
43D4 Hertford County, Eng
94B2 Herzliyya Israel
46C1 Hesbaye Region,
      Belg
46B1 Hesdin France
72B2 Heshui China
22D3 Hesperia USA
12H2 Hess R Can
57B2 Hessen State,
      Germany
22C2 Hetch Hetchy Res
      USA
42C2 Hexham Eng
73C5 He Xian China
73C5 Heyuan China
108B3 Heywood Aust
72D2 Heze China
17B2 Hialeah USA
10A2 Hibbing USA
110C1 Hicks Bay NZ
109C3 Hicks,Pt Aust
23B1 Hidalgo State,
      Mexico
22D3 Hidalgo del Parral
      Mexico
24B2 Hidalgo del Parral
      Mexico
35B1 Hidrolândia Brazil
96A2 Hierro I Canary Is
75C1 Higashine Japan
74B4 Higashi-suidō Str
      Japan
20B2 High Desert USA
19B4 High Island USA
13D1 Highland Region,
      Scot
22D3 Highland USA
22C1 Highland Park Mt
      USA
17B2 Highlands Falls USA
11B3 High Point USA
13D1 High Prairie Can
5G4 High River Can
17B2 High Springs USA
16B2 Hightstown USA
43D4 High Wycombe Eng
39J7 Hiiumaa I Estonia
80B3 Hijāz Region,
      S Arabia
75B2 Hikigawa Japan
75B1 Hikone Japan
110B1 Hikurangi NZ
9C4 Hildago Mexico
24C2 Hildalgo del Parral
      Mexico
56B2 Hildesheim Germany
27R3 Hillaby,Mt Barbados
56C1 Hillerod Den
14B3 Hillsboro Ohio, USA
20B1 Hillsboro Oregon,
      USA
19A3 Hillsboro Texas, USA
44E1 Hillswick Scot
21C4 Hilo Hawaiian Is
93C2 Hilvan Turk
56B2 Hilversum Neth
84D2 Himachal Pradesh
      State, India
82B3 Himalaya Mts Asia
85C4 Himatnagar India
74C4 Himeji Japan
74C3 Himi Japan
92C3 Himş Syria
12E2 Hinchinbrook
      Entrance USA
12E2 Hinchinbrook I USA
85D3 Hindaun India
84B1 Hindu Kush Mts
      Afghan
87B2 Hindupur India
13D1 Hines Creek Can
85D4 Hinganghāt India
69E2 Hinggan Ling Upland
      China
87B3 Hingol R Pak
85D5 Hingoli India
38H5 Hinneya I Nor
16C1 Hinsdale USA
13D2 Hinton Can
34B2 Hipolito Itrogoyen
      Arg

86A2 Hirakud Res India
92B2 Hirfanli Baraji Res
      Turk
87B2 Hirihar India
74E2 Hirosaki Japan
74C4 Hiroshima Japan
46C2 Hirson France
54C2 Hirşova Rom
56B1 Hirtshals Den
84D3 Hisār India
26C3 Hispaniola I
      Caribbean S
94C1 Hisyah Syria
93D3 Hīt Iraq
74E3 Hitachi Japan
75C1 Hitachi-Ota Japan
43D4 Hitchin Eng
38F6 Hitra I Nor
75A2 Hiuchi-nada B Japan
75A2 Hiwasa Japan
56B1 Hjørring Den
76B1 Hka R Burma
97C4 Ho Ghana
76D1 Hoa Binh Viet
76D3 Hoa Da Viet
109C4 Hobart Aust
9C3 Hobbs USA
13C1 Hobro Den
53C2 Hobson L Can
99E2 Hobyo Somalia
76D3 Ho Chi Minh Viet
57C3 Hochkonig Mt
      Austria
54B1 Hódmező'hely Hung
59B3 Hodonin
      Czech Republic
74B2 Hoeryong N Korea
57C2 Hof Germany
38B2 Hofsjökull Mts
      Iceland
74C4 Hōfu Japan
96C2 Hoggar Upland Alg
46D1 Hohe Acht Mt
      Germany
72C1 Hohhot China
6J3 Höhn Iceland
68B3 Hoh Sai Hu L China
68B2 Hoh Xil Shan Mts
      China
99D2 Hoima Uganda
86C1 Hojāi India
75A2 Hojo Japan
110B1 Hokianga Harbour B
      NZ
111B2 Hokitika NZ
74E2 Hokkaidō Japan
90C2 Hokmābad Iran
109C3 Holbrook Aust
9B3 Holbrook USA
19A2 Holdenville USA
87B2 Hole Narsipur India
27R3 Holetown Barbados
26B2 Holguin Cuba
111B2 Holitika NZ
12C2 Holitna R USA
59B3 Hollabrunn Austria
14A2 Holland USA
22B2 Hollister USA
19C3 Holly Springs USA
22C3 Hollywood
      California, USA
17B2 Hollywood Florida,
      USA
4G2 Holman Island Can
38J6 Holmsund Sweden
94B2 Holon Israel
56B1 Holstebro Den
6E3 Holsteinborg
      Greenland
12C2 Holt USA
18A2 Holton USA
12C2 Holy Cross USA
42B3 Holyhead Wales
42D2 Holy I Eng
43B3 Holy I Wales
16C1 Holyoke
      Massachusetts, USA
86C2 Homalin Burma
6D3 Home B Can
12D3 Homer Alaska, USA
19B3 Homer Louisiana,
      USA
111A2 Homer Tunnel NZ
17B1 Homerville USA

Homestead

17B2 **Homestead** USA
17A1 **Homewood** USA
87B1 **Homnābād** India
101C3 **Homoine** Mozam
25D3 **Hondo** R Mexico
25D3 **Honduras, Republic,** Cent America
25D3 **Honduras,G of** Honduras
39G6 **Henefoss** Nor
15C2 **Honesdale** USA
21A1 **Honey L** USA
76C1 **Hong** R Viet
76D1 **Hon Gai** Viet
73A4 **Hongguo** China
73C4 **Hong Hu** L China
72B2 **Honghui** China
73C4 **Hongjiang** China
73C5 **Hong Kong** Colony, S E Asia
68D2 **Hongor** Mongolia
73B5 **Hongshui He** R China
72A3 **Hongyuan** China
72D3 **Hongze Hu** L China
107E1 **Honiara** Solomon Is
77C4 **Hon Khoai** I Camb
76D3 **Hon Lan** I Viet
38K4 **Honningsvåg** Nor
21C4 **Honolulu** Hawaiian Is
77C4 **Hon Panjang** I Viet
74D3 **Honshu** I Japan
20B1 **Hood,Mt** USA
20B1 **Hood River** USA
45C2 **Hook Head** C Irish Rep
12G3 **Hoonah** USA
12A2 **Hooper Bay** USA
101G1 **Hoopstad** S Africa
56A2 **Hoorn** Neth
9B3 **Hoover Dam** USA
12E2 **Hope** Alaska, USA
19B3 **Hope** Arkansas, USA
13C3 **Hope** Can
7D4 **Hopedale** Can
64D2 **Hopen** I Barents S
6D3 **Hopes Advance,C** Can
108B3 **Hopetoun** Aust
100B3 **Hopetown** S Africa
18C2 **Hopkinsville** USA
20B1 **Hoquiam** USA
93D1 **Horasan** Turk
99F1 **Hordiyo** Somalia
47C1 **Horgen** Switz
105H5 **Horizon Depth** Pacific O
91C4 **Hormuz,Str of** Oman/ Iran
59B3 **Horn** Austria
6H3 **Horn** C Iceland
38H5 **Hornavan** L Sweden
19B3 **Hornbeck** USA
20B2 **Hornbrook** USA
111B2 **Hornby** NZ
7B5 **Hornepayne** Can
42D3 **Hornsea** Eng
72B1 **Horn Uul** Mt Mongolia
30E3 **Horqueta** Par
15C2 **Horseheads** USA
56C1 **Horsens** Den
20B1 **Horseshoe Bay** Can
108B3 **Horsham** Aust
43D4 **Horsham** Eng
39G7 **Horten** Nor
4F3 **Horton** R Can
78C2 **Hose Mts** Malay
85D4 **Hoshangābād** India
85D3 **Hoshiārpur** India
87B1 **Hospet** India
29C7 **Hoste** I Chile
82B2 **Hotan** China
19B3 **Hot Springs** Arkansas, USA
8C2 **Hot Springs** S. Dakota, USA
4G3 **Hottah L** Can
46A2 **Houdan** France
72C2 **Houma** China
19B4 **Houma** USA
16C2 **Housatonic** R USA
13B2 **Houston** Can

19C3 **Houston** Mississippi, NZ
19A4 **Houston** Texas, USA
106A3 **Houtman** Is Aust
68B2 **Hovd** Mongolia
68C1 **Hövsgol Nuur** L Mongolia
14A2 **Howard City** USA
12C1 **Howard P** USA
109C3 **Howe,C** Aust
101H1 **Howick** S Africa
44C2 **Hoy** I Scot
39F6 **Høyanger** Nor
59B2 **Hradec-Králové** Czech Republic
59B3 **Hranice** Czech Republic
59B3 **Hron** R Slovakia
73E5 **Hsin-chu** Taiwan
73E5 **Hsüeh Shan** Mt Taiwan
72B2 **Huachi** China
32B6 **Huacho** Peru
72C1 **Huade** China
72D3 **Huaibei** China
72D3 **Huaibin** China
72D3 **Huai He** R China
73C4 **Huaihua** China
73C5 **Huaiji** China
72D3 **Huainan** China
69E4 **Hua Hin** Taiwan
32B5 **Huallaga** R Peru
32B5 **Huallanca** Peru
32B5 **Huamachuco** Peru
100A2 **Huambo** Angola
30C2 **Huanay** Bol
32B5 **Huancabamba** Peru
32B6 **Huancavelica** Peru
32B6 **Huancayo** Peru
73D3 **Huangchuan** China
 Huang Hai = Yellow S
72D2 **Huang He** R China
72B2 **Huangling** China
76D2 **Huanglliu** China
73C3 **Huangpi** China
73D4 **Huangshan** China
73D3 **Huangshi** China
34C3 **Huanguelén** Arg
73E4 **Huangyan** China
74B2 **Huanren** China
32B5 **Huánuco** Peru
30C2 **Huanuni** Bol
72B2 **Huan Xian** China
32B5 **Huaráz** Peru
32B6 **Huarmey** Peru
32B5 **Huascarán** Mt Peru
30B4 **Huasco** Chile
23D1 **Huatusco** Mexico
23B1 **Huauchinango** Mexico
23B2 **Huautla** Mexico
72C2 **Hua Xian** China
24B2 **Huayapan** R Mexico
73C3 **Hubei** Province, China
87B1 **Hubli** India
34C3 **Hucal** Arg
74B2 **Hŭch'ang** N Korea
42D3 **Huddersfield** Eng
39H6 **Hudiksvall** Sweden
17B2 **Hudson** Florida, USA
14B2 **Hudson** Michigan, USA
16C1 **Hudson** New York, USA
16C1 **Hudson** R USA
7B4 **Hudson B** Can
5H4 **Hudson Bay** Can
13C1 **Hudson's Hope** Can
6C3 **Hudson Str** Can
76D2 **Hue** Viet
23B1 **Huejutla** Mexico
50A2 **Huelva** Spain
51B2 **Huércano** Mexico
51B2 **Húercal Overa** Spain
51B1 **Huesca** Spain
23B2 **Huexotla** Hist Site Mexico
107D3 **Hughenden** Aust
12D1 **Hughes** USA
86B2 **Hugli** R India
19A3 **Hugo** USA
73D4 **Hui'an** China

110C1 **Huiarau Range** Mts NZ
74B2 **Huich'ŏn** N Korea
74B2 **Huifa He** R China
32B3 **Huila** Mt Colombia
73D5 **Huilai** China
73A4 **Huili** China
73A4 **Huinan** China
34C2 **Huinca Renancó** Arg
25C3 **Huixtla** Mexico
73A4 **Huize** China
73C5 **Huizhou** China
23B2 **Hujuapan de Léon** Mexico
69F2 **Hulin** China
15C1 **Hull** Can
42D3 **Hull** Eng
58B1 **Hultsfred** Sweden
63D3 **Hulun Nur** L China
69E1 **Huma** China
13E5 **Humaita** Brazil
100B4 **Humansdorp** S Africa
42D3 **Humber** R Eng
42D3 **Humberside** County, Eng
5H4 **Humboldt** Can
20C2 **Humboldt** R USA
20B2 **Humboldt B** USA
6D2 **Humboldt Gletscher** Gl Greenland
21B2 **Humboldt L** USA
108C1 **Humeburn** Aust
109C3 **Hume,L** Aust
100A2 **Humpata** Angola
22C2 **Humphreys** USA
38A1 **Hunaflói** B Iceland
73C4 **Hunan** Province, China
74C2 **Hunchun** China
13C2 **Hundred Mile House** Can
54B1 **Hunedoara** Rom
59B3 **Hungary** Republic, Europe
108B1 **Hungerford** Aust
74B3 **Hŭngnam** N Korea
74B2 **Hunjiang** China
58B2 **Hunsrück** Mts, Germany
109D2 **Hunter** R Aust
13B2 **Hunter** I Can
109C4 **Hunter Is** Aust
14A3 **Huntingburg** USA
43D3 **Huntingdon** Eng
14A2 **Huntington** Indiana, USA
14B3 **Huntington** W Virginia, USA
22C4 **Huntington Beach** USA
22C2 **Huntington L** USA
110C1 **Huntly** NZ
44C3 **Huntly** Scot
12J2 **Hunt,Mt** Can
108A1 **Hunt Pen** Aust
17A1 **Huntsville** Alabama, USA
15C1 **Huntsville** Can
19A3 **Huntsville** Texas, USA
76D2 **Huong Khe** Viet
71F4 **Huon Peninsula** Pen PNG
109C4 **Huonville** Anst
14B1 **Hurd,C** Can
80B3 **Hurghada** Egypt
8D2 **Huron** S. Dakota, USA
14B1 **Huron,L** Can/USA
34A2 **Hurtado** Chile
111B2 **Hurunui** R NZ
38B1 **Húsavik** Iceland
54C1 **Huşi** Rom
39G7 **Huskvarna** Sweden
12C1 **Huslia** USA
93D3 **Husn** Jordan
56B2 **Husum** Aust
109C1 **Hutton,Mt** Aust
72D2 **Hutuo He** R China
46C1 **Huy** Belg
72A2 **Huzhu** China
52C2 **Hvar** I Croatia
100B2 **Hwange** Zim

100B2 **Hwange Nat Pk** Zim
15D2 **Hyannis** USA
68B2 **Hyarvas Nuur** L Mongolia
5E4 **Hydaburg** Can
16C2 **Hyde Park** USA
87B1 **Hyderābād** India
85B3 **Hyderabad** Pak
49D3 **Hyères** France
12J2 **Hyland** R Can
8B2 **Hyndman Peak** Mt USA
38K6 **Hyrynsalmi** Fin
13D1 **Hythe** Can
74C4 **Hyūga** Japan
39J6 **Hyvikää** Fin

I

31C4 **Iaçu** Brazil
54C2 **Ialomiţa** R Rom
54C1 **Iaşi** Rom
97C4 **Ibadan** Nig
32B3 **Ibagué** Colombia
54B2 **Ibar** R Montenegro/ Serbia, Yugos
32B3 **Ibarra** Ecuador
35B1 **Ibiá** Brazil
30E4 **Ibicuí** R Brazil
34D2 **Ibicuy** Arg
51C2 **Ibiza** Spain
51C2 **Ibiza** I Spain
101D2 **Ibo** Mozam
31C4 **Ibotirama** Brazil
91C5 **'Ibrī** Oman
32B6 **Ica** Peru
32D4 **Içá** R Brazil
32D3 **Icana** Brazil
38A1 **Iceland** Republic, N Atlantic O
13C2 **Ice Mt** Can
87A1 **Ichalkaranji** India
74E3 **Ichihara** Japan
75B1 **Ichinomiya** Japan
74E3 **Ichinoseki** Japan
12F3 **Icy B** USA
4B2 **Icy C** USA
19B3 **Idabell** USA
8B2 **Idaho Falls** USA
20B2 **Idanha** USA
46D2 **Idar Oberstein** Germany
95A2 **Idehan Marzūg** Desert Libya
95A2 **Idehan Ubari** Desert Libya
96C2 **Idelès** Alg
68B2 **Iderlym Gol** R Mongolia
95C2 **Idfu** Egypt
55B3 **Idhi Oros** Mt Greece
55B3 **Idhra** I Greece
98B3 **Idiofa** Zaire
12C2 **Iditarod** R USA
92C2 **Idlib** Syria
37C3 **Idritsa** Russian Fed
100B4 **Idutywa** S Africa
55C3 **Ierápetra** Greece
46B1 **Ieper** Belg
63D2 **Iet Oktyobr'ya** Russian Fed
99D3 **Ifakara** Tanz
71F3 **Ifalik** I Pacific O
101D3 **Ifanadiana** Madag
97C4 **Ife** Nig
97C3 **Iférouane** Niger
78C2 **Igan** Malay
35B2 **Igaranava** Brazil
93E2 **Igdir** Iran
39H6 **Iggesund** Sweden
34B2 **Iglesia** Arg
53A3 **Iglesias** Sardegna
6B3 **Igloolik** Can
12C2 **Ignace** Can
55B2 **Igoumenitsa** Greece
61H2 **Igra** Russian Fed
23B2 **Iguala** Mexico
35B2 **Iguape** Brazil
31D3 **Iguatu** Brazil
98A3 **Iguéla** Gabon
101D3 **Ihosy** Madag
74D3 **Iida** Japan
75B1 **Iide-san** Mt Japan
38K6 **Iisalmi** Fin

142

75A2 Iizuka Japan
97C4 Ijebu Ode Nig
56B2 Ijsselmeer S Neth
55C3 Ikaria I Greece
74E2 Ikeda Japan
98C3 Ikela Zaïre
54B2 Ikhtiman Bulg
12D3 Ikolik,C USA
101D2 Ikopa R Madag
79B2 Ilagan Phil
90A3 Ilâm Iran
47C1 Ilanz Switz
13F1 Ile a la Crosse Can
13F1 Ile a la Crosse,L Can
89G8 Ilebo Zaïre
96D1 Ile de Jerba I Tunisia
48B2 Ile de Noirmoutier I France
48B2 Ile de Ré I France
107F3 Ile des Pins I Nouvelle Calédonie
48A2 Ile d'Ouessant I France
48B2 Ile d'Yeu I France
61J3 Ilek R Russian Fed
107F2 Iles Bélep Nouvelle Calédonie
107E2 Iles Chesterfield Nouvelle Calédonie
49D3 Iles d'Hyères I France
43B4 Ilfracombe Eng
92B1 Ilgaz Dağlari Mts Turk
101C3 Ilha Bazaruto I Mozam
33G3 Ilha De Maracá I Brazil
33G4 Ilha de Marajó I Brazil
35B2 Ilha de São Sebastião I Brazil
33G6 Ilha do Bananal Region Brazil
35C2 Ilha Grande I Brazil
35B2 Ilha Santo Amaro I Brazil
96A1 Ilhas Selvegens I Atlantic O
35A2 Ilha Solteira Dam Brazil
31D4 Ilhéus Brazil
12C3 Iliamna I USA
12D2 Iliamna V USA
79B4 Iligan Phil
63C2 Ilim R Russian Fed
63C2 Ilim Russian Fed
63G3 Il'inskiy Russian Fed
55B3 Iliodhrómia I Greece
79B4 Illana B Phil
34A2 Illapel Chile
34A2 Illapel R Chile
97C3 Illéla Niger
47D1 Iller R Germany
4C4 Illiamna L USA
10A2 Illinois State, USA
18B2 Illinois R USA
96C2 Illizi Alg
30B2 Ilo Peru
79B3 Iloilo Phil
38L6 Ilomantsi Fin
97C4 Ilorin Nig
75A1 Imabari Japan
75B1 Imaichi Japan
60C1 Imatra Fin
30G4 Imbituba Brazil
99E2 Imi Eth
20C2 Imlay USA
47D1 Immenstadt Germany
52B2 Imola Italy
31B3 Imperatriz Brazil
52A2 Imperia Italy
98B2 Impfondo Congo
86C2 Imphäl India
47C1 Imst Austria
12B1 Imuruk L USA
75B1 Ina Japan
76C2 In Afahleleh Well Alg
96C2 Inamba-jima I Japan
96C2 In Amenas Alg
38K5 Inari Fin
38K5 Inarijärvi L Fin

75C1 Inawashiro-ko L Japan
96C2 In Belbel Alg
60E5 Ince Burun Pt Turk
92B2 Incekum Burun Pt Turk
74B3 Inch'ón S Korea
96B2 In Dagouber Well Mali
35B1 Indaia R Brazil
38H6 Indals R Sweden
21B2 Independence California, USA
18A2 Independence Kansas, USA
18B2 Independence Missouri, USA
78A3 Inderagiri R Indon
61H4 Inderborskiy Kazakhstan
83B3 India Federal Republic, Asia
14A2 Indiana State, USA
15C2 Indiana USA
104C6 Indian-Antarctic Ridge Indian O
14A3 Indianapolis USA
  Indian Desert = Thar Desert
7E4 Indian Harbour Can
10A84 Indian O
18B1 Indianola Iowa, USA
19B3 Indianola Mississippi, USA
35B1 Indianópolis Brazil
76D2 Indo China Region, S E Asia
70C4 Indonesia Republic, S E Asia
85D4 Indore India
78B4 Indramayu Indon
48C2 Indre R France
85B3 Indus R Pak
60D5 Inebdu Turk
96C2 In Ebeggi Well Alg
96C2 In Ecker Alg
92A1 Inegöl Turk
96D2 In Ezzane Alg
97C3 Ingal Niger
14B2 Ingersoll Can
107D2 Ingham Aust
6D2 Inglefield Land Region Can
11B1 Inglewood NZ
109D1 Inglewood Queensland, Aust
22C4 Inglewood Victoria, Aust
108B3 Inglewood Victoria, Aust
38B2 Ingólfshöfði I Iceland
57C3 Ingolstadt Germany
86B2 Ingrāj Bāzār India
96C3 In-Guezzam Well Alg
101C3 Inhambane Mozam
101C3 Inharrime Mozam
35B1 Inhumas Brazil
32D3 Inírida R Colombia
45A2 Inishbofin I Irish Rep
45A1 Inishkea I Irish Rep
45B2 Inishman I Irish Rep
45B2 Inishmore I Irish Rep
45B1 Inishmurray I Irish Rep
45C1 Inishowen District, Irish Rep
45A2 Inishshark I Irish Rep
45A2 Inishturk I Irish Rep
109C1 Injune Aust
12H3 Inklin Can
12H3 Inklin R Can
12C1 Inland L USA
47D1 Inn R Austria
108B1 Innamincka Aust
68C2 Inner Mongolia Autonomous Region, China
107D2 Innisfail Aust
12C2 Innoko R USA
57C3 Innsbruck Austria
98B3 Inongo Zaïre
58B2 Inowrocław Pol
96C2 In Salah Alg
47B1 Interlaken Switz

24C3 Intexpec Mexico
47C2 Intra Italy
78D3 Intu Indon
75C1 Inubo-saki C Japan
7C4 Inukjuak Can
4E3 Inuvik Can
4F3 Inuvik Region Can
44B3 Inveraray Scot
111A3 Invercargill NZ
109D1 Inverell Aust
13D2 Invermere Can
44B3 Inverness Scot
44C3 Inverurie Scot
108A3 Investigator Str Aust
68A1 Inya Russian Fed
21B2 Inyokern USA
98B3 Inzia R Zaïre
55B3 Ioánnina Greece
18A2 Iola USA
44A3 Iona I Scot
100A2 Iôna Nat Pk Angola
20C1 Ione USA
  Ionian Is = Iónioi Nísoi
55A3 Ionian S Italy/Greece
55B3 Iónioi Nísoi Is Greece
55C3 Ios I Greece
10A2 Iowa R USA
10A2 Iowa State, USA
18B1 Iowa City USA
35B1 Ipameri Brazil
35C1 Ipanema Brazil
61F4 Ipatovo Russian Fed
32B3 Ipiales Colombia
77C5 Ipoh Malay
30F2 Iporá Brazil
55C2 Ipsala Turk
109D1 Ipswich Aust
43E3 Ipswich Eng
16D1 Ipswich USA
30C3 Iquique Chile
32C4 Iquitos Peru
55C3 Iráklion Greece
80D2 Iran Republic, S W Asia
91D4 Iränshahr Iran
23A1 Irapuato Mexico
93D3 Iraq Republic, S W Asia
95A2 Ira Wan Watercourse Libya
94B2 Irbid Jordan
61K2 Irbit Russian Fed
36C3 Ireland Republic, NW Europe
33F3 Ireng R Guyana
74B3 Iri S Korea
71E4 Irian Jaya Province, Indon
95B3 Iriba Chad
79B3 Iriga Phil
99D3 Iringa Tanz
69E4 Iriomote I Japan
33G5 Iriri R Brazil
42B3 Irish S Eng/Irish Rep
12D1 Irkillik R USA
63C2 Irkutsk Russian Fed
65J4 Irlysh R Kazakhstan
108A2 Iron Knob Aust
14A1 Iron Mountain USA
107D2 Iron Range Aust
14A1 Iron River USA
14B3 Irontown USA
10A2 Ironwood USA
10B2 Iroquois Falls Can
75B2 Iro-zaki C Japan
17B1 Irvine Scot
44B3 Irvine Scot
79B4 Isabela Phil
32J7 Isabela I Ecuador
4H2 Isachsen Can
4H2 Isachsen,C Can
6H3 Ísafjörður Iceland
74C4 Isahaya Japan
98C2 Isangi Zaïre
47D1 Isar R Germany
47D1 Isarco R Italy
44E1 Isbister Scot
47D1 Ischgl Austria
53B2 Ischia I Italy
75B2 Ise Japan

47D2 Iseo Italy
46D1 Iserlohn Germany
53B2 Isernia Italy
75B2 Ise-wan B Japan
69E4 Ishigaki I Japan
74E2 Ishikari R Japan
74E2 Ishikari-wan B Japan
65H4 Ishim Russian Fed
65H4 Ishim R Kazakhstan
74E3 Ishinomaki Japan
75C1 Ishioka Japan
84C1 Ishkashim Afghan
14A1 Ishpeming USA
65J4 Isil'kul Russian Fed
99D2 Isiolo Kenya
98C2 Isiro Zaïre
92C2 Iskenderun Turk
92C2 Iskenderun Körfezi B Turk
92B1 Iskilip Turk
65K4 Iskitim Russian Fed
54B2 Iskur R Bulg
12H3 Iskut R Can/USA
23B2 Isla Mexico
34C3 Isla Bermejo I Arg
27E4 Isla Blanquilla Ven
32A2 Isla Coiba I Panama
9B4 Isla de Cedros I Mexico
29B4 Isla de Chiloé I Chile
25D2 Isla de Cozumel I Mexico
25C3 Isla de la Gonâve I Cuba
26A2 Isla de la Juventud I Cuba
34D2 Isla de las Lechiguanas I Arg
3K8 Isla del Coco I Costa Rica
25D3 Isla del Maiz I Caribbean S
23B1 Isla de Lobos I Mexico
29D6 Isla de los Estados I Arg
28E2 Isla de Marajó I Brazil
105L5 Isla de Pascua I Pacific O
26A4 Isla de Providencia I Caribbean S
26A4 Isla de San Andres I Caribbean S
30G4 Isla de Santa Catarina I Brazil
33G2 Isla du Diable I French Guiana
31E2 Isla Fernando de Noronha I Brazil
29C6 Isla Grande de Tierra del Fuego I Arg/Chile
27D4 Isla la Tortuga I Ven
84C2 Islamabad Pak
24A2 Isla Magdalena I Mexico
27E4 Isla Margarita I Ven
34A3 Isla Mocha I Chile
17B2 Islamorada USA
10A1 Island L Can
108A2 Island Lg Aust
110B1 Islands,B of NZ
32A4 Isla Puná I Ecuador
103D6 Isla San Ambrosia I Pacifico O
103D6 Isla San Felix I Pacifico O
24A2 Isla Santa Margarita I Mexico
34A3 Isla Santa Maria I Chile
51C2 Islas Baleares Is Spain
96A2 Islas Canarias Is Atlantic O
51C2 Islas Columbretes Is Spain
25D3 Islas de la Bahia Is Honduras
26A4 Islas del Maiz Is Caribbean S
33E1 Islas de Margarita Is Ven

Islas Diego Ramírez

29C7 **Islas Diego Ramírez**
Is Chile
32J7 **Islas Galapagos** *Is*
Pacific O
30H6 **Islas Juan Fernández**
Chile
32D1 **Islas los Roques** *Is*
Ven
Islas Malvinas =
Falkland Is
105L3 **Islas Revilla Gigedo**
Is Pacific O
29C7 **Islas Wollaston** *Is*
Chile
97A3 **Isla Tidra** *I* Maur
29B5 **Isla Wellington** *I*
Chile
48C2 **Isle** *R* France
104B5 **Isle Amsterdam** *I*
Indian O
43D4 **Isle of Wight** *I* Eng
10B2 **Isle Royale** *I* USA
104B5 **Isle St Paul** *I*
Indian O
104A6 **Isles Crozet** *I*
Indian O
105J4 **Isles de la Société**
Pacific O
105K5 **Isles Gambier** *Is*
Pacific O
101D2 **Isles Glorieuses** *Is*
Madag
104B6 **Isles Kerguelen** *Is*
Indian O
105K4 **Isles Marquises** *Is*
Pacific O
105J5 **Isles Tuamotu** *Is*
Pacific O
22B1 **Isleton** USA
92B3 **Isma'iliya** Egypt
101D3 **Isoanala** Madag
101C2 **Isoka** Zambia
53B3 **Isola Egadi** *I* Italy
52B2 **Isola Ponziane** *I* Italy
53B3 **Isole Lipari** *Is* Italy
52C2 **Isoles Tremiti** *Is* Italy
75B1 **Isosaki** Japan
92B2 **Isparta** Turk
94B2 **Israel** Republic, S W
Asia
51C2 **Issoire** France
48C2 **Issoire** France
94C2 **Issoudun** France
92A1 **Istanbul** Turk
55B3 **Istiáia** Greece
25C3 **Istmo de**
Tehuantepec
Isthmus Mexico
17B2 **Istokpoga,L** USA
52B1 **Istra** *Pen* Croatia
35B1 **Itaberai** Brazil
35C1 **Itabira** Brazil
35C2 **Itabirito** Brazil
31D4 **Itabuna** Brazil
33F4 **Itacoatiara** Brazil
32B2 **Itagui** Colombia
33F4 **Itaituba** Brazil
30G4 **Itajaí** Brazil
35B2 **Itajuba** Brazil
52B2 **Italy** Repubic, Europe
35B1 **Itamaraju** Brazil
35C1 **Itamarandiba** Brazil
35C1 **Itambacuri** Brazil
35C1 **Itambé** *Mt* Brazil
86C1 **Itänagar** India
35B2 **Itanhaém** Brazil
35C1 **Itanhém** *R* Brazil
35C1 **Itaobim** Brazil
35B2 **Itapecerica** Brazil
35C2 **Itaperuna** Brazil
31C5 **Itapetinga** Brazil
35B2 **Itapetininga** Brazil
35B2 **Itapeva** Brazil
31D2 **Itapipoca** Brazil
35B1 **Itapuranga** Brazil
30E4 **Itaqui** Brazil
35C1 **Itarantim** Brazil
35B2 **Itararé** Brazil
35B2 **Itararé** *R* Brazil
35C2 **Itaúna** Brazil
33E6 **Iténez** *R* Brazil/Bol

15C2 **Ithaca** USA
98C2 **Itimbiri** *R* Zaire
35C1 **Itinga** Brazil
6E3 **Itivdleg** Greenland
75B2 **Ito** Japan
74D3 **Itoigawa** Japan
33E6 **Itonomas** *R* Bol
35B2 **Itu** Brazil
35B1 **Itumbiara** Brazil
35A1 **Iturama** Brazil
30C3 **Iturbe** Arg
35B1 **Iturutaba** Brazil
56B2 **Itzehoe** Germany
58D2 **Ivacevichi**
Belorussia
35A2 **Ivaí** *R* Brazil
38K5 **Ivalo** Fin
54A2 **Ivangrad**
Montenegro, Yugos
108B2 **Ivanhoe** Aust
59C3 **Ivano-Frankovsk**
Ukraine
61F2 **Ivanovo** Russian Fed
65H3 **Ivdel'** Russian Fed
98B2 **Ivindo** *R* Gabon
101D3 **Ivohibe** Madag
101D2 **Ivongo Soanierana**
Madag
97B4 **Ivory Coast** Republic,
Africa
52A1 **Ivrea** Italy
6C3 **Ivujivik** Can
74E3 **Iwaki** Japan
74C4 **Iwakuni** Japan
74E2 **Iwanai** Japan
97C4 **Iwo** Nig
69G4 **Iwo Jima** *I* Japan
23B1 **Ixmiquilpa** Mexico
23A2 **Ixtapa** Mexico
23A1 **Ixtlán** Mexico
75A2 **Iyo** Japan
75A2 **Iyo-nada** *B* Japan
65G4 **Izhevsk** Russian Fed
64G3 **Izhma** Russian Fed
91C5 **Izki** Oman
60C4 **Izmail** Ukraine
92A2 **Izmir** Turk
92A1 **Izmit** Turk
55C3 **Izmir Körfezi** *B* Turk
92A1 **Izmit** Turk
92A1 **Iznik** Turk
55C2 **Iznik Golü** *L* Turk
94C2 **Izra'** Syria
23B2 **Izúcar de Matamoros**
Mexico

75B2 **Izumi-sano** Japan
75A1 **Izumo** Japan
74D4 **Izu-shotō** *Is* Japan

J

95B1 **Jabal al Akhdar** *Mts*
Libya
94C2 **Jabal al 'Arab** Syria
95A2 **Jabal as Sawdã** *Mts*
Libya
91B5 **Jabal az Zannah** UAE
94C1 **Jabal Halimah** *Mt*
Leb/Syria
83B3 **Jabalpur** India
59B2 **Jablonec nad Nisou**
Czech Republic
31D3 **Jaboatão** Brazil
35B2 **Jaboticabal** Brazil
51B1 **Jaca** Spain
23B1 **Jacala** Mexico
33F5 **Jacareacanga** Brazil
35B2 **Jacareí** Brazil
35B2 **Jacarezinho** Brazil
29C2 **Jáchal** Arg
35C1 **Jacinto** Brazil
13F2 **Jackfish L** Can
109C1 **Jackson** Aust
22B1 **Jackson** California,
USA
14B2 **Jackson** Michigan,
USA
19B3 **Jackson** Mississippi,
USA
18C2 **Jackson** Missouri,
USA
14B3 **Jackson** Ohio, USA
11B3 **Jackson** Tennessee,
USA
111B2 **Jackson,C** NZ
111A2 **Jackson Head** *Pt* NZ

19B3 **Jacksonville**
Arkansas, USA
17B1 **Jacksonville** Florida,
USA
18B2 **Jacksonville** Illinois,
USA
17C1 **Jacksonville**
N Carolina, USA
19A3 **Jacksonville** Texas,
USA
17B1 **Jacksonville Beach**
USA
26C3 **Jacmel** Haiti
84B3 **Jacobabad** Pak
31C4 **Jacobina** Brazil
23A2 **Jacona** Mexico
Jadotville = Likasi
32B5 **Jaén** Peru
50B2 **Jaén** Spain
Jaffa = Tel Aviv Yafo
108A3 **Jaffa,C** Aust
87B3 **Jaffna** Sri Lanka
86B2 **Jagannathganj Ghat**
Bang
87C1 **Jagdalpur** India
91C4 **Jagin** *R* Iran
87B1 **Jagtial** India
29F2 **Jaguarão** *R* Brazil
35B2 **Jaguarialva** Brazil
91B4 **Jahrom** Iran
85D5 **Jäina** India
72A2 **Jialing** China
85D3 **Jaipur** India
85C3 **Jaisalmer** India
90C2 **Jajarm** Iran
52C2 **Jajce** Bosnia-
Herzegovina
78B4 **Jakarta** Indon
6E3 **Jakobshavn**
Greenland
38J6 **Jakobstad** Fin
23B2 **Jalaca** Mexico
84B2 **Jalal-Kut** Afghan
84D2 **Jalandhar** India
23B2 **Jalapa** Mexico
35A2 **Jales** Brazil
86B1 **Jaleswar** Nepal
85D4 **Jalgaon** India
97B4 **Jalingo** Nig
91B3 **Jalor** S Spain
85C3 **Jälor** India
23A1 **Jalostotitlan** Mexico
86B1 **Jalpaiguri** India
23B1 **Jalpan** Mexico
95B2 **Jalu Oasis** Libya
32A4 **Jama** Ecuador
26B3 **Jamaica** *I*
Caribbean S
26B3 **Jamaica Chan**
Caribbean S
86B2 **Jamalpur** Bang
78A3 **Jambi** Indon
85C4 **Jambussar** India
7B4 **James** *R* Can
5J5 **Jameston** USA
108A2 **Jamestown** Aust
8D2 **Jamestown** N.
Dakota, USA
15C2 **Jamestown** New
York, USA
16D2 **Jamestown** Rhode
Island, USA
23B2 **Jamiltepec** Mexico
87B1 **Jamkhandi** India
84C2 **Jammu** India
84D2 **Jammu and Kashmir**
State, India
85B4 **Jamnagar** India
84C3 **Jampur** Pak
38K6 **Jämsä** Fin
86B2 **Jamshedpur** India
86B1 **Janakpur** Nepal
35C1 **Janaúba** Brazil
90B3 **Jandaq** Iran
109D1 **Jandowae** Aust
81B1 **Jan Mayen** *I*
Norwegian S
35C1 **Januária** Brazil
85D4 **Jaora** India
51 **Japan** Empire,
E Asia
74C3 **Japan,S of** *S* E Asia
104F2 **Japan Trench**
Pacific O

32D4 **Japurá** *R* Brazil
93C2 **Jarãbulus** Syria
35B1 **Jaraguá** Brazil
50B1 **Jarama** *R* Spain
94B2 **Jarash** Jordan
30E3 **Jardim** Brazil
51B2 **Jardin** *R* Spain
26B2 **Jardines de la Reina**
Is Cuba
Jargalant = Hovd
33G3 **Jari** *R* Brazil
86C1 **Jaria Jhánjail** Bang
42C4 **Jarny** France
58B2 **Jarocin** Pol
59C2 **Jaroslaw** Pol
38G6 **Järpen** Sweden
72B2 **Jartai** China
85C4 **Jasdan** India
97C4 **Jasikan** Ghana
91C4 **Jask** Iran
59C3 **Jaslo** Pol
29D6 **Jason Is** Falkland Is
18B2 **Jasper** Arkansas,
USA
13D2 **Jasper** Can
17B1 **Jasper** Florida, USA
14A3 **Jasper** Indiana, USA
19B3 **Jasper** Texas, USA
13D2 **Jasper Nat Pk** Can
58B2 **Jastrowie** Pol
35A1 **Jataí** Brazil
51B2 **Játiva** Spain
35B2 **Jaú** Brazil
32B6 **Jauja** Peru
86A1 **Jaunpur** India
Java = Jawa
87B2 **Javadi Hills** India
Javari = Yavari
70B4 **Java S** Indon
106A2 **Java Trench** Indon
78B4 **Jawa** *I* Indon
71F4 **Jayapura** Indon
94C2 **Jayrūd** Syria
96B2 **Jbel Ouarkziz** *Mts*
Mor
96B1 **Jbel Sarhro** *Mt* Mor
19B4 **Jeanerette** USA
97C4 **Jebba** Nig
93D2 **Jebel 'Abd al 'Aziz**
Mt Syria
95B3 **Jebel Abyad** Sudan
91C5 **Jebel Akhdar** *Mt*
Oman
92C4 **Jebel al Lawz** *Mt*
S Arabia
94B2 **Jebel ash Shaykh** *Mt*
Syria
95C2 **Jebel Asoteriba** *Mt*
Sudan
94B3 **Jebel Ed Dabab** *Mt*
Jordan
94B3 **Jebel el Ata'ita** *Mt*
Jordan
92C3 **Jebel esh Sharqi** *Mts*
Leb/Syria
94B2 **Jebel Ithriyat** *Mt*
Jordan
91C5 **Jebel Ja'lan** *Mt*
Oman
94B2 **Jebel Liban** *Mts* Leb
94C2 **Jebel Ma'lülä** *Mt*
Syria
98C1 **Jebel Marra** *Mt*
Sudan
94C3 **Jebel Mudeisisat** *Mt*
Jordan
95C2 **Jebel Oda** *Mt* Sudan
94B3 **Jebel Qasr ed Deir**
Mt Jordan
94B2 **Jebel Um ed Daraj**
Mt Jordan
95B2 **Jebel Uweinat** *Mt*
Sudan
42C2 **Jedburgh** Scot
Jedda = Jiddah
59C2 **Jedrzejów** Pol
19B3 **Jefferson** Texas,
USA
11A3 **Jefferson City** USA
8B3 **Jefferson,Mt** USA
14A3 **Jeffersonville** USA
60C2 **Jekabpils** Latvia
59B2 **Jelena Gora** Pol
60B2 **Jelgava** Latvia

78C4 Jember *Indon*
57C2 Jena *Germany*
78B2 Jenaja *I Indon*
47D1 Jenbach *Austria*
94B2 Jenin *Israel*
19B3 Jennings *USA*
59B2 Jensenky *Upland Czech Republic*
6F3 Jensen Nunatakker *Mt Greenland*
6B3 Jens Munk *I Can*
108B3 Jeparit *Aust*
31D4 Jequié *Brazil*
35C1 Jequital *R Brazil*
35C1 Jequitinhonha *Brazil*
31C5 Jequitinhonha *R Brazil*
50A2 Jerez de la Frontera *Spain*
50A2 Jerez de los Caballeros *Spain*
94B3 Jericho *Israel*
108C3 Jerilderie *Aust*
48B2 Jersey *I UK*
10C2 Jersey City *USA*
15C2 Jersey Shore *USA*
18B2 Jerseyville *USA*
92C3 Jerusalem *Israel*
109D3 Jervis B *Aust*
13C2 Jervis Inlet *Sd Can*
52B1 Jesenice *Slovenia*
86B2 Jessore *Bang*
11B3 Jesup *USA*
34C2 Jesus Maria *Arg*
16D2 Jewett City *USA*
54A2 Jezerce *Mt Alb*
58C2 Jezioro Mamry *L Pol*
58C2 Jezioro Sniardwy *L Pol*
94B2 Jezzine *Leb*
85C4 Jhabua *India*
85D4 Jhalawar *India*
84C2 Jhang Maghiana *Pak*
85D3 Jhansi *India*
86A2 Jharsuguda *India*
84C2 Jhelum *Pak*
84C2 Jhelum *R Pak*
11C3 J H Kerr L *USA*
84D3 Jhunjhunun *India*
69F2 Jiamusi *China*
73C4 Ji'an *Jiangxi, China*
74B2 Ji'an *Jilin, China*
73D4 Jiande *China*
73B4 Jiang'an *China*
73D5 Jiangbiancun *China*
73A5 Jiangcheng *China*
73B3 Jiang Jiang *R China*
73C5 Jiangmen *China*
72D3 Jiangsu *Province, China*
73C4 Jiangyou *Province, China*
73A3 Jiangyou *China*
72D1 Jianping *China*
73A5 Jianshui *China*
73D4 Jian Xi *R China*
73D4 Jianyang *China*
72E2 Jiaonan *China*
72E2 Jiao Xian *China*
72E2 Jiaozhou Wan *B China*
72C2 Jiaozuo *China*
73E3 Jiaxing *China*
68B3 Jiayuguan *China*
81B3 Jiddah *S Arabia*
72D3 Jieshou *China*
72C2 Jiexiu *China*
72A3 Jiguzi *China*
59B3 Jihlava *Czech Republic*
99E2 Jilib *Somalia*
69E2 Jilin *China*
51B1 Jiloca *R Spain*
99D2 Jima *Eth*
9C4 Jiménez *Coahuila, Mexico*
72D2 Jinan *China*
84D3 Jind *India*
72B2 Jingbian *China*
72C2 Jingdezhen *China*
76C1 Jinghong *China*
73C3 Jingmen *China*
72B2 Jingning *China*
73B4 Jing Xiang *China*

73D4 Jinhua *China*
72C1 Jining *Nei Monggol, China*
72D2 Jining *Shandong, China*
99D2 Jinja *Uganda*
76C1 Jinping *China*
73A4 Jinsha Jiang *R China*
73C4 Jinshi *China*
72E1 Jinxi *China*
72E2 Jin Xian *China*
72E1 Jinzhou *China*
33E5 Jiparaná *R Brazil*
32A4 Jipijapa *Ecuador*
23A2 Jiquilpan *Mexico*
91C4 Jiroft *Iran*
99E2 Jirriban *Somalia*
73B4 Jishou *China*
92C2 Jisr ash Shughûr *Syria*
54B2 Jiu *R Rom*
73D4 Jiujiang *China*
73A4 Jiulong *China*
73D4 Jiulong Jiang *R China*
69F2 Jixi *China*
94B3 Jiza *Jordan*
81C4 Jizan *S Arabia*
97A3 Joal *Sen*
35C1 João Monlevade *Brazil*
31E3 João Pessoa *Brazil*
35B1 João Pirheiro *Brazil*
34B2 Jocoli *Arg*
85C3 Jodhpur *India*
38K6 Joensuu *Fin*
46C2 Joeuf *France*
12D2 Joffre,Mt *Can*
86B1 Jogbani *India*
87A2 Jog Falls *India*
101G1 Johannesburg *S Africa*
21B2 Johannesburg *USA*
6C2 Johan Pen *Can*
12D1 John *R USA*
20C2 John Day *USA*
20C2 John Day *R USA*
44C2 John O'Groats *Scot*
18A2 John Redmond Res *USA*
11B3 Johnson City *Tennessee, USA*
17B1 Johnson *USA*
27N2 Johnston Pt *St Vincent and the Grenadines*
15C2 Johnstown *Pennsylvania, USA*
77C5 Johor Bharu *Malay*
49C2 Joigny *France*
30G4 Joinville *Brazil*
61H3 Jok *R Russian Fed*
38H5 Jokkmokk *Sweden*
93E2 Jolfa *Iran*
11B2 Joliet *USA*
7C5 Joliette *Can*
79B4 Jolo *Phil*
79B4 Jolo *I Phil*
82D2 Joma *Mt China*
58C1 Jonava *Lithuania*
72A3 Joné *China*
11A3 Jonesboro *Arkansas, USA*
19B3 Jonesboro *Louisiana, USA*
6B2 Jones Sd *Can*
58C1 Joniškis *Lithuania*
37J7 Jönköping *Sweden*
11A3 Joplin *USA*
92C3 Jordan *Kingdom, S W Asia*
94B2 Jordan *R Israel*
20C2 Jordan Valley *USA*
86C1 Jorhat *India*
38J5 Jörn *Sweden*
78C3 Jorong *Indon*
39F7 Jørpeland *Nor*
79B3 Jose Panganiban *Phil*
106B2 Joseph Bonaparte G *Aust*
64B3 Jotunheimen *Mt Nor*
94B2 Jouai'ya *Leb*
94B2 Jounié *Leb*

86C1 Jowal *India*
99E2 Jowhar *Somalia*
12H2 Joy,Mt *Can*
5F5 Juan de Fuca,Str of *Can/USA*
101D2 Juan de Nova *I Mozam Chan*
34D3 Juárez *Arg*
31C3 Juàzeiro *Brazil*
31D3 Juazeiro do Norte *Brazil*
99D2 Juba *Sudan*
99E2 Juba *R Somalia*
94B1 Jubail *Leb*
93D3 Jubbah *S Arabia*
96A2 Juby,C *Mor*
51B2 Jucar *R Spain*
23B2 Juchatengo *Mexico*
23A1 Juchipila *R Mexico*
23A2 Juchitán *Mexico*
57C3 Judenburg *Austria*
30B2 Juilaca *Peru*
73C4 Juiling Shan *Hills China*
31C6 Juiz de Fora *Brazil*
30C3 Jujuy *State, Arg*
30C2 Juli *Peru*
33F3 Julianatop *Mt Surinam*
6F3 Julianehab *Greenland*
46D1 Jülich *Germany*
86A1 Jumla *Nepal*
94B3 Jum Suwwana *Mt Jordan*
85C4 Jûnâgadh *India*
72D2 Junan *China*
31B6 Junction City *USA*
31B6 Jundiaí *Brazil*
4E4 Juneau *USA*
107D4 Junee *Aust*
22C2 June Lake *USA*
52A1 Jungfrau *Mt Switz*
16A2 Juniata *R USA*
29D2 Junin *Arg*
73A4 Junlian *China*
31B6 Juquiá *Brazil*
99D2 Jur *R Sudan*
42B2 Jura *I Scot*
49D2 Jura *Mts France*
44B3 Jura,Sound of *Chan Scot*
94B3 Jurf ed Darâwîsh *Jordan*
65K4 Jurga *Russian Fed*
60B2 Jûrmala *Latvia*
32D4 Juruá *R Brazil*
33F6 Juruena *R Brazil*
94C1 Jûsiyah *Syria*
34B2 Justo Daract *Arg*
32D4 Jutaí *R Brazil*
25D3 Juticalpa *Honduras*
90C3 Jûymand *Iran*
56B1 Jylland *Pen Den*
38K6 Jyväskylä *Fin*

K

82B2 K2 *Mt China/India*
90C2 Kaakhka *Turkmenistan*
101H1 Kaapmuiden *S Africa*
71D4 Kabaena *I Indon*
97A4 Kabala *Sierra Leone*
99D3 Kabale *Rwanda*
98C3 Kabalo *Zaire*
98C3 Kabambare *Zaire*
99D2 Kaberole *Uganda*
98C3 Kabinda *Zaire*
90A3 Kabir Kuh *Mts Iran*
100B2 Kabompo *Zambia*
100B2 Kabompo *R Zambia*
98C3 Kabongo *Zaire*
84B2 Kabul *Afghan*
85B4 Kachchh,G of *India*
61K2 Kachkanar *Russian Fed*
63C2 Kachug *Russian Fed*
76B3 Kadan *Burma*
78D3 Kadapongan *I Indon*
85C4 Kadi *India*
108A2 Kadina *Aust*
92B2 Kadinhani *Turk*
87B2 Kadiri *India*

60E4 Kadiyevka *Ukraine*
100B2 Kadoma *Zim*
99C1 Kadugli *Sudan*
97C3 Kaduna *Nig*
97C3 Kaduna *R Nig*
87B2 Kadûr *India*
97A3 Kaédi *Maur*
21C4 Kaena Pt *Hawaiian Is*
74B3 Kaesŏng *N Korea*
97C4 Kafanchan *Nig*
97A3 Kaffrine *Sen*
94C1 Kafrûn Bashûr *Syria*
100B2 Kafue *Zambia*
100B2 Kafue *R Zambia*
100B2 Kafue Nat Pk *Zambia*
74D3 Kaga *Japan*
65H6 Kagan *Kazakhstan*
93D1 Kagizman *Turk*
74C4 Kagoshima *Japan*
90C2 Kahak *Iran*
99D3 Kahama *Tanz*
84B3 Kahan *Pak*
78C3 Kahayan *R Indon*
98B3 Kahemba *Zaire*
46E1 Kahler Asten *Mt Germany*
91C4 Kahnûj *Iran*
18B1 Kahoka *USA*
21C4 Kahoolawe *I Hawaiian Is*
92C2 Kahramanmaraş *Turk*
21C4 Kahuku Pt *Hawaiian Is*
21C4 Kahului *Hawaiian Is*
111B2 Kaiapoi *NZ*
33F2 Kaieteur Fall *Guyana*
72C3 Kaifeng *China*
110B1 Kaikohe *NZ*
111B2 Kaikoura *NZ*
111B2 Kaikoura *NZ*
111B2 Kaikoura Range *Mts NZ*
73B4 Kaili *China*
21C4 Kailua *Hawaiian Is*
71E4 Kaimana *Indon*
75B2 Kainan *Japan*
97C3 Kainji Res *Nig*
110B1 Kaipara Harbour *B NZ*
73C5 Kaiping *China*
96D1 Kairouan *Tunisia*
22C2 Kaiser Peak *Mt USA*
57B3 Kaiserslautern *Germany*
74B2 Kaishantun *China*
58D2 Kaisiadorys *Lithuania*
110B1 Kaitaia *NZ*
111A3 Kaitangata *NZ*
84D3 Kaithal *India*
21C4 Kaiwi Chan *Hawaiian Is*
73B3 Kai Xian *China*
73A5 Kaiyuan *Liaoning, China*
74A2 Kaiyuan *Yunnan, China*
12C2 Kaiyuh Mts *USA*
38K6 Kajaani *Fin*
84B2 Kajaki *Afghan*
99D3 Kajiado *Kenya*
84B2 Kajrān *Afghan*
99D1 Kaka *Sudan*
99D2 Kakamega *Kenya*
75A2 Kake *Japan*
12H3 Kake *USA*
120S Kakhonak *USA*
65E5 Kakhovskoye Vodokhranilische Res *Ukraine*
91B4 Kākī *Iran*
87C1 Kākināda *India*
75A2 Kakogawa *Japan*
4D2 Kaktovik *USA*
75C1 Kakuda *Japan*
Kalaallit Nunaat = *Greenland*
55B3 Kalabáka *Greece*
78D1 Kalabakan *Malay*
100B2 Kalabo *Zambia*
61F3 Kalach *Russian Fed*
61F4 Kalach-na-Donu *Russian Fed*
86C2 Kaladan *R Burma*
21C4 Ka Lae *C Hawaiian Is*

Kalahari Desert

100B3 Kalahari Desert
  Botswana
38J6 Kalajoki Fin
63D2 Kalakan Russian Fed
70A3 Kalakepen Indon
84C1 Kalam Pak
55B3 Kalámai Greece
108Z Kalamazoo USA
84B3 Kalat Pak
92B1 Kalecik Turk
78D3 Kalembau I Indon
99C3 Kalémié Zaïre
38L5 Kalevala Russian Fed
86C2 Kalewa Burma
12D2 Kalgin I USA
106B4 Kalgoorlie Aust
78A4 Kalianda Indon
79B3 Kalibo Phil
98C3 Kalima Zaïre
78C3 Kalimantan Province,
  Indon
55C3 Kálimnos I Greece
86B1 Kálimpang India
60B3 Kaliningrad
  Russian Fed
60C3 Kalinkovichi
  Belorussia
8B2 Kalispell USA
58B2 Kalisz Pol
99D3 Kaliua Tanz
38J5 Kalix R Sweden
100A3 Kalkfeld Namibia
100A3 Kalkrand Namibia
108A1 Kallakoopah R Aust
38K6 Kallävesi L Fin
55C3 Kalloni Kólpos B
  Greece
39H7 Kalmar Sweden
61G4 Kalmytskaya
  Respublika,
  Russian Fed
100B2 Kalomo Zambia
18B1 Kalona USA
13B2 Kalone Peak Mt Can
87A2 Kalpeni I India
85D3 Kālpi India
53A3 Kalsat Khasba
  Tunisia
12B2 Kalskag USA
12C2 Kaltag USA
61H2 Kaluga Russian Fed
39G7 Kalundborg Den
59C3 Kalush Ukraine
87B2 Kalyandurg India
60E2 Kalyazin Russian Fed
61H1 Kama R Russian Fed
74E3 Kamaishi Japan
84C2 Kamalia Pak
110C1 Kamanawa Mts NZ
100A2 Kamanjab Namibia
84D2 Kamard Afghan
87B3 Kamban India
61H2 Kambarka
  Russian Fed
97A4 Kambia Sierra Leone
59D3 Kamenets Podolskiy
  Ukraine
61F3 Kamenka
  Russian Fed
65K4 Kamen-na-Obi
  Russian Fed
61K2 Kamensk-Ural'skiy
  Russian Fed
5H3 Kamilukuak L Can
98C3 Kamina Zaïre
7A3 Kaminak L Can
75C1 Kaminoyama Japan
23E1 Kamo Armenia
75C1 Kamogawa Japan
99D2 Kampala Uganda
77C5 Kampar Malay
78A2 Kampar R Indon
56B2 Kampen Neth
76B2 Kamphaeng Phet
  Thai
77C3 Kampot Camb
91D4 Kamsaptar India
61J2 Kamskoye
  Vodokhranilishche
  Res Russian Fed
85D4 Kamthi India
61G3 Kamyshin
  Russian Fed

61K2 Kamyshlov
  Russian Fed
7C4 Kanaaupscow R Can
98C3 Kananga Zaïre
61G2 Kanash Russian Fed
75B1 Kanayama Japan
74D3 Kanazawa Japan
4C3 Kanbisha USA
87B2 Känchipuram India
84B2 Kandahar Afghan
64E3 Kandalaksha
  Russian Fed
38L5 Kandalakshskaya
  Guba B Russian Fed
97C3 Kandi Benin
109C2 Kandos Aust
87C3 Kandy Sri Lanka
15C2 Kane USA
6C1 Kane Basin B Can
98B1 Kanem Desert
  Region Chad
97B3 Kangaba Mali
92C2 Kangal Turk
6E3 Kangâmiut
  Greenland
91B4 Kangän Iran
77C4 Kangar Malay
106C4 Kangaroo I Aust
6E3 Kangâtsiaq
  Greenland
90A3 Kangavar Iran
72C1 Kangbao China
82C3 Kangchenjunga Mt
  Nepal
73A4 Kangding China
6G3 Kangerdlugssuaq R
  Greenland
6G3 Kangerdlugssvatsaiq
  B Greenland
99D2 Kangetet Kenya
74B2 Kanggye N Korea
7D4 Kangiqsualujjuaq
  Can
6C3 Kangiqsujuaq Can
7C3 Kangirsuk Can
74B3 Kangnüng S Korea
98B2 Kango Gabon
68B4 Kangto Mt China
72B3 Kang Xian China
77D4 Kanh Hung Viet
87B1 Kani Giri India
39J6 Kankaanpää Fin
14A2 Kankakee USA
14A2 Kankakee R USA
97B3 Kankan Guinea
86A2 Känker India
87B3 Kanniyäkumari India
97C3 Kano Nig
74C4 Kanoya Japan
86A1 Känpur India
9D3 Kansas State, USA
18A2 Kansas R USA
10A3 Kansas City USA
73D5 Kanshi China
63B2 Kansk Russian Fed
97C3 Kantchari Burkina
86B2 Kanthi India
12D2 Kantishna USA
12D2 Kantishna R USA
100B3 Kanye Botswana
68D4 Kao-hsiung Taiwan
100A2 Kaoka Veld Plain
  Namibia
97A3 Kaolack Sen
100B2 Kaoma Zambia
21C4 Kapaau Hawaiian Is
98C3 Kapanga Zaïre
6F3 Kap Cort Adelaer C
  Greenland
6H3 Kap Dalton C
  Greenland
39H7 Kapellskär Sweden
6F3 Kap Farvel C
  Greenland
6G3 Kap Gustav Holm C
  Greenland
100B2 Kapiri Zambia
78C2 Kapit Malay
19B3 Kaplan USA
57C3 Kaplice
  Czech Republic
77B4 Kapoe Thai
99C3 Kapona Zaïre

52C1 Kaposvár Hung
6C2 Kap Parry C Can
6H3 Kap Ravn C
  Greenland
78B3 Kapuas R Indon
108A2 Kapunda Aust
84D2 Kapurthala India
7B5 Kapuskasing Can
109D2 Kaputar Mt Aust
93E2 Kapydzhik Mt
  Armenia
6D2 Kap York C
  Greenland
92B1 Karabük Turk
55C2 Karacabey Turk
85B4 Karachi Pak
87A1 Karäd India
60E5 Kara Daglari Mt Turk
54C5 Karadeniz Boğazi Sd
  Turk
68D1 Karaftit Russian Fed
65J5 Karaganda
  Kazakhstan
65J5 Karagayly
  Kazakhstan
87B2 Käraikäl India
90B2 Karaj Iran
92C3 Karak Jordan
65G5 Kara Kalpakskaya
  Respublika,
  Uzbekistan
84D1 Karakax He R China
71D3 Karakelong I Indon
84D1 Karakoram Mts India
84D1 Karakoram P India/
  China
97A3 Karakoro R Maur/
  Sen
65G6 Karakumy Desert
  Russian Fed
94B3 Karama Jordan
92B2 Karaman Turk
65K5 Karamay China
111B2 Karamea NZ
111B2 Karamea Bight B NZ
93B2 Käranja India
92B2 Karapinar Turk
64H2 Kara S Russian Fed
100A3 Karasburg Namibia
38K5 Karasjok Nor
92C2 Karatas Turk
65H5 Kara Tau Mts
  Kazakhstan
76B3 Karathuri Burma
74B4 Karatsu Japan
91B4 Karäz Iran
93D3 Karbalä' Iraq
59C3 Karcag Hung
55B3 Kardhitsa Greece
64E3 Karel'skaya
  Respublika,
  Russian Fed
38J5 Karesvando Sweden
96B2 Karet Desert Region
  Maur
65K4 Kargasok
  Russian Fed
97D3 Kari Nig
100B2 Kariba Zim
100B2 Kariba L Zim/Zambia
100B2 Kariba Dam Zim/
  Zambia
95C3 Karima Sudan
78B3 Karimata I Indon
86C2 Karimganj Bang
99E1 Karin Somalia
39J6 Karis Fin
99C3 Karishimbe Mt Zaïre
55B3 Káristos Greece
87A2 Kärkal India
71F4 Karkar I PNG
90A3 Karkheh R Iran
60D4 Karkinitskiy Zaliv B
  Ukraine
63B3 Karlik Shan Mt
  China
58B2 Karlino Pol
52C2 Karlobag Croatia
52C2 Karlovac Croatia
54B2 Karlovo Bulg
57C2 Karlovy Vary
  Czech Republic

39G7 Karlshamn Sweden
39G7 Karlskoga Sweden
39H7 Karlskrona Sweden
57B3 Karlsruhe Germany
39G7 Karlstad Sweden
12D3 Karluk USA
86C2 Karnafuli Res Bang
84D3 Karnal India
87A1 Karnataka State,
  India
54C2 Karnobat Bulg
100B2 Karoi Zim
99D3 Karonga Malawi
95C3 Karora Sudan
78D3 Karossa Indon
55C3 Kárpathos I Greece
6E2 Karrats Fjord
  Greenland
93D1 Kars Turk
65H4 Karsakpay
  Kazakhstan
58D1 Kärsava Latvia
65J6 Karshi Uzbekistan
38J6 Karstula Fin
94B1 Kartaba Leb
54C2 Kartal Turk
61K3 Kartaly Russian Fed
90A3 Kärün R Iran
86A1 Karwa India
87A2 Kärwär India
68D1 Karymskoye
  Russian Fed
98B3 Kasai R Zaïre
100B2 Kasaji Zaïre
101C2 Kasama Zambia
99D3 Kasanga Tanz
98B3 Kasangulu Zaïre
87A2 Kásaragod India
5H3 Kasba L Can
100B2 Kasempa Zambia
100B2 Kasenga Zaïre
92A2 Kasese Uganda
90B3 Käshän Iran
12C2 Kashegelok USA
82B2 Kashi China
84D3 Käshipur India
74D3 Kashiwazaki Japan
90C2 Käshmar Iran
66D3 Kashmir State, India
61F3 Kasimov Russian Fed
18C2 Kaskaskia R USA
38J6 Kaskinen Fin
61K2 Kasli Russian Fed
5G5 Kaslo Can
98C3 Kasonga Zaïre
100B2 Kasonga-Lunda Zaïre
55C3 Kásos I Greece
  Kaspiyskiy = Lagan'
95C3 Kassala Sudan
56E2 Kassel Germany
96C1 Kasserine Tunisia
100A2 Kassinga Angola
92B1 Kastamonou Turk
55B3 Kastélli Greece
92A2 Kastellorizon I
  Greece
55B2 Kastoría Greece
55C3 Kástron Greece
74D3 Kasugai Japan
75A1 Kasumi Japan
101C2 Kasungu Malawi
84C2 Kasur Pak
100B2 Kataba Zambia
99C3 Katako-kombe Zaïre
4D3 Katalla USA
63G2 Katangli Russian Fed
106A4 Katanning Aust
55B2 Katerini Greece
5E4 Kates Needle Mt
  Can/USA
82D3 Katha Burma
106C2 Katherine Aust
85C4 Käthiawär Pen India
86B1 Kathmandu Nepal
84D2 Kathua India
86B1 Katihär India
100B2 Katima Mulilo
  Namibia
4C4 Katmai,Mt USA
12D3 Katmai Nat Mon
  USA
86A2 Katni India
109D2 Katoomba Aust
59B2 Katowice Pol
39H7 Katrineholm Sweden

97C3 **Katsina** Nig
97C4 **Katsina Ala** Nig
75C1 **Katsuta** Japan
75C1 **Katsuura** Japan
75B1 **Katsuy** Japan
65H6 **Kattakurgan**
      Uzbekistan
39G7 **Kattegat** Str Den/
      Sweden
21C4 **Kauai** I Hawaiian Is
21C4 **Kauai Chan** Hawaiian
      Is
21C4 **Kaulakahi Chan**
      Hawaiian Is
21C4 **Kaunakaki** Hawaiian
      Is
60B3 **Kaunas** Lithuania
97C3 **Kaura Namoda** Nig
38J5 **Kautokeino** Nor
55B2 **Kavadarci** Macedonia
55A2 **Kavajë** Alb
87B2 **Kavali** India
55B2 **Kaválla** Greece
85B4 **Kävda** India
75B1 **Kawagoe** Japan
75B1 **Kawaguchi** Japan
110B1 **Kawakawa** NZ
99C3 **Kawambwa** Zambia
86A2 **Kawardha** India
15C2 **Kawartha Lakes** Can
74D3 **Kawasaki** Japan
110C1 **Kawerau** NZ
110B1 **Kawhia** NZ
97B3 **Kaya** Burkina
12F3 **Kayah I** USA
78D2 **Kayan** R Indon
87B3 **Käyankulam** India
97A3 **Kayes** Mali
92C2 **Kayseri** Turk
1B8 **Kazach'ye**
      Russian Fed
93E1 **Kazakh** Azerbaijan
65G5 **Kazakhstan** Republic,
      Asia
61G2 **Kazan'** Russian Fed
54C2 **Kazanlŭk** Bulg
69G4 **Kazan Retto** Is
      Japan
91B4 **Käzerün** Iran
61H1 **Kazhim** Russian Fed
93E1 **Kazi Magomed**
      Azerbaijan
59C3 **Kazincbarcika** Hung
55B3 **Kéa** I Greece
21C4 **Kealaikahiki Chan**
      Hawaiian Is
8D2 **Kearney** USA
93C2 **Keban Baraji** Res
      Turk
97A3 **Kébémer** Sen
96C1 **Kebili** Tunisia
94C1 **Kebir** R Leb/Syria
38H5 **Kebrekaise** Mt
      Sweden
59B3 **Kecskemét** Hung
58C1 **Kedainiai** Lithuania
97A3 **Kédougou** Sen
12J2 **Keele** R Can
12J2 **Keele Pk** Mt Can
21B2 **Keeler** USA
15D2 **Keene** New
      Hampshire, USA
100A3 **Keetmanshoop**
      Namibia
18C1 **Keewatin** USA
6A3 **Keewatin** Region
      Can
55B3 **Kefallinia** I Greece
94B2 **Kefar Sava** Israel
97C4 **Keffi** Nig
38A2 **Keflavik** Iceland
5G4 **Keg River** Can
76B1 **Kehsi Mansam**
      Burma
75B1 **Keith** Aust
44C3 **Keith** Scot
4F3 **Keith Arm** B Can
6D3 **Kekertuk** Can
85D3 **Kekri** India
77C5 **Kelang** Malay
77C4 **Kelantan** R Malay
84B1 **Kelif** Turkmenistan
92C1 **Kelkit** R Turk
98B3 **Kellé** Congo

4F2 **Kellet,C** Can
20C1 **Kellogg** USA
64D3 **Kelloselka** Fin
45C2 **Kells** Irish Rep
42B2 **Kells Range** Hills
      Scot
58C1 **Kelme** Lithuania
5G5 **Kelowna** Can
5F4 **Kelsey Bay** Can
42C2 **Kelso** Scot
20B1 **Kelso** USA
64E3 **Kem'** Russian Fed
38L6 **Kem'** R Russian Fed
97B3 **Ke Macina** Mali
13B2 **Kemano** Can
65K4 **Kemerovo**
      Russian Fed
38J5 **Kemi** Fin
38K5 **Kemi** R Fin
38K5 **Kemijärvi** Fin
46C1 **Kempen** Region,
      Belg
26B2 **Kemps Bay**
      The Bahamas
109D2 **Kempsey** Aust
57C3 **Kempten** Germany
12D2 **Kenai** USA
12D3 **Kenai Mts** USA
12D2 **Kenai Pen** USA
99D2 **Kenamuke Swamp**
      Sudan
42C2 **Kendal** Eng
109D2 **Kendall** Aust
71D4 **Kendari** Indon
78C3 **Kendawangan** Indon
86B2 **Kendräpära** India
20C1 **Kendrick** USA
97A4 **Kenema** Sierra Leone
98B3 **Kenge** Zaire
76B1 **Kengtung** Burma
100B3 **Kenhardt** S Africa
97A3 **Kéniéba** Mali
96B1 **Kenitra** Mor
45B3 **Kenmare** Irish Rep
45B3 **Kenmare** R Irish Rep
19B4 **Kenner** USA
18C2 **Kennett** USA
16B3 **Kennett Square** USA
20C1 **Kennewick** USA
5F4 **Kenny Dam** Can
7A5 **Kenora** Can
10B2 **Kenosha** USA
43E4 **Kent** County, Eng
20B1 **Kent** Washington,
      USA
14A2 **Kentland** USA
14B2 **Kenton** USA
4H3 **Kent Pen** Can
11B3 **Kentucky** State, USA
11B3 **Kentucky L** USA
19B3 **Kentwood** Louisiana,
      USA
14A2 **Kentwood** Michigan,
      USA
99D2 **Kenya** Republic,
      Africa
Kenya,Mt = Kirinyaga
18B1 **Keokuk** USA
86A2 **Keonchi** India
86B2 **Keonjhargarh** India
71E4 **Kepaluan Tanimbar**
      Arch Indon
6H3 **Keplavik** Iceland
59B2 **Kepno** Pol
78B2 **Kepulauan Anambas**
      Arch Indon
71E4 **Kepulauan Aru** Arch
      Indon
78B2 **Kepulauan Badas** Is
      Indon
71E4 **Kepulauan Banda**
      Arch Indon
71D4 **Kepulauan Banggai** I
      Indon
78B2 **Kepulauan Bunguran
      Seletan** Arch Indon
71E4 **Kepulauan Kai** Arch
      Indon
71D4 **Kepulauan Leti** I
      Indon
78A3 **Kepulauan Lingga** Is
      Indon
70A4 **Kepulauan Mentawi**
      Arch Indon

78A2 **Kepulauan Riau** Arch
      Indon
78D4 **Kepulauan Sabalana**
      Arch Indon
71D3 **Kepulauan Sangihe**
      Arch Indon
71D4 **Kepulauan Sula** I
      Indon
71D3 **Kepulauan Talaud**
      Arch Indon
71E4 **Kepulauan Tambelan**
      Is Indon
71E4 **Kepulauan Tanimbar**
      I Indon
71D4 **Kepulauan Togian** I
      Indon
71D4 **Kepulauan
      Tukambesi** Is Indon
87B2 **Kerala** State, India
108B3 **Kerang** Aust
39K6 **Kerava** Fin
60E4 **Kerch'** Ukraine
71F4 **Kerema** PNG
20C1 **Keremeps** Can
95C3 **Keren** Eritrea
104B6 **Kerguelen Ridge**
      Indian O
99D3 **Kericho** Kenya
70B4 **Kerinci** Mt Indon
99D2 **Kerio** R Kenya
80E2 **Kerki** Turkmenistan
55A3 **Kérkira** Greece
55A3 **Kérkira** I Greece
91C3 **Kerman** Iran
22B2 **Kerman** USA
90A3 **Kermänshäh** Iran
21B2 **Kern** R USA
13F2 **Kerrobert** Can
45B2 **Kerry** County,
      Irish Rep
17B1 **Kershaw** USA
78B3 **Kertamulia** Indon
63D3 **Kerulen** R Mongolia
96B2 **Kerzaz** Alg
55C2 **Keşan** Turk
74E3 **Kesennuma** Japan
38L5 **Kesten 'ga**
      Russian Fed
42C2 **Keswick** Eng
65K4 **Ket** R Russian Fed
97C4 **Kéta** Ghana
78C3 **Ketapang** Indon
5E4 **Ketchikan** USA
97C3 **Ketia** Niger
85B4 **Keti Bandar** Pak
58C2 **Ketrzyn** Pol
43D3 **Kettering** Eng
14B3 **Kettering** USA
20C1 **Kettle** R Can
20C1 **Kettle River Range**
      USA
7C3 **Kettlestone B** Can
90C3 **Kevir-i Namak** Salt
      Flat Iran
14A2 **Kewaunee** USA
14B1 **Key Harbour** Can
17B2 **Key Largo** USA
11B4 **Key West** USA
63C2 **Kezhma** Russian Fed
43D3 **K'teleghazi** Hung
12B2 **Kgun L** USA
94C2 **Khabab** Syria
62H3 **Khabarovsk**
      Russian Fed
85B3 **Khairpur** Pak
85B3 **Khairpur** Region,
      Pak
100B3 **Khakhea** Botswana
55C3 **Khálki** I Greece
55B2 **Khalkidhiki** Pen
      Greece
55B3 **Khalkis** Greece
61G2 **Khalturin**
      Russian Fed
85C4 **Khambhät,G** of India
85D4 **Khämgaon** India
76C2 **Kham Keut** Laos
85C4 **Khammam** India
90A2 **Khamseh** Mts Iran
76C2 **Khan** R Laos
84B1 **Khanabad** Afghan
93E3 **Khänaqin** Iraq
85D4 **Khandwa** India
84C2 **Khanewal** Pak

94C3 **Khan ez Zabib**
      Jordan
77D4 **Khanh Hung** Viet
55B3 **Khania** Greece
84C3 **Khanpur** Pak
65H3 **Khanty-Mansiysk**
      Russian Fed
94B3 **Khan Yunis** Egypt
84D1 **Khapalu** India
68C2 **Khapcheranga**
      Russian Fed
61G4 **Kharabali**
      Russian Fed
86B2 **Kharagpur** India
91C4 **Khärän** Iran
84B3 **Kharan** Pak
91B4 **Khärg** Is Iran
95C2 **Khärga Oasis** Egypt
85D4 **Khargon** India
60E4 **Khar'kov** Ukraine
54C2 **Kharmanli** Bulg
61F2 **Kharovsk**
      Russian Fed
95C3 **Khartoum** Sudan
95C3 **Khartoum North**
      Sudan
74C2 **Khasan** Russian Fed
95C3 **Khashm el Girba**
      Sudan
86C1 **Khasi-Jaintia Hills**
      India
54C2 **Khaskovo** Bulg
1B9 **Khatanga**
      Russian Fed
76B3 **Khawsa** Burma
76C2 **Khe Bo** Viet
85C4 **Khed Brahma** India
55C3 **Khemis** Alg
96B1 **Khenifra** Mor
51D2 **Kherrata** Alg
60D4 **Kherson** Ukraine
63C2 **Khilok** Russian Fed
55C3 **Khios** Greece
55C3 **Khios** I Greece
60C4 **Khmel'nitskiy**
      Ukraine
59C3 **Khodorov** Ukraine
84B1 **Kholm** Afghan
76D3 **Khong** Laos
91B4 **Khonj** Iran
69F2 **Khor** Russian Fed
91A3 **Khoramshahr** Iran
91B5 **Khör Duwayhin** B
      UAE
84C1 **Khorog** Tajikistan
90A3 **Khorramäbad** Iran
90C3 **Khosf** Iran
84B2 **Khost** Pak
60C4 **Khotin** Ukraine
12C2 **Khotol** Mt USA
60C3 **Khoyniki** Belorussia
63F2 **Khrebet Dzhugdzhur**
      Mts Russian Fed
90C2 **Khrebet Kopet Dag**
      Mts Turkmenistan
64H3 **Khrebet Pay-khoy**
      Mts Russian Fed
82C1 **Khrebet Tarbagatay**
      Mts Kazakhstan
63E2 **Khrebet Tukuringra**
      Mts Russian Fed
82A1 **Khudzhand** Tajikistan
86B2 **Khulna** Bang
84D1 **Khunjerab** P China/
      India
90B3 **Khunsar** Iran
91A4 **Khurays** S Arabia
86B2 **Khurda** India
84D3 **Khurja** India
84C2 **Khushab** Pak
94B2 **Khushniyah** Syria
59C3 **Khust** Ukraine
95C3 **Khuwei** Sudan
85B3 **Khuzdar** Pak
90D3 **Khväf** Iran
61G3 **Khvalynsk**
      Russian Fed
90C3 **Khvor** Iran
91B4 **Khvormüj** Iran
92D2 **Khvoy** Iran
84C1 **Khwaja Muhammad**
      Mts Afghan
84C2 **Khyber P** Afghan/Pak

Kiambi

99C3	Kiambi Zaire	106B2	King Leopold Range Mts Aust	59B3	Kiskunhalas Hung	56C1	København Den
19A3	Kiamichi R USA			65F5	Kislovodsk Russian Fed	57B2	Koblenz Germany
12B1	Kiana USA	9B3	Kingman USA			60B3	Kobrin Russian Fed
98B3	Kibangou Congo	98C3	Kingombe Zaire	99E3	Kismaayo Somalia	71E4	Kobroör I Indon
99D3	Kibaya Tanz	108A2	Kingoonya Aust	75B1	Kiso-sammyaku Mts Japan	12C1	Kobuk R USA
98C3	Kibombo Zaire	22C2	Kingsburg USA			54B2	Kočani Macedonia
99D3	Kibondo Tanz	21B2	Kings Canyon Nat Pk USA	163A3	Kissidougou Guinea	76C3	Ko Chang I Thai
99D3	Kibungu Rwanda			17B2	Kissimmee,L USA	86B1	Koch Bihār India
55B2	Kičevo Macedonia	108A3	Kingscote Aust	99D3	Kisumu Kenya	47D1	Kochel Germany
5G4	Kicking Horse P Can	108B2	King Sd Aust	59C3	Kisvárda Hung	6C3	Koch I Can
97C3	Kidal Mali	112C2	King Sejong Base Ant	97B3	Kita Mali		Kochi = Cochin
43C3	Kidderminster Eng			65H6	Kitab Uzbekistan	74C4	Kōchi Japan
97A3	Kidira Sen	14A1	Kingsford USA	75C1	Kitakata Japan	12D3	Kodiak USA
110C1	Kidnappers,C NZ	17B1	Kingsland USA	74C4	Kita-Kyūshū Japan	12D3	Kodiak I USA
56C2	Kiel Germany	43E3	King's Lynn Eng	99D2	Kitale Kenya	87B2	Kodiyakkari India
56C2	Kielce Pol	16C2	Kings Park USA	69G4	Kitalo I Japan	99D2	Kodok Sudan
56C2	Kieler Bucht B Germany	8B2	Kings Peak Mt USA	74E2	Kitami Japan	100A3	Koes Namibia
	Kiev = Kiyev	107C4	Kingston Aust	7B5	Kitchener Can	101G1	Koffiefontein S Africa
80E2	Kifab Uzbekistan	7C5	Kingston Can	99D2	Kitgum Uganda		
97A3	Kiffa Maur	25E3	Kingston Jamaica	55B3	Kithira I Greece	97B4	Koforidua Ghana
89H8	Kigali Rwanda	15D2	Kingston New York, USA	55B3	Kithnos I Greece	74D3	Kōfu Japan
12A2	Kigluaik Mts USA			94A1	Kiti,C Cyprus	75B1	Koga Japan
99C3	Kigoma Tanz	111A3	Kingston NZ	4H3	Kitikmeot Region Can	39G7	Køge Den
75B2	Kii-sanchi Mts Japan	27E4	Kingstown St Vincent and the Grenadines			84C2	Kohat Pak
74C4	Kii-suido B Japan			5F4	Kitimat Can	84B2	Koh-i-Baba Mts Afghan
54B1	Kikinda Serbia, Yugos	9D4	Kingsville USA	38K5	Kitnen R Fin	84B1	Koh-i-Hisar Mts Afghan
		44B3	Kingussie Scot	75A2	Kitsuki Japan		
55B3	Kikládhes Is Greece	4J3	King William I Can	13B1	Kittanning USA	84B2	Koh-i-Khurd Mt Afghan
71F4	Kikori PNG	100B4	King William's Town S Africa	38J5	Kittilä Fin		
98B3	Kikwit Zaire			99D3	Kitunda Tanz	86C1	Kohima India
21C4	Kilauea Crater Mt Hawaiian Is	98A3	Kinkala Congo	13B1	Kitwanga Can	84B1	Koh-i-Mazar Mt Afghan
		39G7	Kinna Sweden	100B2	Kitwe Zambia		
4C3	Kilbuck Mts USA	44D3	Kinnairds Head Pt Scot	57C3	Kitzbühel Austria	84B3	Kohlu Pak
74B2	Kilchu N Korea			47E1	Kitzbühler Alpen Mts Austria	60C2	Kohtla-Järve Estonia
109D1	Kilcoy Aust	75C1	Kinomoto Japan			75B1	Koide Japan
45C2	Kildare County, Irish Rep	44C3	Kinross Scot	57C3	Kitzingen Germany	12A4	Koidern Can
		45B3	Kinsale Irish Rep	99D3	Kiumbi Zaire	77A4	Koihoa Is Nicobar Is
45C2	Kildare Irish Rep	98B3	Kinshasa Zaire	12B1	Kivalina USA	74B4	Köje-do I S Korea
19B3	Kilgore USA	78D3	Kintap Indon	59D2	Kivercy Ukraine	65H4	Kokchetav Kazakhstan
99D3	Kilifi Kenya	42B2	Kintyre Pen Scot	99C3	Kivu,L Zaïre/Rwanda		
99D3	Kilimanjaro Mt Tanz	13D1	Kinuso Can	4C3	Kiwalik USA	39J6	Kokemaki L Fin
99D3	Kilindoni Tanz	99D2	Kinyeti Mt Sudan	60D3	Kiyev Ukraine	38J6	Kokkola Fin
92C2	Kilis Turk	55B3	Kiparissia Greece	61J2	Kizel Russian Fed	107D1	Kokoda PNG
45B2	Kilkee Irish Rep	55B3	Kiparissiakós Kólpos G Greece	92C2	Kizil R Turk	14A2	Kokomo USA
45C2	Kilkenny County, Irish Rep			80D2	Kizyl-Arvat Turkmenistan	71E4	Kokonau Indon
		15C1	Kipawa,L Can			65K5	Kokpekty Kazakhstan
45C2	Kilkenny Irish Rep	99D3	Kipili Tanz	90B2	Kizyl-Atrek Turkmenistan		
55B2	Kilkis Greece	12B3	Kipnuk USA			7D4	Koksoak R Can
45B1	Killala B Irish Rep	45C2	Kippure Mt Irish Rep	57C2	Kladno Czech Republic	100B4	Kokstad S Africa
45B2	Killaloe Irish Rep	100B2	Kipushi Zaire			76C3	Ko Kut I Thai
109D1	Killarney Aust	63C2	Kirensk Russian Fed	57C3	Klagenfurt Austria	38L5	Kola Russian Fed
41B3	Killarney Irish Rep	65J5	Kirghizia Republic, Asia	60B2	Klaipėda Lithuania	71D4	Kolaka Indon
19A3	Killeen USA			8A2	Klamath USA	77B4	Ko Lanta I Thai
12D1	Killik R USA	82B1	Kirgizskiy Khrebet Mts Kirghizia	20B2	Klamath R USA		Kollam = Quilon
44B3	Killin Scot			8A2	Klamath Falls USA	87B2	Kolār India
55B3	Killini Mt Greece	98B3	Kiri Zaire	20B2	Klamath Mts USA	87B2	Kolār Gold Fields India
45B1	Killybegs Irish Rep	105G4	Kiribati Is Pacific O	57C3	Klatovy Czech Republic		
42B2	Kilmarnock Scot	92B2	Kırıkkale Turk			97A3	Kolda Sen
61H2	Kil'mez Russian Fed	99D3	Kirinyaga Mt Kenya	12H3	Klawak USA	39F7	Kolding Den
99D3	Kilosa Tanz	60D2	Kirishi Russian Fed	94B1	Kleiat Leb	87A1	Kolhāpur India
41B3	Kilrush Irish Rep	85B3	Kirithar Range Mts Pak	101G1	Klerksdorp S Africa	12C3	Koliganek USA
99D3	Kilwa Zaire			60E2	Klin Russian Fed	59B2	Kolín Czech Republic
99D3	Kilwa Kisiwani Tanz	55C3	Kirkağaç Turk	58B1	Klintehamn Sweden	56B2	Köln Germany
99D3	Kilwa Kivinje Tanz	90A2	Kirk Bulāg Dāgh Mt Iran	60D3	Klintsy Russian Fed	58B2	Koło Pol
108A2	Kimba Aust			52C2	Ključ Bosnia-Herzegovina	21C4	Koloa Hawaiian Is
12F2	Kimball,Mt USA	42C2	Kirkby Eng			97B3	Kolokani Mali
13D3	Kimberley Can	44C3	Kirkcaldy Scot	58B2	Kłodzko Pol	60E2	Kolomna Russian Fed
101F1	Kimberley S Africa	42B2	Kirkcudbright Scot	12G2	Klondike R Can/USA		
106B2	Kimberley Plat Aust	38K5	Kirkenes Nor	4D3	Klondike Plat Can/USA	60C4	Kolomyya Ukraine
74B2	Kimch'aek N Korea	7B5	Kirkland Lake Can			65K4	Kolpashevo Russian Fed
74B3	Kimch'ŏn S Korea	112A	Kirkpatrick,Mt Ant	59B3	Klosterneuburg Austria		
55B3	Kími Greece	10A2	Kirksville USA			55C3	Kólpos Merabéllou B Greece
60E2	Kimry Russian Fed	93D2	Kirkūk Iraq	12G2	Kluane Can		
70C3	Kinabalu Mt Malay	44C2	Kirkwall Scot	12G2	Kluane L Can	55B2	Kólpos Singitikós G Greece
78D1	Kinabatangan R Malay	18B2	Kirkwood USA	12G2	Kluane Nat Pk Can		
		60D3	Kirov Russian Fed	59B2	Kluczbork Pol	55B2	Kólpos Strimonikós G Greece
14B2	Kincardine Can	61G2	Kirov Russian Fed	12G3	Klukwan USA		
13B1	Kincolith Can	65F5	Kirovakan Armenia	12E2	Klutina L USA	55B2	Kólpos Toronaíos G Greece
19B3	Kinder USA	61J2	Kirovgrad Russian Fed	12E2	Knight I USA		
13F2	Kindersley Can			43C3	Knighton Wales	38L5	Kol'skiy Poluostrov Pen Russian Fed
97A3	Kindia Guinea	60D4	Kirovograd Ukraine	52C2	Knin Croatia		
98C3	Kindu Zaire	61H2	Kirs Russian Fed	106A4	Knob,C Aust	38G6	Kolvereid Nor
61H3	Kinel' Russian Fed	92B2	Kirşehir Turk	46B1	Knokke-Heist Belg	100B2	Kolwezi Zaire
61F2	Kineshma Russian Fed	56C2	Kiruna Sweden	112C9	Knox Coast Ant	1C7	Kolyma R Russian Fed
		75B1	Kiryū Japan	11B3	Knoxville Tennessee, USA		
109D1	Kingaroy Aust	98C2	Kisangani Zaire			54B2	Kom Mt Bulg/Serbia, Yugos
21A2	King City USA	75B1	Kisarazu Japan	6H3	Knud Rasmussens Land Region Greenland		
5F4	Kingcome Inlet Can	86B1	Kishanganj India			99D2	Koma Eth
7C4	King George Is Can	85C3	Kishangarh India	6F3	Kobbermínebugt Greenland	97D3	Komaduga Gana R Nig
107D4	King I Aust	60C4	Kishinev Moldova				
13B2	King I Can	75B2	Kishiwada Japan	74D4	Kobe Japan	59B3	Komárno Slovakia
		99D3	Kisii Kenya			101H1	Komati R S Africa
		99D3	Kisiju Tanz			74D3	Komatsu Japan

75A2	Komatsushima Japan
64G3	Komi Respublika, Russian Fed
70C4	Komodo I Indon
71E4	Komoran I Indon
75B1	Komoro Japan
55C2	Komotini Greece
76D3	Kompong Cham Camb
76C3	Kompong Chhnang Mts Camb
77C3	Kompong Som Camb
76C3	Kompong Thom Camb
76D3	Kompong Trabek Camb
63F2	Komsomol'sk na Amure Russian Fed
65H4	Konda R Russian Fed
99D3	Kondoa Tanz
87B1	Kondŭzkŭr India
6G3	Kong Christian IX Land Region Greenland
6F3	Kong Frederik VI Kyst Mts Greenland
64C2	Kong Karls Land Is Barents S
78D2	Kongkemul Mt Indon
98C3	Kongolo Zaïre
39F7	Kongsberg Den
39G6	Kongsvinger Nor
	Königsberg = Kaliningrad
58B2	Konin Pol
54A2	Konjic Bosnia-Herzegovina
61F1	Konosha Russian Fed
75B1	Konosu Japan
60D3	Konotop Ukraine
59C2	Końskie Pol
49D2	Konstanz Germany
97C3	Kontagora Nig
76D3	Kontum Viet
92B2	Konya Turk
13D3	Kootenay R Can
85C5	Kopargaon India
6J3	Köpasker Iceland
38A2	Köpavogur Iceland
52B1	Koper Slovenia
80D2	Kopet Dag Mts Iran/Turkmenistan
61K2	Kopeysk Russian Fed
77C4	Ko Phangan I Thai
77B4	Ko Phuket I Thai
39H7	Köping Sweden
87B1	Koppal India
52C1	Koprivnica Croatia
85B4	Korangi Pak
87C1	Koraput India
86A2	Korba India
57B2	Korbach Germany
4B3	Korbuk R USA
55B2	Korçë Alb
52C2	Korčula I Croatia
72E2	Korea B China/Korea
74B4	Korea Str S Korea/
59D2	Korec Ukraine
92B1	Körğlu Tepesi Mt Turk
97B4	Korhogo Ivory Coast
85B4	Kori Creek India
55B3	Korinthiakós Kólpos G Greece
55B3	Kórinthos Greece
74E3	Koriyama Japan
61K3	Korkino Russian Fed
92B2	Korkuteli Turk
82C1	Korla China
52C2	Kornat I Croatia
60D5	Köroğlu Tepesi Mt
99D3	Korogwe Tanz
108B3	Koroit Aust
71E3	Koror Palau Is, Pacific O
59C3	Körös R Hung
60C3	Korosten Ukraine
95A3	Koro Toro Chad

12B3	Korovin I USA
69G2	Korsakov Russian Fed
39G7	Korsør Den
46B1	Kortrijk Belg
55C3	Kós I Greece
77C4	Ko Samui I Thai
58B2	Koscierzyna Pol
107D4	Kosciusko Mt Aust
12H3	Kosciusko I USA
74B4	Koshikijima-retto I Japan
59C3	Košice Slovakia
74B3	Kosong N Korea
54B2	Kosovo Aut Republic, Serbia, Yugos
97B4	Kossou L Ivory Coast
101G1	Koster S Africa
99D1	Kosti Sudan
59D2	Kostopol' Ukraine
61F2	Kostroma Russian Fed
56C2	Kostrzyn Pol
59B2	Koszalin Pol
85D3	Kota India
78A4	Kotaagung Indon
78C3	Kotabaru Indon
78D3	Kotabaru Indon
77C4	Kota Bharu Malay
78A3	Kotabum Indon
85C2	Kot Addu Pak
78D1	Kota Kinabalu Malay
87C1	Kotapad India
61G2	Kotel'nich Russian Fed
61F4	Kotel'nikovo Russian Fed
39K6	Kotka Fin
64F3	Kotlas Russian Fed
12B2	Kotlik USA
54A2	Kotor Montenegro, Yugos
60C4	Kotovsk Ukraine
85B3	Kotri Pak
87C1	Kottagüdem India
87B3	Kottayam India
98C2	Kotto R CAR
87B2	Kottüru India
12B1	Kotzebue USA
4B3	Kotzebue Sd USA
97C3	Kouande Benin
98C2	Kouango CAR
97B3	Koudougou Burkina
98B3	Koulamoutou Gabon
97B3	Koulikoro Mali
97B3	Koupéla Burkina
33G2	Kourou French Guiana
97B3	Kouroussa Guinea
98B1	Kousséri Cam
39K6	Kouvola Fin
38L5	Kovdor Russian Fed
60B3	Kovel' Ukraine
	Kovno = Kaunas
61F2	Kovrov Russian Fed
61F3	Kovylkino Russian Fed
60E1	Kovzha R
77C4	Ko Way I Thai
73C5	Kowloon Hong Kong
84B2	Kowt-e-Ashrow Afghan
92A2	Köyceğiz Turk
38L5	Koydor Russian Fed
87A1	Koyna Res India
12B2	Koyuk USA
12C2	Koyukuk R USA
12C1	Koyukuk R USA
92C2	Kozan Turk
55B2	Kozani Greece
61G2	Koz'modemyansk Russian Fed
75B2	Közu-shima I Japan
39F7	Kragerø Nor
54B2	Kragujevac Serbia, Yugos
77B3	Kra,Isthmus of Burma/Malay
	Krakatau = Rakata

94C1	Krak des Chevaliers Hist Site Syria
	Kraków = Cracow
54B2	Kraljevo Serbia, Yugos
60E4	Kramatorsk Ukraine
38H6	Kramfors Sweden
52B1	Kranj Slovenia
61G1	Krasavino Russian Fed
64G2	Krasino Russian Fed
59C2	Kraśnik Pol
61G3	Krasnoarmeysk Russian Fed
60E5	Krasnodar Russian Fed
61J2	Krasnokamsk Russian Fed
61K2	Krasnotur'insk Russian Fed
61J2	Krasnoufimsk Russian Fed
61J3	Krasnousol'-skiy Russian Fed
65G3	Krasnovishersk Russian Fed
65G5	Krasnovodsk Turkmenistan
63B2	Krasnoyarsk Russian Fed
59C2	Krasnystaw Pol
61G3	Krasnyy Kut Russian Fed
60E4	Krasnyy Luch Ukraine
61G4	Krasnyy Yar Russian Fed
76D3	Kratie Camb
6E2	Kraulshavn Greenland
56B2	Krefeld Germany
60D4	Kremenchug Ukraine
60D4	Kremenchugskoye Vodokhranilische Res Ukraine
59D2	Kremenets Ukraine
98A2	Kribi Cam
60D3	Krichev Belorussia
47E1	Krimml Austria
87B1	Krishna R India
87B2	Krishnagiri India
86B2	Krishnanagar India
39F7	Kristiansand Nor
39F7	Kristiansand Sweden
39G7	Kristiansund Nor
38J6	Kristiinankaupunki Fin
55B3	Kríti I Greece
60D4	Krivoy Rog Ukraine
52B1	Krk I Croatia
6G3	Kronpris Frederik Bjerge Mts Greenland
39K7	Kronshtadt Russian Fed
101G1	Kroonstad S Africa
65F5	Kropotkin Russian Fed
101G1	Krugersdorp S Africa
78A4	Krui Indon
55A2	Kruje Alb
58D2	Krupki Belorussia
12B1	Krusenstern,C USA
54B2	Kruševac Serbia, Yugos
39K7	Krustpils Latvia
12G3	Kruzof I USA
65E5	Krym Pen Ukraine
60E5	Krymsk Russian Fed
58B2	Krzyz Pol
96C1	Ksar El Boukhari Alg
96B1	Ksar el Kebir Mor
70A3	Kuala Indon
77C5	Kuala Dungun Malay
77C4	Kuala Kerai Malay
77C5	Kuala Kubu Baharu Malay
77C5	Kuala Lipis Malay
77C5	Kuala Lumpur Malay
77C4	Kuala Trengganu Malay
78D1	Kuamut Malay

74A2	Kuandian China
77C5	Kuantan Malay
93E1	Kuba Azerbaijan
71F4	Kubar PNG
70C3	Kuching Malay
78C4	Kudus Indon
61H2	Kudymkar Russian Fed
57C3	Kufstein Austria
90C3	Kuh Duren Upland Iran
91C4	Kūh e Bazmān Mt Iran
90B3	Kūh-e Dinar Mt Iran
90C2	Kūh-e-Hazār Masjed Mts Iran
91C4	Kūh-e Jebāl Barez Mts Iran
90B3	Kūh-e Karkas Mts Iran
91C4	Kūh-e Laleh Zar Mt Iran
90A2	Kūh-e Sahand Mt Iran
91D4	Kuh e Taftān Mt Iran
90A2	Kūhhaye Sabalan Mts Iran
90A3	Kūhhā-ye Zāgros Mts Iran
38K6	Kuhmo Fin
90B3	Kūhpāyeh Iran
90C3	Kūhpāyeh Mt Iran
91C4	Kūh ye Bashākerd Mts Iran
90A2	Kūh ye Sabalan Mt Iran
100A3	Kuibis Namibia
100A2	Kuito Angola
12H3	Kuiu I USA
74E2	Kuji Japan
75A2	Kuju-san Mt Japan
12C3	Kukaklek L USA
54B2	Kukës Alb
77C5	Kukup Malay
91C4	Kūl R Iran
55C3	Kula I Turk
61J4	Kulakshi Kazakhstan
99D2	Kulal,Mt Kenya
55B2	Kulata Bulg
60B2	Kuldiga Latvia
61H4	Kul'sary Kazakhstan
84D2	Kulu India
92B2	Kulu Turk
65J4	Kulunda Russian Fed
108B2	Kulwin Aust
61G5	Kuma R Russian Fed
75B1	Kumagaya Japan
78C3	Kumai Indon
74C4	Kumamoto Japan
75B2	Kumano Japan
54B2	Kumanovo Macedonia
63E2	Kumara China
97B4	Kumasi Ghana
65F5	Kumayri Armenia
98A2	Kumba Cam
87B2	Kumbakonam India
61J3	Kumertau Russian Fed
74B3	Kümhwa S Korea
39H7	Kumla Sweden
87A2	Kumta India
82C1	Kümüx China
84C2	Kunar R Afghan
39K7	Kunda Estonia
87A2	Kundapura India
85C4	Kundla India
84B1	Kunduz Afghan
98B3	Kunene R Angola
39G7	Kungsbacka Sweden
61J2	Kungur Russian Fed
76B1	Kunhing Burma
82B2	Kunlun Shan Mts China
73A4	Kunming China
74B3	Kunsan S Korea
38K6	Kuopio Fin
52C1	Kupa R Croatia/Bosnia-Herzegovina
106B2	Kupang Indon
107D2	Kupiano PNG
12H3	Kupreanof I USA

60E4 **Kupyansk** Ukraine
82C1 **Kuqa** China
75B1 **Kurabe** Japan
74C4 **Kurashiki** Japan
75A1 **Kurayoshi** Japan
54C2 **Kürdzhali** Bulg
74C4 **Kure** Japan
60B2 **Kuressaare** Estonia
63A1 **Kureyka** *R*
 Russian Fed
65H4 **Kurgan** Russian Fed
88K6 **Kuria Muria Is** Oman
38J6 **Kurikka** Fin
 Kuril Is = Kuril'skoye
 Osrova
69H2 **Kuril'skiye Ostrova**
 Russian Fed
87B1 **Kurnool** India
75C1 **Kuroiso** Japan
1182 **Kurow** NZ
109D2 **Kurri Kurri** Aust
60E3 **Kursk** Russian Fed
 Kurskiy Zaliv =
 Courland Lagoon
82A4 **Kuruktag** *R* China
100B3 **Kuruman** S Africa
74C4 **Kurume** Japan
87C3 **Kurunegala**
 Sri Lanka
65K5 **Kurunktag** *R* China
61J2 **Kusa** Russian Fed
55C3 **Kuşadasi Körfezi** *B*
 Turk
55C2 **Kus Golü** *L* Turk
74D4 **Kushimoto** Japan
74E2 **Kushiro** Japan
86A1 **Kushtia** Bang
61H3 **Kushum** *R*
 Kazakhstan
80E2 **Kushva** Afgan
65G4 **Kushva** Russian Fed
12B2 **Kuskokwim** *R* USA
12B3 **Kuskokwim B** USA
12C2 **Kuskokwim Mts** USA
86A1 **Kusma** Nepal
74E2 **Kussharo-ko** *L*
 Japan
65H4 **Kustanay**
 Kazakhstan
92A2 **Kütahya** Turk
78D3 **Kutai** *R* Indon
59B3 **Kutná Hora**
 Czech Republic
58B2 **Kutno** Pol
96B3 **Kutu** Zaire
86C2 **Kutubdia I** Bang
98C1 **Kutum** Sudan
7C4 **Kuujjuaq** Can
7C4 **Kuujjuarapik** Can
38K5 **Kuusamo** Fin
61J3 **Kuvandyk**
 Russian Fed
93E4 **Kuwait** Kuwait
80C3 **Kuwait** Sheikdom,
 S W Asia
75B1 **Kuwana** Japan
 Kuybyshev = Samara
65J4 **Kuybyshev**
 Russian Fed
61G3 **Kuybyshevskoye**
 Vodokhranilishche
 Res Russian Fed
63C2 **Kuytun** Russian Fed
60E5 **Kuzey Anadolu**
 Daglari *Mts* Turk
61G3 **Kuznetsk**
 Russian Fed
38J4 **Kvaenangen** *Sd* Nor
12C3 **Kvichak** USA
12C3 **Kvichak** *R* USA
12C3 **Kvichak R** USA
38G5 **Kvigtind** *Mt* Nor
38H5 **Kvikkjokk** Sweden
99D3 **Kwale** Kenya
74B3 **Kwangju** S Korea
98B3 **Kwango** *R* Zaire
100B2 **Kwekwe** Zim
12B2 **Kwethluk** USA
12B2 **Kwethluk** *R* USA
58B2 **Kwidzyn** Pol
71E4 **Kwoka** *Mt* Indon
108C3 **Kyabram** Aust
76B2 **Kyaikkami** Burma
76B2 **Kyaikto** Burma

68C1 **Kyakhta** Russian Fed
108A2 **Kyancutta** Aust
76B1 **Kyaukme** Burma
76B1 **Kyauk-padaung**
 Burma
76A2 **Kyaukpyu** Burma
40B2 **Kyle of Lochalsh**
 Scot
46D1 **Kyll** *R* Germany
108B3 **Kyneton** Aust
99D2 **Kyoga** *L* Uganda
109D1 **Kyogle** Aust
74B3 **Kyŏngju** S Korea
74D3 **Kyoto** Japan
 Kyrgyzstan =
 Kirghizia
65H4 **Kyshtym**
 Russian Fed
74C4 **Kyūshū** / Japan
104E3 **Kyushu-Palau Ridge**
 Pacific O
54B2 **Kyustendil** Bulg
68B1 **Kyzyl** Russian Fed
65H5 **Kyzylkum** *Desert*
 Uzbekistan
65H5 **Kzyl Orda**
 Kazakhstan

L

99E2 **Laascaanood**
 Somalia
46E1 **Laasphe** Germany
99E1 **Laasqoray** Somalia
33E1 **La Asunción** Ven
96A2 **Laâyoune** Mor
23A1 **La Barca** Mexico
97A3 **Labé** Guinea
59B2 **Labe** *R*
 Czech Republic
15D1 **Labelle** Can
7A3 **La Belle** USA
12G2 **Laberge,L** Can
78D1 **Labi** Brunei
13E2 **la Biche,L** Can
61F5 **Labinsk** Russian Fed
94C1 **Labouè** Leb
34C2 **Laboulaye** Arg
7D4 **Labrador** *Region*
 Can
7C4 **Labrador City** Can
7E4 **Labrador S**
 Greenland/Can
33E5 **Lábrea** Brazil
78D1 **Labuan** / Malay
78B4 **Labuhan** Indon
76A2 **Labutta** Burma
65H3 **Labytnangi**
 Russian Fed
7C4 **Lac à l'eau Claire**
 Can
46B2 **La Capelle** France
34C2 **La Carlota** Arg
79B3 **La Carlota** Phil
12J1 **Lac Belot** *L* Can
7C4 **Lac Bienville** *L* Can
83B4 **Laccadive Is** India
47B2 **Lac d'Annecy** *L*
 France
4G3 **Lac de Gras** *L* Can
47B1 **Lac de Joux** *L* Switz
47B1 **Lac de Neuchâtel** *L*
 Switz
23A2 **Lac de Patzcuaro** *L*
 Mexico
23A2 **Lac de Sayula** *L*
 Mexico
4F3 **Lac des Bois** *L* Can
47A2 **Lac du Bourget** *L*
 France
25D3 **La Ceiba** Honduras
108A3 **Lacepede B** Aust
48C2 **La Châtre** France
47B1 **La-Chaux-de-Fonds**
 Switz
94B3 **Lachish** *Hist Site*
 Israel
107D4 **Lachlan** *R* Aust
32B2 **La Chorrera** Panama
15D1 **Lachute** Can
7D4 **Lac Joseph** *L* Can
15C2 **Lackawanna** USA
5G4 **Lac la Biche** Can
4G3 **Lac la Martre** *L* Can
5H4 **Lac la Ronge** *L* Can

52A1 **Lac Léman** *L* Switz/
 France
10C1 **Lac Manouane** *L*
 Can
15D1 **Lac Megantic** Can
7C4 **Lac Mistassini** *L* Can
13E2 **Lacombe** Can
15D2 **Laconia** USA
50A1 **La Coruña** Spain
10A2 **La Crosse** USA
9C3 **La Cruces** USA
7A4 **Lac Seul** *L* Can
18B2 **La Cygne** USA
84D2 **Ladakh Range** India
85C3 **Lādnūn** India
73B5 **Ladong** China
60D1 **Ladozhskoye Ozero** *L*
 Ukraine
6B2 **Lady Ann Str** Can
109C4 **Lady Barron** Aust
101G1 **Ladybrand** S Africa
13C3 **Ladysmith** Can
101G1 **Ladysmith** S Africa
71F4 **Lae** PNG
76C3 **Laem Ngop** Thai
56C1 **Laesø** *I* Den
10B2 **Lafayette** Indiana,
 USA
11A3 **Lafayette** Louisiana,
 USA
46B2 **La Fère** France
46B2 **La-Ferté-sous-Jouarre**
 France
97C4 **Lafia** Nig
97C4 **Lafiagi** Nig
46B2 **La Flèche** France
96C1 **La Galite** / Tunisia
61G4 **Lagan'** Russian Fed
56C1 **Lagan** *R* Sweden
31D4 **Lagarto** Brazil
96C1 **Laghouat** Alg
35C2 **Lagoa de Araruama**
 Brazil
29F2 **Lagoa dos Patos** *Lg*
 Brazil
35C2 **Lagoa Feia** Brazil
32B4 **Lago Agrio** Ecuador
35C1 **Lagoa Juparaná** *L*
 Brazil
29D2 **Lagoa mar Chiguita** *L*
 Arg
29F2 **Lagoa Mirim** *L*
 Brazil/Urug
29B6 **Lago Argentino** *L*
 Arg
29B5 **Lago Buenos Aires** *L*
 Arg
29B5 **Lago Cochrane** *L*
 Arg/Chile
29C5 **Lago Colhué Huapi** *L*
 Arg
24B2 **Lago de Chapala** *L*
 Mexico
32A2 **Lago de Chiriqui** *L*
 Panama
23A2 **Lago de Cuitzeo** *L*
 Mexico
29B3 **Lago de la Laja** *L*
 Chile
53A2 **Lago del Coghinas** *L*
 Sardegna
32C2 **Lago de Maracaibo** *L*
 Ven
25D3 **Lago de Nicaragua** *L*
 Nic
32A1 **Lago de Perlas** *L* Nic
52B2 **Lago di Bolsena** *L*
 Italy
52B2 **Lago di Bracciano** *L*
 Italy
52A1 **Lago di Como** *L* Italy
47D2 **Lago d'Idro** *L* Italy
52B1 **Lago di Garda** *L* Italy
47C2 **Lago di Lecco** *L* Italy
47C2 **Lago di Lugano** *L*
 Italy
47D2 **Lago d'Iseo** *L* Italy
47C2 **Lago d'Orta** *L* Italy
29B5 **Lago General Carrera** *L*
 Chile
52A1 **Lago Maggiore** *L*
 Italy
29C5 **Lago Musters** *L* Arg
48B3 **Lagon** France

29B4 **Lago Nahuel Haupi** *L*
 Arg
29B5 **Lago O'Higgins** *L*
 Chile
53A2 **Lago Omodeo** *L*
 Sardegna
30C2 **Lago Poopó** *L* Bol
29B4 **Lago Ranco** *L* Chile
32D6 **Lago Rogaguado** *L*
 Bol
97C4 **Lagos** Nig
50A2 **Lagos** Port
29B5 **Lago San Martin** *L*
 Arg/Chile
24B2 **Lagos de Moreno**
 Mexico
30C2 **Lago Titicaca** Bol/
 Peru
29B5 **Lago Viedma** *L* Arg
8B2 **La Grande** USA
106B2 **Lagrange** Aust
11B3 **La Grange** Georgia,
 USA
14A3 **La Grange** Kentucky,
 USA
19A4 **La Grange** Texas,
 USA
33E2 **La Gran Sabana** *Mts*
 Ven
47B2 **La Grave** France
48B3 **Lagronño** Spain
34A3 **Laguna Aluminé** *L*
 Arg
21B3 **Laguna Beach** USA
34C3 **Laguna Colorada**
 Grande *L* Arg
79B3 **Laguna de Bay** *Lg*
 Phil
25D4 **Laguna de Caratasca**
 Lg Honduras
25D4 **Laguna de Chiriqui** *L*
 Panama
25D3 **Laguna de Managua**
 L Nic
25D3 **Laguna de Nicaragua**
 L Nic
26A4 **Laguna de Perlas** *Lg*
 Nic
23B1 **Laguna de Pueblo**
 Viejo *L* Mexico
24C2 **Laguna de Tamiahua**
 Lg Mexico
25C3 **Laguna de Términos**
 Lg Mexico
23A1 **Laguna de Yuriria** *L*
 Mexico
23A1 **Laguna le Altamira**
 Mexico
24C2 **Laguna Madre** *Lg*
 Mexico
34C2 **Laguna Mar Chiquita**
 L Arg
29B4 **Laguna Nahuel Huapi**
 L Arg
29B4 **Laguna Paiva** Arg
29B4 **Laguna Ranco** Chile
9C4 **Laguna Seca** Mexico
23B1 **Laguna Tortugas** *L*
 Mexico
70C3 **Lahad Datu** Malay
78A3 **Lahat** Indon
38J6 **Lahia** Fin
90B2 **Lahijan** Iran
46D1 **Lahn** *R* Germany
46D1 **Lahnstein** Germany
84C2 **Lahore** Pak
39K6 **Lahti** Fin
23A2 **La Huerta** Mexico
98B2 **Lai** Chad
73B5 **Laibin** China
76C1 **Lai Chau** Viet
100B4 **Laingsburg** S Africa
44B2 **Lairg** Scot
78A3 **Lais** Indon
79C4 **Lais** Phil
72E2 **Laiyang** China
72D2 **Laizhou Wan** *B*
 China
34A3 **Laja** *R* Chile
33E4 **Lajes** Brazil
30F4 **La Jolla** USA
9C3 **La Junta** USA
109C2 **Lake Cargelligo** Aust
11A3 **Lake Charles** USA

17B1 Lake City Florida, USA
17C1 Lake City S Carolina, USA
42C2 Lake District Region, Eng
22D4 Lake Elsinore USA
106C3 Lake Eyre Basin Aust
15C2 Lakefield Can
6D3 Lake Harbour Can
22C3 Lake Hughes USA
16B2 Lakehurst USA
19A4 Lake Jackson USA
13E2 Lake la Biche Can
17B2 Lakeland USA
7A5 Lake of the Woods Can
20B1 Lake Oswego USA
21A2 Lakeport USA
19B3 Lake Providence USA
111B2 Lake Pukaki NZ
109C3 Lakes Entrance Aust
22C2 Lakeshore Can
108B1 Lake Stewart Aust
15C1 Lake Traverse Can
8A2 Lakeview USA
20B1 Lakeview Mt Can
19B3 Lake Village USA
17B2 Lake Wales USA
22C4 Lakewood California, USA
16B2 Lakewood New Jersey, USA
14B2 Lakewood Ohio, USA
17B2 Lake Worth USA
86A1 Lakhimpur India
85B4 Lakhpat India
84C2 Lakki Pak
55B3 Lakonikós Kólpos G Greece
97B4 Lakota Ivory Coast
38K4 Lakseljord Inlet Nor
38K4 Lakselv Nor
34C2 La Laguna Arg
32A4 La Libertad Ecuador
34A2 La Ligua Chile
50A2 La Línea Spain
85D4 Lalitpur India
5H4 La Loche Can
13F1 la Loche,L Can
46C1 La Louvière Belg
26A4 La Luz Nic
7C5 La Malbaie Can
23B2 La Malinche Mt Mexico
50B2 La Mancha Region, Spain
9C3 Lamar Colorado, USA
18B2 Lamar Missouri, USA
19A4 La Marque USA
98B3 Lambaréné Gabon
32A5 Lambayeque Peru
112B10 Lambert Gl Ant
16B2 Lambertville USA
4F2 Lambton,C Can
47C2 Lambro R Italy
76C2 Lam Chi R Thai
50A1 Lamego Port
47B2 La Meije Mt France
32B6 La Merced Peru
21B3 La Mesa USA
55B3 Lamia Greece
42C2 Lammermuir Hills Scot
39G7 Lammhult Sweden
79B3 Lamon B Phil
18B1 Lamoni USA
17F3 Lamotrek I Pacific O
43B3 Lampeter Wales
99E3 Lamu Kenya
47D1 Lana Italy
21C4 Lanai I Hawaiian Is
21C4 Lanai City Hawaiian Is
42C2 Lanark Scot
76B3 Lanbi I Burma
76C1 Lancang R China
42C3 Lancashire County, Eng
21B3 Lancaster California, USA

42C2 Lancaster Eng
18B1 Lancaster Mississippi, USA
15D2 Lancaster New Hampshire, USA
14B3 Lancaster Ohio, USA
10C3 Lancaster Pennsylvania, USA
17B1 Lancaster S Carolina, USA
6B2 Lancaster Sd Can
78B3 Landak R Indon
46E2 Landau Germany
57C3 Landeck Austria
8C2 Lander USA
34C2 Landeta Arg
57C3 Landsberg Germany
4F2 Lands End C Can
43B4 Land's End Pt Eng
57C3 Landshut Germany
39G7 Landskrona Sweden
17A1 Lanett USA
56B2 Langenhagen Germany
47B1 Langenthal Switz
42C2 Langholm Scot
38A2 Langjökull Mts Iceland
77B4 Langkawi I Malay
13C3 Langley Can
108C1 Langlo R Aust
47B1 Langnau Switz
49D2 Langres France
70A3 langsa Indon
68C2 Lang Shan Mts China
76D1 Lang Son Viet
48C3 Languedoc Region, France
29B3 Lanin Arg
79B4 Lanoa,L L Phil
16B2 Lansdale USA
7B4 Lansdowne House Can
16B2 Lansford USA
10B2 Lansing USA
47B2 Lanslebourg France
42C2 Lanzarote I Canary Is
72A2 Lanzhou China
47B2 Lanzo Torinese Italy
79B2 Laoag Phil
76C1 Lao Cai Viet
72D1 Laoha He R China
45C2 Laois County, Irish Rep
46B2 Laon France
32B6 La Oroya Peru
76C2 Laos Republic, S E Asia
49C2 Lapalisse France
32B2 La Palma Panama
96A2 La Palma I Canary Is
34B3 La Pampa State, Arg
33E2 La Paragua Ven
34C2 La Paz Arg
34B2 La Paz Arg
30C2 La Paz Bol
24A2 La Paz Mexico
69G2 La Pérouse Str Japan/Russian Fed
23A1 La Piedad Mexico
20B2 La Pine USA
19B3 Laplace USA
23A2 la Placita Mexico
29E2 La Plata Arg
13F1 La Plonge,L Can
14A2 La Porte USA
39K6 Lappeenranta Fin
38H5 Lappland Region Sweden/Fin
34C3 Laprida Arg
1B8 Laptev S Russian Fed
38J6 Lapua Fin
79B3 Lapu-Lapu Phil
9B4 La Purisima Mexico
95B2 Laqiya Arba'in Well Sudan
30C3 La Quiaca Arg
52B2 L'Aquila Italy
91B4 Lār Iran
96B1 Larache Mor
8C2 Laramie USA

8C2 Laramie Range Mts USA
50B2 Larca Spain
9D4 Laredo USA
91B4 Larestan Region, Iran
Largeau = Faya
47B2 L'Argentière France
17B2 Largo USA
42B2 Largs Scot
90A2 Lāri Iran
30C4 La Rioja Arg
30C4 La Rioja State, Arg
55B3 Lárisa Greece
85B3 Larkana Pak
92B3 Larnaca Cyprus
94A1 Larnaca B Cyprus
45D1 Larne N Ire
50A1 La Robla Spain
46C1 La Roche-en-Ardenne Belg
48B2 La Rochelle France
47B1 La Roche-sur-Foron France
48B2 La Roche-sur-Yon France
51B2 La Roda Spain
27D3 La Romana Dom Rep
5H4 La Ronge Can
5H4 La Ronge,L Can
39F7 Larvik Nor
65J3 Laryak Russian Fed
50B2 La Sagra Mt Spain
15D1 La Salle Can
18C1 La Salle USA
12C3 La Sarre Can
34C1 Las Avispas Arg
34A2 Las Cabras Chile
5G4 Lascombe Can
9C3 Las Cruces USA
26C3 La Selle Mt Haiti
72B2 Lasengmia China
30B4 La Serena Chile
29E3 Las Flores Arg
76B1 Lashio Burma
53C3 La Sila Mts Italy
90B2 Lāsjerd Iran
34A3 Las Lajas Chile
50A2 Las Marismas Marshland Spain
96A2 Las Palmas de Gran Canaria Canary Is
52A2 La Spezia Italy
29C4 Las Plumas Arg
34C2 Las Rosas Arg
20B2 Lassen Peak Mt USA
20B2 Lassen Volcanic Nat Pk USA
23B2 las Tinaí Mexico
98B3 Lastoursville Gabon
52C2 Lastovo I Croatia
24B2 Las Tres Marías Is Mexico
34C2 Las Varillas Arg
9C3 Las Vegas USA
Latakia = Al Lādhiqiyah
53B2 Latina Italy
34B2 La Toma Arg
32D1 La Tortuga I Ven
79B2 La Trinidad Phil
109C4 Latrobe Aust
94B3 Latrun Israel
7C5 La Tuque Can
87B1 Lātūr India
60B2 Latvia Republic, Europe
107D5 Launceston Aust
43B4 Launceston Eng
29B4 La Unión Chile
25D3 La Unión El Salvador
32A4 La Unión Colombia
32B5 La Unión Peru
107D2 Laura Aust
15C3 Laurel Delaware, USA
16A3 Laurel Maryland, USA
11B3 Laurel Mississippi, USA
17B1 Laurens USA
17C1 Laurinburg USA
52A1 Lausanne Switz
78D3 Laut I Indon
29B5 Lautaro Mt Chile

46D2 Lauterecken Germany
15D1 Laval Can
48B2 Laval France
22B2 Lavaega Peak Mt USA
47C2 Laveno Italy
31B6 Lavras Brazil
4A3 Laventiya Russian Fed
101H1 Lavumisa Swaziland
78D1 Lawas Malay
76B1 Lawksawk Burma
18A2 Lawrence Kansas, USA
15D2 Lawrence Massachusetts, USA
111A3 Lawrence NZ
14A3 Lawrenceville Illinois, USA
9D3 Lawton USA
91A5 Layla S Arabia
99D2 Laylo Sudan
23A2 Lázaro Cárdenas Mexico
99E1 Laz Daua Somalia
79B4 Lazi Phil
8C2 Lead USA
13F2 Leader Can
18A2 Leavenworth USA
58B2 Leba Pol
18B2 Lebanon Missouri, USA
20B2 Lebanon Oregon, USA
15C2 Lebanon Pennsylvania, USA
92C3 Lebanon Republic, S W Asia
101C3 Lebombo Mts Mozam/S Africa/Swaziland
58B2 Lebork Pol
47A2 Le Bourg-d'Oisans France
47B1 Le Brassus Switz
29B3 Lebu Chile
47B1 Le Buet Mt France
46B1 Le Cateau France
55A2 Lecce Italy
52A1 Lecco Italy
47D1 Lech R Austria
47D1 Lechtaler Alpen Mts Austria
49C2 Le Creusot France
43C3 Ledbury Eng
13E2 Leduc Can
16C1 Lee USA
45B3 Lee R Irish Rep
41C3 Leeds Eng
43C3 Leek Eng
56B2 Leer Germany
17B2 Leesburg Florida, USA
16A3 Leesburg Virginia, USA
19B3 Leesville USA
109C2 Leeton Aust
56B2 Leeuwarden Neth
106A4 Leeuwin,C Aust
22C2 Lee Vining USA
27E3 Leeward Is Caribbean S
94A1 Lefkara Cyprus
79B3 Legazpi Phil
47D2 Legnago Italy
59B2 Legnica Pol
33F2 Leguan Inlet Guyana
32A4 Leguizamo Colombia
84D2 Leh India
48C2 Le Havre France
16B2 Lehigh R USA
16B2 Lehighton USA
84C2 Leiah Pak
59B3 Leibnitz Austria
43D3 Leicester County, Eng
107C2 Leichhardt R Aust
56A2 Leiden Neth
46B1 Leie R Belg
106C4 Leigh Creek Aust
43D4 Leighton Buzzard Eng

Leine

56B2 Leine *R* Germany
45C2 Leinster Region,
    Irish Rep
57C2 Leipzig Germany
50A2 Leiria Port
39F7 Leirvik Nor
45B1 Leitrim County,
    Irish Rep
73C4 Leiyang China
73B5 Leizhou Bandao *Pen*
    China
73C5 Leizhou Wan *B*
    China
56A2 Lek *R* Neth
96C1 Le Kef Tunisia
19B3 Leland USA
54A2 Lelija *Mt* Bosnia-
    Herzegovina
47B1 Le Locle France
48C2 Le Mans France
6D3 Lemicux Is Can
5C2 Lemmon USA
2182 Lemoore USA
49C2 Lempdes France
86C2 Lemro *R* Burma
52C2 Le Murge Region,
    Italy
63C2 Lena *R* Russian Fed
38L6 Lendery Russian Fed
73C4 Lengshujiang China
    Leningrad = Sankt-
    Peterburg
112B7 Leningradskaya *Base*
    Ant
61H3 Leninogorsk
    Tatarskaya
    Respublika,
    Russian Fed
68A1 Leninogorsk
    Kazakhstan
65K4 Leninsk-Kuznetskiy
    Russian Fed
69F2 Leninskoye
    Russian Fed
65F6 Lenkoran' Azerbaijan
46E1 Lenne *R* Germany
16C1 Lenox USA
46B1 Lens France
63D1 Lensk Russian Fed
53B3 Lentini Italy
76B3 Lenya *R* Burma
52B1 Leoben Austria
43C3 Leominster Eng
16D1 Leominster USA
24B2 León Mexico
25D3 León Nic
50A1 León Region, Spain
50A1 León Spain
100A3 Leonardville
    Namibia
106B3 Leonora Aust
35C2 Leopoldina Brazil
    Léopoldville =
    Kinshasa
60C3 Lepel Belorussia
73D4 Leping China
49C2 Le Puy-en-Velay
    France
98B2 Léré Chad
101G1 Leribe Lesotho
47C2 Lerici Italy
51C1 Lérida Spain
23A1 Lerma *R* Mexico
47D1 Lermoos Austria
55C3 Léros *I* Greece
44E1 Lerwick Scot
46A2 Les Andelys France
26C3 Les Cayes Haiti
47B2 Les Echelles *Mt* France
73A4 Leshan China
54B2 Leskovac Serbia,
    Yugos
48B3 Les Landes Region,
    France
101G1 Leslie S Africa
61H2 Lesnoy Russian Fed
63B2 Lesosibirsk
    Russian Fed
101G1 Lesotho Kingdom,
    S Africa
69F2 Lesozavodsk
    Russian Fed
48B2 Les Sables-d'Olonne
    France

112A Lesser Antarctica
    Region, Ant
27D4 Lesser Antilles *Is*
    Caribbean S
65F5 Lesser Caucasus *Mts*
    Azerbaijan/Georgia
13E1 Lesser Slave L Can
55C3 Lésvos *I* Greece
58B2 Leszno Pol
86C2 Letha Range *Mts*
    Burma
5G5 Lethbridge Can
33F3 Lethem Guyana
59D3 Letichev Ukraine
63D2 Let Oktyobr'ya
    Russian Fed
78B2 Letong Indon
46A1 Le Touquet-Paris-
    Plage France
76B2 Letpadan Burma
48C1 Le Tréport France
47B1 Leuk Switz
57A2 Leuven Belg
55B3 Levádhia Greece
38G6 Levanger Nor
47B2 Levanna *Mt* Italy
71D6 Lévêque,C Aust
46D1 Leverkusen
    Germany
59B3 Levice Slovakia
47D1 Levico Italy
110C2 Levin NZ
7C5 Lévis Can
15D2 Levittown USA
55B3 Lévka *ri Mt* Greece
55B3 Levkás Greece
55B3 Levkás *I* Greece
106B2 Lévêque,C Aust
54C2 Levski Bulg
43E4 Lewes Eng
4082 Lewis *I* Scot
16A2 Lewisburg USA
111B2 Lewis P NZ
8B2 Lewis Range *Mts*
    USA
8B2 Lewiston Idaho, USA
10C2 Lewiston Maine,
    USA
8C2 Lewistown Montana,
    USA
15C2 Lewistown
    Pennsylvania, USA
19B3 Lewisville USA
11B3 Lexington Kentucky,
    USA
18B2 Lexington Missouri,
    USA
15C3 Lexington Park USA
79C3 Leyte G Phil
54A2 Lezhe Alb
82D3 Lhasa China
86B1 Lhazê China
70A3 Lhokseumawe Indon
86C1 Lhozhag China
68B4 Lhunze China
    Liancourt Rocks =
    Tok-do
79C4 Lianga Phil
72B3 Liangdang China
73C5 Lianjiang China
73C5 Lianping China
73C5 Lian Xian China
72D3 Lianyungang China
72E1 Liaodong Bandao *Pen*
    China
72E1 Liaodong Wan *B*
    China
72E1 Liao He *R* China
72E1 Liaoning Province,
    China
72E1 Liaoyang China
72E1 Liaoyuan China
74B2 Liaoyuang China
4F3 Liard *R* Can
4F4 Liard River Can
46C2 Liart France
98B2 Libenge Zaire
9C3 Liberal USA
57C2 Liberec
    Czech Republic
97A4 Liberia Republic,
    Africa
18B2 Liberty Missouri,
    USA

15D2 Liberty New York,
    USA
19B3 Liberty Texas, USA
48B3 Libourne France
23B2 Libres Mexico
98A2 Libreville Gabon
95A2 Libya Republic,
    Africa
95B2 Libyan Desert Libya
95B1 Libyan Plat Egypt
53B3 Licata Italy
43D3 Lichfield Eng
101C2 Lichinga Mozam
101G1 Lichtenburg S Africa
14B3 Licking *R* Can
22B2 Lick Observatory
    USA
60C3 Lida Belorussia
39G7 Lidköping Sweden
53B2 Lido di Ostia Italy
52A1 Liechtenstein
    Principality, Europe
57B2 Liège Belg
58C1 Lielupe *R* Latvia
98C2 Lienart Zaire
57C3 Lienz Austria
60B2 Liepāja Latvia
46C1 Lier Belg
47B1 Liestal Switz
47C1 Lièvre *R* Can
57C3 Liezen Austria
45C2 Liffey *R* Irish Rep
45C1 Lifford Irish Rep
107F3 Lifu *I* Nouvelle
    Calédonie
109C1 Lightning Ridge Aust
46C2 Ligny-en-Barrois
    France
101C2 Ligonha *R* Mozam
47C2 Liguria Region, Italy
52A2 Ligurian S Italy
21C4 Lihue Hawaiian Is
100B2 Likasi Zaire
49E1 Lille France
39C6 Lillehammer Nor
46B1 Lillers France
39G7 Lillestøm Nor
13C2 Lillooet Can
13C2 Lillooet *R* Can
101C2 Lilongwe Malawi
79B4 Liloy Phil
54A2 Lim *R* Montenegro/
    Serbia, Yugos
32B6 Lima Peru
50A1 Lima Spain
10B2 Lima USA
92B3 Limassol Cyprus
45C1 Limavady N Ire
34B3 Limay *R* Arg
34B3 Limay Mahuida Arg
98A2 Limbe Cam
72C2 Limbe Malawi
57B2 Limburg W Gem
31B6 Limeira Brazil
45B2 Limerick County,
    Irish Rep
41B3 Limerick Irish Rep
56B1 Limfjorden *L* Den
106C2 Limmen Bight *B*
    Aust
55C3 Límnos *I* Greece
31D3 Limoeiro Brazil
48C2 Limoges France
25D4 Limón Costa Rica
8C3 Limon USA
48C2 Limousin Region,
    France
79A3 Linapacan Str Phil
29B3 Linares Chile
9D4 Linares Mexico
50B2 Linares Spain
68B4 Lincang China
29D2 Lincoln Arg
18A1 Lincoln California,
    USA
42D3 Lincoln County, Eng
42D3 Lincoln Eng
18C1 Lincoln Illinois, USA
8D2 Lincoln Nebraska,
    USA
15D2 Lincoln New
    Hampshire, USA
111B2 Lincoln NZ
80A Lincoln *S* Greenland

20B2 Lincoln City USA
14B2 Lincoln Park USA
52A2 L'Incudina *Mt* Corse
57B3 Lindau Germany
33F2 Linden Guyana
39F7 Lindesnes *C* Nor
99D3 Lindi Tanz
98C2 Lindi *R* Zaire
101G1 Lindley S Africa
55C3 Líndos Greece
15C2 Lindsay Can
105J3 Line Is Pacific O
72C2 Linfen China
76D2 Lingao China
79B2 Lingayen Phil
56B2 Lingen Germany
78B3 Lingga *I* Indon
73B5 Lingshan China
72C2 Lingshi China
97A3 Linguère Sen
73E4 Linhai Rhejiang,
    China
31D5 Linhares Brazil
72B1 Linhe China
74B2 Linjiang China
39H7 Linköping Sweden
72D2 Linqing China
35B2 Lins Brazil
72A2 Lintao China
47C1 Linthal Switz
68D2 Linxi China
72A2 Linxia China
57C3 Linz Austria
79B3 Lipa Phil
52A2 Lipari *I* Italy
61E3 Lipetsk Russian Fed
54B1 Lipova Rom
56B2 Lippe *R* Germany
46E1 Lippstadt Germany
99D2 Lira Uganda
98B3 Liranga Congo
98C2 Lisala Zaire
50A2 Lisboa Port
    Lisbon = Lisboa
45C1 Lisburn N Ire
45B2 Liscannor B Irish Rep
73D4 Lishui China
73C4 Li Shui *R* China
60E4 Lisichansk Ukraine
48C2 Lisieux France
60E3 Liski Russian Fed
46B2 L'Isle-Adam France
47B1 L'Isle-sur-le-Doubs
    France
107E3 Lismore Aust
45B2 Listowel Irish Rep
73B5 Litang China
94B2 Litani *R* Leb
33G3 Litani *R* Surinam
18C2 Litchfield USA
107E4 Lithgow Aust
60B2 Lithuania Republic,
    Europe
16A2 Lititz USA
69F2 Litovko Russian Fed
19A3 Little *R* USA
11C4 Little Abaco *I*
    The Bahamas
110C1 Little Barrier I NZ
13E2 Little Bow *R* Can
25D3 Little Cayman *I*
    Caribbean S
16B3 Little Egg Harbor *B*
    USA
26C2 Little Inagua *I*
    Caribbean S
77A4 Little Nicobar *I*
    Nicobar Is
11A3 Little Rock USA
22D3 Littlerock USA
13D2 Little Smoky Can
13D2 Little Smoky *R* Can
16A3 Littlestown USA
15D2 Littleton New
    Hampshire, USA
74B2 Liuhe China
73B5 Liuzhou China
55B3 Livanátais Greece
58D1 Līvāni Latvia
12E1 Livengood USA
17B1 Live Oak USA
21A2 Livermore USA
7D5 Liverpool Can
42C3 Liverpool Eng

4E2 Liverpool B Can
42C3 Liverpool B Eng
6C2 Liverpool,C Can
109D2 Liverpool Range Mts
Aust
8B2 Livingston Montana,
USA
19B3 Livingston Texas,
USA
44C4 Livingstone =
Livingstone =
Maramba
19A3 Livingston,L USA
52C2 Livno Bosnia-
Herzegovina
60E3 Livny Russian Fed
14B2 Livonia USA
52B2 Livorno Italy
99D3 Liwale Tanz
52B1 Ljubljana Slovenia
38G6 Ljungan R Sweden
39G7 Ljungby Sweden
39H6 Ljusdal Sweden
38H6 Ljusnan R Sweden
43C4 Llandeilo Wales
43C4 Llandovery Wales
43C3 Llandrindod Wells
Wales
42C3 Llandudno Wales
43B4 Llanelli Wales
43C3 Llangollen Wales
9C3 Llano Estacado Plat
USA
32C2 Llanos Region,
Colombia/Ven
30D2 Llanos de Chiquitos
Region, Bol
Lleida = Lérida
50A2 Llerena Spain
43B3 Lleyn Pen Wales
89E7 Llorin Nig
5H4 Lloydminster Can
30C3 Llullaillaco Mt Arg/
Chile
30C3 Loa R Chile
49C2 Loan France
98B3 Loange R Zaire
100B3 Lobatse Botswana
98B2 Lobaye R CAR
34D3 Loberia Arg
100A2 Lobito Angola
34D3 Lobos Arg
47B2 Locano Italy
47C1 Locarno Switz
44B3 Loch Awe L Scot
44A3 Lochboisdale Scot
44A3 Loch Bracadale Inlet
Scot
44B3 Loch Broom Estuary
Scot
42B2 Loch Doon L Scot
44B3 Loch Earn L Scot
44B2 Loch Ericht Inlet
Scot
44B3 Loch Ericht L Scot
48C2 Loches France
44B3 Loch Etive Inlet Scot
44B3 Loch Ewe Inlet Scot
44B3 Loch Fyne Inlet Scot
44B3 Loch Hourn Inlet
Scot
44B2 Lochinver Scot
44B3 Loch Katrine L Scot
44C3 Loch Leven L Scot
44B3 Loch Linnhe Inlet
Scot
44B3 Loch Lochy L Scot
44B3 Loch Lomond L Scot
44B3 Loch Long Inlet Scot
44A3 Lochmaddy Scot
44B3 Loch Maree L Scot
44B3 Loch Morar L Scot
44C3 Lochnagar Mt Scot
44B3 Loch Ness L Scot
44B3 Loch Rannoch L
Scot
44A2 Loch Roag Inlet Scot
44B3 Loch Sheil L Scot
44B3 Loch Shin L Scot
44A3 Loch Snizort Inlet
Scot
44B3 Loch Sunart Inlet
Scot
44B3 Loch Tay L Scot

44B3 Loch Torridon Inlet
Scot
108A2 Lock Aust
42C2 Lockerbie Scot
15C2 Lock Haven USA
15C2 Lockport USA
76D3 Loc Ninh Viet
53C3 Locri Italy
94B3 Lod Israel
108B3 Loddon R Aust
60D1 Lodeynoye Pole
Russian Fed
84C3 Lodhran Pak
52A1 Lodi Italy
21A2 Lodi USA
98C3 Lodja Zaire
47B1 Lods France
99D2 Lodwar Kenya
58B2 Łódź Pol
38G5 Lofoten Is Nor
8B2 Logan Utah, USA
4D3 Logan,Mt Can
14A2 Logansport Indiana,
USA
19B3 Logansport
Louisiana, USA
50B1 Logroño Spain
86A2 Lohārdaga India
39J6 Lohja Fin
76B2 Loikaw Burma
39J6 Loimaa Fin
48C2 Loir R France
49C2 Loire R France
32B4 Loja Ecuador
50B2 Loja Spain
38K5 Lokan Tekojärvi Res
Fin
46B1 Lokeren Belg
99D2 Lokitaung Kenya
58D1 Loknya Russian Fed
98C3 Lokolo R Zaire
98C3 Lokoro R Zaire
6D3 Loks Land L Can
5C2 Lolland L Den
54B2 Lom Bulg
98C3 Lomami R Zaire
97A4 Loma Mts Sierra
Leone/Guinea
47C2 Lombardia Region,
Italy
71D4 Lomblen I Indon
78D4 Lombok I Indon
79C4 Lomé Togo
98C3 Lomela Zaire
98C3 Lomela R Zaire
60C2 Lomonosov
Russian Fed
47B1 Lomont Region,
France
21A3 Lompoc USA
58C2 Łomza Pol
87A1 Lonāvale India
29B3 Loncoche Chile
7B5 London Can
43D4 London Eng
45C1 Londonderry County,
N Ire
45C1 Londonderry N Ire
29B7 Londonderry I Chile
106B2 Londonderry,C Aust
30C4 Londres Arg
30F3 Londrina Brazil
21B2 Lone Pine USA
11C4 Long I The Bahamas
71F4 Long I PNG
78C2 Long Akah Malay
47E1 Longarone Italy
34A3 Longavi Mt Chile
27H2 Long B Jamaica
17C1 Long B USA
9B3 Long Beach
California, USA
15D2 Long Beach New
York, USA
15D2 Long Branch USA
73D5 Longchuan China
20C2 Long Creek USA
109C4 Longford Aust
45C2 Longford County,
Irish Rep
44D3 Long Forties Region
N Sea
72D1 Longhua China

7C4 Long I Can
10C2 Long I USA
16C2 Long Island Sd USA
78I4 Longlac Can
73B5 Longlin China
8C2 Longmont USA
78D2 Longnawan Indon
29B3 Longquimay Chile
107D3 Longreach Aust
72A2 Longshou Shan
Upland China
42C2 Longtown Eng
15D1 Longueuil Can
34A3 Longuimay Chile
46C2 Longuyon France
11A3 Longview Texas,
USA
8A2 Longview
Washington, USA
46C2 Longwy France
72A3 Longxi China
77D3 Long Xuyen Viet
73D4 Longyan China
73B5 Longzhou China
47D2 Lonigo Italy
49D2 Lons-le-Saunier
France
11C3 Lookout,C USA
99D3 Loolmalasin Mt
Tanz
13D1 Loon R Can
45B2 Loop Hd C Irish Rep
76C3 Lop Buri Thai
98A3 Lopez C Gabon
68B2 Lop Nur L China
30B2 Lora del Rio Spain
10B2 Lorain USA
84B2 Loralai Pak
90B3 Lordegān Iran
107E4 Lord Howe I Aust
105G5 Lord Howe Rise
Pacific O
6A3 Lord Mayor B Can
9C3 Lordsburg USA
35B2 Lorena Brazil
47E2 Loreo Italy
23A1 Loreto Mexico
48B2 Lorient France
44B3 Lorne Aust
57B3 Lörrach Germany
49D2 Lorraine Region
France
9C3 Los Alamos USA
34A2 Los Andes Chile
29B3 Los Angeles Chile
9B3 Los Angeles USA
21A2 Los Banos USA
21A2 Los Gatos USA
52B2 Lošinj I Croatia
29B3 Los Lagos Chile
24B2 Los Mochis Mexico
22B3 Los Olivos USA
34A3 Los Sauces Chile
44C3 Lossiemouth Scot
27E4 Los Testigos Is Ven
29C2 Los Vilos Chile
48C3 Lot R France
34A3 Lota Chile
42C2 Lothian Region, Scot
99D2 Lotikipi Plain Sudan/
Kenya
98C3 Loto Zaire
47B1 Lötschberg Tunnel
Switz
38K5 Lotta R Fin/
Russian Fed
48B2 Loudéac France
97A3 Louga Sen
45C2 Lough Allen L
Irish Rep
45C2 Lough Boderg L
Irish Rep
43D3 Loughborough Eng
45C2 Lough Bowna L
Irish Rep
45C1 Lough Carlingford L
N Ire
41B3 Lough Conn L
Irish Rep
41B3 Lough Corrib L
Irish Rep
41B3 Lough Derg L
Irish Rep

45C2 Lough Derravaragh L
Irish Rep
4H2 Loughead I Can
45C2 Lough Ennell L
Irish Rep
41B3 Lough Erne L N Ire
40B2 Lough Foyle Estuary
N Ire/Irish Rep
40B3 Lough Neagh L N Ire
45C1 Lough Oughter L
Irish Rep
45B2 Loughrea Irish Rep
45C2 Lough Ree L
Irish Rep
45C2 Lough Sheelin L
Irish Rep
42B2 Lough Strangford L
Irish Rep
45C1 Lough Swilly Estuary
Irish Rep
14B3 Louisa USA
70C3 Louisa Reef /
S E Asia
12E2 Louisa,L USA
107E2 Louisiade Arch
Solomon Is
11A3 Louisiana State, USA
17B1 Louisville Georgia,
USA
11B3 Louisville Kentucky,
USA
38L5 Loukhi Russian Fed
48B3 Lourdes France
108C2 Louth Aust
45C2 Louth County,
Irish Rep
42D3 Louth Eng
Louvain = Leuven
48C2 Louviers France
60D2 Lovat R Russian Fed
54B2 Lovech Bulg
21B1 Lovelock USA
52B1 Lòvere Italy
9C3 Lovington USA
38L5 Lovozero
Russian Fed
6B3 Low,C Can
10C2 Lowell
Massachusetts, USA
20B2 Lowell Oregon, USA
16D1 Lowell USA
111B2 Lower Hutt NZ
43E3 Lowestoft Eng
50D2 Łowicz Pol
108B2 Loxton Aust
5F4 Loyd George,Mt Can
54A2 Loznica Serbia,
Yugos
23A2 Loz Reyes Mexico
65H3 Lozva R Russian Fed
100B2 Luacano Angola
98C3 Luachimo Angola
98C3 Lualaba R Zaire
100B2 Luampa Zambia
100B2 Luân Angola
73D3 Lu'an China
98B3 Luanda Angola
100A2 Luando R Angola
100B2 Luanguinga R
Angola
76C1 Luang Namtha Laos
76C2 Luang Prabang Laos
98B3 Luangue R Angola
100C2 Luangwa R Zambia
72D1 Luan He R China
72D1 Luanping China
100B2 Luanshya Zambia
100B2 Luapula R Zaire
50A1 Luarca Spain
98B3 Lubalo Angola
58D2 L'uban Belorussia
79B3 Lubang Is Phil
100A2 Lubango Angola
9C3 Lubbock USA
56C2 Lübeck Germany
98C3 Lubefu Zaire
98C3 Lubefu R Zaire
99C3 Lubero Zaire
98C3 Lubilash R Zaire
59C2 Lublin Pol
60D3 Lubny Ukraine
78C2 Lubok Antu Malay
98C3 Lubudi Zaire
98C3 Lubudi R Zaire

Lubuklinggau

78A3 Lubuklinggau Indon
100B2 Lubumbashi Zaire
98C3 Lubutu Zaire
79B3 Lucban Phil
52B2 Lucca Italy
42B2 Luce B Scot
19C3 Lucedale USA
79B3 Lucena Phil
59B3 Lucenec Slovakia
Lucene = Luzern
37C5 Luchuan China
56C2 Luckenwalde
Germany
101F1 Luckhoff S Africa
86A1 Lucknow India
100B2 Lucusse Angola
46D1 Lüdenscheid
Germany
100A3 Lüderitz Namibia
84D2 Ludhiana India
14A2 Ludington USA
43C3 Ludlow Eng
54C2 Ludogorie Upland
Bulg
17B1 Ludowici USA
54B1 Luduş Rom
39H6 Ludvika Sweden
57B3 Ludwigsburg
Germany
57B3 Ludwigshafen
Germany
56C2 Ludwigslust
Germany
98C3 Luebo Zaire
98C3 Luema R Zaire
98C3 Luembe R Angola
100A2 Luena Angola
100B2 Luena R Angola
72B3 Lüeyang China
73D5 Lufeng China
11A3 Lufkin USA
60C2 Luga Russian Fed
60C2 Luga R Russian Fed
52A1 Lugano Switz
60E4 Lugansk Ukraine
101C2 Lugela Mozam
101C2 Lugenda R Mozam
50A1 Lugo Spain
72A3 Luhuo China
98B3 Lui R Angola
100B2 Luiana Angola
100B2 Luiana R Angola
Luichow Peninsula =
Leizhou Bandao
47C2 Luino Italy
98B2 Luionga R Zaire
72B2 Luipan Shan Upland
China
100B2 Luishia Zaire
68B4 Luixi China
98C3 Luiza Zaire
34B2 Luján Arg
34D2 Luján Arg
73D3 Lujiang China
98B3 Lukenie R Zaire
64E4 Luki Russian Fed
98B3 Lukolela Zaire
58C2 Luków Pol
98C3 Lukuga R Zaire
100B2 Lukulu Zambia
38J5 Lule R Sweden
38J5 Luleå Sweden
54C2 Lüleburgaz Turk
72C2 Lüliang Shan Mts
China
19A4 Luling USA
98C2 Lulonga R Zaire
Luluabourg =
Kananga
100B2 Lumbala Kaquengue
Angola
11C3 Lumberton USA
78D1 Lumbis Indon
86C1 Lumding India
100B2 Lumeje Angola
11A3 Lumsden NZ
39G7 Lund Sweden
101C2 Lundazi Zambia
43B4 Lundy I Eng
56C2 Lüneburg Germany
46D2 Lunéville France
100B2 Lunga R Zambia
86C2 Lunglei India

100A2 Lungue Bungo R
Angola
58D2 Luninec Belorussia
98B3 Luobomo Congo
73B5 Luocheng China
73C5 Luoding China
72C3 Luohe China
72C3 Luo He R Henan,
China
72B2 Luo He R Shaanxi,
China
73C4 Luoxiao Shan Hills
China
72C3 Luoyang China
98B3 Luozi Zaire
100B2 Lupane Zim
101C2 Lupilichi Mozam
La Qu = Tao He
30E4 Luque Par
45C1 Lurgan N Ire
101C2 Lurio R Mozam
90A3 Luristan Region, Iran
100B2 Lusaka Zambia
98C3 Lusambo Zaire
55A2 Lushnjë Alb
99D3 Lushoto Tanz
68B4 Lushui China
72E2 Lüshun China
43D4 Luton Eng
60C3 Lutsk Ukraine
99E2 Luuq Somalia
99C3 Luvua R Zaire
99D3 Luwegu R Tanz
100C2 Luwingu Zambia
71D4 Luwuk Indon
46D2 Luxembourg Grand
Duchy, N W Europe
49D2 Luxembourg Lux
73A5 Luxi China
52C2 Luxor Egypt
61G1 Luza Russian Fed
61G1 Luza R Russian Fed
52A1 Luzern Switz
73B5 Luzhai China
73B4 Luzhi China
73B4 Luzhou China
35B1 Luziânia Brazil
79B2 Luzon I Phil
79B1 Luzon Str Phil
57C3 L'vov Ukraine
44C2 Lybster Scot
38H6 Lycksele Sweden
100B3 Lydenburg S Africa
8B3 Lyell,Mt USA
16A2 Lykens USA
43C4 Lyme B Eng
43C4 Lyme Regis Eng
11C3 Lynchburg USA
108A2 Lyndhurst Aust
15D2 Lynn USA
12G3 Lynn Canal Sd USA
17A1 Lynn Haven USA
5H4 Lynn Lake Can
5H3 Lynx L Can
49C2 Lyon France
12G3 Lyon Canal Sd USA
15C1 Lyons Georgia, USA
106A3 Lyons R Aust
47B2 Lys R Italy
61J2 Lys'va R Russian Fed
111B2 Lyttelton NZ
13C2 Lytton Can
22A1 Lytton USA
58D2 Lyubeshov Ukraine
60E2 Lyublino Russian Fed

M

76C1 Ma R Viet
94B2 Ma'agan Israel
94B2 Ma'alot Tarshiha
Israel
92C3 Ma'an Jordan
73D3 Ma'anshan China
92C2 Ma'arrat an Nu'mān
Syria
46C1 Maas R Neth
46C1 Maaseik Belg
79B3 Maasin Phil
57B2 Maastricht Neth
101C3 Mabalane Mozam
33F2 Mabaruma Guyana
42E3 Mablethorpe Eng
101C3 Mabote Mozam
58C2 Mabrita Belorussia

58D2 M'adel Belorussia
35C2 Macaé Brazil
9D3 McAlester USA
8C4 McAllen USA
101C2 Macaloge Mozam
33G3 Macapá Brazil
35C1 Macarani Brazil
32B4 Macas Ecuador
31D3 Macaú Brazil
73C5 Macau Dependency,
China
98C2 M'Bari R CAR
13C2 McBride Can
12F2 McCarthy USA
13A2 McCauley I Can
42C3 Macclesfield Eng
6B1 McClintock B Can
4H2 McClintock Chan
Can
16A2 McClure USA
22B2 McClure,L USA
4F4 McClure Str Can
19B3 McComb USA
8C2 McCook USA
6C2 Macculloch,C Can
16C1 McCusker,Mt Can
4F4 McDame Can
20C2 McDermitt USA
13E2 Macdonald R Can
106C3 Macdonnell Ranges
Mts Aust
50A1 Macedo de Cavaleiros
Port
55B2 Macedonia Republic,
Europe
31D3 Maceió Brazil
97B4 Macenta Guinea
52B2 Macerata Italy
108A2 Macfarlane,L Aust
19B3 McGehee USA
45B3 MacGillycuddys
Reeks Mts Irish Rep
4C3 McGrath USA
35B2 Machado Brazil
101C3 Machaila Mozam
99D3 Machakos Kenya
32B4 Machala Ecuador
101C3 Machaze Mozam
87B1 Mācherla India
94B2 Machgharab Leb
87C1 Machilipatnam India
32C1 Machiques Ven
32C6 Machu-Picchu Hist
Site Peru
101C3 Macia Mozam
109C1 MacIntyre R Aust
107D3 Mackay Aust
106B3 Mackay,L Aust
14C2 McKeesport USA
13C1 Mackenzie Can
4F3 Mackenzie R Can
4E3 Mackenzie B Can
4G2 Mackenzie King I Can
4E3 Mackenzie Mts Can
14B1 Mackinac,Str of USA
14B1 Mackinaw City USA
12D2 McKinley,Mt USA
19A3 McKinney USA
6C2 Mackinson Inlet B
Can
109D2 Macksville Aust
20B2 Mclaoughlin,Mt USA
109D1 Maclean Aust
100B4 Maclear S Africa
13D2 McLeod R Can
4G3 McLeod B Can
106A3 McLeod,L USA
13C1 McLeod Lake Can
4E3 Macmillan R Can
12H2 Macmillan P Can
20B1 McMinnville Oregon,
USA
112B7 McMurdo Base Ant
13D2 McNaughton L Can
18B1 Macomb USA
53A2 Macomer Sardegna
101C2 Macomia Mozam
11B3 Macon Georgia, USA
18B2 Macon Missouri,
USA
100B2 Macondo Angola
18A2 McPherson USA

104F6 Macquarie Is Aust
109C2 Macquarie R Aust
109C4 Macquarie Harbour B
Aust
109D2 Macquarie,L Aust
17B1 McRae USA
112B11 Mac. Robertson Land
Region, Ant
45B3 Macroom Irish Rep
96C1 M'Sila Alg
4G3 McTavish Arm B
Can
108A1 Macumba R Aust
47C2 Macunaga Italy
4F3 McVicar Arm B Can
59B3 M'yarovár Hung
94B3 Madaba Jordan
95A3 Madadi Well Chad
89J10 Madagascar I
Indian O
95A2 Madama Niger
71F4 Madang PNG
97C3 Madaoua Niger
86C2 Madaripur Bang
90B2 Madau Turkmenistan
15C1 Madawaska R Can
96A1 Madeira I Atlantic O
33E5 Madeira R Brazil
7D5 Madeleine, Isle de la
Can
24B2 Madera Mexico
21A2 Madera USA
87A1 Madgaon India
86B1 Madhubani India
86A2 Madhya Pradesh
State, India
87B2 Madikeri India
98B3 Madimba Zaire
98B3 Madingo Kayes
Congo
98B3 Madingou Congo
10B3 Madison Indiana,
USA
10B2 Madison Wisconsin,
USA
18C2 Madisonville
Kentucky, USA
19A3 Madisonville Texas,
USA
78C4 Madiun Indon
99D2 Mado Gashi Kenya
47D1 Madonna Di
Campiglio Italy
87C2 Madras India
20B2 Madras USA
29A6 Madre de Dios I
Chile
32D6 Madre de Dios R Bol
50B1 Madrid Spain
50B2 Madridejos Spain
47A1 Madura I Indon
87B3 Madurai India
75B1 Maebashi Japan
76B3 Mae Khlong R Thai
77B4 Mae Nam Lunang R
Thai
76C2 Mae Nam Mun R
Thai
76B2 Mae Nam Ping R
Thai
101D2 Maevatanana Madag
101G1 Mafeteng Lesotho
109C3 Maffra Aust
99D3 Mafia I Tanz
101G1 Mafikeng S Africa
30G4 Mafra Brazil
92C3 Mafraq Jordan
32C2 Magangué Colombia
34D3 Magdagachi
24A1 Magdalena Mexico
26C4 Magdalena R
Colombia
78D1 Magdalena,Mt Malay
56C2 Magdeburg Germany
31C6 Magé Brazil
78C4 Magelang Indon
47C1 Maggia R Switz
92B4 Maghâgha Egypt
45C1 Magherafelt N Ire
55A2 Maglie Italy
61J3 Magnitogorsk
Russian Fed
19B3 Magnolia USA
101C2 Magoé Mozam

15D1 Magog Can
23B1 Magosal Mexico
13E2 Magrath Can
7A3 Magwe River Can
76B1 Magwe Burma
90A2 Mahābād Iran
86B1 Mahabharat Range
Mts Nepal
87A1 Mahād India
85D4 Mahadeo Hills India
101D2 Mahajanga Madag
100B3 Mahalapye Botswana
86A2 Mahanadi R India
101D2 Mahanoro Madag
16A2 Mahanoy City USA
87A1 Maharashtra State,
India
86A2 Māhāsamund India
76C2 Maha Sarakham Thai
101D2 Mahavavy R Madag
87B1 Mahbūbnagar India
96D1 Mahdia Tunisia
87B2 Mahe India
85D4 Mahekar India
101D2 Mahéli I Comoros
86A2 Mahendragarh India
99D3 Mahenge Tanz
84C2 Mahesana India
110C1 Mahia Pen NZ
85D3 Mahoba India
51C2 Mahon Spain
12J1 Mahony L Can
96D1 Mahrès Tunisia
85C4 Mahuva India
32C1 Maicao Colombia
47B1 Maîche France
43E4 Maidstone Eng
98B1 Maiduguri Nig
86A2 Maihar India
86C2 Maijdi Bang
76B3 Mail Kyun I Burma
84A1 Maimana Afghan
14B1 Main Chan Can
98B3 Mai-Ndombe L Zaïre
10D2 Maine State, USA
48B2 Maine Region
France
44C2 Mainland I Scot
85D3 Mainpuri India
46A2 Maintenon France
101D2 Maintirano Madag
57B2 Mainz Germany
97A4 Maio I Cape Verde
29C2 Maipó Mt Arg/Chile
34D3 Maipú Arg
32D1 Maiquetía Ven
47B2 Maira R Italy
86C1 Mairābāri India
86C2 Maiskhal I Bang
107E4 Maitland New South
Wales, Aust
108A2 Maitland S Australia,
Aust
112C12 Maitri Base Ant
74D3 Maizuru Japan
70C4 Majene Indon
30B2 Majes R Peru
99D2 Maji Eth
72D2 Majia He R China
Majunga =
Mahajanga
70C4 Makale Indon
86B1 Makalu Mt China/
Nepal
98A3 Makanza Zaïre
52C2 Makarska Croatia
61F2 Makaryev
Russian Fed
Makassar = Ujung
Pandang
78D3 Makassar Str Indon
61H4 Makat Kazakhstan
97A4 Makeni Sierra Leone
60E4 Makeyevka Ukraine
100B3 Makgadikgadi Salt
Pan Botswana
61G5 Makhachkala
Russian Fed
99D3 Makindu Kenya
88H5 Makkah S Arabia
7E4 Makkovik Can
59C3 Makó Hung
98B2 Makokou Gabon
110C1 Makorako,Mt NZ

98B2 Makoua Congo
85C3 Makrāna India
85A3 Makran Coast Range
Mts Pak
96C1 Makthar Tunisia
93D2 Mākū Iran
98C3 Makumbi Zaïre
74C4 Makurazaki Japan
97C4 Makurdi Nig
79B4 Malabang Phil
87A2 Malabar Coast India
89E7 Malabo Bioko
77C5 Malacca,Str of
S E Asia
32C2 Málaga Colombia
50B2 Málaga Spain
101D3 Malaimbandy
Madag
107F1 Malaita I
Solomon Is
99D2 Malakal Sudan
84C2 Malakand Pak
78C4 Malang Indon
98B3 Malange Angola
97C3 Malanville Benin
39H7 Mälaren L Sweden
34B3 Malargüe Arg
12F3 Malaspina Gl USA
93C2 Malatya Turk
101C2 Malawi Republic,
Africa
Malawi,L = Nyasa,L
79C4 Malaybalay Phil
90A3 Malāyer Iran
70B3 Malaysia Federation,
S E Asia
93D2 Malazgirt Turk
58C2 Malbork Pol
58B2 Malchin Germany
18C2 Malden USA
83B5 Maldives Is Indian O
104B4 Maldives Ridge
Indian O
29F2 Maldonado Urug
47D1 Male Italy
85C4 Malegaon India
59B3 Malé Karpaty Upland
Slovakia
101C2 Malema Mozam
84B2 Malestan Afghan
38H5 Malgomaj L Sweden
95B3 Malha Well Sudan
20C2 Malheur L USA
97A3 Mali Republic, Africa
78D1 Malinau Indon
99E3 Malindi Kenya
Malines = Mechelen
40B2 Malin Head Pt
Irish Rep
86A2 Malkala Range Mts
India
85D4 Malkāpur India
55C2 Malkara Turk
54C2 Malko Tŭrnovo Bulg
44B3 Mallaig Scot
95C2 Mallawī Egypt
47D1 Malles Venosta Italy
51C2 Mallorca I Spain
45B2 Mallow Irish Rep
38G6 Malm Nor
38J5 Malmberget Sweden
46D1 Malmédy Germany
43C4 Malmesbury Eng
100A4 Malmesbury S Africa
39G7 Malmö Sweden
61G2 Malmyzh
Russian Fed
79B3 Malolos Phil
15D2 Malone USA
101G1 Maloti Mts Lesotho
38F6 Måløy Nor
28A2 Malpelo I Colombia
34A2 Malpo R Chile
85D3 Malpura India
8C2 Malta Montana, USA
53B3 Malta Chan Malta/
Italy
53B3 Malta I Medit S
100A3 Maltahöhe Namibia
42D2 Malton Eng
39G6 Malung Sweden
87A1 Mālvan India
19B3 Malvern USA
85D4 Malwa Plat India

61G4 Malyy Uzen' R
Kazakhstan
63D2 Mama Russian Fed
61H2 Mamadysh
Russian Fed
99C2 Mambasa Zaïre
71E4 Mamberamo R
Indon
98B2 Mambéré R CAR
98A2 Mamfé Cam
33D6 Mamoré R Bol
97A3 Mamou Guinea
101D2 Mampikony Madag
97B4 Mampong Ghana
94B3 Mamshit Hist Site
Israel
100B3 Mamuno Botswana
97B4 Man Ivory Coast
21C4 Mana Hawaiian Is
101D3 Manabo Madag
33E4 Manacapuru Brazil
51C2 Manacor Spain
71D3 Manado Indon
25D3 Managua Nic
101D3 Manakara Madag
101D2 Mananara Madag
101D3 Mananjary Madag
114J3 Manapouri NZ
111A3 Manapouri,L NZ
86C1 Manas Bhutan
82C1 Manas China
65K5 Manas Hu L China
86A1 Manaslu Mt Nepal
16B2 Manasquan USA
33F4 Manaus Brazil
92B2 Manavgat Turk
93C2 Manbij Syria
42B2 Man,Calf of I Eng
87B1 Mancheral India
9E3 Manchester
Connecticut, USA
42C3 Manchester Eng
10C2 Manchester New
Hampshire, USA
16A2 Manchester
Pennsylvania, USA
69E2 Manchuria Hist
Region, China
91B4 Mand R Iran
101C2 Manda Tanz
35A2 Mandaguari Brazil
39F7 Mandal Nor
76B1 Mandalay Burma
68C2 Mandalgovi
Mongolia
8C2 Mandan USA
14A2 Mandelona USA
99E2 Mandera Eth
26B3 Mandeville Jamaica
101C2 Mandimba Mozam
86A2 Mandla India
101D2 Mandritsara Madag
85D4 Mandsaur India
53C2 Manduria Italy
85B4 Mändvi India
87B2 Mandya India
58D2 Manevichi Ukraine
42D3 Manfield Eng
53C2 Manfredonia Italy
111A3 Manga Desert
Region Niger
110C1 Mangakino NZ
54C2 Mangalia Rom
98B1 Mangalmé Chad
87A2 Mangalore India
101C2 Mange Indon
101D3 Mangoky R Madag
71D4 Mangole I Indon
85B4 Mängral India
63E2 Mangui China
8D3 Manhattan USA
31C6 Manhuacu Brazil
101D2 Mania R Madag
101C2 Manica Mozam
7D5 Manicouagan R Can
91A4 Manifah S Arabia
78D1 Manila Phil
109D2 Manilla Aust
97B3 Maninian Ivory Coast
86C2 Manipur State, India
86C2 Manipur R Burma
92A2 Manisa Turk

41C3 Man,Isle of Irish S
14A2 Manistee USA
14A2 Manistee R USA
14A1 Manistique USA
5H4 Manitoba Province,
Can
5J4 Manitoba,L Can
13F2 Manito L Can
14A1 Manitou Is USA
7B5 Manitoulin I Can
14A2 Manitowoc USA
15C1 Maniwaki Can
32B2 Manizales Colombia
101D3 Manja Madag
106A4 Manjimup Aust
87B1 Mānjra R India
10A2 Mankato USA
97B4 Mankono Ivory Coast
12D2 Manley Hot Springs
USA
110B1 Manly NZ
85C4 Manmad India
78A3 Manna Indon
108A2 Mannahill Aust
87B3 Mannar Sri Lanka
87B3 Mannar,G of India
87B2 Mannārgudi India
57B3 Mannheim Germany
13D1 Manning Can
17B1 Manning USA
108A2 Mannum Aust
97A4 Mano Sierra Leone
71E4 Manokwari Indon
98C3 Manono Zaïre
76B3 Manoron Burma
74B2 Man-wan B Japan
74B2 Manp'o N Korea
84D3 Mānsa India
100B2 Mansa Zambia
6B3 Mansel I Can
19B2 Mansfield Arkansas,
USA
108C3 Mansfield Aust
19B3 Mansfield Louisiana,
USA
16D1 Mansfield
Massachusetts, USA
10B2 Mansfield Ohio, USA
15C2 Mansfield
Pennsylvania, USA
71E2 Mansyu Deep
Pacific O
32A4 Manta Ecuador
79A4 Mantalingajan,Mt
Phil
32B6 Mantaro R Peru
22B2 Manteca USA
48C2 Mantes France
52B1 Mantova Italy
38J6 Mäntta Fin
61F2 Manturovo
Russian Fed
35A2 Manuel Ribas Brazil
79B4 Manukan Phil
110B1 Manukau NZ
71F4 Manus I Pacific O
50B2 Manzanares Spain
26B2 Manzanillo Cuba
24B3 Manzanillo Mexico
63D2 Manzhouli China
94C3 Manzil Jordan
101C3 Manzini Swaziland
98B1 Mao Chad
72A2 Maomao Shan Mt
China
73C5 Maoming China
101C3 Mapai Mozam
71E3 Mapia Is Pacific O
79A4 Mapin I Phil
5H5 Maple Creek Can
101H1 Mapoto Mozam
101H1 Maputo R Mozam
Ma Qu = Huange He
72A3 Maqu China
86B1 Maquan He R China
98B3 Maquela do Zombo
Angola
29C4 Maquinchao Arg
31B3 Marabá Brazil
32C1 Maracaibo Ven
32D1 Maracay Ven
95A2 Marādah Libya
97C3 Maradi Niger
90A2 Marāgheh Iran

Maralal

99D2 **Maralal** Kenya
107F1 **Maramasike** I
 Solomon Is
100B2 **Maramba** Zambia
90A2 **Marand** Iran
31B2 **Maranhõa** State,
 Brazil
109C1 **Maranoa** R Aust
32B4 **Marañón** R Peru
7B5 **Marathon** Can
17B2 **Marathon** Florida,
 USA
78D2 **Maratua** I Indon
23A2 **Maravatio** Mexico
79B4 **Maravi** Phil
34B2 **Marayes** Arg
50B2 **Marbella** Spain
106A3 **Marble Bar** Aust
100B3 **Marblehall** S Africa
16D1 **Marblehead** USA
57B2 **Marburg** Germany
57A2 **Marche** Belg
50A2 **Marchean** Spain
46C1 **Marche-en-Famenne**
 Belg
32J7 **Marchena** I Ecuador
17B2 **Marco** USA
34C2 **Marcos Juárez** Arg
12E2 **Marcus Baker,Mt**
 USA
15D2 **Mary,Mt** USA
84C2 **Mardan** Pak
29E3 **Mar del Plata** Arg
93D2 **Mardin** Turk
99D1 **Mareb** R Eritrea/Eth
16B1 **Margaretville** USA
43E4 **Margate** Eng
76B1 **Marghita** Rom
109C4 **Maria I** Aust
104F3 **Maria** Is Pacific O
13E1 **Mariana Lake** Can
104F3 **Marianas Trench**
 Pacific O
86C1 **Mariani** India
19B3 **Marianna** Arkansas,
 USA
17A1 **Marianna** Florida,
 USA
7G4 **Maria Van Diemen,C**
 NZ
59B3 **Mariazell** Austria
52C1 **Maribor** Slovenia
99C2 **Maridi** Sudan
112B5 **Marie Byrd Land**
 Region, Ant
27E3 **Marie Galante** I
 Caribbean S
39H6 **Mariehamn** Fin
46C1 **Mariembourg** Belg
33G2 **Marienburg** Surinam
100A3 **Mariental** Namibia
39G7 **Mariestad** Sweden
17B1 **Marietta** Georgia,
 USA
14B3 **Marietta** Ohio, USA
19A3 **Marietta** Oklahoma,
 USA
27Q2 **Marigot** Dominica
60B3 **Marijampole**
 Lithuania
31B6 **Marilia** Brazil
98B3 **Marimba** Angola
79B3 **Marinduque** I Phil
10B2 **Marinette** USA
30F3 **Maringa** Brazil
98C2 **Maringa** R Zaire
18B2 **Marion** Arkansas,
 USA
18C2 **Marion** Illinois, USA
10B2 **Marion** Indiana, USA
10B2 **Marion** Ohio, USA
17C1 **Marion** S Carolina,
 USA
11B3 **Marion,L** USA
107E2 **Marion Reef** Aust
21B2 **Mariposa** USA
22B2 **Mariposa** R USA
22B2 **Mariposa Res** USA
60C5 **Marista** R Bulg
60E4 **Mariupol'** Ukraine
61G2 **Mariyskaya**
 Respublika,
 Russian Fed
94B2 **Marjayoun** Leb

58D2 **Marjina Gorki**
 Belorussia
94B3 **Marka** Jordan
99E2 **Marka** Somalia
56C1 **Markaryd** Sweden
43C3 **Market Drayton** Eng
43D3 **Market Harborough**
 Eng
112A **Markham,Mt** Ant
22C1 **Markleeville** USA
16D1 **Marlboro** USA
107D3 **Marlborough** Aust
46B2 **Marle** France
19A3 **Marlin** USA
48C3 **Marmande** France
55C2 **Marmara Adi** I Turk
92A1 **Marmara,S of** Turk
55C3 **Marmaris** Turk
14B3 **Marmet** USA
52B1 **Marmolada** Mt Italy
12D3 **Marmot B** USA
47A1 **Marnay** France
46B2 **Marne** Department,
 France
46B2 **Marne** R France
98B2 **Maro** Chad
101D2 **Maroantsetra** Madag
101C2 **Marondera** Zim
33G3 **Maroni** R French
 Guiana
109D1 **Maroochydore** Aust
98B1 **Maroua** Cam
101D2 **Marovoay** Madag
11B4 **Marquesas Keys** Is
 USA
10B2 **Marquette** USA
46A1 **Marquise** France
109C2 **Marra** R Aust
101H1 **Marracuene** Mozam
96B1 **Marrakech** Mor
106C3 **Marree** Aust
19B4 **Marrero** USA
101C2 **Marromeu** Mozam
101C3 **Marromeu** Mozam
95C2 **Marsa Alam** Egypt
99D2 **Marsabit** Kenya
53B3 **Marsala** Italy
49D3 **Marseille** France
12B2 **Marshall** Alaska,
 USA
14A3 **Marshall** Illinois, USA
14B2 **Marshall** Michigan,
 USA
18B2 **Marshall** Missouri,
 USA
11A3 **Marshall** Texas, USA
105G3 **Marshall Is** Pacific O
18B2 **Marshfield** Missouri,
 USA
26B1 **Marsh Harbour**
 The Bahamas
19B4 **Marsh I** USA
12H2 **Marsh L** Can
76B2 **Martaban,G of** Burma
78A3 **Martapura** Indon
78C3 **Martapura** Indon
15D2 **Martha's Vineyard** I
 USA
49D2 **Martigny** Switz
59B3 **Martin** Slovakia
111C2 **Martinborough** NZ
34B3 **Martin de Loyola** Arg
23B1 **Martínez de la Torre**
 Mexico
27E4 **Martinique** I
 Caribbean S
17A1 **Martin,L** USA
15C3 **Martinsburg** USA
14B2 **Martins Ferry** USA
103G6 **Martin Vaz** I
 Atlantic O
49D3 **Martiques** France
110C2 **Marton** NZ
50B2 **Martos** Spain
78D1 **Marudi** Malay
84B2 **Maruf** Afghan
75A2 **Marugame** Japan
85C3 **Mārwār** India
65H6 **Mary** Turkmenistan
107E3 **Maryborough**
 Queensland, Aust
108B3 **Maryborough**
 Victoria, Aust

5F4 **Mary Henry,Mt** Can
10C3 **Maryland** State, USA
42C2 **Maryport** Eng
21A2 **Marysville** California,
 USA
18A2 **Marysville** Kansas,
 USA
20B1 **Marysville**
 Washington, USA
10A2 **Maryville** Iowa, USA
18B1 **Maryville** Missouri,
 USA
95A2 **Marzuq** Libya
 Masada = Mezada
94B2 **Mas'adah** Syria
99D3 **Masai Steppe**
 Upland Tanz
99D3 **Masaka** Uganda
93E2 **Masally** Azerbaijan
74B3 **Masan** S Korea
101C2 **Masasi** Tanz
25D3 **Masaya** Nic
79B3 **Masbate** Phil
79B3 **Masbate** I Phil
96C1 **Mascara** Alg
23A1 **Mascota** Mexico
35D1 **Mascote** Brazil
101G1 **Maseru** Lesotho
66C3 **Mashad** Iran
84B2 **Mashaki** Afghan
90C2 **Mashhad** Iran
98B3 **Masi-Manimba** Zaïre
99D2 **Masindi** Uganda
99C3 **Masisi** Zaire
90A3 **Masjed Soleyman**
 Iran
101E2 **Masoala** C Madag
10A2 **Mason City** USA
91C5 **Masqat** Oman
52B2 **Massa** Italy
10C2 **Massachusetts** State,
 USA
15D2 **Massachusetts B**
 USA
98B1 **Massakori** Chad
101C3 **Massangena** Mozam
 Massawa = Mits'iwa
15D2 **Massena** USA
98B1 **Massénya** Chad
14B1 **Massey** Can
49C2 **Massif Central** Mts
 France
98B2 **Massif de**
 l'Adamaoua Mts
 Cam
26C3 **Massif de la Hotte**
 Mts Haiti
101D3 **Massif de l'Isalo**
 Upland Madag
98C2 **Massif des Bongo**
 Upland CAR
49D2 **Massif du Pelvoux**
 Mts France
101D2 **Massif du**
 Tsaratanana Mt
 Madag
14B2 **Massillon** USA
97B3 **Massina** Region, Mali
101C3 **Massinga** Mozam
101C3 **Massingir** Mozam
61H4 **Masteksay**
 Kazakhstan
111C2 **Masterton** NZ
74C4 **Masuda** Japan
98B3 **Masuku** Gabon
100C3 **Masvingo** Zim
92C2 **Maşyāf** Syria
98B3 **Matadi** Zaïre
25D3 **Matagalpa** Nic
7C4 **Matagami** Can
9D4 **Matagorda B** USA
110C1 **Matakana I** NZ
100A2 **Matala** Angola
87B3 **Matale** Sri Lanka
97A3 **Matam** Sen
97C3 **Matameye** Niger
24C2 **Matamoros** Mexico
95B2 **Ma'tan as Sarra** Well
 Libya
7D5 **Matane** Can
25D2 **Matanzas** Cuba
34A2 **Mataquito** R Chile
87C3 **Matara** Sri Lanka
106A1 **Mataram** Indon

30B2 **Matarani** Peru
51C1 **Mataró** Spain
111A3 **Mataura** NZ
24B2 **Matehuala** Mexico
27L1 **Matelot** Trinidad
53C2 **Matera** Italy
59C3 **Mátészalka** Hung
79C4 **Mati** Phil
78D3 **Matisiri** I Indon
43D3 **Matlock** Eng
33F6 **Mato Grosso** Brazil
33F6 **Mato Grosso** State,
 Brazil
30E2 **Mato Grosso do Sul**
 State, Brazil
101H1 **Matola** Mozam
91C5 **Matrah** Oman
92A3 **Matrûh** Egypt
74C3 **Matsue** Japan
74E2 **Matsumae** Japan
74D3 **Matsumoto** Japan
74D4 **Matsusaka** Japan
74C4 **Matsuyama** Japan
7B5 **Mattagami** R Can
15C1 **Mattawa** Can
52A1 **Matterhorn** Mt Italy/
 Switz
26C2 **Matthew Town**
 The Bahamas
16C2 **Mattituck** USA
18C2 **Mattoon** USA
84B2 **Matun** Afghan
27L1 **Matura B** Trinidad
86A1 **Mau** India
101C2 **Maúa** Mozam
49C1 **Maubeuge** France
108B2 **Maude** Aust
103J8 **Maud Seamount**
 Atlantic O
21C4 **Maui** I Hawaiian Is
34A3 **Maule** R Chile
14B2 **Maumee** USA
14B2 **Maumee** R USA
100B2 **Maun** Botswana
21C4 **Mauna Kea** Mt
 Hawaiian Is
21C4 **Mauna Loa** Mt
 Hawaiian Is
4F3 **Maunoir** L Can
4F3 **Maunoir,L** Can
48C2 **Mauriac** France
96A2 **Mauritania** Republic,
 Africa
100E3 **Mauritius** I Indian O
100B2 **Mavinga** Angola
86C2 **Mawlaik** Burma
 Mawlamyine =
 Moulmein
112C10 **Mawson** Base Ant
71B3 **Maya** I Indon
63F2 **Maya** R Russian Fed
93D2 **Mayādīn** Syria
11C4 **Mayaguana** I
 The Bahamas
27D3 **Mayagüez** Puerto
 Rico
97C3 **Mayahi** Niger
98B3 **Mayama** Congo
90C2 **Mayamey** Iran
42B2 **Maybole** Scot
10C3 **May,C** USA
109C4 **Maydena** Aust
46D1 **Mayen** Germany
48B2 **Mayenne** France
13D2 **Mayerthorpe** Can
18C2 **Mayfield** USA
61E5 **Maykop** Russian Fed
84B1 **Maymaneh** Afghan
76B1 **Maymyo** Burma
4E3 **Mayo** Can
45B2 **Mayo** County,
 Irish Rep
16A3 **Mayo** USA
45B1 **Mayo,Mts of**
 Irish Rep
79B3 **Mayon** Mt Phil
51C2 **Mayor Mt** Spain
34C3 **Mayor Buratovich**
 Arg
110C1 **Mayor I** NZ
30D2 **Mayor P Lagerenza**
 Par

156

101D2 Mayotte I / Indian O
27H2 May Pen Jamaica
16B3 May Point,C USA
47D1 Mayrhofen Austria
16B3 Mays Landing USA
14B3 Maysville USA
98B3 Mayumba Gabon
100B2 Mazabuka Zambia
84D1 Mazar China
94B3 Mazār Jordan
53B3 Mazara del Vallo Italy
84B1 Mazar-i-Sharif Afghan
24B2 Mazatlán Mexico
60B2 Mazeikiai Lithuania
94B3 Mazra Jordan
101C3 Mbabane Swaziland
98B2 Mbaiki CAR
99D3 Mbala Zambia
100B3 Mbalabala Zim
99D2 Mbale Uganda
98B2 Mbalmayo Cam
98B2 Mbam R Cam
101C2 Mbamba Bay Tanz
98B2 Mbandaka Zaire
98B3 Mbanza Congo Angola
98B3 Mbanza-Ngungu Zaire
99D3 Mbarara Uganda
98B3 Mbènza Congo
98B2 Mbère R Cam
98B3 Mbeya Tanz
98B3 Mbinda Congo
97A3 Mbout Maur
98C3 Mbuji-Mayi Zaire
99D3 Mbulu Tanz
96B2 Mcherrah Region, Alg
101C2 Mchinji Malawi
80D3 Mdrak Viet
9B3 Mead,L USA
5H4 Meadow Lake Can
14B2 Meadville USA
7E4 Mealy Mts USA
109C1 Meandarra Aust
5G4 Meander River Can
45C2 Meath County, Irish Rep
49C2 Meaux France
16C1 Mechanicville USA
56A2 Mechelen Belg
96B1 Mecheria Alg
56C2 Mecklenburg-Vorpommern State Germany
56C2 Mecklenburger Bucht B Germany
101C2 Mecoota Mozam
101C2 Mecubori Mozam
101D2 Mecufi Mozam
101C2 Mecula Mozam
70A3 Medan Indon
34C3 Medanos Arg
34D2 Medanos Arg
7C4 Medecine Hat Can
32B2 Medellín Colombia
96D1 Medenine Tunisia
8A2 Medford USA
54C2 Medgidia Rom
34B2 Media Agua Arg
54B1 Mediaș Rom
20C1 Medical Lake USA
5G5 Medicine Hat Can
35C1 Medina Brazil
80B3 Medina S Arabia
50B1 Medinaceli Spain
50B1 Medina del Campo Spain
50A1 Medina de Rio Seco Spain
86B2 Medinipur India
88E4 Mediterranean S Europe
13F2 Medley Can
61J3 Mednogorsk Russian Fed
86D1 Mêdog China
98B2 Medouneu Gabon
61F3 Medvedista R Russian Fed
64E3 Medvezh'yegorsk Russian Fed

106A3 Meekatharra Aust
84D3 Meerut India
99D2 Méga Eth
55B3 Megalópolis Greece
55B3 Mégara Greece
86C1 Meghālaya State, India
86C2 Meghna R Bang
94B2 Megiddo Hist Site Israel
91B4 Mehrān R Iran
90B3 Mehriz Iran
35B1 Meia Ponte R Brazil
98B2 Meiganga Cam
76B1 Meiktila Burma
47C1 Meiringen Switz
73A4 Meishan China
57C2 Meissen Germany
73D5 Mei Xian China
73D5 Meizhou China
30B3 Mejillones Chile
98B2 Mekambo Gabon
99D1 Mek'elē Eth
86C1 Meknès Mor
76D3 Mekong R Cam
97C3 Mékrou R Benin
77C5 Melaka Malay
104F4 Melanesia Region Pacific O
78C3 Melawi R Indon
107D4 Melbourne Aust
11B4 Melbourne USA
9C4 Melchor Muzquiz Mexico
61J3 Meleuz Russian Fed
98B1 Melfi Chad
53C2 Melfort Can
96B1 Melilla N W Africa
29B4 Melinoyu Mt Chile
34C2 Melincue Arg
34A2 Melipilla Chile
60E4 Melitopol' Ukraine
6D2 Melville Bugt B Greenland
99D2 Melka Guba Eth
101H1 Melmoth S Africa
34C2 Melo Arg
29F2 Melo Urug
22B2 Melones Res USA
12D1 Melozitna R USA
47C1 Mels Switz
43D3 Melton Mowbray Eng
49C2 Melun France
5H4 Melville Can
27Q2 Melville,C Dominica
4F3 Melville Hills Mts Can
106C2 Melville I Aust
4G2 Melville I Can
7E4 Melville,L Can
6B3 Melville Pen Can
45B1 Melvin,L Irish Rep
101D2 Memba Mozam
106A1 Memboro Indon
57C3 Memmingen Germany
78B2 Mempawan Indon
11B3 Memphis Tennessee, USA
19B3 Mena USA
43B3 Menai Str Wales
97C3 Mènaka Mali
14A2 Menasha USA
78C3 Mendawai R Indon
49C2 Mende France
99D2 Mendebo Mts Eth
43C4 Mendip Hills Upland Eng
20B2 Mendocino,C USA
105J2 Mendocino Seascarp Pacific O
22B2 Mendota California, USA
29C2 Mendoza Arg
29C3 Mendoza State, Arg
55C3 Menemen Turk
46B1 Menen Belg
72D3 Mengcheng China
78B3 Menggala Indon
76B1 Menghai China
73A5 Mengla China
76B1 Menglian China
73A5 Mengzi China
107D4 Meninee Aust

108B2 Menindee L Aust
108A3 Meningie Aust
14A1 Menominee USA
14A2 Menomonee Falls USA
100A2 Menongue Angola
51C1 Menorca I / Spain
12F2 Mentasta Mts USA
78B3 Mentok Indon
14B2 Mentor USA
49C2 Ménu France
72A2 Menyuan China
61H2 Menzelinsk Russian Fed
56B2 Meppen Germany
78D2 Merah Indon
18B2 Meramec R USA
52B1 Merano Italy
71F4 Merauke Indon
8A3 Merced USA
8B2 Merced R USA
29B2 Mercedario Mt Chile
29C2 Mercedes Arg
29E2 Mercedes Arg
 Mercedes Buenos Aires, Arg
30E4 Mercedes Corrientes, Arg
29E2 Mercedes Urug
110C1 Mercury B NZ
110C1 Mercury Is NZ
4F2 Mercy B Can
6D3 Mercy,C Can
99E2 Meregh Somalia
76B2 Mergui Burma
76B3 Mergui Arch Burma
25D2 Mérida Mexico
50A2 Mérida Spain
32C2 Mérida Ven
11B3 Meridian USA
109C3 Merimbula Aust
108B2 Meringur Aust
95C3 Merowe Sudan
106A4 Merredin Aust
42B2 Merrick Mt Scot
14A2 Merrillville USA
13C2 Merritt Can
17B2 Merritt Island USA
109D2 Merriwa Aust
99E1 Mersa Fatma Eritrea
51B2 Mers el Kebir Alg
42C3 Mersey R Eng
42C3 Merseyside Metropolitan County, Eng
92B2 Mersin Turk
77C5 Mersing Malay
85C3 Merta India
43C4 Merthyr Tydfil Wales
50A2 Mertola Port
99D3 Meru Mt Tanz
60E5 Merzifon Turk
46D2 Merzig Germany
9B3 Mesa USA
46E1 Meschede Germany
93D1 Mescit Dağ Mt Turk
12C3 Meshik USA
99C2 Meshra Er Req Sudan
47C1 Mesocco Switz
55B3 Mesolóngion Greece
19A3 Mesquite Texas, USA
101C2 Messalo R Mozam
53C3 Messina Italy
100B3 Messina S Africa
55B3 Messini Greece
55B3 Messiniakós Kólpos G Greece
29A3 Mesta R Bulg
52B1 Mestre Italy
32C3 Meta R Colombia
60D2 Meta R Russian Fed
32D2 Meta R Ven
6C3 Meta Incognito Pen Can
19B4 Metairie USA
20C1 Metaline Falls USA
30D4 Metan Arg
101C2 Metangula Mozam
53C2 Metaponto Italy
44C3 Methil Scot
16D1 Methuen USA
111B2 Methven NZ
12H3 Metlakatla USA

18C2 Metropolis USA
87B2 Mettūr India
49D2 Metz France
70A3 Meulaboh Indon
46A2 Meulan France
46C2 Meuse Department, France
49D2 Meuse R France
19A3 Mexia USA
24A1 Mexicali Mexico
24B2 Mexico Federal Republic, Cent America
24C3 México Mexico
23A2 México State, Mexico
18B2 Mexico USA
24C2 México,G of Cent America
94B3 Mezada Hist Site Israel
23B2 Mezcala Mexico
64F3 Mezen' Russian Fed
64G2 Mezhdusharskiy, Ostrov I Russian Fed
85D4 Mhow India
23B2 Miahuatlán Mexico
11B4 Miami Florida, USA
18B2 Miami Oklahoma, USA
11B4 Miami Beach USA
90A2 Miandowāb Iran
101D2 Miandrivazo Madag
90A2 Miāneh Iran
84C2 Mianwali Pak
73A3 Mianyang China
73C3 Mianyang China
73A3 Mianzhu China
72E2 Miaodao Qundao Arch China
73B4 Miao Ling Upland China
61K3 Miass Russian Fed
59C3 Michalovce Slovakia
20C3 Miches Dom Rep
108B2 Michigan State, USA
14A2 Michigan City USA
10B2 Michigan,L USA
7B5 Michipicoten I Can
23A2 Michoacan State, Mexico
54C2 Michurin Bulg
61F3 Michurinsk Russian Fed
104F3 Micronesia Region Pacific O
78B2 Midai I Indon
102F4 Mid Atlantic Ridge Atlantic O
46B1 Middelburg Neth
20B2 Middle Alkali L USA
16D2 Middleboro USA
100B4 Middleburg Cape Province, S Africa
16A2 Middleburg Pennsylvania, USA
101G1 Middleburg Transvaal, S Africa
16B1 Middleburgh USA
15D2 Middlebury USA
15B2 Middlesboro USA
42D2 Middlesbrough Eng
16C2 Middletown Connecticut, USA
16B3 Middletown Delaware, USA
15D2 Middletown New York, USA
14B3 Middletown Ohio, USA
16A2 Middletown Pennsylvania, USA
96B1 Midelt Mor
43C4 Mid Glamorgan County, Wales
104B4 Mid Indian Basin Indian O
104B4 Mid Indian Ridge Indian O
7C5 Midland Can
14B2 Midland Michigan, USA
9C3 Midland Texas, USA
101D3 Midongy Atsimo Madag

Mid Pacific Mts

105G2 **Mid Pacific Mts** Pacific O
20C2 **Midvale** USA
105H2 **Midway Is** Pacific O
18A2 **Midwest City** USA
93D2 **Midyat** Turk
54B2 **Midžor** Mt Serbia, Yugos
59B2 **Mielec** Pol
54C1 **Miercurea-Ciuc** Rom
50A1 **Mieres** Spain
16A2 **Mifflintown** USA
75A2 **Mihara** Japan
72D1 **Mijun Shuiku** Res China
54B2 **Mikhaylovgrad** Bulg
61F3 **Mikhaylovka** Russian Fed
65J4 **Mikhaylovskiy** Russian Fed
38K6 **Mikkeli** Fin
55C3 **Mikonos** I Greece
59B3 **Mikulov** Czech Republic
99D3 **Mikumi** Tanz
74D3 **Mikuni-sammyaku** Mts Japan
75B2 **Mikura-jima** I Japan
32B4 **Milagro** Ecuador
Milan = Milano
51C2 **Milana** Alg
101C2 **Milange** Mozam
52A1 **Milano** Italy
92A2 **Milas** Turk
107C4 **Mildura** Aust
73A5 **Mile** China
93D3 **Mileh Tharthār** L Iraq
107E3 **Miles** Aust
8C2 **Miles City** USA
16C2 **Milford** Connecticut, USA
15C3 **Milford** Delaware, USA
15D2 **Milford** Massachusetts, USA
18A1 **Milford** Nebraska, USA
16B2 **Milford** Pennsylvania, USA
43B4 **Milford Haven** Wales
43B4 **Milford Haven** Sd Wales
18A2 **Milford L** USA
111A2 **Milford Sd** NZ
13E2 **Milk River** Can
49C3 **Millau** France
16C2 **Millbrook** USA
17B1 **Milledgeville** USA
12F2 **Miller,Mt** USA
61F4 **Millerovo** Russian Fed
16A2 **Millersburg** USA
108A1 **Millers Creek** Aust
16C1 **Millers Falls** USA
16C2 **Millerton** USA
22C2 **Millerton L** USA
108B3 **Millicent** Aust
109D1 **Millmerran** Aust
45B2 **Milltown Malbay** Irish Rep
22A2 **Mill Valley** USA
15D3 **Millville** USA
6H2 **Milne Land** I Greenland
21C4 **Milolii** Hawaiian Is
55B3 **Milos** I Greece
107D3 **Milparinka** Aust
16A2 **Milroy** USA
111A3 **Milton** NZ
16A2 **Milton** Pennsylvania, USA
10B2 **Milwaukee** USA
51C2 **Mina** R Alg
91A4 **Mina' al Ahmadi** Kuwait
91C4 **Mināb** Iran
74C4 **Minamata** Japan
78A2 **Minas** Indon
29E2 **Minas** Urug
31B5 **Minas Gerais** State, Brazil
35C1 **Minas Novas** Brazil
25C3 **Minatitlan** Mexico

76A1 **Minbu** Burma
76A1 **Minbya** Burma
34A2 **Mincha** Chile
44A3 **Minch,Little** Sd Scot
44A2 **Minch,North** Sd Scot
40B2 **Minch,The** Sd Scot
12D2 **Minchumina,L** USA
47D2 **Mincio** R Italy
79B4 **Mindanao** I Phil
19B3 **Minden** Louisiana, USA
56B2 **Minden** Germany
108B2 **Mindona L** Aust
79B3 **Mindoro** I Phil
79B3 **Mindoro Str** Phil
45C3 **Mine Hd** C Irish Rep
43C4 **Minehead** Eng
30F2 **Mineiros** Brazil
19A3 **Mineola** USA
23B1 **Mineral de Monte** Mexico
16A2 **Minersville** USA
108B2 **Mingary** Aust
72A2 **Minhe** China
87A3 **Minicoy** I India
73D4 **Min Jiang** R Fujian, China
73A4 **Min Jiang** R Sichuan, China
22C2 **Minkler** USA
97C4 **Minna** Nig
10A2 **Minneapolis** USA
5J4 **Minnedosa** Can
10A2 **Minnesota** State, USA
50A1 **Miño** R Spain
8C2 **Minot** USA
72A2 **Minqin** China
72A3 **Min Shan** Upland China
60C3 **Minsk** Belorussia
58C2 **Minsk Mazowiecki** Pol
12E2 **Minto** USA
4G2 **Minto Inlet** B Can
7C4 **Minto,L** Can
63B2 **Minusinsk** Russian Fed
72A3 **Min Xian** China
7E5 **Miquelon** Can
22D3 **Mirage L** USA
87A1 **Miraj** India
29E3 **Miramar** Arg
84B2 **Miram Shah** Pak
50B1 **Miranda de Ebro** Spain
47D2 **Mirandola** Italy
84B2 **Mir Bachchen Kut** Afghan
78D1 **Miri** Malay
96A3 **Mirik,C** Maur
63A1 **Mirnoye** Russian Fed
63D1 **Mirnyy** Russian Fed
112C9 **Mirnyy** Base Ant
84C2 **Mirpur** Pak
85B3 **Mirpur Khas** Pak
55B3 **Mirtoan S** Greece
74B3 **Miryang** S Korea
86A1 **Mirzapur** India
23B2 **Misantla** Mexico
84C1 **Misgar** Pak
14A2 **Mishawaka** USA
12B1 **Misheguk Mt** USA
75A2 **Mi-shima** I Japan
107E2 **Misima** I Solomon Is
30F4 **Missiones** State, Arg
59C3 **Miskolc** Hung
94C2 **Mismiyah** Syria
71E4 **Misoöl** I Indon
95A1 **Misrātah** Libya
7B5 **Missanabie** R Can
20B1 **Mission City** Can
15C2 **Mississauga** Can
11A3 **Mississippi** State, USA
11A3 **Mississippi** R USA
19C3 **Mississippi Delta** USA
8B2 **Missoula** USA
96B1 **Missour** Mor
11A3 **Missouri** State, USA

10A2 **Missouri** R USA
10C1 **Mistassini,L** Can
30B2 **Misti** Mt Peru
109C1 **Mitchell** Aust
8D2 **Mitchell** R Aust
107D2 **Mitchell** R Aust
11B3 **Mitchell,Mt** USA
45B2 **Mitchelstown** Irish Rep
84C3 **Mithankot** Pak
55C3 **Mitilini** Greece
23B2 **Mitla** Mexico
54B2 **Mitrovica** Serbia, Yugos
95C3 **Mits'iwa** Eritrea
32C3 **Mitu** Colombia
99C3 **Mitumbar Mts** Zaire
98C3 **Mitwaba** Zaire
98B2 **Mitzic** Gabon
75B1 **Miura** Japan
72C3 **Mi Xian** China
69F3 **Miyake** I Japan
75B2 **Miyake-jima** I Japan
69E4 **Miyako** I Japan
74C4 **Miyakonojō** Japan
74C4 **Miyazaki** Japan
75B1 **Miyazu** Japan
74C4 **Miyoshi** Japan
72D1 **Miyun** China
99D2 **Mizan Teferi** Eth
95A1 **Mizdah** Libya
45B3 **Mizen Hd** C Irish Rep
54C1 **Mizil** Rom
86C2 **Mizo Hills** India
86C2 **Mizoram** Union Territory, India
94B3 **Mizpe Ramon** Israel
112B11 **Mizuho** Base Ant
74E3 **Mizusawa** Japan
39H7 **Mjolby** Sweden
100B2 **Mkushi** Zambia
101H1 **Mkuzi** S Africa
58C2 **Mlada Boleslav** Czech Republic
58C2 **Mlawa** Pol
52C2 **Mljet** I Croatia
100B3 **Mmabatho** S Africa
84D2 **Mnadi** India
97A4 **Moa** R Sierra Leone
94B3 **Moab** Region, Jordan
9C3 **Moab** USA
98B3 **Moanda** Congo
98B3 **Moanda** Gabon
98C3 **Moba** Zaire
75C1 **Mobara** Japan
98C2 **Mobaye** CAR
98C2 **Mobayi** Zaire
10A3 **Moberly** USA
11B3 **Mobile** USA
11B3 **Mobile B** USA
8C2 **Mobridge** USA
101D2 **Moçambique** Mozam
76C1 **Moc Chau** Viet
100B3 **Mochudi** Botswana
101D2 **Mocimboa da Praia** Mozam
32B3 **Mocoa** Colombia
30C2 **Mococa** Brazil
34D2 **Mocoreta** R Arg
23B1 **Moctezuma** R Mexico
101C2 **Mocuba** Mozam
47B2 **Modane** France
101G1 **Modder** R S Africa
52B2 **Modena** Italy
46D2 **Moder** R France
8A3 **Modesto** USA
22B2 **Modesto Res** USA
53B3 **Modica** Italy
59B3 **Mödling** Austria
40E **Moe** Aust
47C1 **Moesa** R Switz
42C2 **Moffat** Scot
84D2 **Moga** India
35B2 **Mogi das Cruzes** Brazil
60C3 **Mogilev** Belorussia
60C4 **Mogilev Podolskiy** Ukraine
35B2 **Mogi-Mirim** Brazil
101D2 **Mogincual** Mozam
47E2 **Mogliano** Italy

34B2 **Mogna** Arg
68D1 **Mogocha** Russian Fed
65K4 **Mogochin** Russian Fed
50A2 **Moguer** Spain
110C1 **Mokau** R NZ
86C2 **Mohanganj** Bang
15D2 **Mohawk** R USA
99D3 **Mohoro** Tanz
65J5 **Mointy** Kazakhstan
38G5 **Mo i Rana** Nor
48C3 **Moissac** France
21B2 **Mojave** USA
22D3 **Mojave** R USA
9B3 **Mojave Desert** USA
78C4 **Mojokerto** Indon
86B1 **Mokama** India
110B1 **Mokau** R NZ
22B1 **Mokelumne Aqueduct** USA
22B1 **Mokelumne Hill** USA
22B1 **Mokelumne North Fork** R USA
101G1 **Mokhotlong** Lesotho
96D1 **Moknine** Tunisia
86C1 **Mokokchung** India
98B1 **Mokolo** Cam
74B4 **Mokp'o** S Korea
61F3 **Moksha** R Russian Fed
23B1 **Molango** Mexico
55B3 **Molaoi** Greece
38F6 **Molde** Nor
60C4 **Moldova** Republic, Europe
54B1 **Moldoveanu** Mt Rom
100B3 **Molepolole** Botswana
53C2 **Molfetta** Italy
34A3 **Molina** Chile
30B2 **Mollendo** Peru
60C3 **Molodechno** Belorussia
112C11 **Molodezhnaya** Base Ant
21C4 **Molokai** I Hawaiian Is
61G2 **Moloma** R Russian Fed
109C2 **Molong** Aust
100B3 **Molopo** R Botswana
98B2 **Moloundou** Cam
8D1 **Molson L** Can
71D4 **Molucca S** Indon
71D4 **Moluccas** Is Indon
71D4 **Moma** Mozam
31C3 **Mombaca** Brazil
99D3 **Mombasa** Kenya
98C2 **Mompono** Zaire
56C2 **Mon** I Den
44A3 **Monach Is** Scot
49D3 **Monaco** Principality, Europe
44B3 **Monadhliath Mts** Scot
45C1 **Monaghan** County, Irish Rep
45C1 **Monaghan** Irish Rep
27D3 **Mona Pass** Caribbean S
13B2 **Monarch Mt** Can
5G4 **Monashee Mts** Can
41B3 **Monasterevin** Irish Rep
47B2 **Moncalieri** Italy
31B2 **Monção** Brazil
38L5 **Monchegorsk** Russian Fed
56B2 **Mönchen-gladbach** Germany
24B2 **Monclova** Mexico
7D5 **Moncton** Can
9C4 **Monctova** Mexico
50A1 **Mondego** R Port
52A2 **Mondovi** Italy
27H1 **Moneague** Jamaica
14C2 **Monessen** USA
18B2 **Monett** USA
52B1 **Monfalcone** Italy

50A1 **Monforte de Lemos** Spain
98C2 **Monga** Zaïre
98C2 **Mongala** R Zaïre
99D2 **Mongalla** Sudan
76D1 **Mong Cai** Viet
98B1 **Mongo** Chad
68B2 **Mongolia** Republic, Asia
100B2 **Mongu** Zambia
21B2 **Monitor Range** Mts USA
98C3 **Monkoto** Zaïre
43C4 **Monmouth** Eng
18B1 **Monmouth** USA
13C2 **Monmouth,Mt** Can
97C4 **Mono** R Togo
21B2 **Mono L** USA
53C2 **Monopoli** Italy
51B1 **Monreal del Campo** Spain
19B3 **Monroe** Louisiana, USA
14B2 **Monroe** Michigan, USA
20B1 **Monroe** Washington, USA
18B2 **Monroe City** USA
97A4 **Monrovia** Lib
20D3 **Monrovia** USA
56A2 **Mons** Belg
47D2 **Monselice** Italy
16C1 **Monson** USA
58B1 **Mönsterås** Sweden
101D2 **Montagne d'Ambre** Mt Madag
96C1 **Montagnes des Ouled Nail** Mts Alg
12E3 **Montague I** USA
49C3 **Mont Aigoual** Mt France
48B2 **Montaigu** France
53C3 **Montalto** Mt Italy
8B2 **Montana** State, USA
50A1 **Montañas de León** Mts Spain
49C2 **Montargis** France
48C3 **Montauban** France
15D2 **Montauk** USA
15D2 **Montauk Pt** USA
49D2 **Montbeliard** France
52A1 **Mont Blanc** Mt France/Italy
49C2 **Montceau les Mines** France
51C1 **Montceny** Mt Spain
49D3 **Mont Cinto** Mt Corse
46C2 **Montcornet** France
48B3 **Mont-de-Marsan** France
49C2 **Montdidier** France
30D2 **Monteagudo** Bol
33G4 **Monte Alegre** Brazil
52B2 **Monte Amiata** Mt Italy
47D2 **Monte Baldo** Mt Italy
15C1 **Montebello** Can
106A3 **Monte Bello Is** Aust
47E2 **Montebelluna** Italy
49D3 **Monte Carlo** Monaco
35B1 **Monte Carmelo** Brazil
34D2 **Monte Caseros** Arg
52B2 **Monte Cimone** Mt Italy
52A2 **Monte Cinto** Mt Corse
34B2 **Monte Coman** Arg
52B2 **Monte Corno** Mt Italy
27C3 **Montecristi** Dom Rep
52B2 **Montecristo** I Italy
23A1 **Monte Escobedo** Mexico
53C2 **Monte Gargano** Mt Italy
26B3 **Montego Bay** Jamaica
47D2 **Monte Grappa** Mt Italy
47C2 **Monte Lesima** Mt Italy

49C3 **Montélimar** France
53B2 **Monte Miletto** Mt Italy
50A2 **Montemo-o-Novo** Port
24C2 **Montemorelos** Mexico
26B5 **Montená** Colombia
54A2 **Montenegro** Republic, Yugos
35D1 **Monte Pascoal** Mt Brazil
34A2 **Monte Patria** Chile
53C3 **Monte Pollino** Mt Italy
101C2 **Montepuez** Mozam
8A3 **Monterey** California, USA
15C3 **Monterey** Virginia, USA
8A3 **Monterey B** USA
32B2 **Monteria** Colombia
30D2 **Montero** Bol
47B2 **Monte Rosa** Mt Italy/Switz
22C3 **Monterrey** Mexico
31C5 **Montes Claros** Brazil
50B2 **Montes de Toledo** Mts Spain
29E2 **Montevideo** Urug
52A2 **Monte Viso** Mt Italy
27P2 **Mont Gimie** Mt St Lucia
11B3 **Montgomery** Alabama, USA
96C2 **Mont Gréboun** Niger
46C2 **Montherme** France
47B1 **Monthey** Switz
19B3 **Monticello** Arkansas, USA
15D2 **Monticello** New York, USA
9C3 **Monticello** Utah, USA
53A2 **Monti del Gennargentu** Mt Sardegna
47D2 **Monti Lessini** Mts Italy
53B3 **Monti Nebrodi** Mts Italy
7C5 **Mont-Laurier** Can
48C2 **Montluçon** France
7C5 **Montmagny** Can
46C2 **Montmédy** France
49C3 **Mont Mézenc** Mt France
46B2 **Montmirail** France
50B2 **Montoro** Spain
49D3 **Mont Pelat** Mt France
14B2 **Montpelier** Ohio, USA
10C2 **Montpelier** Vermont, USA
49C3 **Montpellier** France
7C5 **Montréal** Can
48C1 **Montreuil** France
52A1 **Montreux** Switz
47B1 **Mont Risoux** Mt France
8C3 **Montrose** Colorado, USA
40C2 **Montrose** Scot
48B2 **Mont-St-Michel** France
96B1 **Monts des Ksour** Mts Alg
51C3 **Monts des Ouled Neil** Mts Alg
51C2 **Monts du Hodna** Mts Alg
27E3 **Montserrat** I Caribbean S
10C1 **Monts Otish** Mts Can
12B1 **Monument Mt** USA
9B3 **Monument V** USA
98C2 **Monveda** Zaïre
76B1 **Monywa** Burma
52A1 **Monza** Italy
100B2 **Monze** Zambia
101H1 **Mooi** R S Africa
101C1 **Mooi River** S Africa

108B1 **Moomba** Aust
109D2 **Moonbi Range** Mts Aust
108B1 **Moonda L** Aust
109D1 **Moonie** Aust
109C1 **Moonie** R Aust
108A2 **Moonta** Aust
108A4 **Moora** Aust
106A3 **Moore,L** Aust
42C2 **Moorfoot Hills** Scot
8D2 **Moorhead** USA
22C3 **Moorpark** USA
7B4 **Moose** R Can
5H4 **Moose Jaw** Can
5H4 **Moosomin** Can
16D2 **Moosup** USA
101C2 **Mopeia** Mozam
97B3 **Mopti** Mali
30B2 **Moquegua** Peru
39G6 **Mora** Sweden
31D3 **Morada** Brazil
84D3 **Morādābād** India
35B1 **Morada Nova de Minas** L Brazil
101D2 **Morafenobe** Madag
101D2 **Moramanga** Madag
27J2 **Morant Bay** Jamaica
27J2 **Morant Pt** Jamaica
87B3 **Moratuwa** Sri Lanka
59B3 **Morava** R Austria/Slovakia
54B2 **Morava** R Serbia, Yugos
90C2 **Moraveh Tappeh** Iran
40C2 **Moray Firth** Estuary Scot
47C1 **Morbegno** Italy
85C4 **Morbi** India
93D2 **Mor Dağ** Mt Turk
5J5 **Morden** Can
61F3 **Mordovskaya Respublika,** Russian Fed
42C2 **Morecambe** Eng
42C2 **Morecambe B** Eng
107D3 **Moree** Aust
14B3 **Morehead** USA
47C1 **Mörel** Switz
24B3 **Morelia** Mexico
23B2 **Morelos** State, Mexico
85D3 **Morena** India
5E4 **Moresby I** Can
109D1 **Moreton I** Aust
46B2 **Moreuil** France
19B4 **Morez** France
19B4 **Morgan City** USA
22B2 **Morgan Hill** USA
14C3 **Morgantown** USA
101G1 **Morgenzon** S Africa
47B1 **Morges** Switz
46D2 **Morhange** France
74E2 **Mori** Japan
27K1 **Moriatio** Tobago
13B2 **Morice L** Can
13E2 **Morinville** Can
74E3 **Morioka** Japan
109D2 **Morisset** Aust
63D1 **Morkoka** R Russian Fed
48B2 **Morlaix** France
27Q2 **Morne Diablotin** Mt Dominica
106C2 **Mornington** I Aust
85B3 **Moro** Pak
96B2 **Morocco** Kingdom, Africa
79B4 **Moro G** Phil
99D3 **Morogoro** Tanz
23A1 **Moroleon** Mexico
101D3 **Morombe** Madag
26B2 **Moron** Cuba
101D3 **Morondava** Madag
50A2 **Moron de la Frontera** Spain
101D2 **Moroni** Comoros
71D3 **Morotai** I Indon
99D2 **Moroto** Uganda
61F4 **Morozovsk** Russian Fed
42D2 **Morpeth** Eng
19B2 **Morrilton** USA
35B1 **Morrinhos** Brazil

110C1 **Morrinsville** NZ
16B2 **Morristown** New Jersey, USA
15C2 **Morristown** New York, USA
16B2 **Morrisville** Pennsylvania, USA
21A2 **Morro Bay** USA
23A2 **Morro de Papanoa** Mexico
23A2 **Morro de Petatlán** Mexico
101C2 **Morrumbala** Mozam
101C3 **Morrumbene** Mozam
61F3 **Morshansk** Russian Fed
47C2 **Mortara** Italy
34C2 **Morteros** Arg
33G6 **Mortes** R Mato Grosso, Brazil
35C2 **Mortes** R Minas Gerais, Brazil
108B3 **Mortlake** Aust
27L1 **Moruga** Trinidad
103D3 **Moruya** Aust
109C1 **Morven** Aust
44B3 **Morvern** Pen Scot
109C3 **Morwell** Aust
76B3 **Moscos Is** Burma
Moscow = Moskva
20C1 **Moscow** Idaho, USA
56B2 **Mosel** R Germany
46D2 **Moselle** Department, France
46D2 **Moselle** R France
20C1 **Moses Lake** USA
111B3 **Mosgiel** NZ
99D3 **Moshi** Tanz
38G5 **Mosjøen** Nor
63G2 **Moskal'vo** Russian Fed
64E4 **Moskva** Russian Fed
75J1 **Mosquito** R Brazil
39G7 **Moss** Nor
98B3 **Mossaka** Congo
100B4 **Mossel Bay** S Africa
98B3 **Mossendjo** Congo
18B2 **Mossgiel** Aust
31D3 **Mossoró** Brazil
57C2 **Most** Czech Republic
96C1 **Mostaganem** Alg
54A2 **Mostar** Bosnia-Herzegovina
58C2 **Mosty** Belorussia
Mosul = Al Mawşil
39H7 **Motala** Sweden
42C2 **Motherwell** Scot
86A1 **Motihari** India
51B2 **Motilla del Palancar** Spain
50B2 **Motril** Spain
111B2 **Motueka** NZ
111B2 **Motueka** R NZ
47B1 **Moudon** Switz
98B3 **Mouila** Gabon
108B2 **Moulamein** Aust
4G2 **Mould Bay** Can
49C2 **Moulins** France
76B2 **Moulmein** Burma
96B1 **Moulouya** R Mor
17B1 **Moultrie** USA
17C1 **Moultrie,L** USA
18C2 **Mound City** Illinois, USA
18A1 **Mound City** Missouri, USA
98B2 **Moundou** Chad
14B3 **Moundsville** USA
12J1 **Mountain** R Can
17A1 **Mountain Brook** USA
18B2 **Mountain Grove** USA
18B2 **Mountain Home** Arkansas, USA
22A2 **Mountain View** USA
12B2 **Mountain Village** USA
18A1 **Mount Airy** Maryland, USA
16A2 **Mount Carmel** USA
108A1 **Mount Dutton** Aust
108A2 **Mount Eba** Aust
108B3 **Mount Gambier** Aust
16B3 **Mount Holly** USA

Mount Holly Springs

16A2 **Mount Holly Springs** USA
108A2 **Mount Hope** Aust
106C3 **Mount Isa** Aust
108A2 **Mount Lofty Range** Aust
12D2 **Mount McKinley Nat Pk** USA
106A3 **Mount Magnet** Aust
108B2 **Mount Manara** Aust
107E3 **Mount Morgan** Aust
19B3 **Mount Pleasant** Texas, USA
20B1 **Mount Rainier Nat Pk** USA
43B4 **Mounts B** Eng
20B2 **Mount Shasta** USA
11B3 **Mount Vernon** Illinois, USA
19A3 **Mount Vernon** Kentucky, USA
20B1 **Mount Vernon** Washington, USA
45C1 **Mourne Mts** N Ire
98B1 **Moussoro** Chad
86B2 **Mouths of the Ganga** India/Bang
85B4 **Mouths of the Indus** Pak
77D4 **Mouths of the Mekong** Viet
97C4 **Mouths of the Niger** Nig
47B1 **Moûtier** Switz
47B2 **Moûtiers** France
96C2 **Mouydir** Mts Alg
98B3 **Mouyondzi** Congo
96C2 **Mouzon** France
59B3 **M'óvar** Hung
23A1 **Moyahua** Mexico
99D2 **Moyale** Kenya
97A4 **Moyamba** Sierra Leone
96B1 **Moyen Atlas** Mts Mor
100B4 **Moyeni** Lesotho
99D2 **Moyo** Uganda
32B5 **Moyobamba** Peru
84D1 **Moyu** China
101C3 **Mozambique** Republic, Africa
101C3 **Mozambique Chan** Mozm/Madag
61H2 **Mozhga** Russian Fed
60C3 **Mozyr'** Belorussia
99D3 **Mpanda** Tanz
101C2 **Mpika** Zambia
99D3 **Mporokosa** Zambia
100B2 **Mposhi** Zambia
99D3 **Mpulungu** Zambia
99D3 **Mpwapwa** Tanz
60E3 **Mtsensk** Russian Fed
101H1 **Mtubatuba** S Africa
101D2 **Mtwara** Tanz
76C2 **Muang Chainat** Thai
76C2 **Muang Chiang Rai** Thai
76C2 **Muang Kalasin** Thai
76C2 **Muang Khon Kaen** Thai
76B2 **Muang Lampang** Thai
76B2 **Muang Lamphun** Thai
76C2 **Muang Loei** Thai
76C2 **Muang Lom Sak** Thai
76C2 **Muang Nakhon Phanom** Thai
76B2 **Muang Nakhon Sawan** Thai
76C2 **Muang Nan** Thai
76C2 **Muang Phayao** Thai
76C2 **Muang Phetchabun** Thai
76C2 **Muang Phichit** Thai
76C2 **Muang Phitsanulok** Thai
76C2 **Muang Phrae** Thai
76C2 **Muang Roi Et** Thai
76C2 **Muang Sakon Nakhon** Thai
76C3 **Muang Samut Prakan** Thai

76C2 **Muang Uthai Thani** Thai
76C2 **Muang Yasothon** Thai
77C5 **Muar** Malay
78C2 **Muara** Brunei
70B4 **Muara** Indon
78A3 **Muaralakitan** Indon
78A3 **Muaratebo** Indon
78C3 **Muaratewah** Indon
78A3 **Muarenim** Indon
76A2 **Muaungmaya** Burma
99D2 **Mubende** Uganda
100C2 **Muchinga** Mts Zambia
44A3 **Muck** / Scot
109C1 **Muckadilla** Aust
35D1 **Mucuri** Brazil
35C1 **Mucuri** R Brazil
100B2 **Mucusso** Angola
69E2 **Mudanjiang** China
109C2 **Mudgee** Aust
76B2 **Mudon** Burma
101C2 **Mueda** Mozam
107F3 **Mueo** Nouvelle Calédonie
100B2 **Mufulira** Zambia
73C4 **Mufu Shan** Hills China
       Mugadishu = **Muqdisho**
93C4 **Mughayra** S Arabia
92A2 **Muğla** Turk
65G5 **Mugodzhary** Mts Kazakhstan
73A3 **Muguaping** China
93D3 **Mukacheve** Ukraine
57C3 **Mühldorf** Germany
57C2 **Mühlhausen** Germany
38K6 **Muhos** Fin
77C4 **Mui Bai Bung** C Camb
45C2 **Muine Bheag** Irish Rep
100B2 **Mujimbeji** Zambia
59C3 **Mukachevo** Ukraine
78C2 **Mukah** Malay
69G4 **Muko-jima** / Japan
86A1 **Muktinath** Nepal
18B2 **Mulberry** USA
12C2 **Mulchatna** R USA
34A3 **Mulchén** Chile
56C2 **Mulde** R Germany
71F5 **Mulgrave I** Aust
50B2 **Mulhacén** Mt Spain
46D1 **Mülheim** Germany
49D2 **Mulhouse** France
73A4 **Muli** China
44B3 **Mull** / Scot
87C3 **Mullaitvu** Sri Lanka
109C2 **Mullaley** Aust
106A3 **Mullewa** Aust
16B3 **Mullica** R USA
45C2 **Mullingar** Irish Rep
42B2 **Mull of Kintyre** Pt Scot
45C1 **Mull of Oa** C Scot
109D1 **Mullumbimby** Aust
100B2 **Mulobezi** Zambia
84C2 **Multan** Pak
       Mumbai = Bombay
100B2 **Mumbwa** Zambia
61G4 **Mumra** Russian Fed
71D4 **Muna** / Indon
57C3 **München** Germany
14A2 **Muncie** USA
15C2 **Muncy** USA
56B2 **Münden** Germany
109D1 **Mundubbera** Aust
109C1 **Mungallala** Aust
109C1 **Mungallala** R Aust
99C2 **Mungbere** Zaïre
86A2 **Mungeli** India
86B1 **Munger** India
109C1 **Mungindi** Aust
14A1 **Munising** USA
29B6 **Muñoz Gomero,Pen** Chile
45B2 **Munster** Region, Irish Rep

47C1 **Münster** Switz
56B2 **Münster** Germany
54B1 **Muntii Apuseni** Mts Rom
54B1 **Muntii Călimanilor** Mts Rom
54B1 **Muntii Carpații Meridionali** R Rom
54B1 **Muntii Rodnei** Mts Rom
54B1 **Muntii Zarandului** Mts Rom
100B2 **Munyati** R Zim
93C2 **Munzur Silsilesi** Mts Turk
64D3 **Muomio** Fin
76C1 **Muong Khoua** Laos
76D3 **Muong Man** Viet
76D2 **Muong Nong** Laos
76C1 **Muong Ou Neua** Laos
76C1 **Muong Sai** Laos
76C1 **Muong Sen** Viet
76C1 **Muong Sing** Laos
76C1 **Muong Son** Laos
38J5 **Muonio** Fin
38J5 **Muonio** R Sweden/ Fin
99E2 **Muqdisho** Somalia
52B1 **Mur** R Austria
74D3 **Murakami** Japan
29B5 **Murallón** Mt Arg/ Chile
61G2 **Murashi** Russian Fed
93D2 **Murat** R Turk
53A3 **Muravera** Sardegna
75C1 **Murayama** Japan
90B3 **Murcheh Khvort** Iran
111B2 **Murchison** NZ
106A3 **Murchison** R Aust
51B2 **Murcia** Region, Spain
51B2 **Murcia** Spain
54B1 **Mures** R Rom
46E2 **Murg** R Germany
65H6 **Murgab** R Turkmenistan
84B2 **Murgha Kibzai** Pak
109D1 **Murgon** Aust
86B2 **Muri** Aust
98C3 **Muriege** Angola
64E3 **Murmansk** Russian Fed
61F2 **Murom** Russian Fed
74C4 **Muroto** Japan
75A2 **Muroto-zaki** C Japan
20C2 **Murphy** Idaho, USA
22B1 **Murphys** USA
18C2 **Murray** Kentucky, USA
108B2 **Murray** R Aust
13C2 **Murray** R Can
108A3 **Murray Bridge** Aust
71F4 **Murray,L** PNG
17B1 **Murray,L** USA
105J2 **Murray Seacarp** Pacific O
108B2 **Murrumbidgee** R Aust
109C2 **Murrumburrah** Aust
109D2 **Murrurundi** Aust
47B1 **Murten** Switz
108B3 **Murtoa** Aust
110C1 **Murupara** NZ
86A2 **Murwāra** India
109D1 **Murwillimbah** Aust
93D2 **Muş** Turk
54B2 **Musala** Mt Bulg
74B2 **Musan** N Korea
91C4 **Musandam Pen** Oman
       Muscat = Masqat
91C5 **Muscat** Region, Oman
106C3 **Musgrave Range** Mts Aust
98B3 **Mushie** Zaïre
14A2 **Muskegon** USA
14A2 **Muskegon** R USA
18A2 **Muskogee** USA
15C2 **Muskoka,L** Can
95C3 **Musmar** Sudan

99D3 **Musoma** Tanz
8C2 **Musselshell** R USA
100A2 **Mussende** Angola
48C2 **Mussidan** France
55C2 **Mustafa-Kemalpasa** Turk
86A1 **Mustang** Nepal
109D2 **Muswellbrook** Aust
95B2 **Mut** Egypt
101C2 **Mutarara** Mozam
101C2 **Mutare** Zim
101C2 **Mutoko** Zim
101D2 **Mutsamudu** Comoros
100B2 **Mutshatsha** Zaïre
74E2 **Mutsu** Japan
74E2 **Mutsu-wan** B Japan
45B2 **Mutton** / Irish Rep
72B2 **Mu Us Shamo** Desert China
98B3 **Muxima** Angola
63D2 **Muya** Russian Fed
38L6 **Muyezerskiy** Russian Fed
99D3 **Muyinga** Burundi
98C3 **Muyumba** Zaïre
82A1 **Muyun Kum** Desert Kazakhstan
84C2 **Muzaffarabad** Pak
84C2 **Muzaffargarh** Pak
84D3 **Muzaffarnagar** India
86B1 **Muzaffarpur** India
64H3 **Muzhi** Russian Fed
82C2 **Muztag** Mt China
82B2 **Muztagata** Mt China
100C2 **Mvuma** Zim
99D3 **Mwanza** Tanz
98C3 **Mwanza** Zaïre
98C3 **Mweka** Zaïre
98C3 **Mwene Ditu** Zaïre
100C3 **Mwenezi** Zim
99D3 **Mwenga** Zaïre
99C3 **Mweru** L Zaïre
100B2 **Mwinilunga** Zambia
83D4 **Myanaung** Burma
       Myanma = Burma
86D2 **Myingyan** Burma
76B1 **Myinyang** Burma
76B3 **Myinmoletkat** Mt Burma
82D3 **Myitkyina** Burma
76B3 **Myitta** Burma
86C2 **Mymensingh** Bang
69F3 **Myojin** / Japan
39F6 **Myrdal** Nor
38B2 **Myrdalsjökur** Ice Cap Iceland
17C1 **Myrtle Beach** USA
20B2 **Myrtle Creek** USA
39G7 **Mysen** Nor
56C2 **Myślibórz** Pol
64F3 **Mys Kanin Nos** C Russian Fed
59B3 **Myślenice** Pol
61H1 **Mys Lopatka** C Russian Fed
87B2 **Mysore** India
60D5 **Mys Sarych** C Ukraine
16D2 **Mystic** USA
61H5 **Mys Tyub-Karagan** Pt Kazakhstan
63G2 **Mys Yelizavety** C Russian Fed
64H2 **Mys Zhelaniya** C Russian Fed
77D3 **My Tho** Viet
20B2 **Myrtle Point** USA
101C2 **Mzimba** Malawi
101C2 **Mzuzú** Malawi

N

21C4 **Naalehu** Hawaiian Is
39J6 **Naantali** Fin
45C2 **Naas** Irish Rep
75B2 **Nabari** Japan
61H2 **Naberezhnye Chelny** Russian Fed
12F2 **Nabesna** R USA
96D1 **Nabeul** Tunisia
94B2 **Nablus** Israel
101D2 **Nacala** Mozam
20B1 **Naches** USA
101C2 **Nachingwea** Tanz

19B3 Nacogdoches USA
76A3 Nacondam I Indian O
24B1 Nacozari Mexico
85C4 Nadiäd India
50B2 Nador Mor
90B3 Nadushan Iran
59C3 Nadvornaya Ukraine
56C1 Naestved Den
95B2 Näfürah Libya
75A2 Nagahama Japan
82D3 Naga Hills Burma
75B1 Nagai Japan
86C1 Nägaland State, India
74D3 Nagano Japan
74D3 Nagaoka Japan
86C1 Nagaon India
87B2 Nägappattinam India
85C4 Nagar Parkar Pak
74B4 Nagasaki Japan
75B2 Nagashima Japan
75A2 Nagato Japan
85C3 Nägaur India
87B3 Nägercoil India
85B3 Nagha Kalat Pak
84D3 Nagina India
74D3 Nagoya Japan
85D4 Nägpur India
82D2 Nagqu China
59B3 Nagykanizsa Hung
59B3 Nagykörös Hung
69E4 Naha Japan
8A2 Nahaimo Can
84D2 Nähan India
4F3 Nahanni Butte Can
94B2 Nahariya Israel
90A3 Nahävand Iran
46D2 Nahe R Germany
72D2 Nahpu China
72E1 Naimen Qi China
7D4 Nain Can
90B3 Na'in Iran
84D3 Naini Tal India
44C3 Nairn Scot
99D3 Nairobi Kenya
90B3 Najafäbäd Iran
74C2 Najin N Korea
75A2 Nakama Japan
74E3 Nakaminato Japan
75A2 Nakamura Japan
75B1 Nakano Japan
75A1 Nakano-shima I Japan
74C4 Nakatsu Japan
75B1 Nakatsu-gawa Japan
95C3 Nak'fa Eritrea
93E2 Nakhichevan Azerbaijan
92B4 Nakhl Egypt
74C2 Nakhodka Russian Fed
76C3 Nakhon Pathom Thai
76C3 Nakhon Ratchasima Thai
77C4 Nakhon Si Thammarat Thai
12H3 Nakina Can
7B4 Nakina Ontario, Can
12C3 Naknek USA
12C3 Naknek L USA
4C4 Nakrek USA
39G8 Nakskov Den
99D3 Nakuru Kenya
13D2 Nakusp Can
61F5 Nal'chik Russian Fed
87B1 Nalgonda India
87B1 Nallamala Range Mts India
95A1 Nälüt Libya
101H1 Namaacha Mozam
65G6 Namak L Iran
90C3 Namakzar-e Shadad Salt Flat Iran
65J5 Namangan Uzbekistan
101C2 Namapa Mozam
100A4 Namaqualand Region, S Africa
109D1 Nambour Aust
109D2 Nambucca Heads Aust
77D4 Nam Can Viet
82D2 Nam Co L China

76D1 Nam Dinh Viet
101C2 Nametil Mozam
74B4 Namhae-do I S Korea
100A2 Namib Desert Namibia
100A2 Namibe Angola
100A3 Namibia Republic, Africa
82D3 Namjagbarwa Feng Mt China
71D4 Namlea Indon
109C2 Namoi R Aust
13D1 Nampa Can
20C2 Nampa USA
97B3 Nampala Mali
76C2 Nam Phong Thai
74B3 Namp'o N Korea
101C2 Nampula Mozam
38G6 Namsos Nor
76B1 Namton Burma
86D2 Namtu Burma
13B2 Namu Can
101C2 Namuno Mozam
46C1 Namur Belg
100A2 Namutoni Namibia
74B3 Namvon S Korea
13C3 Nanaimo Can
74B2 Nanam N Korea
109D1 Nanango Aust
74D3 Nanao Japan
75B1 Nanatsu-jima I Japan
73B3 Nanbu China
73D4 Nanchang China
73B3 Nanchong China
49D2 Nancy France
87B1 Nänded India
109D2 Nandewar Range Mts Aust
85C4 Nandurbar India
87B1 Nändyäl India
98B2 Nanga Eboko Cam
84C1 Nanga Parbat Mt Pak
78C3 Nangapinoh Indon
78C3 Nangatayap Indon
74B2 Nangnim Sanmaek Mts N Korea
86C1 Nang Xian China
67F3 Nangzhou China
87B2 Nanjangüd India
72D3 Nanjing China
Nanking = Nanjing
75A2 Nankoku Japan
73C4 Nan Ling Region, China
76D1 Nanning R China
73B5 Nanning China
6F3 Nanortalik Greenland
73A5 Nanpan Jiang R China
86A1 Nänpära India
73D4 Nanping China
6A2 Nansen Sd Can
99D3 Nansio Tanz
48B2 Nantes France
13E2 Nanton Can
72C3 Nantong China
10C2 Nantucket I USA
35C1 Nanuque Brazil
72C3 Nanyang China
72C2 Nanyang Hu L China
99D2 Nanyuki Kenya
74D3 Naoetsu Japan
85B4 Naokot Pak
22A1 Napa USA
12B2 Napaiskak USA
15C2 Napanee Can
65K4 Napas Russian Fed
6E3 Napassoq Greenland
76D2 Nape Laos
110C1 Napier NZ
Naples = Napoli
17B2 Naples Florida, USA
19B3 Naples Texas, USA
73B5 Napo China
32C4 Napo R Peru/Ecuador
53B2 Napoli Italy
90A2 Naqadeh Iran
92C4 Naqb Ishtar Jordan
75B2 Nara Japan

97B3 Nara Mali
107D4 Naracoorte Aust
23B1 Naranjos Mexico
87C1 Narasaraopet India
77C4 Narathiwat Thai
86C2 Narayanganj Bang
87B1 Näräyenpet India
49C3 Narbonne France
84D2 Narendranagar India
6C2 Nares Str Can
58C2 Narew R Pol
75C1 Narita Japan
85C4 Narmada R India
84D3 Närmaul India
60E2 Naro Fominsk Russian Fed
99D3 Narok Kenya
84C2 Narowal Pak
107D4 Narrabri Aust
109C1 Narran L Aust
109C2 Narran R Aust
109C2 Narrandera Aust
106A4 Narrogin Aust
109C2 Narromine Aust
87C1 Narsimhapur India
87C1 Narsipatnam India
6F3 Narssalik Greenland
6F3 Narssaq Greenland
6F3 Narssarssuaq Greenland
75C1 Narugo Japan
75A2 Naruto Japan
60C2 Narva Russian Fed
38H5 Narvik Nor
84D3 Närwäna India
64G3 Nar'yan Mar Russian Fed
108B1 Narylico Aust
16D1 Nashua USA
19B3 Nashville Arkansas, USA
11B3 Nashville Tennessee, USA
54A1 Našice Croatia
85D4 Näsik India
99D2 Nasir Sudan
13B1 Nass R Can
26B1 Nassau The Bahamas
16C1 Nassau USA
95C2 Nasser,L Egypt
39G7 Nässjö Sweden
100B3 Nata Botswana
31D3 Natal Brazil
70A3 Natal Indon
101H1 Natal Province, S Africa
90B3 Natanz Iran
7D4 Natashquan Can
7D4 Natashquan R Can
19B3 Natchez USA
19B3 Natchitoches USA
108C3 Nathalia Aust
6H2 Nathorsts Land Region Greenland
13C1 Nation R Can
21B3 National City USA
75C1 Natori Japan
99D3 Natron L Tanz
106A4 Naturaliste,C Aust
47D1 Nauders Austria
56C2 Nauen Germany
16C2 Naugatuck USA
57C2 Naumburg Germany
94B3 Naur Jordan
105G4 Nauru I Pacific O
63C2 Naushki Russian Fed
23B1 Nautla Mexico
9C3 Navajo Res USA
50A2 Navalmoral de la Mata Spain
29C4 Navarino I Chile
51B1 Navarra Province, Spain
34D3 Navarro Arg
19A3 Navasota USA
19A3 Navasota R USA
50A1 Navia R Spain
34A2 Navidad Chile

85C4 Navlakhi India
60D3 Navlya Russian Fed
24B1 Navojoa Mexico
55B3 Návpaktos Greece
55B3 Návplion Greece
85C4 Navsäri India
94C2 Nawä Syria
86B2 Nawäda India
84B2 Nawah Afghan
85B3 Nawrabshah Pak
73B4 Naxi China
55C3 Náxos I / Greece
23A1 Nayar Mexico
90C3 Nay Band Iran
91B4 Näy Band Iran
74E2 Nayoro Japan
94B2 Nazareth Israel
48B2 Nazay France
32C6 Nazca Peru
92A2 Nazilli Turk
63B2 Nazimovo Russian Fed
13C2 Nazko R Can
99D2 Nazret Eth
91C5 Nazwa Oman
65J4 Nazyvayevsk Russian Fed
98B3 Ndalatando Angola
98C2 Ndélé CAR
98C3 Ndendé Gabon
98B1 Ndjamena Chad
98B3 Ndjolé Gabon
100B2 Ndola Zambia
109C1 Neabul Aust
108A1 Neales R Aust
55B3 Neápolis Greece
43C4 Neath Wales
109C1 Nebine R Aust
65G6 Nebit Dag Turkmenistan
8C2 Nebraska State, USA
18A1 Nebraska City USA
13C2 Nechako R Can
19A3 Neches R USA
34D3 Necochea Arg
86C1 Nêdong China
9B3 Needles USA
14A2 Neenah USA
5J4 Neepawa Can
46C1 Neerpelt Belg
63C2 Neftelensk Russian Fed
99D2 Negelê Eth
94B3 Negev Desert Israel
60B4 Negolu Mt Rom
87B3 Negombo Sri Lanka
76A2 Negrais,C Burma
32A4 Negritos Peru
33E4 Negro R Amazonas, Brazil
29C4 Negro R Arg
34D2 Negro R Urug
79B4 Negros I Phil
54C2 Negru Voda Rom
90D3 Nehbändan Iran
73B4 Neijiang China
72B1 Nei Monggol Autonomous Region, China
32B3 Neiva Colombia
99D2 Nejo Eth
99D2 Nek'emté Eth
60D2 Nelidovo Russian Fed
87B2 Nellore India
69F2 Nel'ma Russian Fed
13D3 Nelson Can
111B2 Nelson NZ
7A4 Nelson R Can
108B3 Nelson,C Aust
10A3 Nelson,C USA
12B2 Nelson I USA
97B3 Néma Maur
72A1 Nemagt Uul Mt Mongolia
58C1 Neman R Lithuania
54C1 Nemira Mt Rom
74F2 Nemuro Japan
63E3 Nen R China
41B3 Nenagh Irish Rep
12E2 Nenana USA
12E2 Nenana R USA
43D3 Nene R Eng
69E2 Nenjiang China
18A2 Neodesha USA

Neosho

18B2 **Neosho** USA
63C2 **Nepa** Russian Fed
82C3 **Nepal** Kingdom, Asia
86A1 **Nepalganj** Nepal
45B1 **Nephin** Mt Irish Rep
94B3 **Neqarot** R Israel
34A3 **Nequén** State, Arg
68D1 **Nerchinsk**
Russian Fed
52C2 **Neretva** R Bosnia-Herzegovina/Croatia
71F2 **Nero Deep** Pacific O
38C1 **Neskaupstaður**
Iceland
46B2 **Nesle** France
7E5 **Nesleyville** Can
55B2 **Néstos** R Greece
94B2 **Netanya** Israel
16B2 **Netcong** USA
56B2 **Netherlands**
Kingdom, Europe
3M7 **Netherlands Antilles**
Is Caribbean S
86C2 **Netrakona** Bang
6C3 **Nettilling** L Can
56C2 **Neubrandenburg**
Germany
47B1 **Neuchâtel** Switz
48C2 **Neufchâteau** Belg
48C2 **Neufchâtel** France
46A2 **Neufchâtel-en-Bray**
France
56B2 **Neumünster**
Germany
52C1 **Neunkirchen** Austria
46D2 **Neunkirchen**
Germany
34B3 **Neuquén** Arg
29B4 **Neuquén** State, Arg
34B3 **Neuquén** R Arg
56C2 **Neuruppin** Germany
46D1 **Neuss** Germany
46E2 **Neustadt** Germany
56C2 **Neustadt** Germany
56C2 **Neustrelitz** Germany
46D1 **Neuwied** Germany
8B3 **Nevada** State, USA
18B2 **Nevada** USA
34A3 **Nevada de Chillán**
Mts Arg/Chile
23A2 **Nevada de Colima**
Mexico
23B2 **Nevada de Toluca** Mt
Mexico
94B2 **Nevatim** Israel
60C2 **Nevel'** Russian Fed
49C2 **Nevers** France
109C2 **Nevertire** Aust
27E3 **Nevis** I Caribbean S
58D2 **Nevis** R Belorussia/Lithuania
92B2 **Nevsehir** Turk
61K2 **Nev'yansk**
Russian Fed
101C2 **Newala** Tanz
14A3 **New Albany** Indiana, USA
19C3 **New Albany**
Mississippi, USA
33F2 **New Amsterdam**
Guyana
109C1 **New Angledool** Aust
15C3 **Newark** Delaware, USA
10C2 **Newark** New Jersey, USA
14B2 **Newark** Ohio, USA
43D3 **Newark-upon-Trent**
Eng
15D2 **New Bedford** USA
13B2 **New Bella Bella** Can
20B1 **Newberg** USA
11C3 **New Bern** USA
17B1 **Newberry** USA
26B2 **New Bight**
The Bahamas
14B3 **New Boston** USA
9D4 **New Braunfels** USA
16C2 **New Britain** USA
7D5 **New Brunswick**
Province, Can
16B2 **New Brunswick** USA
16B2 **Newburgh** USA
43D4 **Newbury** Eng

16D1 **Newburyport** USA
16C2 **New Canaan** USA
109D2 **Newcastle** Aust
14A3 **New Castle** Indiana, USA
42B2 **Newcastle** N Ire
14B2 **New Castle**
Pennsylvania, USA
101G1 **Newcastle** S Africa
8C2 **Newcastle** Wyoming, USA
42D2 **Newcastle upon Tyne**
Eng
106C2 **Newcastle Waters**
Aust
45B2 **Newcastle West**
Irish Rep
84D3 **New Delhi** India
109D2 **New England Range**
Mts Aust
12B3 **Newenham,C** USA
43D4 **New Forest,The** Eng
7D4 **Newfoundland**
Province, Can
7E5 **Newfoundland** I
Can
102F2 **Newfoundland Basin**
Atlantic O
18B2 **New Franklin** USA
42B2 **New Galloway** Scot
107E1 **New Georgia** I
Solomon Is
7D5 **New Glasgow** Can
71F4 **New Guinea** SE Asia
12D3 **Newhalen** USA
22C3 **Newhall** USA
10C2 **New Hampshire**
State, USA
101H1 **New Hanover**
S Africa
43E4 **Newhaven** Eng
15D2 **New Haven** USA
13B1 **New Hazelton** Can
19B3 **New Iberia** USA
10C2 **New Jersey** State,
USA
7C5 **New Liskeard** Can
16C2 **New London** USA
106A3 **Newman** Aust
22B2 **Newman** USA
43E3 **Newmarket** Eng
45B2 **Newmarket** Irish Rep
15C3 **New Market** USA
9C3 **New Mexico** State,
USA
16C2 **New Milford**
Connecticut, USA
17B1 **Newnan** USA
109C4 **New Norfolk** Aust
11A3 **New Orleans** USA
16B2 **New Paltz** USA
15D2 **New Philadelphia**
USA
110B1 **New Plymouth** NZ
18B2 **Newport** Arkansas, USA
43D4 **Newport** Eng
14B3 **Newport** Kentucky, USA
20B2 **Newport** Oregon, USA
16A2 **Newport**
Pennsylvania, USA
15D2 **Newport** Rhode
Island, USA
15D2 **Newport** Vermont, USA
43C4 **Newport** Wales
20C1 **Newport**
Washington, USA
22D4 **Newport Beach** USA
11C3 **Newport News** USA
26B1 **New Providence** I
Caribbean S
43B4 **Newquay** Eng
6C3 **New Quebec Crater**
Can
45C2 **New Ross** Irish Rep
45C1 **Newry** N Ire
**New Siberian Is =
Novosibirskye
Ostrova**
17B2 **New Smyrna Beach**
USA

107D4 **New South Wales**
State, Aust
12C3 **New Stuyahok** USA
18A2 **Newton** Kansas,
USA
16D1 **Newton**
Massachusetts, USA
19C3 **Newton** Mississippi,
USA
16B2 **Newton** New York,
USA
43C4 **Newton Abbot** Eng
45C1 **Newton Stewart**
N Ire
42B2 **Newton Stewart**
Scot
43C3 **Newtown** Wales
42B2 **Newtownards** N Ire
16A2 **Newville** USA
5F5 **New Westminster** Can
10C2 **New York** State, USA
10C2 **New York** USA
110 **New Zealand**
Dominion, SW
Pacific O
105G6 **New Zealand Plat**
Pacific O
71F2 **Neya** Russian Fed
91B4 **Neyriz** Iran
90C2 **Neyshābūr** Iran
60D3 **Nezhin** Russian Fed
98B3 **Ngabé** Congo
100B3 **Ngami** L Botswana
110C1 **Ngaruawahia** NZ
110C1 **Ngaruroro** R NZ
110C1 **Ngauruhoe,Mt** NZ
98B3 **Ngo** Congo
76D3 **Ngoc Linh** Mt Viet
98B2 **Ngoko** R Cam
68B3 **Ngoring Hu** L China
99D3 **Ngorongoro Crater**
Tanz
98B3 **N'Gounié** R Gabon
98B1 **Nguigmi** Niger
71E3 **Ngulu** I Pacific O
97D3 **Nguru** Nig
76D3 **Nha Trang** Viet
108B3 **Nhill** Aust
101H1 **Nhlangano**
Swaziland
76D2 **Nhommarath** Laos
106C2 **Nhulunbuy** Aust
97B3 **Niafounké** Mali
14A1 **Niagara** USA
15C2 **Niagara Falls** Can
15C2 **Niagara Falls** USA
70C3 **Niah** Malay
97B4 **Niakaramandougou**
Ivory Coast
97C3 **Niamey** Niger
99C2 **Niangara** Zaïre
98C2 **Nia Nia** Zaïre
70A3 **Nias** I Indon
25D3 **Nicaragua** Republic,
Cent America
53C3 **Nicastro** Italy
49D3 **Nice** France
26B1 **Nicholl's Town**
The Bahamas
83D5 **Nicobar Is** Indian O
92B2 **Nicosia** Cyprus
25D3 **Nicoya,Pen de**
Costa Rica
58C2 **Nidzica** Pol
46D2 **Niederbronn** France
56B2 **Niedersachsen** State,
Germany
99C3 **Niemba** Zaïre
56B2 **Nienburg** Germany
46D1 **Niers** R Germany
97B4 **Niete,Mt** Lib
33F2 **Nieuw Amsterdam**
Surinam
33F2 **Nieuw Nickerie**
Surinam
46B1 **Nieuwpoort** Belg
92B2 **Niğde** Turk
97C3 **Niger** Republic,
Africa
97C4 **Niger** R Nig
97C4 **Nigeria** Federal
Republic, Africa
55B2 **Nigrita** Greece

75C1 **Nihommatsu** Japan
74D3 **Niigata** Japan
74C4 **Niihama** Japan
75B2 **Nii-jima** I Japan
75A2 **Niimi** Japan
74D3 **Niitsu** Japan
94B3 **Nijil** Jordan
56B2 **Nijmegen** Neth
64E3 **Nikel'** Russian Fed
97C3 **Nikki** Benin
74D3 **Nikko** Japan
60D4 **Nikolayevka** Ukraine
61G4 **Nikolayevsk**
Russian Fed
63G2 **Nikolayevsk-na-Amure** Russian Fed
61G2 **Nikol'sk** Russian Fed
61G3 **Nikol'sk** Russian Fed
60D4 **Nikopol** Ukraine
92C1 **Niksar** Turk
91D4 **Nikshahr** Iran
54A2 **Nikšić** Montenegro,
Yugos
71D4 **Nila** I Indon
80B3 **Nile** R N E Africa
14A2 **Niles** USA
87B2 **Nilgiri Hills** India
85C4 **Nimach** India
49C3 **Nîmes** France
109C3 **Nimmitabel** Aust
99D2 **Nimule** Sudan
83B5 **Nine Degree Chan**
Indian O
104C4 **Ninety-East Ridge**
Indian O
109C3 **Ninety Mile Beach**
Aust
73D4 **Ningde** China
73D4 **Ningdu** China
68B3 **Ningjing Shan** Mts
China
76D1 **Ningming** China
73A4 **Ningnan** China
72B2 **Ningxia** Province,
China
72B2 **Ning Xian** China
73B5 **Ninh Binh** Vietnam
107D1 **Ninigo Is** PNG
12D2 **Ninilchik** USA
8D2 **Niobrara** R USA
98B3 **Nioki** Zaïre
97B3 **Nioro du Sahel** Mali
48B2 **Niort** France
5H4 **Nipawin** Can
7B5 **Nipigon** Can
7B5 **Nipigon,L** Can
7B5 **Nipissing** Can
14B1 **Nipissing,L** Can
87B1 **Nirmal** India
86B1 **Nirmāli** India
54B2 **Niš** Serbia, Yugos
81C4 **Nisāb** Yemen
69F4 **Nishino-shima** I
Japan
75A1 **Nishino-shima** I
Japan
75A2 **Nishiwaki** Japan
12G2 **Nisling** R Can
12H2 **Nisutlin** R Can
7C4 **Nitchequon** Can
31C6 **Niterói** Brazil
42C2 **Nith** R Scot
59B3 **Nitra** Slovakia
14B3 **Nitro** USA
78C2 **Niut** Mt Malay
46C1 **Nivelles** Belg
49C2 **Nivernais** Region,
France
38L5 **Nízamábád** Russian Fed
87B1 **Nizāmābād** India
94B3 **Nizana** Hist Site
Israel
61J2 **Nizhniye Sergi**
Russian Fed
65F4 **Nizhniy Novgorod**
Russian Fed
61F3 **Nizhniy Lomov**
Russian Fed
65G4 **Nizhniy Tagil**
Russian Fed
63B1 **Nizhnyaya Tunguska**
R Russian Fed
93C2 **Nizip** Turk
100B2 **Njoko** R Zambia

99D3 **Njombe** Tanz
98B2 **Nkambé** Cam
101C2 **Nkhata Bay** Malawi
98B2 **Nkongsamba** Cam
97C3 **N'Konni** Niger
86C2 **Noakhali** Bang
12B1 **Noatak** USA
12C1 **Noatak** *R* USA
74C4 **Nobeoka** Japan
47D1 **Noce** *R* Italy
23A1 **Nochistlan** Mexico
23B2 **Nochixtlán** Mexico
19A3 **Nocona** USA
24A1 **Nogales** Sonora, Mexico
9B3 **Nogales** USA
23B2 **Nogales** Veracruz, Mexico
47D2 **Nogara** Italy
75A2 **Nogata** Japan
60E2 **Noginsk** Russian Fed
34D2 **Nogoyá** Arg
34D2 **Nogoyá** *R* Arg
84C3 **Nohar** India
75B2 **Nojima-zaki** *C* Japan
98B2 **Nola** CAR
61G2 **Nolinsk** Russian Fed
16D2 **Nomans Land** *I* USA
12A2 **Nome** USA
46D2 **Nomeny** France
72B1 **Nomgon** Mongolia
5H3 **Nonacho L** Can
76C2 **Nong Khai** Thai
101H1 **Nongoma** S Africa
12B1 **Noorvik** USA
13B3 **Nootka Sd** Can
98B3 **Noqui** Angola
7C5 **Noranda** Can
46B1 **Nord** Department, France
64D2 **Nordaustlandet** *I* Barents S
13D2 **Nordegg** Can
38F6 **Nordfjord** *Inlet* Nor
39F8 **Nordfriesische** *Is* Germany
56C2 **Nordhausen** Germany
56B2 **Nordrhein Westfalen** State, Germany
38J4 **Nordkapp** *C* Nor
6E3 **Nordre** Greenland
38H5 **Nord Stronfjället** *Mt* Sweden
1B9 **Nordvik** Russian Fed
45C2 **Nore** *R* Irish Rep
43E3 **Norfolk** County, Eng
8D2 **Norfolk** Nebraska, USA
11C3 **Norfolk** Virginia, USA
107E3 **Norfolk I** Aust
18B2 **Norfolk L** USA
105G5 **Norfolk Ridge** Pacific O
1C10 **Noril'sk** Russian Fed
18C1 **Normal** USA
19A2 **Norman** USA
48B2 **Normandie** Region, France
107D2 **Normanton** Aust
12J1 **Norman Wells** Can
4B3 **Norne** USA
15C2 **Norristown** USA
39H7 **Norrköping** Sweden
39H6 **Norrsundet** Sweden
39H7 **Norrtälje** Sweden
106B4 **Norseman** Aust
63F2 **Norsk** Russian Fed
102J2 **North S** N W Europe
42D2 **Northallerton** Eng
106A4 **Northam** Aust
102E3 **North American Basin** Atlantic O
106A3 **Northampton** Aust
43D3 **Northampton** County, Eng
43D3 **Northampton** Eng
15D2 **Northampton** USA
4G3 **North Arm** *B* Can
17B1 **North Augusta** USA
6D4 **North Aulatsivik** *I* Can

13F2 **North Battleford** Can
7C5 **North Bay** Can
20B2 **North Bend** USA
44C3 **North Berwick** Scot
7D5 **North,C** Can
7G4 **North C** NZ
11B3 **North Carolina** State, USA
20B1 **North Cascade Nat Pk** USA
14B1 **North Chan** Can
42B2 **North Chan** Ire/Scot
8C2 **North Dakota** State, USA
43E4 **North Downs** Eng
14C2 **North East** USA
102H2 **North East Atlantic Basin** Atlantic O
4B3 **Northeast C** USA
40B3 **Northern Ireland** UK
27L1 **Northern Range** *Mts* Trinidad
106C2 **Northern Territory** Aust
44C3 **North Esk** *R* Scot
16C1 **Northfield** Massachusetts, USA
12D2 **North Fork** *R* USA
110B1 **North I** NZ
74B3 **North Korea** Republic, S E Asia
North Land = Severnaya Zemlya
19B3 **North Little Rock** USA
1B4 **North Magnetic Pole** Can
17B2 **North Miami** USA
17B2 **North Miami Beach** USA
8C2 **North Platte** USA
8C2 **North Platte** *R* USA
27R3 **North Pt** Barbados
14B1 **North Pt** USA
40B2 **North Rona** *I* Scot
44C2 **North Ronaldsay** *I* Scot
13F2 **North Saskatchewan** *R* Can
40D2 **North Sea** N W Europe
4D3 **North Slope** Region USA
109D1 **North Stradbroke** *I* Aust
110B1 **North Taranaki Bight** *B* NZ
9C3 **North Truchas Peak** *Mt* USA
44A3 **North Uist** *I* Scot
42C2 **Northumberland** County, Eng
107E3 **Northumberland Is** Aust
7D5 **Northumberland Str** Can
20B1 **North Vancouver** Can
43E3 **North Walsham** Eng
12F2 **Northway** USA
106A3 **North West C** Aust
84C2 **North West Frontier** Province, Pak
7D4 **North West River** Can
4F3 **North West Territories** Can
42D2 **North York Moors Nat Pk** Eng
12B2 **Norton B** USA
12B2 **Norton Sd** USA
112B1 **Norvegia,C** Ant
16C2 **Norwalk** Connecticut, USA
14B2 **Norwalk** Ohio, USA
39F6 **Norway** Kingdom, Europe
5J4 **Norway House** Can
6A2 **Norwegian B** Can
102H1 **Norwegian Basin** Norwegian S
64A3 **Norwegian S** N W Europe
16C2 **Norwich** Connecticut, USA

43E3 **Norwich** Eng
16D1 **Norwood** Massachusetts, USA
14B3 **Norwood** Ohio, USA
54C2 **Nos Emine** *C* Bulg
74D2 **Noshiro** Japan
54C2 **Nos Kaliakra** *C* Bulg
44E1 **Noss** *I* Scot
91D4 **Nostrābād** Iran
101D2 **Nosy Barren** *I* Madag
101D2 **Nosy Bé** *I* Madag
101E2 **Nosy Boraha** *I* Madag
101D3 **Nosy Varika** Madag
58B2 **Noteć** *R* Pol
5G4 **Notikeuin** Can
53C3 **Noto** Italy
39F7 **Notodden** Nor
75B1 **Noto-hantō** *Pen* Japan
7E5 **Notre Dams B** Can
43D3 **Nottingham** County, Eng
43D3 **Nottingham** Eng
6C3 **Nottingham I** Can
6C3 **Nottingham Island** Can
96A2 **Nouadhibou** Maur
97A3 **Nouakchott** Maur
107F3 **Nouméa** Nouvelle Calédonie
97B3 **Nouna** Burkina
107F3 **Nouvelle Calédonie** *I* S W Pacific O
98B3 **Nova Caipemba** Angola
35A2 **Nova Esparança** Brazil
35C2 **Nova Friburgo** Brazil
100A2 **Nova Gaia** Angola
35B2 **Nova Granada** Brazil
35A2 **Nova Horizonte** Brazil
35C1 **Nova Lima** Brazil
Nova Lisboa = Huambo
35A2 **Nova Londrina** Brazil
101C3 **Nova Mambone** Mozam
47C2 **Novara** Italy
7D5 **Nova Scotia** Province, Can
22A1 **Novato** USA
35C1 **Nova Venécia** Brazil
60C3 **Novaya Kakhovka** Ukraine
64G2 **Novaya Zemlya** *I* Barents S
54C2 **Nove Zagora** Bulg
31C2 **Nove Russas** Brazil
54A1 **Nové Zámky** Slovakia
60D2 **Novgorod** Russian Fed
47C2 **Novi Ligure** Italy
54C2 **Novi Pazar** Bulg
54B2 **Novi Pazar** Serbia, Yugos
54A1 **Novi Sad** Serbia, Yugos
61J3 **Novoaleksenyevka** Kazakhstan
61F3 **Novoanninskiy** Russian Fed
61E4 **Novocherkassk** Russian Fed
60C3 **Novograd Volynskiy** Ukraine
58D2 **Novogrudok** Russian Fed
30F4 **Novo Hamburgo** Brazil
65H5 **Novokazalinsk** Kazakhstan
65K4 **Novokuznetsk** Russian Fed
112B12 **Novolazarevskaya** Base Ant
52C1 **Novo Mesto** Slovenia
60E3 **Novomoskovsk** Russian Fed

60E5 **Novorossiysk** Russian Fed
65K4 **Novosibirsk** Russian Fed
1B8 **Novosibirskiye Ostrova** *I* Russian Fed
61J3 **Novotroitsk** Russian Fed
61G3 **Novo Uzensk** Russian Fed
59C2 **Novovolynsk** Ukraine
61G2 **Novo Vyatsk** Russian Fed
60D3 **Novozybkov** Russian Fed
58C2 **Nowy Dwór Mazowiecki** Pol
61K2 **Novvy Lyalya** Russian Fed
61H5 **Novyy Port** Russian Fed
61H5 **Novvy Uzen** Kazakhstan
58B2 **Nowa Sól** Pol
18A2 **Nowata** USA
12D2 **Nowgong** = Nagaon
12D2 **Nowitna** *R* USA
109D2 **Nowra** Aust
90B2 **Now Shahr** Iran
84C2 **Nowshera** Pak
59C3 **Nowy Sącz** Pol
12H3 **Noyes I** USA
46B2 **Noyon** France
97B4 **Nsawam** Ghana
99D1 **Nuba** *Mts* Sudan
81A3 **Nubian Desert** Sudan
84B3 **Nuble** *R* Chile
5D4 **Nueces** *R* USA
5J3 **Nueltin L** Can
26A2 **Nueva Gerona** Cuba
34A3 **Nueva Imperial** Chile
34D2 **Nueva Laredo** Mexico
34D2 **Nueva Palmira** Urug
24B2 **Nueva Rosita** Mexico
26B2 **Nuevitas** Cuba
26B2 **Nuevo Casas Grandes** Mexico
24C2 **Nuevo Laredo** Mexico
99E2 **Nugaal** Region, Somalia
6E2 **Nûgâtsiaq** Greenland
6E2 **Nugssuaq** *Pen* Greenland
6E2 **Nûgussaq** *I* Greenland
108A2 **Nukey Bluff** *Mt* Aust
93D3 **Nukhayb** Iraq
65G5 **Nukus** Uzbekistan
12C2 **Nulato** USA
106B4 **Nullarbor Plain** Aust
97D4 **Numan** Nig
75B1 **Numata** Japan
98C2 **Numatinna** *R* Sudan
74D3 **Numazu** Japan
71E4 **Numfoor** *I* Indon
108C3 **Numurkah** Aust
12B2 **Nunapitchuk** USA
84D2 **Nunkun** *Mt* India
53A2 **Nuoro** Sardegna
91B3 **Nurābād** Iran
47C2 **Nure** *R* Italy
108A2 **Nuriootpa** Aust
84C1 **Nuristan** Upland Afghan
61H3 **Nurlat** Russian Fed
38K6 **Nurmes** Fin
57C3 **Nürnberg** Germany
107C3 **Nurri,Mt** Aust
93D2 **Nusaybin** Turk
12C3 **Nushagak** *R* USA
12C3 **Nushagak B** USA
12C3 **Nushagak Pen** USA
84B3 **Nushki** Pak
7D4 **Nutak** Can
12F2 **Nutzotin Mts** USA
6E2 **Nuuk** = Godthåb
86A1 **Nuwakot** Nepal
87C3 **Nuwara-Eliya** Sri Lanka
6C3 **Nuyukjuak** Can

Nyack

16C2 **Nyack** USA
99D2 **Nyahururu** Kenya
108B3 **Nyah West** Aust
4C3 **Nyai** USA
68B3 **Nyainqentanglha Shan** Mts China
99D3 **Nyakabindi** Tanz
98C1 **Nyala** Sudan
86B1 **Nyalam** China
98C2 **Nyamlell** Sudan
64F3 **Nyandoma** Russian Fed
100C2 **Nyanga** Zim
98B3 **Nyanga** R Gabon
101C2 **Nyasa L** Malawi/ Mozam
76B2 **Nyaunglebin** Burma
61J2 **Nyazepetrovsk** Russian Fed
39G7 **Nyborg** Den
39H7 **Nybro** Sweden
64J3 **Nyda** Russian Fed
6D1 **Nyeboes Land** Region Can
99D3 **Nyeri** Kenya
101C2 **Nyimba** Zambia
82D3 **Nyingchi** China
59C3 **Nyiregyhaza** Hung
99D2 **Nyiru,Mt** Kenya
38J6 **Nykarleby** Fin
39F7 **Nykøbing** Den
39G8 **Nykøbing** Den
39H7 **Nyköping** Sweden
100B3 **Nylstroom** S Africa
109C2 **Nymagee** Aust
39H7 **Nynäshamn** Sweden
109C2 **Nyngan** Aust
47B1 **Nyon** Switz
98B2 **Nyong** R Cam
49D3 **Nyons** France
59B2 **Nysa** Pol
20C2 **Nyssa** USA
63D1 **Nyurba** Russian Fed
99D3 **Nzega** Tanz
97B4 **Nzérékore** Guinea
98B3 **N'zeto** Angola

O

6F3 **Oaggsimiut** Greenland
8C2 **Oahe Res** USA
21C4 **Oahu** I Hawaiian Is
108B2 **Oakbank** Aust
22B2 **Oakdale** Aust
109D1 **Oakey** Aust
21A2 **Oakland** California, USA
20B2 **Oakland** Oregon, USA
14A3 **Oakland City** USA
14A2 **Oak Lawn** USA
22B2 **Oakley** California, USA
20B2 **Oakridge** USA
14C2 **Oakville** Can
111B3 **Oamaru** NZ
112B7 **Oates Land** Region, Ant
109C4 **Oatlands** Aust
23B2 **Oaxaca** Mexico
23B2 **Oaxaca** State, Mexico
65J3 **Ob'** R Russian Fed
75B1 **Obama** Japan
111A3 **Oban** NZ
44B3 **Oban** Scot
75C1 **Obanazawa** Japan
47D1 **Oberammergau** Germany
46D1 **Oberhausen** Germany
47D1 **Oberstdorf** Germany
71D4 **Obi** I Indon
33F4 **Obidos** Brazil
74E2 **Obihiro** Japan
99E1 **Obock** Djibouti
58B2 **Oborniki** Pol
60E3 **Oboyan** Russian Fed
20B2 **O'Brien** USA
61H3 **Obshchiy Syrt** Mts Russian Fed
64J3 **Obskava Guba** B Russian Fed

97B4 **Obuasi** Ghana
17B2 **Ocala** USA
32C2 **Ocana** Colombia
50B2 **Ocaño** Spain
12G3 **Ocean C** USA
15C3 **Ocean City** Maryland, USA
16B3 **Ocean City** New Jersey, USA
5F4 **Ocean Falls** Can
22D4 **Oceanside** USA
19C3 **Ocean Springs** USA
61H2 **Ocher** Russian Fed
44C3 **Ochil Hills** Scot
17B1 **Ochlockonee** R USA
27H1 **Ocho Rios** Jamaica
17B1 **Ocmulgee** R USA
17B1 **Oconee** R USA
14A2 **Oconto** USA
23A1 **Ocotlan** Jalisco, Mexico
23B2 **Ocotlán** Oaxaca, Mexico
97B4 **Oda** Ghana
75A1 **Oda** Japan
38B2 **Ódáðahraun** Region, Iceland
74E2 **Odate** Japan
74D3 **Odawara** Japan
39F6 **Odda** Nor
50A2 **Odemira** Port
55C3 **Odemis** Turk
101G1 **Odendaalsrus** S Africa
39G7 **Odense** Den
56C2 **Oder** R Pol/Germany
9C3 **Odessa** Texas, USA
60D4 **Odessa** Ukraine
20C1 **Odessa** Washington, USA
97B4 **Odenné** Ivory Coast
59B2 **Odra** R Pol
31C3 **Oeiras** Brazil
53C2 **Ofanto** R Italy
94B3 **Ofaqim** Israel
45C2 **Offaly** County, Irish Rep
49D1 **Offenbach** Germany
49D2 **Offenburg** Germany
74D3 **Oga** Japan
99E2 **Ogaden** Region, Eth
74D3 **Ogaki** Japan
8C2 **Ogallala** USA
69G4 **Ogasawara Gunto** Is
97C4 **Ogbomosho** Nig
8B2 **Ogden** Utah, USA
15C2 **Ogdensburg** USA
17B1 **Ogeechee** R USA
12G1 **Ogilvie** Can
4E3 **Ogilvie Mts** Can
17B1 **Oglethorpe,Mt** USA
47D2 **Oglio** R Italy
47B1 **Ognon** R France
97C4 **Ogoja** Nig
98A3 **Ogooué** R Gabon
58C1 **Ogre** Latvia
96B2 **Ogzdiet Khenachich** Well Mali
52C1 **Ogulin** Croatia
111A3 **Ohai** NZ
110C1 **Ohakune** NZ
96C2 **Ohanet** Alg
111A2 **Ohau,L** NZ
10B2 **Ohio** State, USA
14A3 **Ohio** R USA
100A2 **Ohopoho** Namibia
57C2 **Ohre** R Czech Republic
55B2 **Ohrid** Macedonia
55B2 **Ohridsko Jezero** L Macedonia/Alb
110B1 **Ohura** NZ
33G3 **Oiapoque** French Guiana
68B2 **Oijiaojing** China
14C2 **Oil City** USA
21B2 **Oildale** USA
46B2 **Oise** Department, France
49C2 **Oise** R France
74C4 **Oita** Japan
22C3 **Ojai** USA
24B2 **Ojinaga** Mexico

23B2 **Ojitlán** Mexico
75B1 **Ojiya** Japan
30C4 **Ojos del Salado** Mt Arg
23A1 **Ojueloz** Mexico
60E3 **Oka** R Russian Fed
100A3 **Okahandja** Namibia
20C1 **Okanagan Falls** Can
13D2 **Okanagan L** Can
20C1 **Okanogan** Can
20C1 **Okanogan** R USA
20B1 **Okanogan Range** Mts Can/USA
84C2 **Okara** Pak
100A2 **Okavango** R Angola/ Namibia
100B2 **Okavango Delta** Marsh Botswana
74D3 **Okaya** Japan
74C4 **Okayama** Japan
75B2 **Okazaki** Japan
17B2 **Okeechobee** USA
17B2 **Okeechobee,L** USA
17B1 **Okefenokee Swamp** USA
97C4 **Okene** Nig
85B4 **Okha** India
69G1 **Okha** Russian Fed
86B1 **Okhaldunga** Nepal
62J3 **Okhotsk,S of** Russian Fed
69E4 **Okinawa** I Japan
69E4 **Okinawa gunto** Arch Japan
74C3 **Oki-shoto** Is Japan
9D3 **Oklahoma** State, USA
18A2 **Oklahoma City** USA
18A2 **Okmulgee** USA
98B3 **Okondja** Gabon
97C4 **Okpara** R Nig
61J4 **Oktyabr'sk** Kazakhstan
61H3 **Oktyabr'skiy** Russian Fed
74D2 **Okushiri-tō** I Japan
38A2 **Ólafsvik** Iceland
39H7 **Oland** I Sweden
108B2 **Olary** Aust
18B2 **Olathe** USA
29D3 **Olavarria** Arg
53A2 **Olbia** Sardegna
12G1 **Old Crow** Can
56B2 **Oldenburg** Niedersachsen, Germany
56C2 **Oldenburg** Schleswig-Holstein, Germany
15C2 **Old Forge** USA
42C3 **Oldham** Eng
12D3 **Old Harbor** USA
41B3 **Old Head of Kinsale** C Scot
16C2 **Old Lyme** USA
13E2 **Olds** Can
13D3 **Oliver** Can
30C3 **Ollagüe** Chile
30C3 **Ollagüe** Mt Bol
18C2 **Olney** USA
68E1 **Olochi** Russian Fed
39G7 **Olofstrom** Sweden
98B3 **Olombo** Congo
59B3 **Olomouc** Czech Republic

60D1 **Olonets** Russian Fed
79B3 **Olongapo** Phil
48B3 **Oloron Ste Marie** France
68D1 **Olovyannaya** Russian Fed
46D1 **Olpe** Germany
58C2 **Olsztyn** Pol
54B2 **Olt** R Rom
47B1 **Olten** Switz
20B1 **Olympia** USA
20B1 **Olympic Nat Pk** USA
Olympus = Olimbos
20B1 **Olympus,Mt** USA
65J4 **Om'** R Russian Fed
75B1 **Omachi** Japan
75B2 **Omae-zaki** C Japan
45C1 **Omagh** N Ire
18A1 **Omaha** USA
20C1 **Omak** USA
91C5 **Oman** Sultanate, Arabian Pen
91C4 **Oman,G of** UAE
98A3 **Omboué** Gabon
99D1 **Omdurman** Sudan
23B2 **Ometepec** Mexico
99D1 **Om Hajer** Eritrea
13B1 **Omineca** R Can
13B1 **Omineca Mts** Can
75B1 **Omiya** Japan
12H3 **Ommaney,C** USA
4H2 **Ommanney B** Can
99D2 **Omo** R Eth
65J4 **Omsk** Russian Fed
74A2 **Omura** Japan
74C4 **Omuta** Japan
61H2 **Omutninsk** Russian Fed
78D3 **Onang** Indon
14B1 **Onaping L** Can
100A2 **Oncocua** Angola
100A2 **Ondangua** Namibia
59C3 **Ondava** R Slovakia
68D2 **Ondörhaan** Molgolia
83B5 **One and Half Degree Chan** Indian O
64E3 **Onega** Russian Fed
64E3 **Onega** R Russian Fed
15C2 **Oneida L** USA
8D2 **O'Neill** USA
69H2 **Onekotan** I Russian Fed
98C3 **Onema** Zaïre
15D2 **Oneonta** USA
54C1 **Oneşti** Rom
64E3 **Onezhskoye Ozero** L Russian Fed
100A2 **Ongiva** Angola
74B3 **Ongjin** N Korea
72D1 **Ongniud Qi** China
87C1 **Ongole** India
15C2 **Onieda L** USA
101D3 **Onilahy** R Madag
97C4 **Onitsha** Nig
68C2 **Onjüül** Mongolia
75B1 **Ono** Japan
75B2 **Onohara-jima** I Japan
74C4 **Onomichi** Japan
106A3 **Onslow** Aust
17C1 **Onslow B** USA
75B1 **Ontake-san** Mt Japan
22D3 **Ontario** California, USA
20C2 **Ontario** Oregon, USA
7A4 **Ontario** Province, Can
15C2 **Ontario,L** Can/USA
51B2 **Onteniente** Spain
106C3 **Oodnadatta** Aust
106C4 **Ooldea** Aust
18A2 **Oologah L** USA
46B1 **Oostende** Belg
46B1 **Oosterschelde** Estuary Neth
87B2 **Ootacamund** India
13C2 **Ootsa L** Can
64J3 **Opala** Russian Fed
98C3 **Opala** Zaïre
87C3 **Opanake** Sri Lanka
61G2 **Oparino** Russian Fed

59B3 **Opava** Czech Republic	20C1 **Oroville** Washington, USA	16C1 **Otis** Massachusetts, USA	50A1 **Oviedo** Spain
17A1 **Opelika** USA	47B1 **Orsières** Switz	16B2 **Otisville** USA	60C3 **Ovruch** Ukraine
19B3 **Opelousas** USA	65G4 **Orsk** Russian Fed	100A3 **Otjiwarongo** Namibia	63E2 **Ovsyanka** Russian Fed
12C2 **Ophir** USA	38F6 **Ørsta** Nor		111A3 **Owaka** NZ
58D1 **Opochka** Russian Fed	48B3 **Orthez** France	72B2 **Otog Qi** China	75B2 **Owase** Japan
59B2 **Opole** Pol	50A1 **Ortigueira** Spain	110C1 **Otorohanga** NZ	11B3 **Owensboro** USA
Oporto = Porto	47D1 **Ortles** *Mts* Italy	55A2 **Otranto** Italy	21B2 **Owens** *L* USA
110C1 **Opotiki** NZ	27L1 **Ortoire** *R* Trinidad	55A2 **Otranto,Str of** *Chan* Italy/Alb	14B2 **Owen Sound** Can
17A1 **Opp** USA	93E2 **Orūmiyeh** Iran	14A2 **Otsego** USA	107D1 **Owen Stanley Range** *Mts* PNG
38F6 **Oppdal** Nor	30C2 **Oruro** Bol	75B1 **Otsu** Japan	97C4 **Owerri** Nig
110B1 **Opunake** NZ	61J2 **Osa** Russian Fed	39F6 **Otta** Nor	97C4 **Owo** Nig
54B1 **Oradea** Rom	18B2 **Osage** *R* USA	39F7 **Otta** *R* Nor	14B2 **Owosso** USA
38B2 **Oraefajökull** *Mts* Iceland	75B1 **Osaka** Japan	15C1 **Ottawa** Can	20C2 **Owyhee** *R* USA
85D3 **Orai** India	25D4 **Osa,Pen de** Costa Rica	18A2 **Ottawa** Kansas, USA	20C2 **Owyhee Mts** USA
96B1 **Oran** Alg	18C2 **Osceola** Arkansas, USA	15C1 **Ottawa** *R* Can	32B6 **Oxapampa** Peru
30D3 **Orán** Arg	18B1 **Osceola** Iowa, USA	7B4 **Ottawa Is** Can	39H7 **Oxelösund** Sweden
109C2 **Orange** Aust	20C2 **Osgood Mts** USA	7B4 **Otter Rapids** Can	43D4 **Oxford** County, Eng
22D4 **Orange** California, USA	15C2 **Oshawa** Can	6B1 **Otto Fjord** Can	43D4 **Oxford** Eng
49C3 **Orange** France	75B2 **O-shima** *I* Japan	101G1 **Ottosdal** S Africa	16D1 **Oxford** Massachusetts, USA
19B3 **Orange** Texas, USA	10B2 **Oshkosh** USA	18B1 **Ottumwa** USA	19C3 **Oxford** Mississippi, USA
100A3 **Orange** *R* S Africa	97C4 **Oshogbo** Nig	46D2 **Ottweiler** Germany	45B1 **Ox Mts** Irish Rep
17B1 **Orangeburg** USA	7B5 **Oshosh** USA	32B5 **Otusco** Peru	22C3 **Oxnard** USA
101G1 **Orange Free State** Province, S Africa	98B3 **Oshwe** Zaïre	108B3 **Otway,C** Aust	74D3 **Oyama** Japan
17B1 **Orange Park** USA	54A1 **Osijek** Croatia	58C2 **Otwock** Pol	48C2 **Oyen** Can
14B2 **Orangeville** Can	65K5 **Osinniki** Russian Fed	47D1 **Ötz** Austria	98B2 **Oyem** Gabon
56C2 **Oranienburg** Germany	58D2 **Osipovichi** Belorussia	47D1 **Otzal Mts** Austria	44B3 **Oykel** *R* Scot
79C3 **Oras** Phil	18B1 **Oskaloosa** USA	76C1 **Ou** *R* Laos	39F6 **Øyre** Nor
54B1 **Orăstie** Rom	60A2 **Oskarshamn** Sweden	19B3 **Ouachita** *R* USA	109C4 **Oyster B** Aust
54B1 **Oravita** Rom	39G7 **Oslo** Nor	19B3 **Ouachita,L** USA	79A4 **Ozamiz** Phil
52B2 **Orbetello** Italy	92C2 **Osmaniye** Turk	19B3 **Ouachita Mts** USA	17A1 **Ozark** USA
109C3 **Orbost** Aust	56B2 **Osnabrück** Germany	96A2 **Ouadane** Maur	18B2 **Ozark Plat** USA
46B1 **Orchies** France	30F4 **Osório** Brazil	98C2 **Ouadda** CAR	18B2 **Ozarks,L of the** USA
47B2 **Orco** *R* Italy	29B4 **Osorno** Chile	98C1 **Ouaddai** *Desert Region* Chad	59C3 **Ozd** Hung
106B2 **Ord** *R* Aust	50B1 **Osorno** Spain	97B3 **Ouagadougou** Burkina	65K5 **Ozero Alakol** *L* Kazakhstan/Russian Fed
106B2 **Ord,Mt** Aust	20C1 **Osoyoos** Can	97B3 **Ouahigouya** Burkina	65J5 **Ozero Balkhash** *L* Kazakhstan
93C1 **Ordu** Turk	13C1 **Ospika** *R* Can	98C2 **Ouaka** CAR	65J4 **Ozero Baykal** *L* Russian Fed
39H7 **Örebro** Sweden	107D5 **Ossa,Mt** Aust	97C3 **Oualam** Niger	65J4 **Ozero Chany** *L* Russian Fed
8A2 **Oregon** State, USA	16C2 **Ossining** USA	96C2 **Oualên** Alg	69F1 **Ozero Chukchagirskoye** Russian Fed
20B1 **Oregon City** USA	60D2 **Ostashkov** Russian Fed	97C3 **Ouanda Djallé** CAR	69F1 **Ozero Evoron** Russian Fed
39H6 **Oregrund** Sweden	**Ostend = Oostende**	96A2 **Ouarane** Region, Maur	**Ozero Chudskoye = Peipus,L**
60E2 **Orekhovo Zuyevo** Russian Fed	38G6 **Østerdalen** *V* Nor	96C1 **Ouargla** Alg	60D2 **Ozero Il'men** *L* Russian Fed
60E3 **Orel** Russian Fed	38G6 **Östersund** Sweden	98C2 **Ouarra** *R* CAR	38L5 **Ozero Imandra** *L* Russian Fed
61H3 **Orenburg** Russian Fed	56B2 **Ostfriesische Inseln** *Is* Germany	96B1 **Ouarzazate** Mor	82B1 **Ozero Issyk Kul'** *L* Kirghizia
34D3 **Orense** Arg	39H6 **Osthammär** Sweden	51C2 **Ouassel** *R* Alg	69F2 **Ozero Khanka** *L* China/Russian Fed
50A1 **Orense** Spain	53B2 **Ostia** Italy	98B2 **Oubangui** *R* Congo	38L5 **Ozero Kovdozero** *L* Russian Fed
56C1 **Oresund** *Str* Den/Sweden	47D2 **Ostiglia** Italy	46B1 **Oudenaarde** Belg	38L5 **Ozero Kuyto** *L* Russian Fed
111A3 **Oreti** *R* NZ	59B3 **Ostrava** Czech Republic	100B4 **Oudtshoorn** S Africa	38L5 **Ozero Pyazero** *L* Russian Fed
55C3 **Orhaneli** *R* Turk	58B2 **Ostróda** Pol	51B2 **Oued Tlélat** Alg	65H4 **Ozero Tengiz** *L* Kazakhstan
68C2 **Orhon Gol** *R* Mongolia	60C2 **Ostrov** Russian Fed	96B1 **Oued Zem** Mor	38L5 **Ozero Topozero** *L* Russian Fed
23B2 **Oriental** Mexico	64J2 **Ostrov Belyy** *I* Russian Fed	98B2 **Ouesso** Congo	65K5 **Ozero Zaysan** *L* Kazakhstan
108B1 **Orientos** Aust	64H1 **Ostrov Greem Bell** *I* Barents S	96B1 **Ouezzane** Mor	23B1 **Ozuluama** Mexico
51B2 **Orihuela** Spain	64F3 **Ostrov Kolguyev** *I* Russian Fed	98B2 **Ouham** *R* Chad	
15C2 **Orillia** Can	74F2 **Ostrov Kunashir** *I* Russian Fed	97C4 **Ouidah** Benin	**P**
33E2 **Orinoco** *R* Ven	64F2 **Ostrov Mechdusharskiy** *I* Barents S	96B1 **Oujda** Mor	100A4 **Paarl** S Africa
86A2 **Orissa** State, India	90B2 **Ostrov Ogurchinskiy** *I* Turkmenistan	38J6 **Oulainen** Fin	44A3 **Pabbay** *I* Scot
53A3 **Oristano** Sardegna	64G1 **Ostrov Rudol'fa** *I* Barents S	38K5 **Oulu** Fin	58B2 **Pabianice** Pol
38K6 **Orivesi** *L* Fin	64G2 **Ostrov Vaygach** *I* Russian Fed	38K6 **Oulu** *R* Fin	86B2 **Pabna** Bang
33F4 **Oriximiná** Brazil	1B7 **Ostrov Vrangelya** *I* Russian Fed	38K6 **Oulujärvi** *L* Fin	58D2 **Pabrade** Lithuania
23B2 **Orizaba** Mexico	58B2 **Ostrów Wlkp.** Pol	95B3 **Oum Chalouba** Chad	32B5 **Pacasmayo** Peru
35B1 **Orizona** Brazil	59C2 **Ostrowiec** Pol	98B1 **Oum Hadjer** Chad	23B1 **Pachuca** Mexico
44C2 **Orkney** *I* Scot	58C2 **Ostrów Mazowiecka** Pol	95B3 **Oum Haouach** *Watercourse* Chad	105K6 **Pacific-Antarctic Ridge** Pacific O
35B2 **Orlândia** Brazil	50A2 **Osuna** Spain	38K5 **Ounas** *R* Fin	22A1 **Pacific Grove** USA
17B2 **Orlando** USA	15C2 **Oswego** USA	95B3 **Ounianga Kébir** Chad	78C4 **Pacitan** Indon
48C2 **Orléanais** *Region* France	15C2 **Oswego** USA	46D1 **Our** *R* Germany	35C1 **Pacuí** *R* Brazil
48C2 **Orléans** France	43C3 **Oswestry** Eng	35B2 **Ourinhos** Brazil	70B4 **Padang** Indon
63B2 **Orlik** Russian Fed	59B2 **Oświęcim** Pol	35C2 **Ouro Prêto** Brazil	56B2 **Paderborn** Germany
82A3 **Ormara** Pak	75B1 **Ota** Japan	46C1 **Ourthe** *R* Belg	5J3 **Padlei** Can
79B3 **Ormoc** Phil	111B3 **Otago Pen** NZ	42D2 **Ouse** *R* Eng	86C2 **Padma** *R* Bang
17B2 **Ormond Beach** USA	110C2 **Otaki** NZ	43E3 **Ouse** *R* Eng	47D2 **Padova** Italy
46C2 **Ornain** *R* France	74E2 **Otaru** Japan	40B2 **Outer Hebrides** *Is* Scot	9D4 **Padre I** USA
47B1 **Ornans** France	32B3 **Otavalo** Ecuador	22C4 **Outer Santa Barbara** *Chan* USA	
48B2 **Orne** *R* France	100A2 **Otavi** Namibia	100A3 **Outjo** Namibia	
38H6 **Örnsköldsvik** Sweden	75C1 **Otawara** Japan	38K6 **Outokumpu** Fin	
32C3 **Orocué** Colombia	20C1 **Othello** USA	108B3 **Ouyen** Aust	
94B3 **Oron** Israel	55B3 **Óthris** *Mt* Greece	47C2 **Ovada** Italy	
Orontes = 'Asi		34A2 **Ovalle** Chile	
79B4 **Oroquieta** Phil		100A2 **Ovamboland** Region, Namibia	
59C3 **Oroshaza** Hung		61H5 **Ova Tyuleni** *Is* Kazakhstan	
21A2 **Oroville** California, USA		38J5 **Övertorneå** Sweden	

Padstow

43B4 **Padstow** Eng
108B3 **Padthaway** Aust
Padua = Padova
14A3 **Paducah** Kentucky, USA
11B3 **Paducah** USA
38L5 **Padunskoye More** L Russian Fed
74A3 **Paengnyŏng-do** I S Korea
110C1 **Paeroa** NZ
100C3 **Pafuri** Mozam
52B2 **Pag** I Croatia
79B4 **Pagadian** Phil
70B4 **Pagai Selatan** I Indon
70B4 **Pagai Utara** I Indon
71F2 **Pagan** I Pacific O
78D3 **Pagatan** Indon
55C3 **Pagondhas** Greece
110C2 **Pahiatua** NZ
21C4 **Pahoa** Hawaiian Is
17B2 **Pahokee** USA
39K6 **Päijänne** L Fin
21C4 **Pailola Chan** Hawaiian Is
14B2 **Painesville** USA
9B3 **Painted Desert** USA
42B2 **Paisley** Scot
32A5 **Paita** Peru
38J5 **Pajala** Sweden
80E3 **Pakistan** Republic, Asia
76C2 **Pak Lay** Laos
86D2 **Pakokku** Burma
13E2 **Pakowki L** Can
52C1 **Pakrac** Croatia
54A1 **Paks** Hung
76C2 **Pak Sane** Laos
76D2 **Pakse** Laos
99D2 **Pakwach** Uganda
98B2 **Pala** Chad
52C2 **Palagruža** I Croatia
46B2 **Palaiseau** France
Palakhat = Palghat
78C3 **Palangkaraya** Indon
87B2 **Palani** India
85C4 **Palanpur** India
100B3 **Palapye** Botswana
17B2 **Palatka** USA
17E3 **Palau Is** Pacific O
76B3 **Palaw** Burma
79A4 **Palawan** I Phil
79A4 **Palawan Pass** Phil
87B3 **Palayankottai** India
39J7 **Paldiski** Estonia
78A3 **Palembang** Indon
50B1 **Palencia** Spain
94A1 **Paleokhorio** Cyprus
53B3 **Palermo** Italy
19A3 **Palestine** USA
86C2 **Paletwa** Burma
87B2 **Pālghāt** India
85C3 **Pāli** India
85C4 **Pālitana** India
87B3 **Palk Str** India/ Sri Lanka
61G3 **Pallasovka** Russian Fed
38J5 **Pallastunturi** Mt Fin
111B2 **Palliser B** NZ
111C2 **Palliser,C** NZ
101D2 **Palma** Mozam
51C2 **Palma de Mallorca** Spain
31D3 **Palmares** Brazil
26A5 **Palmar Sur** Costa Rica
97B4 **Palmas,C** Lib
26B2 **Palma Soriano** Cuba
17B2 **Palm Bay** USA
17B2 **Palm Beach** USA
22C3 **Palmdale** USA
31D3 **Palmeira dos Indos** Brazil
12E2 **Palmer** USA
112C3 **Palmer** Base Ant
112C3 **Palmer Arch** Ant
112B3 **Palmer Land** Region Ant
111B3 **Palmerston** USA
110C2 **Palmerston North** NZ
16B2 **Palmerton** USA
17B2 **Palmetto** USA

53C3 **Palmi** Italy
32B3 **Palmira** Colombia
107D2 **Palm Is** Aust
21B3 **Palm Springs** USA
18B2 **Palmyra** Missouri, USA
16A2 **Palmyra** Pennsylvania, USA
86B2 **Palmyras Pt** India
22A2 **Palo Alto** USA
78B2 **Paloh** Indon
99D1 **Paloich** Sudan
21B3 **Palomar Mt** USA
70D4 **Palopo** Indon
70C4 **Palu** Indon
93C2 **Palu** Turk
84D3 **Palwal** India
97C3 **Pama** Burkina
78C4 **Pamekasan** Indon
78B4 **Pamengpeuk** Indon
48C3 **Pamiers** France
82B2 **Pamir** Mts China
65J6 **Pamir** R Russian Fed
11C3 **Pamlico Sd** USA
9C3 **Pampa** USA
34B2 **Pampa de la Salinas** Salt pan Arg
34B3 **Pampa de la Varita** Plain Arg
32C2 **Pamplona** Colombia
50B1 **Pamplona** Spain
18C2 **Pana** USA
54B2 **Panagyurishte** Bulg
87A1 **Panaji** India
32B2 **Panamá** Panama
32A2 **Panama** Republic, Cent America
26B5 **Panama Canal** Panama
17A1 **Panama City** USA
21B2 **Panamint Range** Mts USA
21B2 **Panamint V** USA
47D2 **Panaro** R Italy
79B3 **Panay** I Phil
54B2 **Pančevo** Serbia, Yugos
79B3 **Pandan** Phil
87B1 **Pandharpur** India
108A1 **Pandie Pandie** Aust
58C1 **Panevežys** Lithuania
65K5 **Panfilov** Kazakhstan
76B1 **Pang** R Burma
99D3 **Pangani** Tanz
99D3 **Pangani** R Tanz
98C3 **Pangi** Zaïre
78B3 **Pangkalpinang** Indon
6D3 **Pangnirtung** Can
76B1 **Pangtara** Burma
79B4 **Pangutaran Group** Is Phil
84D3 **Panipat** India
84B2 **Panjao** Afghan
74B3 **P'anmunjŏm** N Korea
86A2 **Panna** India
35A2 **Panorama** Brazil
53B3 **Panormoi** I Medit S
23B1 **Pantepec** Mexico
23B1 **Panuco** Mexico
23B1 **Panuco** R Mexico
73A4 **Pan Xian** China
53C3 **Paola** Italy
18B2 **Paola** USA
14A3 **Paoli** USA
110B1 **Papa** Hung
110B1 **Papakura** NZ
23B2 **Papaloapan** R Mexico
23B1 **Papantla** Mexico
44E1 **Papa Stour** I Scot
110B1 **Papatoetoe** NZ
44C2 **Papa Westray** I Scot
107D1 **Papua,G of** PNG
107D1 **Papua New Guinea** Republic, S E Asia
34A2 **Papudo** Chile
76B2 **Papun** Burma
31B2 **Pará** R Brazil
106A3 **Paraburdoo** Aust
32B6 **Paracas,Pen de** Peru
35B1 **Paracatu** Brazil

35B1 **Paracatu** R Brazil
108A2 **Parachilna** Aust
84C2 **Parachinar** Pak
54B2 **Paracin** Serbia, Yugos
35C1 **Pará de Minas** Brazil
21A2 **Paradise** California, USA
18B2 **Paragould** USA
33E6 **Paraguá** R Bol
33E2 **Paragua** R Ven
30E2 **Paraguai** R Brazil
30E4 **Paraguari** Par
30E3 **Paraguay** Republic, S America
30E3 **Paraguay** R Par
31D3 **Paraiba** State, Brazil
35B2 **Paraiba** R Brazil
35C2 **Paraiba do Sul** R Brazil
97C4 **Parakou** Benin
108A2 **Parakylia** Aust
87B3 **Paramakkudi** India
33F2 **Paramaribo** Surinam
69H1 **Paramushir** I Russian Fed
30F3 **Paraná** State, Brazil
34C2 **Paraná** Urug
29E2 **Paraná** R Arg
31B4 **Paraná** R Brazil
35A2 **Paranã** R Brazil
30E2 **Paranaíba** Brazil
35A1 **Paranaíba** Brazil
35A1 **Paranaíba** R Brazil
35A2 **Paranapanema** R Brazil
35A2 **Paranavaí** Brazil
79B4 **Parang** Phil
35C1 **Paraope** R Brazil
110B2 **Paraparaumu** NZ
87B1 **Parbhani** India
94B2 **Pardes Hanna** Israel
34D3 **Pardo** Arg
35D1 **Pardo** R Bahia, Brazil
35A2 **Pardo** R Mato Grosso do Sul, Brazil
35B1 **Pardo** R Minas Gerais, Brazil
35B2 **Pardo** R Sao Paulo, Brazil
59B2 **Pardubice** Czech Republic
69F4 **Parece Vela** Reef Pacific O
10C2 **Parent** Can
70C4 **Parepare** Indon
34C3 **Parera** Arg
33E1 **Pariaman** Indon
33E1 **Paria,Pen de** Ven
48C2 **Paris** France
14B3 **Paris** Kentucky, USA
19A3 **Paris** Texas, USA
14B3 **Parkersburg** USA
109C2 **Parkes** Aust
16B3 **Parkesburg** USA
14A2 **Park Forest** USA
20B1 **Parksville** Can
87B1 **Parli** India
47D2 **Parma** Italy
14B2 **Parma** USA
31C2 **Parnaíba** Brazil
31C2 **Parnaíba** R Brazil
55B3 **Párnon Óros** Mts Greece
60B2 **Pärnu** Estonia
86B1 **Paro** R Bhutan
108B1 **Paroo** R Aust
108B2 **Paroo Channel** R Aust
55C3 **Páros** I Greece
47B2 **Parpaillon** Mts France
34A3 **Parral** Chile
109D2 **Parramatta** Aust
9C4 **Parras** Mexico
6B3 **Parry B** Can
4G2 **Parry Is** Can
7C5 **Parry Sd** Can
14B1 **Parry Sound** Can
52C1 **Parsberg** Germany
5F4 **Parsnip** R Can
18A2 **Parsons** Kansas, USA
14C3 **Parsons** West Virginia, USA

48B2 **Parthenay** France
53B3 **Partinico** Italy
74C2 **Partizansk** Russian Fed
33G4 **Paru** R Brazil
101G1 **Parys** S Africa
19A4 **Pasadena** Texas, USA
22C3 **Pasadena** California, USA
78D3 **Pasangkayu** Indon
76B2 **Pasawing** Burma
19C3 **Pascagoula** USA
54C1 **Paşcani** Rom
20C1 **Pasco** USA
46B1 **Pas-de-Calais** Department, France
39G8 **Pasewalk** Germany
91C4 **Pashú'iyeh** Iran
106B4 **Pasley,C** Aust
29E2 **Paso de los Toros** Urug
29B4 **Paso Limay** Arg
21A2 **Paso Robles** USA
45B3 **Passage West** Irish Rep
16B2 **Passaic** USA
57C3 **Passau** Germany
30E4 **Passo do Los Libres** Arg
47D1 **Passo di Stelvio** Mt Italy
30F4 **Passo Fundo** Brazil
35B2 **Passos** Brazil
47B2 **Passy** France
32B4 **Pastaza** R Peru
34C3 **Pasteur** Arg
5H4 **Pas,The** Can
32B3 **Pasto** Colombia
12B2 **Pastol B** USA
53B3 **Paternò** Italy
16B2 **Paterson** USA
111A3 **Paterson Inlet** B NZ
84D2 **Pathankot** India
Pathein = Bassein
84D2 **Patiala** India
32B6 **Pativilca** Peru
55C3 **Pátmos** I Greece
86B1 **Patna** India
93D2 **Patnos** Turk
63D2 **Patomskoye Nagor'ye** Upland Russian Fed
31D3 **Patos** Brazil
35B1 **Patos de Minas** Brazil
34B2 **Patquia** Arg
55B3 **Pátrai** Greece
35B1 **Patrocinio** Brazil
99E3 **Patta** I Kenya
78D4 **Pattallasang** Indon
77C4 **Pattani** Thai
22B2 **Patterson** California, USA
19B4 **Patterson** Louisiana, USA
12H2 **Patterson,Mt** Can
22C2 **Patterson Mt** USA
14D1 **Pattullo,Mt** Can
31D3 **Patu** Brazil
86C2 **Patuakhali** Bang
25D3 **Patuca** R Honduras
23A2 **Patzcuaro** Mexico
48B3 **Pau** France
4F3 **Paulatuk** Can
31C3 **Paulistana** Brazil
101H1 **Paulpietersburg** S Africa
19A3 **Pauls Valley** USA
76B2 **Paungde** Burma
84D2 **Pauri** India
38H5 **Pauskie** Nor
35C1 **Pavão** Brazil
47C2 **Pavia** Italy
65J4 **Pavlodar** Kazakhstan
61J2 **Pavlovka** Russian Fed

61F2 **Pavlovo** Russian Fed
61F3 **Pavlovsk**
    Russian Fed
78C3 **Pawan** R Indon
18A2 **Pawhuska** USA
16D2 **Pawtucket** USA
47B1 **Payerne** Switz
20C2 **Payette** USA
7C4 **Payne,L** Can
34D2 **Paysandu** Urug
46A2 **Pays-de-Bray** Region,
    France
54B2 **Pazardzhik** Bulg
13D1 **Peace** R Can
17B2 **Peace** R USA
13D1 **Peace River** Can
43D3 **Peak District Nat Pk**
    Eng
108A1 **Peake** R Aust
109C2 **Peak Hill** Aust
71E4 **Peak Mandala** Mt
    Indon
42D3 **Peak,The** Mt Eng
19B3 **Pearl** R USA
21C4 **Pearl City** Hawaiian
    Is
21C4 **Pearl Harbor**
    Hawaiian Is
4H2 **Peary Chan** Can
101C2 **Pebane** Mozam
54B2 **Peć** Serbia, Yugos
35C1 **Peçanha** Brazil
19B4 **Pecan Island** USA
38L5 **Pechenga**
    Russian Fed
64F3 **Pechora** R
    Russian Fed
64G3 **Pechorskoye More** S
    Russian Fed
53C3 **Pecoraro** Mt Italy
9C3 **Pecos** USA
9C3 **Pecos** R USA
59B3 **Pécs** Hung
108A1 **Pedirka** Aust
35C1 **Pedra Azul** Brazil
35B2 **Pedregulho** Brazil
26B3 **Pedro Cays** Is
    Caribbean S
30C2 **Pedro de Valdivia**
    Chile
30E3 **Pedro Juan Caballero**
    Par
34C3 **Pedro Luro** Arg
23B1 **Pedro Mentova**
    Mexico
87C3 **Pedro,Pt** Sri Lanka
108B2 **Peebinga** Aust
42C2 **Peebles** Scot
17C1 **Pee Dee** R USA
16C2 **Peekskill** USA
42B2 **Peel** Eng
12H1 **Peel** R Can
4J2 **Peel Sd** Can
108A1 **Peera Peera Poolanna**
    L Aust
13E1 **Peerless L** Can
71E4 **Peg Arfak** Mt Indon
111B2 **Pegasus B** NZ
83D4 **Pegu** Burma
78A3 **Pegunungan Barisan**
    Mts Indon
78C2 **Pegunungan Iran** Mts
    Malay/Indon
71E4 **Pegunungan Maoke**
    Mts Indon
78D3 **Pegunungan Meratus**
    Mts Indon
78C2 **Pegunungan Muller**
    Mts Indon
78C3 **Pegunungan**
    Schwaner Mts Indon
78A3 **Pegunungan**
    Tigapuluh Mts Indon
76B2 **Pegu Yoma** Mts
    Burma
34C3 **Pehuajó** Arg
    Péipsi Järve =
    Peipus,L
39K7 **Peipus, Lake** Estonia/
    Russian Fed
35A2 **Peixe** R Sao Paulo,
    Brazil
72D3 **Pei Xian** China
78B4 **Pekalongan** Indon

77C5 **Pekan** Malay
78A2 **Pekanbaru** Indon
18C1 **Pekin** USA
    Peking = Beijing
77C5 **Pelabohan Kelang**
    Malay
78D4 **Pelau Pelau Kangean**
    Is Indon
78C4 **Pelau Pelau**
    Karimunjawa Arch
    Indon
78D4 **Pelau Pelau Postilyon**
    Is Indon
54B1 **Peleaga** Mt Rom
63D2 **Peleduy** Russian Fed
14B2 **Pelee I** Can
71D4 **Peleng** I Indon
12G3 **Pelican** USA
69F1 **Peliny Osipenko**
    Russian Fed
34C3 **Pellegrini** Arg
38J5 **Pello** Fin
12H2 **Pelly** R Can
6A3 **Pelly Bay** Can
12C2 **Pelly Crossing** Can
12H2 **Pelly Mts** Can
30F5 **Pelotas** Brazil
30F4 **Pelotas** R Brazil
47B2 **Pelvoux** Region,
    France
78B4 **Pemalang** Indon
78A3 **Pematang** Indon
101D2 **Pemba** Mozam
99D3 **Pemba** I Tanz
13C2 **Pemberton** Can
13D2 **Pembina** R Can
15C1 **Pembroke** Can
17B1 **Pembroke** USA
43B4 **Pembroke** Wales
34A3 **Pemuco** Chile
78D2 **Penambo Range** Mts
    Malay
35A2 **Penápolis** Brazil
50A2 **Peñarroya** Spain
51B1 **Penarroya** Mt Spain
50A1 **Peña Trevina** Mt
    Spain
98B2 **Pende** R Chad
12J3 **Pendelton,Mt** Can
20C1 **Pendleton** USA
20C1 **Pend Oreille** R USA
31D4 **Penedo** Brazil
95D5 **Penganga** R India
73D5 **P'eng-hu Lieh-tao** Is
    Taiwan
72E2 **Penglai** China
73B4 **Pengshui** China
71E4 **Pengunungan Maoke**
    Mts Indon
26C4 **Peninsula de la**
    Guajiri Pen
    Colombia
27E4 **Peninsula de Paria**
    Pen Ven
77C5 **Peninsular Malaysia**
    Malay
10D2 **Péninsule de Gaspé**
    Pen Can
23A1 **Penjamo** Mexico
87B2 **Penner** R India
42C2 **Pennine Chain** Mts
    Eng
16B3 **Penns Grove** USA
10C2 **Pennsylvania** State,
    USA
6D3 **Penny Highlands**
    Can
108B3 **Penola** Aust
44C2 **Penong** Aust
42C2 **Penrith** Eng
11B3 **Pensacola** USA
112A **Pensacola Mts** Ant
78D1 **Pensiangan** Malay
13D3 **Penticton** Can
44C2 **Pentland Firth** Chan
    Scot
42C2 **Pentland Hills** Scot
61G3 **Penza** Russian Fed
43B4 **Penzance** Eng
10B2 **Peoria** USA
78A3 **Perabumulih** Indon
77C5 **Perak** R Malay
78A2 **Perawang** Indon
32B3 **Pereira** Colombia

35A2 **Pereira Barreto** Brazil
61F4 **Perelazovskiy**
    Russian Fed
12D3 **Perenosa B** USA
34C2 **Pergamino** Arg
7C4 **Peribonca** R Can
48C2 **Périqueux** France
25E4 **Perlas Arch de** Is
    Panama
61J2 **Perm'** Russian Fed
    Pernambuco = Recife
31D3 **Pernambuco** State,
    Brazil
108A2 **Pernatty Lg** Aust
54B2 **Pernik** Bulg
46B2 **Péronne** France
23B2 **Perote** Mexico
49C3 **Perpignan** France
22D4 **Perris** USA
17B1 **Perry** Florida, USA
17B1 **Perry** Georgia, USA
18A2 **Perry** Oklahoma,
    USA
4H3 **Perry River** Can
14B2 **Perrysburg** USA
12C3 **Perryville** Alaska,
    USA
18C2 **Perryville** Missouri,
    USA
106A4 **Perth** Aust
15C2 **Perth** Can
44C3 **Perth** Scot
16B2 **Perth Amboy** USA
32C6 **Peru** Republic,
    S America
18C1 **Peru** USA
103E5 **Peru-Chile Trench**
    Pacific O
52B2 **Perugia** Italy
52C2 **Perušic** Croatia
93D2 **Pervari** Turk
61F3 **Pervomaysk**
    Russian Fed
60D4 **Pervomaysk** Ukraine
61J2 **Pervoural'sk**
    Russian Fed
52B2 **Pesaro** Italy
22A2 **Pescadero** USA
    Pescadores = P'eng-
    hu Lieh-tao
52B2 **Pescara** Italy
47D2 **Peschiera** Italy
84C2 **Peshawar** Pak
54B2 **Peshkopi** Alb
14A1 **Peshtigo** USA
60E2 **Pestovo** Russian Fed
94B2 **Petah Tiqwa** Israel
21A2 **Petaluma** USA
46C2 **Pétange** Lux
23A2 **Petatlán** Mexico
101C2 **Petauke** Zambia
108A2 **Peterborough** Aust
15C2 **Peterborough** Can
43D3 **Peterborough** Eng
44D3 **Peterhead** Scot
6D1 **Petermann Gletscher**
    Gl Greenland
106B3 **Petermann Range**
    Mts Aust
29B3 **Peteroa** Mt Arg/Chile
13F1 **Peter Pond L** Can
12H3 **Petersburg** Alaska,
    USA
85C4 **Petläd** India
23B2 **Petlalcingo** Mexico
25D2 **Peto** Mexico
63D2 **Petomskoye**
    Nagor'ye Upland
    Russian Fed
34A2 **Petorca** Chile
14B1 **Petoskey** USA
31C3 **Petrolina** Brazil
65H4 **Petropavlovsk**
    Kazakhstan
35C2 **Petrópolis** Brazil
61G3 **Petrovsk**
    Russian Fed
68C1 **Petrovsk**
    Zabaykal'skiy
    Russian Fed
64E3 **Petrozavodsk**
    Russian Fed
101G1 **Petrus** S Africa
101G1 **Petrusburg** S Africa

1B7 **Pevek** Russian Fed
46D2 **Pfälzer Wald** Region,
    Germany
57B3 **Pforzheim** Germany
84D2 **Phagwara** India
85C3 **Phalodi** India
46D2 **Phalsbourg** France
87A1 **Phaltan** India
77B4 **Phangnga** Thai
76C3 **Phanom Dang** Mts
    Camb
76D3 **Phan Rang** Viet
76D3 **Phan Thiet** Viet
17A1 **Phenix City** USA
76B3 **Phet Buri** Thai
76D3 **Phiafay** Laos
19C3 **Philadelphia**
    Mississippi, USA
16B2 **Philadelphia**
    Pennsylvania, USA
    Philippeville = Skikda
46C1 **Philippeville** Belg
71D2 **Philippine S** Pacific O
71D2 **Philippines** Republic,
    S E Asia
104E3 **Philippine Trench**
    Pacific O
15C2 **Philipsburg**
    Pennsylvania, USA
12E1 **Philip Smith Mts**
    USA
79B2 **Phillipine S** Phil
6B1 **Phillips B** Can
16B2 **Phillipsburg** New
    Jersey, USA
86C1 **Phibots Pen** Can
76C3 **Phnom Penh** Camb
9B3 **Phoenix** Arizona,
    USA
16B2 **Phoenixville** USA
76C1 **Phong Saly** Laos
    Phra Nakhon =
    Bangkok
76C2 **Phu Bia** Mt Laos
76D3 **Phu Cuong** Viet
77B4 **Phuket** Thai
86A2 **Phulbani** India
76C2 **Phu Miang** Mt Thai
76D2 **Phu Set** Mt Laos
76D1 **Phu Tho** Viet
77D4 **Phu Vinh** Viet
47C2 **Piacenza** Italy
109C2 **Pian** R Aust
52C2 **Pianosa** I Italy
52C2 **Pianosa** I Italy
58C2 **Piaseczno** Pol
31C3 **Piatra-Neamt** Rom
31C3 **Piaui** State, Brazil
47E2 **Piave** R Italy
99D2 **Pibor** R Sudan
99D2 **Pibor Post** Sudan
46B1 **Picardie** Region,
    France
19C3 **Picayune** USA
47B2 **Pic de Rochebrune**
    Mt France
34A2 **Pichilemu** Chile
34C3 **Pichi Mahuida** Arg
42D2 **Pickering** Eng
72A4 **Pickle Lake** Can
96A1 **Pico** I Açores
47C1 **Pico Bernina** Mt
    Switz
51C1 **Pico de Anito** Mt
    Spain
24B3 **Pico del Infiernillo** Mt
    Mexico
27C3 **Pico Duarte** Mt
    Dom Rep
31C3 **Picos** Brazil
50B1 **Picos de Europa** Mt
    Spain
109D2 **Picton** Can
111B2 **Picton** NZ
95A2 **Pic Toussidé** Mt
    Chad
35B2 **Piedade** Brazil
22C2 **Piedra** USA
23A2 **Piedras Negras**
    Mexico
38K6 **Pieksämäki** Fin
38K6 **Pielinen** L Fin
47B2 **Piemonte** Region,
    Italy

Pierre

8C2 Pierre USA
59B3 Pieštany Slovakia
101H1 Pietermaritzburg S Africa
100B3 Pietersburg S Africa
101H1 Piet Retief S Africa
60B4 Pietrosu Mt Rom
47E1 Pieve di Cadore Italy
13E2 Pigeon L Can
18B2 Piggott USA
34C3 Piguë Arg
7A4 Pikangikum L Can
8C3 Pikes Peak USA
100A4 Piketberg S Africa
6F3 Pikintaleq Greenland
82B2 Pik Kommunizma Mt Tajikistan
98B2 Pikounda Congo
82C1 Pik Pobedy Mt China/Kirghizia
34D3 Pila Arg
58B2 Piła Pol
30E4 Pilar Par
30D3 Pilcomayo R Arg/Par
84D3 Pilibhit India
59B2 Pilica R Pol
109C4 Pillar,C Aust
55B3 Pilos Greece
12C3 Pilot Point USA
12B2 Pilot Station USA
19C3 Pilottown USA
33F4 Pimenta Brazil
77C4 Pinang I Malay
26A2 Pinar del Rio Cuba
34B2 Pinas Arg
46C1 Pinche Belg
13E2 Pincher Creek Can
20B2 Pindar R USA
55B3 Pindhos Mts Greece
19B3 Pine Bluff USA
106C2 Pine Creek Aust
22C1 Pinecrest USA
22C2 Pinedale California, USA
22C2 Pine Flat Res USA
64F3 Pinega R Russian Fed
16A2 Pine Grove USA
17B2 Pine Hills USA
17B2 Pine I USA
19B3 Pineland USA
17B2 Pinellas Park USA
5G3 Pine Point Can
47E2 Pinerolo Italy
19B3 Pines,Lo'the USA
19B3 Pineville USA
72C3 Pingdingshan China
73B5 Pingguo China
72B2 Pingliang China
72B2 Pingluo China
73D4 Pingtan Dao I China
73E5 P'ing tung Taiwan
72A3 Pingwu China
73B5 Pingxiang Guangxi, China
73C4 Pingxiang Jiangxi, China
31B2 Pinheiro Brazil
70A3 Pini I Indon
55B3 Piniós R Greece
106A4 Pinjarra Aust
13C1 Pink Mountain Can
108B3 Pinnaroo Aust
Pinos,I de, I = Isla de la Juventud
21A2 Pinos,Pt USA
23B2 Pinotepa Nacional Mexico
70C4 Pinrang Indon
60C3 Pinsk Belorussia
32J7 Pinta I Ecuador
61G1 Pinyug Russian Fed
8B3 Pioche USA
52B2 Piombino Italy
6H3 Piórsá Iceland
59B2 Piotrków Trybunalski Pol
44E2 Piper Oilfield N Sea
21B2 Piper Peak Mt USA
10C2 Pipmuacan Res Can
14B2 Piqua USA
35B1 Piracanjuba Brazil
35B2 Piracicaba Brazil

35B2 Piraçununga Brazil
35B2 Piraí do Sul Brazil
55B3 Piraiévs Greece
35B2 Pirajuí Brazil
35A1 Piranhas Brazil
35C1 Pirapora Brazil
35B1 Pirenópolis Brazil
35B1 Pires do Rio Brazil
55B3 Pírgos Greece
Pirineos = Pyrénées
31C2 Piripiri Brazil
46D2 Pirmasens Germany
54A2 Pirot Serbia, Yugos
84C2 Pir Panjāl Range Mts Pak
71D4 Piru Indon
22C3 Piru Creek R USA
49E3 Pisa Italy
32B6 Pisco Peru
57C3 Písek Czech Republic
84B2 Pishin Pak
82A2 Pisis Mt Arg
49E3 Pistoia Italy
50B1 Pisuerga R Spain
20B2 Pit R USA
32B3 Pitalito Colombia
105K5 Pitcairn I Pacific O
38H5 Pite R Sweden
38J5 Piteå Sweden
54B2 Piteşti Rom
63B2 Pit Gorodok Russian Fed
38L6 Pitkyaranta Russian Fed
44C3 Pitlochry Scot
34A3 Pitrutquén Chile
13B2 Pitt I Can
22B1 Pittsburg California, USA
18B2 Pittsburg Kansas, USA
14C2 Pittsburgh USA
18B2 Pittsfield Illinois, USA
16C1 Pittsfield Massachusetts, USA
109D1 Pittsworth Aust
86A1 Piuthan Nepal
47D1 Pizzo Redorta Mt Italy
38B2 Pjórsá Iceland
32A5 Pjura Peru
7E5 Placentia B Can
22B1 Placerville USA
46B1 Plaine des Flandres Plain Belg/France
96C2 Plaine du Tidikelt Desert Region
9C3 Plainview Texas, USA
22B2 Planada USA
30F2 Planalto de Mato Grosso Plat Brazil
31D3 Planalto do Borborema Plat Brazil
31A2 Planalto do Mato Grosso Mts Brazil
19A3 Plano USA
17B2 Plantation USA
17B2 Plant City USA
50A1 Plasencia Spain
61K3 Plast Russian Fed
69F2 Plastun Russian Fed
96C2 Plateau du Tademait Alg
46D2 Plateau Lorrain Plat France
48C2 Plateaux de Limousin Plat France
51C2 Plateaux du Sersou Plat Alg
26C5 Plato Colombia
65G5 Plato Ustyurt Plat Kazakhstan
52B2 Platte R USA
15D2 Plattsburgh USA
18B1 Plattsmouth USA
57C2 Plauen Germany
60E3 Plavsk Russian Fed
23A2 Playa Azul Mexico
32A4 Playas Ecuador
23B2 Playa Vicente Mexico

50A1 Plaza de Moro Almanzor Mt Spain
22B2 Pleasanton California, USA
18B3 Pleasantville USA
14A3 Pleasure Ridge Park USA
76D3 Pleiku Viet
110C1 Plenty,B of NZ
58B2 Pleszew Pol
7C4 Pletipi,L Can
54B2 Pleven Bulg
54A2 Pljevlja Montenegro, Yugos
52C2 Ploče Bosnia-Herzegovina
58B2 Płock Pol
48B2 Ploërmel France
54C2 Ploieşti Rom
60B3 Płońsk Pol
54B2 Plovdiv Bulg
20C1 Plummer USA
12C2 Plummer,Mt USA
100B3 Plumtree Zim
22B1 Plymouth California, USA
14A2 Plymouth Indiana, USA
16D2 Plymouth Massachusetts, USA
15C2 Plymouth Pennsylvania, USA
43B4 Plymouth Sd Eng
43C3 Plynlimon Mt Wales
57C3 Plzeň Czech Republic
58B2 Pniewy Pol
38K6 Pnyäselkä L Fin
97B3 Pô Burkina
47E2 Po R Italy
97C4 Pobé Benin
69G2 Pobedino Russian Fed
82B2 Pocatello USA
15C3 Pocomoke City USA
35B2 Pocos de Caldas Brazil
54A2 Podgorica Montenegro, Yugos
47D2 Po di Volano R Italy
63B1 Podkamennaya Tunguska R Russian Fed
60E2 Podol'sk Russian Fed
59D3 Podol'skaya Vozvyshennost' Upland Ukraine
60D1 Podporozh'ye Russian Fed
61F1 Podyuga Russian Fed
100A3 Pofadder S Africa
74B3 P'ohang S Korea
112C9 Poinsett,C Ant
108C2 Point Aust
27E3 Pointe-à-Pitre Guadeloupe
48B2 Pointe de Barfleur Pt France
98B3 Pointe Noire Congo
98A2 Pointe Pongara Pt Gabon
108B3 Point Fairy Aust
27L1 Point Fortin Trinidad
4B3 Point Hope USA
4G3 Point L Can
12B1 Point Lay USA
16B2 Point Pleasant New Jersey, USA
14B3 Point Pleasant W Virginia, USA
47B2 Point St Bernard Mt France
48C2 Poitiers France
48B2 Poitou Region, France
46A2 Poix France
84A3 Pokaran India
109C1 Pokataroo Aust
64E3 Pokrovsk Russian Fed
63E1 Pokrovsk Russian Fed
58B2 Poland Republic, Europe

92B2 Polatli Turk
78D3 Polewali Indon
47A1 Poligny France
55B2 Políyiros Greece
87B2 Póllachi India
79B3 Polollo Is Phil
59D2 Polonnye Ukraine
58D1 Polotsk Russian Fed
60D2 Poltava Russian Fed
52C1 Pölten Austria
64F3 Poluostrov Kanin Pen Russian Fed
61H5 Poluostrov Mangyshlak Pen Kazakhstan
38L5 Poluostrov Rybachiy Pen Russian Fed
64H2 Poluostrov Yamal Pen Russian Fed
38L5 Polyarnyy Murmansk, Russian Fed
1B8 Polyarnyy Yakutskaya, Russian Fed
105H3 Polynesia Region Pacific O
32B5 Pomabamba Peru
35C2 Pomba R Brazil
22D3 Pomona USA
18A2 Pomona Res USA
17B2 Pompano Beach USA
18A2 Ponca City USA
27D3 Ponce Puerto Rico
17B2 Ponce de Leon B USA
87B2 Pondicherry India
6C2 Pond Inlet Can
50A1 Ponferrade Spain
98C2 Pongo R Sudan
101H1 Pongola R S Africa
87B2 Ponnāni India
86C2 Ponnyadoung Range Mts Burma
13E2 Ponoka Can
64F3 Ponoy Russian Fed
48B2 Pons France
96A1 Ponta da Baleia Pt Brazil
96A1 Ponta Delgada Açores
98B3 Ponta do Padrão Pt Angola
35C2 Ponta dos Búzios Pt Brazil
30F4 Ponta Grossa Brazil
35B2 Pontal Brazil
46D2 Pont-à-Mousson France
30E3 Ponta Pora Brazil
49D2 Pontarlier France
19B3 Pontchartrain,L USA
52B2 Pontedera Italy
52A2 Ponte Leccia Corse
50A1 Pontevedra Spain
18C1 Pontiac Illinois, USA
14B2 Pontiac Michigan, USA
78B3 Pontianak Indon
48B2 Pontivy France
46B2 Pontoise France
19C3 Pontotoc USA
43C4 Pontypool Wales
43C4 Pontypridd Wales
52B2 Ponziane I Italy
Poole Eng
Poona = Pune
108B2 Pooncarie Aust
108B2 Poopelloe,L L Aust
52C2 Poorman USA
3283 Popayán Colombia
46B1 Poperinge Belg
108B2 Popilta L Aust
43B4 Poplar Bluff USA
19C3 Poplarville USA
107D1 Popndetta PNG
23B2 Popocatepetl Mt Mexico
98B3 Popokabaka Zaïre
71F4 Popondetta PNG
54C2 Popovo Bulg
84B2 Porbandar India
13A2 Porcher I Can
12F1 Porcupine R Can/USA

52B1 Poreč Croatia	109D2 Port Macquarie Aust	9B3 Powell,L USA	39K6 Primorsk Russian Fed
35A2 Porecatu Brazil	12B3 Port Moller USA	13C3 Powell River Can	60E4 Primorsko-Akhtarsk Russian Fed
39J6 Pori Fin	107D1 Port Moresby PNG	8C2 Power R USA	13F2 Primrose L Can
111B2 Porirua NZ	100A3 Port Nolloth S Africa	23B1 Powys County, Wales	5H4 Prince Albert Can
38H5 Porjus Sweden	16B3 Port Norris USA	73D4 Poyang Hu L China	4F2 Prince Albert,C Can
69G2 Poronaysk Russian Fed	89E7 Port Novo Benin	92B2 Pozanti Turk	4G2 Prince Albert Pen Can
47B1 Porrentruy Switz	50A1 Porto Port	23B1 Poza Rica Mexico	4G2 Prince Albert Sd Can
38K4 Porsangen Inlet Nor	30F5 Pôrto Alegre Brazil	58B2 Poznań Pol	6C3 Prince Charles I Can
39F7 Porsgrunn Nor	33F6 Pôrto Artur Brazil	30E3 Pozo Colorado Par	112B10 Prince Charles Mts Ant
45C1 Portadown N Ire	30F3 Pôrto E Cunha Brazil	53B2 Pozzuoli Italy	7D5 Prince Edward I Can
8D2 Portage la Prairie Can	52B2 Portoferraio Italy	97B4 Pra R Ghana	13C2 Prince George Can
13C3 Port Alberni Can	27E4 Port of Spain Trinidad	76C3 Prachin Buri Thai	4H2 Prince Gustaf Adolp S Can
50A2 Portalegre Port	47D2 Portomaggiore Italy	76B3 Prachuap Khiri Khan Thai	5E4 Prince of Wales I Can
9C3 Portales USA	97C4 Porto Novo Benin	59B2 Praděd Mt Czech Republic	71F5 Prince of Wales I Aust
100B4 Port Alfred S Africa	20B1 Port Orchard USA	49C3 Pradelles France	4H2 Prince of Wales I Can
13B2 Port Alice Can	20B2 Port Orford USA	35D1 Prado Brazil	4G2 Prince of Wales Str Can
19B3 Port Allen USA	96A1 Porto Santo I Medeira	Prague = Praha	4F2 Prince Patrick I Can
20B1 Port Angeles USA	31D5 Pôrto Seguro Brazil	57C2 Praha Czech Republic	6A2 Prince Regent Inlet Str Can
26B3 Port Antonio Jamaica	53A2 Porto Torres Sardegna	97A4 Praia Cape Verde	13A2 Prince Rupert Can
45C2 Portarlington Irish Rep	53A2 Porto Vecchio Corse	33E5 Prainha Brazil	107D2 Princess Charlotte B Aust
19B4 Port Arthur USA	33E5 Pôrto Velho Brazil	18B2 Prairie Village USA	13B2 Princess Royal I Can
108A2 Port Augusta Aust	111A3 Port Pegasus B NZ	76C3 Prakhon Chai Thai	27L1 Princes Town Trinidad
26C3 Port-au-Prince Haiti	108B3 Port Phillip B Aust	35B1 Prata Brazil	13C3 Princeton Can
14B2 Port Austin USA	108A2 Port Pirie Aust	35B1 Prata R Brazil	18C2 Princeton Kentucky, USA
108B3 Port Campbell Aust	44A3 Portree Scot	Prates = Dongsha Qundao	18B1 Princeton Missouri, USA
86B2 Port Canning India	20B1 Port Renfrew Can	49E3 Prato Italy	16B2 Princeton New Jersey, USA
7D5 Port Cartier Can	27J2 Port Royal Jamaica	16B1 Prattsville USA	4D3 Prince William USA
111B3 Port Chalmers NZ	17B1 Port Royal Sd USA	17A1 Prattville USA	12E2 Prince William Sd Can
17B2 Port Charlotte USA	45C1 Portrush N Ire	48B1 Prawle Pt Eng	97C4 Príncipe I W Africa
16C2 Port Chester USA	92B3 Port Said Egypt	78D4 Praya Indon	20B2 Prineville USA
15C2 Port Colborne Can	17A2 Port St Joe USA	47D1 Predazzo Italy	12E1 Pringle,Mt USA
109C4 Port Davey Aust	45C1 Port St Johns S Africa	63B2 Predivinsk Russian Fed	6F3 Prins Christian Sund Sd Greenland
26C3 Port-de-Paix Haiti	7E4 Port Saunders Can	58C2 Pregolyu R Russian Fed	112B12 Prinsesse Astrid Kyst Region, Ant
77C5 Port Dickson Malay	100C4 Port Shepstone S Africa	76D3 Prek Kak Camb	112B12 Prinsesse Ragnhild Kyst Region, Ant
100C4 Port Edward S Africa	13A2 Port Simpson Can	56C2 Prenzlau Germany	64B2 Prins Karls Forland I Barents S
35C1 Porteirinha Brazil	27Q2 Portsmouth Dominica	76A3 Preparis I Burma	25D3 Prinzapolca Nic
14B2 Port Elgin Can	43D4 Portsmouth Eng	76A2 Preparis North Chan Burma	58D2 Pripet R Belorussia
100B4 Port Elizabeth S Africa	14B3 Portsmouth Ohio, USA	59B3 Přerov Czech Republic	Pripyat' = Pripet
27N2 Porter Pt St Vincent and the Grenadines	11C3 Portsmouth Virginia, USA	23A2 Presa del Infiernillo Mexico	54B2 Priština Serbia, Yugos
21B2 Porterville USA	109D2 Port Stephens B Aust	9B3 Prescott Arizona, USA	56C2 Pritzwalk Germany
107D4 Port Fairy Aust	95C3 Port Sudan Sudan	19B3 Prescott Arkansas, USA	61F3 Privolzhskaya Vozvyshennost' Upland Russian Fed
98A3 Port Gentil Gabon	19C3 Port Sulphur USA	15C2 Prescott Can	54B2 Prizren Serbia, Yugos
19B3 Port Gibson USA	38K5 Porttipahdan Tekojärvi Res Fin	30D4 Presidencia Roque Sáenz Peña Arg	78C4 Probolinggo Indon
12D3 Port Graham USA	50A2 Portugal Republic, Europe	35A2 Presidente Epitácio Brazil	85C2 Proddatūr India
20B1 Port Hammond Can	14A2 Port Washington USA	112C2 Presidente Frei Base Ant	25D2 Progreso Mexico
89E7 Port Harcourt Nig	77C5 Port Weld Malay	23B2 Presidente Alemán L Mexico	20B2 Project City USA
13B2 Port Hardy Can	32D6 Porvenir Bol	35A2 Presidente Prudente Brazil	61F5 Prokhladnyy Russian Fed
7D5 Port Hawkesbury Can	39K6 Porvoo Fin	35A2 Presidente Venceslau Brazil	65K4 Prokop'yevsk Russian Fed
106A3 Port Hedland Aust	30E4 Posadas Arg	59C3 Prešov Slovakia	61F4 Proletarskaya Russian Fed
Port Heiden = Meshik	50A2 Posadas Spain	55B2 Prespansko Jezero L Macedonia, Yugos	64G2 Proliv Karskiye Vorota Str Russian Fed
43B3 Porthmadog Wales	47D1 Poschiavo Switz	10D2 Presque Isle USA	83D4 Prome Burma
7E4 Port Hope Simpson Can	6B2 Posheim Pen Can	42B3 Preston Eng	31D4 Propriá Brazil
22C3 Port Hueneme USA	90C3 Posht-e Badam Iran	31B6 Preston Idaho, USA	20B2 Prospect Oregon, USA
14B2 Port Huron USA	71D4 Poso Indon	18B2 Preston Missouri, USA	107D3 Prosperine Aust
50A2 Portimão Port	58D1 Postavy Belorussia	42B2 Prestwick Scot	59B3 Prostějov Czech Republic
109D2 Port Jackson B Aust	14B2 Post Clinton USA	35B1 Prêto Brazil	6E2 Prøven Greenland
16C2 Port Jefferson USA	100B3 Postmasburg S Africa	101G1 Pretoria S Africa	49D3 Provence Region, France
16B2 Port Jervis USA	52B1 Postojna Slovenia	55B3 Préveza Greece	16D2 Providence USA
109D2 Port Kembla Aust	74C2 Pos'yet Russian Fed	76D3 Prey Veng Camb	15D2 Provincetown USA
14B2 Portland Indiana, USA	101G1 Potchefstroom S Africa	3B3 Price USA	49C2 Provins France
10C2 Portland Maine, USA	19B2 Poteau USA	13B2 Price I Can	8B2 Provo USA
109C2 Portland New South Wales, Aust	53C2 Potenza Italy	60D4 Prichernomorskaya Nizmennost' Lowland Ukraine	
20B1 Portland Oregon, USA	100B3 Potgietersrus S Africa	27M2 Prickly Pt Grenada	
108B3 Portland Victoria, Aust	21D5 Potiskum Nig	58C1 Priekule Lithuania	
27H2 Portland Bight B Jamaica	20C1 Potlatch USA	100B3 Prieska S Africa	
43C4 Portland Bill Pt Eng	15C2 Potomac R USA	20C1 Priest L USA	
109C4 Portland,C Aust	30C2 Potosí Bol	20C1 Priest River USA	
13A1 Portland Canal Can/ USA	30C4 Potrerillos Chile	55B2 Prilep Macedonia, Yugos	
110C1 Portland I NZ	56C2 Potsdam Germany	60D3 Priluki Ukraine	
27H2 Portland Pt Jamaica	16B2 Pottstown USA	34C2 Primero R Arg	
45C2 Port Laoise Irish Rep	16A2 Pottsville USA		
108A2 Port Lincoln Aust	16C2 Poughkeepsie USA		
97A4 Port Loko Sierra Leone	35B2 Pouso Alegre Brazil		
101E3 Port Louis Mauritius	110C1 Poverty B NZ		
108B3 Port MacDonnell Aust	61F3 Povorino Russian Fed		
13B2 Port McNeill Can	7C4 Povungnituk Can		
	8C2 Powder R USA		
	106C2 Powell Creek Aust		

13E2 **Provost** Can
4D2 **Prudhoe Bay** USA
6D2 **Prudhoe Land**
Greenland
58C2 **Pruszkow** Pol
60C4 **Prut** R Romania/
Moldova
60C4 **Prutul** R Romania
18A2 **Pryor** USA
59C3 **Przemyśl** Pol
55C3 **Psará** l Greece
60C2 **Pskov** Russian Fed
58D2 **Ptich** R Belorussia
55B2 **Ptolemais** Greece
32C5 **Pucallpa** Peru
73D4 **Pucheng** China
34A3 **Pucón** Chile
38K5 **Pudasjärvi** Fin
87B2 **Pudukkottai** India
23B2 **Puebla** Mexico
23B2 **Puebla** State, Mexico
50A1 **Puebla de Sanabria**
Spain
50A1 **Puebla de Trives**
Spain
9C2 **Pueblo** USA
34B3 **Puelches** Arg
34B3 **Puelen** Arg
23A2 **Puente Ixbapa**
Mexico
34B2 **Puente del Inca** Arg
32A5 **Puente Aguja** Peru
30B2 **Puerta Coles** Peru
34B2 **Puerta de los Llanos**
Arg
31D3 **Puerta do Calcanhar**
Pt Brazil
32C1 **Puerta Gallinas**
Colombia
23B2 **Puerta Maldonado** Pt
Mexico
32A2 **Puerta Mariato**
Panama
29C5 **Puerta Médanosa** Pt
Arg
23A2 **Puerta Mongrove**
Mexico
25E4 **Puerta San Blas** Pt
Panama
23A2 **Puerta San Telmo**
Mexico
29B5 **Puerto Aisén** Chile
25D4 **Puerto Armuelles**
Panama
33F6 **Puerto Artur** Brazil
32B3 **Puerto Asis**
Colombia
32D2 **Puerto Ayacucho**
Ven
25D3 **Puerto Barrios**
Guatemala
32C2 **Puerto Berrio**
Colombia
32D1 **Puerto Cabello** Ven
25D3 **Puerto Cabezas** Nic
32D2 **Puerto Carreño**
Colombia
25D4 **Puerto Cortes** Costa
Rica
25D3 **Puerto Cortés**
Honduras
96A2 **Puerto del Rosario**
Canary Is
30F3 **Puerto E Cunha**
Brazil
32C1 **Puerto Fijo** Ven
31B3 **Puerto Franco** Brazil
32D6 **Puerto Heath** Bol
25D2 **Puerto Juarez**
Mexico
33E1 **Puerto la Cruz** Ven
50B2 **Puertollano** Spain
27C4 **Puerto Lopez**
Colombia
29D4 **Puerto Madryn** Arg
32D6 **Puerto Maldonado**
Peru
23B2 **Puerto Marquéz**
Mexico
29B4 **Puerto Montt** Chile
30E3 **Puerto Murtinho**
Brazil
29B6 **Puerto Natales** Chile

24A1 **Puerto Peñasco**
Mexico
29D4 **Puerto Pirámides**
Arg
27C3 **Puerto Plata** Dom
Rep
79A4 **Puerto Princesa** Phil
32B3 **Puerto Rico**
Colombia
27D3 **Puerto Rico** l
Caribbean S
27D3 **Puerto Rico Trench**
Caribbean S
23A2 **Puerto San Juan de
Lima** Mexico
33G4 **Puerto Santanga**
Brazil
30E2 **Puerto Suárez** Bol
24B2 **Puerto Vallarta**
Mexico
29B4 **Puerto Varas** Chile
30D2 **Puerto Villarroel** Bol
61G3 **Pugachev**
Russian Fed
84C3 **Pugal** India
51C1 **Puigcerdá** Spain
111B2 **Pukaki,L** NZ
74B2 **Pukch'ŏng** N Korea
110B1 **Pukekobe** NZ
111B2 **Puketeraki Range**
Mts NZ
52B2 **Pula** Croatia
15C2 **Pulaski** New York,
USA
71E4 **Pulau Kolepom** l
Indon
70A4 **Pulau Pulau Batu** ls
Indon
58C2 **Pulawy** Pol
87C2 **Pulicat,L** India
84B1 **Puli-i-Khumri** Afghan
87B3 **Puliyangudi** India
20C1 **Pullman** USA
71E3 **Pulo Anna Merir** l
Pacific O
79B2 **Pulog,Mt** Phil
38L5 **Pulozero** Russian Fed
58C2 **Pultusk** Pol
30C4 **Puna de Atacama**
Arg
86B1 **Punakha** Bhutan
84C2 **Punch** Pak
87A1 **Pune** India
23A2 **Punépen** Mexico
98C3 **Punia** Zaire
34A2 **Punitaqui** Chile
84C2 **Punjab** Province, Pak
84D2 **Punjab** State, India
30B2 **Puno** Peru
24A2 **Punta Abreojos** Pt
Mexico
53C3 **Punta Alice** Pt Italy
34C3 **Punta Alta** Arg
29B6 **Punta Arenas** Chile
24A2 **Punta Baja** Pt
Mexico
34A2 **Punta Curaumilla** Pt
Chile
100A2 **Punta da Marca** Pt
Angola
101C3 **Punta de Barra Falsa**
Pt Mozam
29F2 **Punta del Este** Urug
24A2 **Punta Eugenia** Pt
Mexico
25D3 **Punta Gorda** Belize
17B2 **Punta Gorda** USA
34A1 **Punta Lavapié** Pt
Chile
34A2 **Punta Lengua de
Vaca** Pt Chile
53B2 **Punta Licosa** Pt Italy
34A1 **Punta Poroto** Pt
Chile
9B4 **Punta San Antonia** Pt
Mexico
34A2 **Punta Topocalma**
Chile
73C4 **Puqi** China
64J3 **Pur** R Russian Fed
19A2 **Purcell** USA
12C1 **Purcell Mt** USA
13D2 **Purcell Mts** Can
34A3 **Purén** Chile

86B2 **Puri** India
87B1 **Pūrna** India
86B1 **Pūrnia** India
76C3 **Pursat** Camb
23A1 **Puruandro** Mexico
33E4 **Purus** R Brazil
19C3 **Purvis** USA
78B4 **Purwokerto** Indon
78C4 **Purworejo** Indon
74B2 **Pusad** Indon
74B3 **Pusan** S Korea
60D2 **Pushkin** Russian Fed
58D1 **Pustoshka**
Russian Fed
82D3 **Puta** Burma
34A2 **Putaendo** Chile
110C1 **Putaruru** NZ
16D2 **Putian** China
16D2 **Putnam** USA
87B3 **Puttalam** Sri Lanka
56C2 **Puttgarden** Germany
32B4 **Putumayo** R
Ecuador
78C2 **Putussibau** Indon
38K6 **Puulavesi** L Fin
20B1 **Puyallup** USA
49C2 **Puy de Sancy** Mt
France
111A3 **Puysegur Pt** NZ
99C3 **Pweto** Zaire
87B2 **Pwllheli** Wales
76B2 **Pyapon** Burma
61F5 **Pyatigorsk**
Russian Fed
Pyè = Prome
74B3 **P'yŏngyang** N Korea
108B3 **Pyramid Hill** Aust
21B1 **Pyramid L** USA
111A2 **Pyramid,Mt** NZ
48B3 **Pyrenées** Mts France
58D1 **Pytalovo** Russian Fed
76B2 **Pyu** Burma

Q

94B2 **Qabatiya** Israel
94C3 **Qã'el Hafira** Mud
Flats Jordan
94C3 **Qa'el Jinz** Mud Flats
Jordan
68B3 **Qaidam Pendi** Salt
Flat China
94C2 **Qa Khanna** Salt
Marsh Jordan
99D1 **Qala'en Nahl** Sudan
84B2 **Qalat** Afghan
94C1 **Qal'at al Hisn** Syria
81C3 **Qal'at al Bishah**
S Arabia
93E3 **Qal'at Sãlih** Iraq
68B3 **Qamdo** China
99E1 **Qandala** Somalia
99E2 **Qardho** Somalia
95B2 **Qara** Egypt
90A2 **Qare Shirin** Iran
91A4 **Qaryat al Ulyã**
S Arabia
94C3 **Qasr el Kharana**
Jordan
91D4 **Qasr-e-Qand** Iran
95B2 **Qasr Farafra** Egypt
94C2 **Qatana** Syria
91B4 **Qatar** Emirate,
Arabian Pen
94C3 **Qatrāna** Jordan
95B2 **Qattâra Depression**
Egypt
90C3 **Qãyen** Iran
90A2 **Qazvin** Iran
95C2 **Qena** Egypt
91B4 **Qeydar** Iran
91B4 **Qeys** l Iran
43B2 **Qeziot** Israel
73B5 **Qian Jiang** R China
72E1 **Qian Shan** Upland
China
72E3 **Qidong** China
73B4 **Qijiang** China
84B2 **Qila Saifullah** Pak
84B2 **Qila Saifullah** Pak
68B3 **Qilian Shan** China
72B3 **Qin'an** China
72E2 **Qingdao** China
72A2 **Qinghai** Province,
China

86B3 **Qinghai Hu** L China
72D3 **Qingjiang** Jiangsu,
China
73D4 **Qingjiang** Jiangxi,
China
72B3 **Qing Jiang** R China
72C2 **Qingshuihe** China
72B2 **Qingshui He** R China
72B2 **Qingtonxia** China
72B2 **Qingyang** China
74B2 **Qingyuan** Liaoning,
China
73D4 **Qingyuan** Zhejiang,
China
82C2 **Qing Zang** Upland
China
72D2 **Qinhuangdao** China
72B3 **Qin Ling** Mts China
73B5 **Qinzhou** China
76E2 **Qionghai** China
73A3 **Qionglai Shan**
Upland China
76D1 **Qiongzhou Haixia** Str
China
69E2 **Qiqihar** China
94B2 **Qiryat Ata** Israel
94B3 **Qiryat Gat** Israel
94B2 **Qiryat Shemona**
Israel
94B2 **Qiryat Yam** Israel
94B2 **Qishon** R Israel
63A3 **Qital** China
73C4 **Qiyang** China
72B1 **Qog Qi** China
90B2 **Qoileh-ye Damavand**
Mt Iran
90B3 **Qom** Iran
90B3 **Qomisheh** Iran
Qomolongma Feng =
Everest,Mt
94C1 **Qornet es Saouda** Mt
Leb
6E3 **Qôrnoq** Greenland
91C4 **Qotãbad** Iran
16C1 **Quabbin Res** USA
16B2 **Quakertown** USA
77C3 **Quam Phuoc** l
Viet
76D2 **Quang Ngai** Viet
76D2 **Quang Tri** Viet
77D4 **Quan Long** Viet
73D5 **Quanzhou** Fujian,
China
73C4 **Quanzhou** Guangxi,
China
5H4 **Qu' Appelle** R Can
91C5 **Quarayyãt** Oman
13B2 **Quatsino** Can
90C2 **Quchan** Iran
109C3 **Queanbeyan** Aust
15D1 **Québec** Can
7C4 **Québec** Province,
Can
35B1 **Quebra-Anzol** R
Brazil
34D2 **Quebracho** Urug
30F4 **Quedas do Iguaçu**
Brazil/Arg
16A3 **Queen Anne** USA
13B2 **Queen Bess,Mt** Can
5E4 **Queen Charlotte** Is
Can
13B2 **Queen Charlotte**
Can
13B2 **Queen Charlotte Str**
Can
4H1 **Queen Elizabeth Is**
Can
112B9 **Queen Mary Land**
Region, Ant
4H3 **Queen Maud G** Can
112A **Queen Maud Mts** Ant
16C2 **Queens** Borough,
New York, USA
108B3 **Queenscliff** Aust
107D3 **Queensland** State,
Aust
109C4 **Queenstown** Aust
111A3 **Queenstown** NZ
100B4 **Queenstown** S Africa
16A3 **Queenstown** USA
98B3 **Quela** Angola
101C2 **Quelimane** Mozam

34C3 **Quemuquemú** Arg
13C2 **Quensel L** Can
34D3 **Quequén** Arg
34D3 **Quequén** R Arg
23A1 **Querétaro** Mexico
23A1 **Querétaro** State Mexico
13C2 **Quesnel** Can
84B2 **Quetta** Pak
25C3 **Quezaltenango** Guatemala
79B3 **Quezon City** Phil
100A2 **Quibala** Angola
98B3 **Quibaxe** Angola
32B2 **Quibdó** Colombia
48B2 **Quiberon** France
98B3 **Quicama Nat Pk** Angola
73A4 **Quijing** China
34A2 **Quilima** Chile
34C2 **Quilino** Arg
32C6 **Quillabamba** Peru
30C2 **Quillacollo** Bol
48C3 **Quillan** France
5H4 **Quill L** Can
5H4 **Quill Lakes** Can
34A2 **Quillota** Chile
87B3 **Quilon** India
108B1 **Quilpie** Aust
34A2 **Quilpué** Chile
98B3 **Quimbele** Angola
48B2 **Quimper** France
48B2 **Quimperlé** France
21A2 **Quincy** California, USA
10A3 **Quincy** Illinois, USA
16D1 **Quincy** Massachusetts, USA
34B2 **Quines** Arg
12B3 **Quinhagak** USA
76D3 **Qui Nhon** Viet
50B2 **Quintanar de la Orden** Spain
34A2 **Quintero** Chile
34C2 **Quinto** R Arg
34A3 **Quirihue** Chile
100A2 **Quirima** Angola
109D2 **Quirindi** Aust
101D2 **Quissanga** Mozam
101C3 **Quissico** Mozam
32B4 **Quito** Ecuador
31D2 **Quixadá** Brazil
108A2 **Quorn** Aust
4G3 **Qurlurtuuk** Can
95C2 **Quseir** Egypt
6E3 **Qutdligssat** Greenland
Quthing = Moyeni
73B3 **Qu Xian** Sichuan, China
73D4 **Qu Xian** Zhejiang, China
76D2 **Quynh Luu** Viet
72C2 **Quzhou** China
86C1 **Qüzü** China

R

38J6 **Raahe** Fin
44A3 **Raasay** l Scot
44A3 **Raasay,Sound of** Chan Scot
99F1 **Raas Caseyr** C Somalia
52B2 **Rab** l Croatia
78D4 **Raba** Indon
59B3 **Rába** R Hung
96B1 **Rabat** Mor
94B3 **Rabba** Jordan
80B3 **Rabigh** S Arabia
47B2 **Racconigi** Italy
7E5 **Race,C** Can
94B2 **Rachaya** Leb
57C3 **Rachel** Mt Germany
76D3 **Rach Gia** Viet
14A2 **Racine** USA
59D3 **Rádáuți** Rom
85C4 **Radhanpur** India
27L1 **Radix,Pt** Trinidad
58C2 **Radom** Pol
59B2 **Radomsko** Pol
58C1 **Radviliškis** Lithuania
4G3 **Rae** Can
86A1 **Rãe Bareli** India
6B3 **Rae Isthmus** Can

4G3 **Rae L** Can
110C1 **Raetihi** NZ
34C2 **Rafaela** Arg
94B3 **Rafah** Egypt
98C2 **Rafai** CAR
93D3 **Rafhã Al Jumaymah** S Arabia
91C3 **Rafsanjän** Iran
98C2 **Raga** Sudan
27R3 **Ragged Pt** Barbados
53B3 **Ragusa** Italy
99D1 **Rahad** R Sudan
84C3 **Rahimyar Khan** Pak
90B3 **Rähjerd** Iran
34D2 **Raíces** Arg
87B1 **Rãichur** India
86A2 **Rãigarh** India
108B3 **Rainbow** Aust
17A1 **Rainbow City** USA
20B1 **Rainier** USA
20B1 **Rainier,Mt** USA
10A2 **Rainy L** Can
12D2 **Rainy P** USA
10A2 **Rainy River** Can
86A2 **Rãipur** India
87C1 **Rãjahmundry** India
78C2 **Rajang** R Malay
84B3 **Rajanpur** Pak
85D3 **Rãjapalaiyam** India
85C3 **Rãjasthan** State, India
84D3 **Rãjgarh** India
85D4 **Rãjgarh** State, India
85C4 **Rãjkot** India
86B2 **Rãjmahãl Hills** India
86A2 **Raj Nãndgaon** India
85C4 **Rãjphla** India
86B2 **Rãjshahi** Bang
85D4 **Rãjur** India
111B2 **Rakaia** R NZ
78B4 **Rakata** l Indon
82C3 **Raka Zangbo** R India
59C3 **Rakhov** Ukraine
100B3 **Rakops** Botswana
58C2 **Rakov** Belorussia
11C3 **Raleigh** USA
7A5 **Ralny L** Can
94B2 **Rama** Israel
94B3 **Ramallah** Israel
87B3 **Rãmanãthapuram** India
69G3 **Ramapo Deep** Pacific O
94B2 **Ramat Gan** Israel
46A2 **Rambouillet** France
86B2 **Rãmgarh** Bihar, India
85C3 **Rãmgarh** Rajasthan, India
90A3 **Rãmhormoz** Iran
94B3 **Ramla** Israel
91C5 **Ramlat Al Wahibah** Region, Oman
21B3 **Ramona** USA
84D3 **Rãmpur** India
85D4 **Rãmpura** India
90B2 **Rãmsar** Iran
42B2 **Ramsey** Eng
16B2 **Ramsey** USA
43H4 **Ramsey** I Wales
43E4 **Ramsgate** Eng
94C2 **Ramtha** Jordan
71F4 **Ramu** R PNG
3442 **Rancagua** Chile
86B2 **Rãnchi** India
86A2 **Rãnchi Plat** India
101G1 **Randburg** S Africa
39G7 **Randers** Den
101G1 **Randfontein** S Africa
15D2 **Randolph** Vermont, USA
111B3 **Ranfurly** NZ
86C2 **Rangamati** Bang
111B2 **Rangiora** NZ
110C1 **Rangitaiki** R NZ
110C1 **Rangitäte** R NZ
110C1 **Rangitikei** R NZ
Rangoon = Yangon
86B1 **Rãngpur** India
87B2 **Rãnibennur** India
86A2 **Ranier,Mt** Mt India
84B2 **Rãnipur** India
109C2 **Rankins Springs** Aust
6A3 **Ranklin Inlet** Can

85B4 **Rann of Kachchh** Flood Area India
77B4 **Ranong** Thai
70A3 **Rantauparapat** Indon
18C1 **Rantoul** USA
49D3 **Rapallo** Italy
34A2 **Rapel** R Chile
6D3 **Raper,C** Can
8C2 **Rapid City** USA
14A1 **Rapid River** USA
15C3 **Rappahannock** R USA
47C1 **Rapperswil** Switz
16B2 **Raritan B** USA
95C2 **Ras Abu Shagara** C Sudan
93D2 **Ra's al 'Ayn** Syria
91C5 **Ra's al Hadd** C Oman
91C4 **Ras al Kaimah** UAE
91C4 **Ras-al-Kuh** C Iran
81D4 **Ra's al Madrakah** C Oman
91A4 **Ra's az Zawr** C S Arabia
95C2 **Rãs Bânas** C Egypt
94A3 **Ras Burün** C Egypt
99D1 **Ras Dashan** Mt Eth
90A3 **Ra's-e-Barkan** Pt Iran
92A3 **Ra's el Kenâyis** Pt Egypt
81D4 **Ra's Fartak** C Yemen
95C2 **Rãs Ghârib** C Egypt
99D1 **Rashad** Sudan
94B3 **Rashãdiya** Jordan
92B3 **Rashid** Egypt
90A2 **Rasht** Iran
91C5 **Ra's Jibish** C Oman
99E1 **Ras Khanzira** C Somalia
84B3 **Ras Koh** Mt Pak
95C2 **Rãs Muhammad** C Egypt
96A2 **Ras Nouadhibou** C Maur
69H2 **Rasshua** l Russian Fed
61F3 **Rasskazovo** Russian Fed
91A4 **Ra's Tanãqib** C S Arabia
91B4 **Ra's Tannürah** S Arabia
57B3 **Rastatt** Germany
Ras Uarc = Cabo Tres Forcas
99F1 **Ras Xaafuun** C Somalia
84C3 **Ratangarh** India
76B3 **Rat Buri** Thai
85D3 **Rath** India
56C2 **Rathenow** Germany
45B2 **Rathkeale** Irish Rep
45C1 **Rathlin** l N Ire
45B2 **Rãth Luirc** Irish Rep
85D4 **Ratlãm** India
87A1 **Ratnãgiri** India
87C3 **Ratnapura** Sri Lanka
58C2 **Ratno** Ukraine
47D1 **Rattenberg** Austria
39H6 **Rättvik** Sweden
12H3 **Ratz,Mt** Can
34D3 **Rauch** Arg
100C1 **Raukumara Range** Mts NZ
35C2 **Raul Soares** Brazil
39J6 **Rauma** Fin
86A2 **Raurkela** India
90A3 **Rãvänsar** Iran
90C3 **Rãvar** Iran
59C2 **Rava Russkaya** Ukraine
16C1 **Ravena** USA
52B2 **Ravenna** Italy
57B3 **Ravensburg** Germany
107D2 **Ravenshoe** Aust
42E2 **Ravenspurn** Oilfield N Sea
84C2 **Ravi** R Pak
84C2 **Rawalpindi** Pak
93D2 **Rawãndiz** Iraq
58B2 **Rawicz** Pol
106B4 **Rawlinna** Aust

8C2 **Rawlins** USA
29C4 **Rawson** Arg
78C3 **Raya** Mt Indon
87B2 **Rãyadurg** India
94C2 **Rayak** Leb
7E5 **Ray,C** Can
91C4 **Räyen** Iran
22C2 **Raymond** California, USA
20B1 **Raymond** Washington, USA
109D2 **Raymond Terrace** Aust
12D1 **Ray Mts** USA
23B1 **Rayon** Mexico
90A2 **Razan** Iran
54C2 **Razgrad** Bulg
54C2 **Razim** L Rom
43D4 **Reading** Eng
16B2 **Reading** USA
4G3 **Read Island** Can
16C1 **Readsboro** USA
34B2 **Real de Padre** Arg
34C3 **Realicó** Arg
95B2 **Rebiana** Well Libya
95B2 **Rebiana Sand Sea** Libya
38L6 **Reboly** Russian Fed
106B4 **Recherche,Arch of the ls** Aust
31E3 **Recife** Brazil
107F2 **Récifs D'Entrecasteaux** Nouvelle Calédonie
46D1 **Recklinghausen** Germany
30E4 **Reconquista** Arg
19B3 **Red** R USA
77C4 **Redang** l Malay
16B2 **Red Bank** New Jersey, USA
21A1 **Red Bluff** USA
42D2 **Redcar** Eng
13E2 **Redcliff** Can
109D1 **Redcliffe** Aust
108B2 **Red Cliffs** Aust
13E2 **Red Deer** Can
13E2 **Red Deer** R Can
20B2 **Redding** USA
10A2 **Red L** USA
7A4 **Red Lake** Can
22D3 **Redlands** USA
16A3 **Red Lion** USA
20B2 **Redmond** USA
18A1 **Red Oak** USA
48B2 **Redon** France
22C4 **Redondo Beach** USA
12D2 **Redoubt V** USA
73B5 **Red River Delta** Vietnam
80B3 **Red Sea** Africa/Arabian Pen
13E2 **Redwater** Can
22A2 **Redwood City** USA
14A2 **Reed City** USA
22C2 **Reedley** USA
20B2 **Reedsport** USA
111B2 **Reefton** NZ
93C2 **Refahiye** Turk
35D1 **Regência** Brazil
57C3 **Regensburg** Germany
96C2 **Reggane** Alg
53C3 **Reggio di Calabria** Italy
47D2 **Reggio Nell'Emilia** Italy
54B1 **Reghin** Rom
5H4 **Regina** Can
100A3 **Rehoboth** Namibia
15C3 **Rehoboth Beach** USA
94B3 **Rehovot** Israel
32D1 **Reicito** Ven
43D4 **Reigate** Eng
46C2 **Reims** France
5H4 **Reindeer** R Can
50B1 **Reinosa** Spain
16C3 **Reisterstown** USA
101G1 **Reitz** S Africa
4H3 **Reliance** Can
108A2 **Remarkable,Mt** Aust
78C4 **Rembang** Indon
91C4 **Remeshk** Iran

Remscheid

46D1 **Remscheid** Germany
18C2 **Rend,L** USA
56B2 **Rendsburg** Germany
15C1 **Renfrew** Can
78A3 **Rengat** Indon
34A2 **Rengo** Chile
59D3 **Reni** Ukraine
99D1 **Renk** Sudan
6H2 **Renland** *Pen*
　　Greenland
108B2 **Renmark** Aust
107F2 **Rennell** *I* Solomon Is
48B2 **Rennes** France
21B2 **Reno** USA
47D2 **Reno** *R* Italy
15C2 **Renovo** USA
16C1 **Rensselaer** USA
20B1 **Renton** USA
70D4 **Reo** Indon
35B2 **Reprêsa de Furnas**
　　Dam Brazil
30E3 **Reprêsa Ilha Grande**
　　Dam Brazil
30E3 **Reprêsa Itaipu** *Dam*
　　Brazil
35A2 **Reprêsa Porto**
　　Primavera *Dam*
　　Brazil
35B1 **Reprêsa Três Marias**
　　Dam Brazil
20C1 **Republic** USA
41B3 **Republic of Ireland**
　　NW Europe
6B3 **Repulse Bay** Can
15C1 **Réservoir Baskatong**
　　Res Can
10C1 **Réservoir de la**
　　Grande 2 *Res* Can
10C1 **Réservoir de la**
　　Grande 3 *Res* Can
7C4 **Réservoir de la**
　　Grande 4 *Res* Can
7C5 **Réservoir Cabonga**
　　Res Can
7D4 **Réservoir**
　　Caniapiscau *Res* Can
7C5 **Réservoir Gouin** *Res*
　　Can
10D1 **Réservoir**
　　Manicouagan *Res*
　　Can
90B2 **Reshteh-ye Alborz**
　　Mts Iran
72A2 **Reshui** China
54B1 **Resistencia** Arg
50B1 **Resita** Rom
6A2 **Resolute** Can
111A3 **Resolution I** NZ
6D3 **Resolution Island**
　　Can
101H1 **Ressano Garcia**
　　Mozam
34B2 **Retamito** Arg
46C2 **Rethel** France
55B3 **Réthimnon** Greece
89K10 **Reunion** *I* Indian O
51C1 **Reus** Spain
47C1 **Reuss** *R* Switz
47D1 **Reutte** Austria
61K3 **Revda** Russian Fed
13D2 **Revelstoke** Can
24A3 **Revillagigedo** *Is*
　　Mexico
12H3 **Revillagigedo I** USA
46C2 **Revin** France
94B3 **Revivim** Israel
86A2 **Rewa** India
84D3 **Rewari** India
8B2 **Rexburg** USA
38A2 **Reykjavik** Iceland
24C2 **Reynosa** Mexico
48B2 **Rezé** France
58D1 **Rezekne** Latvia
61K2 **Rezh** Russian Fed
47C1 **Rhätikon** *Mts*
　　Austria/Switz
94B1 **Rhazir** Republic, Leb
56B2 **Rhein** *R* W Europe
56B2 **Rhine** Germany
47B1 **Rheinfelden** Switz
49D2 **Rheinland Pfalz**
　　Region, Germany
47C1 **Rheinwaldhorn** *Mt*
　　Switz

Rhine = Rhein
16C2 **Rhinebeck** USA
10B2 **Rhinelander** USA
47C2 **Rho** Italy
15D2 **Rhode Island** State,
　　USA
16D2 **Rhode Island Sd** USA
　　Rhodes = Ródhos
49C3 **Rhône** *R* France
43C3 **Rhyl** Wales
31D4 **Riachão do Jacuipe**
　　Brazil
50A1 **Ria de Arosa** *B*
　　Spain
50A1 **Ria de Betanzos** *B*
　　Spain
50A1 **Ria de Corcubion** *B*
　　Spain
50A1 **Ria de Lage** *B* Spain
50A1 **Ria de Sta Marta** *B*
　　Spain
50A1 **Ria de Vigo** *B* Spain
84C2 **Riāsi** Pak
50A1 **Ribadeo** Spain
35A2 **Ribas do Rio Pardo**
　　Brazil
42C3 **Ribauê** Mozam
42C3 **Ribble** *R* Eng
35B2 **Ribeira** Brazil
35B2 **Ribeirão Prêto** Brazil
32D6 **Riberalta** Bol
15C2 **Rice L** Can
10A2 **Rice Lake** USA
101H1 **Richard's Bay**
　　S Africa
19A3 **Richardson** USA
12G1 **Richardson Mts** Can
8B3 **Richfield** USA
20C1 **Richland** USA
22A2 **Richland California,**
　　USA
101H1 **Richmond** Natal,
　　S Africa
109D2 **Richmond** New
　　South Wales, Aust
111B2 **Richmond** NZ
107D3 **Richmond**
　　Queensland, Aust
11A3 **Richmond** Virginia,
　　USA
111B2 **Richmond Range** *Mts*
　　NZ
15C2 **Rideau,L** Can
17B1 **Ridgeland** USA
15C2 **Ridgway** USA
27D4 **Riecito** Ven
47D1 **Rienza** *R* Italy
57C2 **Riesa** Germany
29B6 **Riesco** *I* Chile
29H7 **Rimbo** Sweden
52B2 **Rimini** Italy
54C1 **Rîmnicu Sărat** Rom
54B1 **Rîmnicu Vilcea** Rom
10D2 **Rimouski** Can
23A1 **Rincón de Romos**
　　Mexico
39H7 **Ringkøbing** Den
98A2 **Rio Benito** Eq Guinea
32D5 **Rio Branco** Brazil
24B1 **Rio Bravo del Norte**
　　R Mexico/USA
32C1 **Riochacha** Colombia
35B2 **Rio Claro** Brazil
27L1 **Rio Claro** Trinidad
34C3 **Rio Colorado** Arg
34C2 **Rio Cuarto** Arg
31D4 **Rio de Jacuipe** Brazil
35C2 **Rio de Janeiro** Brazil
35C2 **Rio de Janeiro** State,
　　Brazil
29E3 **Rio de la Plata** *Est*
　　Arg/Urug

29C6 **Rio Gallegos** Arg
29C6 **Rio Grande** Arg
30F5 **Rio Grande** Brazil
26A4 **Rio Grande** Nic
25D3 **Rio Grande** *R* Nic
24B2 **Rio Grande** *R*
　　Mexico/USA
23A1 **Rio Grande de**
　　Santiago Mexico
31D3 **Rio Grande do Norte**
　　State, Brazil
30F4 **Rio Grande do Sul**
　　State, Brazil
103G6 **Rio Grande Rise**
　　Atlantic O
26C4 **Riohacha** Colombia
49C2 **Riom** France
32B4 **Riombamba** Ecuador
30C2 **Rio Mulatos** Bol
29C3 **Rio Negro** State, Arg
30F4 **Rio Pardo** Brazil
34C2 **Rio Tercero** Arg
33E6 **Rio Theodore**
　　Roosevelt *R* Brazil
29B6 **Rio Turbio** Arg
35A1 **Rio Verde** Brazil
23A1 **Rio Verde** Mexico
14B3 **Ripley** Ohio, USA
14B3 **Ripley** West Virginia,
　　USA
42D2 **Ripon** Eng
22B2 **Ripon** USA
94B3 **Rishon le Zion** Israel
16A3 **Rising Sun** USA
39F7 **Risør** Nor
6E2 **Ritenberk** Greenland
22C2 **Ritter,Mt** USA
20C1 **Ritzville** USA
34B2 **Rivadavia** Arg
34A1 **Rivadavia** Chile
34C3 **Rivadavia Gonzalez**
　　Moreno Arg
47D2 **Riva de Garda** Italy
34C3 **Rivera** Arg
29E2 **Rivera** Urug
22B2 **Riverbank** USA
97B4 **River Cess** Lib
16C2 **Riverhead** USA
108B3 **Riverina** Aust
11A3 **Riversdale** NZ
22D4 **Riverside** USA
13B2 **Rivers Inlet** Can
111A3 **Riverton** NZ
8C2 **Riverton** USA
17B2 **Riviera Beach** USA
7C4 **Rivière aux Feuilles** *R*
　　Can
7D4 **Rivière de la Baleine**
　　R Can
7D4 **Rivière du Petit**
　　Mécatina *R* Can
46C2 **Rivigny-sur-Ornain**
　　France
93D1 **Rize** Turk
72D2 **Rizhao** China
　　Rizhskiy Zaliv =
　　Riga,G of
39F7 **Rjukan** Nor
46D2 **Roanes Pen** Can
49C2 **Roanne** France
17A1 **Roanoke** Alabama,
　　USA
11C3 **Roanoke** Virginia,
　　USA
11C3 **Roanoke** *R* USA
45B3 **Roaringwater B**
　　Irish Rep
38J6 **Robertsforz** Sweden
19B2 **Robert S Kerr Res**
　　USA
97A4 **Robertsport** Lib
7C5 **Roberval** Can
30H6 **Robinson Crusoe** *I*
　　Chile
108B2 **Robinvale** Aust
13D2 **Robson,Mt** Can
24A3 **Roca Partida** *I*
　　Mexico
103G5 **Rocas** *I* Atlantic O
31E2 **Rocas** *I* Brazil
42C3 **Rochdale** Eng
48B2 **Rochefort** France
5G3 **Rocher River** Can

108B3 **Rochester** Aust
7C5 **Rochester** Can
43E4 **Rochester** Eng
10A2 **Rochester**
　　Minnesota, USA
15D2 **Rochester** New
　　Hampshire, USA
10C2 **Rochester** New York,
　　USA
10B2 **Rockford** USA
11B3 **Rock Hill** USA
10A2 **Rock Island** USA
108B3 **Rocklands Res** Aust
17B2 **Rockledge** USA
8C2 **Rock Springs**
　　Wyoming, USA
110B2 **Rocks Pt** NZ
16C2 **Rockville**
　　Connecticut, USA
16A3 **Rockville** Indiana,
　　USA
16A3 **Rockville** Maryland,
　　USA
14B1 **Rocky Island L** Can
13E2 **Rocky Mountain**
　　House Can
8B1 **Rocky Mts** Can/USA
12B2 **Rocky Pt** USA
56C2 **Rødbyhavn** Den
34B2 **Rodeo** Arg
49C3 **Rodez** France
55C3 **Ródhos** Greece
55C3 **Ródhos** *I* Greece
52C2 **Rodi Garganico** Italy
54B2 **Rodopi Planina** *Mts*
　　Bulg
106A3 **Roebourne** Aust
46C1 **Roermond** Neth
46B1 **Roeselare** Belg
6B3 **Roes Welcome Sd**
　　Can
18B2 **Rogers** USA
14B1 **Rogers City** USA
20B2 **Rogue** *R* USA
85B3 **Rohn** Pak
84D3 **Rohtak** India
58C1 **Roja** Latvia
35A2 **Rolândia** Brazil
50A3 **Ronda** Spain
109C1 **Roma** Aust
52B2 **Roma** Italy
47C2 **Romagnano** Italy
17C1 **Romain,C** USA
54C1 **Roman** Rom
103H5 **Romanche Gap**
　　Atlantic O
71D4 **Romang** *I* Indon
60B4 **Romania** Republic,
　　E Europe
17B2 **Romano,C** USA
49D2 **Romans sur Isère**
　　France
79B3 **Romblon** Phil
　　Rome = Roma
17A1 **Rome** Georgia, USA
15C2 **Rome** New York,
　　USA
49C2 **Romilly-sur-Seine**
　　France
15C3 **Romney** USA
60D3 **Romny** Ukraine
56B1 **Rømø** *I* Den
47B1 **Romont** Switz
48C2 **Romorantin** France
50A2 **Ronda** Spain
31E4 **Rondônia** Brazil
24F6 **Rondônia** State,
　　Brazil
30F2 **Rondonópolis** Brazil
73B4 **Rong'an** China
73B4 **Rongchang** China
72E2 **Rongcheng** China
73B4 **Rongjiang** China
73B4 **Rong Jiang** *R* China
76A1 **Rongklang Range**
　　Mts Burma
39G7 **Rønne** Den
39H7 **Ronneby** Sweden
112B2 **Ronne Ice Shelf** Ant
46B1 **Ronse** Belg
46A1 **Ronthieu** Region,
　　France
9C3 **Roof Butte** *Mt* USA

84D3 Roorkee India
46C1 Roosendaal Neth
112B6 Roosevelt I Ant
106C2 Roper R Aust
33E3 Roraima State, Brazil
33E2 Roraime Mt Ven
38G6 Røros Nor
47C1 Rorschach Switz
38G6 Rørvik Nor
27Q2 Rosalie Dominica
22C3 Rosamond L USA
34C2 Rosario Arg
31C2 Rosário Brazil
34D2 Rosario del Tala Arg
48B2 Roscoff France
45B2 Roscommon County, Irish Rep
41B3 Roscommon Irish Rep
45C2 Roscrea Irish Rep
27E3 Roseau Dominica
109C4 Rosebery Aust
20B2 Roseburg USA
19A4 Rosenberg USA
57C3 Rosenheim Germany
13F2 Rosetown Can
54B2 Roşiori de Vede Rom
39G7 Roskilde Den
60D3 Roslavl' Russian Fed
61E2 Roslyatino Russian Fed
111B2 Ross NZ
12H2 Ross R Can
40B3 Rossan Pt Irish Rep
53C3 Rossano Italy
19C3 Ross Barnet Res USA
15C1 Rosseau L L Can
107E2 Rossel I Solomon Is
112A Ross Ice Shelf Ant
20B1 Ross L USA
13D3 Rossland Can
45C2 Rosslare Irish Rep
111C2 Ross,Mt NZ
97A3 Rosso Maur
45C4 Ross-on-Wye Eng
60E4 Rossosh Russian Fed
4E3 Ross River Can
112B6 Ross S Ant
91B4 Rostãq Iran
56C2 Rostock Germany
Rostov = Rostov-na-Donu
61E4 Rostov-na-Donu Russian Fed
17B1 Roswell Georgia, USA
9C3 Roswell New Mexico, USA
71F2 Rota Pacific O
56B2 Rotenburg Niedersachsen, Germany
46E1 Rothaar-Geb Region Germany
112C3 Rothera Base Ant
42D3 Rotherham Eng
42B2 Rothesay Scot
71D5 Roti I Indon
108C2 Roto Aust
111B2 Rotoiti,L NZ
111B2 Rotorua,L NZ
110C1 Rotorua NZ
110C1 Rotorua,L NZ
56A2 Rotterdam Neth
46B1 Roubaix France
28E2 Rouen France
42E3 Rough Oilfield N Sea
Roulers = Roeselare
101E3 Round I Mauritius
109D2 Round Mt Aust
8C2 Roundup USA
44C2 Rousay I Scot
49C2 Roussillon Region, France
10C2 Rouyn Can
38K5 Rovaniemi Fin
47D2 Rovereto Italy
47D2 Rovigo Italy
52B1 Rovinj Croatia
59D2 Rovno Ukraine
90A2 Row'ān Iran
109C1 Rowena Aust
6C3 Rowley I Can
106A2 Rowley Shoals Aust

79A3 Roxas Palawan, Phil
79B3 Roxas Panay, Phil
111A3 Roxburgh NZ
45C2 Royal Canal Irish Rep
43D3 Royal Leamington Spa Eng
14B2 Royal Oak USA
43E4 Royal Tunbridge Wells Eng
48B2 Royan France
46B2 Roye France
43D3 Royston Eng
59C3 Rožňava Slovakia
46B2 Rozoy France
61F3 Rtishchevo Russian Fed
99D3 Ruaha Nat Pk Tanz
110C1 Ruahine Range Mts NZ
110C1 Ruapehu,Mt NZ
65D3 Rub al Khāli Desert S Arabia
44A3 Rubha Hunish Scot
35A2 Rubinéia Brazil
65K4 Rubtsovsk Russian Fed
12C2 Ruby USA
91C4 Rudan Iran
90A2 Rūdbar Iran
69F2 Rudnaya Pristan' Russian Fed
54B2 Rudoka Planina Mt Macedonia
72E3 Rudong China
14B1 Rudyard USA
46A1 Rue France
48C2 Ruffec France
34C2 Rufino Arg
97A3 Rufisque Sen
100B2 Rufunsa Zambia
43D3 Rugby Eng
39G8 Rügen I Germany
56B2 Ruhr R Germany
73D4 Ruijin China
54B2 Rujen Mt Bulg/Macedonia
99D3 Rukwa L Tanz
44A3 Rum I Scot
54A1 Ruma Serbia, Yugos
91A4 Rumāh S Arabia
98C2 Rumbek Sudan
26C2 Rum Cay I Caribbean S
47A2 Rumilly France
106C2 Rum Jungle Aust
101C2 Rumphi Malawi
111B2 Runanga NZ
110C1 Runaway,C NZ
100C3 Rundi R Zim
100A2 Rundu Namibia
99D3 Rungwa Tanz
99D3 Rungwa R Tanz
99D3 Rungwe Mt Tanz
82C2 Ruoqiang China
68C2 Ruo Shui R China
54C1 Rupea Rom
74C4 Rupert R Can
46D1 Rur R Germany
32D6 Rurrenabaque Bol
101C2 Rusape Zim
54C2 Ruse Bulg
18B1 Rushville Illinois, USA
108B3 Rushworth Aust
19A3 Rusk USA
17B2 Ruskin USA
110B1 Russell NZ
18C2 Russellville Arkansas, USA
18C2 Russellville Kentucky, USA
21A2 Russian R USA
62C3 Russian Fed Asia/Europe
93E1 Rustavi Georgia
101G1 Rustenburg S Africa
19B3 Ruston USA
99C3 Rutana Burundi
46E1 Rüthen Germany
23B2 Rutla Mexico
15D2 Rutland USA
84D2 Rutog China
Ruvu = Pangani

101D2 Ruvuma R Tanz/Mozam
99D2 Ruwenzori Range Mts Uganda/Zaire
101C2 Ruya R Zim
59B3 Ružomberok Slovakia
99C3 Rwanda Republic, Africa
60E3 Ryazan' Russian Fed
61F3 Ryazhsk Russian Fed
60E2 Rybinsk Russian Fed
60E2 Rybinskoye Vodokhranilishche Res Russian Fed
13D1 Rycroft Can
43D4 Ryde Eng
43E4 Rye Eng
20C2 Rye Patch Res USA
60D3 Ryl'sk Russian Fed
61G4 Ryn Peski Desert Kazakhstan
74D3 Ryōtsu Japan
59D3 Ryskany Moldova
69E4 Ryūkyū Retto Arch Japan
59C2 Rzeszów Pol
60D2 Rzhev Russian Fed

S

91B3 Sa'ādatābād Iran
56C2 Saale R Germany
47B1 Saanen Switz
46D2 Saar R Germany
46D2 Saarbrücken Germany
56B3 Saarburg Germany
39J7 Saaremaa I Estonia
46D2 Saarland State, Germany
46D2 Saarlouis Germany
34C3 Saavedra Arg
54A2 Šabac Serbia, Yugos
51C1 Sabadell Spain
75B1 Sabae Japan
78D1 Sabah State, Malay
26C4 Sabanalarga Colombia
70B3 Sabang Indon
87C1 Sabari R India
94B2 Sabastiya Israel
32D2 Sabaya Bol
93C3 Sab'Bi'ār Syria
94C2 Sabhā Jordan
95A2 Sabhā Libya
24B2 Sabinas Mexico
24B2 Sabinas Hidalgo Mexico
19A3 Sabine R USA
19B4 Sabine L USA
91B5 Sabkhat Maţţi Salt Marsh UAE
94A3 Sabkhet El Bardawil Lg Egypt
79B3 Sablayan Phil
7D5 Sable,I C Can
17B2 Sable,C USA
7D5 Sable I Can
90C2 Sabzevār Iran
20C1 Sacajawea Peak USA
10A1 Sackville Can
57C2 Sachsen State, Germany
56C2 Sachsen-Anhalt State, Germany
4F2 Sachs Harbour Can
47B1 Säckingen Germany
22B1 Sacramento USA
22B1 Sacramento R USA
21A1 Sacramento R USA
9C3 Sacramento Mts USA
81C4 Sa'dah Yemen
54B2 Sadanski Bulg
82D3 Sadiya India
50A2 Sado R Port
74D3 Sado-shima I Japan
85D3 Sādri India
Safad = Zefat
84A2 Safed Koh Mts Afghan
39G7 Saffle Sweden
92C3 Safi Jordan
96B1 Safi Mor

St Francis,C

90D3 Safidabeh Iran
94C1 Şāfītā Syria
93E3 Safwān Iraq
75A2 Saga Japan
76B1 Sagaing Burma
75B2 Sagami-nada B Japan
85D4 Sagar India
16C2 Sag Harbor USA
14B2 Saginaw USA
14B2 Saginaw B USA
26B2 Sagua de Tánamo Cuba
26B2 Sagua la Grande Cuba
7C5 Saguenay R Can
51B2 Sagunto Spain
94C3 Sahab Jordan
50A1 Sahagún Spain
96C2 Sahara Desert N Africa
84D3 Saharanpur India
84C2 Sahiwal Pak
93D3 Şahrā al Hijārah Desert Region Iraq
23A1 Sahuayo Mexico
107D1 Saibai I Aust
96C1 Saïda Alg
94B2 Sāida Leb
91B2 Sa'īdābād Iran
51B2 Saidia Spain
86B1 Saidpur India
84C2 Saidu Pak
75A1 Saigō Japan
Saigon = Ho Chi Minh
86C2 Saiha India
68D2 Saihan Tal China
75A2 Saijo Japan
74C4 Saiki Japan
42C2 St Abb's Head Pt Scot
43D4 St Albans Eng
15D2 St Albans Vermont, USA
14B3 St Albans West Virginia, USA
43C4 St Albans Head C Eng
13E2 St Albert Can
46B1 St Amand-les-Eaux France
47A2 St Amand-Mont Rond France
17C2 St Andrew B USA
44C3 St Andrews Scot
17B1 St Andrew Sd USA
27H1 St Ann's Bay Jamaica
7E4 St Anthony Can
108B3 St Arnaud Aust
17D1 St Augustine USA
43B4 St Austell Eng
46D2 St-Avold France
42C2 St Bees Head Pt Eng
47B2 St-Bonnet France
43B4 St Brides B Wales
48B2 St-Brieuc France
15C2 St Catharines Can
27M2 St Catherine,Mt Grenada
17B1 St Catherines I USA
43D4 St Catherines Pt Eng
49C2 St Chamond France
18B2 St Charles Missouri, USA
14B2 St Clair USA
14B2 St Clair,L Can/USA
14B2 St Clair Shores USA
49D2 St Claud France
10A2 St Cloud USA
47B1 St Croix Switz
27E3 St Croix I Caribbean S
43B4 St Davids Head Pt Wales
16B2 St Denis France
101E3 St Denis Réunion
46E2 St Dizier France
12F2 St Elias,Mt USA
12G2 St Elias Mts Can
48B2 Saintes France
49C2 St Étienne France
18B2 St Francis R USA
100B4 St Francis,C S Africa

St Gallen

47C1 **St Gallen** Switz
48C3 **St-Gaudens** France
109C1 **St George** Aust
17B1 **St George** South Carolina, USA
9B3 **St George** Utah, USA
17B2 **St George I** Florida, USA
20B2 **St George,Pt** USA
15D1 **St-Georges** Can
27E4 **St George's** Grenada
45C3 **St George's Chan** Irish Rep/Wales
46A2 **St Germain-en-Laye** France
47B2 **St-Gervais** France
47C1 **St Gotthard** *P* Switz
43B4 **St Govans Head** *Pt* Wales
22A1 **St Helena** USA
103H5 **St Helena** *I* Atlantic O
100A4 **St Helena** S Africa
17B1 **St Helena Sd** USA
109C4 **St Helens** Aust
42C3 **St Helens** Eng
20B1 **St Helens,** USA
20B1 **St Helens,Mt** USA
48B2 **St Helier** Jersey
47B1 **St Hippolyte** France
46C1 **St-Hubert** Belg
7C5 **St-Hyacinthe** Can
14B1 **St Ignace** USA
43B4 **St Ives** Eng
18B2 **St James** Missouri, USA
5E4 **St James,C** Can
15D1 **St Jean** Can
48B2 **St Jean d'Angely** France
47B2 **St-Jean-de-Maurienne** France
10C2 **St Jean,L** Can
15D1 **St-Jérôme** Can
20C1 **St Joe** *R* USA
7D5 **Saint John** Can
7E5 **St John's** Can
14B2 **St Johns** Michigan, USA
17B2 **St Johns** USA
15D2 **St Johnsbury** USA
15D1 **St Joseph** Can
19B3 **St Joseph** Louisiana, USA
14A2 **St Joseph** Michigan, USA
18B2 **St Joseph** Missouri, USA
27L1 **St Joseph** Trinidad
14B2 **St Joseph** *R* USA
14B1 **St Joseph I** Can
7A4 **St Joseph,L** Can
47B1 **St Julien** France
48C2 **St-Junien** France
46B2 **St-Just-en-Chaussée** France
4B2 **St Kilda** *I* Scot
27E3 **St Kitts-Nevis** *Is* Caribbean S
47A1 **St-Laurent** France
7D5 **St Lawrence** *R* Can
7D5 **Saint Lawrence,G of** Can
4A3 **St Lawrence I** USA
15C2 **St Lawrence Seaway** Can/USA
48B2 **St Lô** France
97A3 **St Louis** Sen
11A3 **St Louis** USA
27E4 **St Lucia** *I* Caribbean S
101H1 **St Lucia,L** S Africa
44E1 **St Magnus** *B* Scot
48B2 **St Malo** France
20C1 **St Maries** USA
27E3 **St Martin** *I* Caribbean S
108A2 **St Mary Peak** *Mt* Aust
109C4 **St Marys** Aust
15C2 **St Marys** USA
17B1 **St Marys** *R* USA

46C2 **Ste-Menehould** France
12B2 **St Michael** USA
16A3 **St Michaels** USA
47B2 **St-Michel** France
46C2 **St-Mihiel** France
47C1 **St Moritz** Switz
48B2 **St-Nazaire** France
46C1 **St-Niklaas** Belg
46B1 **St-Omer** France
13E2 **St Paul** Can
10A2 **St Paul** Minnesota, USA
97A4 **St Paul** *R* Lib
17B2 **St Petersburg** USA
7E5 **St Pierre** Can
15D1 **St Pierre,L** Can
46B1 **St-Pol-Sur-Ternoise** France
59B3 **St Pölten** Austria
46B2 **St Quentin** France
49D3 **St Raphaël** France
101D2 **St Sébastien** *C* Madag
17B1 **St Simons I** USA
17B1 **St Stephen** USA
14B2 **St Thomas** Can
49D3 **St-Tropez** France
46C1 **St Truiden** Belg
46A1 **St-Valéry-sur-Somme** France
27E4 **St Vincent and the Grenadines** *Is* Caribbean S
108A2 **St Vincent,G** *I* Aust
46D1 **St-Vith** Germany
46D2 **St Wendel** Germany
71F2 **Saipan** *I* Pacific O
84B2 **Sayābād** Afghan
30C2 **Sajama** *Mt* Bol
74D4 **Sakai** Japan
75A2 **Sakaidi** Japan
75A1 **Sakaiminato** Japan
93D4 **Sakākah** S Arabia
10C1 **Sakami,L** Can
100B2 **Sakania** Zaire
101D3 **Sakaraha** Madag
60D5 **Sakarya** *R* Turk
58C1 **Sakasleja** Latvia
74D3 **Sakata** Japan
97C4 **Sakété** Benin
69G1 **Sakhalin** *I* Russian Fed
69E4 **Sakishima gunto** *Is* Japan
97A4 **Sal** *I* Cape Verde
61F4 **Sal** *R* Russian Fed
39H7 **Sala** Sweden
34D3 **Saladillo** Arg
34C2 **Saladillo** *R* Arg
34D3 **Salado** *R* Buenos Aires, Arg
34B3 **Salado** *R* Mendoza/San Luis, Arg
30D4 **Salado** *R* Santa Fe, Arg
97B4 **Salaga** Ghana
76C3 **Sala Hintoun** Camb
98B1 **Salal** Chad
93D4 **Şalalah** Oman
34A2 **Salamanca** Chile
23A1 **Salamanca** Mexico
50A1 **Salamanca** Spain
15C2 **Salamanca** USA
98B2 **Salamat** *R* Chad
71F4 **Salamaua** PNG
15C2 **Salamonica** USA
78D1 **Salang** Indon
38H5 **Salangen** Nor
30C3 **Salar de Arizaro** Arg
30C3 **Salar de Atacama** *Salt Pan* Chile
30C2 **Salar de Coipasa** *Salt Pan* Bol
30C3 **Salar de Uyuni** *Salt Pan* Bol
47C2 **Salsomaggiore** Italy
61J3 **Salavat** Russian Fed
70D4 **Salayar** Indon
105L5 **Sala y Gomez** *I* Pacific O
34C3 **Salazar** Arg
48C2 **Salbris** France

12E2 **Salcha** *R* USA
100A4 **Saldanha** S Africa
94C2 **Saldhad** Syria
34C3 **Saldungaray** Arg
58C1 **Saldus** Latvia
109C3 **Sale** Aust
18C2 **Salem** Illinois, USA
87B2 **Salem** India
16D1 **Salem** Massachusetts, USA
16B3 **Salem** New Jersey, USA
20B2 **Salem** Oregon, USA
78C4 **Salembu Besar** *I* Indon
39G6 **Salen** Sweden
53B2 **Salerno** Italy
42C3 **Salford** Eng
54A1 **Salgót** Hung
59B3 **Salgótarjan** Hung
31D3 **Salgueiro** Brazil
55C3 **Salihli** Turk
101C2 **Salima** Malawi
39K6 **Salimaa** *L* Fin
18A2 **Salina** Kansas, USA
53B3 **Salina** *I* Italy
23B2 **Salina Cruz** Mexico
30C3 **Salina de Arizato** Arg
34B3 **Salina Grande** *Salt pan* Arg
34B2 **Salina La Antigua** *Salt pan* Arg
35C1 **Salinas** Brazil
22B2 **Salinas** USA
22B2 **Salinas** *R* USA
34B3 **Salinas de Llancanelo** *Salt Pan* Arg
34B2 **Salinas Grandes** *Salt Pan* Arg
19B3 **Saline** *R* Arkansas, USA
27M2 **Salines,Pt** Grenada
31B2 **Salinópolis** Brazil
47A1 **Salins** France
43D4 **Salisbury = Harare**
15C3 **Salisbury** Maryland, USA
6C3 **Salisbury I** Can
43D4 **Salisbury Plain** Eng
38K5 **Salla** Fin
47B2 **Sallanches** France
18B2 **Sallisaw** USA
6C3 **Salluit** Can
86A1 **Sallyana** Nepal
93D2 **Salmas** Iran
38L6 **Salmi** Russian Fed
20C1 **Salmo** Can
13D2 **Salmon Arm** Can
8B2 **Salmon River Mts** USA
39J6 **Salo** Fin
47D2 **Salò** Italy
49D3 **Salon-de-Provence** France
Salonica = Thessaloniki
54B1 **Salonta** Rom
38K6 **Salpausselka** Region, Fin
34B2 **Salsacate** Arg
61F4 **Sal'sk** Russian Fed
94B2 **Salt** Jordan
30C3 **Salta** Arg
30C3 **Salta** State, Arg
22B2 **Saltillo** Mexico
8B2 **Salt Lake City** USA
34C2 **Salto** Arg
34D2 **Salto** Urug
32C3 **Salto Angostura** *Waterfall* Colombia
35D1 **Salto da Divisa** Brazil
33E2 **Salto del Angel** *Waterfall* Ven
30E3 **Salto del Guaira** *Waterfall* Brazil
32C4 **Salto Grande** *Waterfall* Colombia
84C2 **Salt Range** *Mts* Pak
27H2 **Salt River** Jamaica
17B1 **Saluda** USA
47B2 **Saluzzo** Italy

31D4 **Salvador** Brazil
19B4 **Salvador,L** USA
23A1 **Salvatierra** Mexico
91B5 **Salwah** Qatar
76B1 **Salween** *R* Burma
93E2 **Sal'yany** Azerbaijan
57C3 **Salzburg** Austria
56C2 **Salzgitter** Germany
56C2 **Salzwedel** Germany
68B1 **Samagaltay** Russian Fed
79B4 **Samales Group** *Is* Phil
27D3 **Samaná** Dom Rep
92C2 **Samandaği** Turk
84B1 **Samangan** Afghan
79C3 **Samar** *I* Phil
65G4 **Samara** Russian Fed
107E2 **Samarai** PNG
78D3 **Samarinda** Indon
80E2 **Samarkand** Uzbekistan
93D3 **Sāmarrā'** Iraq
79B3 **Samar S** Phil
86A2 **Sambalpur** India
78B2 **Sambas** Indon
101E2 **Sambava** Madag
84D3 **Sambhal** India
78D3 **Sambhar** Indon
59C3 **Sambor** Ukraine
46B1 **Sambre** *R* France
74B3 **Samch'ŏk** S Korea
99D3 **Same** Tanz
47C1 **Samedan** Switz
46A1 **Samer** France
100B2 **Samfya** Zambia
76A1 **Samka** Burma
76C1 **Sam Neua** Laos
55C3 **Sámos** *I* Greece
55C2 **Samothráki** *I* Greece
34C2 **Sampacho** Arg
78A3 **Sampaga** Indon
78C3 **Sampit** Indon
78C3 **Sampit** *R* Indon
19B3 **Sam Rayburn Res** USA
76C3 **Samrong** Camb
56C1 **Samsø** *I* Den
92C1 **Samsun** Turk
97B3 **San** Mali
76D3 **San** *R* Camb
59C2 **San** *R* Pol
81C4 **Şan'ā'** Yemen
98B2 **Sanaga** *R* Cam
34C2 **San Agustin** Arg
79C4 **San Agustin,C** Phil
90A2 **Sanandaj** Iran
22B1 **San Andreas** USA
25C3 **San Andrés Tuxtla** Mexico
9C3 **San Angelo** USA
53A3 **San Antioco** Sardegna
53A3 **San Antioco** *I* Medit S
34A2 **San Antonio** Chile
9C3 **San Antonio** New Mexico, USA
79B2 **San Antonio** Phil
9D4 **San Antonio** *R* Texas, USA
51C2 **San Antonio Abad** Spain
25D2 **San Antonio,C** Cuba
26A2 **San Antonio de los Banos** Cuba
22D3 **San Antonio,Mt** USA
29C4 **San Antonio Oeste** Arg
34D3 **San Agustín** Arg
34B2 **San Agustin de Valle Féril** Arg
85D4 **Sanawad** India
23A1 **San Bartolo** Mexico
24A3 **San Benedicto** *I* Mexico
22B2 **San Benito** *R* USA
22B2 **San Benito Mt** USA
22D3 **San Bernardino** USA
34A2 **San Bernardo** Chile
17A2 **San Blas,C** USA
34A3 **San Carlos** Chile
32A1 **San Carlos** Nic
79B2 **San Carlos** Phil

29B4 **San Carlos de Bariloche** Arg
69E4 **San-chung** Taiwan
61G2 **Sanchursk** Russian Fed
34A3 **San Clemente** Chile
22D4 **San Clemente** *I* USA
21B3 **San Clemente I** USA
34C2 **San Cristóbal** Arg
25C3 **San Cristóbal** Mexico
32C2 **San Cristóbal** Ven
32J7 **San Cristóbal** */* Ecuador
107F2 **San Cristobal** */* Solomon Is
25E2 **Sancti Spiritus** Cuba
78C3 **Sandai** Indon
70C3 **Sandakan** Malay
44C2 **Sanday** */* Scot
9C3 **Sanderson** USA
13F1 **Sandfly L** Can
21B3 **San Diego** USA
92B2 **Sandikli** Turk
84B3 **Sandila** India
39F7 **Sandnes** Nor
38G5 **Sandnessjøen** Nor
98C3 **Sandoa** Zaïre
59C2 **Sandomierz** Pol
38D3 **Sandoy** Føroyar
20C1 **Sandpoint** USA
49D2 **Sandrio** Italy
18A2 **Sand Springs** USA
106A3 **Sandstone** Aust
73C4 **Sandu** China
14B2 **Sandusky** USA
39H6 **Sandviken** Sweden
7A4 **Sandy L** Can
34C2 **San Elcano** Arg
9B3 **San Felipe** Baja Cal, Mexico
34A2 **San Felipe** Chile
34A2 **San Felipe** Guanajuato, Mexico
27D4 **San Felipe** Ven
51C1 **San Feliu de Guixols** Spain
28A5 **San Felix** */* Pacific O
34A2 **San Fernando** Chile
79B2 **San Fernando** Phil
79B2 **San Fernando** Phil
50A2 **San Fernando** Spain
27E4 **San Fernando** Trinidad
22C3 **San Fernando** USA
32D2 **San Fernando** Ven
17B2 **Sanford** Florida, USA
12F2 **Sanford,Mt** USA
34C2 **San Francisco** Arg
27C3 **San Francisco** Dom Rep
22A2 **San Francisco** USA
22A2 **San Francisco B** USA
24B2 **San Francisco del Oro** Mexico
23A1 **San Francisco del Rincon** Mexico
22D3 **San Gabriel Mts** USA
85C5 **Sangameri** India
18C2 **Sangamon** *R* USA
71F2 **Sangan** */* Pacific O
87B1 **Sangaréddi** India
78D4 **Sangeang** */* Indon
22C2 **Sanger** USA
72C2 **Sanggan He** *R* China
78C2 **Sanggau** Indon
98B2 **Sangha** *R* Congo
85B3 **Sanghar** Pak
76B2 **Sangkha Buri** Thai
78D2 **Sangkulirang** Indon
87A1 **Sängli** India
98B2 **Sangmélima** Cam
9B3 **San Gorgonio Mt** USA
9C3 **Sangre de Cristo** *Mts* USA
34C2 **San Gregorio** Arg
22A2 **San Gregorio** USA
84D2 **Sangrür** India
30E4 **San Ignacio** Arg
79B3 **San Isidro** Phil
32B2 **San Jacinto** Colombia
21B3 **San Jacinto Peak** *Mt* USA

34A3 **San Javier** Chile
34D2 **San Javier** Sante Fe, Arg
74D3 **Sanjō** */* Japan
31C6 **São João del Rei** Brazil
22B2 **San Joaquin** *R* USA
22B2 **San Joaquin Valley** USA
32A1 **San José** Costa Rica
25C3 **San José** Guatemala
79B2 **San Jose** Luzon, Phil
79B3 **San Jose** Mindoro, Phil
22B2 **San Jose** USA
34B2 **San José** */* Mexico
30D2 **San José de Chiquitos** Bol
34D2 **San José de Feliciano** Arg
34B2 **San José de Jachal** Arg
34C2 **San José de la Dormida** Arg
31B6 **San José do Rio Prêto** Brazil
24B2 **San José del Cabo** Mexico
34B2 **San Juan** Arg
27D3 **San Juan** Puerto Rico
34B2 **San Juan** State, Arg
27L1 **San Juan** Trinidad
32D2 **San Juan** Ven
26B2 **San Juan** *Mt* Cuba
8C3 **San Juan** *Mts* USA
34B2 **San Juan** *R* Arg
23B2 **San Juan** *R* Mexico
34B2 **San Juan** *R* Nic/ Costa Rica
23B2 **San Juan Bautista** Arg
30E4 **San Juan Bautista** Par
22B2 **San Juan Bautista** USA
25D3 **San Juan del Norte** Nic
27D4 **San Juan de los Cayos** Ven
23A1 **San Juan de loz Lagoz** Mexico
23A1 **San Juan del Rio** Mexico
25D3 **San Juan del Sur** Nic
20B1 **San Juan Is** USA
23A1 **San Juan Tepozcolula** Mexico
29C5 **San Julián** Arg
34C2 **San Justo** Arg
60D2 **Sankt-Peterburg** Russian Fed
98C3 **Sankuru** *R* Zaïre
22A2 **San Leandro** USA
93C2 **Sanliurfa** Turk
32B3 **San Lorenzo** Ecuador
34C2 **San Lorenzo** Arg
22B2 **San Lucas** USA
34B2 **San Luis** Arg
34B2 **San Luis** State, Arg
23A1 **San Luis de la Paz** Mexico
21A2 **San Luis Obispo** USA
23A1 **San Luis Potosi** Mexico
22B2 **San Luis Res** USA
53A3 **Sanluri** Sardegna
34C2 **San Maigualida** *Mts* Ven
34D3 **San Manuel** Arg
34A2 **San Marcos** Chile
23B2 **San Marcos** Mexico
52B2 **San Marino** Republic, Europe
34B2 **San Martin** Mendoza, Arg
112C3 **San Martin** *Base* Ant
47D1 **San Martino di Castroza** Italy
23B2 **San Martin Tuxmelucan** Mexico
22A2 **San Mateo** USA
30E2 **San Matias** Bol
72C3 **Sanmenxia** China

25D3 **San Miguel** El Salvador
22B3 **San Miguel** */* USA
23A1 **San Miguel del Allende** Mexico
34D3 **San Miguel del Monte** Arg
30C4 **San Miguel de Tucumán** Arg
73D4 **Sanming** China
9B3 **San Nicolas** */* USA
34C2 **San Nicolás de los Arroyos** Arg
101G1 **Sannieshof** S Africa
97B4 **Sanniquellie** Lib
59C3 **Sanok** Pol
26B5 **San Onofre** Colombia
22D4 **San Onofre** USA
79B3 **San Pablo** Phil
22A1 **San Pablo B** USA
34D2 **San Pedro** Buenos Aires, Arg
97B4 **San Pédro** Ivory Coast
30D3 **San Pedro** Jujuy, Arg
30E3 **San Pedro** Par
22C4 **San Pedro Chan** USA
9C4 **San Pedro de los Colonias** Mexico
25D3 **San Pedro Sula** Honduras
53A3 **San Pietro** */* Medit S
24A1 **San Quintin** Mexico
34B2 **San Rafael** Arg
22A2 **San Rafael** USA
22C3 **San Rafael Mts** USA
49D3 **San Remo** Italy
34D2 **San Salvador** */* Arg
26C2 **San Salvador** */* Caribbean S
32J7 **San Salvador** */* Ecuador
30C3 **San Salvador de Jujuy** Arg
51B1 **San Sebastian** Spain
53C2 **San Severo** Italy
30C2 **Santa Ana** Bol
25C3 **Santa Ana** Guatemala
22D4 **Santa Ana** USA
22D4 **Santa Ana** USA
34A3 **Santa Ana** Chile
24B2 **Santa Barbara** Mexico
22C3 **Santa Barbara** USA
22C4 **Santa Barbara** */* USA
22B3 **Santa Barbara Chan** USA
22C3 **Santa Barbara Res** USA
22C4 **Santa Catalina** */* USA
22C4 **Santa Catalina,G of** USA
30F4 **Santa Catarina** State, Brazil
26B2 **Santa Clara** Cuba
22B2 **Santa Clara** USA
22C3 **Santa Clara** *R* USA
29C6 **Santa Cruz** Arg
30D2 **Santa Cruz** Bol
34A2 **Santa Cruz** Chile
79B3 **Santa Cruz** Phil
29B5 **Santa Cruz** State, Arg
22A2 **Santa Cruz** USA
22D4 **Santa Cruz** USA
35D1 **Santa Cruz Cabralia** Brazil
22C3 **Santa Cruz Chan** USA
96A2 **Santa Cruz de la Palma** Canary Is
26B2 **Santa Cruz del Sur** Cuba
96A2 **Santa Cruz de Tenerife** Canary Is
100B2 **Santa Cruz do Cuando** Angola
35B2 **Santa Cruz do Rio Pardo** Brazil
22A2 **Santa Cruz Mts** USA
34D2 **Santa Elena** Arg

33E3 **Santa Elena** Ven
34C2 **Santa Fe** Arg
34C2 **Santa Fe** State, Arg
9C3 **Santa Fe** USA
35A1 **Santa Helena de Goiás** Brazil
73B3 **Santai** China
29B6 **Santa Inés** */* Chile
34B3 **Santa Isabel** La Pampa, Arg
34C2 **Santa Isabel** Sante Fe, Arg
107E1 **Santa Isabel** */* Solomon Is
21A2 **Santa Lucia** *Ra* USA
21A2 **Santa Lucia Range** *Mts* USA
97A4 **Santa Luzia** */* Cape Verde
9B4 **Santa Margarita** */* Mexico
22D4 **Santa Margarita** *R* USA
30F4 **Santa Maria** Brazil
26C4 **Santa Maria** Colombia
21A3 **Santa Maria** Arg
96A1 **Santa Maria** */* Açores
23B1 **Santa Maria** *R* Queretaro, Mexico
23A1 **Santa Maria del Rio** Mexico
32C1 **Santa Marta** Colombia
22A2 **Santa Monica** USA
22C4 **Santa Monica B** USA
29E2 **Santana do Livramento** Brazil
32B3 **Santander** Colombia
50B1 **Santander** Spain
51C2 **Santañy** Spain
22C3 **Santa Paula** USA
31C2 **Santa Quitéria** Brazil
33G4 **Santarém** Brazil
50A2 **Santarém** Port
22A1 **Santa Rosa** California, USA
22A1 **Santa Rosa** Honduras
34C3 **Santa Rosa** La Pampa, Arg
34B2 **Santa Rosa** Mendoza, Arg
34B2 **Santa Rosa** San Luis, Arg
22B3 **Santa Rosa** */* USA
24A2 **Santa Rosalia** Mexico
20C2 **Santa Rosa Range** *Mts* USA
31D3 **Santa Talhada** Brazil
35C1 **Santa Teresa** Brazil
53A2 **Santa Teresa di Gallura** Sardegna
22B3 **Santa Ynez** *R* USA
22B3 **Santa Ynez Mts** USA
17C1 **Santee** *R* USA
47C2 **Santhia** Italy
34A2 **Santiago** Chile
27C3 **Santiago** Dom Rep
32A2 **Santiago** Panama
79B2 **Santiago** Phil
32B4 **Santiago** *R* Peru
50A1 **Santiago de Compostela** Spain
26B2 **Santiago de Cuba** Cuba
30D4 **Santiago del Estero** Arg
30D4 **Santiago del Estero** State, Arg
22D4 **Santiago Peak** *Mt* USA
31C5 **Santo** State, Brazil
35A2 **Santo Anastácio** Brazil
30F4 **Santo Angelo** Brazil
97A4 **Santo Antão** */* Cape Verde
35A2 **Santo Antonio da Platina** Brazil
27D3 **Santo Domingo** Dom Rep

Santos

35B2 **Santos** Brazil
35C2 **Santos Dumont** Brazil
30E4 **Santo Tomé** Arg
29B5 **San Valentin** *Mt* Chile
34A2 **San Vicente** Chile
98B3 **Sanza Pomba** Angola
30E4 **São Borja** Brazil
35B2 **São Carlos** Brazil
33G5 **São Félix** Mato Grosso, Brazil
35C2 **São Fidélis** Brazil
35C1 **São Francisco** Brazil
31D3 **São Francisco** *R* Brazil
30G4 **São Francisco do Sul** Brazil
35B1 **São Gotardo** Brazil
99D3 **Sao Hill** Tanz
35C2 **São João da Barra** Brazil
35B2 **São João da Boa Vista** Brazil
35C1 **São João da Ponte** Brazil
35C2 **São João del Rei** Brazil
35C2 **São Joaquim da Barra** Brazil
96A1 **São Jorge** *I* Açores
35B2 **São José do Rio Prêto** Brazil
35B2 **São José dos Campos** Brazil
31C2 **São Luís** Brazil
35C1 **São Marcos** *R* Brazil
35C1 **São Maria do Suaçui** Brazil
35D1 **São Mateus** Brazil
35C2 **São Mateus** *R* Brazil
96A1 **São Miguel** *I* Açores
49C2 **Saône** *R* France
97A4 **São Nicolau** *I* Cape Verde
35B2 **São Paulo** Brazil
35A2 **São Paulo** State, Brazil
31C3 **São Raimundo Nonato** Brazil
35B1 **São Romão** Brazil
35B2 **São Sebastia do Paraiso** Brazil
35A1 **São Simão** Goias, Brazil
35B2 **São Simão** Sao Paulo, Brazil
97A4 **São Tiago** *I* Cape Verde
97C4 **São Tomé** *I* W Africa
97C4 **São Tomé and Principe** Republic, W Africa
96B2 **Saoura** *Watercourse* Alg
35B2 **São Vicente** Brazil
97A4 **São Vicente** *I* Cape Verde
55C2 **Sápai** Greece
78D4 **Sape** Indon
97C4 **Sapele** Nig
74E2 **Sapporo** Japan
53C2 **Sapri** Italy
18A2 **Sapulpa** USA
90A2 **Saqqez** Iran
10C2 **Saquenay** *R* Can
90A2 **Sarab** Iran
54A2 **Sarajevo** Bosnia-Herzegovina
90D2 **Sarakhs** Iran
61J3 **Saraktash** Russian Fed
63A2 **Sarala** Russian Fed
15D2 **Saranac L** USA
15D2 **Saranac Lake** USA
55B3 **Sarandë** Alb
79C4 **Sarangani Is** Phil
61G3 **Saransk** Russian Fed
61H2 **Sarapul** Russian Fed
17B2 **Sarasota** USA
54C1 **Sarata** Ukraine
15D2 **Saratoga Springs** USA

78C2 **Saratok** Malay
61G3 **Saratov** Russian Fed
61G3 **Saratovskoye Vodokhranilishche** *Res* Russian Fed
67F4 **Sarawak** State, Malay
92A2 **Saraykoy** Turk
90C3 **Sarbisheh** Iran
47D1 **Sarca** *R* Italy
95A2 **Sardalas** Libya
90A2 **Sar Dasht** Iran
52A2 **Sardegna** *I* Medit S
Sardinia = Sardegna
38H5 **Sarektjåkkå** *Mt* Sweden
84C2 **Sargodha** Pak
98B2 **Sarh** Chad
90B2 **Sāri** Iran
93D1 **Sarida** *R* Isreal
93D1 **Sarikamiş** Turk
107D3 **Sarina** Aust
47B1 **Sarine** *R* Switz
84B1 **Sar-i-Pul** Afghan
95B2 **Sarir** Libya
95A2 **Sarir Tibesti** *Desert* Libya
74B3 **Sariwŏn** N Korea
48B2 **Sark** *I* UK
92C2 **Sarkişla** Turk
71E4 **Sarmi** Indon
29C5 **Sarmiento** Arg
39G6 **Särna** Sweden
47C1 **Sarnen** Switz
14B2 **Sarnia** Can
58D2 **Sarny** Ukraine
6E2 **Saroaq** Greenland
84B2 **Sarobi** Afghan
78A3 **Sarolangun** Indon
55B3 **Saronikós Kólpos** *G* Greece
47C2 **Saronno** Italy
55C2 **Saros Körfezi** *B* Turk
39G7 **Sarpsborg** Nor
46D2 **Sarralbe** France
46D2 **Sarrebourg** France
46D2 **Sarreguemines** France
46D2 **Sarre-Union** France
51B1 **Sarrion** Spain
85B3 **Sartanahu** Pak
53A2 **Sartène** Corse
48B2 **Sarthe** *R* France
61H4 **Sarykamys** Kazakhstan
65H5 **Sarysu** *R* Kazakhstan
86A2 **Sasarām** India
74B4 **Sasebo** Japan
5H4 **Saskatchewan** Province, Can
5H4 **Saskatchewan** *R* Can
13F2 **Saskatoon** Can
101G1 **Sasolburg** S Africa
61F3 **Sasovo** Russian Fed
97B4 **Sassandra** Ivory Coast
97B4 **Sassandra** *R* Ivory Coast
53A2 **Sassari** Sardegna
56C2 **Sassnitz** Germany
47D2 **Sassuolo** Italy
53A2 **Sastre** Arg
87A1 **Sātāra** India
4G2 **Satellite B** Can
78D4 **Satengar** *Is* Indon
39H6 **Säter** Sweden
17B1 **Satilla** *R* USA
61J2 **Satka** Russian Fed
84D2 **Satluj** *R* India
86A2 **Satna** India
85C4 **Sātpura Range** *Mts* India
54B1 **Satu Mare** Rom
34D2 **Sauce** Arg
39F7 **Sauda** Nor
80C3 **Saudi Arabia** Kingdom, Arabian Pen
46D2 **Sauer** *R* Germany/Lux
46D1 **Sauerland** Region, Germany
38B1 **Sauðárkrókur** Iceland

14A2 **Saugatuck** USA
16C1 **Saugerties** USA
13B2 **Saugstad,Mt** Can
7B5 **Sault Sainte Marie** Can
14B1 **Sault Ste Marie** Can
14B1 **Sault Ste Marie** USA
71E4 **Saumlaki** Indon
48B2 **Saumur** France
98C3 **Saurimo** Angola
27M2 **Sauteurs** Grenada
54A2 **Sava** *R* Serbia, Yugos
97C4 **Savalou** Benin
17B1 **Savannah** Georgia, USA
17B1 **Savannah** *R* USA
76C2 **Savannakhet** Laos
26B3 **Savanna la Mar** Jamaica
7A4 **Savant Lake** Can
76D2 **Savarane** Laos
97C4 **Savé** Benin
101C3 **Save** *R* Mozam
90B3 **Sāveh** Iran
46D2 **Saverne** France
47B2 **Savigliano** Italy
46B2 **Savigny** France
49D2 **Savoie** *Region* France
49D3 **Savona** Italy
38K6 **Savonlinna** Fin
4A3 **Savoonga** USA
38K5 **Savukoski** Fin
71D4 **Savu S** Indon
76A1 **Saw** Burma
85D3 **Sawai Mādhopur** India
78A2 **Sawang** Indon
76B2 **Sawankhalok** Thai
75C1 **Sawara** Japan
12E1 **Sawtooth Mt** USA
106B2 **Sawu** *I* Indon
97C3 **Say** Niger
84B1 **Sayghan** Afghan
91B5 **Sayhūt** Yemen
61G4 **Saykhin** Kazakhstan
68D2 **Saynshand** Mongolia
61H5 **Say-Utes** Kazakhstan
16C2 **Sayville** USA
13B2 **Sayward** Can
57C3 **Sázava** *R* Czech Republic
51C2 **Sbisseb** *R* Alg
42C2 **Scafell Pike** *Mt* Eng
44E1 **Scalloway** Scot
44C2 **Scapa Flow** *Sd* Scot
15C2 **Scarborough** Eng
42D2 **Scarborough** Eng
27E4 **Scarborough** Tobago
44A2 **Scarp** *I* Scot
45B2 **Scarriff** Irish Rep
52A1 **Schaffhausen** Switz
57C3 **Scharding** Austria
57C3 **Scharteberg** *Mt* Germany
7D4 **Schefferville** Can
46B1 **Schelde** *R* Belg
10C2 **Schenectady** USA
47D2 **Schio** Italy
46D1 **Schleiden** Germany
56B2 **Schleswig** Germany
56B2 **Schleswig Holstein** State, Germany
16B1 **Schoharie** USA
71F4 **Schouten** *Is* PNG
7B5 **Schreiber** Can
21B2 **Schurz** USA
16B2 **Schuykill Haven** USA
16B2 **Schuylkill** *R* USA
57B3 **Schwäbische Alb** *Upland* Germany
57B3 **Schwarzwald** *Upland* Germany
12C1 **Schwatka Mts** USA
47C1 **Schwaz** Austria
57C2 **Schweinfurt** Germany
101G1 **Schweizer Reneke** S Africa
56C2 **Schwerin** Germany
47C1 **Schwyz** Switz
53B2 **Sciacca** Italy

14B3 **Scioto** *R* USA
109D2 **Scone** Aust
6H2 **Scoresby Sd** Greenland
103F7 **Scotia Ridge** Atlantic O
103F7 **Scotia S** Atlantic O
44B3 **Scotland** Country, UK
112B7 **Scott** *Base* Ant
13B2 **Scott,C** Can
9C2 **Scott City** USA
112C6 **Scott** *I* Ant
6C2 **Scott Inlet** *B* Can
20B2 **Scott,Mt** USA
108B2 **Scott Reef** Timor S
8C2 **Scottsbluff** USA
17A1 **Scottsboro** USA
109C4 **Scottsdale** Aust
10C2 **Scranton** USA
47D1 **Scuol** Switz
Scutari = Shkodër
5J4 **Seal** *R* Can
108B3 **Sea Lake** Aust
18B2 **Searcy** USA
22B2 **Seaside** California, USA
20B1 **Seaside** Oregon, USA
16B3 **Seaside Park** USA
20B1 **Seattle** USA
22A1 **Sebastopol** USA
58D1 **Sebez** Russian Fed
17B2 **Sebring** USA
111A3 **Secretary** *I* NZ
18B2 **Sedalia** USA
18B2 **Sedan** France
111B2 **Seddonville** NZ
94B3 **Sede Boqer** Israel
94B3 **Sederot** Israel
97A3 **Sédhiou** Sen
94B3 **Sedom** Israel
100A3 **Seeheim** Namibia
111B2 **Sefton,Mt** NZ
77C5 **Segamat** Malay
51B2 **Segorbe** Spain
97B3 **Ségou** Mali
Segovia = Coco
51C1 **Segre** *R* Spain
97B4 **Séguéla** Ivory Coast
96A2 **Seguia el Hamra** *Watercourse* Mor
34C2 **Segundo** *R* Arg
78D2 **Seguntur** Indon
50B2 **Segura** *R* Spain
85B3 **Sehwan** Pak
46D2 **Seille** *R* France
38J6 **Seinäjoki** Fin
48C2 **Seine** *R* France
46B2 **Seine-et-Marne** Department, France
99D3 **Sekenke** Tanz
99D1 **Sek'ot'a** Eth
20B1 **Sekiu** USA
71E4 **Selaru** *I* Indon
78D4 **Selat Alas** *Str* Indon
78B3 **Selat Bangka** *Str* Indon
78A3 **Selat Berhala** *B* Indon
71E4 **Selat Dampier** *Str* Indon
78B3 **Selat Gaspar** *Str* Indon
78D4 **Selat Lombok** *Str* Indon
78D4 **Selat Sape** *Str* Indon
78B4 **Selat Sunda** *Str* Indon
71D4 **Selat Wetar** *Chan* Indon
12B1 **Selawik** USA
12C1 **Selawik** *R* USA
12B1 **Selawik L** USA
92C2 **Selçuk** Turk
12D3 **Seldovia** USA
100B3 **Selebi Pikwe** Botswana
6H3 **Selfoss** Iceland
95B2 **Selima Oasis** Sudan
5J4 **Selkirk** Can
42C2 **Selkirk** Scot

13D2 Selkirk Mts Can
22C2 Selma California, USA
50B2 Selouane Mor
12H2 Selous,Mt Can
78B3 Selta Karimata Str Indon
32C5 Selvas Region, Brazil
107D3 Selwyn Aust
4E3 Selwyn Mts Can
78C4 Semarang Indon
61E2 Semenov Russian Fed
12C3 Semidi Is USA
60E3 Semiluki Russian Fed
19A2 Seminole Oklahoma, USA
17B1 Seminole,L USA
65K4 Semipalatinsk Kazakhstan
79B3 Semirara Is Phil
90B3 Semirom Iran
78C2 Semitau Indon
90B2 Semnan Iran
46C2 Semois R Belg
23B2 Sempoala Hist Site, Mexico
32D5 Sena Madureira Brazil
100B2 Senanga Zambia
19C3 Senatobia USA
74E3 Sendai Honshū, Japan
74C4 Sendai Kyūshū, Japan
85D4 Sendwha India
15C2 Seneca Falls USA
97A3 Senegal Republic, Africa
97A3 Sénégal R Maur Sen
101G1 Senekal S Africa
31D4 Senhor do Bonfim Brazil
52B2 Senigallia Italy
52C2 Senj Croatia
69E4 Senkaku Gunto Is Japan
46B2 Senlis France
99D1 Sennar Sudan
7C5 Sennetere Can
49C2 Sens France
54A1 Senta Serbia, Yugos
98C3 Sentery Zaire
58E1 Sentinel Peak Mt Can
85D4 Seoni India
Seoul = Soul
110B2 Separation Pt NZ
76D2 Sepone Laos
7D4 Sept-Îles Can
95A2 Séquédine Niger
21B2 Sequoia Nat Pk, USA
71D4 Seram I Indon
78B4 Serang Indon
78B4 Serasan I Indon
54A2 Serbia Republic, Yugos
61F3 Serdobsk Russian Fed
77C5 Seremban Malay
99D3 Serengeti Nat Pk Tanz
100C2 Serenje Zambia
59D3 Seret R Ukraine
61G2 Sergach Russian Fed
65H3 Sergino Russian Fed
31D4 Sergipe State, Brazil
60E2 Sergiyev Posad Russian Fed
78C2 Seria Brunei
78C2 Serian Malay
55B3 Sérifos I Greece
47C2 Serio R Italy
95B2 Serir Calanscio Desert Libya
46C2 Sermaize-les-Bains France
71D4 Sermata I Indon
61H3 Sernovodsk Russian Fed
65H4 Serov Russian Fed
100B3 Serowe Botswana
50A2 Serpa Port

60E3 Serpukhov Russian Fed
35B2 Serra da Canastra Mts Brazil
50A1 Serra da Estrela Mts Port
35B2 Serra da Mantiqueira Mts Brazil
35A1 Serra da Mombuca Brazil
35C1 Serra do Cabral Mt Brazil
33F5 Serra do Cachimbo Brazil
35A1 Serra do Caiapó Mts Brazil
35A2 Serra do Cantu Mts Brazil
35C2 Serra do Caparaó Mts Brazil
31C5 Serra do Chifre Brazil
35C1 Serra do Espinhaço Mts Brazil
35B2 Serra do Mar Mts Brazil
35B2 Serra do Mirante Mts Brazil
33G3 Serra do Navio Brazil
35B2 Serra do Paranpiacaba Mts Brazil
33F6 Serra dos Caiabis Mts Brazil
35A2 Serra dos Dourados Mts Brazil
33E6 Serra dos Parecis Brazil
35B1 Serra dos Pilões Mts Brazil
35A1 Serra Dourada Mts Brazil
33F6 Serra Formosa Mts Brazil
55B2 Sérrai Greece
25D3 Serrana Bank Is Caribbean S
51B1 Serrana de Cuenca Mts Spain
35A1 Serranópolis Brazil
33E3 Serra Pacaraima Mts Brazil
33E3 Serra Parima Mts Brazil
33G3 Serra Tumucumaque Brazil
46B2 Serre R France
34B2 Serrezuela Arg
31D4 Serrinha Brazil
6G3 Serrmilik Greenland
35C1 Sertania Brazil
35A2 Sertanópolis Brazil
72A3 Sêrtar China
78C3 Seruyan R Indon
100A2 Sesfontein Namibia
100B2 Sesheke Zambia
47B2 Sestriere Italy
74D2 Setana Japan
49C3 Sète France
35C1 Sete Lagoas Brazil
96C1 Sétif Alg
75B1 Seto Japan
75A2 Seto Naikai S Japan
96B1 Settat Mor
42C2 Setté Cama
5G4 Settler Can
50A2 Sétubal Port
93E1 Sevan,Oz L Armenia
60D5 Sevastopol' Ukraine
7B4 Severn R Can
43C3 Severn R Eng
1B9 Severnaya Zemlya I Russian Fed
63C2 Severo-Baykalskoye Nagorye Mts Russian Fed
60E4 Severo Donets Ukraine
64E3 Severodvinsk Russian Fed
64H3 Severo Sos'va R Russian Fed
8B3 Sevier R USA
8B3 Sevier L USA
50A2 Sevilla Spain

Seville = Sevilla
54C2 Sevlievo Bulg
97A4 Sewa R Sierra Leone
12E2 Seward Alaska, USA
18A1 Seward Nebraska, USA
12A1 Seward Pen USA
13D1 Sexsmith Can
89K8 Seychelles Is Indian O
38C1 Seyðisfjörður Iceland
92C2 Seyhan Turk
60E3 Seym R Russian Fed
108C2 Seymour Aust
16C2 Seymour Connecticut, USA
14A3 Seymour Indiana, USA
46B2 Sézanne France
96D1 Sfax Tunisia
54C1 Sfinto Gheorghe Rom
56A2 's-Gravenhage Neth
72B3 Shaanxi Province, China
98C3 Shabunda Zaire
82B2 Shache China
112C9 Shackleton Ice Shelf Ant
85B3 Shadadkot Pak
91B3 Shādhām R Iran
43C4 Shaftesbury Eng
29G8 Shag Rocks Is South Georgia
90A3 Shāhābād Iran
90A2 Shahbā Syria
91C3 Shahdad Iran
86A2 Shahdol India
90A2 Shāhīn Dezh Iran
90C3 Shāh Kūh Iran
91C3 Shahr-e Bābak Iran
Shahresa = Qomisheh
90B3 Shahr Kord Iran
87B1 Shājābād India
84D3 Shājahānpur India
85D4 Shājāpur India
61F4 Shakhty Russian Fed
62H4 Shakhun'ya Russian Fed
97C4 Shaki Nig
12B2 Shaktoolik USA
61J2 Shamary Russian Fed
99D2 Shambe Sudan
16A2 Shamokin USA
16B1 Shandaken USA
72D2 Shandong Province, China
73C5 Shangchuan Dao I China
72C1 Shangdu China
73E3 Shanghai China
72C3 Shangnan China
100B2 Shangombo Zambia
73D4 Shangra China
73B5 Shangsi China
72C3 Shang Xian China
41B3 Shannon R Irish Rep
72D3 Shanqiu China
74B2 Shansonggang China
63F2 Shantarskiye Ostrova I Russian Fed
73D5 Shantou China
72C2 Shanxi Province, China
72D3 Shan Xian China
73C5 Shaoguan China
73E4 Shaoxing China
73C4 Shaoyang China
44C2 Shapinsay I Scot
94C2 Shaqqā Syria
72A1 Sharhulsan Mongolia
90C2 Sharīfābād Iran
91C4 Sharjah UAE
106A3 Shark B Aust
90C2 Sharlauk Turkmenistan
94B2 Sharon,Plain of Israel
61G2 Sharya Russian Fed
99D2 Shashemenē Eth
73C3 Shashi China

20B2 Shasta L USA
20B2 Shasta,Mt USA
93E3 Shaṭṭ al Gharrat R Iraq
94B3 Shaubak Jordan
13F3 Shaunavon Can
22C2 Shaver L USA
16B2 Shawangunk Mt USA
15D1 Shawinigan Can
19A2 Shawnee Oklahoma, USA
73D4 Sha Xian China
106B3 Shay Gap Aust
94C2 Shaykh Miskin Syria
99E1 Shaykh 'Uthmān Yemen
60E3 Shchekino Russian Fed
60E3 Shchigry Russian Fed
60D3 Shchors Ukraine
65J4 Shchuchinsk Kazakhstan
99E2 Shebele R Eth
74A2 Sheboygan USA
98B2 Shebshi Mts Nig
12F1 Sheenjek R USA
45C1 Sheep Haven Estuary Irish Rep
43E4 Sheerness Eng
94B2 Shefar'am Israel
42D3 Sheffield Eng
84C2 Shekhupura Pak
13B1 Shelagyote Peak Mt Can
16C1 Shelburne Falls USA
14A2 Shelby Michigan, USA
8B2 Shelby Montana, USA
14A3 Shelbyville Indiana, USA
12H2 Sheldon,Mt Can
12D3 Shelikof Str USA
109D2 Shellharbour Aust
111A3 Shelter Pt NZ
20B1 Shelton USA
93E1 Shemakha Azerbaijan
18A1 Shenandoah USA
15C3 Shenandoah R USA
15C3 Shenandoah Nat Pk USA
97C4 Shendam Nig
95C2 Shendi Sudan
72C2 Shenmu China
72E1 Shenyang China
73C5 Shenzhen China
85D3 Sheopur India
59D2 Shepetovka Ukraine
108C3 Shepparton Aust
6B2 Sherard,C Can
43C4 Sherborne Eng
97A4 Sherbro I Sierra Leone
15D1 Sherbrooke Can
85C3 Shergarh India
19B3 Sheridan Arkansas, USA
8C2 Sheridan Wyoming, USA
19A3 Sherman USA
56B2 s-Hertogenbosch Neth
12H3 Sheslay Can
40C1 Shetland Is Scot
Shevchenko = Aktau
91B4 Sheyk Sho'eyb I Iran
69H2 Shiashkotan I Russian Fed
84B1 Shibarghan Afghan
74D3 Shibata Japan
95C1 Shibin el Kom Egypt
75B1 Shibukawa Japan
63C2 Shijiazhuang China
84B3 Shikarpur Pak
67G3 Shikoku I Japan
75A2 Shikoku-sanchi Mts Japan
86B1 Shiliguri India
68D1 Shilka Russian Fed
68D1 Shilka R Russian Fed
16B2 Shillington USA
86C1 Shillong India
61F3 Shilovo Russian Fed
75A2 Shimabara Japan

Shimada

75B2 Shimada Japan
69E1 Shimanovsk
    Russian Fed
74D3 Shimizu Japan
84D2 Shimla India
75B2 Shimoda Japan
87B2 Shimoga India
74C4 Shimonoseki Japan
75B1 Shinano R Japan
91C5 Shinas Oman
74D4 Shingū Japan
75C1 Shinjo Japan
74D3 Shinminato Japan
94C1 Shinshār Syria
99D3 Shinyanga Tanz
74E3 Shiogama Japan
75B2 Shiono-misaki C
    Japan
73A5 Shiping China
16A2 Shippensburg USA
72B3 Shiquan China
75C1 Shirakawa Japan
75B1 Shirane-san Mt
    Japan
75B1 Shirani-san Mt
91B4 Shiraz Iran
90B3 Shir Kūh Iran
75B1 Shirotori Japan
90C2 Shīrvān Iran
12A1 Shishmaref USA
12A1 Shishmaref Inlet
    USA
4B3 Shishmaret USA
72B2 Shitanjing China
14A3 Shively USA
85D3 Shivpuri India
94B3 Shivta Hist Site
    Israel
101C2 Shiwa Ngandu
    Zambia
72C3 Shiyan China
72B2 Shizuishan China
75B1 Shizuoka Japan
21B2 Shoshone Mts USA
60D3 Shostka Ukraine
19B3 Shreveport USA
43C3 Shrewsbury Eng
43C3 Shropshire County,
    Eng
72E1 Shuangliao China
69F2 Shuangyashan
    China
61J4 Shubar-Kuduk
    Kazakhstan
72D2 Shu He R China
73A4 Shuicheng China
84C3 Shujaabad Pak
85D4 Shujālpur India
68B2 Shule He China
54C2 Shumen Bulg
61G2 Shumerlya
    Russian Fed
73D4 Shuncheng China
12C1 Shungnak USA
72C2 Shuo Xian China
91C4 Shūr Gaz Iran
100B2 Shurugwi Zim
13D2 Shuswap L Can
61F2 Shuya Russian Fed
12D3 Shuyak I USA
82D3 Shwebo Burma
76B2 Shwegyin Burma
84A2 Siah Koh Mts
    Afghan
84C2 Sialkot Pak
    Sian = Xi'an
79C4 Siaron I Phil
79B4 Siaton Phil
58C1 Šiauliai Lithuania
65G4 Sibay Russian Fed
101H1 Sibayi L S Africa
52C2 Šibenik Croatia
70A4 Siberut I Indon
84B3 Sibi Pak
68C1 Sibirskoye
    Russian Fed
98B3 Sibiti Congo
99D3 Sibiti R Tanz

54B1 Sibiu Rom
70A3 Sibolga Indon
86C1 Sibsāgār India
78C2 Sibu Malay
79B4 Sibuguey B Phil
98B2 Sibut CAR
79B3 Sibuyan I Phil
79B3 Sibuyan S Phil
73A3 Sichuan Province,
    China
53B3 Sicilia I Medit S
53B3 Sicilian Chan Italy/
    Tunisia
    Sicily = Sicilia
32C6 Sicuani Peru
85C4 Siddhapur India
87B1 Siddipet India
86A2 Sidhi India
95B1 Sidi Barrani Egypt
96B1 Sidi Bel Abbès Alg
96B1 Sidi Kacem Mor
44C3 Sidlaw Hills Scot
112B5 Sidley,Mt Ant
20B1 Sidney I Can
8C2 Sidney Nebraska,
    USA
15C2 Sidney New York,
    USA
14B2 Sidney Ohio, USA
17B1 Sidney Lanier,L
    USA
    Sidon = Säida
58C2 Siedlce Pol
46D1 Sieg R Germany
46D1 Siegburg Germany
46D1 Siegen Germany
76C3 Siem Reap Camb
52B2 Siena Italy
58B2 Sierpc Pol
23B2 Sierra Andrés Tuxtla
    Mexico
34B3 Sierra Auca Mahuida
    Mts Arg
9C3 Sierra Blanca USA
51B1 Sierra de Albarracin
    Mts Spain
50B2 Sierra de Alcaraz
    Spain
34B2 Sierra de Cordoba
    Mts Arg
50A1 Sierra de Gredos Mts
    Spain
50A2 Sierra de Guadalupe
    Mts Spain
50B1 Sierra de
    Guadarrama Mts
    Spain
51B1 Sierra de Guara Mts
    Spain
51B1 Sierra de Gudar Mts
    Spain
23B2 Sierra de Juárez
    Mexico
34C3 Sierra de la Ventana
    Mts Arg
51C1 Sierra del Codi Mts
    Spain
34B2 Sierra del Morro Mt
    Arg
34B3 Sierra del Nevado
    Mts Arg
24B2 Sierra de los
    Alamitos Mts
    Mexico
50B2 Sierra de los Filabres
    Spain
23A1 Sierra de los
    Huicholes Mexico
23B2 Sierra de Miahuatlán
    Mexico
23A1 Sierra de Morones
    Mts Mexico
50A2 Sierra de Ronda Mts
    Spain
34B2 Sierra de San Luis
    Mts Arg
50B2 Sierra de Segura Mts
    Spain
50B1 Sierra de Urbion Mts
    Spain
34B2 Sierra de Uspallata
    Mts Arg
34B2 Sierra de Valle Fértil
    Mts Arg

23B2 Sierra de Zongolica
    Mexico
34C2 Sierra Grande Mts
    Arg
97A4 Sierra Leone
    Republic, Africa
97A4 Sierra Leone,C Sierra
    Leone
79B2 Sierra Madre Mts
    Phil
23A2 Sierra Madre del Sur
    Mts Mexico
24B2 Sierra Madre
    Occidental Mts
    Mexico
24C2 Sierra Madre Oriental
    Mts Mexico
34B2 Sierra Malanzan Mts
    Arg
50A2 Sierra Mojada
    Mexico
50A2 Sierra Morena Mts
    Spain
50B2 Sierra Nevada Mts
    Spain
21A2 Sierra Nevada Mts
    USA
32C1 Sierra Nevada de
    Santa Marta Mts
    Colombia
34B2 Sierra Pié de Palo
    Mts Arg
47B1 Sierre Switz
55B3 Sífnos I Greece
59C3 Sighetu Marmaţiei
    Rom
54B1 Sighişoara Rom
87B1 Sigli Indon
38B1 Siglufjörður Iceland
50B1 Sigüenza Spain
97B3 Siguiri Guinea
    Sihanoukville =
    Kompong Som
85E4 Sihora India
93D2 Siirt Turk
68B3 Sikai Hu L China
85D3 Sikar India
84B2 Sikaram Mt Afghan
97B3 Sikasso Mali
18C2 Sikeston USA
55C3 Síkinos I Greece
55B3 Sikionía Greece
86B1 Sikkim State, India
50A1 Sil R Spain
47D1 Silandro Italy
23A1 Silao Mexico
79B3 Silay Phil
86C2 Silchar India
51B1 Silet Alg
86A1 Silgarhi Nepal
92B2 Silifke Turk
82C2 Siling Co L China
54C2 Silistra Bulg
39F7 Silkeborg Den
47E1 Sillian Austria
18B2 Siloam Springs USA
19B3 Silsbee USA
95A3 Siltou Well Chad
58C1 Silute Lithuania
93D2 Silvan Turk
35B1 Silvania Brazil
85C4 Silvassa India
21B2 Silver City Nevada,
    USA
9C3 Silver City New
    Mexico, USA
20B2 Silver Lake USA
16A3 Silver Spring USA
13B2 Silverthrone Mt Can
108B2 Silverton Aust
47C1 Silvretta Mts
    Austria/Switz
78C2 Simanggang Malay
76C1 Simao China
90A3 Simareh R Iran
55C3 Símav Turk
61G3 Simbirsk
    Russian Fed
15C2 Simcoe,L Can
70A3 Simeulue I Indon
60D5 Simferopol' Ukraine
55C3 Sími I Greece
46D1 Simmern Germany
13B2 Simoon Sound Can

49D2 Simplon Mt Switz
47C1 Simplon P Switz
4C2 Simpson,C USA
106C3 Simpson Desert Aust
6B3 Simpson Pen Can
39G7 Simrishamn Sweden
69H2 Simushir I
    Russian Fed
99E2 Sína Dhaqa Somalia
92B4 Sinai Pen Egypt
32B2 Sincelejo Colombia
17B1 Sinclair,L USA
85D3 Sind R India
85B3 Sindh Region, Pak
55C3 Sindirği Turk
86B2 Sindri India
50A2 Sines Port
99D1 Singa Sudan
77C5 Singapore Republic,
    S E Asia
77C5 Singapore,Str of
    S E Asia
78D4 Singaraja Indon
99D3 Singida Tanz
78B2 Singkawang Indon
109O2 Singleton Aust
78A3 Singtep I Indon
76B1 Singu Burma
53A2 Siniscola Sardgena
93D2 Sinjär Iraq
84B2 Sinkai Hills Mts
    Afghan
95C3 Sinkat Sudan
82C1 Sinkiang
    Autonomous Region,
    China
33G2 Sinnamary French
    Guiana
54B1 Sinoe Turk
54B1 Sintana Rom
78C2 Sintang Indon
50A2 Sintra Port
32B2 Sinú R Colombia
74A2 Sinŭiju N Korea
59B3 Siófok Hung
47B1 Sion Switz
8D2 Sioux City USA
8D2 Sioux Falls USA
10A2 Sioux Lookout Can
79B4 Sipalay Phil
27L1 Siparia Trinidad
69E2 Siping China
112B3 Siple Base Ant
112B5 Siple I Ant
79B3 Sipocot Phil
70A4 Sipora Indon
79B4 Siquijor I Phil
87B2 Sira India
53C3 Siracusa Italy
86B2 Sirajganj Bang
13C2 Sir Alexander,Mt Can
91B5 Sir Bani Yäs I UAE
106C2 Sir Edward Pellew
    Group Is Aust
54C1 Siret R Rom
12J2 Sir James
    McBrien,Mt Can
87B2 Sir Kālahasti India
13D2 Sir Laurier,Mt Can
93D2 Şirnak Turk
85C4 Sirohi India
87B1 Sironcha India
85D4 Sironj India
55B3 Síros I Greece
91B4 Sirri I Iran
84D3 Sirsa India
13D2 Sir Sandford,Mt Can
87A2 Sirsi India
95A1 Sirte Desert Libya
95A1 Sirte,G of Libya
52C1 Sisak Croatia
76C2 Sisaket Thai
76C3 Sisophon Camb
46B2 Sissonne France
90D3 Sīstan Region, Iran/
    Afghan
49D3 Sisteron France
63B2 Sistig Khem
    Russian Fed
86A1 Sītāpur India
55C3 Sitía Greece
4E4 Sitka USA
12D3 Sitkalidak I USA
12D3 Sitkinak I USA

178

76B2 **Sittang** R Burma
46C1 **Sittard** Neth
86C2 **Sittwe** Burma
78C4 **Situbondo** Indon
92C2 **Sivas** Turk
93C2 **Siverek** Turk
92B2 **Sivrihisar** Turk
95B2 **Siwa** Egypt
84D2 **Siwalik Range** *Mts* India
86A1 **Siwalik Range** *Mts* Nepal
72D3 **Siyang** China
56C1 **Sjælland** I Den
39G7 **Skagen** Den
39F7 **Skagerrak** *Str* Nor/ Den
20B1 **Skagit** R USA
20B1 **Skagit Mt** Can
4E4 **Skagway** USA
39G7 **Skara** Sweden
59C2 **Skarzysko-Kamienna** Pol
5F4 **Skeena** R Can
13B1 **Skeena** R USA
4D3 **Skeenjek** R USA
42E3 **Skegness** Eng
38H5 **Skellefte** R Sweden
38J6 **Skellefteå** Sweden
55B3 **Skiathos** I Greece
45B3 **Skibbereen** Irish Rep
5E4 **Skidegate** Can
58C2 **Skierniewice** Pol
39F7 **Skien** Nor
96C1 **Skikda** Alg
74C4 **Shikoku** I Japan
42D3 **Skipton** Eng
55B3 **Skiros** I Greece
39F7 **Skive** Den
56B1 **Skjern** Den
6F3 **Skjoldungen** Greenland
14A2 **Skokie** USA
55B3 **Skópelos** I Greece
54B2 **Skopje** Macedonia
39G7 **Skövde** Sweden
63E2 **Skovorodino** Russian Fed
4C3 **Skwentna** USA
58B2 **Skwierzyna** Pol
40B2 **Skye** I Scot
39G7 **Slagelse** Den
45C2 **Slaney** R Irish Rep
54B2 **Slatina** Rom
78C4 **Slaung** Indon
5G3 **Slave** R Can
13E1 **Slave Lake** Can
65J4 **Slavgorod** Russian Fed
59D2 **Slavuta** Ukraine
60E4 **Slavyansk** Ukraine
44B3 **Sleat,Sound of** *Chan* Scot
12C2 **Sleetmute** USA
45C2 **Sleeve Bloom** *Mts* Scot
19C3 **Slidell** USA
16B2 **Slide Mt** USA
45B1 **Sligo** County, Irish Rep
41B3 **Sligo** Irish Rep
41B3 **Sligo** B Irish Rep
54C2 **Sliven** Bulg
54C2 **Slobozia** Rom
13D3 **Slocan** Can
58D2 **Slonim** Belorussia
43D4 **Slough** Eng
22B2 **Slough** R USA
59B3 **Slovakia** Republic, Europe
52B1 **Slovenia** Republic, Europe
56C2 **Slubice** Pol
59D2 **Sluch'** R Ukraine
58D2 **Słupsk** Pol
58D2 **Slutsk** Belorussia
58D2 **Slutsk** R Belorussia
41A3 **Slyne Head** *Pt* Irish Rep
63C2 **Slyudyanka** Russian Fed
7D4 **Smallwood Res** Can
54B2 **Smederevo** Serbia, Yugos

54B2 **Smederevska Palanka** Serbia, Yugos
60D4 **Smela** Ukraine
15C2 **Smethport** USA
13E1 **Smith** Can
4F3 **Smith Arm** B Can
13B2 **Smithers** Can
7C3 **Smith I** Can
13B2 **Smith Sd** Can
15C2 **Smiths Falls** Can
109C4 **Smithton** Aust
13D1 **Smoky** R Can
109D2 **Smoky C** Aust
13E2 **Smoky Lake** Can
38F6 **Smøla** I Nor
60D3 **Smolensk** Russian Fed
55B2 **Smólikas** *Mt* Greece
54B2 **Smolyan** Bulg
58D2 **Smorgon'** Belorussia
16B3 **Smyrna** Delaware, USA
17B1 **Smyrna** Georgia, USA
42B2 **Snaefell** *Mt* Eng
38B2 **Snaefell** *Mt* Iceland
8B2 **Snake** R USA
8B2 **Snake River Canyon** USA
56B2 **Sneek** Neth
45B3 **Sneem** Irish Rep
22B2 **Snelling** USA
59B2 **Snežka** *Mt* Pol/ Czech Republic
38F6 **Snøhetta** *Mt* Nor
20B1 **Snohomish** USA
20B1 **Snoqualmie P** USA
76D3 **Snoul** Camb
43B3 **Snowdon** *Mt* Wales
43B3 **Snowdonia Nat Pk** Wales
4G3 **Snowdrift** Can
5H4 **Snow Lake** Can
108A2 **Snowtown** Aust
109C3 **Snowy Mts** Aust
9C3 **Snyder** USA
7B4 **Soan-kundo** I S Korea
99D2 **Sobat** R Sudan
31C2 **Sobral** Brazil
58C2 **Sochaczew** Pol
61E5 **Sochi** Russian Fed
9C3 **Socorro** USA
24C1 **Socorro** I Mexico
34A2 **Socos** Chile
81D4 **Socotra** I Yemen
38K5 **Sodankylä** Fin
99D2 **Soda Springs** USA
39H6 **Soderhamn** Sweden
39H7 **Södertälje** Sweden
99C1 **Sodiri** Sudan
99D2 **Sodo** Eth
46E1 **Soest** Germany
101C2 **Sofala** Mozam
Sofia = Sofiya
54B2 **Sofiya** Bulg
69G4 **Sofu Gan** I Japan
32C2 **Sogamoso** Colombia
39F6 **Sognefjorden** *Inlet* Nor
82D2 **Sog Xian** China
95C2 **Sohâg** Egypt
84D3 **Sohipat** India
46B1 **Soignies** Belg
46B2 **Soissons** France
85C3 **Sojat** India
74A3 **Sōjosōn-man** B N Korea
92A2 **Söke** Turk
97C4 **Sokodé** Togo
61E2 **Sokol** Russian Fed
58C2 **Sokolka** Pol
97B3 **Sokolo** Mali
6H3 **Sekongens Øy** I Greenland
99D1 **Sokota** Eth
97C3 **Sokoto** Nig
97C3 **Sokoto** R Nig
111A3 **Solander** I NZ
79B2 **Solano** Phil
87B1 **Solapur** India
47D1 **Solbad Hall** Austria
47D1 **Sölden** Austria
12D2 **Soldotna** USA
26C4 **Soledad** Colombia

43D4 **Solent** *Sd* Eng
46B1 **Solesmes** France
58D2 **Soligorsk** Belorussia
61J2 **Solikamsk** Russian Fed
32C4 **Solimões** R Peru
46D1 **Solingen** Germany
38H6 **Sollefteå** Sweden
61H3 **Sol'Iletsk** Russian Fed
70B4 **Solok** Indon
105G4 **Solomon** *Is* Pacific O
47B1 **Solothurn** Switz
39F8 **Soltau** Germany
22B3 **Solvang** USA
42C2 **Solway Firth** *Estuary* Eng/Scot
100B2 **Solwezi** Zambia
75C1 **Sōma** Japan
55C3 **Soma** Turk
81C5 **Somalia** Republic, E Africa
54A1 **Sombor** Serbia, Yugos
107D2 **Somerset** County, Eng
43C4 **Somerset** County, Eng
16D2 **Somerset** Massachusetts, USA
15C2 **Somerset** Pennsylvania, USA
100B4 **Somerset East** S Africa
6A2 **Somerset I** Can
16B3 **Somers Point** USA
16B2 **Somerville** USA
19A3 **Somerville Res** USA
54B1 **Somes** R Rom
46B2 **Somme** Department, France
46B2 **Somme** R France
46C2 **Sommesous** France
86A2 **Son** R India
74A3 **Sonch'ŏn** N Korea
39F8 **Sønderborg** Den
6E3 **Søndre Strømfjord** Greenland
47C1 **Sondrio** Italy
76D3 **Song Ba** R Viet
76D3 **Song Cau** Viet
101C2 **Songea** Tanz
72E3 **Songjiang** China
77C4 **Songkhla** Thai
74B3 **Songnim** N Korea
77C5 **Sông Pahang** R Malay
72A3 **Songpan** China
72C1 **Sonid Youqi** China
76C1 **Son La** Viet
85B3 **Sonmiani** Pak
85B3 **Sonmiani Bay** Pak
22A1 **Sonoma** USA
22B2 **Sonora** California, USA
24A2 **Sonora** R Mexico
9B3 **Sonoran Desert** USA
22C1 **Sonora P** USA
25D3 **Sonsonate** El Salvador
71E3 **Sonsorol** I Pacific O
10B2 **Soo Canals** Can/USA
13C3 **Sooke** Can
58B2 **Sopot** Pol
59B3 **Sopron** Hung
22B2 **Soquel** USA
53B2 **Sora** Italy
94B3 **Sored** R Israel
15D1 **Sorel** Can
109C4 **Sorell** Aust
92C2 **Sorgun** Turk
50B1 **Soria** Spain
38J5 **Sørkjosen** Nor
64C2 **Sørksop** R Barents S
61H4 **Sor Mertvyy Kultuk** *Plain* Kazakhstan
35B2 **Sorocaba** Brazil
61H3 **Sorochinsk** Russian Fed
71F3 **Soroi** I Pacific O
60C4 **Soroki** Moldova
71E4 **Sorong** Indon
71E4 **Sorong** Province, Indon
99D2 **Soroti** Uganda

38J4 **Sørøya** I Nor
53B2 **Sorrento** Italy
38K5 **Sorsatunturi** *Mt* Fin
38H5 **Sorsele** Sweden
79B3 **Sorsogon** Phil
38L6 **Sortavala** Russian Fed
74B3 **Sōsan** S Korea
59B2 **Sosnowiec** Pol
65H4 **Sos'va** Russian Fed
98B2 **Souanké** Congo
97B4 **Soubré** Ivory Coast
16B2 **Souderton** USA
27P2 **Soufrière** St Lucia
27N2 **Soufrière** *Mt* St Vincent and the Grenadines
48C3 **Souillac** France
96C1 **Souk Ahras** Alg
74B3 **Souk** S Korea
51C2 **Soummam** R Alg
Sour = Tyr
101G1 **Sources,Mt aux** Lesotho
31D3 **Sousa** Brazil
96D1 **Sousse** Tunisia
100B4 **South Africa** Republic, Africa
16B2 **Sonbo** USA
14B2 **Southampton** Can
43D4 **Southampton** Eng
16C2 **Southampton** USA
6B3 **Southampton I** Can
28F6 **South Atlantic** O
7D4 **South Aulatsivik I** Can
106C3 **South Australia** State, Aust
104E5 **South Australian Basin** Indian O
19C3 **Southaven** USA
17B2 **South Bay** USA
14B1 **South Baymouth** Can
14A2 **South Bend** Indiana, USA
20B1 **South Bend** Washington, USA
16D1 **Southbridge** USA
South Cape = Ka Lae
11B3 **South Carolina** State, USA
70C2 **South China S** S E Asia
8C2 **South Dakota** State, USA
16C1 **South Deerfield** USA
43D4 **South Downs** Eng
109C4 **South East C** Aust
111A2 **Southern Alps** *Mts* NZ
5H4 **Southend** Can
43E4 **Southend-on-Sea** Eng
111A2 **Southern Alps** *Mts* NZ
106A4 **Southern Cross** Aust
5J4 **Southern Indian L** Can
27H2 **Southfield** Jamaica
105G5 **South Fiji Basin** Pacific O
12D2 **South Fork** R Alaska, USA
22B1 **South Fork** California, USA
28F8 **South Georgia** I S Atlantic O
43C4 **South Glamorgan** County, Wales
14A2 **South Haven** USA
5J3 **South Henik L** Can
104F3 **South Honshu Ridge** Pacific O
111A2 **South I** NZ
16C2 **Southington** USA
74B3 **South Korea** Republic, S E Asia
21A2 **South Lake Tahoe** USA
112C8 **South Magnetic Pole** Ant
17B2 **South Miami** USA
16A3 **South Mt** USA

4F3	**South Nahanni** *R* Can
26G1	**South Negril Pt** Jamaica
103F8	**South Orkney** *Is* Atlantic O
8C2	**South Platte** *R* USA
80E	**South Pole** Ant
42C3	**Southport** Eng
27R3	**South Pt** Barbados
16B2	**South River** USA
44C2	**South Ronaldsay** *I* Scot
103G7	**South Sandwich Trench** Atlantic O
22A2	**South San Francisco** USA
5H4	**South Saskatchewan** *R* Can
42D2	**South Shields** Eng
11D1	**South Taranaki Bight** *B* NZ
44A3	**South Uist** *I* Scot
	South West Africa = *Namibia*
107D5	**South West C** Aust
105J5	**South West Pacific Basin** Pacific O
45H	**South West Peru Ridge** Pacific O
43D3	**South Yorkshire** County, Eng
58C1	**Sovetsk** Russian Fed
61G2	**Sovetsk** Russian Fed
101G1	**Soweto** S Africa
98B3	**Soyo Congo** Angola
60D3	**Sozh** *R* Belorussia
46C1	**Spa** Belg
50A1	**Spain** Kingdom
	Spalato = *Split*
42C3	**Spalding** Eng
14B1	**Spanish** *R* Can
26B3	**Spanish Town** Jamaica
21B2	**Sparks** USA
11B3	**Spartanburg** USA
55B3	**Sparti** Greece
69F2	**Spassk Dal'niy** Russian Fed
27R3	**Speightstown** Barbados
12E2	**Spencer** USA
14A3	**Spencer** Indiana, USA
8D2	**Spencer** Iowa, USA
6A3	**Spencer B** Can
108A3	**Spencer,C** Aust
108A2	**Spencer G** Aust
6C3	**Spencer I** Can
111B2	**Spenser Mts** NZ
45C1	**Sperrin Mts** N Ire
44C3	**Spey** *R* Scot
57B3	**Speyer** Germany
27K1	**Speyside** Tobago
12F1	**Spike Mt** USA
20C1	**Spirit Lake** USA
5G4	**Spirit River** Can
	Spitsbergen = *Svalbard*
64C2	**Spitsbergen** *I* Barents S
57C3	**Spittal** Austria
38F6	**Spjelkavik** Nor
52C2	**Split** Croatia
47C1	**Splügen** Switz
20C1	**Spokane** USA
55C3	**Sporádhes** *Is* Greece
22A2	**Spray** USA
56C2	**Spree** *R* Germany
100A3	**Springbok** S Africa
18B2	**Springdale** USA
10B3	**Springfield** Illinois, USA
10C2	**Springfield** Massachusetts, USA
18B2	**Springfield** Missouri, USA
14B3	**Springfield** Ohio, USA
20B2	**Springfield** Oregon, USA
15D2	**Springfield** Vermont, USA
100B4	**Springfontein** S Africa
101G1	**Springs** S Africa
41D3	**Spurn Head** *Pt* Eng
13C3	**Squamish** Can
60E3	**Sredne-Russkaya Vozvyshennost** *Upland* Russian Fed
63B1	**Sredne Sibirskoye Ploskogorye** *Tableland* Russian Fed
61J2	**Sredniy Ural** *Mts* Russian Fed
76D3	**Srepok** *R* Camb
68D1	**Sretensk** Russian Fed
76C3	**Sre Umbell** Camb
83C5	**Sri Lanka** Republic, S Asia
84C2	**Srinagar** Pak
87A1	**Srivardhan** India
58B2	**Šroda Wlk.** Pol
30H6	**Sta Clara** / Chile
32J7	**Sta Cruz** / Ecuador
56B2	**Stade** Germany
44A3	**Staffa** / Scot
43C3	**Stafford** County, Eng
16C2	**Stafford Springs** USA
	Stalingrad = *Volgograd*
6A1	**Stallworthy,C** Can
59C2	**Stalowa Wola** Pol
32J7	**Sta Maria** / Ecuador
16C2	**Stamford** Connecticut, USA
16B1	**Stamford** New York, USA
100A3	**Stampriet** Namibia
101G1	**Standerton** S Africa
14B2	**Standish** USA
101H1	**Stanger** S Africa
22B2	**Stanislaus** *R* USA
54B2	**Stanke Dimitrov** Bulg
109C4	**Stanley** Aust
29E6	**Stanley** Falkland Is
87B2	**Stanley Res** India
	Stanleyville = *Kisangani*
25D3	**Stann Creek** Belize
63E2	**Stanovoy Khrebet** *Mts* Russian Fed
47C1	**Stans** Switz
109D1	**Stanthorpe** Aust
59C2	**Starachowice** Pol
54B2	**Stara Planiná** *Mts* Bulg
60D2	**Staraya Russa** Russian Fed
54C2	**Stara Zagora** Bulg
58B2	**Stargard Szczecinski** Pol
19C3	**Starkville** USA
57C3	**Starnberg** Germany
58B2	**Starogard Gdanski** Pol
59D3	**Starokonstantinov** Ukraine
43C4	**Start Pt** Eng
60E3	**Staryy Oskol** Russian Fed
15C2	**State College** USA
16B2	**Staten I** USA
17B1	**Statesboro** USA
15C3	**Staunton** USA
39F7	**Stavanger** Nor
46C1	**Stavelot** Belg
61F4	**Stavropol'** Russian Fed
108B3	**Stawell** Aust
58B2	**Stawno** Pol
20B2	**Stayton** USA
12B2	**Stebbins** USA
12F2	**Steele,Mt** USA
16A2	**Steelton** USA
20C2	**Steens Mt** USA
6E2	**Steenstrup Gletscher** *Gl*
4H2	**Stefansson I** Can
101H1	**Stegi** Swaziland
47D1	**Steinach** Austria
8D2	**Steinbach** Can
38G6	**Steinkjer** Nor
13C2	**Stein Mt** Can
23B2	**Stemaco** Mexico
47D2	**Stenay** France
56C2	**Stendal** Germany
110B2	**Stephens,C** NZ
108B2	**Stephens Creek** Aust
14A1	**Stephenson** USA
12H3	**Stephens Pass** USA
7E5	**Stephenville** Can
100B4	**Sterkstroom** S Africa
8C2	**Sterling** Colorado, USA
14B2	**Sterling Heights** USA
61J3	**Sterlitamak** Russian Fed
13E2	**Stettler** Can
14B2	**Steubenville** USA
4D3	**Stevens Village** USA
13B1	**Stewart** Can
21B2	**Stewart** USA
12G2	**Stewart** *R* Can
12G2	**Stewart Crossing** Can
111A3	**Stewart I** NZ
107F1	**Stewart Is** Solomon Is
4E3	**Stewart River** Can
16A3	**Stewartstown** USA
101G1	**Steyn** S Africa
57C3	**Steyr** Austria
12G3	**Stika** USA
12H3	**Stikine** *R* Can
12H3	**Stikine Ranges** *Mts* Can
18A2	**Stillwater** Oklahoma, USA
21B2	**Stillwater Range** *Mts* USA
108A2	**Stirling** Aust
44C3	**Stirling** Scot
16C1	**Stockbridge** USA
59B3	**Stockerau** Austria
39H7	**Stockholm** Sweden
42C3	**Stockport** Eng
22B2	**Stockton** California, USA
42D2	**Stockton** Eng
18B2	**Stockton L** USA
43C3	**Stoke-on-Trent** Eng
38A2	**Stokkseyri** Iceland
38G5	**Stokmarknes** Nor
39K8	**Stolbtsy** Belorussia
58D2	**Stolin** Belorussia
16B3	**Stone Harbor** USA
44C3	**Stonehaven** Scot
19A3	**Stonewall** USA
12D2	**Stony** *R* USA
38H5	**Storavan** *L* Sweden
38G6	**Støren** Nor
109C4	**Storm B** Aust
44A2	**Stornoway** Scot
59D3	**Storozhinets** Ukraine
16C2	**Storrs** USA
38G6	**Stors168jon** *L* Sweden
38H5	**Storuman** Sweden
16D1	**Stoughton** USA
43E3	**Stowmarket** Eng
45C1	**Strabane** N Ire
109C4	**Strahan** Aust
42B2	**Stralsund** Germany
38F6	**Stranda** Nor
39H7	**Strängnäs** Sweden
42B2	**Stranraer** Scot
49D2	**Strasbourg** France
15C3	**Strasburg** USA
14B2	**Stratford** Can
16C2	**Stratford** Connecticut, USA
110B1	**Stratford** NZ
43D3	**Stratford-on-Avon** Eng
108A3	**Strathalbyn** Aust
42B2	**Strathclyde** Region, Scot
13E2	**Strathmore** Can
18C1	**Streator** USA
47C2	**Stresa** Italy
53C3	**Stretto de Messina** *Str* Italy/Sicily
38D3	**Streymoy** Føroyar
53C3	**Stroboli** / Italy
6E3	**Stromfjord** Greenland
44C2	**Stromness** Scot
18A1	**Stromsburg** USA
38H6	**Stromsund** Sweden
38G6	**Ströms Vattudal** *L* Sweden
44C2	**Stronsay** / Scot
43C4	**Stroud** Eng
16B2	**Stroudsburg** USA
54B2	**Struma** *R* Bulg
43B3	**Strumble Head** *Pt* Wales
55B2	**Strumica** Macedonia
59C3	**Stryy** Ukraine
59C3	**Stryy** *R* Ukraine
108B1	**Strzelecki Creek** *R* Aust
17B2	**Stuart** Florida, USA
13C2	**Stuart** *R* Can
12B2	**Stuart I** USA
13C2	**Stuart L** Can
47D1	**Stubaier Alpen** *Mts* Austria
76D3	**Stung Sen** Camb
76D3	**Stung Treng** Camb
5A2	**Stura** *R* Italy
112C7	**Sturge I** Ant
14A2	**Sturgeon Bay** USA
14C1	**Sturgeon Falls** Can
18C2	**Sturgis** Kentucky, USA
14A2	**Sturgis** Michigan, USA
106B2	**Sturt Creek** *R* Aust
108B1	**Sturt Desert** Aust
100B4	**Stutterheim** S Africa
19B3	**Stuttgart** USA
57B3	**Stuttgart** Germany
38A1	**Stykkishólmur** Iceland
59D2	**Styr'** *R* Ukraine
35C1	**Suaçui Grande** *R* Brazil
81B4	**Suakin** Sudan
73E5	**Su-ao** Taiwan
34C2	**Suardi** Arg
78B2	**Subi** / Indon
54A1	**Subotica** Serbia, Yugos
60C4	**Suceava** Rom
45B2	**Suck** *R* Irish Rep
30C2	**Sucre** Bol
35A1	**Sucuriú** *R* Brazil
98C1	**Sudan** Republic, Africa
14B1	**Sudbury** Can
43E3	**Sudbury** Eng
99C2	**Sudd** *Swamp* Sudan
33F2	**Suddie** Guyana
98C2	**Sue** *R* Sudan
4H2	**Suerdrup Is** Can
92B4	**Suez** Egypt
92B3	**Suez Canal** Egypt
92B4	**Suez,G of** Egypt
16B2	**Suffern** USA
43E3	**Suffolk** County, Eng
109D2	**Sugarloaf Mt** Aust
91C5	**Suhar** Oman
68C1	**Sühbaatar** Mongolia
84B3	**Sui** Pak
72C2	**Suide** China
69E2	**Suihua** China
73B3	**Suining** China
46C2	**Suippes** France
41B3	**Suir** *R* Irish Rep
73C3	**Sui Xian** China
72E1	**Suizhong** China
85C3	**Sujángarth** India
78B4	**Sukabumi** Indon
78C3	**Sukadana** Borneo, Indon
78B4	**Sukadana** Sumatra, Indon
74E3	**Sukagawa** Japan
78C3	**Sukaraja** Indon
60E3	**Sukhinichi** Russian Fed
61F2	**Sukhona** *R* Russian Fed
61F5	**Sukhumi** Georgia
6E3	**Sukkertoppen** Greenland

6E3 Sukkertoppen L Greenland
38L6 Sukkozero Russian Fed
85B3 Sukkur Pak
87C1 Sukma India
95A2 Súknah Libya
100A3 Sukses Namibia
75A2 Sukumo Japan
13C1 Sukunka R Can
60E3 Sula R Russian Fed
84B3 Sulaiman Range Mts Pak
70C4 Sulawesi I Indon
54C1 Sulina Rom
38H5 Sulitjelma Nor
32A4 Sullana Peru
18B2 Sullivan USA
13B2 Sullivan Bay Can
13E2 Sullivan L Can
52B2 Sulmona Italy
19B3 Sulphur Louisiana, USA
19A3 Sulphur Oklahoma, USA
19A3 Sulphur Springs USA
86A1 Sultānpur India
79B4 Sulu Arch Phil
70C3 Sulu S Philip
30D4 Sumampa Arg
70B4 Sumatera I Indon
70C4 Sumba I Indon
70D4 Sumbawa I Indon
70D4 Sumbawa Besar Indon
99D3 Sumbawanga Tanz
100A2 Sumbe Angola
44E2 Sumburgh Head Pt Scot
78C4 Sumenep Indon
69G3 Sumisu I Japan
13D3 Summerland Can
5F4 Summit Lake Can
21B2 Summit Mt USA
111B2 Sumner,L NZ
75A2 Sumoto Japan
17B1 Sumter USA
60D3 Sumy Ukraine
16A2 Sunbury USA
34C2 Sunchales Arg
74B3 Sunch'ŏn N Korea
74B4 Sunch'ŏn S Korea
86A2 Sundargarh India
86B2 Sunderbans Swamp India
42D2 Sunderland Eng
13E2 Sundre Can
15C1 Sundridge Can
38H6 Sundsvall Sweden
38D3 Suduroy Føroyar
78D3 Sungaianyar Indon
78A3 Sungaisalak Indon
20A2 Sunnyside USA
21A2 Sunnyvale USA
63D1 Suntar Russian Fed
97B4 Sunyani Ghana
75A2 Suō-nada B Japan
38K6 Suojoki Fin
86B1 Supaul India
18A1 Superior Nebraska, USA
10A2 Superior Wisconsin, USA
10B2 Superior,L Can/USA
76C3 Suphan Buri Thai
93D2 Süphan Dağ Turk
71E4 Supiori I Indon
93E3 Suq ash Suyukh Iraq
72D3 Suqian China
Suqutra = Socotra
91C5 Sūr Oman
61G3 Sura R Russian Fed
78C4 Surabaya Indon
75B2 Suraga-wan B Japan
78C4 Surakarta Indon
109C1 Surat Aust
85C4 Surat India
84C3 Surātgarh India
77B4 Surat Thani Thai
85C4 Surendranagar India
16B3 Surf City USA
64J3 Surgut Russian Fed
87B1 Suriapet India
49D2 Sürich Switz

79C4 Surigao Phil
76C3 Surin Thai
33F3 Surinam Republic, S America
43D4 Surrey County, Eng
47C1 Sürsee Switz
95A1 Surt Libya
38A2 Surtsey I Iceland
78A3 Surulangun Indon
47B2 Susa Italy
75A2 Susa Japan
75A2 Susaki Japan
21A1 Susanville USA
47D1 Süsch Switz
12E2 Susitna R USA
16A3 Susquehanna R USA
16B2 Sussex USA
43D4 Sussex West Eng
13B1 Sustut Peak Mt Can
100B4 Sutherland S Africa
84C2 Sutlej R Pak
21A2 Sutter Creek USA
14B3 Sutton USA
12C3 Sutwik I USA
74D3 Suwa Japan
58C2 Suwałki Pol
17B2 Suwannee R USA
94B2 Suweilih Jordan
74B3 Suwŏn S Korea
72D3 Su Xian China
75B1 Suzaka Japan
72C3 Suzhou China
74D3 Suzu Japan
75B2 Suzuka Japan
75B1 Suzu-misaki C Japan
64C2 Svalbard Is Barents S
59C3 Svalyava Ukraine
38G5 Svartisen Mt Nor
76D3 Svay Riêng Camb
38G6 Sveg Sweden
39G7 Svendborg Den
Sverdlovsk = Yekaterinburg
6A1 Sverdrup Chan Can
69F2 Svetlaya Russian Fed
58C2 Svetlogorsk Russian Fed
39K6 Svetogorsk Russian Fed
54B2 Svetozarevo Serbia, Yugos
54C2 Svilengrad Bulg
58D2 Svir' Belorussia
59B3 Svitavy Czech Republic
69E1 Svobodnyy Russian Fed
38G5 Svolvaer Nor
107E3 Swain Reefs Aust
17B1 Swainsboro USA
100A3 Swakopmund Namibia
42D2 Swale R Eng
70C3 Swallow Reef I S E Asia
87B2 Swamihalli India
25D3 Swan I Honduras
43D4 Swanage Eng
108B3 Swan Hill Aust
13D2 Swan Hills Can
13D2 Swan Hills Mts Can
26A3 Swan I Caribbean S
5H4 Swan River Can
43C4 Swansea Wales
43C4 Swansea B Wales
101G1 Swartruggens S Africa
Swatow = Shantou
101H1 Swaziland Kingdom, S Africa
39G7 Sweden Kingdom, N Europe
20B2 Sweet Home USA
9C3 Sweetwater USA
100B4 Swellendam S Africa
59B2 Świdnica Pol
58B2 Świdwin Pol
58B2 Świebodzin Pol
58B2 Świecie Pol
5H4 Swift Current Can
43D4 Swindon Eng
45B2 Swinford Irish Rep

56C2 Świnoujście Pol
49D2 Switzerland Federal Republic, Europe
45C2 Swords Irish Rep
109D2 Sydney Aust
7D5 Sydney Can
64G3 Syktyvkar Russian Fed
17A1 Sylacauga USA
38G6 Sylarna Mt Sweden
86C2 Sylhet Bang
56B1 Sylt I Germany
14B2 Sylvania USA
112C11 Syowa Base Ant
Syracuse = Siracusa
15C2 Syracuse USA
65H5 Syr Darya R Kazakhstan
93C2 Syria Republic, S W Asia
61J2 Sysert' Russian Fed
61G3 Syzran' Russian Fed
56C2 Szczecin Pol
58B2 Szczecinek Pol
58C2 Szczytno Pol
59C3 Szeged Hung
59B3 Székesfehérvár Hung
59B3 Szekszard Hung
59B3 Szolnok Hung
59B3 Szombathely Hung
58B2 Szprotawa Pol

T

90C3 Tabas Iran
23A1 Tabasco Mexico
32D4 Tabatinga Brazil
56B3 Tabelbala Alg
76C3 Tabeng Camb
13E2 Taber Can
79B3 Tablas I Phil
100A4 Table Mt S Africa
18B2 Table Rock Res USA
78B3 Taboali Indon
57C3 Tábor Czech Republic
99D3 Tabora Tanz
97B4 Tabou Ivory Coast
90A2 Tabriz Iran
92C4 Tabūk S Arabia
23A2 Tacámbaro Mexico
82C1 Tacheng China
79C3 Tacloban Phil
30B2 Tacna Peru
8A2 Tacoma USA
99E1 Tadjoura Djibouti
87B2 Tādpatri India
74B3 Taebaek Sanmaek Mts S Korea
74B3 Taegu S Korea
74B4 Taehŭksan I S Korea
74B3 Taejŏn S Korea
51B1 Tafalla Spain
96C2 Tafasaset Watercourse Alg
43C4 Taff R Wales
94B3 Tafila Jordan
60E4 Taganrog Ukraine
97A3 Tagant Region, Maur
79B4 Tagbilaran Phil
96B2 Taguenout Hagguerete Well Maur
107E2 Tagula I Solomon Is
79C4 Tagum Phil
Tagus = Tejo
96C2 Tahat Mt Alg
105J4 Tahiti I Pacific O
18A2 Tahlequah USA
21A2 Tahoe City USA
21A2 Tahoe,L USA
97C3 Tahoua Niger
71D3 Tahuna Indon
72D2 Tai'an China
72B3 Taibai Shan Mt China
72D1 Taibus Qi China
73E5 T'ai-chung Taiwan
111B3 Taieri R NZ
72C2 Taihang Shan China
110C1 Taihape NZ
72E3 Tai Hu L China
108A3 Tailem Bend Aust
44B3 Tain Scot

73E5 T'ai-nan Taiwan
35C1 Taiobeiras Brazil
73E5 T'ai pei Taiwan
77C5 Taiping Malay
75C1 Taira Japan
78A3 Tais Indon
75A1 Taisha Japan
29B5 Taitao,Pen de Chile
73E5 T'ai-tung Taiwan
38K5 Taivalkoski Fin
69E4 Taiwan Republic, China
Taiwan Haixia = Formosa Str
72C2 Taiyuan China
72D3 Taizhou China
81C4 Ta'izz Yemen
82A2 Tajikistan Republic, Asia
50B1 Tajo R Spain
76B2 Tak Thai
74D3 Takada Japan
75A2 Takahashi Japan
110B2 Takaka NZ
74C4 Takamatsu Japan
74D3 Takaoka Japan
110B1 Takapuna NZ
75B1 Takasaki Japan
75B1 Takayama Japan
74D3 Takefu Japan
70A3 Takengon Indon
76C3 Takeo Camb
75A2 Takeo Japan
Take-shima = Tok-do
90A2 Takestān Iran
75A2 Taketa Japan
4G3 Takijvak L Can
99D1 Takkaze R Eritrea/Eth
13B1 Takla L Can
13B1 Takla Landing Can
12B2 Taklesluk L USA
12H2 Taku Arm R Can
23A1 Tala Mexico
59B3 Talabanya Hung
84C2 Talagang Pak
34A2 Talagante Chile
87B3 Talaimannar Sri Lanka
97C3 Talak Desert Region, Niger
78A3 Talangbetutu Indon
32A4 Talara Peru
50B2 Talavera de la Reina Spain
34A3 Talca Chile
34A3 Talcahuano Chile
86B2 Tālcher India
82B1 Taldy Kurgan Kazakhstan
71D4 Taliabu Indon
84B1 Taligan Afghan
99D2 Tali Post Sudan
78D4 Taliwang Indon
12E2 Talkeetna USA
17A1 Talladega USA
93D2 Tall 'Afar Iraq
17B1 Tallahassee USA
94C1 Tall Bisah Syria
60B2 Tallinn Estonia
92C3 Tall Kalakh Syria
19B3 Tallulah USA
60D4 Tal'noye Ukraine
58C2 Talpaki Russian Fed
30B4 Taltal Chile
109C1 Talwood Aust
78D1 Tamabo Range Mts Malay
97B4 Tamale Ghana
96C2 Tamanrasset Alg
96C2 Tamanrasset Watercourse Alg
16B2 Tamaqua USA
Tamatave = Toamasina
23A2 Tamazula Jalisco, Mexico
23B2 Tamazulápan Mexico
23B1 Tamazunchale Mexico
97A3 Tambacounda Sen
61F3 Tambov Russian Fed
50A1 Tambre R Spain
98C2 Tambura Sudan

Tamchaket

97A3 Tamchaket Maur
50A1 Tamega R Port
23B1 Tamiahua Mexico
87B2 Tamil Nadu State, India
76D2 Tam Ky Viet
17B2 Tampa USA
17B2 Tampa B USA
39J6 Tampere Fin
23B1 Tampico Mexico
68D2 Tamsagbulag Mongolia
86C2 Tamu Burma
23B1 Tamuis Mexico
109D2 Tamworth Aust
43D3 Tamworth Eng
38K4 Tana Nor
99D1 Tana L Eth
99E3 Tana R Kenya
38K5 Tana R Nor/Fin
75B2 Tanabe Japan
38K4 Tanafjord Inlet Nor
78D3 Tanahgrogot Indon
71E4 Tanahmerah Indon
12D1 Tanana USA
12E2 Tanana R USA
Tananarive = Antananarivo
47C2 Tanaro R Italy
74B2 Tanch'ŏn N Korea
34D3 Tandil Arg
78B2 Tandjong Datu Pt Indon
71E4 Tandjung d'Urville C Indon
78D3 Tandjung Layar C Indon
78B3 Tandjung Lumut C Indon
78D2 Tandjung Mangkalihet C Indon
78D3 Tandjung Sambar C Indon
78C2 Tandjung Sirik C Malay
71E4 Tandjung Vals C Indon
85B3 Tando Adam Pak
85B3 Tando Muhammad Khan Pak
108B2 Tandou L Aust
87B1 Tandür India
110C1 Taneatua NZ
76B2 Tanen Range Mts Burma/Thai
96B2 Tanezrouft Desert Region Alg
91C4 Tang Iran
99D3 Tanga Tanz
60E4 Tangarog Russian Fed
99C3 Tanganyika,L Tanz/Zaire
96B1 Tanger Mor
82C2 Tanggula Shan Mts China
Tangier = Tanger
78A2 Tangjungpinang Indon
82C2 Tangra Yumco L China
72D2 Tangshan China
79B4 Tangub Phil
63C2 Tanguy Russian Fed
Tanintharyi = Tenasserim
79B4 Tanjay Phil
101D3 Tanjona Ankaboa C Madag
101D2 Tanjona Babaomby C Madag
101D2 Tanjona Vilanandro C Madag
101D3 Tanjona Vohimena C Madag
78C4 Tanjong Bugel C Indon
78B4 Tanjong Cangkuang C Indon
78C3 Tanjong Puting C Indon
78C3 Tanjong Selatan C Indon
78D3 Tanjung Indon

70A3 Tanjungbalai Indon
78A3 Tanjung Jabung Pt Indon
78B3 Tanjungpandan Indon
78B4 Tanjung Priok Indon
78D2 Tanjungredeb Indon
78D2 Tanjungselor Indon
84C2 Tank Pak
68B1 Tannu Ola Mts Russian Fed
97B4 Tano R Ghana
97C3 Tanout Niger
23B1 Tanquián Mexico
73E4 Tan-shui Taiwan
86A1 Tansing Nepal
95C1 Tanta Egypt
96A2 Tan-Tan Mor
4B3 Tanunak USA
99D3 Tanzania Republic, Africa
72A3 Tao He R China
72B2 Taole China
96B1 Taourirt Mor
60C2 Tapa Estonia
25C3 Tapachula Mexico
33F4 Tapajós R Brazil
34C3 Tapalquén Arg
72B4 Tapan Indon
11A3 Tapanui NZ
32D5 Tapauá R Brazil
85D4 Tapi R India
86B1 Taplejung Nepal
111B2 Tapuaenuku Mt NZ
35B2 Tapuaritinga Brazil
79B4 Tapul Group Is Phil
33E4 Tapurucuara Brazil
109D1 Tara Aust
65J4 Tara Russian Fed
65J4 Tara R Russian Fed
54A2 Tara R Bosnia-Herzegovina/Montenegro, Yugos
97D4 Taraba R Nig
30D2 Tarabuco Bol
Tarābulus = Tripoli
50B1 Taracón Spain
110C1 Taradale NZ
78D2 Tarakan Indon
44A3 Taransay I Scot
53C2 Taranto Italy
32B5 Tarapoto Peru
49C2 Tarare France
110C2 Tararua Range Mts NZ
96C2 Tarat Alg
110C1 Tarawera NZ
51B1 Tarazona Spain
44C3 Tarbat Ness Pen Scot
84C2 Tarbela Res Pak
42B2 Tarbert Strathclyde, Scot
44A3 Tarbert Western Isles, Scot
48C3 Tarbes France
106C4 Tarcoola Aust
109C2 Tarcoon Aust
109D2 Taree Aust
96A2 Tarfaya Mor
95A1 Tarhūnah Libya
91B5 Tarif UAE
30D3 Tarija Bol
87B2 Tarikere India
81C4 Tarim Yemen
99D3 Tarime Tanz
82C1 Tarim He R China
82C2 Tarim Pendi Basin China
84B2 Tarin Kut Afghan
18A1 Tarkio USA
79B2 Tarlac Phil
32B6 Tarma Peru
49C3 Tarn R France
59C2 Tarnobrzeg Pol
59C3 Tarnów Pol
107D3 Taroom Aust
51C1 Tarragona Spain
109C4 Tarraleah Aust
51C1 Tarrasa Spain
16C2 Tarrytown USA
92B2 Tarsus Turk
44D2 Tartan Oilfield N Sea

47D2 Tartaro R Italy
60C2 Tartu Estonia
92C3 Tartūs Syria
35C1 Tarumirim Brazil
70A3 Tarutung Indon
52B1 Tarvisio Italy
80D1 Tashauz Turkmenistan
86C1 Tashigang Bhutan
82A1 Tashkent Uzbekistan
65K4 Tashtagol Russian Fed
63A2 Tashtyp Russian Fed
79B4 Tasikmalaya Indon
94B2 Tasīl Syria
6E2 Tasiussaq Greenland
95A3 Tasker Well Niger
110B2 Tasman B NZ
107D5 Tasmania I Aust
111B2 Tasman Pen Aust
109C4 Tasman Pen Aust
107E4 Tasman S NZ Aust
92C1 Taşova Turk
96C2 Tassili du Hoggar Desert Region, Alg
96C2 Tassili N'jjer Desert Region, Alg
72A2 Tata Mor
96D1 Tataouine Tunisia
65K4 Tatarsk Russian Fed
69G2 Tatarskiy Proliv Str Russian Fed
61G2 Tatarstan Russian Fed
75B1 Tateyama Japan
5G3 Tathlina L Can
12E2 Tatitlek USA
13C2 Tatla Lake Can
59B3 Tatry Mts Pol/Slovakia
75A2 Tatsuno Japan
85B4 Tatta Pak
35B2 Tatuí Brazil
93D2 Tatvan Turk
31C3 Tauá Brazil
35B2 Taubate Brazil
110C1 Taumarunui NZ
101F1 Taung S Africa
76B2 Taungdwingyi Burma
76B1 Taung-gyi Burma
76A2 Taungup Burma
84C2 Taunsa Pak
43C4 Taunton Eng
16D2 Taunton USA
46E1 Taunus Region, Germany
110B1 Tauroa Pt NZ
7A3 Tavani Can
7A3 Tavani Can
65H4 Tavda R Russian Fed
43B4 Tavistock Eng
76B3 Tavoy Burma
76B3 Tavoy Pt Burma
92A2 Tavsanli Turk
111B2 Tawa NZ
19A3 Tawakoni,L USA
14B2 Tawas City USA
70C3 Tawau Malay
98C1 Taweisha Sudan
79B4 Tawitawi I Phil
79B4 Tawitawi Group Is Phil
23B2 Taxco Mexico
23B2 Taxcoco Mexico
44C3 Tay R Scot
76C3 Tay Indon
12B1 Taylor Alaska, USA
13C1 Taylor Can
82D2 Taylor Michigan, USA
19A3 Taylor Texas, USA
18C2 Taylorville USA
80B3 Taymāʾ S Arabia
63B1 Taymyr R Russian Fed
76D3 Tay Ninh Viet
63B2 Tayshet Russian Fed

68B2 Tayshir Mongolia
44C3 Tayside Region, Scot
79A3 Taytay Phil
90D3 Tayyebāt Iran
71A Taza Mor
93B2 Tazirbū Libya
12E2 Tazlina,L USA
64J3 Tazovskiy Russian Fed
65F5 Tbilisi Georgia
98B3 Tchibanga Gabon
95A2 Tchigai,Plat du Niger
97C3 Tchin Tabaradene Niger
98B2 Tchollire Cam
58B2 Tczew Pol
111A3 Te Anau NZ
111A3 Te Anau,L NZ
110C1 Te Aroha NZ
110C1 Te Awamutu NZ
23A2 Tebessa Alg
23A2 Teboman Mexico
23A2 Tecaitlán Mexico
23B1 Tecate Mexico
61K2 Techa R Russian Fed
23A1 Tecolotlán Mexico
23A2 Tecpan Mexico
54C1 Tecuci Rom
18A1 Tecumseh USA
80E2 Tedzhen Turkmenistan
65H6 Tedzhen R Turkmenistan
42D2 Tees R Eng
42D2 Tefé Brazil
88B4 Tegal Indon
78B4 Teginneng Indon
25D3 Tegucigalpa Honduras
21B3 Tehachapi Mts USA
21B3 Tehachapi P USA
4J3 Tehachapi P USA
90B2 Tehrān Iran
23B2 Tehuacán Mexico
23B2 Tehuantepec Mexico
23B2 Tehuitzingo Mexico
43B3 Teifi R Wales
7A R Port
23A2 Tejupilco Mexico
111B2 Tekapo,L NZ
82B1 Tekeli Kazakhstan
92A1 Tekirdağ Turk
55C2 Tekir Dağlari Mts Turk
19C3 Teknaf Bang
110C1 Te Kuiti NZ
16C Tela Honduras
94B2 Tel Aviv Yafo Israel
34B3 Telén Arg
21B2 Telescope Peak Mt USA
33F5 Teles Pires R Brazil
47D1 Telfs Austria
63A2 Teli Russian Fed
94B3 Tell el Meise Mt Jordan
12A1 Teller USA
87B2 Tellicherry India
77C5 Telok Anson Malay
78D2 Telok Darvel Malay
71E4 Telok Flamingo C
78C3 Telok Kumai B Indon
78B4 Telok Pelabuanratu B Indon
78D4 Telok Saleh B Indon
78C3 Telok Sampit B
78B3 Telok Sukadona B Indon
23B2 Teloloapán Mexico
64G3 Tel'pos-iz Mt Russian Fed
58C1 Telšiai Lithuania
78C3 Telukbatang Indon
71E4 Teluk Berau B Indon
78B4 Telukbetung Indom
70D4 Teluk Bone B Indon
71E4 Teluk Cendrawasih B Indon
78D3 Teluk Mandar B Indon
71D4 Teluk Tolo B Indon

70D3 **Teluk Tomini** *B* Indon
71D3 **Téluk Weda** *B* Indon
14B1 **Temagami,L** Can
23B2 **Temascal** Mexico
78A3 **Tembesi** *R* Indon
78A3 **Tembilahan** Indon
27F5 **Temblador** Ven
77C5 **Temerloh** Malay
65G5 **Temir** Kazakhstan
65J4 **Temirtau** Kazakhstan
15C1 **Temiscaming** Can
109C2 **Temora** Aust
9B3 **Tempe** Aust
19A3 **Temple** USA
45C2 **Templemore** Irish Rep
23B1 **Tempoal** Mexico
34A3 **Temuco** Chile
111B2 **Temuka** NZ
32B4 **Tena** Ecuador
87C1 **Tenäli** India
23B2 **Tenancingo** Mexico
76B3 **Tenasserim** Burma
43B4 **Tenby** Wales
99E1 **Tendaho** Eth
83D5 **Ten Degree Chan** Indian O
98B1 **Ténéré** *Desert Region* Niger
96A2 **Tenerife** *I* Canary Is
76B1 **Teng** *R* Burma
78D3 **Tenggarong** Indon
72A2 **Tengger Shamo** *Desert* China
112C2 **Teniente Jubany** *Base* Ant
112C2 **Teniente Rodolfo Marsh Martin** *Base* Ant
87B3 **Tenkäsi** India
100B2 **Tenke** Zaire
97B3 **Tenkodogo** Burkina
106C2 **Tennant Creek** Aust
11B3 **Tennessee** *State,* USA
18C2 **Tennessee** *R* USA
34A2 **Teno** Chile
78D1 **Tenom** Malay
25C3 **Tenosique** Mexico
109D1 **Tenterfield** Aust
17B2 **Ten Thousand Is** USA
23A1 **Teocaltiche** Mexico
35C1 **Teofilo Otôni** Brazil
23B2 **Teotihuacan** Hist Site, Mexico
23B2 **Teotitlan** Mexico
23A1 **Tepatitlan** Mexico
24B2 **Tepehuanes** Mexico
23B2 **Tepeji** Mexico
23A1 **Tepic** Mexico
57C2 **Teplice** Czech Republic
110C1 **Te Puke** NZ
23A1 **Tequila** Mexico
23B2 **Tequistepec** Mexico
51C1 **Ter** *R* Spain
97C3 **Téra** Niger
75B1 **Teradomari** Japan
52B2 **Teramo** Italy
96A1 **Terceira** *I* Açores
59D3 **Terebovlya** Ukraine
31C3 **Teresina** Brazil
35C2 **Teresópolis** Brazil
92C1 **Terme** Turk
80E2 **Termez** Uzbekistan
52B2 **Termoli** Italy
71D3 **Ternate** Indon
52B2 **Terni** Italy
59D3 **Ternopol** Ukraine
13B2 **Terrace** Can
53B2 **Terracina** Italy
100B3 **Terrafirma** S Africa
112C8 **Terre Adélie** Region, Ant
19B4 **Terre Bonne B** USA
14A3 **Terre Haute** USA
19A3 **Terrell** USA
56B2 **Terschelling** *I* Neth
51B1 **Teruel** Spain
4C2 **Teshekpuk L** USA
4C2 **Teshekpuk L** USA
74E2 **Teshio** *R* Japan

68B2 **Tesiyn Gol** *Mts* Mongolia
12H2 **Teslin** Can
12H3 **Teslin** *R* Can
12H2 **Teslin L** Can
63B3 **Teslyn Gol** *R* Mongolia
96C2 **Tessalit** Mali
97C3 **Tessaoua** Niger
101C2 **Tete** Mozam
23A2 **Tetela** Mexico
96B1 **Tetouan** Mor
61G2 **Tetyushi** Russian Fed
30D3 **Teuco** *R* Arg
23A1 **Teúl de Gonzalez Ortega** Mexico
71D4 **Teun** *I* Indon
52B2 **Tevere** *R* Italy
52C2 **Teviot** *R* Scot
65J4 **Tevriz** Russian Fed
111A3 **Te Waewae B** NZ
78C3 **Tewah** Indon
109D1 **Tewantin** Aust
72A3 **Têwo** China
19B3 **Texarkana** USA
19B3 **Texarkana,L** USA
109D1 **Texas** Aust
9C3 **Texas** *State,* USA
19B4 **Texas City** USA
56A2 **Texel** *I* Neth
19A3 **Texoma,L** USA
101G1 **Teyateyaneng** Lesotho
23B2 **Teziutlán** Mexico
86C1 **Tezpur** India
76C1 **Tha** Laos
101G1 **Thabana Ntlenyana** *Mt* Lesotho
101G1 **Thaba Putsoa** *Mt* Lesotho
76B3 **Thagyettaw** Burma
76D1 **Thai Binh** Viet
76C2 **Thailand** Kingdom, S E Asia
76C3 **Thailand,G of** Thai
76D1 **Thai Nguyen** Viet
76C2 **Thakhek** Laos
84C2 **Thal** Pak
76C4 **Thale Luang** *L* Thai
109C1 **Thallon** Aust
110C1 **Thames** NZ
43E4 **Thames** *R* Eng
76D2 **Thanh Hoah** Viet
87B2 **Thanjavur** India
76D1 **Thanlwin = Salween**
85C3 **Thar Desert** India
108B1 **Thargomindah** Aust
55B2 **Thásos** *I* Greece
8C2 **Thermopolis** USA
4F2 **Thesiger B** Can
14B1 **Thessalon** Can
55B2 **Thessaloniki** Greece
43E3 **Thetford** Eng
15D1 **Thetford Mines** Can
101G1 **Theunissen** S Africa
19B4 **Thibodaux** USA
5J4 **Thicket Portage** Can
8D2 **Thief River Falls** USA
20B2 **Thielsen,Mt** USA
49C2 **Thiers** France
43B1 **Thiès** Sen
99D3 **Thika** Kenya
86B1 **Thimphu** Bhutan
49D2 **Thionville** France
55C3 **Thira** *I* Greece
42D2 **Thirsk** Eng
Thiruvananthapuram = Trivandrum
39F7 **Thisted** Den
55B3 **Thívai** Greece
48C2 **Thiviers** France
17B1 **Thomaston** Georgia, USA

45C2 **Thomastown** Irish Rep
17B1 **Thomasville** Georgia, USA
6A2 **Thom Bay** Can
5J4 **Thompson** Can
18B1 **Thompson** *R* USA
4G3 **Thompson Landing** Can
13C2 **Thompson** *R* Can
16C2 **Thompsonville** USA
17B1 **Thomson** USA
107D3 **Thomson** *R* Aust
76C3 **Thon Buri** Thai
76B2 **Thongwa** Burma
47B1 **Thonon-les-Bains** France
42C2 **Thornhill** Scot
48B2 **Thouars** France
15C2 **Thousand Is** Can/ USA
13E2 **Three Hills** Can
7G4 **Three Kings Is** NZ
76B2 **Three Pagodas P** Thai
14A2 **Three Rivers** Michigan, USA
20B2 **Three Sisters** *Mt* USA
6D2 **Thule** Greenland
47B1 **Thun** Switz
10B2 **Thunder Bay** Can
47B1 **Thuner See** *L* Switz
77B4 **Thung Song** Thai
47C1 **Thur** *R* Switz
57C2 **Thüringen** State, Germany
57C2 **Thüringer Wald** *Upland* Germany
45C2 **Thurles** Irish Rep
71F5 **Thursday I** Aust
44C2 **Thurso** Scot
112B4 **Thurston I** Ant
47C1 **Thusis** Switz
108B1 **Thylungra** Aust
73B5 **Tiandong** China
73B5 **Tian'e** China
72D2 **Tianjin** China
73B5 **Tianlin** China
82C1 **Tiãn Shan** *Mts* C Asia
72B3 **Tianshui** China
72A2 **Tianzhu** China
96C1 **Tiaret** Alg
35A2 **Tibagi** *R* Brazil
94B2 **Tiberias,L** Israel
Tiber,R = Tevere,R
95A2 **Tibesti** *Mountain Region* Chad
82C2 **Tibet** Autonomous Region, China
108B1 **Tibooburra** Aust
86A1 **Tibrikot** Nepal
24A2 **Tiburón** *I* Mexico
97B3 **Tichitt** Maur
96A2 **Tichla** Mor
47C2 **Ticino** *R* Italy/Switz
15D2 **Ticonderoga** USA
25D2 **Ticul** Mexico
97A3 **Tidjikja** Maur
47C1 **Tiefencastel** Switz
74A2 **Tieling** China
46B1 **Tielt** Belg
46C1 **Tienen** Belg
65J5 **Tien Shan** *Mts* China/Kirghizia
72D2 **Tientsin** China
39H6 **Tierp** Sweden
23B2 **Tierra Blanca** Mexico
23B2 **Tierra Colorada** Mexico
29C6 **Tierra del Fuego** Territory, Arg
28C8 **Tierra del Fuego** *I* Arg/Chile
35B2 **Tietê** Brazil
35A2 **Tiete** *R* Brazil
14B2 **Tiffin** USA
17B1 **Tifton** USA
32B3 **Tigre** *R* Peru
33E2 **Tigre** *R* Ven
93E3 **Tigris** *R* Iraq
23B1 **Tihuatlán** Mexico

21B3 **Tijuana** Mexico
85D4 **Tikamgarh** India
60D2 **Tikhin** Russian Fed
61F4 **Tikhoretsk** Russian Fed
93D3 **Tikrit** Iraq
1B8 **Tiksi** Russian Fed
46C1 **Tilburg** Neth
43E4 **Tilbury** Eng
30C3 **Tilcara** Arg
108B1 **Tilcha** Aust
76A1 **Tilin** Burma
97C3 **Tillabéri** Niger
20B1 **Tillamook** USA
97C3 **Tillia** Niger
55C3 **Tílos** *I* Greece
108B2 **Tilpa** Aust
32B3 **Tiluá** Colombia
64G3 **Timanskiy Kryazh** Russian Fed
111B2 **Timaru** NZ
60E4 **Timashevsk** Russian Fed
55B3 **Timbákion** Greece
19B4 **Timbalier B** USA
97B3 **Timbédra** Maur
Timbuktu = Tombouctou
97B3 **Timétrine Monts** *Mts* Mali
97C3 **Timia** Niger
96C2 **Timiş** *R* Rom
96C2 **Timişoara** Rom
10B2 **Timmins** Can
10B1 **Timor** *I* Indon
106B2 **Timor S** Aust/Indon
34C3 **Timote** Arg
27D5 **Tinaca Pt** Phil
87B2 **Tindivanam** India
96B2 **Tindouf** Alg
96C2 **Tin Fouye** Alg
6F3 **Tingmiarmiut** Greenland
32B5 **Tingo Maria** Peru
97B3 **Tingréla** Ivory Coast
86B1 **Tingri** China
71F2 **Tinian** Pacific O
30C4 **Tinogasta** Arg
55C3 **Tinos** *I* Greece
43B4 **Tintagel Head** *Pt* Eng
96C2 **Tin Tarabine** *Watercourse* Alg
108B3 **Tintinara** Aust
96C2 **Tin Zaouaten** Alg
22C2 **Tioga P** USA
77C5 **Tioman** *I* Malay
47D1 **Tione** Italy
45C2 **Tipperary** County, Irish Rep
41B3 **Tipperary** Irish Rep
18B2 **Tipton** Missouri, USA
87B2 **Tiptur** India
23A2 **Tiquicheo** Mexico
55A2 **Tiranë** Alb
47D1 **Tirano** Italy
60C4 **Tiraspol** Moldova
87B2 **Tirchchirāppalli** India
55C3 **Tire** Turk
93C1 **Tirebolu** Turk
44A3 **Tiree** *I* Scot
54C2 **Tîrgovişte** Rom
54B1 **Tîrgu Jiu** Rom
54B1 **Tîrgu Mureş** Rom
54C1 **Tirich Mir** *Mt* Pak
96A2 **Tiris** Region, Mor
61J3 **Tirlyanskiy** Russian Fed
54B1 **Tîrnáveni** Rom
55B3 **Tírnavos** Greece
85D4 **Tirodi** India
47D1 **Tirol** Province, Austria
53A2 **Tirso** *R* Sardegna
87B3 **Tiruchchendur** India
87B3 **Tirunelveli** India
87B2 **Tirupati** India
87B2 **Tiruppattūr** India
87B2 **Tiruppur** India
87B2 **Tiruvannāmalai** India
19A3 **Tishomingo** USA

Tisīyah

94C2 Tisīyah Syria
59C3 Tisza R Hung
86A2 Titlagarh India
54B2 Titov Veles Macedonia
98C2 Titule Zaire
17B2 Titusville USA
43C4 Tiverton Eng
52B3 Tivoli Italy
23B2 Tixtla Mexico
99E2 Tiyeglow Somalia
23B2 Tizayuca Mexico
25D2 Tizimin Mexico
96C1 Tizi Ouzou Alg
96B2 Tiznit Mor
23A1 Tizpan el Alto Mexico
23B2 Tlacolula Mexico
23B2 Tlacotalpan Mexico
23A2 Tlalchana Mexico
23B2 Tlalnepantla Mexico
23B2 Tlalpan Mexico
23A1 Tlaltenango Mexico
23B2 Tlancualpican Mexico
23B2 Tlapa Mexico
23B2 Tlapacoyan Mexico
23A1 Tlaquepaque Mexico
23B2 Tlaxcala Mexico
23B2 Tlaxcala State, Mexico
23B2 Tlaxiaco Mexico
96B1 Tlemcen Alg
101D2 Toamasina Madag
34C3 Toay Arg
75B2 Toba Japan
84B2 Toba and Kakar Ranges Mts Pak
27E4 Tobago I Caribbean S
13C2 Toba Inlet Sd Can
71D3 Tobelo Indon
14B1 Tobermory Can
44A3 Tobermory Scot
71E3 Tobi I Pacific O
21B1 Tobin,Mt USA
65H4 Tobol R Kazakhstan
70D4 Toboli Indon
65H4 Tobol'sk Russian Fed
Tobruk = Tubruq
31B2 Tocantins R Brazil
31B3 Tocantins State, Brazil
17B1 Toccoa USA
47C1 Toce R Italy
30B3 Tocopilla Chile
30C3 Tocorpuri Mt Chile
32D1 Tocuyo R Ven
85D3 Toda India
47C1 Tödi Mt Switz
75A1 Todong S Korea
9B4 Todos Santos Mexico
13E2 Tofield Can
13B3 Tofino Can
12B3 Togiak USA
12B3 Togiak B USA
97C4 Togo Republic, Africa
72C1 Togtoh China
12F2 Tok USA
74E2 Tokachi R Japan
75B1 Tokanan(ki Japan
95C3 Tokar Sudan
69E4 Tokara Retto Arch Japan
92C1 Tokat Turk
74B3 Tökchok-kundo Arch S Korea
75A1 Tok-do I S Korea
82B1 Tokmak Kirghizia
110C1 Tokomaru Bay NZ
12H3 Toku R Can/USA
78C3 Tokung Indon
69E4 Tokuno I Japan
74C4 Tokushima Japan
75A2 Tokuyama Japan
74D3 Tökyö Japan
110C1 Tolaga Bay NZ
101D3 Tôlanaro Madag
30F3 Toledo Brazil
50B2 Toledo Spain
14B2 Toledo USA
19B3 Toledo Bend Res USA

101D3 Toliara Madag
23B1 Toliman Mexico
32B3 Tolina Mt Colombia
51B1 Tolosa Spain
29B3 Toltén Chile
23B2 Toluca Mexico
61G3 Tol'yatti Russian Fed
74E2 Tomakomai Japan
78D1 Tomani Malay
58C2 Tomaszów Mazowiecka Pol
11B3 Tombigbee R USA
98B3 Tomboco Angola
35C2 Tombos Brazil
97B3 Tombouctou Mali
100A2 Tombua Angola
34A3 Tomé Chile
50B2 Tomelloso Spain
50A2 Tomer Port
106B3 Tomkinson Range Mts Aust
63E2 Tommot Russian Fed
55B2 Tomorrit Mt Alb
65K4 Tomsk Russian Fed
16B3 Toms River USA
25C3 Tonalá Mexico
20C1 Tonasket USA
15C2 Tonawanda USA
105H4 Tonga Is Pacific O
101H1 Tongaat S Africa
73D3 Tongcheng China
72B2 Tongchuan China
72A2 Tongde China
46C1 Tongeren Belg
76E2 Tonggu Jiao I China
73A5 Tonghai China
74B2 Tonghua China
74B3 Tongjosŏn-man N Korea
76D1 Tongkin,G of China/Viet
72E1 Tongliao China
73D3 Tongling China
108B2 Tongo Aust
34A2 Tongoy Chile
73B4 Tongren Guizhou, China
72A2 Tongren Qinghai, China
86C1 Tongsa Bhutan
76B1 Tongta Burma
68B3 Tongtian He R China
44B2 Tongue Scot
72D2 Tong Xian China
72B2 Tongxin China
73B4 Tongzi China
9C4 Tonich Mexico
99C2 Tonj Sudan
85D3 Tonk India
18A2 Tonkawa USA
76C3 Tonle Sap L Camb
21B2 Tonopah USA
12E2 Tonsina USA
8B2 Tooele USA
109D1 Toogoolawah Aust
108B1 Toompine Aust
109D1 Toowoomba Aust
22C1 Topaz L USA
18A2 Topeka USA
9C4 Topolobampo Mexico
20B1 Toppenish USA
99D2 Tor Eth
55C3 Torbali Turk
90C2 Torbat-e-Heydariyeh Iran
90C2 Torbat-e Jäm Iran
12D2 Torbert,Mt USA
50A1 Tordesillas Spain
56C2 Torgau Germany
46B1 Torhout Belg
69G3 Tori I Japan
47B2 Torino Italy
99D2 Torit Sudan
35A1 Torixoreu Brazil
50A1 Tormes R Spain
13E2 Tornado Mt Can
38J5 Torne L Sweden
38H5 Torneträsk Sweden
7D4 Torngat Mts Can
38J5 Tornio Fin
34C3 Tornquist Arg
15C2 Toronto Can

60D2 Toropets Russian Fed
99D2 Tororo Uganda
92B2 Toros Dağlari Mts Turk
43C4 Torquay Eng
22C4 Torrance USA
50A2 Torrão Port
51C1 Torreblanca Spain
53B2 Torre del Greco Italy
50B1 Torrelavega Spain
50B2 Torremolinos Spain
108A2 Torrens,L Aust
24B2 Torreón Mexico
47B2 Torre Pellice Italy
107D2 Torres Str Aust
50A2 Torres Vedras Port
16C2 Torrington Connecticut, USA
8C2 Torrington Wyoming, USA
9C4 Torrón Mexico
38D3 Tórshavn Føroyar
47C2 Tortona Italy
51C1 Tortosa Spain
90C2 Torüd Iran
45C2 Tory I Irish Rep
60D2 Torzhok Russian Fed
75A2 Tosa Japan
74C4 Tosa-shimizu Japan
74C4 Tosa-wan B Japan
75B2 To-shima I Japan
Toshkent = Tashkent
60D2 Tosno Russian Fed
74C2 Tosu Japan
92B1 Tosya Turk
61F1 Tot'ma Russian Fed
43C4 Totnes Eng
33F2 Totness Surinam
23B2 Totolapan Mexico
51B2 Totona Spain
109C2 Tottenham Aust
74C3 Tottori Japan
97B4 Touba Ivory Coast
97A3 Touba Sen
96B1 Toubkal Mt Mor
97B3 Tougan Burkina
96C1 Touggourt Alg
97A3 Tougué Guinea
46C2 Toul France
49D3 Toulon France
48C3 Toulouse France
97B4 Toumodi Ivory Coast
76B2 Toungoo Burma
46B1 Tourcoing France
96A2 Tourine Maur
46B1 Tournai Belg
48C2 Tours France
74E2 Towada Japan
74E2 Towada-ko L Japan
15C2 Towanda USA
107C2 Townsville Aust
16A3 Towson USA
43C4 Towy R Wales
74D3 Toyama Japan
75B1 Toyama-wan B Japan
75B2 Toyohashi Japan
75B2 Toyonaka Japan
75B1 Toyooka Japan
74D3 Toyota Japan
96C1 Tozeur Tunisia
46D2 Traben-Trarbach Germany
93C1 Trabzon Turk
22B2 Tracy California, USA
34A3 Traiguén Chile
13D3 Trail Can
41B3 Tralee Irish Rep
45C2 Tralee B Irish Rep
45C2 Tramore Irish Rep
39G7 Tranås Sweden
77B4 Trang Thai
71E4 Trangan I Indon
109C2 Trangie Aust
12E2 Transalaskan Pipeline USA
100B3 Transvaal Province, S Africa
Transylvanian Alps = Munţii Carpaţii Meridionali
53B3 Trapani Italy

109C3 Traralgon Aust
97A3 Trarza Region, Maur
76C3 Trat Thai
108B2 Traveller's L Aust
56C2 Travemünde Germany
14A2 Traverse City USA
12C1 Traverse Peak Mt USA
111B2 Travers,Mt NZ
47C2 Trebbia R Italy
59B3 Trebič Czech Republic
54A2 Trebinje Bosnia-Herzegovina
57C3 Trebon Czech Republic
29F2 Treinta y Tres Urug
29C4 Trelew Arg
39G7 Trelleborg Sweden
43B3 Tremadog B Wales
15D1 Tremblant,Mt Can
13C2 Trembleur L Can
16A2 Tremont USA
59B3 Trenčin Slovakia
34C3 Trenque Lauquén Arg
43D3 Trent R Eng
47D1 Trentino Region, Italy
47D1 Trento Italy
15C2 Trenton Can
18B1 Trenton Missouri, USA
16B2 Trenton New Jersey, USA
7E5 Trepassey Can
34C3 Tres Arroyos Arg
35B2 Tres Corações Brazil
30F3 Três Lagoas Brazil
34C3 Tres Lomas Arg
22B2 Tres Pinos USA
35C2 Três Rios Brazil
47C2 Treviglio Italy
47C2 Treviso Italy
47C2 Trezzo Italy
87B2 Trichūr India
108C2 Trida Aust
46D2 Trier Germany
52B1 Trieste Italy
45C2 Trim Irish Rep
87C3 Trincomalee Sri Lanka
33E6 Trinidad Bol
29E2 Trinidad Urug
9C3 Trinidad USA
34C3 Trinidad I Arg
27E4 Trinidad I
103G6 Trindade I Atlantic O
27E4 Trinidad & Tobago Republic Caribbean S
19A3 Trinity USA
9D3 Trinity R USA
7E5 Trinity B Can
12D3 Trinity Is USA
17A1 Trion USA
94B1 Tripoli Leb
95A1 Tripoli Libya
55B3 Tripolis Greece
86C2 Tripura State, India
103H6 Tristan da Cunha Is Atlantic O
87B3 Trivandrum India
59B3 Trnava Slovakia
107E1 Trobriand Is PNG
15D1 Trois-Rivières Can
65H4 Troitsk Russian Fed
39G7 Trollhättan Sweden
38F6 Trollheimen Mt Nor
90B3 Tromelin I Indian O
38H5 Tromsø Nor
38G6 Trondheim Nor
38G6 Trondheimfjord Inlet Nor
42B2 Troon Scot
102J3 Tropic of Cancer
103J6 Tropic of Capricorn
96B2 Troudenni Mali
7A1 Trout L Ontario, Can
17A1 Troy Alabama, USA
16C1 Troy New York, USA
14B2 Troy Ohio, USA
54B2 Troyan Bulg

49C2	**Troyes** France
91B5	**Trucial Coast** Region, UAE
21A2	**Truckee** *R* USA
25D3	**Trujillo** Honduras
32B5	**Trujillo** Peru
50A2	**Trujillo** Spain
32C2	**Trujillo** Ven
109C2	**Trundle** Aust
7D5	**Truro** Can
43B4	**Truro** Eng
68B2	**Tsagaan Nuur** *L* Mongolia
68B1	**Tsagan-Tologoy** Russian Fed
101D2	**Tsaratanana** Madag
100B3	**Tsau** Botswana
99D3	**Tsavo** Kenya
99D3	**Tsavo Nat Pk** Kenya
65J4	**Tselinograd** Kazakhstan
100A3	**Tses** Namibia
68C2	**Tsetserleg** Mongolia
97C4	**Tsévié** Togo
100B3	**Tshabong** Botswana
100B3	**Tshane** Botswana
98B3	**Tshela** Zaïre
98C3	**Tshibala** Zaïre
98C3	**Tshikapa** Zaïre
98C3	**Tshuapa** *R* Zaïre
101D3	**Tsihombe** Madag
61F4	**Tsimlyanskoye Vodokhranilishche** *Res* Russian Fed
	Tsinan = Jinan
	Tsingtao = Qingdao
101D2	**Tsiroanomandidy** Madag
13B2	**Tsitsutl Peak** *Mt* Can
58D2	**Tsna** *R* Belorussia
72B1	**Tsogt Ovoo** Mongolia
68C2	**Tsomog** Mongolia
75B2	**Tsu** Japan
75B1	**Tsubata** Japan
74E3	**Tsuchiura** Japan
74E2	**Tsugaru-kaikyo** *Str* Japan
100A2	**Tsumeb** Namibia
100A3	**Tsumis** Namibia
75B1	**Tsuruga** Japan
74D3	**Tsuruga** Japan
74D3	**Tsuruoka** Japan
75B4	**Tsushima** Japan
74C3	**Tsuyama** Japan
50A1	**Tua** *R* Port
45B2	**Tuam** Irish Rep
60E5	**Tuapse** Russian Fed
111A3	**Tuatapere** NZ
30G4	**Tubarão** Brazil
94B2	**Tubas** Israel
79A4	**Tubbataha Reefs** *Is* Phil
57B3	**Tübingen** Germany
95B1	**Tubruq** Libya
16B3	**Tuckerton** USA
9B3	**Tucson** USA
30C4	**Tucumán** State, Arg
34B2	**Tucunuco** Arg
33E2	**Tucupita** Ven
51B1	**Tudela** Spain
93C3	**Tudmur** Syria
101H1	**Tugela** S Africa
109D2	**Tuggerah** *L* Aust
12D3	**Tugidak I** USA
79B2	**Tuguegarao** Phil
63F2	**Tugur** Russian Fed
72D2	**Tuhai He** *R* China
4E3	**Tuktoyaktuk** USA
58C1	**Tukums** Latvia
99D3	**Tukuyu** Tanz
84B1	**Tukzar** Afghan
60E3	**Tula** Russian Fed
23B1	**Tulancingo** Mexico
78A3	**Tulangbawang** *R* Indon
32B3	**Tulcán** Colombia
60C5	**Tulcea** Rom
100B3	**Tuli** Zim
94B2	**Tulkarm** Israel
48C2	**Tulle** France
19B3	**Tullos** USA
45C2	**Tullow** Irish Rep
18A2	**Tulsa** USA
93C3	**Tulūl ash Shāmīyah** *Desert Region* Syria/S Arabia
63C2	**Tulun** Russian Fed
78C4	**Tulungagung** Indon
32B3	**Tumaco** Colombia
109C3	**Tumbarumba** Aust
32A4	**Tumbes** Ecuador
108A2	**Tumby Bay** Aust
74B2	**Tumen** China
87B2	**Tumkūr** India
77C4	**Tumpat** Malay
85D4	**Tumsar** India
97B3	**Tumu** Ghana
109C3	**Tumut** Aust
109C3	**Tumut** *R* Aust
27L1	**Tunapuna** Trinidad
92C2	**Tunceli** Turk
99D3	**Tunduma** Zambia
101C2	**Tunduru** Tanz
54C2	**Tundzha** *R* Bulg
87B1	**Tungabhadra** *R* India
68D4	**Tung-Chiang** Taiwan
38B2	**Tungnafellsjökull** *Mts* Iceland
12J2	**Tungsten** Can
63B1	**Tunguska** *R* Russian Fed
87C1	**Tuni** India
96D1	**Tunis** Tunisia
88E4	**Tunisia** Republic, N Africa
32C2	**Tunja** Colombia
12B2	**Tuntutuliak** USA
12B2	**Tununak** USA
34B2	**Tunuyán** Arg
34B2	**Tunuyán** *R* Arg
22C2	**Tuolumne Meadows** USA
35A2	**Tupã** Brazil
35B1	**Tupaciguara** Brazil
19C3	**Tupelo** USA
30C3	**Tupiza** Bol
15D2	**Tupper Lake** USA
34B2	**Tupungato** Arg
29C2	**Tupungato** *Mt* Arg
86C1	**Tura** India
63C1	**Tura** Russian Fed
90C2	**Turan** Iran
63B2	**Turan** Russian Fed
93C3	**Turayf** S Arabia
80E3	**Turbat** Pak
75B0	**Turbo** Colombia
54B1	**Turda** Rom
63A3	**Turfan Depression** China
65H4	**Turgay** Kazakhstan
63B3	**Turgen Uul** *Mt* Mongolia
54C2	**Turgovishte** Bulg
92A2	**Turgutlu** Turk
39K7	**Türi** Estonia
51B2	**Turia** *R* Spain
	Turin = Torino
61K2	**Turinsk** Russian Fed
69F2	**Turiy Rog** Russian Fed
99D2	**Turkana,L** Kenya/Eth
80E1	**Turkestan** Region, C Asia
82A1	**Turkestan** Kazakhstan
92C2	**Turkey** Republic, W Asia
80D1	**Turkmenistan** Republic, Asia
90B2	**Turkmenskiy Zaliv** *B* Turkmenistan
27C2	**Turks Is** Caribbean S
39J6	**Turku** Fin
99D2	**Turkwel** *R* Kenya
22B2	**Turlock** USA
22B2	**Turlock L** USA
110C2	**Turnagain,C** NZ
25D3	**Turneffe I** Belize
16C1	**Turners Falls** USA
46C1	**Turnhout** Belg
54B2	**Turnu Măgurele** Rom
63A3	**Turpan** China
26B2	**Turquino** *Mt* Cuba
80E1	**Turtkul'** Uzbekistan
18A2	**Turtle Creek Res** USA
13F2	**Turtle L** Can
63A1	**Turukhansk** Russian Fed
68C1	**Turuntayevo** Russian Fed
35A1	**Turvo** *R* Goias, Brazil
35B2	**Turvo** *R* São Paulo, Brazil
58C2	**Tur'ya** *R* Ukraine
19C3	**Tuscaloosa** USA
18C2	**Tuscola** USA
90C3	**Tusharik** Iran
	Tutera = Tudela
87B3	**Tuticorin** India
54C2	**Tutrakan** Bulg
57B3	**Tuttlingen** Germany
68C2	**Tuul Gol** *R* Mongolia
105G4	**Tuvalu** *Is* Pacific O
63B2	**Tuvinskaya Respublika,** Russian Fed
23A2	**Tuxpan** Jalisco, Mexico
24B2	**Tuxpan** Nayarit, Mexico
23B1	**Tuxpan** Veracruz, Mexico
23B2	**Tuxtepec** Mexico
25C3	**Tuxtla Gutiérrez** Mexico
50A1	**Túy** Spain
76D3	**Tuy Hoa** Viet
92B2	**Tuz Gölü** *Salt L* Turk
93D3	**Tuz Khurmātū** Iraq
54A2	**Tuzla** Bosnia-Herzegovina
60E2	**Tver'** Russian Fed
42C2	**Tweed** *R* Eng/Scot
109D1	**Tweed Heads** Aust
42C2	**Tweedsmuir Hills** Scot
7E5	**Twillingate** Can
8B2	**Twin Falls** USA
14A2	**Two Rivers** USA
63E2	**Tygda** Russian Fed
19A3	**Tyler** USA
65K3	**Tym** *R* Russian Fed
69G1	**Tyrnovskoye** Russian Fed
42D2	**Tyne** *R* Eng
42D2	**Tyne and Wear** Metropolitan County, Eng
42D2	**Tynemouth** Eng
38G6	**Tynset** Nor
12D3	**Tyonek** USA
94B2	**Tyr** Leb
	Tyre = Tyr
45C1	**Tyrone** County, N Ire
108B3	**Tyrrell,L** Aust
53B2	**Tyrrhenian S** Italy
65H4	**Tyumen'** Russian Fed
43B3	**Tywyn** Wales
55B3	**Tzoumérka** *Mt* Greece
99E2	**Uarsciek** Somalia
35C2	**Ubá** Brazil
35C1	**Ubaí** Brazil
35C1	**Ubangi** *R* CAR
47B2	**Ubaye** *R* France
75A2	**Ube** Japan
50B2	**Úbeda** Spain
6E2	**Ubekendt Ejland** *I* Greenland
35B1	**Uberaba** Brazil
35B1	**Uberlândia** Brazil
76C2	**Ubon Ratchathani** Thai
58D2	**Ubort** *R* Belorussia
32C5	**Ucayali** *R* Peru
84C3	**Uch** Pak
63F2	**Uchar** *R* Russian Fed
74E2	**Uchiura-wan** *B* Japan
63B2	**Uda** *R* Russian Fed
85C4	**Udaipur** India
86B1	**Udaipur Garhi** Nepal
34D3	**Udaquoila** Arg
39G7	**Uddevalla** Sweden
38H5	**Uddjaur** *L* Sweden
87B1	**Udgir** India
84D2	**Udhampur** India
61H2	**Udmurtskaya Respublika,** Russian Fed
76C2	**Udon Than** Thai
63F2	**Udskaya Guba** *B* Russian Fed
87A2	**Udupi** India
75B1	**Ueda** Japan
99C2	**Uele** *R* Zaïre
56C2	**Uelzen** Germany
98C2	**Uere** *R* Zaïre
61J3	**Ufa** Russian Fed
61J2	**Ufa** *R* Russian Fed
100A3	**Ugab** *R* Namibia
99D3	**Ugaila** *R* Tanz
12D3	**Ugak B** USA
99D2	**Uganda** Republic, Africa
12C3	**Ugashik B** USA
12C3	**Ugashik L** USA
47B2	**Ugine** France
69G2	**Uglegorsk** Russian Fed
60E2	**Uglich** Russian Fed
60E3	**Ugra** *R* Russian Fed
44A3	**Uig** Scot
98B3	**Uige** Angola
61H4	**Uil** Kazakhstan
8B2	**Uinta Mts** USA
100B4	**Uitenhage** S Africa
59C3	**Ujfehértó** Hung
75B2	**Uji** Japan
30C3	**Ujina** Chile
85D4	**Ujjain** India
70C4	**Ujung Pandang** Indon
99D3	**Ukerewe I** Tanz
86C1	**Ukhrul** India
21A2	**Ukiah** California, USA
20C1	**Ukiah** Oregon, USA
58C1	**Ukmerge** Lithuania
60C4	**Ukraine** Republic, Europe
68C2	**Ulaanbaatar** Mongolia
68B2	**Ulaangom** Mongolia
72C1	**Ulaan Uul** Mongolia
82C1	**Ulangar Hu** *L* China
68C1	**Ulan Ude** Russian Fed
68B3	**Ulan Ul Hu** *L* China
34B2	**Ulapes** Arg
74B3	**Ulchin** S Korea
54A2	**Ulcinj** Montenegro, Yugos
68B2	**Uldz** Mongolia
68B2	**Uliastay** Mongolia
58D1	**Ulla** *R* Lithuania
100D3	**Ulladulla** Aust
44B3	**Ullapool** Scot
38H5	**Ullsfjorden** *Inlet* Nor
74C2	**Ullswater** *L* Eng
74C3	**Ullung-do** *I* S Korea
57C3	**Ulm** Germany
108A1	**Uloowaranie,L** Aust
74B3	**Ulsan** S Korea
45C1	**Ulster** Region, N Ire
65K5	**Ulungur He** *R* China
65K5	**Ulungur Hu** *L* China
44A3	**Ulva** *I* Scot
42C2	**Ulverston** Eng
109C4	**Ulverstone** Aust
63G2	**Ulya** *R* Russian Fed
60D4	**Uman** Ukraine
6E2	**Umanak** Greenland
86A2	**Umaria** India
85B3	**Umarkot** Pak
108A1	**Umaroona,L** Aust
20C1	**Umatilla** USA
38L5	**Umba** Russian Fed
99D3	**Umba** *R* Tanz
38H6	**Ume** *R* Sweden
38J6	**Umeå** Sweden
101H1	**Umfolozi** *R* S Africa
4C3	**Umiat** USA
91C4	**Umm al Qaiwain** UAE

Umm as Samīm

91C5 **Umm as Samīm** *Salt Marsh* Oman
99C1 **Umm Bell** Sudan
98C1 **Umm Keddada** Sudan
99D1 **Umm Ruwaba** Sudan
91B5 **Umm Sa'id** Qatar
20B2 **Umpqua** *R* USA
85D4 **Umred** India
100B4 **Umtata** S Africa
35A2 **Umuarama** Brazil
52C1 **Una** *R* Bosnia-Herzegovina/Croatia
35B1 **Unai** Brazil
12B2 **Unalakleet** USA
80C3 **Unayzah** S Arabia
16C2 **Uncasville** USA
101G1 **Underberg** S Africa
60D3 **Unecha** Russian Fed
94B3 **Uneisa** Jordan
7D4 **Ungava B** Can
30F4 **União de Vitória** Brazil
34B3 **Unión** Arg
18B2 **Union** Missouri, USA
17B1 **Union** S Carolina, USA
14C2 **Union City** Pennsylvania, USA
17A1 **Union Springs** USA
15C3 **Uniontown** USA
91B5 **United Arab Emirates** Arabian Pen
36C3 **United Kingdom** Kingdom, W Europe
2H4 **United States of America**
6B1 **United States Range** *Mts* Can
13F2 **Unity** Can
20C2 **Unity** USA
46D1 **Unna** Germany
86A1 **Unnão** India
44E1 **Unst** *I* Scot
13A1 **Unuk** *R* USA
92C1 **Unye** Turk
61F2 **Unzha** *R* Russian Fed
33E2 **Upata** Ven
98C3 **Upemba Nat Pk** Zaire
6E2 **Upernavik** Greenland
22D3 **Upland** USA
100B3 **Uplington** S Africa
14B2 **Upper Arlington** USA
18C2 **Upper Arrow L** Can
111C2 **Upper Hutt** NZ
20B2 **Upper Klamath L** USA
20B2 **Upper L** USA
45C1 **Upper Lough Erne** *L* N Ire
27L1 **Upper Manzanilla** Trinidad
39H7 **Uppsala** Sweden
72B1 **Ural Qiangi** China
91A4 **Urairah** S Arabia
61H3 **Ural** *R* Kazakhstan
109D2 **Uralla** Aust
61H3 **Ural'sk** Kazakhstan
65G4 **Uralskiy Khrebet** *Mts* Russian Fed
5H4 **Uranium City** Can
75B1 **Urawa** Japan
18C1 **Urbana** Illinois, USA
14B2 **Urbana** Ohio, USA
52B2 **Urbino** Italy
42C2 **Ure** *R* Eng
61G2 **Uren'** Russian Fed
80E1 **Urgench** Uzbekistan
84B2 **Urgun** Afghan
55C3 **Urla** Turk
54B2 **Uroševac** Serbia, Yugos
31B4 **Uruçu** Brazil
23A2 **Uruapan** Mexico
35B1 **Urucuia** *R* Brazil
30E4 **Uruguaiana** Brazil
29E2 **Uruguay** Republic, S America
29E2 **Uruguay** *R* Urug
82C1 **Urümqi** China
69H2 **Urup** *I* Russian Fed
84B2 **Uruzgan** Afghan
61F3 **Uryupinsk** Russian Fed
61H2 **Urzhum** Russian Fed
54C1 **Urziceni** Rom
82C1 **Usa** China
75A2 **Usa** Japan
64G3 **Usa** *R* Russian Fed
92A2 **Uşak** Turk
100A3 **Usakos** Namibia
99D3 **Ushashi** Tanz
65J5 **Ush Tobe** Kazakhstan
29C6 **Ushuaia** Arg
63E2 **Ushumun** Russian Fed
43C4 **Usk** *R* Wales
92A1 **Usküdar** Turk
63C2 **Usolye Sibirskoye** Russian Fed
34B2 **Uspallata** Arg
69F2 **Ussdaryisk** Russian Fed
47C1 **Uster** Switz
53B3 **Ustica** *I* Italy
57C2 **Usti nad Labem** Czech Republic
65J4 **Ust'Ishim** Russian Fed
58B2 **Ustka** Pol
65K5 **Ust'-Kamenogorsk** Kazakhstan
63C2 **Ust Karabula** Russian Fed
61J2 **Ust'Katav** Russian Fed
63C2 **Ust'-Kut** Russian Fed
61E4 **Ust Labinsk** Russian Fed
63F1 **Ust'Maya** Russian Fed
1C8 **Ust'Nera** Russian Fed
63E2 **Ust'Nyukzha** Russian Fed
63C2 **Ust'Ordynskiy** Russian Fed
64G3 **Ust'Tsil'ma** Russian Fed
63F2 **Ust'Umal'ta** Russian Fed
75A2 **Usuki** Japan
25C3 **Usulutan** El Salvador
101H1 **Usutu** *R* Swaziland
8B3 **Utah** State, USA
8B3 **Utah L** USA
58D1 **Utena** Russian Fed
85B3 **Uthal** Pak
10C2 **Utica** USA
51B2 **Utiel** Spain
13D1 **Utikuma L** Can
56B2 **Utrecht** Neth
101H1 **Utrecht** S Africa
50A2 **Utrera** Spain
38K5 **Utsjoki** Fin
74D3 **Utsunomiya** Japan
76C2 **Uttaradit** Thai
86A1 **Uttar Pradesh** State, India
16H4 **Uva** Russian Fed
107F3 **Uvéa** *I* Nouvelle Calédonie
99D3 **Uvinza** Tanz
99C3 **Uvira** Zaire
6E2 **Uvkusigssat** Greenland
39J6 **Uvsikaupunki** Fin
68B1 **Uvs Nuur** *L* China
74C4 **Uwajima** Japan
72B2 **Uxin Qi** China
63B2 **Uyar** Russian Fed
30C3 **Uyuni** Bol
80E1 **Uzbekistan** Republic, Asia
48C2 **Uzerche** France
59C3 **Uzhgorod** Ukraine
54A2 **Užice** Serbia, Yugos
60E3 **Uzlovaya** Russian Fed
92A1 **Uzunköprü** Turk

V

101F1 **Vaal** *R* S Africa
101G1 **Vaal Dam** *Res* S Africa
100B3 **Vaalwater** S Africa
38J6 **Vaasa** Fin
59B3 **Vác** Hung
30F4 **Vacaria** Brazil
35C1 **Vacaria** *R* Minas Gerais, Brazil
21A2 **Vacaville** USA
85C4 **Vadodara** India
38K4 **Vadsø** Nor
47C1 **Vaduz** Leichtenstein
38D3 **Vágar** Føroyar
29E3 **Va Gesell** Arg
59B3 **Váh** *R* Slovakia
87B2 **Vaigai** *R* India
65K3 **Vakh** *R* Russian Fed
60B4 **Válcea** Rom
29C4 **Valcheta** Arg
47D2 **Valdagno** Italy
60D2 **Valday** Russian Fed
60D2 **Valdayskaya Vozvyshennost'** *Upland* Russian Fed
32D2 **Val de la Pascua** Ven
50A2 **Valdepeñas** Spain
12E2 **Valdez** USA
29B3 **Valdivia** Chile
46B2 **Val d'Oise** *Department* France
17B1 **Valdosta** USA
20C2 **Vale** USA
13D2 **Valemount** Can
31D4 **Valença** Bahia, Brazil
35C2 **Valença** Rio de Janeiro, Brazil
49C3 **Valence** France
51B2 **Valencia** Region, Spain
51B2 **Valencia** Spain
32D1 **Valencia** Ven
45A3 **Valencia** *I* Irish Rep
50A2 **Valencia de Alcantara** Spain
46B1 **Valenciennes** France
47C2 **Valenza** Italy
32C2 **Valera** Ven
39K7 **Valga** Estonia
54A2 **Valjevo** Serbia, Yugos
Valka = Valga
39J6 **Valkeakoski** Fin
25D2 **Valladolid** Mexico
50B1 **Valladolid** Spain
47B2 **Valle d'Aosta** Region, Italy
27D5 **Valle de la Pascua** Ven
23A1 **Valle de Santiago** Mexico
47B2 **Valle d'Isère** France
32C1 **Valledupar** Colombia
97C3 **Vallée de l'Azaouak** *V* Niger
97C3 **Vallée Tilemsi** *V* Mali
18C3 **Valle Grande** Bol
22A1 **Vallejo** USA
30B4 **Vallenar** Chile
53B3 **Valletta** Malta
8D2 **Valley City** USA
20B2 **Valley Falls** USA
15D1 **Valleyfield** Can
13D1 **Valleyview** Can
47E2 **Valli di Comacchio** *Lg* Italy
51C1 **Valls** Spain
58D1 **Valmiera** Latvia
35A2 **Valparaiso** Brazil
34A2 **Valparaiso** Chile
23A1 **Valparaiso** Mexico
17A1 **Valparaiso** USA
101G1 **Vals** *R* S Africa
85C4 **Valsád** India
60E3 **Valuyki** Russian Fed
50A2 **Valverde del Camino** Spain
38J6 **Vammala** Fin
93D2 **Van** Turk
63C1 **Vanavara** Russian Fed
18B2 **Van Buren** Arkansas, USA
13C3 **Vancouver** Can
20B1 **Vancouver** USA
5F5 **Vancouver I** Can
12G2 **Vancouver,Mt** Can
18C2 **Vandalia** Illinois, USA
14B3 **Vandalia** Ohio, USA
13C2 **Vanderhoof** Can
106C2 **Van Diemen G** *Gulf* Aust
39G7 **Vänern** *L* Sweden
39G7 **Vänersborg** Sweden
101D3 **Vangaindrano** Madag
93D2 **Van Gölü** *Salt L* Turk
76C2 **Vang Vieng** Laos
9C3 **Van Horn** USA
15C1 **Vanier** Can
1C6 **Vankarem** Russian Fed
38H6 **Vännäs** Sweden
48B2 **Vannes** France
47B2 **Vanoise** *Mts* France
100A4 **Vanrhynsdorp** S Africa
6B3 **Vansittart I** Can
105G4 **Vanuatu** *Is* Pacific O
14B2 **Van Wert** USA
47C2 **Varallo** Italy
90B2 **Varamin** Iran
86A1 **Vārānasi** India
38K4 **Varangerfjord** *Inlet* Nor
38K4 **Varangerhalvøya** *Pen* Nor
52C1 **Varazdin** Croatia
39G7 **Varberg** Sweden
39F7 **Varde** Nor
38L4 **Vardø** Nor
58C2 **Varena** Lithuania
47C2 **Varenna** Italy
47C2 **Varese** Italy
35B2 **Varginha** Brazil
58B1 **Varkaus** Fin
54C2 **Varna** Bulg
39G7 **Värnamo** Sweden
17B1 **Varnville** USA
35C1 **Várzea da Palma** Brazil
47C2 **Varzi** Italy
50B1 **Vascongadas** Region, Spain
60D3 **Vasil'kov** Ukraine
14B2 **Vassar** USA
39H7 **Västerås** Sweden
39H7 **Västervik** Sweden
52B2 **Vasto** Italy
65J4 **Vasyugan** *R* Russian Fed
38B2 **Vatnajökull** *Mts* Iceland
38A1 **Vatneyri** Iceland
54C1 **Vatra Dornei** Rom
39G7 **Vättern** *L* Sweden
9C3 **Vaughn** USA
32C3 **Vaupés** *R* Colombia
13C2 **Vauxhall** Can
87C3 **Vavuniÿa** Sri Lanka
39G7 **Växjö** Sweden
64G2 **Vaygach, Ostrov** *I* Russian Fed
34C2 **Vedia** Arg
38G5 **Vega** *I* Nor
13E2 **Vegreville** Can
50A2 **Vejer de la Frontera** Spain
39F7 **Vejle** Den
52C2 **Velebit** *Mts* Croatia
52C1 **Velenje** Slovenia
35C1 **Velhas** *R* Brazil
47C2 **Velikaya** *R* Russian Fed
60D2 **Velikiye Luki** Russian Fed
61G1 **Velikiy Ustyug** Russian Fed
54C2 **Veliko Tŭrnovo** Bulg
97A3 **Vélingara** Sen
61F1 **Vel'sk** Russian Fed
87B3 **Vembanad L** India
34C2 **Venado Tuerto** Arg
31B6 **Venâncio Aures** Brazil
49C2 **Vendôme** France
12E1 **Venetie** USA
47D2 **Veneto** Region, Italy
47E2 **Venezia** Italy

32D2 Venezuela Republic, S America
87A1 Vengurla India
12C3 Veniaminof V USA
Venice = Venezia
87B2 Venkatagiri India
56B2 Venlo Neth
58C1 Venta *R* Latvia
101G1 Ventersburg S Africa
58C1 Ventspils Latvia
32D3 Venturari *R* Ven
22C3 Ventura USA
60D1 Vepsovskaya Vozvyshennost' *Upland* Russian Fed
30D4 Vera Arg
51B2 Vera Spain
23B2 Veracruz Mexico
23B1 Veracruz State, Mexico
85C4 Veräval India
47C2 Verbania Italy
47C2 Vercelli Italy
35A1 Verde *R* Goias, Brazil
23A1 Verde *R* Jalisco, Mexico
35A1 Verde *R* Mato Grosso do Sul, Brazil
23B2 Verde *R* Oaxaca, Mexico
Verde,C = Cap Vert
35C1 Verde Grande *R* Brazil
34C3 Verde,Pen Arg
49D3 Verdon *R* France
46C2 Verdun France
101G1 Vereeniging S Africa
61H2 Vereshchagino Russian Fed
97A3 Verga,C Guinea
34D3 Vergara Arg
50A1 Verin Spain
63D2 Verkh Angara *R* Russian Fed
61J3 Verkhneural'sk Russian Fed
63E1 Verkhnevilyuysk Russian Fed
1C8 Verkhoyansk Russian Fed
35A1 Vermelho *R* Brazil
13E2 Vermilion Can
10C2 Vermont State, USA
22B2 Vernalis USA
13D2 Vernon Can
46A2 Vernon France
9D3 Vernon USA
17B2 Vero Beach USA
54B3 Veroia Greece
47D2 Veronanuova Italy
47D2 Verona Italy
46B2 Versailles France
101H1 Verulam S Africa
46C1 Verviers Belg
46C1 Vervins France
46A2 Vesle *R* France
49D2 Vesoul France
38G5 Vesterålen *Is* Nor
38G5 Vestfjorden *Inlet* Nor
38A2 Vestmannaeyjar Iceland
53B2 Vesuvio *Mt* Italy
59B3 Veszprém Hung
39H7 Vetlanda Sweden
61F2 Vetluga *R* Russian Fed
46B1 Veurne Belg
47B1 Vevey Switz
46A2 Vexin Region, France
47A2 Veynes France
50A1 Viana do Castelo Port
Viangchan = Vientiane
49E3 Viareggio Italy
39F7 Viborg Den
53C3 Vibo Valentia Italy
Vic = Vich
112C2 Vicecomodoro Marambio *Base* Ant
52B1 Vicenza Italy
51C1 Vich Spain
32D3 Vichada *R* Colombia
61F2 Vichuga Russian Fed

49C2 Vichy France
19B3 Vicksburg USA
35C2 Vicosa Brazil
106C4 Victor Harbour Aust
34C2 Victoria Arg
13C3 Victoria Can
34A3 Victoria Chile
78D1 Victoria Malay
108B3 Victoria State, Aust
9D4 Victoria USA
106C2 Victoria *R* Aust
26B2 Victoria de las Tunas Cuba
100B2 Victoria Falls Zambia/Zim
4G2 Victoria I Can
108B2 Victoria,L Aust
99D3 Victoria,L C Africa
112B7 Victoria Land Region, Ant
86C2 Victoria,Mt Burma
99D2 Victoria Nile *R* Uganda
111B2 Victoria Range *Mts* NZ
106C2 Victoria River Downs Aust
4H3 Victoria Str Can
55C3 Victoriaville Can
100B4 Victoria West S Africa
34B3 Victorica Arg
21B3 Victorville USA
34A2 Vicuna Chile
34C2 Vicuña Mackenna Arg
17B1 Vidalia USA
54B2 Videle Rom
54C2 Vidin Bulg
85D4 Vidisha India
58D1 Vidzy Belorussia
29D4 Viedma Arg
26A4 Viejo Costa Rica
Vielha = Viella
51C1 Viella Spain
Vienna = Wien
18C2 Vienna Illinois, USA
14B3 Vienna W Virginia, USA
49C2 Vienne France
48C2 Vienne *R* France
76C2 Vientiane Laos
47C1 Vierwaldstätter See *L* Switz
48C2 Vierzon France
53C2 Vieste Italy
70B2 Vietnam Republic, S E Asia
76D1 Vietri Viet
27P2 Vieux Fort St Lucia
79B2 Vigan Phil
47C2 Vigevano Italy
48B3 Vignemale *Mt* France
50A1 Vigo Spain
87C1 Vijayawäda India
55A2 Vijosë *R* Alb
38B2 Vik Iceland
54B2 Vikhren *Mt* Bulg
13E2 Viking Can
38G6 Vikna *I* Nor
101C2 Vila da Maganja Mozam
101C2 Vila Machado Mozam
101C3 Vilanculos Mozam
Vilanova i la Geltrú = Vilanova-y-Geltrú
50A1 Vila Real Port
101C2 Vila Vasco da Gama Mozam
35C2 Vila Velha Brazil
58D2 Vileyka Belorussia
38H6 Vilhelmina Sweden
33E6 Vilhena Brazil
60C2 Viljandi Estonia
101G1 Viljoenskroon S Africa
9C3 Villa Ahumada Mexico
50A1 Villa Atuel Arg
50A1 Villaba Spain
23A2 Villa Carranza Mexico

52B1 Villach Austria
34B2 Villa Colon Arg
34C2 Villa Constitución Arg
34C2 Villa de Maria Arg
23A1 Villa de Reyes Mexico
34B2 Villa Dolores Arg
47D2 Villafranca di Verona Italy
34C2 Villa General Mitre Arg
34B2 Villa General Roca Arg
34D2 Villaguay Arg
25C3 Villahermosa Mexico
23A1 Villa Hidalgo Mexico
34C2 Villa Huidobro Arg
34C3 Villa Iris Arg
34C3 Villa Maria Arg
30D3 Villa Montes Bol
23A1 Villanueva Mexico
50A1 Villa Nova de Gaia Port
50A2 Villanueva de la Serena Spain
51C1 Villanueva-y-Geltrú Spain
34B3 Villa Regina Arg
51B2 Villarreal Spain
29B3 Villarrica Chile
30E4 Villarrica Par
50B2 Villarrobledo Spain
34C2 Villa San José Arg
34C2 Villa Valeria Arg
32C3 Villavicencio Colombia
49C2 Villefranche France
7C5 Ville-Marie Can
51B2 Villena Spain
46B2 Villeneuve-St-Georges France
48C3 Villeneuve-sur-Lot France
19B3 Ville Platte USA
46B2 Villers-Cotterêts France
34A2 Villurbanne France
101G1 Villiers S Africa
87B2 Villupuram India
58D2 Vilnius Lithuania
63D1 Vilyuy *R* Russian Fed
63E1 Vilyuysk Russian Fed
34A2 Viña del Mar Chile
51C1 Vinaroz Spain
14A3 Vincennes USA
38H5 Vindel *R* Sweden
85D4 Vindhya Range *Mts* India
16B3 Vineland USA
16D2 Vineyard Haven USA
76D2 Vinh Viet
76D3 Vinh Cam Ranh *B* Viet
77D4 Vinh Loi Viet
77D3 Vinh Long Viet
18A2 Vinita USA
54A1 Vinkovci Croatia
60C4 Vinnitsa Ukraine
112B3 Vinson Massif *Upland* Ant
100A3 Vioolsdrift S Africa
47D1 Vipiteno Italy
79B3 Virac Phil
87B2 Virddhächalam India
100A2 Virei Angola
35C1 Virgem da Lapa Brazil
101G1 Virginia S Africa
10C3 Virginia State, USA
10A2 Virginia USA
21B2 Virginia City USA
27E3 Virgin Is Caribbean S
52C1 Virovitica Croatia
46C2 Virton Belg
87B3 Virudunagar India
52C2 Vis *I* Croatia
21B2 Visalia USA
79B3 Visayan S Phil
39H7 Visby Sweden
4H2 Viscount Melville Sd Can

54A2 Višegrad Bosnia-Herzegovina
50A1 Viseu Port
83C4 Vishakhapatnam India
47B1 Visp Switz
49C1 Vissingen Neth
21B3 Vista USA
Vistula = Wisla
53C3 Vitavia *R* Czech Republic
87A1 Vite India
60D2 Vitebsk Belorussia
52B2 Viterbo Italy
50A1 Vitigudino Spain
63D2 Vitim *R* Russian Fed
50B1 Vitora Spain
31C6 Vitória Brazil
31C4 Vitória da Conquista Brazil
48B2 Vitre France
46C2 Virty-le-Francois France
38J5 Vittangi Sweden
53B3 Vittoria Italy
47E2 Vittorio Veneto Italy
69H2 Vityaz Depth Pacific O
50A1 Vivero Spain
63B1 Vivi *R* Russian Fed
34D3 Vizcacha Arg
63C2 Vizhne-Angarsk Russian Fed
83C4 Vizianagaram India
54B1 Vlädeasa *Mt* Rom
61F5 Vladikavkaz Russian Fed
Vladimir Russian Fed
59C2 Vladimir Volynskiy Ukraine
74C2 Vladivostok Russian Fed
56A2 Vlieland *I* Neth
46B1 Vlissingen Neth
55A2 Vlorë Alb
57C3 Vöcklabruck Austria
76D3 Voeune Sai Camb
47C2 Voghera Italy
101D2 Vohibinany Madag
101E2 Vohimarina Madag
99D3 Voi Kenya
97B4 Voinjama Lib
49D2 Voiron France
54A1 Vojvodina *Aut Republic* Serbia, Yugos
26A5 Volcán Baru *Mt* Panama
23B2 Volcán Citlaltepetl *Mt* Mexico
30C3 Volcán Lullaillaco *Mt* Chile
34A3 Volcáno Copahue *Mt* Chile
34A3 Volcáno Domuyo *Mt* Arg
Volcano Is = Kazan Retto
29B3 Volcáno Lanin *Mt* Arg
30C3 Volcán Ollagüe *Mt* Chile
34A3 Volcáno Llaima *Mt* Chile
34A3 Volcáno Maipo *Mt* Arg
34A3 Volcáno Peteroa *Mt* Chile
34B3 Volcáno Tromen *V* Arg
23A2 Volcán Paracutin *Mt* Mexico
32B3 Volcán Puräce *Mt* Colombia
34A2 Volcán Tinguiririca *Mt* Arg/Chile
61J2 Volchansk Russian Fed
61G4 Volga *R* Russian Fed
61F4 Volgodonsk Russian Fed

Volgograd

61F4 **Volgograd**
   Russian Fed
61G3 **Volgogradskoye**
   Vodokhranilishche
   Res Russian Fed
60D2 **Volkhov** Russian Fed
60D2 **Volkhov** *R*
   Russian Fed
58C2 **Volkovysk** Belorussia
101G1 **Volksrust** S Africa
61F2 **Vologda** Russian Fed
48B2 **Vologues** France
55B3 **Vólos** Greece
61G3 **Vol'sk** Russian Fed
22B2 **Volta** USA
97B3 **Volta Blanche** *R*
   Burkina
97B4 **Volta,L** Ghana
97B3 **Volta Noire** *R*
   Burkina
35C2 **Volta Redonda** Brazil
97B3 **Volta Rouge** *R*
   Burkina
61F4 **Volzhskiy**
12D2 **Von Frank Mt** USA
6J3 **Vopnafjörður** Iceland
47C1 **Voralberg** Province,
   Austria
47C1 **Vorder Rhein** *R*
   Switz
56C1 **Vordingborg** Den
64H3 **Vorkuta** Russian Fed
39G6 **Vorma** *R* Nor
60E3 **Voronezh**
   Russian Fed
38M5 **Voron'ya** *R*
   Russian Fed
39K7 **Võru** Estonia
49D2 **Vosges** *Mt* France
39F6 **Voss** Nor
63B2 **Vostochnyy Sayan**
   Mts Russian Fed
112B9 **Vostok** *Base* Ant
61H2 **Votkinsk**
   Russian Fed
46C2 **Vouziers** France
60D4 **Voznesensk** Ukraine
54B2 **Vranje** Serbia, Yugos
54B2 **Vratsa** Bulg
54A1 **Vrbas** Serbia, Yugos
52C2 **Vrbas** *R* Serbia,
   Yugos
52B1 **Vrbovsko** Bosnia-
   Herzegovina
101G1 **Vrede** S Africa
33F2 **Vreed en Hoop**
   Guyana
54B1 **Vršac** Serbia, Yugos
52C2 **Vrtoče** Bosnia-
   Herzegovina
100B3 **Vryburg** S Africa
101H1 **Vryheid** S Africa
54A1 **Vukovar** Croatia
13E2 **Vulcan** Can
53B3 **Vulcano** *I* Italy
77D3 **Vung Tau** Viet
38J5 **Vuollerim** Sweden
38L6 **Vyartsilya**
   Russian Fed
61H2 **Vyatka** *R*
   Russian Fed
69F2 **Vyazemskiy**
   Russian Fed
60D2 **Vyaz'ma** Russian Fed
61F2 **Vyazniki** Russian Fed
60C1 **Vyborg** Russian Fed
64G3 **Vym'** *R* Russian Fed
43C3 **Vyrnwy** *R* Wales
60D2 **Vyshiy Volochek**
   Russian Fed
59B3 **Vyškov**
   Czech Republic
60E1 **Vytegra** Russian Fed

W

97B3 **Wa** Ghana
13E1 **Wabasca** Can
5G4 **Wabasca** *R* Can
13E1 **Wabasca L** Can
14A2 **Wabash** USA
14A3 **Wabash** *R* USA
5J4 **Wabowden** Can
7D4 **Wabush** Can

17B2 **Waccasassa B** USA
16D1 **Wachusett Res** USA
19A3 **Waco** USA
85B3 **Wad** Pak
95A2 **Waddān** Libya
5F4 **Waddington,Mt** Can
93E4 **Wadi al Batin**
   Watercourse Iraq
93D3 **Wadi al Ghudāf**
   Watercourse Iraq
94C2 **Wadi al Harir** *V* Syria
93D3 **Wadi al Mirah**
   Watercourse Iraq/
   S Arabia
93D3 **Wadi al Ubayyid**
   Watercourse Iraq
93D3 **Wadi Ar'ar**
   Watercourse
   S Arabia
91A5 **Wadi as Hsaba'**
   Watercourse
   S Arabia
92C3 **Wadi as Sirhān** *V*
   Jordan/S Arabia
94C2 **Wadi az Zaydi** *V*
   Syria
94C3 **Wadi edh Dhab'i** *V*
   Jordan
94A3 **Wadi el 'Arish** *V*
   Egypt
94C3 **Wadi el Ghadaf** *V*
   Jordan
94B3 **Wadi el Hasa** *V*
   Jordan
94C3 **Wadi el Janab** *V*
   Jordan
94B3 **Wadi el Jeib** *V* Israel/
   Jordan
95B3 **Wadi el Milk**
   Watercourse Sudan
92A3 **Wadi el Natrun**
   Watercourse Egypt
94B3 **Wadi es Sir** Jordan
94B3 **Wadi Fidan** *V* Jordan
94B3 **Wadi Hareidin** *V*
   Egypt
93D3 **Wadi Hawran** *R* Iraq
95B3 **Wadi Howa**
   Watercourse Sudan
98C1 **Wadi Ibra**
   Watercourse Sudan
94C2 **Wadi Luhfi**
   Watercourse Jordan
94B3 **Wadi Mujib** *V*
   Jordan
94B3 **Wadi Qitaiya** *V*
   Egypt
80B3 **Wadi Sha'it**
   Watercourse Egypt
99D1 **Wad Medani** Sudan
93E4 **Wafra** Kuwait
6B3 **Wager B** Can
6A3 **Wager Bay** Can
109C3 **Wagga Wagga** Aust
106A4 **Wagin** Aust
95A2 **Wāha** Libya
21C4 **Wahiawa** Hawaiian Is
18A1 **Wahoo** USA
8D2 **Wahpeton** USA
87A1 **Wai** India
111B2 **Waiau** NZ
111A3 **Waiau** *R* NZ
111B2 **Waiau** *R* NZ
71E3 **Waigeo** *I* Indon
110C1 **Waihi** NZ
110C1 **Waikaremoana,L** NZ
110C1 **Waikato** *R* NZ
108A2 **Waikerie** Aust
111B3 **Waikouaiti** NZ
21C4 **Wailuku** Hawaiian Is
111B2 **Waimakariri** *R* NZ
111B2 **Waimate** NZ
21C4 **Waimea** Hawaiian Is
106B1 **Waingapu** Indon
13E2 **Wainwright** Can
4B2 **Wainwright** USA
111B2 **Waipara** NZ
110C2 **Waipukurau** NZ
111C2 **Wairarapa,L** NZ
111B2 **Wairau** *R* NZ
110C1 **Wairoa** NZ
110C1 **Wairoa** *R* NZ
111B2 **Waitaki** *R* NZ
110B1 **Waitara** NZ

110C1 **Waitomo** NZ
110B1 **Waiuku** NZ
75B1 **Wajima** Japan
99E2 **Wajir** Kenya
75B1 **Wakasa-wan** *B*
   Japan
111A3 **Wakatipu,L** NZ
74D4 **Wakayama** Japan
42D3 **Wakefield** Eng
27H1 **Wakefield** Jamaica
16D2 **Wakefield** Rhode
   Island, USA
76B2 **Wakema** Burma
69G2 **Wakkanai** Japan
108B3 **Wakool** *R* Aust
59B2 **Walbrzych** Pol
109D2 **Walcha** Aust
59B2 **Walcz** Pol
46D1 **Waldbröl** Germany
16B2 **Walden** USA
43C3 **Wales** Country, UK
12A1 **Wales** USA
6B3 **Wales I** Can
109C2 **Walgett** Aust
112B4 **Walgreen Coast**
   Region, Ant
99C3 **Walikale** Zaire
21B2 **Walker L** USA
14B2 **Walkerton** Can
8B2 **Wallace** USA
108A2 **Wallaroo** Aust
109C3 **Walla Walla** Aust
20C1 **Walla Walla** USA
16C2 **Wallingford** USA
105H4 **Wallis and Futuna** *Is*
   Pacific O
20C1 **Wallowa** USA
20C1 **Wallowa Mts** *Mts*
   USA
109C1 **Wallumbilla** Aust
18B2 **Walnut Ridge** USA
110C1 **Walouru** NZ
43D3 **Walsall** Eng
9C3 **Walsenburg** USA
9C3 **Walsenburgh** USA
111B3 **Walterboro** USA
17A1 **Walter F George Res**
   USA
16D1 **Waltham** USA
100A3 **Walvis Bay** Namibia
103J6 **Walvis Ridge**
   Atlantic O
97C4 **Wamba** Nig
98B3 **Wamba** *R* Zaire
18A2 **Wamego** USA
84B2 **Wana** Pak
108B1 **Wanaaring** Aust
111A2 **Wanaka** NZ
111A2 **Wanaka,L** NZ
14B1 **Wanapitei L** Can
109C1 **Wandoan** Aust
108B3 **Wanganella** Aust
110C1 **Wanganui** NZ
110C1 **Wanganui** *R* NZ
109C3 **Wangaratta** Aust
99E2 **Wanle Weyne**
   Somalia
76E2 **Wanning** China
87B1 **Wanparti** India
73B3 **Wanxian** China
73B3 **Wanyuan** China
13D2 **Wapiti** *R* Can
18B2 **Wappello,L** USA
16C2 **Wappingers Falls**
   USA
87B1 **Warangal** India
109C4 **Waratah** Aust
108C3 **Waratah B** Aust
108C3 **Warburton** Aust
108A1 **Warburton** *R* Aust
109C1 **Warbreccan** Aust
97A4 **Warder** Eth
85D4 **Wardha** India
111A3 **Ward,Mt** NZ
5F4 **Ware** Can
16C1 **Ware** USA
16D2 **Wareham** USA
109D1 **Warialda** Aust
76C2 **Warin Chamrap**
   Thai
100B3 **Warmbad** S Africa
16B2 **Warminster** USA
21B2 **Warm Springs** USA

56C2 **Warnemünde**
   Germany
20B2 **Warner Mts** USA
17B1 **Warner Robins** USA
108B3 **Warrackabeal** Aust
108A1 **Warrandirinna,L** Aust
107D3 **Warrego** *R* Aust
19B3 **Warren** Arkansas,
   USA
109C2 **Warren** Aust
16D2 **Warren**
   Massachusetts, USA
14B2 **Warren** Ohio, USA
15C2 **Warren**
   Pennsylvania, USA
45C1 **Warrenpoint** N Ire
18B2 **Warrensburg** USA
101F1 **Warrenton** S Africa
15C3 **Warrenton** USA
97C4 **Warri** Nig
108A1 **Warrina** Aust
42C3 **Warrington** Eng
108B3 **Warrnambool** Aust
58C2 **Warsaw = Warszawa**
58C2 **Warszawa** Pol
59B2 **Warta** *R* Pol
109D1 **Warwick** Aust
43D3 **Warwick** County,
   Eng
43D3 **Warwick** Eng
16B2 **Warwick** New York,
   USA
16D2 **Warwick** Rhode
   Island, USA
8B3 **Wasatch Range** *Mts*
   USA
101H1 **Wasbank** S Africa
21B2 **Wasco** USA
4H2 **Washburn L** Can
85D4 **Wāshim** India
10C3 **Washington** District
   of Columbia, USA
17B1 **Washington** Georgia,
   USA
14A3 **Washington** Indiana,
   USA
18B2 **Washington**
   Missouri, USA
16B2 **Washington** New
   Jersey, USA
14B2 **Washington**
   Pennsylvania, USA
8A2 **Washington** State,
   USA
14B3 **Washington Court**
   House USA
6D1 **Washington Land**
   Can
15D2 **Washington,Mt** USA
43E3 **Wash,The** Eng
85A3 **Washuk** Pak
12E2 **Wasilla** USA
7C4 **Waskaganish** Can
26A4 **Waspán** Nic
70D4 **Watampone** Indon
16C2 **Waterbury** USA
45C2 **Waterford** County,
   Irish Rep
41B3 **Waterford** Irish Rep
45C2 **Waterford Harbour**
   Irish Rep
46C1 **Waterloo** Belg
10A2 **Waterloo** USA
15C2 **Watertown** New
   York, USA
101H1 **Waterval-Boven**
   S Africa
10D2 **Waterville** Maine,
   USA
16C1 **Watervliet** USA
13E2 **Waterways** Can
43D4 **Watford** Eng
15C2 **Watkins Glen** USA
8C1 **Watrous** Can
99C2 **Watsa** Zaire
12J2 **Watson Lake** Can
22B2 **Watsonville** USA
71F4 **Wau** PNG
99C2 **Wau** Sudan
7B5 **Wau** USA
109D2 **Wauchope** Aust
17B2 **Wauchula** USA
14A2 **Waukegan** USA
10B2 **Wausau** USA

14A2 **Wauwatosa** USA
106C2 **Wave Hill** Aust
43E3 **Waveney** R Eng
14B3 **Waverly** Ohio, USA
46C1 **Wavre** Belg
10B2 **Wawra** Can
95A2 **Wāw Al Kabir** Libya
95A2 **Wāw an Nāmūs** Well Libya
22C2 **Wawona** USA
19A3 **Waxahachie** USA
17B1 **Waycross** USA
17B1 **Waynesboro** Georgia, USA
19C3 **Waynesboro** Mississippi, USA
16A3 **Waynesboro** Pennsylvania, USA
15C3 **Waynesboro** Virginia, USA
18B2 **Waynesville** Missouri, USA
84B2 **Wazi Khwa** Afghan
43E4 **Weald,The** Upland Eng
42C2 **Wear** R Eng
19A3 **Weatherford** Texas, USA
20B2 **Weaverville** USA
14B1 **Webbwood** Can
16D1 **Webster** USA
18B2 **Webster Groves** USA
29D6 **Weddell** Falkland Is
112C2 **Weddell S** Ant
13C2 **Wedge Mt** Can
20B2 **Weed** USA
101H1 **Weenen** S Africa
109C2 **We Waa** Aust
72D1 **Weichang** China
57C3 **Weiden** Germany
72D2 **Weifang** China
72E2 **Weihai** China
72C3 **Wei He** R Henan, China
72C2 **Wei He** R Shaanxi, China
109C1 **Weilmoringle** Aust
73A4 **Weining** China
107D2 **Weipa** Aust
14B2 **Weirton** USA
20C2 **Weiser** USA
72D3 **Weishan Hu** L China
57C2 **Weissenfels** Germany
17A1 **Weiss L** USA
99D1 **Weldiya** Eth
101G1 **Welkom** S Africa
15C2 **Welland** Can
43D3 **Welland** R Eng
106C2 **Wellesley Is** Aust
12G2 **Wellesley L** Can
43D3 **Wellingborough** Eng
109C2 **Wellington** Aust
18A2 **Wellington** Kansas, USA
111B2 **Wellington** NZ
6A2 **Wellington Chan** Can
13C2 **Wells** USA
43C4 **Wells** Eng
110B1 **Wellsford** NZ
106B3 **Wells,L** Aust
57C3 **Wels** Austria
43C3 **Welshpool** Wales
13D1 **Wembley** Can
7C4 **Wemindji** Can
20B1 **Wenatchee** USA
20C1 **Wenatchee** R USA
97B4 **Wenchi** Ghana
72E2 **Wenden** China
73E4 **Wenling** China
32J7 **Wenman** I Ecuador
73A5 **Wenquan** China
107D4 **Wenthaggi** Aust
108B2 **Wentworth** Aust
72A3 **Wen Xian** China
73C4 **Wenzhou** China
73C4 **Wenzhou** China
101G1 **Wepener** S Africa
12G1 **Wernecke Mts** Can
57C2 **Werra** R Germany
109D2 **Werris Creek** Aust
56B2 **Wesel** Germany
56B2 **Weser** R Germany
106C2 **Wessel Is** Aust

14A2 **West Allis** USA
104C4 **West Australian Basin** Indian O
104C5 **West Australian Ridge** Indian O
19C3 **West B** USA
86B2 **West Bengal** State, India
43D3 **West Bromwich** Eng
16B3 **West Chester** USA
56B2 **Westerburg** Germany
56B2 **Westerland** Germany
16D2 **Westerly** USA
106A3 **Western Australia** State, Aust
87A1 **Western Ghats** Mts India
44A3 **Western Isles** Scot
96A2 **Western Sahara** Region, Mor
105H4 **Western Samoa** Is Pacific O
46B1 **Westerschelde** Estuary Neth
46D1 **Westerwald** Region, Germany
49D1 **Westfalen** Region, Germany
29D6 **West Falkland** I Falkland Is
16C1 **Westfield** Massachusetts, USA
16A3 **Westfield** New York, USA
18C2 **West Frankfort** USA
109C1 **Westgate** Aust
43C4 **West Glamorgan** County, Wales
102E3 **West Indies** Is Caribbean S
13E2 **Westlock** Can
14B2 **West Lorne** Can
45C2 **Westmeath** County, Irish Rep
18B2 **West Memphis** USA
43D3 **West Midlands** County, Eng
43D4 **Westminster** Eng
16A3 **Westminster** Maryland, USA
17B1 **Westminster** S Carolina, USA
100B3 **West Nicholson** Zim
78D1 **Weston** Malay
14B3 **Weston** USA
43C4 **Weston-super-Mare** Eng
17B2 **West Palm Beach** USA
18B2 **West Plains** USA
22B1 **West Point** California, USA
19C3 **West Point** Mississippi, USA
16C2 **West Point** New York, USA
12F2 **West Point** Mt USA
45B2 **Westport** Irish Rep
111B2 **Westport** NZ
40C2 **Westray** I Scot
13C2 **West Road** R Can
42E3 **West Sole** Oilfield N Sea
11B3 **West Virginia** State, USA
22C1 **West Walker** R USA
109C2 **West Wyalong** Aust
42D3 **West Yorkshire** County, Eng
71D4 **Wetar** I Indon
13E2 **Wetaskiwin** Can
99D3 **Wete** Tanz
46E1 **Wetzlar** Germany
Wevok = Cape Lisburne
71F4 **Wewak** PNG
19A2 **Wewoka** USA
45C2 **Wexford** County, Irish Rep
45C2 **Wexford** Irish Rep
5H5 **Weyburn** Can
43C4 **Weymouth** Eng
16D1 **Weymouth** USA

110C1 **Whakatane** NZ
110C1 **Whakatane** R NZ
44E1 **Whalsay** I Scot
110B1 **Whangarei** NZ
42D3 **Wharfe** R Eng
19A4 **Wharton** USA
111B2 **Whataroa** NZ
16A3 **Wheaton** Maryland, USA
8B3 **Wheeler Peak** Mt Nevada, USA
9C3 **Wheeler Peak** Mt New Mexico, USA
14B2 **Wheeling** USA
13C3 **Whistler** Can
15C2 **Whitby** Can
42D2 **Whitby** Eng
18B2 **White** R Arkansas, USA
12F2 **White** R Can
14A3 **White** R Indiana, USA
8C2 **White** R S Dakota, USA
7E4 **White B** Can
108B2 **White Cliffs** Aust
40C2 **White Coomb** Mt Scot
13D2 **Whitecourt** Can
14A1 **Whitefish Pt** USA
7D4 **Whitegull L** Can
15D2 **Whitehall** New York, USA
16B2 **Whitehall** Pennsylvania, USA
42C2 **Whitehaven** Eng
12G2 **Whitehorse** Can
110C1 **White I** NZ
19B4 **White L** USA
109C4 **Whitemark** Aust
21B2 **White Mountain Peak** USA
12E1 **White Mts** Alaska, USA
15D2 **White Mts** New Hampshire, USA
99D1 **White Nile** R Sudan
16C2 **White Plains** USA
7B5 **White River** Can
15D2 **White River Junction** USA
White S = Beloye More
13B2 **Whitesail L** Can
20D1 **White Salmon** USA
17C1 **Whiteville** USA
97B4 **White Volta** R Ghana
42B2 **Whithorn** Scot
17B1 **Whitmire** USA
21B2 **Whitney,Mt** USA
12E2 **Whittier** Alaska, USA
22C4 **Whittier** California, USA
5H3 **Wholdia L** Can
108A2 **Whyalla** Aust
14B2 **Wiarton** Can
84B2 **Wichita** USA
9D3 **Wichita Falls** USA
44C2 **Wick** Scot
45C2 **Wicklow** County, Irish Rep
45C3 **Wicklow** Irish Rep
45C2 **Wicklow Mts** Irish Rep
109C1 **Widgeegoara** R Aust
46D1 **Wied** R Germany
59B2 **Wielun** Pol
59B3 **Wien** Austria
59B3 **Wiener Neustadt** Austria
58C2 **Wieprz** R Pol
46E1 **Wiesbaden** Germany
42C3 **Wigan** Eng
19C3 **Wiggins** USA
42B2 **Wigtown** Scot
42B2 **Wigtown B** Scot
47C1 **Wil** Switz
20C1 **Wilbur** USA
108B2 **Wilcannia** Aust
21B2 **Wildcat Peak** Mt USA
47B1 **Wildhorn** Mt Switz

13E2 **Wild Horse** Can
47D1 **Wildspitze** Mt Austria
17B2 **Wildwood** Florida, USA
16B3 **Wildwood** New Jersey, USA
101G1 **Wilge** R S Africa
56B2 **Wilhelmshaven** Germany
15C2 **Wilkes-Barre** USA
112B8 **Wilkes Land** Ant
13F2 **Wilkie** Can
20B2 **Willamette** R USA
108B2 **Willandra** R Aust
20B1 **Willapa B** USA
9C3 **Willcox** USA
27D4 **Willemstad** Curaçao
108A1 **William Creek** Aust
108B3 **William,Mt** Aust
21A2 **Williams** California, USA
13C1 **Williams Lake** Can
15C2 **Williamsport** USA
16C1 **Williamstown** Massachusetts, USA
14B3 **Williamstown** W Virginia, USA
16C2 **Willimantic** USA
16B2 **Willingboro** USA
13D2 **Willingdon,Mt** Can
107E2 **Willis Group** Is Aust
17B2 **Williston** Florida, USA
100B4 **Williston** S Africa
13C1 **Williston L** Can
8D2 **Willmar** USA
108A3 **Willoughby,C** Aust
13C2 **Willow** R Can
20B2 **Willow Ranch** USA
21A2 **Willows** USA
18B2 **Willow Springs** USA
108A2 **Wilmington** Aust
16B3 **Wilmington** Delaware, USA
17C1 **Wilmington** N Carolina, USA
7A5 **Wilnona** USA
11C3 **Wilson** USA
108B1 **Wilson** R Aust
6B3 **Wilson,C** Can
22C3 **Wilson,Mt** California, USA
20B1 **Wilson,Mt** Oregon, USA
109C3 **Wilsons Promontory** Pen Aust
43D4 **Wiltshire** County, Eng
46C2 **Wiltz** Lux
14A2 **Winamac** USA
101G1 **Winburg** S Africa
16C1 **Winchendon** USA
15C1 **Winchester** Can
43D4 **Winchester** Eng
16C1 **Winchester** New Hampshire, USA
15C3 **Winchester** Virginia, USA
42C2 **Windermere** Eng
100A3 **Windhoek** Namibia
107D3 **Windorah** Aust
8C2 **Wind River Range** Mts USA
109D2 **Windsor** Aust
16C2 **Windsor** Connecticut, USA
43D4 **Windsor** Eng
7D5 **Windsor** Nova Scotia, Can
14B2 **Windsor** Ontario, USA
15D1 **Windsor** Quebec, Can
17B1 **Windsor Forest** USA
16C2 **Windsor Locks** USA
27E4 **Windward Is** Caribbean S
26C3 **Windward Pass** Caribbean S
13E1 **Winefred L** Can
18A2 **Winfield** Kansas, USA
109D2 **Wingham** Aust

189

Winifreda

34C3 Winifreda Arg
7B4 Winisk *R* Can
7B4 Winisk L Can
76B2 Winkana Burma
20B1 Winlock USA
97B4 Winneba Ghana
14A2 Winnebago,L USA
20C2 Winnemucca USA
19B3 Winfield USA
5J4 Winnipeg Can
5J4 Winnipeg,L Can
5J4 Winnipegosis Can
4J4 Winnipegosis,L Can
15D2 Winnipesaukee,L USA
10A2 Winona Minnesota, USA
19C3 Winona Mississippi, USA
15D2 Winooski USA
9B3 Winslow USA
16C2 Winsted USA
11B3 Winston-Salem USA
46E1 Winterberg Germany
17B2 Winter Garden USA
17B2 Winter Park USA
22B1 Winters USA
47C1 Winterthur Switz
107D3 Winton Aust
111A3 Winton NZ
43E3 Wisbech Eng
10B2 Wisconsin State, USA
7B5 Wisconsin Rapids USA
12D1 Wiseman USA
58B2 Wisla *R* Pol
56C2 Wismar Germany
33F2 Witagron Surinam
101G1 Witbank S Africa
9D3 Witchita Falls USA
43D3 Witham *R* Eng
42E3 Withernsea Eng
43D4 Witney Eng
46D1 Witten Germany
56C2 Wittenberg Germany
106A3 Wittenoom Aust
46D1 Wittlich Germany
58B2 Wladyslawowo Pol
58B2 Wloclawek Pol
58C2 Wlodawa Pol
109C3 Wodonga Aust
47C1 Wohlen Switz
71E4 Wokam Indon
43D4 Woking Eng
71F3 Woleai *I* Pacific O
20B2 Wolf Creek USA
8C2 Wolf Point USA
57C3 Wolfsberg Austria
56C2 Wolfsburg Germany
5H4 Wollaston L Can
5H4 Wollaston Lake Can
4G3 Wollaston Pen Can
109D2 Wollongong Aust
101G1 Wolmaransstad S Africa
59B2 Wolow Pol
108B3 Wolseley Aust
43C3 Wolverhampton Eng
16A2 Womelsdorf USA
109D1 Wondai Aust
13C3 Wonju S Korea
108B2 Wonomirta *R* Aust
13C1 Wonowon Can
74B3 Wônsan N Korea
108C3 Wonthaggi Aust
108A2 Woocalla Aust
16B3 Woodbine USA
15C3 Woodbridge USA
5G4 Wood Buffalo Nat Pk Can
109D1 Woodburn Aust
20B1 Woodburn USA
16B3 Woodbury USA
12F1 Woodchopper USA
21A2 Woodland California, USA
20B1 Woodland Washington, USA
107E1 Woodlark *I* PNG
106C4 Woomera Aust
106C3 Woodroffe,Mt Aust
14B2 Woodstock Ontario, Can

16B3 Woodstown USA
110C2 Woodville NZ
19B3 Woodville USA
108A2 Woomera Aust
15D2 Woonsocket USA
14B2 Wooster USA
43C3 Worcester Eng
100A4 Worcester S Africa
16D1 Worcester USA
47E1 Wörgl Austria
42C2 Workington Eng
8C2 Worland USA
46E2 Worms Germany
43B4 Worms Head *Pt* Wales
43D4 Worthing Eng
8D2 Worthington USA
71D4 Wowoni *I* Indon
12H3 Wrangell USA
12H3 Wrangell I USA
12F2 Wrangell Mts USA
40B2 Wrath,C Scot
43C3 Wrexham Wales
17B1 Wrightsville USA
22D3 Wrightwood USA
4F3 Wrigley Can
59B2 Wrocław Pol
58B2 Wrzesnia Pol
69E2 Wuchang China
76E1 Wuchuan China
72C2 Wuding He *R* China
72A3 Wudu China
73C4 Wugang China
72B2 Wuhai China
73C3 Wuhan China
73D3 Wuhu China
73D5 Wuhua China
84D2 Wüjang China
72B1 Wujia He *R* China
73B4 Wu Jiang *R* China
97C4 Wukari Nig
73B4 Wuling Shan *Mts* China
97D4 Wum Cam
73A4 Wumeng Shan Upland China
46D1 Wuppertal Germany
72B2 Wuqi China
72D2 Wuqing China
57B3 Würzburg Germany
57C2 Wurzen Germany
72C2 Wutai Shan *Mt* China
71F4 Wuvulu *I* Pacific O
72A2 Wuwei China
73E3 Wuxi China
73E3 Wuxing China
72C2 Wuyang China
73D4 Wuyi Shan *Mts* China
72B1 Wuyuan China
76D2 Wuzhi Shan *Mts* China
72B2 Wuzhong China
73C5 Wuzhou China
14B2 Wyandotte USA
109C1 Wyandra Aust
43C4 Wye Eng
43C4 Wylye *R* Eng
43E3 Wymondham Eng
108B2 Wyndham Aust
18B2 Wynne USA
4G2 Wynniatt B Can
109C4 Wynyard Aust
8C2 Wyoming State, USA
14A2 Wyoming USA
109D2 Wyong Aust

X

84D1 Xaidulla China
72D1 Xai Moron He *R* China
101C3 Xai Xai Mozam
23B2 Xaltinguis Mexico
100A2 Xangongo Angola
46D1 Xanten Germany
55B2 Xánthi Greece
100B3 Xau,L Botswana
14B3 Xenia USA
72A2 Xiahe China
73D5 Xiamen China
72B3 Xi'an China

73B4 Xianfeng China
73C3 Xiangtan China
73C4 Xiang Jiang *R* China
73C4 Xiangtan Province, China
73C4 Xianning China
72B3 Xianyang China
73C4 Xiao Shui *R* China
73D4 Xiapu China
73A4 Xichang China
23B1 Xicotepec Mexico
76C2 Xieng Khouang Laos
73B4 Xifeng China
86B1 Xigazê China
72A1 Xi He *R* China
72B2 Xiji China
73C5 Xi Jiang *R* China
72E1 Xiliao He *R* China
73B5 Xilin China
23B1 Xilitla Mexico
73C4 Xinfeng China
72C1 Xinghe China
73D5 Xingning China
73B4 Xingren China
72C2 Xingtai China
33G4 Xingu *R* Brazil
68B2 Xingxingxia China
73A4 Xingyi China
72A2 Xining China
72E2 Xinjin Liaoning, China
73A3 Xinjin Sichuan, China
72D2 Xinwen China
72B2 Xin Xian China
72C2 Xinxiang China
73C3 Xinyang China
73C5 Xinyi Guangdong, China
72D3 Xinyi Jiangsu, China
72D1 Xi Ujimqin Qi China
74A2 Xiuyan China
23B2 Xochimilco Mexico
73D3 Xuancheng China
73B3 Xuanhan China
72D1 Xuanhua China
73A4 Xuanwei China
72C3 Xuddur Somalia
72A2 Xunhua China
73C5 Xun Jiang *R* China
69E2 Xunke China
73D5 Xunwu China
73C4 Xupu China
76E1 Xuwen China
73B4 Xuyong China
72D3 Xuzhou China

Y

73A4 Ya'an China
108B3 Yaapeet Aust
98B2 Yabassi Cam
68C1 Yablonovvy Khrebet *Mts* Russian Fed
94C2 Yabrūd Syria
20B2 Yachats USA
30D3 Yacuiba Bol
87B1 Yādgir India
95A1 Yafran Libya
23A1 Yahualica Mexico
72B2 Yahuma Zaire
75B1 Yaita Japan
75B2 Yaizu Japan
73A4 Yajiang China
20B1 Yakima USA
20B1 Yakima *R* USA
97B3 Yako Burkina
98C2 Yakoma Zaire
74E2 Yakumo Japan
12G3 Yakutat USA
12G3 Yakutat B USA
63E1 Yakutsk Russian Fed
77C4 Yala Thai
12B2 Yalalag Mexico
98C2 Yalinga CAR
109C3 Yallourn Aust
68B3 Yalong *R* China
73A4 Yalong Jiang *R* China
54C2 Yalova Turk
60D5 Yalta Ukraine
74B2 Yalu Jiang *R* China
74D3 Yamagata Japan
74C4 Yamaguchi Japan

68D1 Yamarovka Russian Fed
109D1 Yamba New S Wales, Aust
108B2 Yamba S Australia, Aust
99C2 Yambio Sudan
54C2 Yambol Bulg
71E4 Yamdena *I* Indon
Yam Kinneret = Tiberias,L
108B1 Yamma Yamma,L Aust
97B4 Yamoussoukro Ivory Coast
85D3 Yamuna *R* India
86C1 Yamzho Yumco *L* China
63F1 Yana *R* Russian Fed
108B3 Yanac Aust
75A2 Yanagawa Japan
87C1 Yanam India
72B2 Yan'an China
80B3 Yanbu'al Bahr S Arabia
108B2 Yancannia Aust
72E3 Yancheng China
72B2 Yanchi China
108B1 Yandama *R* Aust
98C2 Yangambi Zaire
72C1 Yang He *R* China
73C5 Yangjiang China
76B2 Yangon Burma
72C2 Yangquan China
73C5 Yangshan China
73C3 Yangtze Gorges China
72E3 Yangtze,Mouths of the China
72D3 Yangxin China
73B4 Yanhe China
74B2 Yanji China
108C3 Yanko *R* Aust
8D2 Yankton USA
68A2 Yanqqi China
72D1 Yan Shan *Hills* China
108B1 Yantabulla Aust
72E2 Yantai China
72D2 Yanzhou China
98B2 Yaoundé Cam
71E4 Yapen *I* Indon
71E3 Yap Is Pacific O
24B2 Yaqui *R* Mexico
61G2 Yaransk Russian Fed
32C3 Yari *R* Colombia
74D3 Yariga-dake *Mt* Japan
82B2 Yarkant He *R* China
86C1 Yarlung Zangbo Jiang *R* China
7D5 Yarmouth Can
94B2 Yarmūk *R* Syria/Jordan
61E2 Yaroslavl' Russian Fed
94B2 Yarqon *R* Israel
109C3 Yarram Aust
109D1 Yarraman Aust
109C3 Yarrawonga Aust
60D2 Yartsevo Russian Fed
63B1 Yartsevo Russian Fed
32B2 Yarumal Colombia
97C3 Yashi Nig
97C3 Yashikera Nig
61F4 Yashkul' Russian Fed
84C1 Yasin Pak
54C2 Yasinya Ukraine
109C2 Yass Aust
109C2 Yass *R* Aust
75A1 Yasugi Japan
94C2 Yates Center USA
98C2 Yatolema Zaire
74C4 Yatsushiro Japan
94B3 Yatta Israel
32C4 Yavari Peru
74B4 Yavatmāl India
74C4 Yawatahama Japan
76D2 Ya Xian China
90B3 Yazd Iran
90B3 Yazd-e Khvāst Iran
19B3 Yazoo *R* USA

19B3 Yazoo City USA
76B2 Ye Burma
59D3 Yedintsy Moldova
108A2 Yeelanna Aust
60E3 Yefremov Russian Fed
61F4 Yegorlyk R Russian Fed
99D2 Yei Sudan
65H4 Yekaterinburg Russian Fed
60E3 Yelets Russian Fed
44E1 Yell I Scot
87C1 Yellandu India
Yellow = Huang He
8B1 Yellowhead P Can
4G3 Yellowknife Can
5G4 Yellowmead P Can
109C2 Yellow Mt Aust
69E3 Yellow Sea China/Korea
8C2 Yellowstone R USA
8B2 Yellowstone L USA
6B1 Yelverton B Can
97C3 Yelwa Nig
81C4 Yemen Republic, Arabian Pen
76C1 Yen Bai Viet
97B4 Yendi Ghana
76B1 Yengan Burma
63B2 Yeniseysk Russian Fed
63B1 Yeniseyskiy Kryazh Ridge Russian Fed
64J2 Yeniseyskiy Zal B Russian Fed
12D2 Yentna R USA
43C4 Yeo R Eng
109C2 Yeoval Aust
43C4 Yeovil Eng
63C1 Yerbogachen Russian Fed
65F5 Yerevan Armenia
21B2 Yerington USA
21B3 Yermo USA
69E1 Yerofey-Pavlovich Russian Fed
94B3 Yeroham Israel
61G3 Yershov Russian Fed
Yerushalayim = Jerusalem
92C1 Yesil R Turk
94B2 Yesud Hama'ala Israel
109D1 Yetman Aust
96B2 Vetti Maur
93E1 Yevlakh Azerbaijan
60D4 Yevpatoriya Ukraine
72E2 Ye Xian China
60E4 Yeysk Russian Fed
55B2 Yiannitsá Greece
73A4 Yibin China
73C3 Yichang China
69E2 Yichun China
72B2 Yijun China
54C2 Yildiz Dağlari Upland Turk
92C2 Yildizeli Turk
73A5 Yiliang China
72B2 Yinchuan China
72D3 Ying He R China
72E1 Yingkou China
73D3 Yingshan Hubei, China
72B3 Yingshan Sichuan, China
73C3 Yingtan China
82C1 Yining China
72B1 Yin Shan Upland China
99D2 Yirga Alem Eth
99D2 Yirol Sudan
63D3 Yirshi China
73B5 Yishan China
72D2 Yishui China
55B3 Yithion Greece
38J6 Yivieska Fin
73C4 Yiyang China
38K5 Yli-Kitka L Fin
38J5 Ylilornio Sweden
19A4 Yoakum USA
23B2 Yogope Mexico
78C4 Yogyakarta Indon

13D2 Yoho Nat Pk Can
98B2 Yokadouma Cam
75B2 Yokkaichi Japan
75B1 Yokohama Japan
75B1 Yokosuka Japan
74C3 Yonago Japan
74E3 Yonezawa Japan
72A2 Yong'an China
72A3 Yongchang China
74B3 Yongch'on S Korea
73B4 Yongchuan China
72A2 Yongdeng China
73D5 Yongding China
72D2 Yongding He R China
74B3 Yŏngdŏk S Korea
74B3 Yŏnghŭng N Korea
74B3 Yongji S Korea
72B2 Yongning China
16C2 Yonkers USA
49C2 Yonne R France
42D3 York Eng
18A1 York Nebraska, USA
16A3 York Pennsylvania, USA
107D2 York,C Aust
108A2 Yorke Pen Aust
108A3 Yorketown Aust
7A4 York Factory Can
41C3 Yorkshire Moors Moorland Eng
42D2 Yorkshire Wolds Upland Eng
5H4 Yorkton Can
22B2 Yosemite L USA
22C1 Yosemite Nat Pk USA
75A2 Yoshii R Japan
75A2 Yoshino R Japan
61G2 Yoshkar Ola Russian Fed
74B3 Yŏsu S Korea
41B3 Youghal Irish Rep
45C3 Youghal Harb Irish Rep
73B5 You Jiang R China
109C2 Young Aust
34D2 Young Urug
111A2 Young Range Mts NZ
13E2 Youngstown Can
14B2 Youngstown Ohio, USA
22A1 Yountville USA
73B4 Youyang China
92B2 Yozgat Turk
22D2 Yreka USA
39G7 Ystad Sweden
43C3 Ystwyth R Wales
44C3 Ythan R Scot
73C4 Yuan Jiang R Hunan, China
73A5 Yuan Jiang R Yunnan, China
72C2 Yuanping China
21A2 Yuba City USA
74E2 Yūbari Japan
25D3 Yucatan Pen Mexico
25D2 Yucatan Chan Mexico/Cuba
72C2 Yuci China
63F2 Yudoma R Russian Fed
73D4 Yudu China
73A4 Yuexi China
73C4 Yueyang China
54A2 Yugoslavia Republic, Europe
73B5 Yu Jiang R China
12C2 Yukon R Can/USA
4E3 Yukon Territory Can
76E1 Yulin Guangdong, China
73C5 Yulin Guangxi, China
72B2 Yulin Shaanxi, China
9B3 Yuma USA
72D3 Yumen China
72D2 Yunan China
34A3 Yungay Chile
73C5 Yunkai Dashan Hills China
108A2 Yunta Aust
72C3 Yunxi China

72C3 Yun Xian China
73B3 Yunyang China
32B5 Yurimaguas Peru
73E5 Yu Shan Mt Taiwan
38L6 Yushkozero Russian Fed
82D2 Yushu Tibet, China
73A5 Yuxi China
74F2 Yuzhno-Kuril'sk Russian Fed
69G2 Yuzhno-Sakhalinsk Russian Fed
61J3 Yuzh Ural Mts Russian Fed
46A2 Yvelines Department, France
47B1 Yverdon Switz

Z
56A2 Zaandam Neth
93D2 Zāb al Babir R Iraq
93D2 Zāb as Şaghir R Iraq
68D2 Zabaykal'sk Russian Fed
59B3 Zabreh Czech Republic
59B2 Zabrze Pol
23A2 Zacapu Mexico
24B2 Zacatecas Mexico
23B2 Zacatepec Morelos, Mexico
23B2 Zacatepec Oaxaca, Mexico
23B2 Zacatlan Mexico
23A1 Zacoalco Mexico
23B1 Zacualtipan Mexico
52C2 Zadar Croatia
76B3 Zadetkyi I Burma
50A2 Zafra Spain
95C1 Zagazig Egypt
96B1 Zagora Mor
52C1 Zagreb Croatia
91D4 Zāhedān Iran
94B2 Zahle Leb
92C3 Zahrez Chergui Marshland Alg
61H2 Zainsk Russian Fed
98C3 Zaire Republic, Africa
98B3 Zaire R Zaire/Congo
54B2 Zaječar Yugos
68C1 Zakamensk Russian Fed
93D2 Zakho Iraq
55B3 Zákinthos I Greece
59B3 Zakopane Pol
59B3 Zalaegerszeg Hung
54B1 Zalău Rom
56C2 Zalew Szczeciński Lg Pol
92C2 Zalingei Sudan
63F2 Zaliv Akademii B Russian Fed
65G5 Zaliv Kara-Bogaz Gol B Turkmenistan
74C2 Zaliv Petra Velikogo B Russian Fed
69G2 Zaliv Turpeniya B Russian Fed
95A2 Zaltan Libya
88H9 Zambesi R Mozam
100B2 Zambezi Zambia
100B2 Zambezi R Zambia
100B2 Zambia Republic, Africa
79B4 Zamboanga Phil
79B4 Zamboanga Pen Phil
52C2 Zambrów Pol
32B4 Zamora Ecuador
23A2 Zamora Mexico
50A1 Zamora Spain
59C2 Zamość Pol
72A3 Zamtang China
98B3 Zanaga Congo
50B2 Záncara R Spain
84D2 Zanda China
14B3 Zanesville USA
84D2 Zangla India
90A2 Zanjān Iran
84B2 Zanjitas Arg
34B2 Zanjon R Arg
99D3 Zanzibar Tanz
99D3 Zanzibar I Tanz
96C2 Zaouatallaz Alg

72D3 Zaozhuang China
93D2 Zap R Turk
39K7 Zapadnaja Dvina R Russian Fed
65H3 Zapadno-Sibirskaya Nizmennost' Lowland Russian Fed
63B2 Zapadnyy Sayan Mts Russian Fed
34A3 Zapala Arg
60E4 Zaporozh'ye Ukraine
93C2 Zara Turk
23A1 Zaragoza Mexico
50B1 Zaragoza Spain
90B2 Zarand Iran
90C3 Zarand Iran
80E2 Zaranj Afghan
93D2 Zarara Ven
58D1 Zarasai Lithuania
34D2 Zárate Arg
90B3 Zard Kuh Mt Iran
12H3 Zarembo I USA
84B2 Zarghun Shahr Afghan
84B2 Zargun Mt Pak
92C3 Zaria Nig
92C3 Zarqa Jordan
94B2 Zarqa R Jordan
32B4 Zaruma Ecuador
58B2 Zary Pol
96D1 Zarzis Tunisia
84D2 Zāskār Mts India
84D2 Zāskār R India
94C2 Zatara R Jordan
Zatoka Gdańska = Gdansk,G of
69E1 Zavitinsk Russian Fed
59B2 Zawiercie Pol
63C2 Zayarsk Russian Fed
65K5 Zaysan Kazakhstan
82D3 Zayü China
68B4 Zayü Mt China
58B2 Zduńska Wola Pol
46B1 Zeebrugge Belg
94B3 Zefat Israel
101G1 Zeerust S Africa
94B2 Zefat Israel
97C3 Zeguerem Watercourse Mali
99E1 Zeila Somalia
57C2 Zeitz Germany
61G2 Zelenodol'sk Russian Fed
39K6 Zelenogorsk Russian Fed
47D1 Zell Austria
98C2 Zemio CAR
64F1 Zemlya Aleksandry I Barents S
64F2 Zemlya Frantsa Iosifa Is Barents S
64F1 Zemlya Georga I Barents S
64H1 Zemlya Vil'cheka I Barents S
73B4 Zenning China
47B1 Zermatt Switz
63E2 Zeya Russian Fed
63E2 Zeya R Russian Fed
50A1 Zêzere R Port
94B1 Zghorta Leb
58B2 Zgierz Pol
73D2 Zhangjiakou China
73D4 Zhangping China
72D2 Zhangwei He R China
72E1 Zhangwu China
72A2 Zhangye China
73D5 Zhangzhou China
73C5 Zhanjiang China
73A4 Zhanyi China
73C5 Zhaoqing China
73A4 Zhaotong China
72D2 Zhaoyang Hu L China
61J4 Zharkamys Russian Fed
63E1 Zhatay Russian Fed
73D4 Zhejiang Province, China
67F3 Zhengou China

Zyyi

72C3 **Zhengzhou** China	73C4 **Zhuzhou** China	57C2 **Zittau** Germany	100C2 **Zumbo** Mozam
72D3 **Zhenjiang** China	72D2 **Zibo** China	72D2 **Ziya He** *R* China	23B2 **Zumpango** Mexico
73A4 **Zhenxiong** China	106C3 **Ziel,Mt** Aust	72A3 **Ziyang** China	97C4 **Zungeru** Nig
73B4 **Zhenyuan** China	58B2 **Zielona Góra** Pol	61J2 **Zlatoust**	73B4 **Zunyi** China
61F3 **Zherdevka**	76A1 **Zigaing** Burma	Russian Fed	76D1 **Zuo** *R* China
Russian Fed	73A4 **Zigong** China	59B3 **Zlin** Czech Republic	73B5 **Zuo Jiang** *R* China
73C3 **Zhicheng** China	97A3 **Ziguinchor** Sen	65K4 **Zmeinogorsk**	47C1 **Zürich** Switz
68C1 **Zhigalovo**	23A2 **Zihuatanejo** Mexico	Russian Fed	47C1 **Zürichsee** *L* Switz
Russian Fed	94B2 **Zikhron Ya'aqov**	58B2 **Znin** Pol	95A1 **Zuwārah** Libya
73B4 **Zhijin** China	Israel	59B3 **Znoimo**	95A2 **Zuwaylah** Libya
58D2 **Zhitkovichi**	59B3 **Žilina** Slovakia	Czech Republic	61H2 **Zuyevka**
Belorussia	95A2 **Zillah** Libya	100B3 **Zoekmekaar**	Russian Fed
60C3 **Zhitomir** Ukraine	47D1 **Ziller** *R* Austria	S Africa	100B4 **Zvishavane** Zim
60D3 **Zhlobin** Belorussia	47D1 **Zillertaler Alpen** *Mts*	47B1 **Zofinger** Switz	59B3 **Zvolen** Slovakia
60C4 **Zhmerinka** Ukraine	Austria	72A3 **Zoigê** China	54A2 **Zvornik** Bosnia-
84B2 **Zhob** Pak	58D1 **Zilupe** Russian Fed	59D3 **Zolochev** Ukraine	Herzegovina
58D2 **Zhodino** Latvia	63C2 **Zima** Russian Fed	101C2 **Zomba** Malawi	97B4 **Zwedru** Lib
72B2 **Zhongning** China	23B1 **Zimapan** Mexico	98B2 **Zongo** Zaïre	46D2 **Zweibrücken**
112C10 **Zhongshan** *Base* Ant	23B2 **Zimatlan** Mexico	92B1 **Zonguldak** Turk	Germany
73C5 **Zhongshan** China	100B2 **Zimbabwe** Republic,	97B4 **Zorzor** Lib	47B1 **Zweisimmen** Switz
72B2 **Zhongwei** China	Africa	96A2 **Zouerate** Maur	57C2 **Zwickau** Germany
68B4 **Zhougdian** China	94B3 **Zin** *R* Israel	54B1 **Zrenjanin** Serbia,	56B2 **Zwolle** Neth
73E3 **Zhoushan Quandao**	23B2 **Zinacatepec** Mexico	Yugos	58C2 **Zyrardów** Pol
Arch China	23A2 **Zinapécuaro** Mexico	47C1 **Zug** Switz	65K5 **Zyryanovsk**
72E2 **Zhuanghe** China	97C3 **Zinder** Niger	47D1 **Zugspitze** *Mt*	Kazakhstan
72A3 **Zhugqu** China	73C4 **Zi Shui** China	Germany	59B3 **Żywiec** Pol
73C3 **Zhushan** China	23A2 **Zitácuaro** Mexico	50A2 **Zújar** *R* Spain	94A1 **Zyyi** Cyprus